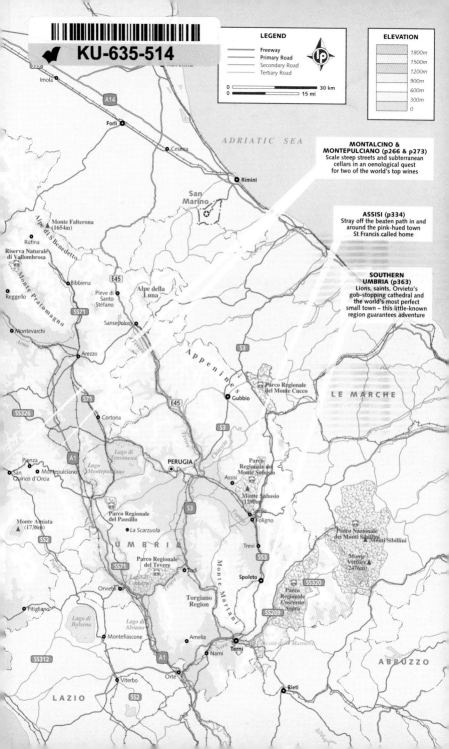

KU-635-514

LEGEND

Freeway
Primary Road
Secondary Road
Tertiary Road

0   30 km
0   15 mi

ELEVATION

1800m
1500m
1200m
900m
600m
300m
0

**MONTALCINO &
MONTEPULCIANO (p266 & p273)**
Scale steep streets and subterranean
cellars in an oenological quest
for two of the world's top wines

ASSISI (p334)
Stray off the beaten path in and
around the pink-hued town
St Francis called home

**SOUTHERN
UMBRIA (p363)**
Lions, saints, Orvieto's
gob-stopping cathedral and
the world's most perfect
small town – this little-known
region guarantees adventure

ADRIATIC SEA

Imola

Forlì

Cesena

Rimini

San
Marino

Monte Falterona
(1654m)

Alpe di S Benedetto

Rùfina

Riserva Naturale
di Vallombrosa

Bibbiena

Pieve di
Santo
Stéfano

Alpe della
Luna

Reggello

Monte Pratomagno

Montevarchi

Sansepolcro

Arezzo

Arno

Appenines

Parco Regionale
del Monte Cucco

LE MARCHE

Cortona

Gubbio

Lago di
Trasimeno

Lago di
Montepulciano

PERUGIA

Chiascio

Parco Regionale del
Monte Subasio

Pienza

Montepulciano

Assisi

San
Quirico d'Orcia

Monte Subasio
(1290m)

Spello

Monte Amiata
(1738m)

Parco Regionale
del Pausillo

La Scarzuola

Foligno

UMBRIA

Parco Nazionale
dei Monti Sibillini

Monti Sibillini

Trevi

Monte
Vettore
(2476m)

Parco Regionale
del Tevere

Todi

Spoleto

Parco
Regionale
Coscerno
Aspra

Orvieto

Lago di
Corbara

Torgiano
Region

Monte Martani

Pitigliano

Lago di
Bolsena

Lago di
Alviano

Montefiascone

Amelia

Nera

Terni

Cascata delle Marmore

ABRUZZO

Viterbo

Narni

Orte

Rieti

LAZIO

On the Road

NICOLA WILLIAMS Coordinating Author

It's the smell of white truffles that seduces. My tastebuds went wild when we shaved them onto buttered pasta and then a *bistecca alla fiorentina* (loin steak) for lunch. Hot date: truffle hunting in December at Barbialla Nuova (p170) in the San Miniato hills, west of Florence.

ALEX LEVITON

Salvatore, the famous chef of the well-known restaurant Il Bacco Felice (p347), is known for his rather unconventional ways. My fiancé Matt had just arrived in Italy the night before, so I figured Salvatore's mecca of Umbrian cuisine was the perfect welcome.

LEIF PETTERSEN

Distended and woozy after yet another two-lunch day: I selflessly forced down countless stomach-stretching meals, with no regard for my dwindling sex appeal, to ensure that eating options in my territory were something special.

ALISON BING

Here I am on the border of Lazio and Tuscany, purchasing half a priest's house…no, really. My partner Marco's family is from the region, and this medieval town in truffle country immediately felt (and tasted) like home. We found and bought our place that afternoon.

MILES RODDIS

To break up the research, we invited the family to fly out and join us for a long weekend in Tuscany. The grandchildren love nothing more than clambering over rocks, so we took them up to the marble quarries, in the hills behind Carrara, where they spent a happy couple of hours romping.

See full author biographies on page 435

TUSCANY & UMBRIA

Be it unravelling a thousand Tuscan tales in the devilishly steep streets of a hill-top town, revelling in Florence's city-sophisticate pageant of Renaissance masterpieces or committing yourself truly, madly, deeply to Umbria's savage soul, these regions are disproportionately rich – in art, in food, in passion.

It is Italy's iconic land of myth and legend: Dante, David, Puccini, the Renaissance, Hepburn's Vespa, da Vinci…they were all born here against a fiery fresco of Etruscan gods, equestrian battles, bonfire-mad monks and marble mountain peaks. Tramping through trees for truffles, touring on a free-spirited Vespa, frolicking at village festivals or revelling in the simple peasantry of Tuscan cuisine: try it alfresco.

Italian Icons

Positively sparkling with grand-slam sights and experiences, this region says more about Italy than any other. Whether you are touring the Tuscan countryside on the back of a 1950s Vespa, admiring next season's collection in Florence's drawing room or getting lost in the Renaissance (p46), the dazzling region of Tuscany and Umbria is an iconic masterpiece.

'The world's greatest engineering cockup'

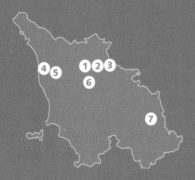

'Creative, elegant, liberating: the world's most famous two-wheeler'

Author's Tip
Only 40 people are allowed up Pisa's Leaning Tower at a time. To avoid disappointment, book in advance or sprint to a ticket office upon arrival in Pisa to book a slot for later that day. The same goes for *David's* Galleria dell'Accademia (p105).

1 David (p120)
The world's most famous sculpture: but why the small appendage? And what's that crack on his left arm? Find out why as you stroll through the art of this elegant Renaissance city.

2 Florence's Duomo (p105)
The dome of the world's fourth-largest cathedral – a Renaissance masterpiece dominating Florence's skyline – screams drama, intrigue and a thousand and one tales. It's best seen inside out.

3 Gucci (p151)
No label screams 'Made in Italy!' louder than Gucci, creator of scandal and fashion since 1921. Shopping in Florence for fashion is irresistible.

4 Leaning Tower of Pisa (p185)
Pisano's stump of a tower already had a noticeable lean three tiers in: the world's greatest engineering cockup, Italy would not be Italy without Pisa's Torre Pendente.

5 Vespa (p191)
Creative, elegant, liberating: the world's most famous two-wheeler (b 1946) is *the* icon of Italian design. Visit the factory in northwest Tuscany where it was born.

6 Chianti (p74)
Cheap 1970s, raffia-wrapped bottled Chianti might not compete with the new millennium Supertuscans, but it remains the wine everyone knows and loves.

7 St Francis of Assisi (p338)
He spoke to the animals and spiritual souls. The sleepy Umbrian town of soft pink-hued stone where St Francis was born, now a World Heritage Site (p27), has scarcely changed since.

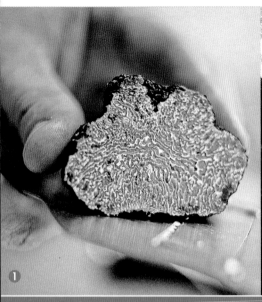

Natural Wonders

When Renaissance man's brilliance sends heads spinning, flee to Mother Nature. Be it tramping through Tuscan woods on damp autumnal mornings to hunt grubby white truffles, rising with the larks to hike around legends in Umbria's magnificent Sybilline Mountains, or plunging into sea-blue waters, this green part of Italy has ample natural beauty for you to experience.

'Stunning sea views, windy caves and soothing spa waters are what these mountains are all about'

❶ & ❷ White & Black Truffles (p71)
Sadly for *tartufi* (truffles) aficionados in this world, how this aphrodisiac grows or how to grow it remains a mystery. Revel in the hunt in the hills of San Miniato (p170) and Norcia (p385).

❸ Carrara Marble (p207)
Michelangelo rummaged through dusty workshops in search of the dream block, as do contemporary artists, equally mad about the world's best-known *marmo bianco* (white marble) cut out of Carrara's Marble Mountain.

❹ Apuane Alps (p204)
Great walking (p84), stunning sea views, windy caves and soothing spa waters (p88) are what these mountains are all about. Stride out.

❺ Isola d'Elba (p223)
Napoleon would think twice about fleeing from Elba today. This island is an uplifting orgy of beach, sea, mountains and mouth-watering seafood. Stretch out and relax.

❻ Pitigliano (p290)
Sure it's man-made, as are the other zillion hill-top towns in this region, but the mountainous cliff face on which this ancient Etruscan village sits is a definitive natural wonder. Tombs pit its volcanic innards.

❼ Lake Trasimeno (p356)
Frolic around its idyllic islands, honeymoon in a blanket of flowers and follow its never-ending trails. Italy's largest natural, non-Alpine lake in northern Umbria is charming.

❽ Monti Sibillini (p386)
Dance with wolves and red deer, skip with fairies or dip your toes in icy streams beneath falcon-pricked skies in Umbria's wild-spirited Sybilline Mountains, protected by a national park and sugar-iced year-round with snow.

❾ Cascata delle Marmore (p387)
Smashing down from a mighty height of 165m, these magnificent waterfalls in southern Umbria – Europe's highest – appear more natural wonder than Roman creation. Catching sight of them from the back of a river raft is especially thrilling.

La Cucina Caldesi

An abundance of fresh herbs and vegetables is the chief attraction of Tuscan cuisine for London's Tuscan chef Giancarlo Caldesi and wife Katie (pictured on p11), whose cooking school – in the limelight since starring in the BBC TV documentary *Return to Tuscany* – winters in Marylebone and summers in Torrita di Siena, 15km north of Giancarlo's native Montepulciano. 'Tuscan recipes are based upon seasonal local ingredients – something we're all trying to imitate in modern city dining. Yet this is for real! If you seek artichokes or even chilli at the wrong time of year, it's just not possible to buy them,' commented Katie, in between disclosing her and Giancarlo's Tuscan culinary highlights.

Katie's Tip

Get the locals to recommend their favourite restaurant. Look for *Cucina Tipica Toscana* signs and, on the menu, *pasta fatta in casa* (no, it doesn't mean there's a large guy in the house, just the pasta is home-made!). Good menus should always include *ribollita, pappardelle, pici* and the enormous *bistecca alla fiorentina* (p68).

❶ & ❷ Pici & Pinci

A real family favourite: we love making and eating these long lengths of hand-rolled pasta found mainly in Montepulciano (*pici*) and Montalcino (*pinci*).

❸ La Botte Piena

An *enoteca* (wine bar) with a vast array of local wines to try and buy, **Osteria La Botte Piena** (☎ 0577 66 94 81; www.labottepiena.com; Piazza Dionisa Cinughi 12, Montefollonico) has beautifully prepared dishes and local *affettati* (cured meats) to go with them. Find it 12km northwest of Montepulciano in Montefollonico.

❹ Il Conte Matto

A very good local restaurant in Trequanda (22km northwest of Montepulciano), **Ristorante Il Conte Matto** (☎ 0577 62 20 79; www.contematto.it; Via Taverne 40, Trequanda) has a wonderful alfresco dining area with views over the Tuscan countryside. We take our students there to sample Tuscan cooking; try the wild boar with cocoa or the *ribollita*.

❺ Porcini Mushrooms

Katie on hunting for Porcini mushrooms in the mountains outside Siena: 'I was taught where to look for the precious treasures and it was so exciting; I came away with a basket to cook at home, which would have cost a fortune in a shop'.

❻ Sagre

It amazes me how Tuscans make festivals out of things as bizarre as snails, *crostini* (toasted sliced bread), polenta and so on. Local to us is Torrita di Siena's Sagra della Porchetta, when pork is cooked in a variety of ways and served, often for very little money, with local wines. There is always a great spirit and you get a real sense of belonging.

❼ Olive Oil

We get ours from friends who produce just enough for them and a little for us. Their oil is dark green, gutsy in flavour, and makes a real impact when swirled in a bean soup or used to dress a *bistecca alla fiorentina*.

❽ Babbo's Eggs

Our family favourite for breakfast: *babbo* is Tuscan for dad or daddy and this is the way Giancarlo's father used to cook them. Reheat your leftover pasta tomato *sugo* (sweet tomato sauce) in a large frying pan and drop in an egg per person, taking care they don't touch. Delicious served with fresh bread.

Contemporary Art

Contemporary Tuscan masters like Massimo Bartolini and Gianfranco Masi (p54) are proof that artistic inspiration is alive and kicking across a mix of mediums – sculpture, site-specific installation, digital, performance photography and so on. Can't hack another Madonna or Magi adoration? Turn to a genius of today.

Author's Tip

Biennial exhibitions that have contemporay art focus: Florence's Biennale Internazio dell'Arte Contemporanea (www.florencebiennale.org) and Il Chianti's Tusciaelecta (www.tusciaelecta.it). Hideouts of contemporary art include Florence's JK Place (p135), Gallery Art & Continentale (p136) and farm Podere Castellare (p165 and p309).

❶ Galleria Continua (p257)

Don't follow the tourists in San Gimignano. Dive instead into this often-overlooked contemporary art gallery, in the medieval town.

❷ Il Giardino dei Tarocchi (p289)

An absolute must for Niki de Saint Phalle buffs: Jean Tinguely makes lightning strike the tower of Babel in the artist's Tarot Garden – for her 'a garden of joy, a little corner of paradise'. Find it near Lago di Burano, southern Tuscany.

❸ Fattoria di Celle (p162)

Cutting-edge art installations mingle with 19th-century follies at this private open-air sculpture park near Pistoia; guided visits are fabulous three- to four-hour hikes around art.

❹ Parco Sculture del Chianti (p168)

A green wooded sculpture park with dozens of funky site-specific installations created in situ by famous Italian and international artists, in Pievasciata, located 13km north of Siena.

Contents

Regional Map Contents

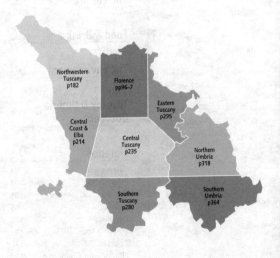

Northwestern
Tuscany
p182

Florence
pp96–7

Eastern
Tuscany
p295

Central
Coast &
Elba
p214

Central
Tuscany
p235

Northern
Umbria
p318

Southern
Tuscany
p280

Southern
Umbria
p364

Destination Tuscany & Umbria

If you get it right, travelling in Tuscany and Umbria is one of those rare experiences in life – like a perfect spring day or the power of first love – that cannot be overrated. Despite incessant praise, the *bellezza* (beauty) of this region continues to defy description, for Tuscany and Umbria, it seems, really do have it all: extraordinary art and architecture (p41); colourful *feste* (festivals; p22); a season-driven cuisine emulated the world over (p66); and a never-ending landscape of olive groves, vineyards and poplars. In few places do art and life intermingle so completely.

Big city–sophisticate dame, younger country-bumpkin boy, Tuscany and Umbria drum up a quintessential Italian experience. Pilgrims have not stopped flocking to *carceri* (hermit retreats in caves) in Assisi since St Francis converted souls there in the 13th century. Meanwhile Florence has been a fashionable stop on European grand tours since the 19th century, when privileged young men mixed with wealthy nobles on Via de' Tornabuoni between gulps of Renaissance art at the Uffizi. Take in Giotto's action-packed frescoes in Assisi's Basilica di San Francesco, Signorelli's sunny scenes of eternal damnation in Orvieto's striped cathedral and Pisano's mesmerising marble friezes in Perugia – yes, there's exceptional art all over the place (p52).

From the foot of *David* to the wild heights of Valnerina or savage peaks of Umbria's Monti Sibillini, a staunch conservatism stamps the entire region. Unswervingly dedicated to living life well rather than blazing new trails, Tuscans and Umbrians rank among Italy's most furious nationalists (you try blending into that quintessential Umbrian village where grown men still live at home with mama and nothing has changed for, oh, 400 years).

Yet conversely, the provinces have almost always been politically left-leaning, making the place surprisingly internationally minded in parts, too. Tunisian-born, bilingual Italian-French Claudio Martini, a fervent fan of globalisation and AFC Fiorentina, heads up Tuscany's left-wing regional government, and one of Italy's few female presidents, Maria Rita Lorenzetti, sits at the helm of Umbria's regional government.

Increasing urban congestion has seen the wealthier turn to greener scapes in recent years – unfortunately prompting a marked increase in ugly construction projects, say Italian environmentalists who, despite strict laws governing land management and development (p83), still believe traditional hill towns and the very character of the region are threatened. New housing intended for local people is being snapped up instead by Italians from elsewhere and an increasing number of foreigners. This trend, born in the 1980s with John Mortimer's legendary 'Chiantishire', is evident today even in landlocked Umbria's remotest parts. Get in quick, in fact: prices in this still relatively cheap, undiscovered region of prairie-like expanses, savage peaks and lake-side frolics are set to rise as more sunseekers cotton on to the popularity of Umbria as a second-home destination.

For local country folk, reaping a living from agriculture is fostered through low-interest loans and other financial incentives that ensure farmers stay in business. Earning an extra crust from *agriturismo*

FAST FACTS

Combined population: 4.5 million

Foreign population: around 6%

GDP per capita: Tuscany €26,280, Umbria €22,830

Inflation: 2.3%

Unemployment: Tuscany 4.8%, Umbria 6.1%

Land area: 31,430 sq km

Vineyard area: 108,000 hectares

Annual wine production: 4 million hectolitres

(farm-stay accommodation) is fine, providing it remains less profitable than the farmstead's traditional activity (for further details see the Agriturismi chapter, p309). Forever keen to promote their green nature, more farms are organic or – like the new €8-million solar-panel park planned to generate energy for around 500 homes in Tuscany's Grosseto province – turning to renewable energy sources. Clearly the way of the future for this privileged part of Italy.

From farming to frescoes, Tuscans and Umbrians demonstrate a savage attention to life's fine print. A surprising number of people here care deeply about the floral aftertastes of sheep's cheese, the correct way to cut marble and the nuances of a Gregorian chant. Lurking behind the *disinvoltura* – the appearance of effortlessness – is a cool calculation that leaves nothing to chance. It's no accident that double-entry accounting was invented here during the Renaissance. This may be the land of Dante, Michelangelo, Brunelleschi and Botticelli, but this is also the home of Salvatore Ferragamo and Fabio Picchi. Food, fashion, art and architecture – you'll quickly learn that at the root of Tuscan and Umbrian pathology is an unswerving dedication to living life well. So take a leaf out their book and start learning how to live the good life.

Getting Started

Tuscany is a place everyone wants to be. Whether it be to view world-class art in Florence or flop between cypresses outside an old stone farmhouse framed by vines, the hordes are here. Few know that much about Umbria (despite it being touted for a while as the new Tuscany), bar it has even more soul-stirring rolling hills wedged between hill-top villages than its more manicured, Brit-loved neighbour.

Several budget airlines fly into Pisa's Galileo Galilei airport, the major entry point. Florence, Siena, Pisa and the Chianti wine region hit the list of many a city break and are the region's most expensive spots. Umbria overall is cheaper. Main towns are interlinked by train or bus, but wheels – car or bike – are essential in the countryside.

WHEN TO GO

The region is busy year-round, although most visit May to September. August is best avoided: the weather is hot and clammy, especially inland; huge numbers of Italians take holidays at this time, filling up coastal resorts; and loads of restaurants and many shops in Florence close for two or three weeks.

Low season – March to early May and late September to October – is the best time to visit. The weather is warm, prices are lower and tourists are less. Be warned: hotels' definitions of low and high season do vary; check when planning where to stay.

The Parco Nazionale delle Foreste Cantinesi and the Apuane Alps provide relief from the summer heat but are not immune from torrid weather. The Alps also happen to be Tuscany's wettest zone; see p401.

One of the many festivals studding the Tuscan and Umbrian calendar (p22) is as good a reason as any around which to plan a trip.

COSTS & MONEY

Accommodation is the biggest expense, Florence being particularly pricey: expect to pay up to €70 for a budget hotel double room with bathroom, up to €150 for a midrange double room with bathroom and anything upwards of €150 for a palatial top-end pad. The region's growing number of midrange B&Bs are not necessarily cheaper but do offer excellent value for money.

LONELY PLANET INDEX

Litre of unleaded 95 petrol €1.30

Litre of water in shop/restaurant €0.80/1.50

Bottle of run-of-the-mill Chianti Classico €7

Souvenir T-shirt €15

Pizza €5-10

HOW MUCH?

Cappuccino standing up/sitting down in Florence €1.10/3.50

Cappuccino elsewhere €0.80

Two-scoop gelato €1.80

Italian-flag *David* boxer shorts €6

Half- /full-day bike hire €7/14

Public transport ticket €1.20

DON'T LEAVE HOME WITHOUT...

- Valid travel insurance (p405)
- ID card or passport and visa if required (p410)
- Your credit-, debit-card PIN number (p407)
- Sunglasses, hat and something to cover shoulders in churches
- Sturdy walking shoes or trainers to combat cobbles
- Lonely Planet's *Italian Phrasebook*
- Sun screen and mosquito repellent
- Picnic-friendly pocket knife with corkscrew
- An adventurous appetite and a thirst for good wine (p66)

At the lower end of the scale, a few hotels have doubles with bathroom for around €45, and a hostel dorm bed costs €15 to €30.

Parking is a painful business in central Florence, where extortionate overnight parking fees range from €15 to €50; bigger cars pay more. In other Tuscan towns and in Umbria overnight parking averages around €10.

Dining prices listed in this guide – up to €20 for a budget meal, up to €45 for a midrange meal and upwards of €45 for a top-end meal – are the average you can expect to pay for a *primo* (first course, usually of pasta), *secondo* (main course), dessert and house wine. It is quite acceptable to only order an *antipasto* (starter) and *primo*, for example, or just a *secondo*. Then, of course, there are cheaper pizzas and tripe *panini* aplenty.

Public transport is relatively economical, while museum prices, by no means dirt cheap, are reasonable compared to what is charged in the UK, for example.

> 'Sit down at a table and the price instantly doubles or even triples'

Cutting Costs

Avoid paying for breakfast at your hotel (usually between €5 and €15). You'll get much better value at a local café – providing you stand and drink your cappuccino at the bar. Sit down at a table and the price instantly doubles or even triples.

Read the fine print on menus to check the *coperto* (cover charge) and *servizio* (service fee). Both are the norm, so you usually need to factor in between €1.50 and €3 per head before you even open your mouth to order.

Check museums for free or discounted entrance fees. EU citizens aged under 18 or over 65 often get in free, while a student card invariably yields a discount.

If you're staying in a city for several days and using public transport, consider a weekly (or monthly for longer periods) bus pass.

TRAVEL LITERATURE

Tuscany and Umbria have inspired reams of writing. For history and culture books, see p28 and p56; for food and wine, see p66.

A Small Place in Italy (Eric Newby) A witty, engaging account by this classic travel writer of life in I Castagni (The Chestnuts), the farmhouse he and his feisty Italian wife Wanda bought in 1967.

After Hannibal (Barry Unsworth) An astute evocation of 21st-century manners and morals in the Booker Prize winner's adopted Umbria (where Hannibal defeated the Romans, hence the title).

The Lady in the Palazzo: At Home in Umbria (Marlena De Blasi) Colourful portrait of the town and folk of Orvieto interwoven in the tale of how the American author renovates a crumbling old medieval palazzo in the cliff-top Umbrian town.

My House in Umbria (William Trevor) Tender tear-jerker by the well-known Anglo-Irish writer. The train a romantic novelist is travelling on is bombed by terrorists, after which she returns home to Umbria to recuperate with three survivors.

Songbirds, Truffles and Wolves: An American Naturalist in Italy (Gary Paul Gabhan) Written a decade ago but one of a kind: the naturalist and poet walks from Florence to Assisi, recounting food, folklore, people and nature he encounters.

Too Much Tuscan Sun: Confessions of a Chianti Tour Guide (Dario Castagno) Clever marketing and natural wit has made this comic flipside of the coin told by a Tuscan bestseller; look out for his next book *Too Much Tuscan Wine* (2008) and see more at www.toomuchtuscansun.com.

Under the Tuscan Sun, Bella Tuscany and In Tuscany (Frances Mayes) Compulsory reading; the trio of bestsellers recounts Mayes' experience restoring an old rural Tuscan villa, and her musings on local life, love, cuisine and history.

INTERNET RESOURCES

Bella Umbria (www.bellaumbria.net) A comprehensive guide to the region, including accommodation reservations online, last-minute offers and travel itineraries.

Lonely Planet (www.lonelyplanet.com) Concise information, travellers' postcards and the Thorn Tree bulletin board, first-stop shop for advice before you go.
Trenitalia (www.trenitalia.com) Italy's national railways website.
Turismo in Toscana (www.turismo.toscana.it) Official Tuscany tourist board website.
Tuscan Journey (www.tuscanjourney.org) Tuscan recipes, events, itineraries, legends, gardens and more: well-written guide to less-travelled Tuscany.
Umbria: the Green Heart of Italy (www.umbria-turismo.it) Official Umbrian tourist board website.

TRAVELLING RESPONSIBLY

Since our inception in 1973, Lonely Planet has encouraged our readers to tread lightly, travel responsibly and enjoy the magic independent travel affords. International travel is growing at a jaw-dropping rate, and we still firmly believe in the benefits it can bring – but, as always, we encourage you to consider the impact your visit will have on both the global environment and the local economies, cultures and ecosystems.

Your journey isn't environmentally significant on the grand scale but it's one of 700 million holidays taken worldwide each year. So what can you do to leave a shallower environmental footprint? Tuscany and Umbria have a good rail network; if you're just covering major cities, simply hop on the train. Buses also link main towns and reach deep into the hinterland, while much of rural Tuscany and Umbria is idyllic cycling terrain. If you're renting, a compact car is cheaper and has less impact.

Seek out eco-friendly places to stay; many *agriturismi* (farm-stay accommodation; p309) are just that. And when you shop for food, poke around local markets and small shops rather than supermarkets, which tend to source from far afield.

UK-based sustainable travel body **The Travel Foundation** (www.thetravelfoundation .org.uk) gives tips and guidance on travelling responsibly.

Fly Less, Stay Longer

Budget airlines are here to stay and bring in a large percentage of visitors to Umbria and Tuscany. Mile for mile, the amount of carbon dioxide emitted for one person driving a car is much the same as for one passenger on a plane. The problem with flying is that the carbon and other greenhouse gases spewed out at high altitude have a significantly greater effect on climate change.

Accommodation

It's not always easy to tell. Green is fashionable. As more and more places seek to exploit the green label, it can be hard to differentiate between the

---

A DRINKING PROBLEM

Water is an Italian problem. No, not desertification but simply how to rehydrate without resorting to bottled H_2O, extracted, transported and the source of hundreds of thousands of redundant plastic bottles each year. Buy just one and then refill and re-refill it. Even better, invest in a heavier-duty kind that can last a lifetime. Restaurants present a special difficulty; waiters tend to regard you as eccentric or a cheapskate if you insist on tap water, which is pure and potable throughout the region. Go on, brazen it out!

H_2O in a different form also travels the globe as the major constituent of wines and beers. So buy local. There are enough palatable Tuscan and Umbrian wines for a different tipple every night. Beer? Well, quaff the sparkling Italian fizz and wait until you return home for something with real taste.

TOP 10

France TUSCANY & UMBRIA Sea

Green Forays

Peace, tranquillity and outdoor adventure reign in these green havens off the tourist track.

- Stroll through the manicured grounds of Florence's Giardini Bardini (p125).
- Horse-trek, hike or bike amid wild beauty in Garfagnana (p207) and neighbouring Lunigiana (p211).
- Cycle up the steep flanks of long-extinct volcano, Monte Amiata (p278).
- Romp around remote Gorgona Island (p219).
- Hop aboard the Nature Train in Siena (p244) and loop through the Crete Senese (p250).
- Mellow like a monk at Camaldoli (p303), where tree planting, herbal products and vegetarianism are a way of life.
- Ramble in eastern Tuscany's Parco Nazionale delle Foreste Casentini, Monte Falterona e Campigna (p303).
- Cruise down a long and dusty dirt road to La Scarzuola (p372).
- Rub shoulders with wolves, boars and golden eagles in Umbria's best untouched natural scenery (p387).
- Play *Robinson Crusoe* on Isola Polvese (p357).

Romantic Propositions

Florence ranks among Europe's top honeymoon cities. There is no question about it – this region is romantic.

- Wake up with a view over Florence – the city's top B&Bs (p134), Hotel Scoti (p134), Palazzo Magnani Feroni (p136) and Albergo Torre di Bellosguardo (p136) can't be beaten.
- Pop champagne on the banks of Florence's Arno; on the stone 'seats' on the Ponte Santa Trinità (p117) are the hottest in town.
- Indulge in afternoon tea or a candle-lit dinner on the loggia of Fiesole's Villa San Michele (p156).
- Live the blue-blooded life in a villa with infinity pool on the wine- and olive oil–rich estate of Rignana (p166) in Il Chianti.
- Wine and dine with stunning terrace views at Le Vecchie Mura, San Gimignano (p259).
- Swoop through Tuscan skies in a hot-air balloon (p266).
- Honeymoon in Umbria (p361).
- Picnic under the Tree of Good and Evil in Perugia's Medieval Gardens (p324).
- Stroll with your sweetheart down 'Girl-Kissing Alley' in Amelia (p394).
- Honour Terni's (p390) patron saint, St Valentine on 14 February.

Cheap Thrills

Giggles and a good time are guaranteed for very little dosh.

- Watch night fall in Florence over Ponte Vecchio from the sturdy stone bridge supports of Ponte Santa Trinità (p117).
- Down a tripe *panino* at Nerbone in Florence's central market or at a tripe cart near Piazza Sant' Ambrogio (p137).
- Fill up on a banquet of complimentary appetisers for the price of a drink at one of Florence's fashionable aperitif bars (p146).
- Two-wheel ride atop Lucca's city walls (p191).
- Prop up Pisa's Leaning Tower (p183).
- Catch Siena's Il Palio (p246): the investment of time and planning is exorbitant, but watching the hair-raising spectacle *is* free!
- Bathe in sulphurous, hot water cascading outside the entrance to Terme di Saturnia (p290).
- Savour the *passeggiata* (traditional evening stroll; p322) in Orvieto (p364), Perugia (p318) or Foligno (p347).
- Marvel the day away with world-shaping art in the churches of Assisi (p334).
- Catch a film beneath stars at Citta di Castello's CinaCitta' di Castello Estate (p355).

genuinely ecofriendly and the opportunist. The eco-labelling scheme **Legambiente Turismo** (www.legambienteturismo.it) certifies hotels, judging them on features such as their use of water and energy resources and reduced waste production, and whether they offer good local cuisine. Look out for its green swan sign. To contribute maximally to the local economy, seek out family-run B&Bs and, in particular, *agriturismi* – Umbria and Tuscany have an excellent network.

Slow Food

Italians have always had a healthy penchant for long, relaxed meals where food is to be savoured, not scoffed. And it was in Italy that the **Slow Food Movement** (www.slowfood.com) originated. With the snail as its symbol, it champions traditional cuisine, the use of local seasonal ingredients and sustainable agriculture. It now has over 80,000 members in more than 100 countries and has spawned a sister, Slow City movement (p370). Arm yourself with its English-language *Osterie & Locande d'Italia: A Guide to Traditional Places to Eat & Stay in Italy,* a guide reviewing plenty of trattorie, *osterie* (restaurants focussing on wine), restaurants, B&Bs, hotels and *agriturismi* in both Tuscany and Umbria.

Events Calendar

A vibrant affair indeed is this region's rich cultural calendar – a magnetic merry-go-round of age-old traditional celebrations with a religious and/or historical flavour, performing arts *feste* (festivals) and gastronomic *sagre* (feasts). In the family home, Easter and Christmas remain the most important events of the year, while for those in the countryside it is the natural cycle of harvests – olives, grapes, chestnuts and so on – that is the master of ceremony.

JANUARY

UMBRIA JAZZ WINTER   End Dec-early Jan
Many of the world's great names in jazz take the stage in Orvieto (p368) with this spectacular New Year's Eve event that actually lasts a few days.

FEBRUARY

CARNEVALE   Period before Ash Wednesday
Prior to the start of Lent, many towns stage carnivals and enjoy their last opportunity to indulge before four weeks of fasting. The biggest and best carnival is in Viareggio (see p202) on the Tuscan coast, second-to-none after Venice for its riots of floats and party spirit.

MOSTRA MERCATA DEL   Last weekend Feb,
TARTUFO NERO   1st weekend Mar
Umbrian eating capital, Norcia, plies its precious black truffle on lucky visitors. See p385.

MARCH–APRIL

SETTIMANA SANTA   Easter
Solemn processions and passion plays mark Holy Week in various cities. In Florence, Easter Sunday sees a cart full of fireworks explode with a big bang at noon on Piazza del Duomo during the Scoppio del Carro (Explosion of the Cart), a tradition dating to the Crusades; the better the explosion, the better the omen for the city.

MAY

CORSA ALL'ANELLO   2nd Sunday
Named for the Race of the Ring held in Narni (p393), these two weeks leading up to the equestrian joust filled with singing baroque choirs dressed in traditional garb and feasts.

CORSA DEI CERI   15 May
Three neighbourhoods in Gubbio (p350) jostle against one another carrying gigantic 'candles' through the city streets.

PALIO DELLA BALESTRA   Last Sunday
The men of Gubbio (p350) and its Tuscan neighbour Sansepolcro battle it out in medieval costume with antique crossbows.

JUNE

CENA MEDIEVALE   Early Jun
Festive open-air medieval dinner with 500 new friends in Certaldo (p169); a shared table is set up in the town square and €38 buys you a party-mad evening of traditional dishes, music and dancing.

L'INFIORATA DEL CORPUS   21 Jun
DOMINI
The best place to celebrate Corpus Domini is in Spello (p342), where locals decorate the streets with colourful flower-petal designs.

FESTA DI SAN GIOVANNI   24 Jun
Medieval football matches end with a fireworks display over Piazzale Michelangelo in Florence (p132) on St John's Day, otherwise known as Midsummer's Day.

PALIO DEI RIONI   Third Sunday
Gastronomic fair celebrating local produce held in Castignion Fiorentino, Arezzo (p304).

GIOCO DEL PONTE   Last Sunday
Two teams in medieval garb contend for the Ponte di Mezzo in Pisa (p188).

PALIO DELLE QUATTRO ANTICHE REPUBBLICHE MARINARE
This ancient race between the four old-time maritime republics – Genoa, Amalfi, Pisa (p188) and Venice – is as much a procession of boats and events and serious competition. A race that rotates between the cities, it next sails into Pisa in 2010.

JULY

IL PALIO   2 Jul
One of Italy's most famous festivals, this is a dangerous and competitive bareback horse race through
a piazza in Siena (p246), preceded by a colourful
parade of traditionally costumed supporters.

SPOLETO FESTIVAL   Early to mid-Jul
This international performing arts event in Spoleto (p381) features music, theatre, dance, art and
courtroom re-creations.

UMBRIA JAZZ   10 days in mid-Jul
The crème de la crème of jazz flock to this international festival featuring traditional jazz, soul,
experimental and New Orleans brass bands in
Perugia (p324).

SUMMER FESTIVAL
The best of international contemporary music
shows up for this very reasonably priced Luccan
music festival (p196). Acts have included Youssou
N'Dour, Jamiroquai and Van Morrison.

SAGRA DEL PESCE   Last weekend
Typical local seafood dishes are prepared in
Piombino (p223), culminating on the Sunday with
a giant feed-the-masses frying pan of fried fish for
all the townsfolk to enjoy.

PALIO DEI COLUMBI   End Jul-early Aug
The culminating event of this festival, dating from
1346, pairs a 'knight' on horseback with a cross-
bowman aiming at a target to free a dove, but
for two weeks Amelia (p395) proffers medieval
demonstrations and taverns.

AUGUST

SAGRE DEL BOMBOLONE   1-3 Aug
Celebration of the famous *bombolone* (sweet doughnut) in Sillicano-Camporgiano, Lucca (p191).

SAGRE DELLE OLIVE CON   14 & 15 Aug
CONIGLIO E POLENTA
Local Bagni di Lucca (p208) festival celebrating
the traditional local dish: olives with rabbit and
polenta.

FERRAGOSTO   15 Aug
You can practically hear the crickets chirping as
virtually every Italian man, woman and child heads
out of the cities to the coast or country, closing
many of their shops and restaurants behind them
(thus, a good time to stay away from either spot).

SEPTEMBER

GIOSTRO DEL SARACINO   1st Sun
This event in Arezzo ushers in a medieval jousting
competition. See boxed text, p298.

PALIO DELLA BALESTRA   1st Sun
Sansepolcro (p301) holds a rematch to Gubbio's
May competition, Palio della Balestra.

FESTA DELL'UVA E DEL VINO   3rd weekend
Open-air dinners with live entertainment and
local wine in Arezzo (p295).

SAGRA MUSICALE UMBRIA   Mid- to late Sep
World-renowned conductors and musicians play
at this music festival (p324), one of Europe's oldest, in Perugia.

GRAPE HARVEST   Late Sep & Oct
Called Vendemmia in Chianti, late September and
October is the prime season to sample the new
wines, olive oils and cheeses.

OCTOBER–NOVEMBER

MARCIA DELLA PACE   1st week Oct
Europe's largest peace march has seen pilgrims
walk 24km between Perugia and Assisi (p338).

EUROCHOCOLATE   Around 3rd week Oct
Charlie would be in heaven. For eight days in October, the streets and squares of Perugia (p324)
become one giant chocolate factory – tasting
workshops, chocolate sculptures etc.

SAGRA DELLA LUMACA   Last two weeks Oct
Molluscs invade medieval Cantalupo di Bevagna
(p345), northern Umbria, during this entire festival devoted to snail dishes.

MOSTRA DEL TARTUFO   Last three
BIANCO   weekends Nov
White truffle fair in San Miniato, west of Florence.
See p171.

DECEMBER

NATALE
During the weeks before Christmas there are many
processions and religious events regionwide.

SAGRA DEL VINE BRULÈ   30 Dec
Come 9pm in Abetone, Pistoia (p160), a giant caul-
dron of mulled wine is made, and most people
arrive on skis.

Itineraries

CLASSIC ROUTES

ONLY THE BEST
10 Days/Florence roundtrip

Florence (p92) heads any 'best of' tour. Squeeze in the best of this intensely absorbing city (diary note: return next year) in three days, and move on to **Lucca** (p191), light on heavy-weight museums but loaded with laid-back provincial charm. Next day hit packed **Pisa** (p182) to scale its Leaning Tower, lunch and leave by dusk for a quintessential Tuscan farmhouse in **Il Chianti** (p164) or the **San Miniato Hills** (p171). Check in for two nights to day-trip next morning to **San Gimignano** (p254), with its ground-breaking Galleria Continua.

Siena (p235) is the next best thing to take in. Then step into Umbria and head to **Assisi** (p334), where Giotto frescoed a basilica to stunning effect, stopping for a dip and a fish lunch around **Lake Trasimeno** (p356). **Spello** (p341) gives a quick fix of typical small-town charm and **Spoleto** (p378) is Umbria's unbeatable hiking 'n biking base. Carry on to hill-top **Narni** (p390), where you can catch the highway back to **Perugia** (p318) and Florence, breaking the return journey in **Arezzo** (p295).

Only a fool would tear around at this speed! Florence to Perugia clocks up a breathtaking 1000km that can be done in a whirlwind 10 days, but merits much more time. For those determined to go slow, detours abound, not to mention a flurry of islands.

HILL-TOP HAPPY   Five Days/Monteriggioni to Perugia

There's no finer than the justifiably famous, walled medieval stronghold of **Monteriggioni** (p252) and **Volterra** (p261), a pretty run due west where lunch beckons. Then follow the crowd to **San Gimignano** (p254), your overnight stop, along the picturesque back road (p261). Next morning, abandon your vehicle in lower **Certaldo** (p169) and ride the funicular up to the old part of town. Stroll the sights and have lunch, before putting your foot on the pedal south of Siena to vine-rich **Montalcino** (p266) and **Montepulciano** (p273) – essential musts for hill top–happy wine buffs. Taste, drink, dine and sleep well. Next day, zip to another Tuscan classic, wickedly steep **Cortona** (p305) and feast on steep medieval alleys, Renaissance art and stunning views.

Forget those aching calves. Cross into Umbria where yet more ancient stone town walls and arches slumber in the sun at **Todi** (p373), **Amelia** (p394) and **Narni** (p390). Wind your way through Terni to the SS209 and meander through the scenery mecca of the **Valnerina** (p387). Cross the mountain to **Spoleto** (p378), filled with centuries-old staircases and a Roman theatre, then hit **Trevi** (p346), mired in a mix of afternoon naps, greying olive trees and vistas of the Spoleto Valley.

Last stop, drink your way along the **Strada del Sagrantino** (trail of Sagrantino wine; p359) through the impossibly charming wine towns of **Montefalco** (p344), **Bevagna** (p345) and **Spello** (p341), then make your way to the most cosmopolitan of preserved hill-top towns, **Perugia** (p318).

It might be one relentlessly giddying zig-zag up and down, up and down, but this hill-top tour – 530km in all – rewards with stunning vistas, superb motoring, sensational dining and more history than you can ever absorb. For those who long never go home, there is another idyllically set agriturismo (farm stay) around every corner.

GASTRO-MOTORING IN UMBRIA   Four Days/Perugia to Orvieto

Start the day on a sweet note with a hazelnut kiss smothered in chocolate in **Perugia** (p328) and a tour of its **chocolate factory** (p324). Lunch and play away the afternoon on Lake Trasimeno where **Castiglione del Lago's La Cantina** (p361) dishes up local specialities fish, *fagiolina* (white beans) and tasting (olive-oil and wine); or consider dropping in to Umbria's most famous winemaking family in **Torgiano** (p331). Come dusk, the **world's first hotel dedicated to chocolate** (p326), with its choc-fuelled restaurant and shop selling choco-gadgets as well as the real thing, ensures sweet dreams – although nearby **Relais Borgo Brufa** (p329), with its spa and sensuous restaurant, is less twee.

Swill, sniff and spit the next morning away in **Montefalco's enoteche** or well-known **Arnaldo Caprai** (p344) winery in search of the perfect red Sagrantino, then set aside several hours for lunch with **Salvatore** (p329) in **Foligno** (p347). Spend the smidgen of afternoon remaining in slow-city **Trevi** (p346) savouring Italy's best olive oil and tracking down **black celery** (p66).

Ciangiale (wild boar) in the **Valnerina** (p387) are mad about black truffles. Feast on both around **Norcia** (p383); **Ristorante Piermarini** (p329) is a tasty address and runs cooking classes to boot. For vegetarians, **Castelluccio** (p387), with its delicately thin-skinned lentils and hearty cuisine based on locally grown lentils, spelt and ricotta cheese, is an obvious overnight stop; **Locanda dè Senari** (p387) has beds and tucker.

Looping southwest, there are sweet *fichi girotti* (fig and chocolate snack) to salivate over in **Amelia** (p394) and Orvieto Classico to taste/buy by the barrelful in **Orvieto** (p364).

Eating your way around Umbria on this 450km-long itinerary touches the very best of Italy's green heart. Linger a little in this untamed land and you're quite likely to fall quite madly in love, not to mention loosen your belt a notch.

TAILORED TRIPS

WORLD HERITAGE SITES

The region has its fair share of world gems. Start with a serious slug of Renaissance splendour in the historic heart of **Florence** (p92), then head towards **Pisa** (p182), where that oh-so-famous Leaning Tower is but one of a trio of heady medieval masterpieces on Piazza dei Miracoli. Head southeast next, stopping off in **Volterra** (p51) should you fancy a spot of non-Heritage DIY discovery (track down that mad old asylum with its hidden wall carvings), en route to **San Gimignano** (p254). Stay until the crowds get too much in this tourist-packed hilltop town then hightail it to the historic centre of **Siena** (p235), where the Gothic treats of this city with its famous Piazza del Campo deserve at least two days. **Pienza** (p271) by contrast, is a tiny jewel of a village so small you can walk from one end to another in just 15 minutes. Take a cultural breather in the gentle countryside of **Val d'Orcia** (p270), then head south to **Assisi** (p334) and its spiritual orgy of medieval masterpieces, especially magic at dusk after the coach tour has left.

FINE WINE

If you don't get further than **Florence** (p92), you'll still get some great tipples at the city's plethora of *enoteche* (wine bars); **Enoteca Pinchiorri** (p144) is deemed the crème de la crème of Florentine wine bars (prices to match). For tasting between vines, follow the **Strada dei Vini Chianti Rùfina** (p165) east of Florence or bear south to another part of **Il Chianti** (p164); tasting like crazy in **Le Cantine di Greve in Chianti** (p164) and touring the historic wine cellars of Tuscany's most famous wine-making family in **Badia di Passignano** (p166) are highlights. The Ricasoli family's **Castello di Brolio** (p168) – a real castle – is pretty famous, too.

Weave your way southeast to **Massa Marittima** (p282), surrounded by vineyards, and treat your wine cellar to a couple of bottles of Vino Monteregio. From here, it's a hop to **San Gimignano** (p254), with its wine museum and licking, biting, thrusting, stinging **Vernaccia** (p258). Nearby, in **Montalcino** (p266) excruciatingly velvety Brunello is stashed in a fortress. Next stop: **Montepulciano** (p273), home of the deliciously snooty Vino Nobile, which you can try at several cellars.

Southeast is Umbria's main wine-producing area of **Torgiano** (p331), south of Perugia. Look for the aromatic Rubesco Riserva, one of Italy's finest wines.

This trip is recommended by car and, as it involves countless hectolitres of vino, with a designated driver.

History

Any truthful account of Tuscan and Umbrian life over the past three millennia is more than just a history – it's an opera, and we're all still humming its tune. You're probably already familiar with its famous libretto, which goes something like this:

I Drinking gives way to nefarious intrigues
II Debauchers denounce their wicked ways and promise reform
III Tragedy meets heroism and beasts find beauty
IV Offence is taken and treasures stolen
V Ideals are lost, found and misplaced
VI The cast gathers on stage for an encore

No overture is needed; the action is already well under way.

WINE, WOMEN & THE OPEN ROAD

Italy's oldest known wine is Chianti Classico, with favourable reviews from way back in the 14th century and a growing region clearly defined by 1716.

No one knows exactly why the ancient Etruscans headed to Tuscany and Umbria from parts east (probably Anatolia) in the 9th century BC, but Etruscan artefacts give some idea why they stayed: dinner. The wild boar that still roam the hills of Umbria and Tuscany were a favourite Etruscan menu item, and boar hunts are a recurring theme on Etruscan ceramics, tomb paintings, even bronze hand mirrors. Just in case the odd boar bristle might tickle the throat or a truffle shaving might head down the windpipe, Etruscans washed their meals down with plenty of wine, introducing viticulture to Italy.

Tomb paintings show Etruscan women keeping pace with men in banquets so decadent, they scandalised even orgy-happy Romans. Many middle-class and aristocratic women had the means to do what they wished, which apparently included music, romance, politics and ordering about a vast underclass of servants. Roman military histories boast of conquests of Etruscan women along with Etruscan territory starting in the 3rd century BC, but these accounts are probably exaggerated. According to recent genetic tests, Etruscans did not mingle much with their captors – their genetic material is distinct from modern Italians, the descendants of ancient Romans.

Etruscans didn't take kindly to Roman authority, nor were they keen on being enslaved to establish Roman plantations. They secretly allied with Hannibal to bring about the ignominious defeat of the Romans at Lake Trasimeno, where some 16,000 Roman soldiers were lost in about three hours. Afterwards Rome began to take a more hands-off approach with the Etruscans, granting them citizenship in 88 BC to manage their own affairs in the new provinces of Umbria and Tuscia (Tuscany), and in return securing safe passage along the major inland Roman trade route of Via Flaminia.

TIMELINE

9th century BC	265 BC	59 BC
Etruscans bring wine, women and song to the hills of Tuscany and Umbria, but fail to invite the Romans; war ensues	Etruria falls to Rome, but remains unruly and conspires with Hannibal against Rome during the Punic wars; Roman headaches are solved by making Etruscans Roman citizens in 88 BC	After winning an election by ballot box–stuffing means that would make the Bush administration seem honest, Julius Caesar establishes a soldier-retiree resort called Florentia

Little did the Romans suspect when they paved the road that they were also paving the way for their own replacements in the 5th to 8th centuries AD: first came German emperor Theodoric, then Byzantine Emperor Justinian, then the Lombards and finally Charlemagne in 800.

MAROZIA & MATILDA: HOW TO MAKE (& BREAK) POPES

Social standing was hard to maintain with medieval power constantly changing hands, but a couple of women managed to pull it off. The daughter of a Roman senator and a notorious prostitute-turned-senatrix, Marozia already had one illegitimate son by her lover Pope Sergius III and was pregnant again when she married the Lombard Duke of Spoleto, Alberic I in 909 AD. He was hardly scrupulous himself: he'd achieved his position by murdering the previous duke, and soon had Sergius III deposed. When Alberic was killed in turn, Marozia married Guy of Tuscany and conspired with him to smother Pope John X and install (in lethally rapid succession) Pope Leo VI and Stephen VIII.

After Guy's death, she wooed his half-brother Hugh of Arles, the new King of Italy. No matter that he was already married: by then Marozia's son had been named Pope John XI, and Hugh's previous marriage was soon annulled. But at the wedding ceremony, the happy couple was arrested by the Marozia's son, Alberic II, who was reportedly scandalised that his mother and grandmother had turned the papacy into a 'pornocracy'. Marozia spent the rest of her life in prison, but her legacy lived on: no less than five popes were her direct descendants.

Another woman who wielded power effectively despite frequent medieval power shifts was Countess Matilda of Tuscany (1046–1115). Rumour has it that she was more than just an ally to Pope Gregory VII, but there's no doubt that she was a formidable strategist on and off the battlefield. To consolidate her family's Tuscan holdings, she married her own stepbrother, Godfrey the Hunchback. She soon arranged for him to be sent off to Germany, annulled the marriage, and found herself a powerful prince 26 years her junior to marry.

When Matilda's ally Pope Gregory VII excommunicated Holy Roman Emperor Henry IV in 1077 for threatening to replace him with an Antipope, the emperor showed up outside her castle barefoot and kneeling in the snow to beg the pope's forgiveness – and Matilda kept him waiting there for three days. Henry retaliated by conspiring with Matilda's neighbours to seize her property, and even turned her trophy husband against her – but Matilda soon dislodged Henry's power base in the north with the support of his son Conrad. Henry's wife also joined the feud, claiming that her husband had forced her to participate in orgies and satanic rituals. In 1106 Henry died disgraced by his own family and humbled on the battlefield by a woman, and was left buried in unconsecrated ground until his term of excommunication was revoked. Matilda outlived him by nine years, and at her death

Learn to speak Etruscan at Etruscology Online: http://www.etruskisch .de/pgs/vc.htm. Favourite words: *netshvis* (a fortune-teller who reads animal entrails) and *thuta* (which can mean either 'chaste' or 'only married once').

AD 476	570–774	773–74
German king Odovacar (aka Odoacer) snatches Rome out from under Romulus Augustulus, and becomes the first of many foreign kings of Italy	The Lombards rule Italy as far south as Florence, and manage to turn the tiny Duchy of Spoleto into a booming trade empire	Charlemagne makes his move on Italy, and grants himself the modest title Holy Roman Emperor with a crown to match on Christmas Day in 800 AD

left behind her substantial holdings to the Church, a line that would claim among its descendants one Michelangelo Buonarroti, and mortal remains to be interred at St Peter's in Rome. Her husband never remarried, and died childless not long after Matilda.

AGONY & ECSTASY

Lashings, starvation, solitary confinement: in the middle ages, it wasn't always easy to distinguish religious practices from criminal punishments. Among the privileged classes it became a mark of distinction to renounce worldly ties for a life of piety – not to mention a handy way to winnow the number of eligible heirs to a title. A nobleman from Norcia named Benedict set the example and started a monastery-building spree in AD 500, when he ditched his studies to seek a higher purpose among hermits in the hills. His rule of peace, prayer and work was taken up by Benedictine religious orders, which limited food intake and downtime but didn't require the vows of silence, fasting or hard labour practised by more hermetic believers. Some Benedictine orders even had help tilling their fields from tenant farmers and hired workers, freeing up monks for reading and creative tasks like manuscript illumination and wine-making. Benedictine communities were founded by noble patrons, such as the widowed *margravise* (marquise) Willa of Tuscany, who in 978 founded Badia Fiorentina, Florence's first abbey (p108).

But not all medieval monks and nuns whiled away the hours with a good book and a nice glass of wine. 'Hair shirts' woven of scratchy sackcloth, horsehair or chain mail became all the rage among the aristocracy after Holy Roman Emperor Charlemagne (c AD 742–814) was buried in his. The first known case of religious self-flagellation dates from the mid-13th century in Perugia, when a strange spontaneous parade of believers began whipping themselves while singing. By 1260 roving bands of Flagellants appeared in major cities across Umbria and Tuscany, stripped to the waist, hooded and ecstatically whipping themselves while singing *laudi*, songs about the passion of Christ. They made quite an impression in Florence, Siena and Gubbio, where adherents formed *scuole di battuti* (schools of beatings) to build Case di Dio (Houses of God) that served as charity centres and hospices and also hosted mass flagellation sessions using specialised equipment.

The sudden popularity of mortification of the flesh may be tied to the popular outpouring of grief at the death of St Francis of Assisi in 1226 – legend has it that even his trusty donkey wept to see him go. Although he did practise strict poverty and periodic fasting and wore chafing friar's robes, the gentle Francis was apparently too preoccupied with caring for the sick, needy and animals to make a conspicuous display of his own personal suffering, even when going blind.

The Church remained neutral on the issue until the fledgling Flagellants claimed that like scratching an itch, their activities could grant temporary relief from sin. This posed direct competition for the Church's practice

The undisputed master of pious masochism was Umbrian Benedictine monk San Domenico Loricato, who in a single week is said to have all but flayed himself with 300,000 lashes while reciting psalms.

1082	1084	1136
Florence picks a fight with Siena over ownership of the Chianti region, starting a bitter rivalry that will last the next 400 years – sure, it sounds extreme, but there was some really good wine at stake	Henry IV gets himself crowned Holy Roman Emperor by a specially appointed Antipope, only to be scolded by Countess Matilda of Tuscany that it doesn't count, and he'd better apologise	Scrappy seafaring Pisa adds Amalfi to its conquests, which also included Jerusalem, Valencia, Tripoli and Mallorca, plus colonies in Constantinople and Cairo, among others

of confession, not to mention its steady business in indulgences, pardons and tithes. The Flagellant movement was banned in 1262, only to regain momentum a century later during the plague and recur periodically until the 15th century, when the Inquisition subjected Flagellants to the ultimate mortification of the flesh: burning at the stake. But self-flagellation processions continued to be held in Tuscany under the Church's guidance into the late 19th century, and self-flagellation continues to be practised privately by zealous penitents today.

DEMOCRACY AMONG DEVIANTS

Not all agony came with a side order of religious ecstasy in medieval Tuscany and Umbria. Legal records indicate that no one was exempt from violence: leaders of powerful families were stabbed by rivals while attending Mass, peasants were ambushed by brigands roaming the deceptively bucolic landscape and bystanders were maimed in neighbourhood disputes that all too easily escalated to kill-or-be-killed brawls.

But if crime seemed vicious, medieval criminal justice was often worse. Even petty crimes such as theft were subject to some combination of steep fines, corporal punishment and public humiliation, such as public flogging or mutilation. Nobles could demand satisfaction for the rather capriciously defined crime of *laesa maiestas*, or insulting nobility, but an alarming number skipped such legal niceties and kidnapped or suffocated the children of their rivals instead. Jails were rare, since suspects received only cursory trials and incarceration was deemed insufficient to extract true penitence. The earliest known jail in the region (and among the first in Europe) was Le Stinche prison, founded in Florence in 1297. Niccolò Machiavelli (1469–1527) endured six rounds of interrogation on Le Stinche's notorious rack for an alleged plot to overthrow the government, and amazingly survived to describe the place. Apparently Stinche was indeed stinky, and also swarming with vermin that attacked shackled prisoners waiting their turn at the rack.

By the 13th century, many Tuscan and Umbrian communities were plenty ready for change. Farmers who had painstakingly reclaimed their fields wanted to get their produce to market alive, merchants needed peaceful piazzas to conduct their business and the populace at large began to entertain hopes of living past age 40. *Comuni* (town councils) were established in cities and towns such as Gubbio, Siena and Perugia, with representatives drawn from influential families, guilds and the merchant classes in a new power-sharing arrangement. Across Umbria and Tuscany, ambitious building projects were undertaken to give citizens a new sense of shared purpose and civic identity. Hospitals and public charities helped serve the city's needy, and new public squares, marketplaces and town halls became crucial meeting places and testing grounds for civic society. Law and order was kept (relatively speaking) by a podesta, an independent judiciary often brought in from outside the city for limited terms of office to prevent corruption.

Born an Assisi heiress, introduced to the joys of poverty by St Francis himself and cofounder of the first Franciscan abbey, St Clare gained another claim to fame in 1958 as the patron saint of TV.

Il Principe (The Prince) is Niccolò Machiavelli's allegory of absolute power – but was it a cautionary tale against the Medici who'd had him tortured for suspected treason, or an instructional manual to get back in the Medici good graces? Five centuries later, the debate continues.

1167	1223	1314–21
The *comune* (town council) of Siena establishes a written constitution, declaring that elected terms should be short and money should be pretty; it's soon amended to guarantee Sienese public boxing matches	Franciscan order founded in Assisi, with strict vows of poverty and lifelong manual labour requirements – and monasteries are soon overflowing with new recruits	Dante Alighieri makes a classical allegory shockingly modern in his *Divina Commedia*, told in the first person and the familiar Tuscan dialect instead of the usual formal Latin, and peppered with political satire, pathos, adventure and light humour

'Book curses' in the margins of medieval library books warned borrowers that failure to return a book was a grave offence, subject to fatal attacks of giant bookworms and eternal damnation.

Each *comune* (town council) developed its own style of government, but the most imaginative was Siena. To curb bloody turf battles among its *contrade* (neighbourhoods), Siena channelled that fighting spirit into organised boxing matches, bullfights and Il Palio, the annual horse race still run today (see the boxed text, p246). Anyone who broke the peace was subject to heavy fines, and the city's coffers soon swelled with monies collected for cursing in the city's *osterie* (pubs). After Florence won yet another battle against Siena by cutting off the town's water supply, Siena's *comune* was faced with a funding choice: either build an underground aqueduct to fend off Florence, or build a cathedral that would establish Siena as a creative capital of the medieval world. The council voted unanimously for the cathedral. Work began almost immediately in 1215 and continued for more than three centuries, through bouts of famine, banking disasters and plague that nearly wiped out the city. But from these dark days emerged a magnificent Duomo and an expressive, eerily glowing style of painting known as the Sienese School, which is recognised as a precocious precursor to the Renaissance.

DISASTERS & SAVING GRACES

'Midway on our life's journey, I found myself in dark woods, the right road lost…' So begins the ominous year 1300 in Dante Alghieri's *Inferno*, where our hero Dante escapes from one circle of hell only to tumble into the next. Gloomy? Certainly – but also uncannily accurate. In the 14th century, Dante and his fellow Tuscans would face a harrowing sequence of events, including famine, economic collapses, plague, war and tyranny. Umbrians had all this to contend with plus a series of earthquakes, not to mention lowlands that tended to revert to marsh when not diligently drained. It's no small miracle that anyone in the region survived the 14th century – but it's an even greater wonder that the early Renaissance emerged from this hellish scenario.

For Dante with a pop-culture twist, check out Sandow Birk and Marcus Sanders' satirical, slangy translation of *The Divine Comedy*, which sets *Inferno* in hellish Los Angeles traffic, *Purgatorio* in foggy San Francisco and *Paradiso* in New York.

When medieval mystics predicted that the year 1300 would bring certain doom for all but the few, they were only off by about 50 years. Half to two-thirds of the population were decimated in cities across Tuscany and Umbria in the bubonic plague outbreak of 1348, and since the carriers of the plague (fleas and rats) weren't correctly identified and eradicated, the Black Death repeatedly ravaged the area for decades afterwards. Blame for the disease was placed on the usual suspects – lepers, immigrants, gypsies, heretics, Jewish communities, women of loose morals – but no amount of scapegoating could cure the afflicted. Entire hospital and monastery populations were wiped out, leaving treatment to opportunists promising miracle cures. Indulging in flagellation, liquor, sugar or spices were prescribed, as was abstaining from bathing, fruit and olive oil – all to no avail. Florentine author and 1348 plague eyewitness Giovanni Boccaccio writes of entire families left to starve under quarantine, sick children abandoned by parents and family members hastily dumped still breathing in mass graves.

1348–50	1353–57	1375-1406
Black Death ravages Tuscany and Umbria, wiping out two-thirds to three-quarters of the population in dense urban areas, and it doesn't stop there: 40 more outbreaks are recorded in Umbria before 1500	Cardinal Gil de Albornoz exerts Church control across central Italy. Where appeals to faith fail to convince locals, he just barges in with troops and sets up a fortified castle atop the town.	Philosopher-politician Colluccio Salutati serves as chancellor of Florence, promoting a new secular civic identity to trump old feudal tendencies – a bold new model of citizenship for Europe that occasionally even works

But amid the ample evidence of human failings there were also more reassuring signs of humanity. Meals were shared, and orphans cared for by strangers. Doctors and devout clergy who cared for the sick were the most obvious heroes of the day – though they lacked the medical knowledge to save plague victims, they knowingly risked their own lives just to provide a dignified death for their patients. At age 19, St Catherine of Siena overruled her family's understandable objections and dedicated her life to serving the plague ridden. She also wrote long, eloquent letters to the pope and heads of powerful families in the region, imploring them to reconsider their warring ways and allow the troubled region a moment's peace.

MACHIAVELLI'S MANOEUVRES

Born in 1469 into a poor offshoot of one of Florence's leading families, Niccolò Machiavelli got off to a bad start. His father, an impoverished, small-time lawyer, was continually in debt, but was at least rich in books, which his son devoured.

Somehow the young Machiavelli managed to swing a post in the city's second chancery at the age of 29 and so embarked on a colourful career as a Florentine public servant. Our man must have shown early promise, as by 1500 he was in France on his first diplomatic mission in the service of the Republic.

Impressed by the martial success of Cesare Borgia and the centralised state of France, Machiavelli came to the conclusion that Florence needed a standing army.

The city, like many others on the Italian peninsula, used to employ mercenaries to fight its wars. The problem was that mercenaries had few reasons to fight and die for anyone. They took their pay and often did their best to avoid mortal combat. Machiavelli convinced the Republic of the advantages of a conscripted militia, which he formed in 1506. Three years later it was blooded in battle against the rebellious city of Pisa, whose fall was mainly attributed to the troops led by the wily statesman.

The return to power of the Medici family in 1512 was a blow for Machiavelli, who was promptly removed from office. Suspected of plotting against the Medici, he was even thrown into the dungeon in 1513 and tortured. He maintained his innocence and, once freed, retired to his little property outside Florence a poor man.

It was in these years, far from political power, that he did his greatest writing. *Il Principe (The Prince)* is his classic treatise on the nature of power and its administration, a work reflecting the confusing and corrupt times in which he lived and a desire for strong and just rule in Florence and beyond.

Machiavelli never got back into the mainstream of public life. He was commissioned to write an official history of Florence, the *Istorie Fiorentine*, and towards the end of his life he was appointed to a defence commission to improve the city walls and join a papal army in its ultimately futile fight against imperial forces. By the time the latter had sacked Rome in 1527, Florence had again rid itself of Medici rule. Machiavelli hoped that he would be restored to a position of dignity, but by now he was suspected almost as much by the Medici opponents as he had been years before by the Medici. He died in 1527 frustrated and, as in his youth, on the brink of poverty.

1378	1469–92	1478–80
The *signoria* (city government) ignores a petition from *ciompi* (wool-carders) for fairer representation: cue the Revolt of Ciompi. *Ciompi* overrun government, with numbers in minor guilds but divisions exploited by major guilds that ban *ciompi*.	Lorenzo de' Medici unofficially rules Florence, despite the 1478 Pazzi Conspiracy overthrow attempt that left his brother Giuliano torn to shreds in the Duomo. Before his death at 43, Lorenzo commissions great artistic masterpieces.	A confusing set of overlapping wars break out among the papacy, Siena, Florence, Venice, Milan and Naples, as individual families broker secret pacts and the dwindling Tuscan population pays the price

Boccaccio's *The Decameron* (1348–53) is the story of 10 young women and men who escape plague-ridden Florence, and tell bawdy, tragic and satirical tales to pass 10 days in a Tuscan villa.

Painful though those days must have been to record, writers such as Dante (1265–1321), Boccaccio (1313–75) and Marchione di Coppo Stefani (c 1336–85) wrote frank assessments of their time, believing that their critiques might one day serve the greater good. More than any painterly tricks of perspective or shading, it's this more rounded view of humanity that brought truth to Renaissance art.

Yet this legacy was nearly lost in another disaster, the 1966 Great Flood of Florence, which deluged the city with more than 4m of water, left thousands of people homeless, and buried three million rare manuscripts and thousands of works of arts under some 500,000 tonnes of mud, stone and sewage. But thousands of people arrived from across Italy and around the world to rescue the city and its treasures from the mud, and today these heroes are honoured as *gli angeli del fango* (angels of mud).

BETWEEN BELLIGERENCE & BEAUTY

Find photos of Florence's 'mud angels' in action and hear stories of survival in the aftermath of the 1966 flood at http://www.angelidelfango.it/english/index_e.html.

The Renaissance was a time of great art and great tyrants, not to mention an uneasy relationship between the two. The careful balance of power of the *comuni* became a casualty of the plague in the 14th century, since political control was mostly left to those who managed to survive and were either strong enough or unscrupulous enough to claim it. Cardinal Albornoz (1310–67) seized the moment to extend Church control across central Italy, building fortifications for new religious authorities in formerly independent secular municipalities such as Perugia. In *comuni* such as Florence and Siena, powerful families assumed control of the *signoria,* the city council ostensibly run by guild representatives and merchants.

Most unelected Renaissance rulers weren't great tyrants but rather petty ones, obsessed with accumulating personal power and wealth, and their lasting contributions to civic life were costly wars of conquest and internal strife. Cities, commercial entities and individual families took sides with either the Rome-backed Guelphs or the imperial Ghibellines, loyalists of the Holy Roman Empire. Since each of these factions was eager to put itself on the map, this competition might have meant a bonanza for artists and architects – but shifting fortunes in the battlefield meant funds for pet art projects could disappear just as quickly as they appeared.

Tuscany began to resemble a chess game, with feudal castles appearing only to be overtaken, powerful bishops aligning with nobles before being toppled and the occasional rise to power of minor players backed by key commercial interests. Nowhere was the chess game harder to follow than in the Ghibelline *comune* of Pistoia: first it was conquered by the Florentine Guelphs, then it split into White and Black Guelph splinter groups, then it was captured by Lucca before being reclaimed by the Florentines.

The Medici family were by no means exempt from the usual failings of Renaissance tyrants, but early on in his rise to power, Cosimo il Vecchio (1389–1464) revealed a surprisingly enlightened self-interest and an excep-

1494	**1498**	**1527–30**
The Medici are expelled by Charles VIII of France, and Savonarola declares a theocratic republic with his Consiglia di Cinquecento – a kind of religious Red Guard that denounces neighbours for owning books	To test Savonarola's beliefs, rival Franciscans invite him to a trial by fire. Savonarola sends a representative to be burned instead, who is saved when the event gets rained out. Instead, Savonarola is tortured, hung and burned as heretic.	Florentines run the Medici out of town, having enough of their costly wars and unelected leadership. The Republic of Florence holds out for three years, until the emperor's and pope's combined cannon power reinstalls the Medici.

tional eye for art. Although he held no elected office, he served as ambassador for the Church, and through his behind-the-scenes diplomacy skills managed to finagle a rare 25-year stretch of relative peace for Florence. When a conspiracy led by competing banking interests exiled him from Florence in 1433, some of Cosimo's favourite artists split town with him, including Donatello and Fra Angelico. But they weren't gone long: Cosimo's banking interests were too important to Florence, and he returned triumphant after just a year to crush his rivals, exert even greater behind-the-scenes control and sponsor such masterpieces as Brunelleschi's legendary dome for Florence's Duomo.

But sponsorship from even the most enlightened and powerful patrons had its downsides: their whims could make or break artists, and they attracted powerful enemies. Lorenzo de' Medici (aka Lorenzo the Magnificent; 1449–92) was a legendary supporter of the arts and humanities, providing crucial early recognition and support for Leonardo da Vinci, Sandro Botticelli and Michelangelo Buonarroti, among others. But after Lorenzo narrowly escaped an assassination attempt by a conspiracy among the rival Florentine Pazzi family, the King of Naples and the pope, the artists he supported had to look elsewhere for sponsorship until Lorenzo could regain his position. Religious reformer Savonarola took an even darker view of Lorenzo and the classically influenced art he promoted, viewing it as a sinful indulgence in a time of great need and suffering. When Savonarola ousted the Medici in 1494, he decided their decadent art had to go, too, and Botticellis, Michelangelos and other works went up in flames in massive 'bonfires of the vanities'.

THE SUN & OTHER TOUCHY SUBJECTS

Savonarola's theocratic rule over Florence lasted just four years, until his denunciation of decadence got him excommunicated and executed by Pope Alexander VI (1431–1503), who didn't appreciate Savonarola critiquing his extravagant spending, illegitimate children and pursuit of personal vendettas. But Savonarola's short reign would have an impact on Tuscany and Umbria for centuries to come. The church now saw the need to exert more direct control over the independent-minded region, and guard against humanist philosophies that might contradict the Church's divine authority. The Inquisition made heretical ideas punishable by death, which had an understandably chilling effect on intellectual inquiry. The celebrated universities in Pisa, Perugia and Siena were subject to close scrutiny, and the University of Pisa was effectively closed for about 50 years until Cosimo I de' Medici reinaugurated it in 1543.

One of the most notable faculty members at the revitalised University of Pisa was a professor of mathematics named Galileo Galilei (1564–1642). To put it in mathematical terms, Galileo was a logical paradox: a Catholic who fathered three illegitimate children; a man of science with a poetic streak, who lectured on the dimensions of hell according to Dante's *Inferno*; and an

In *The Rise and Fall of the House of Medici*, Christopher Hibbert takes on the Medici in all their might, melodrama and dastardly genius – don't expect much on the artists they sponsored beyond namedropping, though.

The Medici have nothing to hide – at least, not anymore. Dig your own dirt on Florence's dynamic dynasty in the archives at www .medici.org.

1571	1633	1656
Painters are no longer obliged to belong to guilds, so individual artistic expression no longer means you have to pay your dues first	Galileo Galilei is condemned for heresy in Rome, over the objections of Europe's nascent scientific community. True to Galileo's observations of a pendulum in motion, the Inquisition's extreme measures yielded an opposite reaction: Enlightenment.	Oh no, not again: the plague kills at least 300,000 people across central and southern Italy; roughly three times as many as are killed in the 1655–66 Great Plague of London

Explore Galileo's life, times, religious context and scientific advances at The Galileo Project: http://galileo.rice.edu.

He needed that one for the Inquisitors: see Galileo's preserved middle finger in Florence's Museum of the History of Science (p111).

inventor of telescopes whose head was quite literally in the clouds, yet who kept in close contact with many friends who were the leading intellectuals of their day.

Galileo's meticulous observations of the physical universe attracted the attention of the Church, which by the 16th century had a conflicted relationship to the stars. Pope Paul III kept several astrologers on hand, and no major papal initiative or construction project could be undertaken without first searching the sky with an astrolabe for auspicious signs. Yet theologian (and sometime astrologer) Tomasso Campanella was found guilty of heresy for dissenting views that emphasised observation. Research into the universe's guiding physical principles was entrusted by Paul III to his consulting theologians, who determined from close examination of the scriptures that the sun must revolve around the earth.

Equipped with telescopes that he'd adjusted and improved, Galileo came to a different conclusion. His observations supported Nicolaus Copernicus' theory that the planets revolved around the sun, and a cautious body of Vatican Inquisitors initially allowed him to publish his findings as long as he also presented a case for the alternate view. But when Galileo's research turned out to be dangerously convincing, the Vatican reversed its position and tried him for heresy. By then Galileo was quite ill, and his weakened state and widespread support may have spared him the usual heresy sentence of execution. Under official threat of torture, Galileo stated in writing that he may have overstated the case for the Copernican view of the universe, and was allowed carry out his prison sentence under house arrest. Pope Urban VIII alternately indulged his further studies and denied him access to doctors, but Galileo kept on pursuing scientific research even after he began losing his sight. Meanwhile, Tomasso Campanella was taken out of prison and brought to Rome, where he became Urban VIII's personal astrologer in 1629.

GOING FOR BAROQUE

With his astrologers on hand, the pope might have seen Italy's foreign domination coming. Far from cementing the Church's authority, the Inquisition created a power vacuum on the ground while papal authorities were otherwise occupied with lofty theological matters. While local Italian nobles and successful capitalists vied among themselves for influence as usual, the Austrian Holy Roman Empress Maria Theresa took charge of the situation in 1737, and set up her husband Francis as the Grand Duke of Tuscany.

The mother of 16 children (including the now-notorious Marie Antoinette) and self-taught military strategist soon put local potentates in check, and pushed through reforms that curbed witch burning, outlawed torture, established mandatory education and allowed Italian peasants to keep a modest share of their crops. She also brought the Habsburgs' signature flashy style to Tuscany and Umbria, and kicked off a frenzy of redecoration with flamboyant frescoes packed with cherubs, ornate architectural details that

1737	1765–90	1796–1801
Maria Theresa makes her move on the Medici, and ends their dynastic rule by installing her husband Francis of Lorraine as Grand Duke of Tuscany. She remains the brains of the operation, reforming and bilking Tuscany from behind the scenes.	Enlightenment leader Leopold I continues his mother's reforms in Tuscany. Moved by Cesare Beccaria's case for criminal justice reform in *On Crime and Punishment*, Leopold makes Tuscany the first sovereign state to outlaw the death penalty.	Italy becomes a battleground between Napoleon, the Habsburgs and their Russian allies, and Tuscans and Umbrians witness much of their cultural patrimony divvied up as spoils of war

are surely a nightmare to dust, and gilding whenever and wherever possible. Perhaps fearing that her family's priceless art collection might factor into Maria Theresa's redecorating plans, Medici heiress Anna Maria Luisa de' Medici willed everything to the city of Florence upon her death in 1743, on the condition that it all must remain in the city.

Naturally the glint of gold captured the attention of Napoleon Bonaparte, who took over swathes of Tuscany and Umbria in 1799. So appreciative was Napoleon of the area's cultural heritage, in fact, that he decided to take as much as possible home with him. The rest he gave as gifts to various relatives – never mind that all those Tuscan villas and church altarpieces were not technically his to give. When Habsburg Ferdinando III took over the title of Grand Duke of Tuscany in 1814, Napoleon's sister Elisa Bonaparte and various other relations refused to budge from the luxe Luccan villas they had usurped, and concessions had to be made to accommodate them all.

Still more upscale expats arrived in Tuscany and Umbria with the inauguration of Italy's cross-country train lines in 1840. Soon no finishing-school education would be complete without a Grand Tour of Italy, and the landmarks and museums of Tuscany and Umbria were required reading. Trainloads of debutantes, dour chaperones and career bachelors arrived, setting the stage for EM Forster novels, Tuscan timeshare investors and George Clooney wannabes.

> To see a complete list of the alleged P2 members found on Licio Gelli's Rolodex in 1981, see http://www.namebase .org/sources/dE.html.

RED & BLACK: A CHEQUERED PAST

While an upper-crust expat community was exporting Romantic notions about Italy, the country was facing some harsh realities. Commercial agriculture provided tidy sums to absentee royal Austrian landlords, but reduced peasants to poverty and created stiff competition for small family farms. In rural areas, three-quarters of the family income was spent on a meagre diet of mostly grains. The promise of work in the burgeoning industrial sector lured many to cities, where long working hours and dangerous working conditions seemed another dead end: 70% of family income was still spent on food. Upward mobility was rare, since university admissions were strictly limited, and the Habsburgs were cautious about allowing locals into their imperial army or bureaucratic positions. Increasingly, the most reliable means for Tuscans and Umbrians to support their families was emigration to the Americas.

Austrian rule provided a common enemy that, for once, united Italians across provinces and classes. The Risorgimento (reunification period) was not so much a reorganisation of some previously unified Italian state (which hadn't existed since Roman times) as a revival of city-state ideals of an independent citizenry. The secret societies that had flourished right under the noses of the French as a local check on colonial control soon formed a network of support for nationalist sentiment. In 1848-49 revolution broke

1805–14	**1860**	**1915**
Napoleon establishes himself as King of Italy, with the military assistance of Italian soldiers he'd conscripted yearly since 1802 – but when fortunes turn and conscripts desert, Napoleon loses Tuscany to Grand Duke Ferdinando III in 1814	Two decades of insurrections culminate in a new Italian government, with a parliament and a king. Florence becomes Italy's capital in 1865, despite extensive poverty and periodic bread riots; the capital moves to Rome in 1871.	Italy enters WWI fighting a familiar foe: the Austro-Hungarian Empire. War casualties, stranded POWs, heating oil shortages and food rationing make for a hard-won victory by 1917.

out, and a radical government was temporarily installed in Florence. Nervous that Austrians would invade, conservative Florentine leaders invited Habsburg Leopold II to return as Archduke of Tuscany (1797–1870, Grand Duke of Tuscany from 1824 to 1859). But when rural unrest in Tuscany made Austria's return to power difficult, Austrian retaliation and brutal repression galvanised nationalist sentiment in the region. Although the country was united under one flag in 1861, that early split decision between radicals and conservatives would define the region's political landscape in the years ahead.

Unification didn't end unemployment or unrest, since only 2% of Italy's population gained the right to vote in 1861 – the same 2% that controlled most of the country's wealth. Strikes were held across the country to protest working conditions, and their brutal suppression gave rise to a new Socialist Party in 1881. The new Italian government's money-making scheme to establish itself as a colonial power in Ethiopia and Eritrea proved a costly failure – 17,000 Italian soldiers were lost near Adowa in 1896, in the worst defeat by any European colonial power in Africa. When grain prices were

BEYOND SECRET HANDSHAKES

With so many despots and inquisitors constantly within earshot, 17th-century Italians had to watch their words – let slip a tax complaint or scientific fact and you might end up charged with treason or heresy. Hence the initial appeal of secret societies, where early Enlightenment thinkers could speak freely among like-minded people without fear of reprisal. Freemasonry is one of the better-known secret societies to take root in Enlightenment-era Italy, but the group's inner workings remain murky today. Initially membership was secret, meetings were clandestine and cloaked in ritual, records were written in code, and members took strict loyalty oaths to protect the proceedings and fellow members. Papal authorities banned Freemasonry in 1738 and an Italian variant known as the Carbonari in 1821, assuming (not incorrectly) that secret societies were fomenting opposition to theocratic and imperial dictates.

But after the new Italian Republic was established, a new secret society was founded in 1877 called Propaganda Due, or P2. In the years after WWII, members took it upon themselves to define a new direction for Italy that looked eerily like its old one under Fascism. According to documents found by police in a 1981 raid of the home of Tuscan banker, P2 leader and former Blackshirt Licio Gelli, the 'plan for democratic rebirth' involved suppressing trade unions and civil liberties and consolidating the media to promote a unified national outlook. Police also found a P2 membership list that included some familiar names: members of Parliament, heads of Italy's secret services, journalists and one Silvio Berlusconi. Pursued on charges of bank fraud and implicated in the 'strategy of tension' that terrorised Italy during the 1970s, Gelli escaped to Switzerland, where he was found but escaped from prison. He fled to South America, where he had friends among the Argentine military junta. Finally he gave himself up in 1987 in Switzerland and was extradited to Italy, where he was sentenced to 12 years for embezzlement. He then fled to the French Riviera, but was extradited from France in 1998 to serve his sentence.

1921	1940–43	1943–45
Mussolini forms the Fascist Party, and Tuscan supporters fall in line by 1922. The 1924 elections are 'overseen' by Fascist *squadristi*, and Fascists win a Parliamentary majority.	The Fascist Italian Empire joins Axis ally Germany in declaring war on Great Britain and France. Italy loses battles abroad and at home before surrendering in 1943 – but Mussolini refuses to comply, and war continues.	The Italian Resistance joins Allied Forces in fighting Mussolini's forces and the Nazis, and with Allied forces liberates Tuscany in 1944. When Italy's civil warfare ends in 1945, a coalition government is formed and the monarchy abolished.

raised in 1898, many impoverished Italians could no longer afford to buy food, and riots broke out. Rural workers unionised, and when a strike was called in 1902, 200,000 rural labourers came out en masse.

Finally, Italian politicians began to take the hint, and initiated some reforms. Child labour was banned, working hours were set and the right to vote was extended to all men over 30 by 1912 (women would have to wait for their turn at the polls until 1945). But right after the government promised the Socialists to fund an old-age pension scheme, it reneged, and opted to invade Tunisia instead. Then Italy got more war than it had budgeted for in 1914, when WWI broke out. A young Socialist firebrand named Mussolini led the call for Italy to intervene, though most Socialists were opposed.

By 1917, Italy had won the war, but few Italians were in the mood to celebrate. In addition to war casualties, 600,000 Italians served time as prisoners of war (POWs), and 100,000 died due primarily to the Italian government's failure to send food, clothing and medical supplies to its own soldiers. Wartime decrees that extended working hours and outlawed strikes had made factory conditions so deplorable that women led mass strikes even under penalty of prison. Bread shortages spread nationwide, along with bread riots. Mussolini found support for his call to order in the Tuscan countryside, and by 1922 his black-shirted squads could be seen parading through Florence, echoing Mussolini's call for the ouster of his former colleagues and the purging of communists.

But no amount of purging prevented the country from plunging into recession in the 1930s after Mussolini demanded (and obtained) a revaluation of the Italian *lira*. While the free fall of wages won Mussolini allies among industrialists, it created further desperation among his power base. New military conquests in Libya and Ethiopia initially provided a feeble boost to the failing economy, but when the enormous bill came due in the late 1930s, Mussolini hastily agreed to an economic and military alliance with Germany. Contrary to the bold claims of Mussolini's propaganda machine, Italy was ill prepared for the war it entered in 1940.

A powerful Resistance movement soon emerged in Mussolini's former stomping grounds in the Tuscan countryside – tragically, not soon enough to prevent hundreds of thousands of Italian casualties, plus an as-yet-unknown number of Italians shipped off to 23 Italian concentration camps (including one near Arezzo) and death camps in Germany. A new Italian government surrendered to the Allies in 1943, but Mussolini refused to concede defeat, and dragged Italy through two more years of civil war, Allied campaigns and German occupation. Tuscany and Umbria emerged from these black years redder than ever, and Tuscany in particular became a staunch Socialist power base – though later government investigations would reveal that Fascists lingered on in the ranks of bureaucracy well into the 1970s.

Lion of the Desert (1981) follows two decades of resistance to Mussolini's occupation of Libya, with an international cast headed by Anthony Quinn as resistance leader Omar Mukhtar, filmed entirely in Libya by Syrian-American director Moustapha Akkad.

1946	**1959–63**	**1969**
In a hotly contested vote, a national referendum establishes a republic and ousts the Italian monarchy, which had enabled Mussolini's rise to power and briefly rallied under metrosexual Umberto II and his leftist wife Marie-José	Italy's Economic Miracle revives post-war economy via industrialisation, entrepreneurship and US Marshall Plan investments to stop Italy from joining the Soviet Bloc. Florence revives its textile industry and becomes Italy's first fashion capital.	Mass strikes of the *autunno caldo* (hot autumn) join ongoing university student uprisings demanding social change, and promote sweeping reforms not just in working conditions but also housing, social services, pensions and civil rights.

THE BIKER, THE FRIAR & THE ACCOUNTANT

Unbelievable though it may sound, this trio became heroes of the Italian Resistance. Giorgio Nissim was a Jewish accountant in Pisa who belonged to a secret Tuscan Resistance group helping Jewish Italians escape from Fascist Italy. The network was discovered by the Fascists, and everyone involved was sent to concentration camps except Giorgio, who was never discovered. It seemed nowhere was safe for Jewish refugees – until Franciscan friar Rufino Niccacci helped organise the Assisi Underground, which hid hundreds of Jewish refugees from all over Italy in convents and monasteries across Umbria in 1943–44. In Assisi nuns who'd never met anyone Jewish before learned to cook kosher meals for their guests, and locals risked their lives to provide shelter to total strangers.

The remaining problem was how to get forged travel documents to the refugees, and quick. Enter Gino Bartali, world-famous Tuscan cyclist, Tour de France winner and three-time champion of the Giro d'Italia. After his death in 2003, documents revealed that during his 'training rides' during the war years, Bartali had carried Resistance intelligence and falsified documents to transport Jewish refugees to safe locations. Suspected of involvement, Bartali was once interrogated at the dreaded Villa Triste in Florence, where political prisoners were held and tortured – but he revealed nothing. Until his death he refused to discuss his efforts to save Jewish refugees even with his children, saying, 'One does these things, and then that's that'.

ONCE MORE, WITH FEELING

Today the region's true colours are neither red nor black, but more of a trendy neutral. Since Silvio Berlusconi's right-wing government was ousted in 2006 by the centrist coalition government led by Romano Prodi, the region seems to have joined the rest of the country in wait-and-see mode.

Granted, both Tuscany and Umbria still have their dark sides. Italy's postwar economic miracle brought an influx of wealth but also unregulated real estate developments to these rolling hills, and the violent activities of neo-Fascist and Red Brigade operatives in the area during the Anni di Piombo (Years of Lead) still cast a long shadow over today's political scene. The Mani Pulite (Clean Hands) task force charged with exposing connections between politicians and mafia figures after the Tangentopoli (Bribesville) scandal of 1992 are still at it today, thanks to the delaying tactics of Silvio Berlusconi and other implicated politicians.

But if the history of Tuscany and Umbria is an opera, the last verse is a coda. Today agriculture and travel are once again the defining features of the region, just as they were three millennia ago – and just like way back then, you never know who'll take the stage next.

In 1993, a car bomb at the Uffizi killed five people. The Mafia was suspected, but never successfully indicted. That year 200,000 people protested Mafia violence, demanding reform through the Mani Pulite (Clean Hands) task force.

1970s-80s	1993	2006
The *Anni di Piombo* (Years of Lead) terrorise the country with extremist violence and reprisals; police kill anarchist Franco Serantini in a 1972 protest in Pisa, and Red Brigades kill Florence's mayor Lando Conti in 1986	A string of Mafia-motivated bombings that killed five people and caused US$10 million damage to irreplaceable works of art in Florence's Uffizi galvanises the country against Mafia and spurs Mani Pulite (Clean Hands) reformers	Romano Prodi's centrist government defeats Berlusconi's right-wing coalition. After 12 years of power, corruption, scandals and unpopular moves (such as supporting war in Iraq), Berlusconi is ousted from government but still operates his media empire.

Art & Architecture

Renaissance palazzo city halls in Poland, Tuscan villa restaurants in Macau and American refrigerators studded with magnets of Michelangelo's *David* dressed in a Hawaiian shirt: the cultural influence of Tuscany and Umbria is such a given that it's hard to imagine how our world might have looked otherwise. What if these hill-top towns hadn't been founded, town hall meetings were never convened, villas had seemed like too much upkeep and nobles decided to show off by throwing a party instead of commissioning art? There might be less democracy on display, fewer masterpieces to stretch our imaginations and a whole lot more Paris Hilton (perish the thought).

The treasury of architectural styles and artistic expression that is Tuscany and Umbria was not the work of one supremely enlightened dictator or artistic genius, but a motley cast of characters worthy of its own fresco cycle. Picture it: party boys get religion and found monasteries; peasants storm castles and demand their basic rights, plus sewage systems and public art; squadrons of artists stay up all night working pigment and fresh ideas into wet plaster; and religious authorities become their biggest fans and worst enemies. All this attracts admirers to the area and its art and architecture, which Napoleon's troops decided made nice souvenirs and Mussolini's minions agreed should be the template for the new Italy – minus a few centuries' worth of architectural details.

But improbably enough, the region's art and architecture survived plague, war, Fascism, earthquakes and a rather nasty rash of post-war housing projects. In small towns, cathedrals and municipal museums across the region, unfold the story of a people whose stubborn independent mindedness and ingenuity bordering on insanity left a legacy like none other.

ELEGANT DEATH: THE ETRUSCANS

About 2800 years before you started dreaming of a hill-top getaway in Tuscany or Umbria, the Etruscans had a similar idea. Dotting the countryside are hill-top towns (p25) founded by the Etruscans to keep a watchful eye on their crops below – and their neighbours across the valley. Perugia has kept much of its character as an Etruscan gated community, with its Arco Etrusco (p323) in the ancient city walls and an Etruscan well in the town centre, just in case the neighbours got nasty and cut off the water supply downhill.

From the 8th to the 3rd century BC, Etruscan towns held their own against friends Romans, and countrymen, worshipped their own gods and goddesses, and farmed lowlands with sophisticated drainage systems of their own invention. How well the Etruscans lived between sieges and war is unclear, but they sure knew how to throw a funeral: a wealth of jewellery, ceramics and other creature comforts for the afterlife have been found in the Etruscan stone tombs of Ipogeo dei Volumni near Perugia (p324) and Crocifisso del Tufo outside Orvieto (p368).

Despite the tantalising clues they left behind, no-one seems to know who the Etruscans were or where they came from. Recent studies of their genetic material suggest they have more in common with Anatolia than with modern Italians, and early Roman historians suggested a connection with Asia Minor. Come up with your own theories at the Museo Claudio Faina e Civico in Orvieto (p367) and the Museo Archeologico Nazionale dell'Umbria in Perugia (p323), where you'll notice that Etruscan ceramic urns and iron horses seem distinctly Greek, while their scarab-beetle jewellery and tomb paintings look oddly Egyptian.

Become an aficionado on Umbrian art in Umbria – check out university-level classes in Italian culture available at University for Foreigners Perugia at www.unistrapg .it/english.

Romans knew a good thing when they plundered it. After conquering swathes of Etruscan territory in Umbria and Tuscany in the 3rd century BC, the Etruscans' highly refined, geometric style seen in artefacts at Spoleto's Museo Archeologico e Teatro Romano (p379) was incorporated into Roman art and architecture. But even after another 800 years of trying, Rome never entirely succeeded in establishing its authority throughout Etruscan territory. This would become a recurring theme, with local municipal authorities battling with papal emissaries from Rome for control over the region right through the 15th century AD.

WELCOME, PILGRIMS: RELIGIOUS ATTRACTIONS

Roman centurions may have failed to make much of an impression, but Christianity began to take hold in Etruscan territory when a lovelorn young man from Norcia named Benedict abandoned his studies and a promising career in the Roman nobility to join the growing community of hermits in the hills of Umbria c AD 500. Fledgling monasteries nearby sought his spiritual leadership, but his appointment as abbot didn't go so well – the monks tried to poison him twice.

He miraculously survived, and monasteries sprang up in the valley beyond his cave as word of his piety spread. Founded by Longobard Duke of Spoleto Faroaldo II after St Peter commanded him in a dream to build a church, San Pietro in Valle (p389) features five Roman sarcophagi and 8th-century Romanesque frescoes on the upper part of the nave, showing scenes from the Old Testament and crusaders galloping through arches on a couple of pin-headed horses and a camel. Not to be outdone, the nearby monastery of Sant'Eutizio (p387) set itself apart through manuscript illumination c AD 1000 and Eutizio's own hair shirt, a relic with the mystical ability to bring rain when duly venerated.

These buildings and others in the area helped establish the blend of Lombard and Roman style known as Romanesque as the décor scheme of choice for local ecclesiastical structures. The basic template was simple: a stark nave stripped of extra columns ending in a domed apse, surrounded by chapels usually donated by wealthy patrons. Gone were the colonnaded Roman façades seen on earlier buildings, such as the 4th century Tempietto del Clitunno near Spoleto (p378); the new look was more spare and austere, befitting a place where hermits might feel at home and nobles may feel inspired to surrender worldly possessions.

While Umbria kept the architecture relatively simple in local *tufo* volcanic stone, Tuscany couldn't resist showing off just a bit. In the 11th century, the grand colonnade and loggia in Lucca's duomo (p192) and two-tone striped marble nave of Pisa's cathedral (p185) gave Romanesque a Tuscan makeover, and this new look was applied to Carrara's cathedral (p205) and Chiesa di San Miniato al Monte in Florence (p127). Alison Pisano's marble pulpit for the baptistry in Pisa (p186) was another spectacle in marble: a hexagonal structure embodying fellow Pisan Leonardo Fibonacci's mathematical theories about harmonious proportions, covered with deep reliefs of Old and New Testament characters who are almost twisting free of the picture plane.

Siena was not about to be outdone by its neighbours and rivals in Florence and Pisa, and in 1215 its city council approved a no-expenses-spared programme to rebuild and redecorate its greenish-black-and-white striped marble cathedral (p240). They got what they paid for in the 13th century with bronze baptistry doors by Andrea Pisano, a pulpit by Alison Pisano, a rose window designed by Duccio di Buoninsegna and an *Annunciazione* by his star pupil Simone Martini (now in the Uffizi; see p112), plus storytelling inlaid marble floors at the receiving end of many a dropped jaw. Since Flor-

How come tourists are the only ones in Italian churches on Sunday? Satirist Beppe Severgnini shares his theories on this and Italy's other cultural developments in English at www.beppesevergnini.com/articles.htm and in Italian at www.corriere.it/solferino/severgnini.

> **KEEP YOUR EYE ON THE DONKEY**
>
> At first glance, the medieval galleries of **Siena's Pinacoteca Nazionale** (p243) may look like a forest of Madonnas on thrones and Jesuses on crosses. But take a closer look at details jumping out from those fields of frozen poses and beatific expressions, and you'll see the Renaissance coming. Grand Gothic gestures give way to a range emotions in Taddeo di Bartolo's 1405 *Adorazione del Magi* (Adoration of the Magi) – note the tender expression of the donkey watching as the wise men kiss the feet of the somewhat blasé baby Jesus and his delighted mother. The figures in the background of Giovanni di Paolo's mid-15th-century *Flight into Egypt* may loom unnaturally large over the Gothic buildings, but his plodding, demoralised donkey gives the whole scene a relatable quality.

ence continued to best Siena rather mercilessly on the battlefield, Siena was determined to outdo Florence with religious spectacle, and commissioned a cathedral that included a Tuscan Gothic façade by Giovanni Pisano, a dome with a cupola by Bernini and the crowning glory by Sienese artist Pinturicchio: the Piccolomini Library frescoes (p241), which tell the life story of Sienese Pope Pius II in jewel-like colours. The plan to outshine Florence worked for about 150 years, until the Florentines picked up a few cues from Sienese painters, and started a little something called the Renaissance.

But while Tuscany's churches were becoming quite spectacular, nothing prepared pilgrims for what they would find inside the upper and lower churches in Assisi (p334). Not long after St Francis' death in 1226, an all-star team of artists was hired to decorate the churches in his honour: Cimabue, Giotto, Pietro Lorenzetti and Simone Martini captured the life and gentle spirit of St Francis while his memory was still fresh in the minds of the faithful. For medieval pilgrims not accustomed to multiplexes and special effects, entering a space covered floor to ceiling with stories told in living colour must have been a dazzling, overwhelming experience. Painter, art historian and Renaissance man Giorgio Vasari praised Cimabue for setting the standard for realistic modelling and perspective with his Lower Church frescoes, which you can still make out despite the extensive damage wrought over the years by earthquakes – not to mention art thieves who plundered fresco fragments after the devastating 1997 quake.

But the most startling achievement here is Giotto's fresco cycle, which shows Francis not just rolling up but tearing off his sleeves to provide aid to lepers and the needy, as onlookers and family members gasp and look away in shock. These images had an emotional, immediate impact on viewers, creating a much more theatrical setting for church services. Chants and solos added to the liturgy provided a surround-sound component to the fresco cycles, and the drama reached fever pitch with passion plays and other theatrical elements. Even while it was still in progress in the 13th century, the Basilica at Assisi drew hundreds of thousands of pilgrims each year; today annual attendance figures top four million.

Wonder what art might inspire ordinary people to self-flagellate, or brave the Assisi crowds in July? Find out what art moves people most and why in Kenyon College's *Pilgrimage Art* magazine, online at http://peregrinations.kenyon.edu/current.html.

ENLIGHTENED DARK AGES: THE RISE OF THE COMUNE

But while communities sprang up around hermits and holy men in the hinterlands, cities began taking on a life of their own in the 13th and 14th century. Some public facilities were holdovers from Roman times: the aqueducts at Narni (p391), the baths of Volterra (p263) and the theatre in Spoleto (up and running each year during the Spoleto Festival; see p381). Road networks also served as handy trade routes starting in the 11th century, and farming estates and villas began to spring up outside major trading centres as a new middle class of merchants, farmers and skilled craftspeople emerged. Taxes and donations sponsored the building of hospitals such, as Filippo Brunelleschi's Spedale degli Innocenti (p121), which is considered the earliest Florentine Renaissance building (1419–36). Streets were paved, town walls erected and sewage systems were built to accommodate an increasingly sophisticated urban population not keen on sprawl or squalor.

Once townsfolk came into some money they weren't necessarily keen to part with it, and didn't always agree how their tax dollars should be spent. Town councils were formed to represent the various interests of merchants, guilds and competing noble families, and the first order of business on the agenda in major medieval cities like Perugia, Todi, Siena, Florence and Gubbio was the construction of an impressive town hall reflecting the importance and authority of the *comune*, or municipality. Surprisingly, these democratic monuments don't look as though they were designed by committee, and Siena's Palazzo Comunale (p237) has become a global icon of civic pride with its pointed Sienese arches, a splendid marble loggia contributed by Sienese Black Plague survivors, and the tall Torre del Mangia clock tower that serves as the compass needle orienting the entire city.

But in addition to being savvy political lobbyists and fans of grand architecture projects that kept their constituents gainfully employed, medieval *comune* were masters of propaganda. Perugia's carved-relief Fontana Maggiore (p321) by Alison and Giovanni Pisano in the city's central piazza and the frescoed town council hall in the Palazzo dei Priori (now called the Sala dei Notari; p322) were part of a brilliant chamber-of-commerce-style PR campaign positioning Perugia as the embodiment of ancient virtues and Christian belief, with imagery that blended ancient mythology, Biblical themes and Perugia's contemporary history.

Better and bigger than any political billboard is Ambrogio Lorenzetti's *Effetti del Buon e del Cattivo Governo* (The Allegories of Good and Bad Government) in Siena's Palazzo Comunale (p237). In *Good Government*, townsfolk make their way through town in an orderly fashion, pausing to do business, greet one another, join hands and dance a merry jig. In *Bad Government*, a horned, fanged Tyrannia rules over a scene of chaos surrounded by winged vices, while Justice lies unconscious, her scales shattered. Like the best campaign speeches, this cautionary tale was brilliantly rendered, but not always heeded.

> Ouch, that had to hurt: all those gorgeously painted but weirdly gory details are explained in *The Thief, the Cross, and the Wheel: Pain and the Spectacle of Punishment in Medieval and Renaissance Europe* by Mitchell B Merback.

TRADING UP: IMPORTS & COSMOPOLITAN INFLUENCES

When they weren't busy politicking, late medieval farmers, craftspeople and merchants did quite well for themselves in Umbria and Tuscany. Enterprising Umbrians drained marshlands to grow additional crops for sale, and the elegant ceramics, tile and marbles showcased in churches, villas and workshops across Tuscany and Umbria became all the rage throughout

---

ARCHITECTURE, TECHNICALLY SPEAKING

Entablature Atop a row of columns on a classical façade, this includes an architrave, a long slab that holds the columns in place, the decorative frieze atop that and the triangular pediment to cap it off; see the façade of Basilica di Santa Maria Novella, Florence (p115)

Pietra serena Greenish-grey 'serene stone'; see the columns at Basilica di San Lorenzo, Florence (p118)

Rustification Stone with a chiselled, rough-hewn look; see the 1st floor of Florence's Palazzo Medici-Riccardi (p118)

Sgraffito A surface covered with plaster, then scratched away to create a three-dimensional trompe-l'oeil effect of carved stone or brick; see the façade of Pisa's Palazzo della Carovana on Piazza dei Cavalieri (p187)

Spolia Creative reuse of ancient monuments in new structures; see the Arco d'Etrusco, Perugia (p323)

Europe and the Mediterranean. Artisans were kept busy applying their skills to civic works projects and churches, which had to be expanded and updated to keep up with the growing numbers and rising expectations of pilgrims in the area.

With outside interest came outside influence, as local styles adapted to international markets. Florence, Deruta and Orvieto became famous for lustrous, tin-glazed *maiolica* (Majolica ware) tiles and plates painted with vibrant metallic pigments inspired by the Islamic ceramics of Majorca, Spain. Ceramic reliefs by the prolific Florentine della Robbia family are now enshrined at the Museo del Bargello (p108), including Lorenzo de Medici's favourite *Madonna della Mele* (c 1460). Modest Romanesque cathedrals were given an International Gothic makeover befitting their appeal to pilgrims of all nations, but the Italian take on the French style was both more colourful and more subdued than the grey-stone spires and flying buttresses of Paris. Italian Gothic in the region often featured a simple layout and striped stone naves fronted by multilayer birthday-cake façades, which might be frosted with pink paint, glittering mosaics and rows of arches that are capped with sculptures. Particularly fabulous examples of this confectionary approach are the duomos in Siena, Orvieto and Florence. The last two were tricked out by Arnolfo di Cambio, also known for his work in Florence's Palazzo Vecchio (p110). Santa Croce in Florence (p121) is more restrained and gorgeously proportioned, with a broad, window-lined nave that gives a sense of effortless grandeur.

The evolution from solid Romanesque to airy Gothic to a Yin-Yang balance of the two can be witnessed in several standout buildings in the region. The Gothic trend started while the upper church of the Basilica di San Francesco in Assisi (p334) was under construction, and the resulting blend of a relatively austere Romanesque exterior with high Gothic drama indoors set a new ecclesiastical architecture standard exported by Franciscan monks all over Europe. The pointed arches on the lower half of the façade of Santa Maria Novella (p115) reveal a Gothic underbelly below the lofty classical proportions of the Corinthian columns and pediment added by Leon Battista Alberti in 1470, with ingenious side scrolls to pull the look together. But while humanist and religious idioms and cross-cultural influences were seamlessly blended in lofty Renaissance architecture, the reality on the ground looked quite different.

UNFRIENDLY COMPETITION: RIVALRIES TO THE DEATH
By the 14th century, the smiling Sienese townsfolk of Ambroggio Lorenzetti's *Allegory of Good Government* and the placid Umbrian countryside backdrop of the Basilica di San Francesco frescoes must've seemed like figments of fertile imaginations. The Black Death swept through cities in Umbria and left communal government hobbled, giving Church authorities and warlords an excuse to impose new and decidedly less democratic authority. To quell uprisings by workers in Perugia, the pope's French emissary Gerard de Puy built a new citadel in 1371, which was overrun by unimpressed townsfolk five years later. But while municipalities fended off tyranny, fields returned to swampland, roads became toll-collecting opportunities for thugs, and merchants abandoned the region for greener, safer pastures. The Assisi fresco painters who miraculously survived the plague would not live to see their work finished, due to some rather unkindly acts of God: major earthquakes erupted in Umbria every 20 years for some 250 years.

Meanwhile in Tuscany, the great medieval arts capital of Siena was suffering. After a major famine in 1329 and a bank collapse, the municipality

Can you imagine Florence without the art? Neither could the 'mud angels', young people who arrived en masse after the Florence Flood of 1966 to rescue thousands of irreplaceable artworks and manuscripts.

If you think the architecture in Arezzo and Terni looks cinematic, you and Roberto Begnini have something in common: the Tuscan actor/director filmed his Oscar-winning, box office-busting *La vita é bella* (Life Is Beautiful) in these two cities.

For the bigger picture on Italian medieval and Renaissance art, visit the Virtual Uffizi at www .virtualuffizi.com/uffizi /index1.htm for listings searchable by artist or era.

went into debt to maintain roads, continue work on the Duomo, help the needy and jumpstart the local economy. But just when Siena seemed set for a comeback, the plague devastated the city in 1348. Three-quarters of Siena's population was soon dead, and virtually all economic and artistic activity ground to a halt. The *comune* rallied with tough fines on lawbreakers, new business taxes and rules against wearing black mourning attire (too depressing), and within five years Siena was going strong. But when another plague in 1374 killed 80,000 Sienese, followed by a famine, the city never entirely recovered. It did find a new heroine and patron saint in St Catherine, whose devotion to the sick, dying, criminals and lepers is captured in Andrea Vanni's 15th-century fresco in San Domenico (p244) and in frescoes in her childhood home (p244).

Florence was also hit by the plague in 1348, and despite fervent public prayer rituals, 96,000 Florentines died in just seven months. Those who survived experienced a crisis of faith, making Florence fertile territory for humanist ideals – not to mention macabre superstition, attempts to raise the dead, and a fascination with corpses that the likes of Leonardo da Vinci would call science and others morbid curiosity. Power struggles also ensued among Florence's great families, many of whom had well-placed relatives at the Vatican to make their case for power. Florence's booming post-plague textile trade helped fund military campaigns against its comparatively weaker neighbours Arezzo, Pisa and Cortona, and even brought commercial power players Lucca and Siena into the Florentine sphere of influence.

More to the right, please: Mussolini tried to set the left-leaning Tower of Pisa straight by pouring concrete around its base, which only sunk the tower further into the ground.

A building boom ensued as Church and secular authorities competed to become the defining fixtures of the local landscape. In Florence, Cosimo il Vecchio commissioned Michelozzo di Bartolomeo Michelozzi to build Palazzo Medici-Riccardi (p118), an imposing three-storey building on a base of rough-hewn, 'rusticated' stone. Medici archnemesis Filippo Strozzi promptly hired Benedetto da Maiano to build him a bigger, better palazzo (p117), with higher ceilings, an airy arcaded courtyard and a more impressive cornice. Too bad the Strozzis didn't get to stay in their new palazzo for long: after Filippo supported an insurrection against the Medici he retreated to Venice until the latest Medici leader was murdered. When he tried to return to Florence, he was captured and tortured to the point where suicide seemed an attractive alternative.

THE RENAISSANCE: PICTURING AN IMPERFECT WORLD, PERFECTLY

So who actually came out ahead of all this jockeying for position? Oddly enough, architects. To put an end to the competing claims of the Tuscan Ghibelline faction allied with the Holy Roman Empire (for the often gory details, see p28), the Rome-backed Guelph faction marked its territory with

---

RENAISSANCE ART SMARTS

Chiaroscuro A three-dimensional effect created with contrasting highlights and dark shading; Leonardo da Vinci was the master of this illusion

Contrapposto Shifting weight in a casual pose, so that a figure is balanced; Michelangelo was able to make it work with colossal statues

Perspective The relationship and proportions of elements in a picture, so that ones that are large and low seem close and those small and high seem far; Raphael got this down to a science

Sfumato Shading built up with layers of translucent colour instead of hard lines; again, see Leonardo da Vinci

Vanishing point The spot in an image where all lines perpendicular to the picture plane converge, tricking the eye into believing that you're seeing into the distance; the astonishing early master is Masaccio

impressive new landmarks. Guelph Florence hired Giotto to design the city's iconic 85m-tall square *campanile* (bell tower; p107), one-upping the 57m-tall tower under construction in Ghibelline Pisa that was already looking a bit off kilter. Pisa battled with Florence throughout the 14th and 15th centuries, and was otherwise too preoccupied with shoring up its sagging political position and its Leaning Tower (p185) to keep up with its construction-happy Guelph neighbours. Eventually Pisa conceded architectural defeat, giving its Piazza dei Cavalieri (p187) a Florentine facelift with the *sgriffito* (scratched-plaster) façade of Palazzo della Carovana by Giorgio Vasari, chief decorator of Florence's Palazzo degli Uffizi.

Mess with Florence, and you take on Rome: This was the not-so-subtle hint delivered by Florentine architecture, which made frequent reference to the glories of ancient Rome. Filippo Brunelleschi and Michelangelo Buonarotti recycled the coffered ceiling of the Parthenon in Rome for the Basilica di San Lorenzo (p118), with Andrea del Verocchio providing the Roman-style Medici family sarcophagus. The Roman-inspired Florentine style became known as Renaissance or 'rebirth' – but there was also much to Renaissance architecture that was truly novel. Red-carpet appearances can't compare with entrances made on the grand staircase at the Biblioteca Medicea Laurenziana (Laurentian Library) at San Lorenzo, which Michelangelo framed for dramatic effect with two curving stairways.

Meanwhile, Florentine artists enjoyed a bonanza of commissions to paint heroic battle scenes, fresco private chapels and carve busts of the latest power players – works that sometimes outlived their patrons' clout. The Peruzzi family rose to prominence in 14th-century Florence as bankers with interests reaching from London to the Middle East, and set the trend for art patronage by commissioning Giotto to fresco the family's memorial chapel in Santa Croce, completed in 1320 (p121). When Peruzzi client King Edward III of England defaulted on loans and war with Lucca interfered with business, the Peruzzi went bankrupt – but as patrons of Giotto's precocious experiments in perspective and Renaissance illusionism, their legacy set the tone for the artistic flowering of Florence.

One Florentine family to follow the Petrucci's lead were the prominent Brancaccis, who commissioned a chapel in the Basilica di Santa Maria del Carmine in Florence (p126), to be painted by Masolino and his precocious assistant Masaccio, whose work after his death at 27 was completed by Fra Filippo Lippi. In these dramatic frescoes framed in astonishingly convincing architectural sets, select scenes from the life of St Peter allude to pressing Florentine concerns of the day: the new income tax, unfair imprisonment and hoarded wealth. Masaccio's image of expulsion of Adam and Eve from the Garden of Eden proved especially prophetic: the Brancaccis were allied with the Strozzi family, and were similarly exiled by the Medici before they could see the work completed. But Fra Filippo Lippi came out ahead, and went on to complete major commissions, including the fresco cycles of John the Baptist and St Stephen in the choir or the Prato Duomo (p158). Yet he died poor, apparently having given away much of his money to the needy and, by some accounts, various mistresses.

But the patrons with the greatest impact on the course of art history were the Medici. Patriarch Cosimo il Vecchio was exiled in 1433 by a consortium of Florentine families who considered him a triple threat: powerful banker, ambassador of the Church, and consummate politician with the savvy to sway emperors and popes. But the flight of capital from Florence after his departure created such a fiscal panic that the exile was hastily rescinded and within a year the Medici were back in Florence. To announce his return in grand style, Cosimo funded the 1437 rebuilding of the Convento di San Marco by

Rebel Artemesia Gentileschi shattered the 17th-century glass ceiling for women artists by excelling in Caravaggio's workshop, taking on historical and religious themes, exchanging ideas with Galileo Galilei and becoming the first woman member of Florence's Academy of Art and Design.

Was it a genius gene, or something in the water? In *Painting and Experience in 15th Century Italy*, Michael Baxandall takes a close look at Renaissance paintings and the 15th-century society that made so much impossibly genius seem entirely possible.

MADONNA WANNABES

An ageless international star who's an inspiration to Italian fashion designers: can you blame Umbrian towns for wanting their own *Sistine Madonna*? Raphael's leading lady locks eyes with some two million visitors a year at the Old Masters Picture Gallery in Dresden, Germany, putting the town devastated by WWII bombings back on the cultural map and bored cherubs on T-shirts. Most other Raphael Madonnas left behind Raphael's early stomping grounds in Umbria long ago without so much as a backward glance, which for centuries has left the Umbrian communities that provided crucial early support for the orphaned Raphael trying not to feel somehow slighted. Some Madonnas have kept a mysteriously low profile: a Madonna known as the *de Brécy Tondo* hung over a cottage fireplace in Wales for 100 years before it was identified as a probable Raphael in February 2007. Meanwhile, Umbria has had to be content with the damaged 1505 *Holy Trinity* at Capella di San Severo in Perugia, begun by Raphael at age 16 but finished by his tutor Perugino after Raphael's death in 1521. But in 2003, big news hit the tiny Umbrian town of Cerqueto (population 500), when the frescoes in the town's shrine were identified as the work of 17-year-old Raphael. Look out, Madonna: you never know when a young unknown will come out of nowhere to steal your thunder.

Michelozzo, and commissioned Fra Angelico to fresco the monks' quarters with scenes from the life of Christ. Another artist pleased with Cosimo's return was Donatello, who had completed his lithe bronze statue of *David* with Cosimo's patronage, and was able to complete the pulpit he'd been commissioned to create with Michelozzo for the Prato duomo (p158).

Through such commissions, early Renaissance innovations in perspective, closely observed realism, and the play of light and dark (*chiaroscuro*) began to catch on throughout Tuscany and Umbria. Cosimo's grandson Lorenzo de' Medici gave an early and important nod of approval to Cortona-born painter Luca Signorelli, who took foreshortening to expressive extremes in his *Last Judgment* in Orvieto with up-the-nostril angles on angels and creepy between-the-toes peeks at demons (p366). A painter from Sansepolcro named Piero della Francesca earned a reputation for figures glowing with otherworldly light, caught in personal predicaments that seem somehow relatable: Roman soldiers snoozing on the job, crowds left goggle-eyed by miracles bystanders distressed to witness cruel persecution (p301).

THE GREAT DEBATE: SCANDAL, SCIENCE & CENSORSHIP

The High Renaissance is often seen as a kind of university faculty meeting, with genteel, silver-haired sages engaged in a collegial exchange of ideas. A bar brawl might be closer to the metaphorical truth, with artists, scientists, politicians and clergy mixing it up and everyone emerging bruised. The debate was never as simple as church versus state, science versus art or seeing versus believing; in those days, politicians could be clergy, scientists could be artists, and artists could be clergy. Nor was debate strictly academic: any statement, however artistic, could mark a person as a menace, a has-been, a heretic or a dead man.

Giorgio Vasari's gossipy *Lives of the Artists* (1st edition 1550) documents shocking behaviour from his Renaissance contemporaries that may not have happened quite as he describes, yet is entirely possible given what we know of those tumultuous times. Legal records show that after being exiled from Florence for stabbing a man with a wooden stake, Pietro Vanucci attracted more positive notice for frescoing the better part of the city of Perugia c 1500 under the pseudonym Perugino. He also gained fame as the tutor of a promising young painter named Raphael, who promptly stole papal commissions right out from under him. But you'd never guess this back story

Cimabue was a primary-school dropout, Rapahel died young because of a sex-induced fever and scary-obsessive Michelangelo sculpted until his shoes disintegrated: Renaissance art star–maker Giorgio Vasari wrote *Lives of the Artists* centuries before the era of fact checking and libel suits, so he dishes better dirt than any tabloid.

to look at Perugino's serene figures of Justice, Prudence, Temperance and Fortitude in Perugia's Collegio del Cambio (p322). They're painted under the same starry sky as Biblical figures, suggesting that the universe might be able to accommodate both secular and sacred ideals – an idea ahead of its time in 1503. A dispute over salt taxes led to a clash between Perugia's ruling Baglioni family and Pope Paul III, and the ensuing Salt War ended Perugia's relative independence from papal authority in 1540. Papal forces levelled the homes of the Baglioni and with them untold art treasures, though the Collegio was left mercifully intact.

War wasn't the only danger to Renaissance art. Inspired by Masaccio, tutored by Fra Filippo Lippi and backed by Lorenzo de' Medici, Sandro Botticelli was a rising art star who'd worked alongside Perugino and was sent to Rome to paint a fresco celebrating papal authority in the Sistine Chapel. The golden boy who'd painted the Venus with the golden hair for Lorenzo de' Medici's private villa in 1485 (p113) could do no wrong, until he was accused of sodomy in 1501. The charges didn't stick but the rumours did, and Botticelli's work was critiqued as too decadently sensual for religious subjects. When religious reformer Savonarola ousted the Medici and began to purge Florence of decadent excess in the face of surely imminent Armegeddon, Botticelli paintings went up in flames in the massive 'Bonfire of the Vanities'. Botticelli repudiated mythology and turned his attention to Madonnas, some of whom bear a marked family resemblance to his Venus.

Another artist whose classically inspired work was alternately admired and rejected was Michelangelo. Lorenzo de' Medici personally took charge of the young sculptor's schooling from age 13, and he remained the darling of Florence until the Medici were ousted by Savonarola in 1494. By some accounts, Savonarola tossed rare early paintings by Michelangelo onto his bonfires (ouch). Without his Medici protectors, Michelangelo seemed unsure of his next move: he briefly hid in the basement of San Lorenzo and roamed around Italy. In Rome he carved a Bacchus for Cardinal Raffaele Riaro that the patron deemed unsuitable – which only seemed to spur Michelangelo to make a bigger and still more sensuous statue of *David* in 1501 (p120).

Although he was the one artist who Vasari positively gushed about, Michelangelo was by all other accounts fiercely competitive, denigrating the work of Perugino, openly gloating when his rival Leonardo da Vinci failed to complete a commission, and accusing Raphael and Bramante of setting him an impossible task with his Sistine Chapel commission. The magnificent ceiling frescoes took him four years, and the altarpiece was still incomplete in 1534 when an ailing Medici Pope Clement VII called on him to complete the work. But Michelangelo had grown estranged from the Medici for the misery their power plays had caused Florence, so he painted for his old friend a terrifying *Last Judgment* that caused a scandal for violence and nudity that was painted over by another artist for modesty's sake.

As the Church consolidated its control across Tuscany and Umbria in the 16th and 17th century, science at odds with scriptures became more risqué than sensual. Pisa-born mathematician and devout Catholic Galileo Galilei had three illegitimate children, but did not incur the wrath of the Church until his astronomy research demonstrated that Copernicus was right, and earth really did revolve around the sun – contrary to then-current interpretation of Biblical phrases. Although Church authorities allowed him to make a published case for and against heliocentrism, Galileo was found guilty of heresy and spent the rest of his life under house arrest, studying physics even while going blind. The Church reversed its ruling posthumously and Galileo's remains are now fittingly interred at Florence's Santa Croce,

Architect, sculptor, poet, incurable romantic: yet again, Michelangelo defines the term Renaissance man with *Complete Poems and Selected Letters of Michelangelo*, translated by Creighton Gilbert.

A team of Leonardo da Vinci scholars led by Oxford University's Martin Kemp provide the latest scientific and historical thinking about the elusive genius at www .universalleonardo.org.

DA VINCI MYSTERY SOLVED

And you thought the new guy at your office was a weirdo: Botticelli and Perugino once worked in the same workshop as an audacious teenager who filled notebooks with wild theories about painting, music, engineering and warfare – in mirror-image handwriting, no less. He also admitted to robbing graves of some 30 human cadavers so that he could dissect them, which at the time was a punishable offence of desecration, and still sounds pretty creepy. But Lorenzo de' Medici was so impressed with this young man of many talents that he sent him as an ambassador to broker peace with Ludovico Sforza of Milan. Today few of Leonardo da Vinci's 13,000 pages of notes remain in Florence, and 72 pages of wild, scribbled theories about fossils and moon glow are privately owned by Bill Gates, who bought them for $30 million. But in 2005, another priceless treasure surfaced: the artist's Florence workshop, hidden behind the walls of Santissima Annunziata monastery. If this sacred ground was the site of Leonardo's stolen cadaver experiments, the Church must have been more understanding than anyone imagined. Sure makes doodling and daydreaming on the job seem forgivable, and possibly even a savvy career move.

where Brunelleschi's rational architecture blends harmoniously with Giotto's devotional frescoes (p121).

The constraints imposed by papal emissaries and petty tyrants created a creative backlash in the 16th century, as 'mannerist' artists explored darker visions and eerie special effects in the manner of the High Renaissance. Scenes of *Il Deposizione* (the Deposition, where Jesus' body is taken down from the cross) provided the ideal opportunity to explore extreme perspective and twisting, restless bodies in works from the 1520s at the Cattedrale di Volterra in Arezzo by Il Rosso Fiorentino (aka the Redhead from Florence) and at Santa Felicità in Florence (p123) by Jacopo Pontormo. In both works, the figures seem lit by a camera flashbulb and their bodies boneless under layers of drapery – movie magic ahead of its time. The Sienese painter known as 'Il Sodomo' (for reasons unknown but rather nastily insinuated by Vasari) combined Leonardo's High Renaissance illusionism with moody Sienese drama in his 1542 *Saint Sebastian with Madonna and Angels* (now at Pisa's Museo Nazionale di San Matteo; p188). The same year, the Inquisition arrived in Italy, marking a definitive end to the Renaissance exploration of humanity, in all its glorious imperfections.

OUR SUMMER PLACE: COLONIAL POWER & INFLUENCE

Who says you can't take a villa home with you? Discover all the architectural elements that make a home quintessentially Tuscan in Alexandra Black's *Tuscan Elements*, and turn your cold-water flat into the most desirable destination this side of Lucca.

In the centuries that followed the sack of Rome by Charles V in 1527, artistic production in Tuscany and Umbria came to be defined by passing trends, imperial excess and periodic pillaging. Umbria began to reclaim its farms from marshlands and make a comeback in the late 15th century, but regular looting by passing armies made it slow going. Deruta and Gubbio struggled to regain their reputations as ceramics centres, but a steady stream of pilgrims and tourists en route to Rome helped keep Umbrian artistic traditions limping along. But anything that wasn't nailed down was lifted by Napoleonic forces in the 18th century, making artistic progress from this time period hard to track.

Tuscany had the rather more dubious luck of being the holiday destination of choice for despots, generals and imperial relations. Imported Roman baroque touches started to make an appearance on the Florentine cityscape in the 17th century: Gherardo Silvani's bodaciously curvy, sculpture-bedizened façade for San Gaetano (p117), and Pietro da Cortona's ornately obsequious frescoes at the Palazzo Pitti (p123) celebrating the four ages of man – and the power of the Medici through them all. But Cortona's prediction did not hold, and the Medici power waned despite Maria de' Medici's convenient and turbulent marriage to King Henry IV of France in 1600.

Lucca in particular began to look distinctly French, with wide boulevards, neoclassical buildings and more than 300 baroque villas. As a consolation prize for separating from her husband, Elisa Baciocchi was dubbed by her brother Napoleon Bonaparte the Duchess of Tuscany, and soon established the trend for Italian vacation villas with her Villa Reale near Lucca (p199). When Napoleon lost Tuscany in 1814, former Grand-Duke of Tuscany Ferdinando III was briefly reinstated, only to lose Lucca in a treaty to Elisa in 1815. But the Bourbon Queen Maria Luisa of Etruria (western Tuscany) had an eye on a villa herself, and through treaty negotiations took control of Lucca in 1817.

A 'Grand Tour' of Italy became an obligatory display of culture and class status by the 18th century, and Tuscany and Umbria were key stops on the itinerary. German and English artists enraptured with Michelangelo, Perugino and other early High Renaissance painters took the inspiration home. This resulted in the high-octane romanticism of Henry Fuseli (1741–1825), the Swiss-German naturalised British painter best known for his unruly horses, and the moody, craft-conscious Pre-Raphaelite movement of Dante Gabriel Rosetti (1828–82), William Morris and friends. Conversely, Italian artists picked up on artistic trends making a splash in Northern Europe

---

MASSIMO BARTOLINI

The acclaimed conceptual artist responsible for dreamlike spaces and out-of-body experiences, toast of biennials (Venice, Shanghai, Frankfurt etc) and proof that artistic inspiration is alive and well and (still) living in Tuscany.

Why he lives and works in a small Tuscan town It's not just for the food. I was born here and honestly, I would rather return here.

Where the Renaissance meets installation art Piero's *Pregnant Madonna* in Monterchi, at the border with Umbria. This Madonna is hosted inside the former elementary school of the town, and the inside is like a home, it's domestic. There's a welcome mat, townsfolk that chat in the atrium, and people in the town still bring flowers to the Madonna to protect pregnancies, though they're forced to put them behind the big glass that protects the painting. That vase of little flowers behind that monolith of technology is a memorable vision, just as this elementary school is the most beautiful museum I've ever visited.

How the Renaissance obsession with light and dark figures into his own work I like to associate light with actions and objects. Light adds painting to sculpture, and it creates a landscape that contains sculpture, hosting it and shaping it.

Favourite landscape features I like the pine woods and little bars in hill-top towns. I'm sorry that in Tuscany there are no deserts, which are my favourite natural landscapes, but it seems that soon I'll be indulged [with global warming].

Hidden gem due for discovery The insane asylum in Volterra, where about 10 pavilions from the beginning of the 1900s are left in disrepair, but it's a place of incredible beauty. In a cloister of one of these pavilions, there's about 100m of wall carved with writings and drawings by one of the patients with a belt buckle in the 1960s.

What it's like to be a contemporary artist surrounded by Old Masters Warhol was surrounded by famous actresses and canned soup and he made masterworks from it. I try not to worsen the landscape that surrounds me, the masterpieces I see every day. [laughs] I made sculptures of mountains inspired by the mountains painted by Fra Angelico. A masterwork becomes nature; the artefact disappears, so you're free to look at it just as you look at the sea, a beautiful machine, a rock.

ARTISTS DIRECTORY:
25 LATE, GREAT TUSCAN & UMBRIAN ARTISTS

Artist	Known for...	As seen in...
Ambrogio Lorenzetti	riveting tales starring flat but expressive characters caught in compromising positions, in glowing colours Hollywood can't match	*Effetti del buon e del cattivo governo* (The Allegories of Good and Bad Government), c1290–1348, in Siena's Palazzo Comunale (p237)
Andrea della Robbia	taking ceramics way beyond teacups with (1435–1525) eye-catching, sometimes garish high-contrast reliefs; where Wedgwood found its blue-and-white inspiration	*Madonna della mele* (Madonna of the apple), Museo del Bargello, Florence (p108)
Artemesia Gentileschi (1593–1653)	turbulent, violent mythological scenes revealed by otherworldly spotlighting; think *Pulp Fiction* meets *Citizen Kane* in oil paint	*Giuditta che decapita Oloferne* (Judith Beheading Holofernes), Uffizi, Florence (p112)
Cimabue (Cenni di Pepi; c 1240–1302)	frescoes of religious figures with steady gazes, elegant poses worthy of a supermodel and the intimate quality of a family portrait	Lower church frescos at Basilica di San Francesco, Assisi (p334)
Domenico Ghirlandaio (1449–94)	crisp, revealing portraits capturing every last detail with a lively line, blending the earthiness of his peer Fra Filippo Lippi and the elegance of Sandro Botticelli	Sassetti chapel altarpiece in Galleria dell'Accademia, Florence (p119)
Donatello (1386–1466)	taut, lithe, twisting figures that set the standard for *contropposto* (shifting weight in a casual pose, so that a figure is balanced) and Renaissance hunks	*David* statue in Florence's Palazzo del Popolo (p108); pulpit for Prato cathedral (p158)
Duccio di Buoninsegna (c 1255–1318)	the Sienese school: ethereal, riveting figures with level gazes and pale-green skin against glowing gold backgrounds, like elegant aliens	*Maesta* (Madonna and Child Enthroned with 20 Angels and 19 Saints) at Siena's Museo dell'Opera della Metropolitana (p241)
Fra Angelico (Guido di Pietro Trosini, also known as Beato Angelico; 1395–1455)	frescoes of relatable religious figures with wry expressions and casual poses, with a light that seems to come from within – makes a laborious fresco look like that one great snapshot you get between posed photos	frescoes at Museo di San Marco, Florence (p119)
Fra Filippo Lippi (1406–69)	pure charm and uncanny empathy: moon-faced Madonnas, squirming baby Jesuses, and crowd scenes where you can read the minds of each person	fresco cycles of John the Baptist and St Stephen in the choir of Prato Cathedral (p158)
Giotto (1267–1337)	kick-starting the Renaissance with action-packed frescoes that you'll swear are in motion; each character pinpoints emotions with facial expressions and poses that need no translation	Life of St Francis fresco cycle at Basilica di San Francesco in Assisi (p334); frescoes in Santa Croce (p121)
Leonardo da Vinci (1452–1519)	genius so flabbergasting, the term polymath (aka 'Renaissance man') had to be coined to explain him, and new painting terms defined to describe his style (*sfumato, chiaroscuro,* see boxed text, p46)	*Annuaciazione* (Annunciation) at the Uffizi, Florence (p112); workshop at Santissima Annunziata (p121)

Artist	Known for...	As seen in...
Lorenzo Ghiberti (1378–1455)	precise, dynamic reliefs that look like jewels and read like comic books, with strong diagonals to keep the plot moving	*Gates of Paradise* bronze doors at Florence Baptistry (p107)
Luca Signorelli (1455–1523)	bringing irresistible beauty to the grotesque, with sunny scenes of eternal damnation and eerie, contrasting-colour shading	*Last Judgment*, Orvieto Cathedral (p366)
Masaccio (1401–28)	putting painting into perspective, framing figures in architectural settings of astonishingly correct mathematical scale and proportion	Cappella Brancacci frescoes, Basilica di Santa Maria del Carmine, Florence (p126)
Michelangelo Buonarotti (1475–1564)	turning raw marble into imposing figures with impeccable balance, muscular movements and subtle emotion; he wasn't kidding when he claimed he saw the angel in the marble, and set it free	*David* at Galleria dell'Accademia, Florence (p119)
Alison Pisano (c 1220–84)	Roman-inspired marble friezes writhing with more activity than an ant farm, without losing the plot	Pisa baptistry doors (p186); Fontana Maggiore in Perugia (p321)
Paolo Uccello (1397–1475)	vast battle scenes with a distant vanishing point and such high-contrast highlights that the horses seem lit by lightning	*Battle of San Romano* at the Uffizi, Florence (p112)
Perugino (Pietro di Cristoforo Vannucci; 1446–1524)	ideal 'can't we all just get along?' visions of wind-blown philosophers, modern virtues and curious cherubs flitting through sublime classical architecture	Collegio del Cambio frescoes, Perugia (p322)
Piero della Francesca (1412–92)	luminous figures with lovely, limpid eyes and penetrating gazes that seem to follow you across the room and into your next life	*Legend of the True Cross* frescoes at San Francesco in Arezzo (p296); *Pregnant Madonna* at Montevarchi (p300)
Pinturicchio (Bernardino di Betto; 1452–1513)	centuries before the first Milan fashion week, he pictured a world where everyone glowed in vibrant colours and distinctive good looks	Piccolomini Library frescoes in Siena (p241)
Pontormo (1494–1557)	gorgeously dishevelled boneless beauties in distress whose unfurrowed brows could be an advert for Botox	*Il Deposizione* at Chiesa di Santa Felicità, Florence (p123)
Raphael (1483–1520)	Madonnas with skin as immaculate as conception holding court with angels, in simple settings and restrained colour schemes	*Annuciation* at the Uffizi, Florence (p112)
Rosso Fiorentino (1494–1540)	crowd scenes that come alive with ingenious stage lighting and eerie colour contrasts achieved centuries before digital effects	*Il Deposizione* at the Pinacoteca Comunale, Arezzo (p295)
Sandro Botticelli (c 1444–1510)	the world's loveliest nudes: translucent, floating figures that glide across the canvas and glow from within	*Birth of Venus*, at the Uffizi, Florence (p112)
Simone Martini (c 1284–1344)	surprising expressions in spectacular gilded Gothic settings: cranky Madonna, pushy angels, furious toddlers	*Annunciation* from Pisa cathedral, now at the Uffizi, Florence (p112)

without having to leave home. Impressionism, plein-air-painting and romanticism became trendy among Italian artists, as witnessed in the collection at Florence's Galleria d'Arte Moderna (p124). But the most fascinating case of artistic import-export is Italian Art Nouveau, named Liberty after the London store that put William Morris' Italian-inspired visual ideals into commercial action.

Get the scoop on the Renaissance artist with the biggest cult following at www.pierodellafranc esca.it.

SHOCKS TO THE SYSTEM: WAR, FUTURISM & FASCISM

After centuries under the thumbs of popes and sundry imperial powers, Tuscany and Umbria had acquired a certain forced cosmopolitanism, and local artists could identify with Rome or Paris in addition to their own *campanile* (bell tower). The wave of nationalism that came with Italian unification didn't have a clear, immediate artistic effect within Tuscany or Umbria, whose biggest star in the early 20th century was Livorno-born painter and sculptor Amedeo Modigliani (1884–1920), who lived most of his adult life in Paris. A precocious and precarious talent, Modigliani made pilgrimages to the Uffizi, read Nietzsche, seduced maids and smoked hashish – all of which have been suggested as possible inspirations for his iconic long-faced, blank-eyed female figures.

Forward momentum for the local scene was provided by futurism and Gerardo Dottori's 1914 *Ciclista*, which echoed experiments in picturing movement by Umberto Boccioni and seems to have been the working prototype Fortunato Depero's famous 1924 futurist poster for Bianchi Bicycles. But what started out as a radical experiment in *aeropittura*, the sensation of flight, became codified into a staunch nationalist aesthetic under the Fascists, and Dottori became better known for his 1933 portrait of Il Duce, aka Benito Mussolini. The Fascists also took quite a shine to the striking medieval buildings of Umbria, and decreed that all Umbrian buildings should be stripped of post-medieval ornament – a decision thankfully not put into practice, since soon thereafter the Fascists became otherwise occupied with losing the war. Still, Mussolini got his wish with austere, rationalist tower blocks that sprang up in the suburbs of Terni, Spoleto and Foligno, which have since been disparaged as only marginally liveable.

Cracks in the futurist fabric were memorably rendered by Alberto Burri (1915–95), who was born in Città di Castello, went to Africa as a doctor, got captured by the Americans and started to paint while in a prisoners of war (POW) camp in Texas. His abstract works combine oil paint and lowly materials like burlap and salvaged wood – an instinct shared by radical 1970s Arte Povera (Poor Art) artists, who used only materials they could get for free or on the cheap. Burri's earthy, exposed-seam works proved the ideal foil to Victor Vasarely's giddy, airtight Op art at the 1965 Sao Paolo Biennial, where the artists jointly landed the top prize. To judge for yourself, head to Città di Castello to see two galleries warehousing his work (p354).

During the Renaissance, the average artist earned about a third of the salary of a lawyer –today, it's about a fifth.

CONTEMPORARY ART: WHAT'S PAST IS PROLOGUE

Tuscany and Umbria can still draw crowds just with past glories, with 120 museums in Umbria and 1.5 million visitors annually to the Uffizi alone in Tuscany. But though 2800 years of rich artistic tradition means job security for legions of art conservation specialists and art historians, it can have a stultifying effect on artists attempting to create something wholly new. But look beyond the usual etchings of key landmarks and the inevitable sunflowers, and you'll find contemporary art in progress.

Most notable is Massimo Bartolini (b 1962), who radically alters the local landscape with just a few deceptively simple (and quintessentially Tuscan) adjustments of light and perspective that fundamentally change our experience: a bedroom where all the furniture appears to be sinking into the floor, Venice style, or a gallery where the viewer wears special shoes that subtly change the lighting in the gallery with each step. Bartolini has also changed the local flora of the tiny Tuscan town of Cecina near Livorno where he lives and works, attracting colourful flocks of contemporary art collectors and curators. These days you might be more likely to find his work at the Shanghai or Venice Biennale, but his installations can occasionally be found interrupting the countryside at the biennial Tuscia Electa arts festival (www .tusciaelecta.it).

Another artist who works with local material is Florentine Gianfranco Masi (b 1979), whose digital videos show the ever-changing configurations of clouds and tourists that define the Tuscan landscape. Check out his work online at www.etraarte.com, and find out about other upcoming contemporary art events. As long as Tuscany and Umbria exist, there will be no lack of art.

The Culture

Find Umbria online at www.regione.umbria.it (in Italian)

The land is the essence: just as Florentine perfumer Lorenzo Villaresi finds inspiration for his finely crafted fragrances in the Tuscan countryside (opposite), so it is the natural scape of cypress trees and vines that creates this region's strong cultural backbone.

Deeply attached to their patch of land, people in this rural neck of the woods with a sugar dusting of small towns are not simply Italian or Tuscan or Umbrian. Harking back to centuries of coexistence as rival political entities with their own style of architecture, school of painting and so on, it is the *paese* (hometown) or, in the case of Siena, the *contrada* (neighbourhood), in which one is born that reigns supreme. People from Florence, Pisa, Perugia and so on wear their authentic 'Made in …' labels with overwhelming pride.

What single word best describes the Tuscan lifestyle?

Passion (p268).

Hence the strong local rivalry, albeit one that, when the chips are down, is light-hearted(ish): 'Tuscans are more or less similar no matter where they come from, in so far as they speak the same language, share the same turn of phrase', believes Francesco Carlo Griccioli (p59), typical of the many whose family trees create split loyalties. 'Florentines are witty; they like to joke, they have a strong sense of humour…it can be a very nasty sense of humour, (derisive) comments that touch an exposed raw nerve. Sienese are rougher (less sophisticated) in a way' he continues, concluding 'yet apart from this local rivalry, their likes and dislikes are really the same'.

The standard form of greeting is the handshake. Kissing on both cheeks is generally reserved for people who already know one another, sometimes after only a relatively brief acquaintance.

Passionate, proud, reserved, hard-working, family-oriented, fond of food and wine (p66), pernickety about their appearance and thrifty are characteristics attributed to Tuscans across the board. With their gargantuan artistic heritage and tradition of master craftsmanship (opposite), Florentines are known for their attention to detail, quest for perfection, appreciation of beauty and deep respect for the past. Brash, no, but they do like to make it known where they stand in Florentine society: from oversized doorknobs to sculpted stonework, overt statements of wealth and power are everywhere in this class-driven city, whose Florentine – penned for the world to read by literary greats Dante, Boccaccio and Petrarch in the 14th century – is deemed the purest form of Italian.

Landlocked Umbria has always had to lean on its own land for sustenance and remains devout to its past as a port-less place unaccustomed to foreign influences. Self-reliant, honest and unabashedly direct are Umbrians who

---

TALK OF THE TOWN

Tune into the underbelly of what people are thinking NOW with these locally generated blogs.

Bytes of Italy (www.bytesofitaly.com) 'Random Pieces of Italian Culture, Food, Products and Travel' is the strapline of this brilliant Italy-wide blog.

Florence Night & Day (http://lovingflorence.blogspot.com) Diary of a 30-something Florentine gal, in English.

Living in Florence (www.melindagallo.com/blog) An American moves to Florence.

Tuscany Blog (www.tuscanyblog.com) Crammed with useful links, recommendations and advice, this is a one-stop shop for tracking down food and wine, real estate, farm accommodation, B&Bs, upcoming events and so on.

Tuscany Travel (http://tuscany-travel.blogspot.com) Useful info on where to go, what to see, sleeping, eating, events and so on in Tuscany

Tuscany.Podtravels.tv (http://tuscany.podtravels.tv) Videoblogs covering everything from Tuscany's grape harvest to pig breeding and futuristic sonic gardens.

THE FINE ART OF CRAFTSMANSHIP

An intense respect for Tuscany's fine art of craftsmanship drives **Lorenzo Villoresi** (☎ 055 234 11 87; www.lorenzovilloresi.it; Via de' Bardi 14; ⏰ 9am-1pm & 2-5pm Mon-Fri), a Florentine perfumer who crafts unique fragrances in an elegant rooftop atelier on the Oltrarno with panoramic river views.

'We have revived materials like marble, silver, other stones, olive wood etc that always belonged to the art and tradition of perfumery but disappeared in the last 50 years,' explained Mr Villoresi. His unusual, highly sensual olfactory collection is as much about natural cotton sachets filled with Tuscan herbs, scented wood bundles, ebony bathroom accessories and olive-oil bodycare products as exquisite custom-made perfumes stars flock to Florence for. Visits are by appointment only and cost from €2500 to €3000 for a two-hour session and a bottle of perfume.

'Alabaster, typical to southern Tuscany, is special. It has been used since ancient times as a vessel of fragrance and of light, for lamps and chandeliers. But we have created scented candles in alabaster jars,' said Mr Villoresi, citing his use of statuary marble to craft grooming accessories and white or red travertine marble to make potpourri jars as other examples of his unexpected use of traditional materials.

Mr Villoresi has travelled the world, greatly admires the traditional hospitality and sensuality that greeted him in India, Egypt, Morocco, Jordan, the Middle and Far East, and sees his perfume house as timeless, aspiring to no specific style, Florentine or other. The 16 fragrances in his prêt à porter range (€90 to €120 for a 100ml bottle) – split into classical and fantasy and designed for either gender – draw their names from several languages, French, Latin, Persian and Akkadian included. Some (such as Alamut) are earthy, opulent, aromatic and immediately transport your olfactory senses to the Orient. Acqua di Colonia recalls the age-old use of natural essential oils; while others simply recreate familiar aromas much-loved by all – the scent of a freshly powdered face (Teint de Neige), a freshly cut meadow (Yerbamate), a Tuscan herb garden (Spezie).

Despite the exotic influence of far-flung lands, a childhood spent in a villa near Florence plays its part in the art of this highly revered nose who won the coveted Prix François Coty in Europe's perfume-making capital, Grasse, in southern France in 2006.

'In the countryside where I grew up there were wild poppies in the fields; all the herbs and spices of the garden, those used for cooking, tomatoes, and so on, laurel and many other sources of odours and colour.'

'I use galbanum, especially in Yerbamate, a scent similar to that of wild poppy. In Uomo (Man – the first fragrance crafted by Mr Villoresi and the one he wears) and Dilmun I use laurel; if you take a laurel leaf and break it – a child especially does it – the smell is fantastic. Also in my family home, there were oranges, bitter oranges, 6m high, full of blossoms – an incredible smell.'

And if Florence were a fragrance: 'It would be a spring kind of fragrance, between April and May. It would be the fragrance of trees in the city, the magnolia trees, also wisteria, mimosa, other flowers and the green part of the city too made by the Cascine park.'

Mr Villoresi's next fragrance, Mare Nostrum, will reflect Tuscany's heady mix of mountain and seaside.

---

have little time for vanity or conceit – no messing here luv, what you see is what you get. That said, Umbrians are Italian, too (albeit salt-of-the-earth Italians) and, even in the pokiest of towns, they still don big sunglasses when it's cloudy.

The quintessential Umbrian never travels, lives in the same place for 400 years and has little worldliness to share. He is aloof, distant and will give you the warmest welcome when you leave. Those in walled, impenetrable Perugia will quickly realise it has yet to shake off its city-under-siege mentality.

LA DOLCE VITA

Life is *dolce* (sweet) for this privileged pocket of Italy – two of the country's wealthiest regions – where the family reigns supreme, and tradition and quality reign over quantity. From the great names in viticulture to the flower-producing industry of Pescia and Umbria's small-scale farms, it is family-run businesses handed between generations that form the backbone of this proud, strong region.

In Florence – the only city with a whiff of cosmopolitan air wafting through it (still pinprick tiny and scarcely multicultural compared to London, New York or any other real city) – daily life is the fastest paced. City-slick Florentines rise early, drop kids at school by 8am then flit from espresso standing up in the same *caffè* to the office by 9am. Lunch is a lengthy affair for these food- and wine-mad people, as is the early-evening *aperitivi* enjoyed in a bar with friends to whet appetites for dinner (around 9pm). Smokers – fast dwindling – puff on pavements outside.

Theatre, concerts, art exhibitions and *il calcio* (football) entertain after hours. Indeed, the region's two top-flight professional football clubs ACF Fiorentina and less lucky Perugia Calcio enjoy fanatical fan bases. Weekends see many flee their city apartments for less urban climes where the din of *motorini* (scooters) whizzing through the night is less, space and light more: green countryside is a 15-minute getaway from lucky old Florence, unlike many urban centres where industrial sprawl really sprawls.

Tuscans and Umbrians by their very nature travel little (many spend a lifetime living in the town of their birth) and place great importance on their family home – at 75% home ownership, Italy is among Europe's highest. An increasing chunk of Florentine society owns the countryside home they weekend in: €80,000 gets you a ramshackle fixer-upper on a hectare of land with olive trees near Terni; €200,000 buys the chance of a dream home in an abandoned 70 sq m deconsecrated stone church atop a hill near Città di Castello; and €4 million is the price to pay for a 16th-century Medici hunting lodge with orchard, camellia garden and manicured grounds near Pisa (some work required). At one time the domain of Tuscany's substantial well-off British population (there's good reason why playwright John Mortimer dubbed Chianti 'Chiantishire' in his 1989 TV adaptation, *Summer Lease*), the region's bounty of stylish stone villas and farmhouses with terracotta floors, wood-burning fireplace and terrace with view are as much in the hands of Tuscans eagerly rediscovering their countryside today as foreigners.

Rural lifestyle, particularly in Umbria, is slavishly driven by close-knit, ancient communities in small towns and villages where local matters and gossip are more important than national or world affairs. Everyone knows everyone to the point of being clannish, making assimilation for outsiders hard – if not impossible. Farming is the self-sufficient way of life, albeit

Florence is one of Italy's biggest centres of Buddhism, which counts 5000-odd followers throughout Tuscany; the city has small Jewish and Muslim populations, too.

Peep into a Tuscan home with Frances Mayes' beautifully illustrated, glossy coffee-table book *Bringing Tuscany Home: Sensuous Style from the Heart of Italy*.

A PEASANT LIFE

Mezzadria (share cropping), a medieval form of land management in place until 1979, was the key to success in the Tuscan countryside.

Contadini (peasants) lived and worked on the land, receiving in return a home for their traditionally large families (typically 10 – the more hands the better) and 50% of the crops or profit reaped from the land they worked. The other half went to the *padrone* (land owner), who often did not live on his *fattoria* (agricultural estate) but in the city.

Post-WWII industrialisation saw the birth of the tractor and the first shift in the equal balance between landowner and peasant: farmers had no money to buy tractors, obliging owners to invest instead and so upsetting the apple cart in terms of who gave how much. Gradually farm workers gravitated towards towns in search of better-paid jobs, the 1960s witnessing a particularly large exodus and so prompting the eventual collapse of share cropping and many a Tuscan farm with it.

A NOBLE LIFE

Sitting in the smaller of two lounges, hunting prints on one wall, line-up of past presidents on another, a white-gloved waiter in dovetail jacket brings two glasses of white wine on a silver tray. This, I later learn, is the 'foreign part' of the club where lady guests like myself (why, oh why, didn't I don a skirt this morning and leave my Adidas messenger bag at home) can tread: the games room, library, billiard table, ballroom and reading room with the day's newspapers are reserved strictly for members of Florence's exclusive, elusive Circolo dell' Unione (club of nobles to you and me), enthroned since 1852 in a *palazzo* (palace) on Florence's most aristocratic street, Via de' Tournabuoni.

You don't need 'a crown on your head' to join the club. But it helps, as Francesco Carlo Griccioli, *nobile* (nobleman) of both Florence and Siena (and the best-dressed, spriteliest 85-year-old in town), explains over lunch (in the guests' dining room; blue-blooded members lunch elsewhere).

'Names are examined, families, connections and all that, and the New Members' Commission gives its judgement to the board of directors – one black ball annuls five white balls', says Mr Griccioli, quickly explaining the club's self-perpetuating black-balling means of election, typical to many a gentlemen's club, as a perplexed look flashes across my face. Not hereditary, member-ship costs (a lot). Most of its 410 members (some female since five years ago) are, as Mr Griccioli delicately puts it, 'family members': 60% bear a title, albeit titles unrecognised by the Italian state since 1948 following the fall of the Italian monarchy.

From the 12th century until the Renaissance when wealth and ability overtook aristocratic ranking, titles of nobility – prince, duke, marques, count, viscount, baron, patrician and noble – ruled the roost. 'Florentine nobility derives mainly from bankers and merchants who made Flor-ence what it is,' says Mr Griccioli whose family – silk weavers – originated in Florence but moved to Siena in the 16th century where it acquired property. 'The titles of count and baron belong to feudal families, not merchants, who lived in castles and properties outside Florence', he says, citing the wine-making Ricàsoli family from Il Chianti as an example.

An army officer's son educated at home by British governesses, Mr Griccioli perfected his flawless English public-school accent during WWII attached to the British 8th army as Italian intelligence liaison officer. After a lifetime career working for Italian motor giant FIAT in India and the US, Mr Griccioli returned home, living first in a farmhouse outside Florence (Pisan wife Carla's dowry) and later moving into town when country life became too difficult.

'We like to have open house and always had guests and friends coming and going. Until 10 years ago it was fairly easy to get (domestic) assistance', says Mr Griccioli as the club's 'invisible' waiter glides silently towards our table, silver platter of veal in hand.

'I don't know if it is good or bad but when I was 20, 30 and 40 there was a separation between classes. Today, when I speak to my nephews, it is clear they mix with everyone. Yes, our club is exclusive, but outside of here the world is open.'

'If you can imagine we had servants galore and we had influence, prestige, position and all that, and this today doesn't exist any longer,' says Mr Griccioli good-naturedly. For him, patriot-ism, Roman Catholicism, the upkeep of tradition, gracious living and 'presenting oneself with a straight face to the rest of the world' matter most.

On Florence as one of the world's great cultural capitals: 'I always maintain the mayor of Florence can pick up the phone and call his counterpart in London or New York and they will listen.'

one that is becoming increasingly difficult – hence the mushrooming of *agriturismi* (farm-stay accommodation; p309) as farmers stoically utilise every resource they have to make ends meet.

Urban or rural, children typically remain at home until they reach their 30s, often only fleeing the nest to wed. In line with national trends, Tuscan and Umbrian families are small – two or three kids, with one third of Tuscan families childless. Despite increasing numbers of women working, chau-vinistic attitudes remain well entrenched in more rural areas where career opportunities have always been less or nonexistent.

TUSCAN DESIGN

Never has Italian design been so expressive as in 1963 when Piaggio in Pontedera (p191), 25km east of Pisa, launched the Vespa 50, a motorised scooter requiring no driving license. Overnight it became a 'must-have' item as Italy's young things snapped up the machine and the freedom and independence it gave. All of Europe's Vespas are still made in the Tuscan plant where the original 'wasp' was born in 1946.

While Audrey Hepburn was cruising around Rome side-saddle on a Vespa for Hollywood, a group of anti-establishment artists and architects were busy building a reputation for Florence as the centre of 1960s avant-garde design: design groups Radical Design, Archizoom and Superstudio were all founded in Florence in 1966, and included hot-shot Florentines Massimo Morozzi (b 1941; buy his pasta set from Alessi) and Andrea Branzi (b 1938), whose furniture designs are timeless.

As with fashion, the design scene moved to Milan in the 1970s starving Tuscany of its cutting edge.

E' QUI LA FESTA?

It's here the party? Delve into the mindset of a Tuscan or Umbrian and a holy trinity of popular folklore, agricultural tradition and religious rite of passage dances before your eyes. No cultural agenda is more jam-packed with ancient festivity than theirs: patron saints alone provide weeks of celebration given every village, town, profession, trade and social group has a saint they call their own and venerate religiously.

Festivities climax (twice!) with Siena's soul-stirring Il Palio (p246), a hot-blooded horse race conceived in the 12th century to honour the Virgin Mary and revamped six centuries on to celebrate the miracles of the Madonna of Provenzano (2 July) and Assumption (16 August). Deeply embroiled in its religious roots is fierce *contrada* rivalry, not to mention a fervent penchant for dressing up and a widespread respect of tradition that sees horses blessed before the race, jockeys riding saddleless, a local Sienese artist designing August's winning silk banner and a non-Sienese artist doing July's etc. Legend says that a Sienese bride marrying in far-off lands took earth from her *contrada* with her to put beneath the legs of her marital bed to ensure her offspring would be conceived on home soil. Atypical only to Siena, other folkloric festivals such as Arezzo's Giostra del Saracino (p298) and Pisa's Gioco del Ponte (p188) reflect the same historic division of cities and all-consuming *campanilismo* (literally, loyalty to one's bell tower).

No ritual is more agrarian in origin than Carnevale (p202), celebrated with gusto in Viareggio around Mardi Gras.

By no means the social force it was, Catholicism (the religion of 85% of the region) and its religious rituals play a key role in daily lives: first communions, church weddings and religious feast days are an integral part of Tuscan and Umbrian society.

LA BELLA FIGURA

A sense of style is vital to Tuscans who take great pride in their dress and appearance – not surprising given this is where the Italian fashion industry was born. Gucci and Salvatore Ferragamo (p151) got the haute-couture ball rolling in the 1920s with boutiques in Florence.

But it was in 1951 when a well-heeled Florentine nobleman called Giovanni Battista Giorgini held a fashion soiree in his Florence home that Italy's first prêt-a-porter fashion shows were spawned. The catwalk quickly shifted to Florence's Palazzo Pitti where Europe's most prestigious fashion shows dazzled until 1971 when Milan stole the show – for women's wear. Top designers

Smoking in all enclosed public places in Italy has been banned since 2005. Fines for maverick puffers range from €27.50 to €275, with higher penalties still for those who light up in the presence of pregnant women, lactating mothers and *bambini* (kids) under 12.

'Better a death in the family than a Pisan at the door' so goes an old Florentine proverb.

still leg it to Florence twice a year to unveil their menswear collections at the Pitti Immagine Uomo fashion shows and their creations for *bambini* (kids) at Pitti Bimbo; both events waltz around Fortezza da Basso. Florentine designers to look for include Roberto Cavelli, Enrico Coveri, Pucci and Ermanno Daeilli, the creative energy behind the Ermano Scervino label.

Indisputably beautiful is *la bella figura* of Umbrian-born model-turned-actress Monica Bellucci (b 1968), better known as Mary Magdelene in Mel Gibson's *The Passion of the Christ* (2004) than the face of *Elle*. Most recently, six months pregnant, she posed nude for *Vanity Fair* to express her disgust at an Italian law restricting in vitro fertilization to married couples and preventing the use of donor sperm.

Style tips: dress up, not down – shorts, flip-flops (thongs) and tacky T-shirts are no go in restaurants, cafés, clubs and bars in towns and attract plenty of stares elsewhere. Cover yourself well when entering a church (no shorts, short skirts or sleeveless tops) and at least a little when sunbathing on a beach; topless bathing is not *de rigueur* and nude sunbathing offends anywhere other than on a few remote beaches.

> Prato is one of Europe's major textile production centres; some 9000 factories employ around 45,000 people.

ARTS
Painting, sculpture and architecture is covered in Art & Architecture (p41).

Literature
The stirrings of Italian literature written in the vernacular began in Tuscany and Umbria in the beginning of the 13th century. One of the genres first created was spiritual poetry, concentrated in Assisi after the death of St Francis.

The first writer of real stature was Dante Alighieri (1265–1321), who wrote equally comfortably in both Italian and Latin. Born in Florence to a wealthy family, he received a rounded education, then became active in Florentine politics allying himself with the Guelph faction. Flexing his literary muscles,

> www.greatdante.net explains all you wanted to know about the great poet, his life and works.

TOP 10 NOVELS WITH A TUSCAN OR UMBRIAN SETTING

Travel literature aside, there are reams of novels with a local setting to pick from, ranging from 20th-century classics to comic contemporary works of fiction.

A Room with a View (EM Forster; 1908) A comedy of manners exploring the emotional awakening of a prim young English lady as she encounters Florence.

Aaron's Rod (DH Lawrence; 1921) A coal miner from the Midlands abandons his wife and children to pursue his dream of becoming a professional flautist in 1920s Florence.

The Birth of Venus (Sara Dunant; 2004) The glory – and gore – of Renaissance Florence is painted with extraordinary potency in this gripping bestseller.

The Custom of the Country (Edith Wharton; 1913) A honeymoon near Siena.

Indian Summer (Williams Dean Howells; 1886) A 40-something American newspaper publisher pursues his dream of living in Florence in this comic American-literature classic.

Innocence (Penelope Fitzgerald; 1986) The romantic adventures of an Italian noble family in the 16th and 20th centuries; short-listed for the Booker Prize.

My House in Umbria (William Trevor; 1991) A tender novel about the relationships between the survivors of a terrorist bomb attack as they recuperate in the Umbrian countryside. In 2003 it was made into a film starring Dame Maggie Smith.

Renato's Luck (Jeff Shapiro; 2001) Strife for the head of the local waterworks in sleepy Sant'Angelo d'Asso when a dam threatens to submerge the town.

Tuscany for Beginners: A Novel (Imogen Edward-Jones; 2005) Boisterous, racy, easy-on-the-brain story of life in a Tuscan B&B, with more than a touch of *Fawlty Towers*.

Where Angels Fear to Tread (EM Forster; 1905) 'Clash-of-cultures' tale about Lilia who marries an Italian gigolo in 'Monteriano', a fictionalised version of San Gimignano.

LOVE-LOCKED LOVERS

Any real Italian Romeo knows what to do when in Florence – head to the most famous bridge across the Arno where love-locked lovers declare their eternal love for another by locking a padlock, marked in felt-tip pen with the date and their initials, to the railings around a statue of Renaissance Florentine sculptor Benvenuto Cellini. Then they toss the key in the river.

In mid-2006 police cornered off part of Ponte Vecchio to remove 5500 *lucchetti d'amore* (love locks) from the railings. Just months later, they were smothered with hundreds more. The fine for love-locked lovers caught in the act is €50.

---

he began to write in different styles and genres, covering everything from philosophy and politics to love. He was exiled from Florence in 1301 when the opposing group, the Ghibellines (p34), took the reigns of power. He spent most of the rest of his life wandering Europe and composing, among much else, his *Divina Commedia* (Divine Comedy), the first great work written in Italian to stand the test of time.

Dante does not stand completely alone. Together with two fellow Tuscans, he formed the triumvirate that laid down the course for the development of a rich literature in Italian.

Petrarch (Francesco Petrarca; 1304–74), born in Arezzo to Florentine parents who had been exiled from their city at about the same time as Dante, wrote more in Latin than in Italian. *Il Canzoniere* is the distilled result of his finest poetry. Although the core subject is his unrequited love for a girl called Laura, the whole breadth of human grief and joy is treated with a lyrical quality hitherto unmatched. His influence spread far and across time: the Petrarchan sonnet form, rhyme scheme and even subject matter was adopted by the English Metaphysical poets of 17th-century England, such as John Donne.

The Florentine Giovanni Boccaccio (1303–75), who ended his days in Certaldo, was a friend of Petrarch. His masterpiece, *Decameron,* was written in the years following the plague of 1348, which he survived in Florence. Each of his 10 characters recounts a story featuring a vast panorama of personalities, events and symbolism.

During the second half of the 15th century, Lorenzo il Magnifico, the Medici ruler of Florence and patron of the arts *par excellence,* was handy with a pen in his own right. Just as importantly, his enlightened approach to learning and the arts created a healthy atmosphere for writers to flourish.

Another outstanding writer of the Florentine Renaissance is Niccolò Machiavelli (1469–1527; see p33), known above all for his work on power and politics, *Il Principe*. His *Mandragola* is a lively piece of comic theatre and a virtuoso example of Italian literature.

Tuscany and Umbria took a literary break during the 17th to 19th centuries, although Tuscany did give birth to Carlo Lorenzini (1826–90), creator of *Le Avventure di Pinocchio* (p200).

19TH CENTURY ONWARDS

Giosue Carducci (1835–1907) was one of the key figures of 19th-century Tuscan literature. Born in the Maremma, he spent the second half of his life in Bologna. The best of his poetry, written in the 1870s, ranged in tone from pensive evocation of death (such as in *Pianto Antico*) or memories of youthful passion *(Idillio Maremmano)* to an historic nostalgia harking back to the glories of ancient Rome.

Florence's Aldo Palazzeschi (1885–1974) was in the vanguard of the Futurist movement during the pre-WWI years. In 1911 he published arguably

Locally published *The Tuscany Lifestyle* by Pier Francesco Listri is a detailed portrait of just that: the Tuscans, their living space, their art of making and cuisine.

For spot-on, humorous anecdotes on local Tuscan culture seen from a female perspective, read Linda Falcone's entertaining *Italian Dance & I'm a Wallflower.*

his best work, *Il Codice di Perelà* (Perelà's Code), an at times bitter allegory that in part becomes a farcical imitation of the life of Christ.

By the 1920s and '30s Florence was bubbling with activity as a series of literary magazines flourished in spite of the Fascist regime. Magazines such as *Solaria,* which lasted from 1926 to 1934, its successor *Letteratura* (which began circulating in 1937) and *Il Frontespizio* (1929–40) gave writers from across Italy a platform from which to launch and discuss their work. One of its founding authors, Alessandro Bonsanti (1904–84) wrote essays and literary criticism. Guglielmo Petroni (1911–93), from Lucca, was another contributor to *Letteratura.* Although a poet of some note, he's chiefly recognised for his novel *Il Mondo è una Prigione* (The World Is a Prison; 1948), a vivid account of a political prison and the Italian Resistance. Mario Tobino (1910–91), from Viareggio, used his experience as director of a lunatic asylum to great effect in *Le Donne Libere di Magliano* (Free Women of Magliano).

One of Italy's leading post-war poets was the Florentine Mario Luzi (1914–2005), whose poetry expressed the anguish arising from the contrast between the individual and the broader universe.

Few women writers reached the limelight in Tuscany but an important exception was Anna Banti (1895–1985). Her approach to her characters was psychological, while simultaneously analysing the position of women in society.

Dacia Maraini (b 1936), for many years the partner of author Alberto Moravia, is Tuscany's most prominent contemporary female author, with some 10 novels and a fistful of plays to her credit. An interesting one is *Voci* (Voices), a mystery laced with disturbing social comment, where the main character, a female journalist, embarks on the investigation of a murder.

Pisa-born Antonio Tabucchi (b 1943) has written more than a dozen novels, plus volumes of short stories. One such story is *Sostiene Pereira* (translated into English and titled, bizarrely, *Pereira Declares* for the US market and *Declares Pereira* in the UK), set in prewar Lisbon.

> Gem up on local politics with the website of Tuscany's regional government at www .regione.toscana.it

Cinema

Tuscany's first claim to fame in the world of cinema is as the place where the film projector was invented, a year before the Lumière brothers patented theirs in Paris; poor Filoteo Alberini created his *kinetografo* (cinema projector) in Florence in 1895 but everyone ignored him.

TOP 10 FILMS SET HERE

Tuscany and Umbria remain a favourite location for English-language film directors.

- *A Room with a View* (1986)
- *The English Patient* (1996)
- *Much Ado About Nothing* (1993)
- *Life Is Beautiful* (1998)
- *Tea with Mussolini* (1999)
- *Gladiator* (2000)
- *Hannibal* (2001)
- *Under the Tuscan Sun* (2003)
- *My House in Umbria* (2003)
- *Portrait of a Lady* (2003)

The biggest name is Franco Zeffirelli (b 1923), whose career has taken him from radio and theatre to opera production and film. He created the TV blockbuster *Jesus of Nazareth* (1977) and many film adaptations of operas, along with film hits such as *Romeo and Juliet* (1968), *Hamlet* (1990) and the semiautobiographical *Tea with Mussolini* (1999).

Director and spirited actor Roberto Benigni (b 1952), a child of the village of Misericordia near Arezzo, picked up three Oscars and created a genre all of his own – Holocaust comedy – with *La Vita é Bella* (Life Is Beautiful; 1998), a film that prompted Charlie Chaplin's daughter, Geraldine, to declare that Benigni had inherited her father's cinematic poetry. Parts of *La Vita é Bella* and Begnini's less successful rendition of *Pinocchio* (2002) were shot at Papigno, a factory converted into movie studios near Terni.

Umbria hasn't seen much in the way of the film industry; Zeffirelli's 1972 *Brother Sun, Sister Moon* (about the lives of St Francis and St Clare) was shot in Assisi.

Theatre

Comic actress Maria Cassi, on stage for 25 years, is no fool; she can really make people laugh. Born of peasant stock in the house opposite the church on top of the hill in San Domenico di Fiesole, she is much loved all over Italy

---

DANIELE'S PLAYLIST

A high-flying events organiser, self-confessed reggae junkie and world traveller, Milan-born Daniele Palladini left for Jamaica when he was 18, has worked in Toronto, Boston and Rome, and arrived in Florence in 2005 to open Plasma (p146). As manager and art director of the region's most experimental music and video-art space, he knows the beat. Daniele says a wholly Tuscan sound is hard to pinpoint.

'Kids all over the world are connected with things like MySpace and You Tube. It's a huge melting pot and in the Western world there's been a standardisation of styles, making it difficult to tell if a band is from the UK, Italy or Finland, let alone Tuscany!'

'Tuscany is quite good for indies. But big bands only stop in Milan and sometimes Rome. The big problem is Italy's getting old and it's increasingly difficult for young people to find spaces to express themselves. Yes, Italy does have the biggest arts patrimony in the world, but we cannot live forever in the Renaissance.'

Despite all the odds, Tuscany does yield a diverse line-up ('the soil for musicians here is rich') as Daniele's playlist of the region's most interesting sounds now reveals.

Appaloosa (www.appaloosarock.com) Rebellious Livorno's much-loved band.

Elton Junk (www.myspace.com/eltonjunk) Psychedelic punk trio from Siena.

Ether (www.myspace.com/3ther) Electronic IDM sound, a tad experimental, from Florence; independent indie label.

evanicetrip (www.myspace.com/evanicetrip) Florentine rock band looking for a label.

Jealousy Party (www.myspace.com/jealousyparty) Florentine free jazz trio dedicated to improvisation.

Miranda (www.mirandamiranda.it) Florence-based noise/experimental-punk trio, brilliant live, with two albums to date; *Rectal Explorations* (2006; from SCRATCH records) is the latest.

Moleskin (www.moleskin.it) Post-rock from Città di Castello.

O.B.O (www.oboism.com) oshinOko Bunker Orchestra: noise'n'roll in Florence.

Samuel Katarro (www.myspace.com/samuelkatarro) Modern one-man band from Pistoia.

Train de Vie (www.traindevie.net) Florentine popfolk fusing a violin, flute, guitar and voice with strong Afro-Latin and folk-rock rhythms hammered on bass and drums; its third album was recorded live in Florence's Teatro di Rifredi in 2007.

TV Lumière (www.tvlumiere.it) Dark melodic melancholic post-rock sound from Terni; self-produced its first album, *TV Lumière* (2005).

Zenerswoon (www.zenerswoon.com) Three-piece indie rock band from Florence with one album to date, *There In the Sun* (2005).

for her strong Tuscan humour, mime and expression, which she gets from her dad: 'He had a strong sense of narration, of telling a tale with gestures to make it stronger,' she says with a smile. For Ms Cassi, artistic director at Florence's ground-breaking Teatro del Sale (p141), theatre in Tuscany has never been so innovative: the region boasts more than 200 theatres, many 'more like workshops, constantly producing, evolving'.

No theatre better reflects Tuscany's peasant roots than Monticchiello's Teatro di Povero (p273), near Pienza in central Tuscany. Each summer and at Christmas, villagers stage a series of plays inspired by the traditions, trials and tribulations of their tiny Tuscan village, home to some 300 people.

Music

Far and away Tuscany's most famous musical figure is Lucca-born Giacomo Puccini (1858–1924), composer of opera classics *Madame Butterfly*, *Tosca* and *La Bohème* (p195).

On a different note, one of Italy's former leading pop bands Litfiba was a Florentine product – its ex-singer Pero Pelù, now continues solo – and both Jovanotti, the country's most popular rap singer, and the singer Irene Grandi are also Tuscan. Siena-born Gianna Nannini is an internationally acclaimed and politically active Italian artist whose work ranges from rock albums to film soundtracks.

Tuscany has produced plenty of bands and musicians, ranging from Marasco – a gritty, folksy singer from Florence big in the 1950s – through to Dirotto Su Cuba, a trip-hop band. In Umbria, jazz has an enormous following thanks to Umbria Jazz and the Spoleto Festival, major events on the European jazz calendar.

If you read Italian, www .cultura.toscana.it bursts with up-to-the-minute information on Tuscany's cultural scene, theatre, music, literature and dance.

Food & Drink

Ask any Tuscan who created French cuisine and they'll say Tuscany: in 1533 Catherine de' Medici wed the Duke of Orleans in Marseille, taking an entourage of master cooks, pastry makers and meat men with her from Florence.

Be it shopping for fresh produce at Florence's central market (p143), snacking on a tripe burger (p137), sinking your teeth into a *bistecca alla fiorentina* (p68) or sniffing out truffles (p170), this region cooks up a feast of gastronomic experiences.

'To cook like your mother is good, to cook like your grandmother is better,' says the Tuscan proverb. And indeed, it is age-old recipes passed between generations that form the backbone of contemporary Tuscan and Umbrian cuisine. Ever faithful to its humble rural roots, it is a peasant fare based on beans, bread and other cheap, abundant essentials that these *mangiafagioli* ('bean eaters' as Tuscans are known by other Italians) thrive on…and are envied the world over.

During the 13th and 14th centuries when Florence prospered and the wealthy started using silver cutlery instead of fingers, simplicity remained the hallmark of dishes cooked up at the lavish banquets held by feuding families as a show of wealth. During the Renaissance the Medici passion for flaunting the finer things in life gave Tuscan cuisine a fanciful kick as spectacular sculptures of sugar starred alongside spit-roasted suckling pig on the banquet table.

Yet for ordinary Tuscans and town trattorie, it was the region's age-old 'poor dishes' that kept hunger at bay. These dishes were dictated by each season, used fresh local produce or leftovers, and were savoured around a shared table. Contemporary Tuscan and Umbrian cuisine continues this tradition.

THE COUNTRY KITCHEN

It was over an open wood fire in *la cucina contadina* (the farmer's kitchen) that Tuscan and Umbrian cuisine was cooked up. Its basic premise: don't waste a crumb.

THE ARK OF TASTE

Save the Zolfino bean and the Cetica red potato (makes a mean gnocchi)! Bake more Casola chestnut bread! Breed more Zeri lambs!

An international project born and headquartered in Florence, the Ark of Taste is essentially a list of endangered food products drawn up by the Slow Food Foundation for Biodiversity in partnership with the Region of Tuscany. It covers the world and protects indigenous edibles threatened with extinction by industrialisation, globalisation, hygiene laws, environmental dangers and so on.

In Tuscany 32 items make it onto the list (including Colonnata lard, Certaldo onions, Garfagnana potato bread, Carmignano dried figs, Londa Regina peaches, Pistoian Mountain *pecorino* cheese and *bottarga* – made from the salted roe of red mullet). Umbria has three endangered items (sweet red Cannara onions, Trevi black celery and Lake Trasimeno beans).

Tuscan cured meats are particularly plentiful on the endangered list: *maleggato* (blood sausage from San Miniato), *mortadella* (made dull pink with drops of alkermes liqueur), Siennese *buristo* (pig's blood salami), Valdarno *tarese* (a 50cm- to 80cm-long pancetta spiced with red garlic, orange peel and covered in pepper), Florentine *bardiccio* (fresh fennel-flavoured sausage encased in a natural skin of pig intestine and eaten immediately) and *biroldo* (spiced sausage made from pig's head and blood in Garfagnana).

Dining on or sampling any of these items when in the region guarantees an authentic, delicious, tasting experience. For a full list see www.fondazioneslowfood.it.

Meat & Game

The icon of Tuscan cuisine is Florence's *bistecca alla fiorentina*, a loin steak legendary not only for its gluttonous size but because it was at one time outlawed (see p68).

Tuscan markets conjure up an orgy of animal parts most wouldn't even dream of digesting. In the past the prime beef cuts were only the domain of the wealthy. Offal was the prime fare of peasants who cooked tripe in the pot for hours with onions, carrots and herbs to make *lampredotto* or with tomatoes and herbs to make *trippa alla fiorentina* – two Florentine classics still going strong.

Fortunately *pasto*, a particularly gruesome mix of cows lungs (*picchiante*) and chopped potatoes, is not even a gastronomic curiosity these days – unlike *cibrèo* (chicken's kidney, liver, heart and cockscomb stew) and *colle ripieno* (stuffed chicken's neck), two dishes not for the faint-hearted that can still be sampled at Trattoria Cibrèo in Florence (p141). Another fabulous golden oldie (cooked by the Etruscans no less as many a fresco illustrates) still going strong is *pollo al mattone* – boned chicken splattered beneath a brick, rubbed with herbs and baked beneath the brick. The end result: handsomely crispy.

Wild boar, hunted in autumn, is turned into sausages (*salsicce di cinghiale*) or simmered for hours to make a rich stew.

Pork reigns supreme in Umbria, where every last morsel of the family pig was eaten. Butchers from Norcia (p383) were so well known for their craft in medieval times that, to this day, a pork butcher anywhere in Italy is known as a *norcino* and works in a *norcineria*. Pigs are roasted whole on a spit to become *la porchetta* (suckling pig), or slaughtered, butchered and conserved (to eat in the long hard winter traditionally) as *prosciutto di Norcia*, a coarse salty cured ham. Other porky Umbrian specialities include *capocollo* (seasoned cured pork sausage), *barbozzo* (pig-cheek bacon) and *mazzafegati* (pork liver, orange peel and sultana sausages).

In Tuscany the family pig invariably ended up on the plate as a salty slice of *soprassata* (head, skin and tongue boiled, chopped and spiced with garlic, rosemary etc), *finocchiona* (fennel-spiced sausage), *prosciutto* (from Casentino is the best), nearly black *mallegato* (blood sausage spiked with nutmeg, cinnamon, raisins and pine kernels from San Miniato) or *mortadella* (salami speckled with cubes of white fat). Butcher legend Dario Cecchini (p166) in Il Chianti is the most fun man to taste these with and buy them from. *Lardo di Colonnata* (tasty pig fat aged in salt and herbs for at least six months) is among the Tuscan food products safeguarded by Slow Food's Ark of Taste (opposite).

> The strap line of Bill Buford's hilarious *Heat* says it all: an amateur's adventures as kitchen slave, line cook, pasta maker and – most significantly – an apprentice for six months to Il Chianti's legendary Dante-quoting butcher (p166).

Fish

Livorno leads the region in seafood, fishy *cacciucco* (one 'c' for each type of fish thrown into it) being its signature dish. Deriving its name from the Turkish *kukut*, meaning 'small fry', *cacciucco* is a stew of five fish simmered with tomatoes and red peppers, and served atop stale bread. *Triglie alla Livornese* is red or white mullet cooked in tomatoes and *baccalà alla Livornese*, also with tomatoes, features cod traditionally salted aboard the ships en route to the old Medici port. Salt cod, not to be confused with unsalted air-dried stockfish (*stoccofisso*), is a Tuscan trattoria mainstay – served as tradition demands on Friday.

The area around Lake Trasimeno in Umbria is another *pesce* (fish) hot spot, where you can fish and eat your own catch (p359), or dine out on *carpa regina in porchetta* (carp cooked in a wood oven with loads of fennel and garlic) and *tegamaccio* (a kind of soupy stew of the best varieties of local lake

THE ETIQUETTE OF BISTECCA ALLA FIORENTINA

'There is only one way to cook a *bistecca alla fiorentina*. If you ask for it blue or well done you are asking for something else', says Umberto Montana between antipasti bites of *soprassata* (head, skin and tongue boiled, chopped and spiced with garlic, rosemary etc) and *finocchiona* (fennel-spiced sausage) over lunch at Osteria del Caffè Italiano (p140), his *osteria* which cooks traditional Tuscan cuisine.

'Burnt outside and completely raw inside…that is not a *bistecca alla fiorentina*. It should be pink in the middle; just the finest slither is blue', he continues enthusiastically, illustrating the required rainbow of colours with two slices of bread as I savour a sweet Tuscan artichoke and eye up the 45 different bottles of olive oil vying to be tested on a dresser opposite.

Florence's legendary hunk of a beef cut sits on the T-bone, is between 3cm and 4cm to 5cm thick and easily feeds two. It comes from Tuscany's beautiful cream-coloured Chianina cattle aged at least 15 months old and the loin must hang for a minimum of 10 days.

'Good meat and a good fire' are the secrets to a perfect *bistecca alla fiorentina* says Mr Montana, who pays a good deal more for his meat to hang for at least 25 days, preferably 40, thus ensuring it arrives in his restaurant mouth-melting tender. He cooks it straight – no salt ('dries the meat, makes it tough'), no olive oil ('fat in the meat already') – and cooks it on all three sides ('turn it thrice') above an exactly controlled fire of moderate temperature ('too hot, it will burn'). Total cooking time: 15 to 20 minutes; salt and pepper before serving.

Bistecca alla fiorentina, banned by the EU for fear of mad-cow disease in 2001 and back on the menu since 2006, is priced by *l'etto* (100g). Pay around €45 per kilo.

---

fish – eel, whiting, perch, trout and so on – simmered in olive oil, white wine and herbs).

Pulses, Grains & Vegetables

Poor man's meat was precisely what pulses were to Tuscans and Umbrian centuries ago. Jam-packed with protein, cheap and available year-round (eaten fresh in summer, dried in winter), pulses (beans, peas and lentils) – of which an incredible variety exist – make some of the region's most traditional dishes, *minestra di fagioli* (bean soup) and *pasta e ceci* (chickpea pasta) included. Throw the other dirt-cheap staple, bread, into the pot and what do you get – *minestra di pane* (bread and bean soup) and *ribollita* (a 'reboiled' bean, vegetable and bread soup with black cabbage, left to sit for a day before being served).

White *cannellini* beans drizzled in olive oil are an inevitable accompaniment to meat. Amid the dozens of different bean varieties, *cannellini* and dappled *borlotti* are the most common, the round yellow *zolfino* and silky smooth *sorano* bean the most prized. The greenish *verdino di Cave* and yellowish *giallo di Cave* cultivated for at least century in Cave, a hamlet near Foligno in northern Umbria, is harvested and the entire crop sold at the village's Sagra del fagiolo di Cave in October. Another Umbrian variety, the small white *fagiolo del purgatorio* (purgatorial bean), alludes to the centuries-old Lenten tradition of eating beans on Ash Wenesday to purge sins.

Lenticchie (green lentils) from Castelluccio, near Norcia in Umbria, are another source of local pride, as are the 18 local varieties of *farro dicocco* (emmer wheat), an ancient grain cultivated in the Valnerina area and around Spoleto, southern Umbria. Of a similar age to emmer but with a tougher husk is *farro della Garfagnana* (spelt), a grain grown in Central Europe as early as 2500 BC and one that has never died out in the Garfagnana, northwest Tuscany.

The Tuscan vegetable garden is lush, strictly seasonal, and one that sees medieval vegetables cultivated alongside tomatoes, zucchini, mushrooms

Enjoy great website design and plenty of recipes and extensive descriptions of regional Tuscan and Umbrian specialities at www .italianmade.com.

and others common to most European tables: wild fennel, black celery (braised as a side dish), sweet red onions (delicious oven baked), artichokes and zucchini flowers (both stuffed and oven baked), black cabbage, broad beans, chicory, chard, thistle-like cardoons and green tomatoes are among the more unusual to look out for.

Practically an antique and prized the world over as one of the most expensive spices, saffron is fast becoming all the rage again, particularly around San Gimignano where it was enthusiastically traded in medieval times. A fiery red and as fine as dust by the time it reaches the kitchen,

---

INTERVIEW WITH FABIO PICCHI

Deeply rooted in tradition yet full of surprises best describes the cuisine of Tuscany's most well-known chef, Fabio Picchi, who famously serves no pasta in his fabled Florentine trattoria (p141) – itself named after one of his most ancestral dishes, *cibrèo*.

'It is an old family recipe – chicken kidney, liver, heart and cockscomb. It may be stewed, but the best way is with spinach and parmesan flan, in the middle of which you throw the *cibrèo*', says the Florentine with a wide smile. He casually throws in that stuffed chicken's neck (which, incidentally, is served head on plate) is another memorable family heirloom recipe.

Fabio Picchi smiles a lot. A large burly man with handsome white hair, full beard, he has an enormously gentle, charismatic manner. He exudes passion – passion for the Renaissance city where he was born, for food, for his four children (two of whom, 20-year-old Duccio and 25-year-old Giulio, work with him) and for his own childhood, of which five months of the year was idyllically spent on Isola d'Elba.

'My father, a professional scuba-diving fisherman, tried not to become rich but to simply do what he loved, and that was fishing. At home there was always lots of fish for my mother to cook.' Fabio cites two of his most poignant culinary memories as shellfish cooked with tomatoes, and particularly fatty fish – such as *sgombro* (mackerel) or *sugarelli* (scad) – combined with rosemary, sage, garlic, olive oil and 'other things found on the rocks', then cooked in vinegar to annul the fat.

The other is *arrosto di agnello* (leg of lamb), a traditional Tuscan family feast served at Easter and, depending on the family, a handful of other times a year.

'For me it wasn't so much the lamb as the way of eating it. I realised I was an adult the day my father gave me the roasting tin to mop up the juices with bread!' says the larger-than-life chef. On the day I lunched there, his Teatro del Sale (p141) kitchen cooked up an inventive mouth-watering mix of spit-roasted meat cuts, sausage and, most notably, hunks of baguette-type bread dunked in oil before cooking. The result – dished up in a roasting tin – was divine.

For Fabio Picchi, food and taste is a happy, emotional affair, nurtured by the extraordinary love his own parents exhibited so passionately towards one another and expressed today in the chef's culinary philosophy of combining simple flavours.

'Mayonnaise – a combination of egg, olive oil and lemon juice – is a perfect example of this, of creating a fourth element completely different from the original three.' One of his personal favourites served at Cibrèo (p141) – a simple ricotta and potato flan – gets its kick from the puddles of *ragù* (meat sauce), olive oil and dusting of grated parmesan it is served with. His star *primo*, so much in demand that he deliberately doesn't always serve it to ensure appetites stay whetted, is *passato di peperoni gialli* (yellow bell-pepper soup).

'So why no pasta?' I ask this Slow Food–hailed chef for whom Tuscan cuisine is an age-old tradition that scarcely changes ('there's a big difference between Tuscan cuisine and Tuscan restaurants'). Is it, as the press says, a deliberate move on his part to uphold a true Tuscan culinary tradition?

'No. Pasta is as traditional to Tuscany as it is to Naples. When I opened Cibrèo in 1979 I was 24 and only had a wood stove, and to keep water boiling all day on a wood stove was a problem. So I decided no pasta. And the next day everyone was talking about this Italian restaurant in Florence with no pasta. It was my fortune!' he laughs.

saffron in its rawest state is, in fact, the dried flower stigma of the saffron crocus. Should you want to learn how it is grown, stay at Podere Castellare (p165).

Pasta

Florentine chef Fabio Picchi (p69) says it is a fallacy to say that pasta is not part of Tuscan cuisine: he has a good giggle every time the press yet again cites the absence of pasta in his Florence trattoria as a reflection of true Tuscan gastronomy. Indeed, no Tuscan banquet would be quite right without a *primo* of home-made *maccheroni* (wide flat ribbon pasta), *pappardelle* (wider flat ribbon pasta) or Siennese *pici* (ultrathin strands of spaghetti-like pasta dried in *tagliatelle*-style nests) served with a duck, hare, rabbit or boar sauce.

Umbria has its own pasta: round stringlike *umbricelli* (also spelled *ombricelli*), fatter than spaghetti, and *strangozzi* (*strozzapreti* in some towns), which is like *umbricelli* but with a rougher surface to better absorb the accompanying meat, tomato or (culinary orgasm alert!) black-truffle sauce.

Bread

One bite and the difference strikes – *pane* (bread) here is unsalted, creating a disconcertingly bland taste many a bread lover might never learn to love.

Yet it is this centuries-old staple, deliberately unsalted to ensure it lasted for a good week and to compliment the region's salty cured meats, that forms the backbone of Tuscany's most famous dishes: *pappa al pomodoro* (a thick bread and tomato soup, eaten hot or cold), *panzanella* (a tomato and basil salad mixed with a mush of bread soaked in cold water) and *ribollita*. None sound or look particularly appetising, but their depth of flavour is extraordinary.

Thick-crusted *pane Toscana* (also known as *pane casalingo*) is the basis of two antipasti delights, traditionally served on festive occasions but appearing on most menus today – *crostini* (lightly toasted slices of bread topped with liver pate) and *fettunta* (also called *crogiantina* or *bruschetta;* toast fingers doused in garlic, salt and olive oil).

Cheese

So important was cheese-making in the past, it was deemed a dowry skill. Still highly respected, the *pecorino* (sheep's milk cheese) crafted in Pienza, a Tuscan town near the Umbrian border, ranks among Italy's greatest *pecorini*: taste it young and mild in the company of fava beans; or more mature and tangier, spiked with *toscanello* (black pepper corns) or *pecorino di tartufo* (black-truffle shavings). *Pecorino* massaged with olive oil during the ageing process turns red and is called *rossellino*.

Pecorino is commonly served region wide as a first course with either fresh pear or chestnuts and honey. Mild-tasting *caciotta* is made from cow's milk and laced with truffle shavings by Umbrians to become *caciotta al tartufo*. Shepherds in the Umbrian hills traditionally salted ricotta (*ricotta salata*) to preserve it.

Any dish *alla livornese* is tomato red, Livorno apparently being Europe's first city in the 16th century to cook with tomatoes (imported from the USA).

'In Tuscany the bread has to be eaten and if it can't be eaten, you cook it.'
UMBERTO MONTANA, ALLE MURATE (P139), FLORENCE

AN APPETITE FOR UMBRIA

The best cookbook on Umbria right now is *An Appetite for Umbria* by Christine Smallwood (£19.99; Bonny Day Publishing). Smallwood has compiled recipes from the best restaurants in Umbria – Il Bacco Felice in Foligno, La Fornace di Mastro Giorgio in Gubbio etc – along with a beautiful guide to Umbrian food and wine. Available for sale in several of the restaurants listed and from the website www.appetiteforumbria.com.

PIG UGLY BUT PRECIOUS

From Etruscan truffle hunts to hunting with Imperio and a dog called Toby (p170), how *tartufi* (truffles) grow remains a mystery. They're not a plant, they don't spawn like a mushroom and cultivating them is impossible.

The known facts are that they grow in symbiosis with an oak tree; come in 'white' (actually a mouldy old yellowish colour) or black; and are sniffed out by highly trained dogs (traditionally it was a pig) from late November to early January in two privileged pockets of Tuscany (around San Giovanni d'Asso near Siena and San Miniato west of Florence), and Norcia and Spoleto in Umbria.

Pig ugly but precious, these highly sought-after lumps of fungus are certainly worth their weight in gold. They are typically served with simple mild-tasting dishes (a plate of pasta? perfect!) to give the palate full opportunity to revel in their subtle flavour. Yet it is the pungent aroma of these knobbly lumps that is the most extraordinary (it can even be aphrodisiacal according to some).

Olive Oil

Olive oil heads the culinary trinity (bread and wine are the other two) and epitomises the earthy simplicity that Tuscan and Umbrian cuisine is all about: dipping chunks of bread into pools of this liquid gold or biting into a slice of oil-doused *fettunta* are sweet pleasures in life here.

The Etruscans were the first to cultivate olive trees and press the fruit to make oil, a process later refined by the Romans. As with wine, strict rules govern when and how olives are harvested (October through to 31 December), the varieties used and so on. Extra virgin oil originating from the terraced hillsides in Umbria is covered by one state-regulated Denomination of Protected Origin (DOP), while the best Tuscan oils bear a Chianti Classico DOP or Terre di Siena DOP label and an IGP certificate of quality issued by the region's Consortium of Tuscan Olive Oil.

In *Around the Tuscan Table*, renowned food scholar and academic Carole Counihan takes an anthropological look at family and food and how it has changed over the decades in 20th-century Florence.

Sweets, Chocolate & Ice

Be it the simple honey, almond and sugar-cane sweets traditionally served at the start of 14th-century banquets in Florence or the sugar sculptures made to impress at the flamboyant 16th- and 17th-century feasts of the power-greedy Medici, *dolci* (sweets) have always been reserved for festive occasions. In more humble circles street vendors sold *bamboloni* (doughnuts) and *pandiramerino* (rosemary-bread buns), while carnival (p73) in Florence was marked by *stiacchiata* (Florentine flat bread made from eggs, flour, sugar and lard, then dusted with icing sugar).

As early as the 13th century, servants at the Abbazia di Montecelso near Siena paid tax to the nuns in the form of *panpepato* (a pepper and honey flat bread), although legend tells a different tale: following a siege in Siena, the good-hearted Sister Berta baked a revitalising flat cake of honey, dried fruit, almonds and pepper to pep up the city's weakened inhabitants. Subsequently sweetened with spices, sprinkled with icing sugar and feasted on once a year at Christmas, Siena's *panforte* (literally 'strong bread') – a flat, hard cake with nuts and candied fruit – is eaten year-round today. An old wives tale says it stops couples quarrelling.

Unsurprisingly it was at the Florentine court of Catherine de' Medici that Italy's most famous product, gelato (ice cream), first appeared thanks to court maestro Bernardo Buontalenti (1536–1608), who engineered a way of freezing sweetened milk and egg yolks together; the ice house he designed still stands in the Boboli Gardens (p124). For centuries, ice cream and sherbets – a mix of shaved ice and fruit juice served between courses at Renaissance banquets to aid digestion – only appeared on wealthy tables.

In Tuscany there are some six million olive trees studding 55,000 hectares, framed by 10,000 olive-oil producers.

Tuscan *biscotti* (biscuits) – served with candied fruits and sugared almonds at the start of and between courses at Renaissance banquets – are dry, crisp and often double baked. *Cantucci* are traditionally studded with almonds but spiked with anything from chocolate to apricots these days. *Brighidini di Lamporecchio* are small round aniseed-flavoured wafers; *ricciarelli* are almond biscuits, sometimes with candied orange; and pine kernels stud *lardpinocchiati*. All these biscuits are best sampled when dipped in a glass of *Vin Santo* (p74). In Lucca *buccellato*, a treat that is given by godparents to their godchild on their first Holy Communion, is sweetness and light (p198).

Umbrian chocolate is legendary – the world-famous *baci* (hazelnut 'kisses' covered with chocolate) being made at the now Nestlé-owned Perugina chocolate factory (p324), which can be visited in Perugia.

TUTTI A TAVOLA

Walk into a trattoria or restaurant half an hour before opening time and the chatter of its entire staff merrily dining around a communal table strikes you instantly.

For where to eat and drink, typical restaurant opening hours, dining with kids, drinks other than wine, vegetarians and vegans and so on, see p403.

Tutti a tavola (the shared table) is an integral part of culinary culture. Traditionally gathering for a hearty *pranzo* (lunch) around noon, families – during the working week at least – tend to share the main family meal in the evening now. Sunday lunch does, however, remain sacred. *Colazione* (breakfast), a quick dash in a bar or *caffé* on the way to work for a cappuccino and *cornetto* (croissant), scarcely counts as a meal.

An everyday *cena* (dinner) comprises a *primo* (first course) and *secondo* (second course), usually accompanied by a *contorno* (vegetable side dish) and a piece of fruit as dessert. The traditional Italian, belt-busting five-course whammy of *antipasto* (appetiser), *primo, secondo* with *contorno, insalata* (salad) and *dolci* (dessert) generally only happens on Sunday and feast days. In true Italian style, coffee – as in a short sharp espresso shot and *nothing* else (no cappuccino please) – is only ever served at the end of a meal alongside, on special occasions, a digestive of grappa (p74) or other fiery liqueur. Bread flows but don't expect a side plate; put it on the table (sauce-mopping is not allowed) and know you'll pay for it – restaurants charge a fixed €1.50 to €3 per head *coperto* (cover).

On the volatile subject of pasta, Italians don't go to restaurants to eat pasta – every Italian thinks he can cook pasta better at home. It is not locals therefore who eat *lasagne* and *spaghetti Bolognese* in restaurants, rather tourists, meaning places with these dishes are essentially tourist traps. Should your pasta involve fish don't ask for parmesan, and if it happens to be long and thin, twirling it around your fork as if you were born twirling is the only way. Should you be confronted with a long piece dangling, bite rather than suck.

Dress decently when dining and strike a pose by resting your forearms or wrists (never elbows) on the table. Finally, if you want to avoid dishes tampered to suit tourist tastebuds, avoid the fixed-price *menù turistico*. Good value as it might appear, it is a pale reflection of authentic fare consumed by locals.

Smoking is illegal in all public places, cafés and restaurants included.

BUONE FESTE

Be it the start of a harvest, a wedding, birth or religious holiday, traditional celebrations are intrinsically woven into Tuscan culinary culture. By no means as raucous as festivals of the past when an animal was sacrificed, most remain meaty affairs. As integral to the festive calendar as these madcap days of overindulgence are the days of eating *magro* (lean) – fasting days, usually preceding every feast day and in place for 40 days during Lent.

Tuscans have baked simple breads and cakes like ring-shaped *berlingozzo* (Tuscan sweet bread) and *schiacciata alla fiorentina* (a flattish spongey bread-cum-cake best made with old-fashioned lard) for centuries during Carnevale, the period of merrymaking leading up to Ash Wednesday. Fritters are another sweet Carnevale treat: *cenci* are plain twists (literally 'rags') of fried sweet dough sprinkled with icing sugar; *castagnole* look like puff-up cushions; and *fritelle di mele* (apple fritters) are slices of apple battered, deep fried and eaten warm with plenty of sugar.

Pasqua (Easter) is big. On Easter Sunday, families take baskets of hard-boiled white eggs covered in a white-cloth napkin to church to be blessed and return home to a luncheon feast of roast lamb gently spiced with garlic and rosemary, pre-empted by the blessed eggs. In Umbria, *ciaramicola* is the traditional Easter cake. Shaped in a ring with five humps representing Perugia's five historical quarters, it comes iced in white and sprinkled with multicoloured hundreds-and-thousands.

September's grape harvest sees grapes stuck on top of *schiacciata* to make *schiacciata con l'uva* (grape cake), and autumn's chestnut harvest brings a flurry of chestnut festivals and *castagnaccio* (chestnut cake baked with chestnut flower, studded with raisins, topped with a rosemary sprig and delicious served with a slice of ricotta) to the Tuscan table. Come *Natale* (Christmas), a *bollito misto* (boiled meats) with all the trimmings is the traditional festive dish in many families: various meaty animal parts, trotter et al, are thrown in the cooking pot and simmered for hours with a vegetable and herb stock. The meat is later served with mustard, salsa verde and other sauces. A whole pig, notably the recently revived ancient white-and-black Cinta Senese (Siena belted) breed, roasted on a spit is the other option.

Elizabeth Romer's *The Tuscan Year* is a beautiful and extremely informative account of Tuscan farm life in a valley, seen through the eyes of a committed foodie; recipes add extra zest.

A typical Chianti Classico stays on the table and is part of the food. As a child I remember my grandfather putting the *fiasche* (flask) on the table and it stayed there for every meal.

COSIMO GERICKE, CHIANTI WINE PRODUCER, FATTORIA DI RIGNANA (P312)

MESSAGE IN A BOTTLE

Call yourself a rock star? Then show us your wine label! While Bob Dylan's scrawl of an autograph graces the etiquette of the full-bodied red Planet Waves, produced from a Montepulciano and Merlot grape mix at the Fattoria La Terrazza (www.fattorialeterrazze.it), 100km east of Umbria, Sting has plumped for the Tuscan heart – Il Chianti. His private label, limited and signed, is a Chianti Colli Aretini known as Il Serrestori, named after the silk-weaving family who once ruled the vast wine-producing estate near Figline Valdarno that the ageing rocker snapped up for a mere €6 million in 2002.

HOT DATES

Dedicated oenophiles could plan a trip around the last weekend in May when dozens of wine-producing estates in Tuscany and Umbria open their cellars to wine-tasters during **Cantine Aperte**, an annual festival organised by Italy's dynamic **Wine Tourism Movement** (www .movimentoturismovino.it).

Other hot dates to consider include **Benvenuta Vendemmia** (Welcome Harvest), a grape-harvest festival on a September Sunday; **Novello in Cantina**, an opportunity to taste the new wines in November; and the festive **Calici di Stelle** on 10 August which ushers in wine, dance and folk music to town squares.

Food festivals – a great excuse to dine well, drink and sometimes dance 'til dawn – stud the region's rich cultural calendar (see p22).

WINE

There's much more to this vine-rich region than cheap, raffia-wrapped bottled Chianti – *that* was the 1970s darling. Something of a viticulture powerhouse in Italy today, Tuscany and Umbria provides plenty of excitement for visiting oenophiles.

Vin santo (literally 'holy wine') is sweet to both regions. Sip the golden syrupy dessert wine at Mass (!) or as a dessert with a plate of almond-studded *cantucci* (p71).

Wine tasting is an endless pleasure in both regions where myriad *enoteche* (wine bars) and *cantine* (wine cellars) ensure tastebuds stay titillated. Trattorie wine lists feature a limited selection generally, but most midrange and top-end restaurants stock a gambit of price ranges and geographical origins.

When selecting, remember a *vino da tavola* (table wine) could well be so simply because its producer has chosen not to adhere to the regulations governing production, thus does not bear a state-issued Denominazione di Origine Controllata (DOC) or Denominazione d'Origine Controllata e Garantita (DOCG) classification typically associated with quality. *Superiore* on the label denotes DOC wines above the general standard (perhaps with greater alcohol or longer ageing) and *Riserva* is applied only to DOC or DOCG wines aged for a specified amount of time.

This said, ordering a glass or jug of *vino della casa* (house wine) costs no more than €6 a litre and will not disappoint.

> Indispensable for any expert or lover of Italian wines is *Italian Wines* (Gambero Rosso & Slow Food Editore), an annual wine guide in English with detailed reviews of 2200 wine producers and 16,000 wines across 1000 pages.

Tuscany

> American food, wine and travel writer Kyle Phillips, wed to a Florentine and living in Tuscany, produces two excellent websites reviewing Italian cuisine at http://italianfood.about .com and wine at www .italianwinereview.com

Tuscany is largely about reds, Brunello di Montalcino being up there at the top with Italy's most prized: count on €5 a glass, €20 to €100 for an average bottle and €5000 for a 1940s collectible. Intense and complex with an ethereal fragrance, it is the product of Sangiovese grapes grown south of Siena; must spend at least two years ageing in oak; and is best paired with game, wild boar and roasts. See p258 for more detail. Brunello grape rejects go into Rossi di Montalcino, Brunello's substantially cheaper and wholly drinkable kid sister.

Prugnolo Gentile grapes (a clone of Sangiovese) form the backbone of the distinguished Vino Nobile di Montepulciano (2006 was an exceptional year). Its intense but delicate nose and a dry vaguely tannic taste make it the perfect companion to red meat and mature cheese.

Then there's Chianti, a cheery full and dry red fellow known the world over, easy to drink, suited to any dish and wholly affordable. More famous than it was good in the 1970s, contemporary Chianti gets the thumbs up

from wine critics today. Produced in seven sub-zones from Sangiovese
and a mix of other grape varieties, Chianti Classico – the traditional heart
of this longstanding wine-growing area – is the best known with a DOCG
guarantee of quality and a Gallo Nero (Black Cockerel) emblem that once
symbolised the medieval Chianti League. Young fun Chianto Colli Senesi
from the Siena hills is the largest sub-zone; Chianti Colli Pisane is light
and soft in style, and Chianti Rùfina (p165) comes from the hills east of
Florence.

One result of Chianti's 'cheap wine for the masses' reputation in the 1970s
was the realisation by some Tuscans – including the Antinoris, Tuscany's
most famous wine-producing family – that wines with a rich, complex, internationally acceptable taste following the New World tradition of blending
mixes could be sold for a lot more than local wines. Thus, innovative exciting
wines were developed and cleverly marketed to appeal to buyers in both New
York and Florence. And when an English-speaking scribe dubbed the end
product 'Super Tuscans' the name stuck. Sassacaia, Tignanello and Solaia
are super-hot Super Tuscans.

Tuscan whites amount to one label loved by popes and artists alike during
the Renaissance: Vernaccia di San Gimignano (p258).

Umbria

Umbria was first recognised for its whites, most notably the dry Orvieto
Classico, as gorgeous as the southern Umbrian town that bears its name
and where Etruscans first cultivated vines. Ironically, some of the most
prestigious wines from this area, such as the fruity well-structured Cervaro
della Sala (literally 'Stag of the Hall', made from grechetto and chardonnay
grapes) and the sweet golden dessert wine Muffato della Sala (a blend of
four grapes), are made by Tuscany's Antinori family. The Antinoris bought
Castello della Sala in Ficulle, 18km from Orvieto, in 1940 and slowly made
the centuries-old estate complete with 52 hectares of vines and olive groves,
29 farms and a dilapidated 14th-century castle into the highly respected
label it is today. The man behind the transformation: Umbrian-born Renzo
Cotarella.

Queen of Umbrian wine is Chiari Lungarotti, whose family transformed
Torgiano, south of Perugia, into the royal wine-making area it is today:
Torgiano was the first wine-producing area of Umbria to gain both the DOC
(1968) and DOCG (1990) quality recognitions. Lungarotti wine production
is vast and covers the whole gambit of wine today – white, red, rosé and

Tuscany produces six
DOCG wines and 30-plus
DOC wines. Umbria's
twinset of DOCGs stand
alongside a dozen or so
DOC wines.

Packed with fascinat-
ing facts and insights
on Umbrian culinary
products and the best for
learning about Umbrian
food is Umbria's Centro
Agro Alimentare dell'
Umbria at http://english
.umbriadoc.com

THE WINE ROADS

There is nothing quite so idyllic or so perfect an opportunity to glimpse the traditional farming
lifestyle as following Le Strade del Vino, well-marked wine trails that take motorists and cyclists
along scenic Tuscan and Umbrian back roads, past a plethora of vineyards and vintner's wine
cellars (look for the sign *'cantine aperte'*) where you can taste and buy wine.

Each *strada* has its own distinct emblem; look for a sign that has something resembling a
bunch of grapes and you're probably on the right track. Every *strada* has its own map, with listings of wineries and sometimes *agriturismi* (farm-stay accommodation), restaurants, wine-tasting
enoteche (wine bars), and even open olive mills or other gastronomic delights.

To date 14 Tuscan and four Umbrian *strade* have been marked crisscrossing famous wine-
production areas like Rùfina and Montepulciano in Tuscany, and Umbria's Colli del Trasimeno
and Strada dei Vini Etrusco Romana between Narni and Orvieto. Tourist offices have maps
and information, as does www.terreditoscana.regione.toscana.it and www.umbriadoc.com (in
Italian).

TOP FIVE VIRTUAL TUSCAN KITCHENS

Peek into a Tuscan kitchen with these excellent food-driven blogs:

Delicious Italy (www.deliciousitaly.com) 'Bite-sized portions of information for the independent traveller' (who likes to eat well): click on the map to reach excellent dining and food-shopping recommendations, itineraries etc for Tuscany and Umbria.

Faith Willinger (www.faithwillinger.com) Florence is home for hugely successful author, food critic and chef, Faith Willinger.

Luculian Delights – An Italian Experience (http://lucullian.blogspot.com) Tip-top food-driven blog with loads of recipes tried and tested by Swedish Ilva living with Marco, three children and a dog in a farmhouse near Pistoia.

Mestolando (www.mestolando.com) Recipes, including videoblogs, from a kitchen in Florence by Florentine Claudia and expat Brian.

Over a Tuscan Stove (http://divinacucina.blogspot.com) Food-focused blog cooked up by a cooking school in Florence.

---

sparkling. Its Museo del Vino (p331) and neighbouring *cantina* (wine bar) provides prime opportunity to discover Umbrian viticulture and taste its wine, as does the extraordinary wine list in the top-notch restaurant and hotel (p331) the family owns: Torgiano Rosso Riserva DOCG is its most renowned appellation.

Bevagna (p345) and Montefalco (p344), east of Perugia, make up the other wealthy wine area thanks to the Sagrantino di Montefalco, which comes as a *passito* (sweet) or *secco* (dry) white – best drunk with sweet biscuits and venison or roasts respectively – or as a red. Taste all three at numerous points along the well-marketed Strada del Sagrantino (www.stradadelsagrantino.it; p75).

WINE & COOKERY COURSES

The website www.italycookingschools.com has hundreds of possibilities to consider.

Badia a Coltibuono (☎ 0577 74 48 32; www.coltibuono.com) Rolls-Royce course with prices to match, founded by author of 30-odd cookbooks Lorenza de' Medici (of *those* de' Medicis) over 20 years ago and continued today by her son, Guido: the art of Tuscan cuisine in an 11th-century abbey at Badia a Coltibuono, 38km northeast of Siena in Il Chianti; one-, three- and five-day courses.

Cordon Bleu (Map pp100-1; ☎ 055 234 54 68; www.cordonbleu-it.com; Via di Mezzo 55r) Chocolate, cakes, pastry, Christmas specialities, cooking courses for kids and other sessions aimed at more serious, gourmet cooks; you'll find the school in Florence.

Cordon Bleu Perugia (☎ 075 592 50 12 in Italian, 075 692 02 49 in English; www.cordonbleu perugia.com) Three-hour beginners' class to week-long pro chef courses at this cooking school near Perugia (p324), northern Umbria.

La Cucina Caldesi (☎ 0207 487 0570; www.lacucinacaldesi.com) Famously featured in the BBC TV series, *Return to Tuscany*, this cooking school run by Tuscan-born Giancarlo and wife Katie during winters in Marylebone, London, and summers in Tuscany at Torrita di Siena near Pienza.

La Cucina del Garga (☎ 055 21 13 96; www.garga.it) Hands-on Tuscan cookery courses, from one-day Florence classes to eight days in southern Tuscany, run by the team from Trattoria Garga (p138).

Faith Willinger (www.faithwillinger.com) Wednesday morning-long market-to-table sessions in an 18th-century home in central Florence and longer Food Lover tours with the author of *Adventures of An Italian Food Lover* and other bestselling titles.

Organic Tuscany (☎ 347 328 93 33; www.organictuscany.org; hamlet of La Selva, 5km from Certaldo) Week-long organic cooking courses with Florentine Riccardo, Shilpa and Manuela in an ecofriendly farmhouse; includes visits to local biodynamic and organic farms, wine tasting and accommodation. Highlight: vegetarian cooking course during the September grape harvest.

...toscaneggiando (☎ 348 644 24 63; www.toscaneggiando.it; Via Villa Fontana 90, San Colombano, Capannori) 'Simple cooking lessons in a familiar atmosphere' is how this small, enterprising and highly imaginative team markets itself. Lessons in central Lucca or surrounding countryside (one/two people €110/160).

Villa San Michele (p156) To-die-for thematic cookery courses (for kids aged eight to 14 years, aristocratic Florentine cuisine, recipes for single diners etc) in a to-die-for venue on the hills overlooking Florence; morning courses followed by lunch with the villa's own Tuscan chef, too.

EAT YOUR WORDS

For pronunciation guidelines, see p426.

Useful Phrases

I'd like to reserve a table.

Vorrei riservare un tavolo.　vo·*ray* ree·ser·*va*·re oon *ta*·vo·lo

I'd like the menu, please.

Vorrei il menù, per favore.　vo·*ray* eel me·*noo* per fa·*vo*·re

Do you have a menu in English?

Avete un menù (scritto) in inglese?　a·*ve*·te oon me·*noo*
(*skree*·to) een een·*gle*·ze

What would you recommend?

Cosa mi consiglia?　*ko*·za mee kon·*see*·lya

Please bring the bill.

Mi porta il conto, per favore.　mee *por*·ta eel *kon*·to per fa·*vo*·re

I'm a vegetarian.

Sono vegetariano/a.　*so*·no ve·je·ta·*rya*·no/a

I'm a vegan.

Sono vegetaliano/a.　*so*·no ve·je·ta·*lya*·no/a

Food Glossary

AT THE TABLE

aceto	a·*che*·to	vinegar
coltello	kol·*tel*·lo	knife
cucchiaio	koo·*kya*·yo	spoon
forchetta	for·*ke*·ta	fork
olio	*o*·lyo	oil
pepe	*pe*·pe	pepper
sale	*sa*·le	salt

STAPLES

aglio	*a*·lyo	garlic
burro	*boo*·ro	butter
formaggio	for·*ma*·jo	cheese
miele	*mye*·le	honey
pane	*pa*·ne	bread
panna	*pa*·na	cream
riso	*ree*·zo	rice
soya	*soy*·ya	soy
tartufo	tar·*too*·fo	truffle
uovo/uova	*wo*·vo/*wo*·va	egg/eggs
zucchero	*tsoo*·ke·ro	sugar

DRINKS

acqua	a·kwa	water
birra	bee·ra	beer
caffè	ka·fe	coffee
tè	te	tea
vino (rosso/bianco)	vee·no (ross·o/byan·ko)	wine (red/white)

MEAT & SEAFOOD

agnello	a·nye·lo	lamb
aragosta	a·ra·go·sta	lobster
carpaccio	kar·pa·cho	very fine slices of raw meat
coniglio	ko·nee·lyo	rabbit
cozze	ko·tse	mussels
frutti di mare	froo·tee dee ma·re	seafood
gamberoni	gam·be·ro·nee	prawns
granchio	gran·kyo	crab
pollo	pol·lo	chicken
polpi	pol·po	octopus
prosciutto	pro·shoo·to	cured ham
salsiccia	sal·see·cha	sausage
tonno	tonn·o	tuna
trippa	tree·pa	tripe
vitello	vee·te·lo	veal

VEGETABLES

asparagi	as·pa·ra·jee	asparagus
carciofi	kar·cho·fee	artichokes
carota	ka·ro·ta	carrot
cavolo	ka·vo·lo	cabbage
fagiolini	fa·jo·lee·nee	green beans
finocchio	fee·no·kyo	fennel
funghi	foon·gee	mushrooms
insalata	in·sa·la·ta	salad
melanzane	me·lan·dza·ne	eggplant/aubergine
olive	o·lee·va	olive
patate	pa·ta·te	potatoes
peperoni	pe·pe·ro·nee	capsicums/peppers
piselli	pee·ze·lee	peas
pomodori	po·mo·do·ree	tomatoes
rucola	roo·ko·la	rocket
spinaci	spee·na·chee	spinach

GELATO FLAVOURS & FRUIT

amarena	a·ma·re·na	wild cherry
arancia	a·ran·cha	orange
bacio	ba·cho	chocolate and hazelnuts
ciliegia	chee·lye·ja	cherry
cioccolata	cho·ko·la·ta	chocolate
cono	ko·no	cone
coppa	ko·pa	cup
crema	kre·ma	cream
fragola	fra·go·la	strawberry
frutta di bosco	froo·ta dee bos·ko	fruit of the forest (wild berries)
limone	lee·mo·ne	lemon
mela	me·la	apple

melone	me·*lo*·ne	melon
nocciola	no·*cho*·la	hazelnut
pere	*pe*·ra	pear
pesca	*pe*·ska	peach
uva	*oo*·va	grapes
vaniglia	va·*nee*·lya	vanilla
zuppa inglese	tsoo·pa een·gle·ze	'English soup', trifle

The Environment

THE LANDSCAPE

If you think of Tuscany's coast as the base, the region forms a rough triangle covering 22,990 sq km. Crammed within that triangle is a remarkable variety of land forms, from mountains in the north and east to flat plains in the south, from islands off the coast to the hill country of the interior.

Much of the coast facing the Tyrrhenian and Ligurian Seas is flat, except for a stretch immediately south of Livorno and parts of the Monte Argentario peninsula.

In all, two-thirds of Tuscany is mountainous or hilly. The Apennines, shared with Emilia (part of the Emilia-Romagna region), close off the northern flank of Tuscany and run roughly from east to west (with a gradual southward drop). The Apuane Alps (p204), an offshoot that rises from the coastal plain up in the region's northwestern corner, are renowned for their white marble deposits (see p207).

The gentle rounded hills of Il Chianti and Le Crete contrast with the wildness of the mountains. Their undulating, richly fertile slopes have been shaped as much by humans as by the forces of nature. It's a satisfying, mathematically correct landscape of sweeping fields, olive groves and vineyards, where even the sparse lines of cypress trees have been planted by previous generations.

On either side of them sprawl Monte Albano south of Pistoia, and Monte Pratomagno in the province of Arezzo to the east.

It takes a full 5kg of olives to produce 1L of virgin oil.

The most extensive lowlands are the inland Maremma Pisana, one-time swamps south of Pisa, and the main Maremma, which extends down the coast and over the regional boundary with Lazio.

The River Arno, all 240 winding kilometres of it, is Tuscany's main river. It rises in Monte Falterona in the Apennines, flows south to Arezzo and then meanders northwest for a while. By the time it passes through Florence it is on a westwards course towards Pisa and finally the Ligurian Sea. It was once an important trade artery, but river traffic today is virtually nonexistent.

Of the seven islands scattered off Tuscany's coast, the central and eastern parts of Elba (p223), along with Giannutri (p289) and parts of Giglio (p289), are reminders of a great Apennine wall that collapsed into the sea millions of years ago. Capraia (p219), Montecristo (p233), western Elba and parts of Giglio were forced up by volcanic activity. The islands vary considerably, from the unexciting flatness of Pianosa (p233) to the rugged and rocky coastline of much of Elba.

Neighbouring Umbria is an undulating, landlocked region with an area of more than 8400 sq km. Around 53% of its terrain is mountainous and most of the rest is decidedly hilly. The massive Umbrian-Marche Apennines are dominated by the Monti Sibillini (p386), whose highest peak, Monte Vettore, rears up to nearly 2500m. Other notable ranges include the Gubbio Apennines, the Monti Martani, and the lower yet still impressive peaks of the Amerini and Spoleto clusters.

Less than 10% of Umbria is low lying. Through it, curling from north to southwest and bisecting the region, runs the Tiber River, navigable for centuries. The second-longest river is the Nera. As it meets its Velino tributary, it forms the Cascata delle Marmore (Marmore Waterfalls; p388), a spectacular sight when the nearby hydro station lets water flow their way.

Umbria is also rich in both natural and artificial lakes. Lake Trasimeno (p356), in the west, is the largest lake in central-southern Italy. Lake Corbara and Lago di Alviano (p396), these days more of a marshland, are artificial.

FLORA & FAUNA

The flowers of Tuscany and Umbria, especially if you're around in springtime, are spectacular. In the mountains, alpine and sub-alpine varieties abound, while wild flowers common to the Mediterranean world thrive in the hills and intensively cultivated plains, flourishing thanks to a relatively low use of pesticides. Wild animals, by contrast, have a hard time of it in a land where it's almost a badge of masculinity to go hunting with your mates.

Animals

Cinghiale (wild boar) has been on Tuscan menus since the days of the Etruscans, and the rural areas of the region still teem with them. The only difference is that today most are the offspring of Eastern European boar, imported to make up for the depletion of local species. They also roam many of the regional nature parks in Umbria. Although they're common enough, you'll be lucky to spot them on walks in the countryside; they are busy avoiding their most dangerous predator – the armed hunter.

Among other animals fairly common in the Tuscan and Umbrian countryside are squirrels, rabbits, foxes, martens, weasels and hares. The badger and the black-and-white-quilled *istrice*, a porcupine supposedly imported from North Africa by the ancient Romans for the dinner table, are rarer. In parks such as the Parco Regionale della Maremma (p285), there's a good chance of spotting roe deer, grazing at dawn or dusk.

Wolves – the prey of both feral dogs and unscrupulous hunters, despite their protected status – are making something of a comeback with an estimated 150 animals roaming the more remote upland areas in small packs. Sightings are extremely rare. The wildcat is another predator that roams the scarcely populated areas of Tuscany and Umbria, but it too is rare and hardly ever seen.

On a more slithery note, you can encounter several kinds of snakes. Most are harmless and will glide out of your way. The only poisonous one is the viper, identified by its diamond markings. Rocky areas and the island of Elba are among its principal habitats.

Bird life is varied in Tuscany. The best time of year for twitchers is from November to March, when many migratory species linger in coastal nature reserves such as Lago di Burano (p289), Laguna di Orbetello (p287) and Monti dell'Uccellina (p285). As many as 140 species call Tuscany home or use it as a stopover. They include the black-winged stilt, buzzard, falcon, hawk, hoopoe, jay, kestrel, kingfisher, osprey, thrush, woodpecker and wren.

Umbria is also a great place to see a wide variety of bird life. Its extensive marshlands are an important stopping-off place for migratory species, such as the grey heron, purple heron, bittern and spoonbill. In other parts of the region birds of prey, such as the golden eagle, goshawk, peregrine falcon, eagle owl and osprey, circle the skies.

Plants

Tuscan and Umbrian farmland is a visually pleasing mix of orderly human intervention and nature left more or less to itself. Everywhere, long lines of vines stripe the countryside, alternating with olive groves (olives were introduced in Etruscan times from the Middle East).

Tall, slender cypress and the odd flattened *pino marittimo* (cluster pine, found mainly on the coast) are among the most striking of the regions' trees. The cypress was introduced from Asia Minor in Roman times precisely for its decorative qualities.

Beech trees thrive in the cooler mountainous territory of the Apuane Alps, often competing for light and space with chestnuts. Thereabouts, hunting for

The Dunarobba Fossil Forest, near Avigliano, is one of the oldest woods in the world, thought to date back almost two million years.

Where to Watch Birds in Italy, published by the Italian Bird Protection League (LIPU), highlights over 100 recommendations for species spotting.

Birds of Britain & Europe with North Africa & the Middle East by Herman Heinzel et al, *Birds of Britain & Europe* by John Gooders and the exquisitely illustrated *Birds of Europe* by Lars Jonsson make excellent guides for spotters.

chestnuts then roasting them is a favourite pastime on November weekends. In the Casentino (p303) and Vallombrosa areas of eastern Tuscany, deep, thick forests of pine, oak (one species of which is the cork oak, its bark important to the wine industry) and beech still cover large tracts of otherwise little-touched land. Other species include maple, hazelnut, alder and imported eucalyptus.

www.blueflag.org lists Tuscany's cleanest beaches.

In Umbria, other trees of note down in the plains include willows, poplars and the black alder. Water lilies flourish in the rich marshlands, while rare flowers such as the yellow poppy discreetly survive in Parco Nazionale dei Monti Sibillini (p386).

Springtime, of course, is the brightest time of year in Tuscany and Umbria; whole valley floors and upland plains are awash in a technicolour sea of wild flowers, including jonquils, crocuses, anemones, gentians and orchids.

Down by the sea, Tuscan coastal and island areas boast typical Mediterranean *macchia* (dry, prickly scrubland).

NATIONAL PARKS

Three of Italy's 24 national parks are within Tuscany.

For further information on national parks and other protected areas in Tuscany and Umbria visit www.parks.it. The World Wide Fund for Nature (WWF) has an Italian chapter at www.wwf.it.

The Parco Nazionale dell'Arcipelago Toscano (p217), Europe's largest marine park, embraces the islands of Montecristo, Gorgona, Giannutri, Pianosa, and part of Capraia, Elba and Giglio. It protects both their fragile coastlines and the wild, mountainous hinterland.

Within the Parco Nazionale delle Foreste Casentinesi, Monte Falterona e Campigna (p303), on the border with Emilia-Romagna, is Italy's most extensive and best-preserved forest. Deep inside the woods of chestnut and beech, threaded by ancient mule tracks, a few wolves are re-establishing themselves. You won't see them but you may well spot another predator, the golden eagle, as it planes above you.

To the west and also shared with Emilia-Romagna, the recently created Parco Nazionale dell'Appennino Tosco-Emiliano protects the fragile mountain environment of the Apennines. Below its highest peaks – Prado, Cusna and Alpe di Succiso, each above 2000m – are glinting lakes, rocky cliffs and grasslands.

Tuscany also has three regional parks, one in the Apuane Alps, one in the Maremma and one on the heavily urbanised coast near Livorno.

Umbria has just one national park, the Parco Nazionale dei Monti Sibillini (p386), which takes its name from the principal mountain range in the area. An amazing 1800 varieties of plant, including the Apennine edelweiss and several strains of orchid, populate its deeply incised north-facing valleys and jagged upper slopes.

Legambiente (www .legambiente.com in Italian) is Italy's largest environmental organisa- tion, with over 1000 local branches. Look out for its green swan insignia, indicating ecofriendly places.

On a more modest scale, Umbria has a fistful of regional parks: Parco Regionale di Colfiorito, Parco Regionale del Trasimeno, Parco Regionale del Monte Cucco (p351), Parco Regionale del Monte Subasio, Parco Regionale del Fiume Nera and Parco Regionale del Tevere.

Other protected areas and places of naturalistic interest include La Valle Nature Oasis, La Cascata delle Marmore (p388), Fonti del Clitunno (Clitunno Springs) and Foresta Fossile di Dunarobba (Dunarobba Fossil Forest).

ENVIRONMENTAL ISSUES

In a recent poll organised by *National Geographic Traveler* magazine, Tuscany was rated 9th equal among 115 major tourist destinations. Criteria, on all of which the region scored highly, included a place's ecological and environmental quality, its aesthetic appeal and the sensitivity of its tourism development.

But not everything's rosy. One of the greatest ecological issues in the region is marble extraction in the mountains of the Apuane Alps. The great white scars, which from the seaside look almost like snowfalls, are the result of many centuries' work.

TOUGH TUSCAN LOVE

Bureaucrats tend to get bad press worldwide and Tuscans, like all of us, enjoy a good moan from time to time. But big brother restrictions, which the farmer or home owner may perceive as petty, have done wonders in preserving the region's countryside, saving it from the blight of overdevelopment that poisons so many Mediterranean lands where tourism rules.

Tuscany imposes some of Europe's strictest building regulations and land-use restrictions (why, there are even limitations on the colour you can paint the exterior of your house). New construction is limited to two storeys so buildings retain their traditional squat, low profile. Most importantly, land cannot be subdivided. So, since plots remain intact, the region is spared the ugly rows of identical terraced housing or clone villas that elsewhere scar not only the coastline but, increasingly, inland too.

Agriturismo, in the form of rural home stays and B&Bs, is actively fostered and funded so that small farms can stay in business. Here, there are also restrictions on getting too big for your boots and regulations ensuring that they retain their mud: should the family income from tourism exceed the earnings of the farm, the farmer's low-interest loans and tax concessions will be snatched away.

Not everything's perfect, of course, and Tuscans find ways of slipping around restrictions they regard as inconvenient. There's concern over the number of properties, new and old, that function as second homes, occupied for only a few weeks each year. And the temptations are great. If you're a cash-strapped mayor, it's difficult to resist the siren song of property developers who might promise to repair the streets, build a community centre or sports hall if you'd nod, wink and just sign here, *signor...*

Before WWII, the level of incursion was much slighter and marble miners eased blocks down to nearby villages with complex pulley systems. But today, the pace of removal has accelerated. About 1.5 million tonnes per year are scraped out and trundled away on heavy trucks. The extraction is disfiguring part of a nature reserve, the waste produced creates disposal problems and the heavy truck traffic is invasive. However, few voices seriously object to this prestigious industry. Carrara marble (p207) is sought after worldwide by everyone from architects to sculptors and the industry is a significant local employer.

Heavy industry never really came to Tuscany or Umbria, so the associated problems of air and water pollution elsewhere in Italy are not as great here. That said, the medium- and light-industrial areas of Livorno, Piombino, suburban Florence, Perugia and along the Arno and Tiber Rivers are far from hazard free. Heavy road traffic makes clean air a distant dream in much of the densely populated Prato-Pistoia area. Noise pollution can also be a problem in cities.

Umbria, where farming remains a significant occupation, is much less affected. The introduction of several hydroelectric plants and the manufacturing of chemicals, iron, steel and processed food have all taken their toll on the countryside, but on a much smaller scale and with a less detrimental impact on the environment.

The landscape of Tuscany and Umbria appears something of a work of art, with farmers alternating a patchwork quilt of farmland with stretches of forest. The post-WWII crisis in agriculture saw many farmers leave the land and in more remote spots, where wringing results from the earth was always a challenge at best, forest or scrub is reclaiming its territory. Sometimes this uncontrolled regrowth has a downside, helping propagate bushfires.

Regional government bodies in both Tuscany and Umbria are now taking a tougher line concerning the environment, partly in response to EU directives. Initiatives include reforestation and the promotion of environmentally friendly agricultural methods.

Flower spotters will enjoy *Mediterranean Wild Flowers* by M Blamey and C Grey Wilson. *Trees of Britain & Europe* also makes a handy companion, while Paul Sterry's *Complete Mediterranean Wildlife* is a good general guide to the flora and fauna of the region.

Tuscany & Umbria Outdoors

The gorgeous landscapes of Tuscany and Umbria beg to be explored and savoured, slowly. Those who tear through the countryside on the highways miss out on a rich variety of outdoor activities that underscore the area's splendour.

Because Tuscany and Umbria are year-round destinations, there's something to do in every season, from adrenaline-inducing winter skiing to leisurely countryside strolls. Families will be delighted to discover how accessible these activities are, while those in search of more demanding pursuits won't be disappointed either. There will still be plenty of time left to lounge around the villa and sip Chianti – which tastes all the better after a day in the region's fresh open air.

WALKING

Tuscany and Umbria are eminently suited to walking. Indeed, a common sight throughout the region is large hiking groups, mostly from the UK and frequently distinguishable at 200m by the floppy white sunhats they so often seem to sport.

The patchwork countryside of the centre, the wilder valleys and mountains in the south and northwest and, even more dramatically, the Apuane Alps and Apennine ranges all offer colourful variety.

A truly ambitious trekker could undertake the 24-stage Grande Escursione Appenninica, an arc that takes you from the Due Santi pass above La Spezia southeast all the way to Sansepolcro. Alternatively Umbria's Monti Sibillini is superb for walkers using Castelluccio as a base, with a choice of demanding backpack hikes to the summit or casual day hikes.

People have been crisscrossing Tuscany for millennia, creating paths and trails as they went. One of the most important pilgrim routes in Europe during the Dark Ages was the Via Francigena (or Via Romea), in its time a veritable highway across Tuscany. Starting in the Magra River valley and winding through the wild Lunigiana territory of the northwest, the trail hugged the coast for a while before cutting inland to Siena via San Gimignano and then turning south to Rome, capital of Christianity. Parts of the route can still be walked today and there's a movement afoot to restore even more of it as a resource for hikers.

Edizione Multigraphic produces good maps of Tuscany and the Apennines at 1:25,000.

Best Time of Year

Spring is the prettiest time, while the colours of autumn have their own mellow appeal. Since summertime lingers into late October, you have plenty of daylight for longer walks. After Tuscany's mad summer tourist rush, things begin to ease off by late September – all the more so out in the countryside.

If you're planning to go walking in the Apuane Alps or other mountain areas (such as Monte Vettore or the small Orecchiella reserve), the most pleasant time is in summer. August, though, the month when most Italians take their holidays and trails get busy, is best avoided if you can be flexible. Lower terrain, by contrast, is best left untrodden in high summer as the heat can be oppressive, making even a crawl to the nearest air-conditioned bar a strain.

What to Take

For your average walks in the Tuscany-Umbria area you will need only a minimum of items. For easy, undemanding outings, a pair of comfortable trainers (runners) is usually quite adequate. Otherwise, pull on either comfortable walking shoes or sturdy boots, depending on what kind of terrain you are planning to cover. A small daypack should contain an extra layer of clothing, in case temperatures drop, and some kind of wet-weather gear. Depending on the season, sunscreen, sunglasses and a hat are recommended. Obviously you need a map of the area, and a compass too if you're planning some serious stuff off the beaten track. Whatever the season, pack at least one bottle of water, calculating for at least 1.5L per walker for a summer day walk. A fistful or two of light, high-nutrition, easily assimilated food such as power bars, dried fruit or nuts can stave off hunger pangs and impart a quick kick of energy.

For slip-in-the-pocket reference books about flowers, trees, birds and bigger mammals, check the sidebars in the Environment chapter (p80).

Wild camping is not permitted in the high mountains. That may seem like bad news to some, as you will need to plan your overnight stops around the availability of beds in *rifugi* (mountain huts). The upside is that you can leave tents, cooking gear and the like at your base accommodation. Bring your sleeping bag along as extra insurance against the cold.

It's not just the cold – be prepared for all kinds of weather in the mountains. The day may start in splendid sunshine and heat, but that can easily change to chillingly cold, wet and clammy. Bear in mind that the Apuane Alps get the greatest concentration of rainfall in all Tuscany.

Prime Spots

Il Chianti (p164) is a favourite among walkers of all levels. One of the classic walks takes you rambling over several days (perhaps as many as five or six) from Florence to Siena. *Chianti Classico: Val di Pesa-Val d'Elsa*, a map at 1:25,000 published by Edizioni Multigraphic (see www.edizionimultigraphic .it – in Italian – for its full map catalogue), covers most of the area and has hiking trails superimposed.

Smart multiday hikers walk with only a daypack, having signed up with one of the many outdoor adventure companies that transport your luggage from stage to stage.

Another area within easy reach of Florence for a day's walking is Il Mugello (p163), northeast of the city and extending to the border with Emilia-Romagna. *Sorgenti Firenze Trekking* (SOFT; Florence Springs Trekking) are a network of signed day or half-day trails crisscrossing the area. *Mugello, Alto Mugello, Val di Sieve,* produced by SELCA, is a decent map for hikers at 1:70,000.

For a day of history and hiking you could walk from San Gimignano to Volterra or vice versa. Both your point of departure and your goal are fascinating medieval towns, each of which has reasonable transport links and plenty of accommodation.

History buffs may want to walk in the tracks of the Etruscans, basing themselves in Suvereto or Campiglia Marittima. In a more structured way, at the Parco Archeologico di Baratti e Populonia (p222) you can follow the Via delle Cave, an undemanding, signed two-hour walk that passes by a series of tombs and the quarries from which their building blocks were hewn.

Back on the spine of the Apennines, the Garfagnana (p207), up in the northwest, and Lunigiana (p211), spilling into Liguria, both offer exciting medium-mountain walking. Castelnuovo (p210) makes a good base and its **Centro Visite Parco Alpi Apuane** (www.parks.it/parco.alpi.apuane) is well stocked with information and maps.

You can enjoy these two areas in their own right or do a couple of limbering-up treks, then attack the Apuane Alps (p204). The serious hikes are stunning and challenging, but there are also possibilities for less arduous itineraries. *The Alps of Tuscany: Selected Hikes in the Apuane Alps, the Cinque*

Terre and Portofino by Francesco Greco presents many enjoyable multiday routes. For gourmets and gourmands, it also recommends restaurants and local dishes to tempt you at the end of each walk. Edizioni Multigraphic's *Parco delle Alpi Apuane* map at 1:50,000 covers the whole of the range. If your Italian is up to it, you might go for one of several Italian guides to the mountains, such as the *Guida al Parco delle Alpi Apuane* edited by Giuliano Valdes or Angelo Nerli's *Alta Via del Parco Alpi Apuane*.

The island of Elba is especially well geared for short walks and you will generally be able to plan your own routes quite easily. For more information, contact **Il Genio del Bosco – Centro Trekking Isola d'Elba** (☎ 0565 93 08 37; www .geniodelbosco.it in Italian).

In Umbria, hiking in the scenic Monti Sibillini (p386) is wonderful, although there are relatively few marked trails. For information, contact the **Ente Parco Nazionale Monti Sibillini** (☎ 0737 97 27 11; www.sibillini.net). A good base for shorter day hikes is Castelluccio, with a choice of trails threading from the village. One of the most popular leads to the Lago di Pilato under Monte Vettore; here, legend tells, Pontius Pilate is buried. The Club Alpino Italiano (CAI) map *Parco Nazionale dei Monti Sibillini* covers the park at 1:25,000, as does the Edizioni Multigraphic alternative of the same name.

Information
MAPS & BOOKS

> If maps leave you flustered, tackle one of Tuscany's signed trails, such as the three-day Piglione Trekking, starting from Metato, Apuane Trekking, a four- to eight-stage circuit from Carrara, or, further north, the 10-day Garfagnana Trekking.

Edizioni Multigraphic publishes a couple of series of maps that are designed for walkers and mountain-bike riders (*mulattiere*, or mule trails, are especially good for mountain bikes). The *Carte dei Sentieri* series is at 1:25,000, while the *Carte Turistica e dei Sentieri* maps are at a scale of either 1:25,000 or 1:50,000.

In addition to Edizioni Multigraphic and the CAI, the German cartographers Kompass produce 1:25,000 scale, walker-friendly maps of various parts of Italy, including Tuscany and Umbria.

Walking in Tuscany, by Gillian Price, is an excellent guide that describes over 50 walks and hikes of a none-too-strenuous nature (the text spills over into neighbouring Umbria and Lazio). Its ample selection takes you from Chianti country to the island of Elba, and to plenty of less explored parts of the Tuscan region as well. However, it doesn't cover the more arduous trekking possibilities in the Apuane Alps in Tuscany's northwest.

The series of *Guide dei Monti d'Italia*, grey hardbacks published by the Touring Club Italiano (TCI) and CAI, are exhaustive walking guides containing maps. *Walking and Eating in Tuscany and Umbria* by James Lasdun and Pia Davis embraces two of the region's most delightful activities, offering 40 varied itineraries across these two central regions of Italy and plenty of tips for restaurants and overnight stays.

Organised Walking Holidays

Most major British adventure travel companies offer guided walking holidays in Tuscany, and usually Umbria, too. Established players include the following:

ATG Oxford (☎ 01865 315 678; www.atg-oxford.co.uk; 69-71 Banbury Rd, Oxford OX2 6PJ) Also offers cycling holidays.

Explore (☎ 0870 333 4001; www.explore.co.uk; Nelson House, 55 Victoria Rd, Farnborough GU14 7PA) Also offers cycling holidays.

Headwater (☎ 01606 720 033; www.headwater-holidays.co.uk; The Old School House, Chester Rd, Northwich CW8 1LE) Also offers cycling holidays.

HF Holidays (☎ 020 8905 9558; www.hfholidays.co.uk; Imperial House, The Hyde, Edgeware Rd, London NW9 5AL) Also offers cycling holidays in Umbria.

Inntravel (☎ 01653 617 459; www.inntravel.co.uk; Inntravel Ltd, Nr Castle Howard, York YO60 7JU) Also offers cycling holidays.

Ramblers Holidays (☎ 01707 331 133; www.ramblersholidays.co.uk; Lemsford Mill, Lemsford Village, Welwyn Garden City AL8 7TR) With this offshoot of the nonprofit Ramblers Association, in business for over 60 years, you can sign up for a straight hiking holiday or opt for its hybrid walking and cooking Tuscany option.

Sherpa Expeditions (☎ 020 8577 2717; www.sherpaexpeditions.com; 131a Heston Rd, Hounslow TW5 0RF) Also offers cycling holidays.

Walks Worldwide (☎ 01524 242 000; www.walksworldwide.com; 12 The Square, Ingleton, Carnforth LA6 3EG)

World Walks (☎ 01242 254 353; www.worldwalks.com; 30 Imperial Sq, Cheltenham GL50 1QZ)

> Hidden Italy (www .hiddenitaly.com.au) is an Australian outfit that sets up self-guided walking tours in Tuscany and Umbria.

CYCLING

Italy is generally a cycle-friendly country and Tuscany and Umbria are no exception. Although most historic town and city centres are closed to motorised traffic, cyclists are free to wobble around at will. There are plenty of places where you can rent a bike, buy your colour-coordinated Lycra, and obtain advice on routes and itineraries. Whether you're out for a day's gentle pedalling around town with the children in tow, a sybaritic weekend winery tour in Il Chianti with a bunch of friends or a serious workout on that muscle tone with a week or more of pedal power, Tuscany and Umbria provide plenty of cycling scope.

Cycling to Suit You

Matching the varied landscape, there is also a wide choice of roads and routes. Paved roads are particularly suited to high-tech racing bikes (watch out for the Sunday swarm of identically clad riders from the local club as the peloton sweeps by) or travelling long distances on touring bikes. Country roads, known as *strade bianche,* have dirt surfaces covered with gravel for stability.

Back roads and trails are a further option if you are fairly fit and have a multigear mountain bike, as this is mainly hilly terrain. There are also plenty of other challenges for the more ambitious cyclist: Monte Amiata is the perfect goal for aspiring hill climbers, while hilly itineraries with short but challenging climbs beckon from Umbria through to Il Chianti and Le Crete. Don't despair; there are also plenty of itineraries with gentler slopes for amateur cyclists and even for families with children.

Best Time of Year

The best time of year for serious pedalling is spring, not only because of the obvious advantage of a cooler temperature, but also because the scenery is at its most breathtaking at this time of year, with valleys drenched in poppies and wildflowers. However, Easter and the days either side of 25 April and 1 May, both national holidays, are best avoided because of the crowds that infiltrate the region.

Autumn is also a good season, although there's a greater chance of rain, which can lead to slippery roads and poor visibility.

What Type of Bike?

The most versatile bicycle for most of the roads of Umbria and Tuscany is a comfortable all-terrain bike capable of travelling over both paved and country roads and, even more importantly, able to climb hills without forcing you to exert yourself excessively. Ideally, it should give you a relaxed riding posture, have front suspension and be equipped with a wide range of gears, similar to a mountain bike.

If you are bringing your own bike from home, check in advance with your airline if there's a fee and how much, if any, disassembling and packing it requires. Bikes can be transported by train in Italy, either with you or to arrive within a couple of days.

www.parks.it is an excellent site, full of information about Tuscany and Umbria's national and regional parks, nature reserves and other protected areas.

Prime Spots

IL CHIANTI

The picturesque SS222, also known as the Strada Chiantigiana, runs between Florence and Siena, cleaving right through Chianti country. Although it is far from traffic free, you'll find it's a scenic and justifiably popular cycling route.

More importantly, there are over 400km of traffic-free roads and plans are underway to develop cycle touring further with more trails and special cycle signposts to indicate directions, as well as offering information about accommodation, mechanical assistance and bicycle rental.

Edizioni Multigraphic's map *Chianti e le Colline Senesi* has mountain-bike trails superimposed.

Parco Ciclistico del Chianti (☎ 0577 74 94 11; www.parcociclisticodelchianti.it), based in Gaiole in Chianti, is an ecologically committed local cycling organisation that offers both tailor-made and 'ready-to-ride' tours.

AROUND SIENA

The hills around San Gimignano and Colle di Val d'Elsa are another favourite venue for cyclists. One challenging route starts from Casole d'Elsa, following the road as it climbs to Monteguidi, then descending to cross the Cecina River before reaching the village of Montecastelli in the province of Pisa. An easier ride starts with a panoramic circuit around the town walls of Monteriggioni, carrying on to Colle di Val d'Elsa, and continuing towards San Gimignano and Volterra.

LE CRETE & VAL D'ORCIA

The rolling landscape here is similar to Il Chianti's, except that instead of pedalling through woodlands, you pass between vast swathes of wheat fields. Among the most stunning routes are the Monte Sante Marie road from Asciano to Torre a Castello and the Pieve a Salti road from Buonconvento to San Giovanni d'Asso. Both are unpaved and require all-terrain or mountain bikes. An alternative for cyclists with touring bikes is the legendary Lauretana road from Siena to Asciano and onwards towards Chiusure, Mont Oliveto Maggiore and Buonconvento.

WINDING DOWN, SOAKING IT UP

After a day on the hoof or in the saddle, nothing rivals a good long soak to ease the stiffness. From the hills of Tuscany and Umbria bubble restorative waters that people hereabouts have been using ever since Roman times. Nowadays the emphasis is upon curing and beauty treatments, but many spas also offer wellness programmes or simply the chance to dunk yourself in water fresh from their springs.

Following an active day in the Garfagnana you can relax in the thermal waters at Bagni di Lucca (p208). If you're heading back to the plains, the grander resort of Montecatini Terme (p163) has a huge choice of hotels and several health establishments. After walking or biking in Le Crete and the Val d'Orcia, a dip in the large pool at lovely little Bagno Vignoni (p270) rounds the day off nicely or, if you prefer more bustle, Chianciano Terme (p276) has spas and hotels aplenty. Umbria's main spa is at Terme di Fontecchio (p355), near Città di Castello, while Nocera Umbra (p351), not far from Gubbio, is a smaller but no less attractive option.

MONTE AMIATA

Only die-hard peddlers should attempt to climb the steep flanks of this 1738m long-extinct volcano. The good news is that, at a mere 1370m, you'll come across a restaurant (Prato Le Macinaie) to revive you, roughly a 4km ride from the peak. You can also spend the night here, should your exertions have exhausted you. You can attack the mountain by several routes: the easiest are those leading up from Arcidossa and Abbadia San Salvatore; the latter is a 14km uphill ride with a steady but reasonably slight gradient. The most difficult approach is via Castel del Piano, 15km of unremitting uphill work with a steady, steep 7% gradient for the first 10km. But, oh, the exhilarating joy of whooshing down without a single turn of the pedals…

UMBRIA

The broad valleys of the Umbria region around Orvieto, Spello and Lago di Trasimeno are not too physically demanding. They're well suited for cyclists who want to experience the beauty of the unique and varied landscape at a leisurely pace.

Information
MAPS & BOOKS
Bicycle Touring in Tuscany by David Cleveland describes eight multiday tours, each with a detailed route map. In defiance of its title, it also embraces cycle trips in Umbria and Le Marche. *Garfagnana by Bicycle* by Lucia and Bruno Giovannetti has detailed descriptions of key route features, a contour map, 27 itineraries for mountain bikes and five touring maps.

The *Guida Cicloturistica del Chianti* by Fabio Masotti and Giancarlo Brocci has 20 cycling itineraries and 32 detailed maps of the Chianti region. Another excellent planning resource, though older, is the two volumes of Sergio Grillo and Cinzia Pezzani's *Toscana in Mountain Bike,* between them they cover 69km of off-road itineraries throughout the region. Both are in Italian but very visual with explicit maps.

CYCLING ASSOCIATIONS
The Siena-based **Amici Della Bicicletta** (☎ 0577 4 51 59; www.adbsiena.it in Italian) is an active, ecologically minded group that promotes cycling as a daily form of urban transport and organises day-long and sometimes more extensive bike trips. It also dedicates considerable effort to developing and promoting cycling paths and itineraries for visiting cyclists.

Cycling Tours
From Florence, a handful of operators offer one-day cycling excursions into Il Chianti, complete with cycle rental, often with lunch and sometimes with a visit to a winery thrown in. For more details, see p131. From Arezzo, **Alessandro Madiai** (☎ 338 649 14 81; torrequebrada@virgilio.it), himself a passionate cyclist, runs day and overnight tours around the enchanting southern Tuscany countryside.

Several UK-based outdoor travel companies organise cycling tours of Tuscany and Umbria, whether accompanied or wheeling free. Among them are most of those we suggest for walking tours (see p86). Each does bike tours in either Umbria or Tuscany and, in most cases, both. Also well worth considering is the wondrously named **The Chain Gang** (www.thechaingang.co.uk), specialists in two-wheel travel.

In the US, both **Ciclismo Classico** (www.ciclismoclassico.com) and **ExperiencePlus** (www.experienceplus.com) offer cycle tours in Umbria and Tuscany.

Il Cornacchino (www.cornacchino.it) is a very special *agriturismo* on the slopes of Monte Amiata, east of Grosseto (p316). With more than 50 horses from the gentle and docile to friskier mounts, Ezio, Gulio and Fabio, supported by their international, multilingual team, offer lessons, treks and fun in the saddle.

SKIING

The region's skiing scene centres upon **Abetone** (www.abetone.com), on the border with the region of Emilia-Romagna. While the Apennines are smaller and less majestic than the Alps, they have a charm of their own. Abetone and the neighbouring, much smaller resort of Cutigliano have between them some 50km of downhill pistes. Abetone has a couple of cross-country trails, while Cutigliano offers a more demanding, more attractive 15km circuit.

Best Time of Year

The ski season generally runs from December to late March. Abetone gets pretty busy during weekends as skiers head up here from Florence and other nearby cities, such as Lucca and Pisa, by the bus and car load.

If you are here in late March, you may catch Pinocchio Sugli Sci, a keenly contested ski competition for children.

Prime Spots

A couple of shops on the main square in Abetone hire boots and skis – you'll have to supply your own woolly hat. From here it is a couple of minutes' walk to the chairlift that takes you to the top of Monte Selletta (1711m). Here, there's a good choice of blue runs and a couple of red, although the latter should pose little problem to even relatively novice skiers. On the contrary, they are exhilarating with dips that allow you to pick up speed, followed by slower, flat sections where you can regain control.

Once you've warmed up with a couple of easy runs, ski across the face of the ridge to lift 17, then take lift 15 and whoosh down the trail to lift 18. This is the heart of the ski area with trails leading into all the valleys on the Tuscan side. It's also the access point for the Val di Luce (Valley of Light), a beautiful, appropriately named valley that has most of the area's more rewarding intermediate trails. If you head to the Alpe Tre Potenze (1940m), you will be rewarded with gorgeous panoramic views stretching all the way to the Tuscan coast.

> Lake Trasimeno abounds with water sports and outdoor activities. Ask for *Tourist Itineraries in the Trasimeno District*, a booklet of walking and horse-riding tracks, at the tourist office (www .castiglionedellago.it).

Information

For ski-lift passes and more information contact the **Ufficio Centrale Biglietti** (☎ 0573 6 05 56; Piazza Piramidi, Abetone; 1-day weekday/weekend €28/33, 3-day weekdays €72, 1 week €135). You can sign up for lessons with a trio of ski schools. **Scuola Zeno Colò** (☎ 0573 6 00 32), **Scuola Sci Montegomito** (☎ 0573 6 03 92) and **Scuola Sci Colò** (☎ 0573 60 70 77). Over the mountain in Cutigliano, Scuola Amerigo **Colò** (☎ 0573 62 93 91) is your only option.

WATER SPORTS

Enjoying the water needn't involve any special effort, equipment or out-lay but, if you are keen on more than an idle paddle or swim, there are plenty of activities that are on offer. Diving facilities are generally of a high standard, and scuba-diving courses are not that expensive, with good rental gear widely available. Snorkelling, the low-tech alternative, still allows you to get dramatically close to fascinating aquatic life. Although there are several areas, such as Monte Argentario (Porto Ercole), that are excellent for diving, the island of Elba is where most divers of all levels head. The main tourist office in Portoferraio carries a list of schools and courses that are available.

If you're into wrecks, you can dive at Pomonte where the *Elvisco* cargo boat is submerged at a depth of 12m. Alternatively, a Junker 52, a German plane from WWII, lies on the seabed near Portoferraio at a more challenging depth of 38m.

Typical prices are: one dive with guide €35; six dives €190; introductory snorkelling €50; PADI course €220; and open-water diving course €350.

The coves of the Tuscan archipelagos and around Monte Argentario are superb for sailing, as well as windsurfing, kite surfing and sea kayaking. You can rent equipment and receive instruction at the major resorts. A six-day sailing or windsurfing/kite surfing course (1½ hours' instruction per day) costs from €170.

Windsurfing is also very popular on the Costa Fiorita near Livorno. For information on sailing and windsurfing courses here, contact **Costa Fiorita Booking Centre** (☎ 0586 75 90 59; www.costafiorita.it in Italian). Further up the coast, Viareggio holds several annual sailing regattas, including the Coppa di Primavera in March and the Vela Mare Cup in May. For more information, check out the website www.circolovelamare.it (in Italian).

Fishing in the sea is unlikely to lead to a very plentiful catch because of commercial overfishing that, in turn, has led to occasional fishing bans. For a more certain catch, you are better off heading for the trout farms and artificial lakes and streams of the interior. Before you cast your line in fresh water, you will need a permit, available from the **Federazione Italiano della Pesca Sportiva ed Attività Subacquee** (www.fipsas.it in Italian), which has offices in every province.

Best Time of Year
In Monte Argentario and Elba it's possible to enjoy most water sports, including diving, throughout autumn and winter as the water temperature remains relatively temperate year-round. For diving, however, you'll shiver without a semidry wetsuit between November and May, but you can switch to a regular wet suit for summer.

Florence

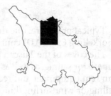

Return time and again and you still won't see it all. Stand on a bridge over the Arno several times in a day, and the light, the mood and the view change every time. Surprisingly small as it is, this city is like no other. Cradle of the Renaissance and of the masses of globe-trotting tourists who flock here to feast on world-class art and extraordinary architecture, Florence (Firenze) is magnetic, romantic, unrivalled and too busy. A visit here is madness, in fact, for anyone who can remain completely unmoved after viewing Botticelli's *Spring*, Michelangelo's muscular warrior, or the Brancacci Chapel's emotive frescoes of Adam and Eve being hurled out of Paradise.

Yet there's more to this river-side city than priceless masterpieces. Strolling its narrow streets evokes a thousand tales of the past: medieval dyers coloured wool in *caldaie* (vats) on Via delle Caldaie; Renaissance *calzaiuoli* (hosiers) hand-crafted fine shoes in workshops on Via dei Calzaiuoli; tanners made a stink in *conce* (tanneries) on Via delle Conce; and yes, those Medici did keep caged *leoni* (lions), although nothing caused quite a stir as the giraffe given to Lorenzo the Magnificent by an Egyptian sultan in 1486.

Plush, decadent and equally exotic is contemporary Florence's flamboyant line-up of designer boutiques around Via de' Tornabuoni. Gucci was born here, as was fashion designer Roberto Cavalli who, like many a smart Florentine, hangs out in the wine-rich hills around Florence today. After a little while in this intensely absorbing city, you might just want to do the same.

HIGHLIGHTS

- Marvel at the world's greatest Renaissance art in the **Uffizi** (p112)

- View the Duomo, baptistry and campanile from atop Brunelleschi's famous red-brick **dome** (p105)

- Do a *David* tour: Michelangelo's original in the **Galleria dell'Accademia** (p119), the famous copies on **Piazza della Signoria** (p108) and **Piazzale Michelangelo** (p127), and those by Donatello and Andrea Verrocchio in **Museo del Bargello** (p108)

- See the *bistecca alla fiorentina* (loin steak or T-bone steak), alongside other Florentine specialities in the city's colourful **food market** (p143), then sample one at **Trattoria Mario** (p137) or **Trattoria Angiolino** (p141)

- Flee the city for a breath of fresh air in **Fiesole** (p154)

- Hunt white truffles and learn about Chianina cattle on an estate near **San Miniato** (p170)

- Swill and spit some of Italy's finest wines on a tasting tour through **Il Chianti** (p164)

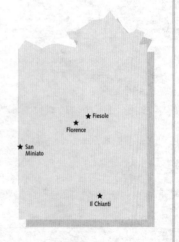

HISTORY

Florence's history stretches to the time of the Etruscans, who based themselves in Fiesole. Julius Caesar founded the Roman colony of Florentia around 59 BC, making it a strategic garrison on the narrowest crossing of the Arno so he could control the Via Flaminia linking Rome to northern Italy and Gaul.

After the collapse of the Roman Empire, Florence fell to invading Goths, followed by Lombards and Franks. The year AD 1000 marked a crucial turning point in the city's fortunes when Margrave Ugo of Tuscany moved his capital from Lucca to Florence. In 1110 Florence became a free *comune* (city-state) and by 1138 was ruled by 12 consuls, assisted by the Consiglio di Cento (Council of One Hundred), whose members were drawn mainly from the prosperous merchant class. Agitation among differing factions in the city led to the appointment in 1207 of a foreign head of state called the *podestà*, aloof in principle from the plotting and wheeler-dealing of local cliques and alliances.

Medieval Florence was a wealthy dynamic *comune*, one of Europe's leading financial, banking and cultural centres, and a major player in the international wool, silk and leather trades. The sizable population of mon-eyed merchants and artisans began forming guilds and patronising the growing number of artists who found lucrative commissions in this burgeoning city. But a political crisis was on the horizon.

Struggles between the pro-papal Guelphs (Guelfi) and the pro-Holy Roman Empire Ghibellines (Ghibellini) started in the mid-13th century, with power yo-yoing between the two for almost a century. Into this fractious atmosphere were born revolutionary artist Giotto and outspoken poet Dante Alighieri, whose family belonged to the Guelph camp. After the Guelphs split into two factions, the Neri (Blacks) and Bianchi (Whites), Dante went with the Bianchi – the wrong side – and was expelled from his native city in 1302, never to return.

In 1348 the Black Death spirited away almost half the population. This dark period in the city's history was used as a backdrop by Boccaccio for his *Decameron*.

The history of Medici Florence begins in 1434, when Cosimo il Vecchio (the Elder, also known simply as Cosimo de' Medici), a patron of the arts, assumed power. His eye for talent

and tact in dealing with artists saw the likes of Alberti, Brunelleschi, Luca della Robbia, Fra Angelico, Donatello and Filippo Lippi flourish under his patronage.

In 1439 the Church Council of Florence, aimed at reconciling the Catholic and Eastern churches, brought to the city Byzantine scholars and craftsmen, who they hoped would impart the knowledge and culture of classical antiquity. The Council, attended by the pope, achieved nothing in the end, but it did influence what was later known as the Renaissance. Under the rule of Cosimo's popular and cultured grandson, Lorenzo il Magnifico (1469–92), Florence became the epicentre of this 'Rebirth', with artists such as Michelangelo, Botticelli and Domenico Ghirlandaio at work.

But Florence's golden age was not to last, effectively dying along with Lorenzo in 1492. Just before his death, the Medici bank had failed, and, two years later, the Medici were driven out of Florence. In a reaction against the splendour and excess of the Medici court, the city fell under the control of Girolamo Savonarola, a humourless Dominican monk who led a stern, puritanical republic. In 1497 the likes of Botticelli gladly consigned their 'immoral' works and finery to the flames of the infamous 'Bonfire of the Vanities'. The following year Savonarola fell from public favour and was burned as a heretic.

The pro-French leanings of the subsequent republican government brought it into conflict with the pope and his Spanish allies. In 1512 a Spanish force defeated Florence and the Medici were reinstated. Their tyrannical rule endeared them to few, and when Rome, ruled by the Medici pope Clement VII, fell to the emperor Charles V in 1527, the Florentines took advantage of this low point in the Medici fortunes to kick the family out again. Two years later, though, imperial and papal forces besieged Florence, forcing the city to accept Lorenzo's great-grandson, Alessandro de' Medici, a ruthless transvestite whom Charles made Duke of Florence. Medici rule continued for another 200 years, during which time they gained control of all of Tuscany, though after the reign of Cosimo I (1537–74), Florence drifted into steep decline.

The last male Medici, Gian Gastone, died in 1737, after which his sister, Anna Maria, signed the grand duchy of Tuscany over to the House of Lorraine (at the time effectively under Austrian control). This situation remained unchanged, apart from a brief interruption under Napoleon from 1799 to 1814, until the duchy was incorporated into the Kingdom of Italy in 1860. Florence briefly became the national capital a year later, but Rome assumed the mantle permanently in 1871.

Florence was badly damaged during WWII by the retreating Germans, who blew up all its bridges except Ponte Vecchio. Devastating floods ravaged the city in 1966, causing inestimable damage to its buildings and artworks. However, the salvage operation led to the widespread use of modern restoration techniques that have saved artworks throughout the country. In 1993 the Mafia exploded a massive car bomb, killing five, injuring 37 and destroying a part of the Uffizi. Just over a decade later, this world-class gallery amid a fair amount of controversy embarked on its biggest-ever expansion, set to double its exhibiting area by 2012 if it's lucky.

ORIENTATION

Central train station Stazione di Santa Maria Novella is a good reference point. Budget hotels and *pensioni* (small hotels) are concentrated east of it around Via Nazionale and south around Piazza di Santa Maria Novella. The main route to the city centre (a 10-minute walk) is Via de' Panzani then Via de' Cerretani. Spot the Duomo and you're there.

Most major sights are within easy walking distance. From Piazza di San Giovanni around the baptistry, Via Roma leads to Piazza della Repubblica and beyond to Ponte Vecchio. From Piazza del Duomo follow Via de' Calzaiuoli for Piazza della Signoria, the historic seat of government. The Uffizi is on the piazza's southern edge, near the Arno. The trendy, less touristy area south of the river is known as Oltrarno.

Maps

Tourist offices dole out free maps and bookshops sell Touring Club Italiano's *Florence* (1:12,500), with a city-centre cutaway (1:6500).

INFORMATION
Bookshops

BM Bookshop (Map p103; ☎ 055 29 45 75; Borgo Ognissanti 4r) British and American books in a pleasing old-fashioned environment.

THE RED & THE BLACK

Florence has two parallel street-numbering systems: red or brown numbers (which usually have 'r' for *rosso*, or red, after the number) indicate commercial premises, whereas black or blue numbers are for private residences.

Black/blue numbers may denote whole buildings, while each red/brown number refers to one commercial entity – and a building may have several. It can turn you purple if you're hunting for a specific address in a hurry.

Edison (Map pp100-1; ☎ 055 21 31 10; Piazza della Repubblica 27r; ☯ 9am-midnight Mon-Sat, 10am-midnight Sun) Stocks maps, travel guides and reference books on Florence and Tuscany; novels and nonfiction in English.

McRae Books (Map pp100-1; ☎ 055 238 24 56; www .mcraebooks.com; Via de' Neri 32r; ☯ 9am-7.30pm Mon-Sun) English-language bookshop covering the whole gambit of genres; brilliantly organised.

Mel Bookstore (Map pp100-1; ☎ 055 28 73 39; www .melbookstore.it; Via de' Cerretani 16r) Tuscan travel literature, guides, reference books and maps.

Paperback Exchange (Map pp100-1; ☎ 055 29 34 60; www.papex.it; Via dell Oche 4r) Anglo-American bookshop, new and second-hand.

Emergency

Police Station (Questura; Map pp98-9; ☎ 055 4 97 71; Via Zara 2; ☯ 24hr) Report thefts at the foreigners' office here.

Tourist Police (Polizia Assistenza Turistica; Map pp100-1; ☎ 055 20 39 11; Via Pietrapiana 50r, Piazza dei Ciompi; ☯ 8.30am-6.30pm Mon-Fri, 8.30am-1pm Sat)

Internet Access

Internet Pitti (Map pp100-1; www.internetpitti.com; Piazza Pitti 7; per hr €4; ☯ 11am-11pm Mon-Sun) Excellent bulletin board crammed with ads for flatmates, room rentals etc.

Internet Train (www.internettrain.it) Via Porta Rossa 38r (Map pp100-1; per hr €4.30; ☯ 9.30am-midnight Mon-Sat, 10am-midnight Sun); Borgo San Jacopo 30r (Map pp100-1; per hr €3.20; ☯ 11am-10pm Mon-Fri, noon-10pm Sat & Sun); Via dell'Oriuolo 40r (Map pp100-1; per hr €3.20; ☯ 10am-10.30pm Mon-Fri, noon-8pm Sat, 3-7pm Sun); Via Guelfa 24 (Map pp98-9; per hr €3.20; ☯ 9am-midnight Mon-Fri, 11am-9pm Sat & Sun) In all, 10-odd branches.

Internet Resources

Locally generated blogs are also useful; see p56.

City of Florence (www.comune.firenze.it) City information.

Firenze-Oltrarno (www.firenze-oltrarno.net) Loadsa' links south of the river.

Firenze Net (http://english.firenze.net) Up-to-the-minute information on city life.

Florence for Fun (www.florenceforfun.org) Practical info aimed at international students in Florence.

The Florentine (www.theflorentine.net) English-language newspaper.

Studentsville (www.studentsville.it) Everything about studying, living and lodging in this student-busy city.

viviFirenze (www.vivifirenze.it) Another student perspective: practical guide to living and studying in Florence.

Laundry

Wash & Dry (wash or dry €3.50; ☽ 8am-10pm) Via de' Serragli 87r (**Map p103**); Borgo San Frediano 39r (**Map p103**); Via dei Servi 105r (**Map pp98-9**); Via del Sole 29r (**Map pp100-1**); Via della Scala 52-54r (**Map pp98-9**); Via Nazionale 129 (**Map pp98-9**)

Left Luggage

Stazione di Santa Maria Novella (Map pp98-9; per item for 5hr €3.80, for every hr thereafter €0.60; ☽ 6am-midnight) Find it on platform 16.

Medical Services

24-Hour Pharmacy (Map pp98-9; ☎ 055 21 67 61; Stazione di Santa Maria Novella) Inside the main train station.

Dr Stephen Kerr (Map pp100-1; ☎ 055 28 80 55; www .dr-kerr.com; Via Porta Rossa 1; ☽ 3-5pm Mon-Fri) Resident British doctor, by appointment or open clinic.

Emergency Doctor (Guardia Medica; ☎ 055 28 77 88) For a doctor at night or on a public holiday.

Farmacia all'Insegna del Moro (Map pp100-1; ☎ 055 21 13 43; Piazza di San Giovanni 20r; ☽ 24hr) Pharmacy in business since 1521.

Farmacia Molteni (Map pp100-1; ☎ 055 28 94 90; Via de' Calzaiuoli 7; ☽ 24hr) Pharmacy.

Ospedale di Santa Maria Nuova (Map pp100-1; ☎ 055 2 75 81; Piazza di Santa Maria Nuova 1)

Tourist Medical Service (Map pp98-9; ☎ 055 47 54 11; Via Lorenzo il Magnifico 59; ☽ clinic 11am-noon & 5-6pm Mon-Sat) English-speaking doctors on call 24 hours.

Money

American Express (Map pp100-1; ☎ 055 5 09 81; Via Dante Alighieri 22r; ☽ 9am-5.30pm Mon-Fri)

Post

Central Post Office (Map pp100-1; Via Pellicceria)

Tourist Information

Comune di Firenze Tourist Office Train Station (Map pp98-9; ☎ 055 21 22 45; www.comune.fi.it in Italian; Piazza della Stazione 4; ☽ 8.30am-7pm Mon-Sat, 8.30am-1.30pm Sun); Santa Croce (Map pp100-1; ☎ 055 234 04 44; Borgo Santa Croce 29r; ☽ 9am-7pm Mon-Sat, 9am-2pm Sun) Information on the city, run by Florence's city council.

Florence Tourist Board (Map pp100-1; ☎ 055 233 20; www.firenzeturismo.it; Via Manzoni 16; ☽ 9am-1pm Mon-Fri)

Provincia di Firenze Tourist Office City Centre (Map pp98-9; ☎ 055 29 08 32/3; www.provincia .firenze.it in Italian, www.firenzeturismo.it; Via Cavour 1r; ☽ 8.30am-6.30pm Mon-Sat, 8.30am-1.30pm Sun); Florence Airport (Map pp96-7; ☎ 055 31 58 74; infoaeroporto@aeroporto.firenze.it; ☽ 8.30am-8.30pm) Information on the city and province of Florence: stocks lists of recommended guided tours, updated museum opening hours and accommodation; sells books and maps. Also runs the **SOS Turista phoneline** (☎ 055 276 03 82) for tourists in trouble (disputes over hotel bills etc).

Travel Agencies

CTS (Map pp98-9; ☎ 055 28 95 70; www.cts.it in Italian; Via de' Ginori 25r) Florence branch of national youth-travel organisation.

DANGERS & ANNOYANCES

Florence's most annoying feature is its crowds, closely followed by street vendors flogging tack.

Solo travellers should avoid the area around Stazione di Santa Maria Novella and Parco delle Cascine, frequented by pimps and prostitutes after dark. Pickpockets are active in crowds and on buses and Florence has many bag snatchers. Watch out for the 'You-have-gunk-on-your-suitcase!' scam (p402).

Readers warn women not to walk/jog alone along the Forte di Belevedere footpath.

SIGHTS

Florence seriously overwhelms. Its wealth of museums and galleries house many of the world's most important and exquisite examples of Renaissance art and its architecture is unrivalled. Yet the secret is not to feel pressured to see and do everything: combining your personal pick of the major sights with ample meandering through the city's warren of narrow streets is the trick.

In true Italian fashion, state museums and monuments (Uffizi and Galleria Accademia

(Continued on page 104)

A B C D

To Villa Medicea
di Castello (3km);
Teatro della
Limonaia (4km)

1
Area Ex-FIAT

To Aeroporto di
Firenze (5km);
Pistoia (30km)

Ponte
di Mezzo

6 ☐
Via M Mercati

To Villa Medicea
di Careggi (1km)

Via Stibbert

Parco di
Villa Fabbricotti

Via Vittorio Emanuele II

🏛 3

Piazza
GB Giorgini

Piazza P
Leopoldo

Via F Gianni

See Stazione & Around Map (pp98–9)

To Tenax
(8km)

Ponte
di S
Donato

Ponte
alle
Mosse

Viale Francesco Redi

**San
Jacopino**

Via Benedetto Marcello

Via del Ponte alle Mosse

Viale Belfiore

Viale Filippo Strozzi

Viale dello Statuto

Torrente Mugnone

Viale Spartaco Lavagnini

Via San Gallo

Giardino
dell's
Orticltura

Ponte
Rosso

**Piazza dell
Libertà**

2

Torrente Terzolle

Canale Macinante

Parco delle Cascine

To Piscina Le
Pavoniere (200m)

3

Stazione
Porta al
Prato

Ex-Stazione
Leopolda

Viale Fratelli Rosselli

Porta al
Prato

Piazza
del
Crocifisso

Palazzo
degli
Affari

Stazione di
Santa Maria
Novella

Mercato
Centrale

Via de' Ginori

Palazz
Cappo

Piazza P
Uccella

Via del Sansovino

To Car Pound (2km); Pisa (40km);
Pisa International Airport
Galileo Galilei (42km)

Pignone

Via Bronzino

Ponte
della
Vittoria

2•

Lungarno Amerigo Vespucci

Piazza
dell'Unità
Italiana

Via Valfonda

Via de' Cerretani

Duomo

4

Lungarno di S Rosa

A R N O

**Piazza
Pier
Vettori**

Viale A Aleardi Ariosto

Monticelli

**San
Frediano**

Ponte
alla
Carraia

Lungarno Guicciardini

Via de' Tornabuoni

Piazza delle
Repubblica

Via de' Benci

Ponte
Vecchio

**Santo
Spirito**

Lungarno Torrigiani

5

Viale Francesco Petrarca

**Giardino
Torrigiani**

Via de' Serragli

Via Romana

Via dell'Agnolo

Via de' Guicciardini

**Giardino di
Boboli
(Boboli Gardens)**

Bellosguardo

Isolotto

Istituto
d'Arte

Piazzale
di Porta
Romana

Via Senese

Viale del Poggio Imperiale

**San
Niccolò**

Viale Nicolò Machiavelli

Via della Torre del Gallo

See Oltrarno & Nearby
Quarters Map (p103)

6

To Certosa di Firenze (3km); Trattoria Bibe
(3km); Guesthouse Villino Giulia (3km)

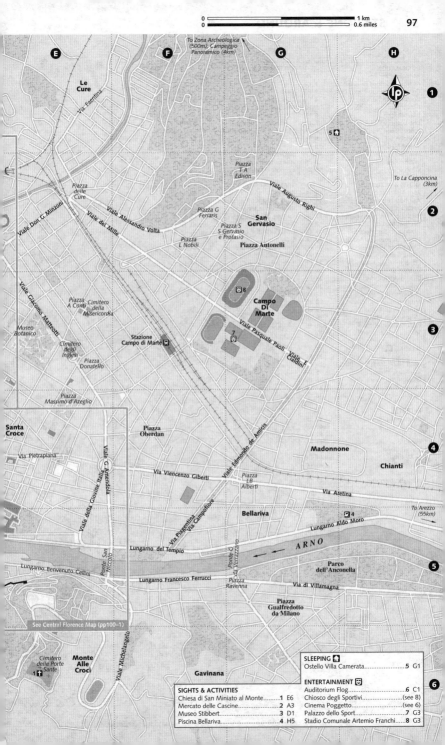

0 — 1 km
0 — 0.6 miles

E **F** **G** **H**

1 **2** **3** **4** **5** **6**

Le Cure

Via Faentina

To Zona Archeologica
(500m); Campeggio
Panoramico (4km)

Piazza
T A
Edison

5 🏠

Viale Augusto Righi

To La Capponcina
(3km)

Piazza
delle
Cure

Viale Don G. Minzoni

Viale Alessandro Volta

Viale dei Mille

Piazza G
Ferraris

Piazza S
S Gervasio
e Protasio

San
Gervasio

Piazza
L Nobili

Piazza Antonelli

Viale Giacomo Matteotti

Piazza
A Conti

Cimitero
della
Misericordia

Museo
Botanico

Cimitero
degli
Inglesi

Piazza
Donatello

Stazione
Campo di Marte 🚉

8 🏟

Campo Di
Marte

7 🏟

Viale Pasquale Paoli

Viale F Gioberti

Piazza
Massimo d'Azeglio

Santa
Croce

Piazza
Oberdan

Madonnone

Chianti

Via Pietrapiana

Viale G. Amendola

Via Vincenzo Gioberti

Viale Edmondo de Amicis

Piazza
LB
Alberti

Via Aretina

To Arezzo
(55km)

Viale della Giovine Italia

Via Piagentina

Via Campofiore

Bellariva

4 🏟

Lungarno Aldo Moro

Lungarno del Tempio

*Ponte G
da Verrazzano*

A R N O

Parco
dell'Anconella

Ponte San
Niccolò

Lungarno Benvenuto Cellini

Lungarno Francesco Ferrucci

Piazza
Ravenna

Via di Villamagna

See Central Florence Map (pp100–1)

Piazza
Gualfredotto
da Milano

Cimitero
delle Porte
Sante

1 🏛

Monte
Alle
Croci

Gavinana

Viale Michelangelo

SIGHTS & ACTIVITIES
Chiesa di San Miniato al Monte......1 E6
Mercato delle Cascine.....................2 A3
Museo Stibbert..............................3 D1
Piscina Bellariva............................4 H5

SLEEPING 🏠
Ostello Villa Camerata....................5 G1

ENTERTAINMENT 🎭
Auditorium Flog.............................6 C1
Chiosco degli Sportivi..................(see 8)
Cinema Poggetto.........................(see 6)
Palazzo dello Sport.........................7 G3
Stadio Comunale Artemio Franchi......8 G3

A **B** **C** **D**

Piazza B
Tanucci

INFORMATION
24-Hour Pharmacy...........................1 D6
Agenzie 365 Hotel Reservation.........2 D6
Comune di Firenze Tourist Office......3 E6
Consorzio ITA................................4 D6
CTS..5 F6
Internet Train................................6 F5
Left-Luggage Office.........................7 D6
Police Station.................................8 G4
Provincia di Firenze Tourist Office....9 F6
Tourist Medical Service..................10 F3
Wash & Dry..................................11 G6
Wash & Dry..................................12 F5
Wash & Dry..................................13 D6

SIGHTS & ACTIVITIES
Alice Atelier.................................14 E6
Amici del Turismo.........................15 G6
Basilica di San Lorenzo..................16 F6
Basilica di Santa Maria Novella.......17 E6
Cappelle Medicee..........................18 F6
Cenacolo di Sant'Apollonia............19 G5
Centro Lorenzo de' Medici.............20 E6
Chiesa della SS Annunziata.............21 H5
Chiesa Russa Ortodoss...................22 F3
City Sightseeing Firenze.................23 E6
Fortezza da Basso..........................24 D4
Galleria dell'Accademia..................25 G5
Galleria dell'Accademia Entrance.....26 G5
La Bottega dei Ragazzi...................27 H6
Mondobimbo................................28 H2
Museo Archeologico......................29 H6
Museo di San Marco......................30 G5
Palazzo Medici-Riccardi..................31 F6
Spedale degli Innocenti..................32 H6

SLEEPING
Hotel Casci..................................33 F6
Hotel Morandi alla Crocetta...........34 H6
Johanna & Johlea..........................35 G4
Ostello Archi Rossi........................36 E5
Ostello Gallo d'Oro.......................37 H4
Palazzo Alfani..............................38 G6

EATING
Antico Forno Santi........................39 E5
Carabè..40 G6
Da Sergio....................................41 F6
Divino...42 F6
Il Vegetariano..............................43 G4
La Mescita...................................44 G6
Mercato Centrale..........................45 F6
Nerbone......................................46 F6
Trattoria Mario.............................47 F6

ENTERTAINMENT
Be Bop Music Club........................48 G6
Box Office....................................49 C5
Central Park.................................50 A6
Ex-Stazione Leopolda....................51 B5
Meccanò Club..............................52 A6
Palazzo dei Congressi
  (Open-air Cinema).......................53 E5
Teatro del Maggio Musicale
  Fiorentino..................................54 B6

SHOPPING
Arte Liutaria................................55 G6
Le Spose di Laila...........................56 G4

TRANSPORT
Alinari..57 E5
ATAF Ticket & Information Office.....58 F6
Biciclette a Noleggio......................59 D6
CAP & COPIT Bus Station...............60 E5
Florence by Bike...........................61 G4
Lazzi Bus Station...........................62 E5
SITA...63 D6
Terravision Bus Stop......................64 D6
Ticket Office................................65 D6
Train Information Office..................66 D6

Via C Guasti

Via del Romito

Via E Fabbri

Via G Richa

Via Crimea

Via Cosseria

Viale Filippo Strozzi

Piazza F
Baldinucci

Via delle Cascine

Via Maragliano

Viale Filippo Strozzi

Via delle Porte Nuove

Via Benedetto Marcello

Via del Ponte alle Mosse

Via Belfiore

Via Cittadella

Via Guido Monaco

Via I Pensieri

Viale Fratelli Rosselli

Viale Belfiore

Via Jacopo da Diacceto

Via Luigi Alamanni

Via Valfonda

49 C5

P

P

24

Piazza
Adua

Stazione
Santa Maria
Novella

Stazione
Porta al Prato

Ex-Stazione Leopolda
51

Canale Macinante

Via Fosso Macinante

Parco
delle
Cascine

Piazzale
Porta
al Prato

Porta
al
Prato

50

Via Montebello

Via Maggia

Via Il Prato

Via Bernardo Rucellai

Via della Scala

13

66 **65**
7 1
2
4 1

59

Viale degli Olmi
52

63
64 **64**

Via de' Panzani

Via Santa Caterina
da Siena

Cappellone
degli
Spagnoli

Ponte
della
Vittoria

Lungarno Amerigo Vespucci

Corso Italia

Via G Garibaldi

Via Maggia

Via Palazzuolo

Via degli Orti Oricellari

54

See Oltrarno & Nearby Quarters Map (p103)

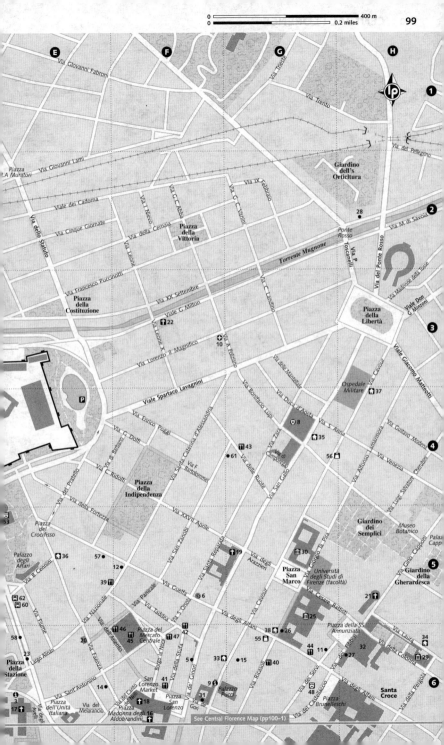

0   400 m
0   0.2 miles

E **F** **G** **H**

1

Via Giovanni Fabroni

Via Trieste

Via Trento

Via del Pellegrino

Piazza
A. Muratori

Via Giovanni Lami

Giardino
dell's
Orticltura

Via IX Febbraio

28

2

Viale dei Cadorna

Via G. C. Abba

Piazza
della
Vittoria

Ponte
Rosso

Via M. di Savoia

Via Cinque Giornate

Via della Cernaia

Via G. Niccoli

Via C. C. Vanini

Via del Ponte Rosso

Via Madonna della Tosse

Via dello Statuto

Torrente Mugnone

Via Leone

Via P. Toscanelli

Piazza
della
Costituzione

Via Francesco Pucchotti

Via XX Settembre

Viale G. Milton

Via C. Landino

Piazza
della
Libertà

Viale Don
G. Minzoni

3

Via Leone X

🚻22

Via Lorenzo Il Magnifico

⊕
10

Via A. Poliziano

Via delle Mantellate

Via Cavour

Viale Giacomo Matteotti

Viale Spartaco Lavagnini

Via Duca d'Aosta

Ospedale
Militare 🏨37

Via Enrico Poggi

Via C. Dolfi

Via Bonifacio Lupi

Via S. Anna

🔘 8

35🏨

Via Gustavo Modena

4

Via G. Bartolini

Via di Barbano

Via Santa Caterina d'Alessandria

🍴43

Via Zara

Via di
Campolisse

56 🏨

Via Alfonso Lamarmora

Via Venezia

Via del Pratello

Via C. Ridolfi

Piazza
della
Indipendenza

Via F.
Bartolomei

61 ●

Via delle Ruote

Via San Gallo

Via Luigi Salvatore Cherubini

Via della Fortezza

Via XXVII Aprile

Giardino
dei
Semplici

Museo
Botanico

Palazo
Capp

Piazza
del
Crocifisso

Palazzo
degli
Affari

🏨36

57 ●

12 ●

🍴19

Via degli
Arazzieri

🏛30

Piazza
San Marco

Via Giorgio La Pira

Via Gino Capponi

Giardino
della
Gherardesca

5

Via B. Cennini

39 🍴

Via San Zanobi

Via Santa Reparata

Via Cavour

Università
degli Studi di
Firenze (facoltà)

21 🏨

⊟62
⊟60

Via Panicale

Via Nazionale

Via Guelfa

@ 6

Via Cesare Battisti

Via Laura

6

Via Fiume

58 ●

20

🏨46

Piazza del
Mercato
Centrale

Via dell'Ariento

Via Taddea

Via S. Orsola

🍴47

🍴42

Via degli Alfani

38 ● ● 26

55 🏨

🏛25

Piazza della SS.
Annunziata

34 🏨
29 🏨

32

Via della Pergola

Via Faenza

45

Borgo la Noce

5 ●

33 🏨

● 15

🍴40

44
11 ● 🏨

48

27 ●

Via della Colonna

Piazza
della
Stazione

23 ●

Largo Alinari

Via Sant'Antonino

14 ●

San
Lorenzo
Market

41 🍴

18

Via de' Ginori

9 ●

31

Palazzo
Pucci

Via de' Servi

Piazza
Brunelleschi

Santa
Croce

ℹ
17 🏨

Piazza
dell'Unità
italiana

Via del Melarancio

Via del Canto
de' Nelli

Piazza
Madonna degli 16
Aldobrandini 🏨

Piazza
San
Lorenzo

Via de' Gori

Via del Castellaccio

Via degli Alfani

See Central Florence Map (pp100–1)

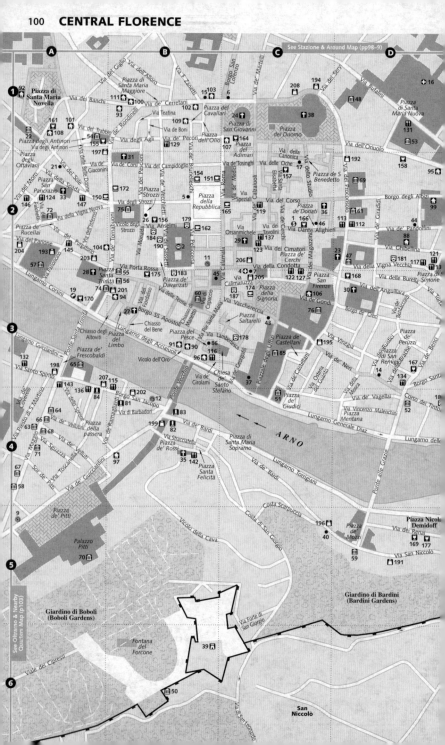

See Stazione & Around Map (pp98–9)

A **B** **C** **D**

Piazza di
Santa Maria
Novella

Piazza di
Santa Maria
Maggiore

Piazza degli Antinori

Piazza degli Antinori

Piazza
degli
Ottaviani

Piazza della
Spada
San
Pancrazio

Piazza di
Rucellai

Via del Parione

Piazza
Santa
Trinita

Lungarno Corsini

Piazza di
San Giovanni

Piazza
del Duomo

Piazza
di Santa
Maria Nuova

Piazza del
Cavallari

Piazza del
Adimari

Piazza
dell'Olio

Piazza S Benedetto

Borgo degli Albizi

Piazza
della
Repubblica

Piazza
Orsanmichele

Piazza de'
Donati

Via de' Pandolfini

Via Chibellina

Piazza de'
Davanzati

Piazza della
Signoria

Piazza San
Firenze

Piazza di
Sinione

Chiasso
del Bene

Piazza
del
Limbo

Piazza del
Pesce

Piazza
Saltarelli

Piazza de'
Castellani

Piazza de'
Peruzzi

Piazza
di San
Remigio

Piazza de'
Frescobaldi

Via Santo Spirito

Chiesa di
santo
Stefano

Piazzale degli Uffizi

Piazza
de'
Giudici

Lungarno Generale Diaz

Via de' Vellutini

Piazza
della
passera

Piazza di
Santa Maria
Sopramo

Piazza
de' Rossi

Piazza
Santa
Felicità

ARNO

Lungarno Torrigiani

Ponte alle Grazie

Piazza Nicola
Demidoff

Piazza
de'
Mozzi

Via San Niccolò

Piazza
de' Pitti

Costa Scarpuccia

Palazzo
Pitti

Costa di San Giorgio

Vicolo della Cava

See Oltrarno & Nearby
Quarters Map (p103)

Giardino di Boboli
(Boboli Gardens)

Giardino di Bardini
(Bardini Gardens)

Fontana
del
Forcone

Via Forte di
San Giorgio

Viale dei Cipressi

San
Niccolò

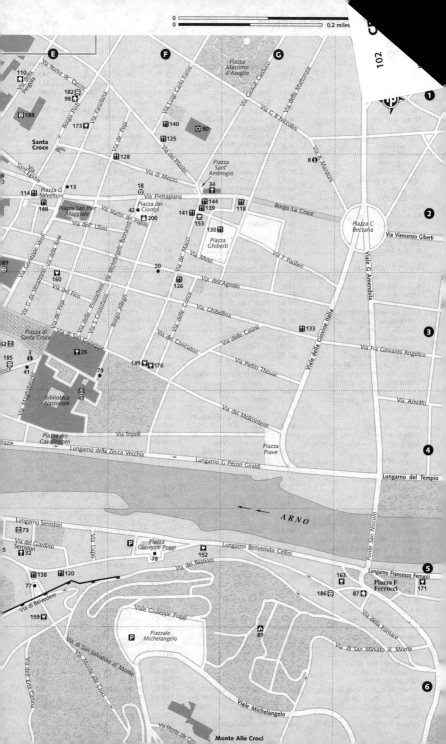

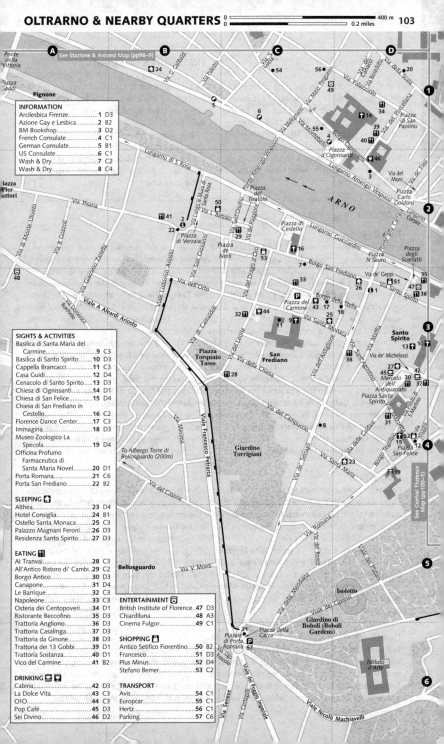

See Stazione & Around Map (pp98–9)

Pignone

INFORMATION
Arcilesbica Firenze	**1** D3
Azione Gay e Lesbica	**2** B2
BM Bookshop	**3** D2
French Consulate	**4** C1
German Consulate	**5** B1
US Consulate	**6** C1
Wash & Dry	**7** C2
Wash & Dry	**8** C4

SIGHTS & ACTIVITIES
Basilica di Santa Maria del Carmine	**9** C3
Basilica di Santo Spirito	**10** D3
Cappella Brancacci	**11** C3
Casa Guidi	**12** D4
Cenacolo di Santo Spirito	**13** D3
Chiesa di Ognissanti	**14** D1
Chiesa di San Felice	**15** D4
Chiesa di San Frediano in Cestello	**16** C2
Florence Dance Center	**17** C3
Immagina	**18** D3
Museo Zoologico La Specola	**19** D4
Officina Profumo Farmaceutica di Santa Maria Novel	**20** D1
Porta Romana	**21** C6
Porta San Frediano	**22** B2

SLEEPING
Althea	**23** D4
Hotel Consiglia	**24** B1
Ostello Santa Monaca	**25** C3
Palazzo Magnani Feroni	**26** D3
Residenza Santo Spirito	**27** D3

EATING
Al Tranvai	**28** C3
All'Antico Ristoro di' Cambi	**29** C2
Borgo Antico	**30** D3
Canapone	**31** D4
Le Barrique	**32** C3
Napoleone	**33** C3
Osteria dei Centopoveri	**34** D1
Ristorante Beccofino	**35** D1
Trattoria Angliono	**36** D3
Trattoria Casalinga	**37** D3
Trattoria da Ginone	**38** D3
Trattoria dei 13 Gobbi	**39** D1
Trattoria Sostanza	**40** D1
Vico del Carmine	**41** B2

DRINKING
Cabiria	**42** D3
La Dolce Vita	**43** C3
OIO	**44** C3
Pop Café	**45** D3
Sei Divino	**46** D2

ENTERTAINMENT
British Institute of Florence	**47** D3
Chiardiluna	**48** A3
Cinema Fulgor	**49** C1

SHOPPING
Antico Setificio Fiorentino	**50** B2
Francesco	**51** D3
Plus Minus	**52** D4
Stefano Bemer	**53** C2

TRANSPORT
Avis	**54** C1
Europcar	**55** C1
Hertz	**56** C1
Parking	**57** C6

ARNO

Giardino di Boboli (Boboli Gardens)

Giardino Torrigiani

Bellosguardo

Isolotto

Istituto d'Arte

See Central Florence Map (pp100–1)

FLORENCE

(Continued from page 95)

included) close on Monday. But Florence is a year-round destination and there are plenty of major sights open whichever day of the week you are in town. Note that museum ticket offices usually shut 30 minutes before closing time.

Most churches enforce a strict dress code for visitors: no shorts, sleeveless shirts or plunging necklines.

FREE ENTRY & DISCOUNTS

Those with an EU passport (have it on you as ID) aged under 18 and over 65 get into Florence's state museums for free. EU citizens who are aged between 18 and 25 pay half-price.

For one week of the year (usually some time in spring), admission to state museums is free of charge; dates change making it impossible to plan a trip around this, but keep your eyes open.

FLORENCE IN...

Two Days

If you don't have prebooked tickets for the Uffizi and Galleria dell'Accademia, race straight to a ticket office (opposite) to book slots for later that day and day two. Then concentrate on enjoying yourself, starting with a cappuccino in **Caffè Gilli** (p143). Explore the splendid **Duomo** (opposite) and adjoining **Baptistry** (p107) and, assuming you have a head for heights (and no heart problems), scale either **Brunelleschi's dome** (p107) or the **Campanile** (p107). When hunger beckons, zip north for a speed lunch to remember at **Trattoria Mario** (p137) near Florence's central food market – but get there by noon at the latest to ensure a table; if you're too late, nip into the Mercato Central for a tripe sandwich at **Nerbone** (p137) instead.

Devote the afternoon to **Piazza della Signoria** (p111) and the neighbouring **Uffizi** (p112). Recover afterwards with a stroll along the Arno, crossing **Ponte Vecchio** (p123) for a glimpse of the Oltrarno district, where you could dine in one of the traditional Tuscan restaurants along Via Santo Spirito. Should a spot of theatre appeal, dine at **Teatro del Sale** (p141).

Start day two with the **Fra Angelico frescoes** (p177) in the **Museo di San Marco** (p119), followed by the **Galleria dell'Accademia** (p119), home to Michelangelo's *David*, and a simple lunch at **La Mescita** (p137). Take a break from museums in the afternoon: go **shopping** (p149), discover the fine art of **Florentine craftsmanship** (p150) or enjoy a green stroll through the **Boboli and Bardini Gardens** (p124) instead. End the day with an all-essential Florentine **aperitivo** (p146) or a spot of **wine-tasting** (p144).

Four Days

Follow the above itinerary for the first two days. Use the morning of day three to discover Renaissance sculpture in the **Museo del Bargello** (p108), followed by lunch at either **Osteria del Caffé Italiano** (p140), **La Canova di Gustavino** (p139) or the more upmarket **Gustavino** (p139). Spend the afternoon outside the city in **Fiesole** (p154), enjoying fantastic views over Florence, exploring its Roman and Etruscan remains, walking in the hills, and relaxing in the cafés and restaurants on its main square. Back in Florence, **Alle Murate** (p139) is a smart sightseeing dinner choice.

Next day, visit **Basilica di Santa Croce** (p121), followed by a long lazy lunch over an English-language newspaper or art magazine at Fabio Picchi's **Teatro del Sale** (p141). In the afternoon cross the river and hike up to **Piazzale Michelangelo** (p127) and **Chiesa di San Miniato al Monte** (p127) for feisty views, then descend for dinner at one of the Oltrarno's many excellent eating choices (p141).

One Week

Follow the previous itinerary, and on the fifth day consider heading north of the old city to the Medici villas (p128) or making a day trip to **Il Chianti** (p164). Spend your last day scooping up the bits you missed or back-tracking to bits that left you wishing you had more time to explore. Otherwise, **Palazzo Vecchio** (p110) is fun to tour; or what about the **Basilica di Santa Maria Novella** (p115) and **Basilica di San Lorenzo** (p118), followed by a peek in the **Cappelle Medicee** (p118).

One date that doesn't shift is 18 February, the day Anna Maria Louisa de' Medici (1667–1743) died. In honour of the last of the Medici family who bequeathed the city its vast cultural heritage, admission to all state museums is free on this day.

Duomo & Around

As the city's most iconic landmark, not to mention an icon of Italy alongside Pisa's Leaning Tower and Rome's Colosseum, the **Duomo** (Cathedral; Map pp100-1; ☎ 055 230 28 85; ⊙ 10am-5pm Mon-Wed & Fri, 10am-4pm Thu, 10am-4.45pm Sat, 10am-3.30pm 1st Sat of month, mass in English 5pm Sat) thrills. Its famous red-tiled dome dominating Florence's skyline is packed with drama and intrigue, while the sheer size and vivacity of its breathtaking pink, white and green marble façade – as you approach the building from the piazza – turns you into a very tiny Alice in Wonderland.

Begun in 1296 by Sienese architect Arnolfo di Cambio, the world's fourth-largest cathedral took almost 150 years to complete. Its neo-Gothic façade was designed in the 19th century by architect Emilio de Fabris to replace the uncompleted original, torn down in the 16th century. The oldest and most clearly Gothic part of the cathedral is its south flan[k] by **Porta dei Canonici** (Canons' Door), a [?] century High Gothic creation (you ente[r] [?] climb up inside the dome). Wander around the trio of apses, designed to appear as the flowers on the stem that is the nave of the church and so reflecting its proper name – Cattedrale di Santa Maria del Fiore (St Mary of the Flower).

DOME

When Michelangelo went to work on St Peter's in Rome, he reportedly said: 'I go to build a greater dome, but not a fairer one'. One of the finest masterpieces of the Renaissance, Florence's famous cathedral **dome** (adult/under 6yr €6/free; ⊙ 8.30am-7pm Mon-Fri, 8.30am-5.40pm Sat) is indeed a feat of engineering and one that cannot be fully appreciated without staggering up the 463 stone steps inside it.

At the first stop for breath on the ascent – one of four decorative exedrae around the octagonal drum already completed in 1417 – winches used to build it bring home just how much of a gargantuan task 15th-century builders faced. No supporting frame was used during construction of the dome (1420–36), actually two concentric domes built from red

---

CUT THE QUEUE

In summer and busy periods such as Easter, ridiculously long queues to get into key museums can mean a hot and sticky wait of four to seven hours! Booking ahead, however, slashes waiting time to zero (or, in the case of the Uffizi at peak times, an hour or so).

For a fee of €3 per ticket, tickets can be reserved up to one day in advance to all 13 *musei statali* (state museums), including the Uffizi, Galleria dell'Accademia (where *David* lives), Palazzo Pitti, Museo del Bargello, Museo Archeologico and the Medici chapels (Cappelle Medicee). Free tickets for those aged under 18 also incur the €3 booking fee. Make yourself a coffee then call **Firenze Musei** (Florence Museums; ☎ 055 29 48 83; www.firenzemusei.it; ⊙ ticket reservations 8.30am-6.30pm Mon-Fri, 8.30am-12.30pm Sat) and loiter in the inevitable phone queue. Once connected with a real person, you'll be allotted a date and time to visit and a booking number, which you need to quote when you arrive at the sight to pay for your ticket. At the Uffizi, signs point pre-booked ticket holders to a different entrance; in summer you might well have to queue twice – first to pay for/collect your ticket then again to actually get into the museum.

In Florence, tickets can likewise be prebooked at **Firenze Musei information desks** (⊙ 8.30am-7pm Tue-Sun) at the Uffizi (p112) and Palazzo Pitti (p123) – for travellers in town for a few days, reserving tickets on day one for one or two days hence is the savvy thing to do. For those with no Uffizi ticket in hand, set the alarm for 6am to be ready and waiting in the queue outside the gallery by 7am; when the doors open at 8.15am, you should be among the stream of visitors that swing through with the first flush.

Online, museum tickets can also be booked through **Weekend a Firenze** (www.weekendafirenze .com), a web service for booking museums, galleries, shows and tours (commission €5.70). Reserve at least one day in advance, print out the email confirmation and present it at the cashier's desk on the day of your visit.

Many hotels and B&Bs also prebook museum tickets for guests.

TOP FIVE TRICKS TO FLEE THE CROWDS

Mission impossible it might seem, but play your cards right and it is possible to get away from everyone else – or at least the vast majority. Our top tricks:

- Forget the big sights; instead, devote time to tracking down hidden treasures such as Michelangelo's curvaceous staircase and vestibule in the Biblioteca Laurenziana Medicea (p118)

- To visit the Boboli Gardens (p123), skip the main entrance (and horrid queue) it shares with Palazzo Pitti. Enter the gardens instead from neighbouring **Giardino Bardini** (☎ 055 261 22 14; Via dei Bardi 1r; adult/concession incl Boboli Gardens & Silver Museum €6/3; ☽ 8.15am-4.30pm Jan, Feb, Nov & Dec, to 5.30pm Mar, to 6.30pm Apr, May, Sep & Oct, to 7.30pm Jun-Aug), allowing plenty of time to stroll around these smaller but substantially better-kept gardens first.

- When prebooking your ticket for the Uffizi (p105), take a slot for the late afternoon when there are supposedly less people.

- If you succeed in getting into Florence's infamous **Corridoio Vasariano** (Map pp100–1; ☎ 055 29 48 83; ☽ guided tour on special request), you'll leave the crowds behind you. Only a privileged few are allowed into this enclosed walkway commissioned by Cosimo I in 1565 as a private promenade between Palazzo Vecchio with Palazzo Pitti and strung with art today.

- Forget Piazzale Michelangelo (p127) with its ticky tacky souvenir stalls; continue higher to Chiesa di San Miniato al Monte (p127) to watch the sun set over the city.

brick to designs by Brunelleschi. Though he was initially commissioned with arch-rival Ghiberti to build what would be, at the time, the world's largest church dome, he quickly took the lead on a project that had defeated every architect before him. More than a decade on, the Florentine maestro had to prove himself again when authorities threw open the crowning lantern to competition – which Brunelleschi won, only to die months later; see his tomb in the cathedral crypt.

From the exedrae, steps spiral relentlessly up to a balustrade at the base of the 91m-high and 45.5m-wide dome, from where you get an aerial view of the octagonal **coro** (choir) of the cathedral below and the seven round stained-glass windows piercing the octagonal drum. Look up and study the mesmerising late-16th-century frescoes by Giorgio Vasari and Frederico Zuccari, depicting the *Giudizio Universale* (Last Judgment), that blaze a fiery trail of colour across the interior of the dome.

Continuing up (puff puff), snapshots of Florence flash past through small windows as the gruelling maze of narrow stone steps and airless passageways cut from the outer to inner wall of the double-walled dome. The final leg – a straight flight up the curve of the inner dome – rewards with an unforgettable 360-degree panorama of one of Europe's most beautiful cities. Allow yourself at least half an hour up here to enjoy (and recuperate).

INTERIOR

After the visually tumultuous façade and extraordinary frescoes of the dome, the sparse decoration of the cathedral's vast interior, 155m long and 90m wide, comes as a surprise. It is also unexpectedly secular in places (a reflection of the sizeable chunk of the cathedral not paid for by the church): down the left aisle two immense frescoes of equestrian statues portray two *condottieri* (mercenaries) – left Niccolò da Tolentino by Andrea del Castagno and right Sir John Hawkwood by Uccello – who fought in the service of Florence in the 14th century; while 'divine' poet Dante is honoured with Domenico di Michelino's *Dante e I Suoi Mondi* (Dante and His Worlds).

From the central choir beneath the frescoed dome, the two wings of the transept and the rear apse spread out, each containing five chapels. The pillars delimiting the entrance into each wing and the apse are fronted by statues of Apostles, as are the two hefty pillars just west of the choir stalls.

Between the left (north) arm of the transept and the apse is the **Sagrestia delle Messe** (Mass Sacristy), its panelling a marvel of inlaid wood carved by Benedetto and Giuliano da Maiano. The fine bronze doors were executed by Luca della Robbia – his only known work in the material. Above the doorway is his glazed terracotta *Resurrezione* (Resurrection).

Throughout, stained-glass windows by Donatello, Andrea del Castagno, Paolo Uccello and Lorenzo Ghiberti positively glow.

A stairway near the main entrance of the cathedral leads down to the **crypt** (admission €3; ☻ 10am-5pm Mon-Fri, 10am-4.45pm Sat), where excavations have unearthed parts of the 5th-century Chiesa di Santa Reparata, which originally stood on the site. There's a small display of Roman pottery, architectural fragments and sections of the original mosaic floor, typical of early Italian churches. Brunelleschi's tomb is also here, beside the gift shop.

CAMPANILE

Equally physical is the heady 414-step climb up the graceful, 82m-high **bell tower** (adult/under 6yr €6/free; ☻ 8.30am-7.30pm), another escapade not recommended for the faint-hearted (literally).

Architect Giotto died before the building of the bell tower was complete, leaving Andrea Pisano and Francesco Talenti to finish it. The first tier of bas-reliefs around the base of the campanile are copies of those carved by Pisano, but possibly designed by Giotto, depicting the Creation of Man and the *attività umane* (arts and industries). Those on the second tier depict the planets, the cardinal virtues, the arts and the seven sacraments. The sculptures of the Prophets and Sibyls in the niches of the upper storeys are copies of works by Donatello and others; see the originals in the Museo dell'Opera del Duomo.

MUSEO DELL'OPERA DEL DUOMO

Light, airy and surprisingly overlooked by the crowds, the **Cathedral Museum** (Map pp100-1; Piazza del Duomo 9; www.operaduomo.firenze.it; admission €6; ☻ 9am-7.30pm Mon-Sat, 9am-1.40pm Sun) behind the cathedral safeguards treasures once adorning the Duomo, baptistry and campanile.

Make a beeline for the glass-topped courtyard with its awe-inspiring display of seven of the original 10 panels from Ghiberti's glorious masterpiece – the *Porta del Paradiso* (Doors of Paradise) designed for the baptistry – that took 27 painstaking years to complete. The remaining three panels, currently on tour in the US, will return to the Museo dell' Opera del Duomo by this book's publication.

The main room is devoted to statuary from Arnolfo di Cambio's original never-to-be-completed Gothic façade. Pieces include several by Arnolfo – *Pope Boniface VIII, The Virgin and Child* and *Santat Reparata* – and Donatello's *St John,* which, with its long flowing beard, stands out among the four mighty evangelist statues.

On the mezzanine is the museum's best-known piece, Michelangelo's *Pietà,* a work he intended for his own tomb. Vasari recorded in his *Lives of the Artists* that, dissatisfied with both the quality of the marble and of his own work, Michelangelo broke up the unfinished sculpture, destroying the arm and left leg of the figure of Christ. A student of Michelangelo's later restored the arm and completed the figure.

Continue upstairs, a pair of exquisitely carved *cantorie* (singing galleries) – one by Donatello, the other by Luca della Robbia – face each other. Originally in the cathedral's sacristy, their scenes of musicians and children at play add a refreshingly frivolous touch amid so much sombre piety. Most striking of several carvings by Donatello are the haunted gaze of his *Prophet Habakkuk,* originally in the bell tower, and, dramatically placed in the centre of an adjoining room, his wooden representation of a gaunt, desperately desolate *Mary Magdalene.*

BAPTISTRY

Ghiberti and Brunelleschi competed for domes…and doors, as the gilded bronze doors at the eastern entrance of this wonderful, 11th-century Romanesque **baptistry** (admission €3; ☻ noon-7pm Mon-Sat, 8.30am-2pm Sun) testify. An octagonal striped structure of white and green marble (hard to make out these days amid the thick black dirt covering the façade), it was built on the site of a Roman temple.

The baptistry has three sets of doors, conceived as a series of panels in which the story of humanity and the Redemption would be told. The earliest by Andrea Pisano (1336) illustrate the life of St John the Baptist. Lorenzo Ghiberti sculpted the second and third, following a contest in 1401 between six leading artists, including Brunelleschi, who cast the Old Testament tale of the sacrifice of Isaac in bronze. A victorious Ghiberti spent the next 20 years completing the northern doors: the top 20 panels recount episodes from the New Testament, and the eight lower ones show the four Evangelists and four fathers of the Church.

Decades of toil for Ghiberti climaxed with the eastern doors. Another 28 years of work, they depict scenes from the Old Testament in 10 panels. So extraordinary were the bas-reliefs that, many years later, Michelangelo stood before the doors in awe and declared them fit to be the Porta del Paradiso (Gate of Paradise), hence their name. What you see are copies (in turn, pawed so much they too have been taken away for restoration); turn to the Museo dell'Opera Duomo for the originals.

The grubby two-coloured marble on the baptistry's façade continues inside (less grubby) where mosaics form the single most arresting decorative feature. Those in the apse were started in 1225 and the glittering dome spectacle was designed by Tuscan artists, including Cimabue, and carried out by Venetian craftsmen over 32 years towards the end of the 12th century. The stars of this vibrant ceiling are its *Christ in Majesty* and *Last Judgment*.

To the right of the apse lies the magnificent tomb of Baldassare Cossa (1370–1419) sculpted by Donatello. Better known as the antipope John XXIII, Cossa was hardly a saint, but as antipope he had helped Giovanni di Bicci de' Medici (1360–1429) – the Medici credited with making the Medici rich – break into papal banking. So when Cossa asked in his will to be buried in the baptistry, it was the least Giovanni could do.

From the Duomo to Piazza della Signoria
VIA DEL PROCONSOLO
Bernardo Buontalenti started work on the **Palazzo Nonfinito** (literally 'Unfinished Palace', Map pp100–1), a residence for members of the Strozzi family, in 1593. Buontalenti and others completed the 1st floor and courtyard, which is Palladian in style, but the upper floors were never completely finished, hence the building's name.

On the other side of Borgo degli Albizi stands the equally proud **Palazzo dei Pazzi** (Map pp100–1), constructed a century earlier and clearly influenced by Palazzo Medici-Riccardi. It's used as offices these days, but you can peek into the courtyard.

BADIA FIORENTINA
Recently restored 10th-century **Badia Fiorentina** (Florence Abbey; Map pp100-1; Via del Proconsolo; ☙ frescoed cloister 3-6pm Mon, church 7am-6pm Tue-Sat & Sun pm) was founded by Willa, the mother of Margrave Ugo of Tuscany. Ugo continued her work after experiencing a hellish vision of the punishment awaiting him in the afterlife should he

not repent his sins. Visit simply to see Filippino Lippi's *Appearance of the Virgin to St Bernard* (1485), to the left as you enter the church through the small Renaissance cloister. At the left end of the transept is Mino da Fiesole's monument to Margrave Ugo. Stairs to the right of the altar lead up to an open gallery overlooking the cloister, decorated with 15th-century frescoes illustrating the life of St Benedict. The bell tower and front cloister remain closed for renovation.

PALAZZO DEL BARGELLO
It was inside the gaunt exterior of Palazzo del Bargello (Map pp100–1), Florence's earliest public building also called Palazzo del Podestà, that the *podestà* (governing magistrate) meted out justice from the late 13th century until 1502. As the **Museo del Bargello** (Map pp100-1; ☎ 055 238 86 06; Via del Proconsolo 4; admission €4, audioguide for 1/2 €5.50/7; ☙ 8.15am-1.50pm Tue-Sat, 2nd & 4th Sun of the month) today, the place houses Italy's most comprehensive collection of Tuscan Renaissance sculpture.

Crowds claw to see *David* but few rush to see his creator's early works in the Bargello. Michelangelo was just 22 when a cardinal commissioned him to create the drunken grape-adorned *Bacchus* displayed in the ground-floor hall devoted to Michelangelo and 16th-century sculpture. Unfortunately the cardinal didn't like the result and sold it to a banker. The artist's large roundel of the Madonna and Child with the infant St John, the *Tondo Pitti,* portrays the halo-bare pair in a very human light.

After Michelangelo left Florence in 1534, sculpture was dominated by Baccio Bandinelli (see his *Adam & Eve* here) and Benvenuto Cellini, whose playful marble *Ganimede* (Ganymede) feeding a falcon meat is uplifting. In the same room, exponent of the Renaissance's later mannerism, Vincenzo Danti, demonstrates how a sculpture should be able to be viewed from all angles with his magnificent *Honour Triumphs over Deceit* (1560), a powerful portrayal of dominance notable for being carved from a single block of marble. Giambologna's *Florence Triumphs over Pisa* – Florence portrayed as a woman, Pisa as a bearded man – is equally impressive. Moving upstairs to the Loggia, Giambologna's portrayals of Architecture, Geometry and a menagerie of animals jostle for the limelight with *Jason* (1589), the formidable late-mannerist sculpture of his pupil Pietro Francavilla; note the detail of the dead ewe's fleece.

Keen to discover Renaissance sculpture in chronological order? Save the Michelangelo hall until last and start instead with the Sala di Donatello on the 1st floor. Here, in the majestic Salone del Consiglio Generale where the city's general council met, works by Donatello and other early-15th-century sculptors can be enjoyed. Originally on the façade of Chiesa di Orsanmichele and now within a tabernacle at the hall's far end, Donatello's *San Giorgio* (St George; 1416) brought a new sense of perspective and movement to Italian sculpture.

Yet it is Donatello's two versions of David, a favourite subject for sculptors, which really fascinate: Donatello fashioned his slender, youthful dressed image in marble in 1409 and his fabled bronze between 1440 and 1450. The latter is extraordinary – the more so when you consider it was the first free-standing naked statue to be sculpted since classical times. Compare these two early boyish Davids with the *David* (1465) – Goliath's decapitated, heavily bearded head at his feet – sculpted 15 years later by Andrea Verrocchio, another Renaissance master whose Florence workshop took on a 17-year-old Leonardo as apprentice in 1469. The deft hand of the young maestro is said to be seen in Verrocchio's *Noblewoman with Bouquet* (1475–80), a highlight of the museum's last 15th-century collection.

Criminals received their last rites before execution in the palace's 1st-floor Capella del Podestà, also known as the Mary Magdalene Chapel, where *Hell* and *Paradise* are finely frescoed on the walls. These frescoes by Giotto were not discovered until 1840 when the chapel was turned into a store room and prison. All the more remarkable was Giotto's portrait of Dante, standing as part of a crowd, in *Paradise*.

The 2nd floor moves into the 16th century with a superb collection of terracotta pieces by the prolific della Robbia family, including some of their best-known works, such as Andrea's *Ritratto Idealizia di Fanciullo* (Bust of a Boy; c 1475) and Giovanni's *Pietà* (1514). Instantly recognisable, Giovanni's works are more elaborate and flamboyant than either father Luca's or cousin Andrea's, using a larger palette of colours.

MUSEO CASA DI DANTE & AROUND

The **Museo Casa di Dante** (Dante's Museum House; Map pp100-1; ☎ 055 21 94 16; Via Santa Margherita 1; admission €3; ☼ 10am-5pm Tue-Sat, 10am-1pm Sun, 10am-4pm 1st Sun of month, closed last Sun of month) was built in 1910 above the foundations of Dante's dwelling, so don't believe any claims that he lived in it! Those with a special interest in the poet may find the limited display inside mildly diverting.

Up the road, 11th-century **Chiesa di Santa Margherita** (Map pp100-1; Via Santa Margherita), also known as the **Chiesa di Dante**, is where the poet first spied muse Beatrice Portinari and married Gemma Donati; both women are buried in the church.

CHIESA DI ORSANMICHELE

Unusually the arcades of an old grain market were walled in during the 14th century to create a church. The *signoria* (city government) ordered the guilds to finance its decoration and commissioned sculptors to erect statues of their patron saints in niches and tabernacles around the building's exterior.

These statues, commissioned over the 15th and 16th centuries, represent the work of some of the greatest Renaissance artists; many are in the Museo del Bargello, but several such as Ghiberti's bronze *San Matteo* (St Matthew; in the middle on Via Arte della Lana) remain in the **Chiesa e Museo di Orsanmichele** (Map pp100-1; ☎ 055 2 38 85; Via Arte della Lana; admission free; ☼ 10am-5pm Tue-Sun). The main feature of the interior is the splendid Gothic tabernacle, decorated with coloured marble, by Andrea Orcagna.

PIAZZA DELLA REPUBBLICA

Originally the site of a Roman forum and the heart of medieval Florence, this people-busy square was created in the 1880s as part of an ambitious plan of 'civic improvements' involving the demolition of the old market, Jewish ghetto and surrounding slums. Vasari's **Loggia del Pesce** (Fish Market; Map pp100–1) was saved and re-erected on Via Pietrapiana (see p123). Several of the city's oldest cafes (p143) flank the square today.

MERCATO NUOVO

A stroll south down Via Calimala brings you to this loggia, built in the mid-16th century to protect merchandise such as wool, silk and gold traded at the **Mercato Nuovo** (New Market; Map pp100-1; Via Porta Rossa). Sadly it now only shelters tacky souvenir and leather stalls.

At its southern end is the **Fontana del Porcellino** (Piglet Fountain) and the bronze statue of a boar, an early-17th-century copy of the Greek marble original in the Uffizi. Rub the porker's snout, throw a coin into the fountain and – so goes the legend – you're bound to return to Florence.

Piazza della Signoria

The hub of the city's political life throughout the centuries and surrounded by some of its most celebrated buildings, this lovely café-lined piazza pierced at its centre with an equestrian statue of Cosimo I by Giambologna has witnessed more events in Florentine history than any other.

Whenever Florence entered one of its innumerable political crises, the people would be called here as a *parlamento* (people's plebiscite) to rubber-stamp decisions that frequently meant ruin for some ruling families and victory for others. Scenes of great pomp and circumstance alternated with those of terrible suffering: it was here that vehemently pious preacher-leader Savonarola set light to the city's art – books, paintings (Botticelli and Michelangelo both hurled a couple of pieces onto the pyre), musical instruments, mirrors, fine clothes and on – on his famous **Bonfire of Vanities** in 1497, and where the Dominican monk was hung in chains and burnt as a heretic along with two other supporters a year later.

The same spot where both fires burnt is marked by a bronze plaque embedded in the ground in front of Ammannati's **Fontana di Nettuno** (Neptune Fountain). With its pinheaded bronze satyrs and divinities frolicking at its edges, this huge fountain is hardly pretty and is much mocked as *il biancone* (the big white thing), not to mention a waste of good marble, by many a Florentine.

No, the much-photographed **David** guarding the entrance to Palazzo Vecchio since 1910 is *not* the original (which stood here until 1873 but is now in the Galleria dell'Accademia; p120). Ditto for Donatello's *Marzocco*, the heraldic Florentine lion (for the original see Museo del Bargello; p108) and *Giuditta e Oloferne* (Judith and Holofernes; original inside Palazzo Vecchio).

PALAZZO VECCHIO

The traditional seat of government, Florence's imposing fortress palace with its striking crenellations and 94m-high **Torre d'Arnolfo** is as much a symbol of the city as the Duomo. It was designed by Arnolfo di Cambio between 1298 and 1314 for the *signoria* that ruled medieval and Renaissance Florence, hence its original name Palazzo della Signoria. During their short time in office the nine *priori* – guild members picked at random – in the *Signoria* lived in the palace. Every two months nine new names were pulled out of the hat, ensuring ample comings and goings.

In 1540 Cosimo I made the place his ducal residence and centre of government, commissioning Vasari to renovate and decorate the interior – to the horror of his snooty wife, Eleonora de Toledo, who turned her nose up at the result and persuaded her consort to buy Palazzo Pitti instead.

But it took time to fit out Palazzo Pitti just the way the demanding Eleonora wanted. Ironically, and with a dash of poetic justice, she died before the work was finished, but the Medici family moved in anyway in 1549. From then onwards, the ducal palace was called **Palazzo Vecchio** (Old Palace; Map pp100-1; ☎ 055 276 82 24; Piazza della Signoria; adult/18-25yr/3-17yr €6/4.50/2, visit plus guided tour adult/18-25yr/3-17yr €8/6.50/3, each additional tour €1, family of 4/5 €14/16; ☼ 9am-7pm Fri-Wed, 9am-2pm Thu). It remains the seat of the city's power, home to the mayor's office and the municipal council.

The best way to discover this den of political drama and intrigue is by thematic guided tour: there are several for children (p130) and the best of the adult bunch is the secret-passage tour. Groups of 12 are led along the **secret staircase** built between the palace's super-thick walls in 1342 as an escape route (emerging at a tiny door on Via della Ninna) for French Duke of Athens Walter de Brienne who seized the palace and nominated himself Lord of Florence, only to be sent packing back to France by the Florentines a year later.

Another narrow stone staircase links the **tesoretto** (treasury) of Cosimo I – a tiny room no larger than a cupboard for his private collection, entered by one carefully concealed door and exited by another – with the equally intimate but substantially more sumptuous **studiolo** (study) of his introverted, alchemy-mad son Francesco I. Cosimo commissioned Vasari and a team of top Florentine mannerist artists to decorate the study, Francesco appearing in one of the 34 emblematic paintings covering the walls, not as a prince, but as an inconsequential scientist experimenting with gunpowder. The lower paintings concealed 20 cabinets in which the young prince hid his shells, stones, crystals and other curious treasures.

Completely oversized by contrast is the magnificent 53m-long, 22m-wide **Salone dei Cinquecento** (16th-Century Room), created within the original building in the 1490s to accommodate the Consiglio dei Cinquecento (Council of 500) that ruled Florence at the end of the 15th century. Star of the show at floor level is Michelangelo's sculpture *Genio della Vittoria* (Genius of Victory), destined for Rome and Pope Julius II's tomb, but left unfinished in the artist's studio when he died.

What impresses most about this room though, sheer size aside, are the swirling battle scenes, painted floor to ceiling by Vasari and his apprentices, which glorify Florentine victories by Cosimo I over arch rivals Pisa and Siena: unlike the Sienese, the Pisans are depicted bare of armour (play 'Spot the Leaning Tower'). To top off this unabashed celebration of his own power, Cosimo had himself portrayed as a god in the centre of the exquisite panelled ceiling – but not before commissioning Vasari to raise the original ceiling 7m in height. Viewing the result from above – from between the 25 hefty firwood trusses reached by yet another hidden staircase accessible only to secret-passage tours – is a staggering experience. It took Vasari and his school, in consultation with Michelangelo, just two years to construct the ceiling and paint the 34 gold-leafed panels, which rest simply on a wooden frame. The effect is mesmerising.

Across the balcony taking you above the hall, Cosimo's fractious wife comes to life in the **Quartiere di Eleonora di Toledo.** The private apartments for both her and her ladies-in-waiting bear the same heavy-handed décor blaring the glory of the Medici as the rest of the palace. Of note is the ceiling in the Camera Verde (Green Room) by Ridolfo del Ghirlandaio, inspired by designs from Nero's *Domus Aurea* in Rome; and the vibrant frescoes by Bronzino in the chapel. In all, Eleonara had 11 children with Cosimo, dying so the story goes from a broken heart in 1562 at the age of 40 after one of her sons stabbed the other, only for the other to be stabbed to death by Cosimo: investigations have since proved that all three died from malaria.

In the **Sala dei Gigli**, named after its frieze of fleur-de-lys, representing the Florentine Republic, that decorates three of the walls, look at the remarkable coffered ceiling and enjoy Donatello's powerful carving of *Guiditta e Oloferne* (Judith and Holofernes). Domenico Ghirlandaio's fresco on the far wall, depicting figures from Roman history, was meant to be one of a series by other artists, including Botticelli.

A small study off the hall is the chancery, where Machiavelli plotted for a while. The other room, **Sala delle Carte Geografiche** (Map Room), houses Cosimo I's fascinating collection of 16th-century maps, often rudimentary and of varying degrees of accuracy, charting everywhere in the known world at the time, from the polar regions to the Caribbean.

LOGGIA DELLA SIGNORIA

Built in the late 14th century as a platform for public ceremonies, this **loggia** (Map pp100–1) subsequently assumed the name of Loggia dei Manzi when Cosimo I stationed his Swiss mercenaries, armed with lances, here to remind people who was in charge. It shelters sculptures and tourists from the rain today.

To the left of the steps stands Benvenuto Cellini's magnificent bronze statue of *Perseus* (1545) brandishing the head of Medusa. To the right is Giambologna's Mannerist *Ratto delle Sabine* (Rape of the Sabine; 1583), his final work. Inside the loggia is another of Giambologna's works, *Ercole col Centauro Nesso* (Hercules with the Centaur Nessus), which originally stood near the southern end of Ponte Vecchio.

MUSEO DI STORIA DELLA SCIENZA

Telescopes, instruments for the measurement of distance, time and space, and a room full of wax and plastic cutaway models of the various stages of childbirth are highlights in the bizarre collection of the **Museum of the History of Science** (Map pp100-1; ☎ 055 26 53 11; www.imss.fi.it; Piazza de' Giudici 1; adult/concession €6.50/4; ⏱ 9.30am-

FLORENCE

4.30pm Mon-Fri, 9am-1pm Sat). But the *pièce de résistance*, preserved like a saintly relic, is Galileo's desiccated middle finger, raised skywards, as if a timeless riposte to his Inquisition accusers.

The Uffizi

Forget the world-famous masterpieces for a second: just the ridiculous (is it *really* necessary?) circus of snagging a ticket (p105) casts an immediate awe-inspiring mystique over this world-famous art gallery that every visitor to Florence, art lover or not, feels obliged to visit. Incredibly really, given getting in invariably involves setting the alarm for 6am and standing in line for several hours. The actual visit moreover, depending on how many tour groups you jostle with, works temporarily on loan to other museums etc, can be a real anticlimax.

Yet that is the power of the **Galleria degli Uffizi** (Uffizi Gallery; Map pp100–1; Piazzale degli Uffizi 6; ☎ 055 238 86 51; adult/18-25yr with EU passport/under 18yr €6.50/3.25/free, 85-min audioguide for 1/2 €5.50/8; ☯ 8.15am-6.35pm Tue-Sun), a legend in its own

right up there with the Hermitage, Louvre and Tate. Filling the vast, oversized U-shaped **Palazzo degli Uffizi**, its sheer size alone impresses (don't dream of viewing the 50-plus rooms and 1555 masterpieces properly in one visit – preselect which artists or period of art interests you most).

Should you have the mental stamina to spend the day here, the Uffizi has a lovely **rooftop café** (only accessible once you're in) serving light snacks (pizza/panini €3.50/4.50, cappuccino standing up/sitting down €1.60/4.50) and fabulous views. During the grand old days of the duke, this was the terraced hanging garden where the Medici clan gathered to listen to music performances on the square below.

THE PALACE
Cosimo I commissioned Vasari to design and build this gargantuan U-shaped palace – a government-office building (*uffizi* means offices) for the city's administrators, judiciary and guilds – on the banks of the Arno in 1560.

THE UFFIZI: FACE OF THE FUTURE

The lighting in places is atrocious; the vital statistics of some works are not even marked, let alone explained in English; and world-class masterpieces jostle for limited wall space. Historic, vast, world famous and rammed to the rafters with the very best of the Renaissance it might be, but Italy's iconic art gallery sucks in terms of museum design and efficiency.

In short, the Uffizi urgently needs a facelift. Yet this in itself is not the issue (a €49 million revamp project pledging to more than double the 5400-sq-m state gallery in size was announced way back in 1997); implementing it is the problem. Eventually, finally, years too late, the first crane hit the Florence skyline in early 2007. Hoped-for completion date: 2010, maybe, possibly, don't hold your breath.

'The backbone of the gallery, the sequence of current rooms, will remain the same', said Dr Angelo Tartuferi, chief curator of the Uffizi's medieval to 15th-century art collection. 'But we will have many new rooms, for example a new room for the 13th-century Italian paintings and so on', he added referring to the greater period of art history the so-called Nuovi Uffizi (literally 'New Uffizi'; www.nuoviuffizi.eu in Italian; and a constant 'work in progress') will embrace. For years hundreds if not thousands of art works have been kept under wraps in storage, simply because of lack of display space.

Asked if new media would play a part: 'The traditional way of presentation is important; new media distracts from the originals', continued Dr Tartuferi, shaking his head dogmatically at the preposterous idea of interactive exhibits aiding visitors in their navigation of some of the world's most priceless art.

Indeed tradition seems determined to doggedly reign over the Uffizi: the startlingly modern and cutting-edge exit designed for the 16th-century gallery on Piazza Castellani by Japanese artist Arata Isozaki in 2000 was shelved five years later after bulldozers dug up archaeological ruins of medieval Florence – much to the glee of critics who'd already slammed it as an 'abandoned bed frame'. Isozaki's wise response: a contemporary, cutting-edge reflection of Florence's historic Loggia della Signoria framing the other side of the Uffizi on Piazza della Signoria.

Vasari was also the design brain behind the **Corridoio Vasariano** (p106), a private corridor begun a year later than the Uffizi to link Palazzo Vecchio and Palazzo Pitti, cutting through the Uffizi and across Ponte Vecchio en route.

Following Vasari's death in 1564, architects Alfonso Parigi and Bernando Buontalenti took over the Uffizi project, Buontalenti modifying the upper floor of the palace to house the works of art keenly collected by Francesco I, a passion inherited from his father. In 1580 the building was finally complete. By the time the last of the Medici family died in 1743, the family's private art collection was enormous – and the fortune of lucky old Florence who inherited it from Anna Maria when she died, the deal being the collection should never-leave the city. Florence's fate as bearer of the world's single greatest collection of Italian and Florentine art was sealed.

Over the years, sections of the collection have been moved to the Museo del Bargello and the Museo Archeologico, and other collections in turn have been moved here. Several artworks were destroyed or badly damaged in 1993 when a car bomb planted by the Mafia exploded outside the gallery's west wing, killing five people. Documents cataloguing the collection were also destroyed.

THE COLLECTION

Arranged in chronological order by school, the collection spans the whole gambit of art history from ancient Greek sculpture to 18th-century Venetian paintings. But it is its masterpiece-rich Renaissance and mannerist collections that are the most striking.

As in the 16th century, works are displayed on the 3rd floor in a series of numbered rooms off two dramatically long corridors – east *(corridoio di levante)* and west *(corridoio di ponente)*. They are linked at one end by a loggia *(secondo corridoio)*, from where you can enjoy the finest view in Florence of crowded Ponte Vecchio and the mysterious Corridoio Vasariano. A good hour can be spent in these corridors, admiring the grotesques decorating the ceiling and the Medici family portraits hanging in the east corridor where the seeds of the Uffizi were sown in 1580. The portraits and antique sculptures line the west corridor that was turned into gallery space in the late 17th century.

As expansion plans slowly come to fruition, some rooms are likely to be temporarily closed and the contents of others changed; the main area affected will be the 1st-floor hang-out of Caravaggio and his chiaroscuro cronies.

Upon arrival at the gallery, boards at the ticket booth and at the main entrance say what's closed that day. For an updated room-by-room breakdown, visit www.polomuseale.firenze.it/English; search the gallery catalogue at www.virtualuffizi.com.

Tuscan Masters: 12th Century to 14th Century

Three large altarpieces from Florentine churches viewed in chronological order – *Madonna in Maestà* (Madonna Enthroned) by Tuscan masters Duccio di Buoninsegna, Cimabue and Giotto – and a polyptych by Giotto likewise featuring the Madonna enthroned in room 2 clearly reflect the transition from Gothic to the precursor of the Renaissance. Note the overtly naturalistic realism overtones in Giotto's portrayal of the Madonna and child among angels and saints, painted some 25 years after that of Buoninsegna and Giotto master Cimabue.

Dating to the same period, Simone Martini's shimmering *Annunciazione* (Annunciation; 1333) sets the Madonna in a sea of gold and is a masterpiece of the Sienese school of the 14th century – the focus of room 3. Also of note is the triptych *Madonna col Bambino e Santi* (Madonna with Child and Saints) by Ambrogio Lorenzetti, which demonstrates the same realism as Giotto; unfortunately both Ambrogio and his artistic brother Pietro died from the plague in Siena in 1348.

Masters in 14th-century Florence paid as much attention to detail as their Siennese counterparts, as works in room 4 demonstrate: savour the depth of realism and extraordinary gold-leaf work of *San Reminio Pietà* (1360–65) – displayed in the Uffizi since 1851 – by gifted Giotto pupil, Giottino (otherwise known as Giotto di Stefano).

Renaissance Pioneers

A concern for perspective was a hallmark of the early-15th-century Florentine school (room 7) that pioneered the Renaissance. The one panel (the other two are in the Louvre and London's National Gallery) from Paolo Uccello's striking *La Battaglia di San Romano* (Battle of San Romano) shows the artist's efforts to create perspective with amusing effect as he directs the lances, horses and soldiers to a central disappearing point: the painting celebrates Florence's victory over Siena.

Piero della Francesca's famous profile portraits (1465; room 8) of the crooked-nosed, red-robed Duke and Duchess of Urbino – the former always painted from the left side after losing his right eye in a jousting accident and the latter painted a deathly white reflecting the posthumous portrait the diptych was – are wholly humanist in spirit. So, too, is the portrait of solemn humanity reflected in *Madonna col Bambino* (Madonna with Child) painted jointly by Masaccio and Masolino.

Carmelite monk Filippo Lippi had an unfortunate soft spot for earthly pleasures, marrying a nun from Prato and causing huge scandal. Search for the artist's self-portrait as a podgy friar in *Coronation of the Virgin* (1439–47), which hangs alongside works by his son Filippino.

Another related pair, brothers Antonio and Piero del Pollaiolo, fill room 9, where their seven cardinal and theological values

of 15th-century Florence – commissioned for the merchant's tribunal in Piazza della Signoria – burst forth with fantastic energy: Charity holds a burning flame as a baby boy suckles at her breast; Faith bears a cross and chalice; Prudence poses with a mirror and a serpent; and Temperence is traditionally portrayed pouring liquid from one vessel to another. *Fortezza* (Strength; 1470) – an elegant young woman dressed in shining armour, cloak draped across her knee – is the first documented work by Botticelli, the clarity of line and light, and the humanity in the face, setting it apart from Pollaiolo's. In their haste to reach the next room wholly devoted to Botticelli, most visitors miss the twin set of Botticelli's miniatures depicting a sword-bearing Judith returning from the Camp of Holofernes and the Discovery of the Decapitated Holofernes in his Tent displayed in a glass cabinet in room 9.

The spectacular Sala del Botticelli, numbered 10 to 14, but one large hall in fact – a

---

FIVE TOP FIVES

Ditch the traditional room-by-room audio guide: set yourself an alternative tour.

■ Masterpieces: Botticelli's *Primavera* (Spring) and *La Nascita di Venere* (Birth of Venus; rooms 10–14); Titian's *Flora* (room 28); Ruben's *Enrico IV alla Battaglia di Ivry* and *Ingresso Trionfale di Enrico IV a Parigi* portraying French King Henri IV at the Battle of Ivry and his triumphal march into Paris (room 41); Rembrandt's *Self-Portrait*, *Portrait of an Old Man* and *Self-Portrait as an Old Man* (room 44); and Caravaggio's *Sacrificio d'Isacco* (Sacrifice of Isaac; Sala del Caravaggio).

■ Hidden Treasures: Leonardo da Vinci's *Annunciazione* (room 15), painted when he was a student of Verrocchio; Botticelli's twin set of miniature panels (room 9) starring warrior Judith and Hercules' decapitated head; the ceiling frescoes (1588) of weapon and gunpowder workshops by Ludovico Buti in the Sala di Mantegna e di Correggio (room 23); the secret entrance to the mysterious Corridoio Vasariano, wedged between room 25 and 34 at the far end of the west wing; and the world's second-largest collection of miniatures comprising 472 small portraits shown off in the small oval room built to house the dowry of Ferdinando I's wife.

■ Adoration of the Magi: Gentile Da Fabriano (International Gothic Style; rooms 5 and 6); Filippino Lippi (Renaissance; room 8); Botticelli (Renaissance; rooms 10–14); Ghirlandaio (Renaissance; rooms 10–14); Leonardo da Vinci (Renaissance; room 15); and Dürer (German Renaissance; room 20).

■ Madonna and Child: *Madonna col Bambino e due Angeli* (Madonna with Child and Two Angels) by Filippo Lippi (room 8); Sarto's *Madonna col Bambino* (room 26); Raffaello's *Madonna del Cardellino* (Madonna of the Goldfinch; room 26); Titian's *Madonna delle Rose* (Madonna of the Roses; room 28); and Parmigianino's *Madonna col Bamino e Angeli* (Madonna with Child and Angels), otherwise known as *Madonna dal Collo Lungo* (Madonna with the Long Neck; room 29).

■ Nudes: *Medici Venus* (La Tribuna); *Sleeping Hermaphrodite* (room 17); Lukas Cranach's *Adamo* (Adam) & *Eva* (Eve; both room 20); Titian's *Urbino Venus* (room 28); and Tintoretto's *Leda e il cigno* (Leda and the Swan; room 32).

former Medici theatre, hence the fine high beamed ceiling – gets packed: it is a definitive Uffizi highlight. Of the 15 works by the Renaissance master known for his ethereal figures, *Nascita di Venere* (Birth of Venus), *Primavera* (Spring) and the deeply spiritual *Annunciazione* (Annunciation) are the best known. Contrast these with *Calunnia* (Calumny): for some, a disturbing reflection of Botticelli's loss of faith in human potential as he aged; for others, a deliberate reining in of his free spirit in order not to invite the attentions of the puritanical Savonarola.

La Tribuna

It was in this exquisite octagonal-shaped treasure trove (room 18), created by Francesco I, that the Medici clan stashed away their most precious masterpieces. Today their family portraits hang on the red upholstered walls (red evoking the element of fire) and a walkway leads visitors around the edge of the stunning mosaic marble floor (representing earth). Delicate mother-of-pearl (water) inlays make the domed ceiling a feast for the eyes, crowned with a lantern (representing air).

The celebrated *Medici Venus*, a 1st-century-BC copy of a 4th-century-BC work by the Greek sculptor Praxiteles and part of the Medici collection since 1688, takes pride of place in the Tribuna. Several other lovely classical statues (frustratingly unlabelled) serenade the famous nude, including *The Wrestlers*, a 1st-century AD copy of a 3rd-century BC work.

High Renaissance to Mannerism

Arriving in the west wing, Michelangelo dazzles with his brilliant *Tondo Doni*, a depiction of the Holy Family that steals the High Renaissance show in room 25 hands down. The composition is unusual, Joseph holding an exuberant Jesus on his muscled mother's shoulder as she twists round to gaze at him, the colours as vibrant as when they were first applied in 1506. It was painted for wealthy Florentine merchant Agnolo Doni (who hung it above his bed) and bought by the Medici for Palazzo Pitti in 1594.

Raphael (1483–1520) and Andrea del Sarto (1486–1530) rub shoulders in room 26, where Sarto's classical *Madonna col Bambino* (1517) fills the room with terror: a distressed Madonna sits on a pedestal smothered in horrid winged creatures ('the harpies') with bloated

tummies, bony legs and cries of distress ripping across their monstrous faces. The work of Florence's two main mannerist masters, Pontormo and Rosso Fiorentino, represented in the next room, are often equally disquieting.

Previous works by Tuscan masters can be compared with the greater naturalism inherent in the work of their Venetian counterparts in room 28 where – in another defining Uffizi moment – 11 Titians kick in. Masterpieces include the world's most powerful nude (opposite), painted in 1538 and hung disguised with a cover portraying *Sacred Love* in the Uffizi's Tribuna from 1736; the highly sensual *Flora* (1515); and an exquisitely tender study of *Madonna delle Rose* (Madonna of the Roses), in which the Christ child plays with flowers proffered by the infant John the Baptist, Mary observing with a hint of amusement on her face.

Painter of portraits with a penchant for the more figurative thought of an older face, Tintoretto was the Venetian school's greatest mannerist painter. His *Ritratto di Ammiraglio Veneziano* (Portrait of a Venetian Admiral) in the Sala al Bassano e del Tintoretto (room 32) is astonishing: the admiral's dark solemn eyes peer out from a canvas that is almost entirely black bar a hint of rich purple velvet and a pair of hands.

Baroque & Neoclassicism

Downstairs on the 1st floor (something of a building site as the Uffizi revamps itself; p112), intense, dramatic, invariably bloody and loaded with tension are the baroque hallmarks of Caravaggio (1573–1610), leading exponent of the baroque movement, and his admirers. Take one look at Artemisia Gentileschi's gruesome *Judith Slaying Holofernes* (1620–21) – dead man's eyeballs strewn, dagger thrust in bloody throat – in the Sala del Caravaggio and you get the picture. One of the first female artists to be acclaimed in post-Renaissance Italy, Artemisia Gentileschi (1593–1653), victim in a highly scandalous seven-month rape trial, painted strong women seeking revenge on evil males. Like Caravaggio, she used *chiaroscuro* (contrast of light and dark) to full dramatic effect.

Santa Maria Novella & Around

BASILICA DI SANTA MARIA NOVELLA

Just south of Stazione di Santa Maria Novella, this **church** (Map pp98-9; ☎ 055 21 59 18; Piazza di Santa

Maria Novella; admission €2.50; 9am-5pm Mon-Thu, 1-5pm Fri) was begun in the late 13th century as the Dominican order's Florentine base. Although it was mostly completed by around 1360, work on the façade and embellishment of the interior continued well into the 15th century. It was here that the Church Council of Florence was held in 1439. The tomb of the Patriarch of Constantinople, who died in the city, is near the **Cappella Rucellai**.

The lower section of the green-and-white marble façade is transitional from Romanesque to Gothic, while the upper section and the main doorway were designed by Alberti and completed around 1470. Halfway along the north aisle, the highlight of the Gothic interior is Masaccio's superb fresco *Trinità* (Trinity; 1428), one of the first artworks to use the then newly discovered techniques of perspective and proportion.

The first chapel to the right of the altar, **Cappella di Filippo Strozzi**, features spirited frescoes by Filippino Lippi, depicting the lives of St John the Evangelist and St Philip the Apostle. Domenico Ghirlandaio's series of frescoes behind the main altar was painted with the help of artists who may have included the young Michelangelo. Relating the lives of the Virgin Mary, St John the Baptist and others, the frescoes are notable for their depiction of Florentine life during the Renaissance, and feature portraits of members of the Tornabuoni family, who commissioned them. Brunelleschi's crucifix hangs above the altar in the **Cappella Gondi**, the first chapel left of the choir. Giotto's crucifix (c 1288) hangs above the centre of the nave.

To reach the **Chiostro Verde** (Green Cloister), which takes its name from the green earth base used for its frescoes, go out of the church and follow signs for the *museo*. Three of its four walls are decorated with fading frescoes recounting Genesis. The most interesting artistically, by Paolo Uccello, are those on the party wall with the church. *Il Diluvio Universale* (Great Flood) is outstanding.

Off the next side of the cloister is the **Cappellone degli Spagnoli** (Spanish Chapel), set aside for the Spanish retinue that accompanied Eleonora de Toledo, Cosimo I's wife. It contains some well-preserved frescoes by Andrea di Bonaiuto.

On the west side of the cloister, a **museum** (055 28 21 87; adult/concession €2.70/2; 9am-5pm Mon-Thu & Sat) showcases ecclesiastical relics.

MUSEO NAZIONALE ALINARI DELLA FOTOGRAFIA

Thoughtfully laid out inside a former Leopoldine convent, the **Alinari National Photography Museum** (Map pp100-1; 055 21 63 10; www.alinarifondazione.it; Piazza Santa Maria Novella 14a; adult/child €9/6; 9.30am-7.30pm Tue-Fri, Sun & Mon, 9.30am-11.30pm Sat) provides a snapshot of photography from its early-19th-century origins to contemporary art. Temporary exhibits add an up-to-the-minute angle and there's an itinerary for blind visitors.

OFFICINA PROFUMO-FARMACEUTICA DI SANTA MARIA NOVELLA

Take a step back in time to Renaissance Florence at this venerable **perfumery-pharmacy** (Map p103; 055 21 62 76; www.smnovella.com; Via della Scala 16), in business since 1612. The fruit of cures concocted from medicinal herbs grown by Dominican friars at the monastery here since 1221, the pharmacy continues to honour its natural roots in the many fragrances and face- and body-care products it carefully crafts today. Particularly fun are the old-fashioned Renaissance remedies it still sells (acqua di Santa Maria Novella to cure hysterics, acqua di Melissa to aid digestion, and smelling salts) and the dietary supplements available in the herbalist shop (dandelion to purify, devil's claw to aid joint function etc, bladderwrack algae to spur on weight loss etc). Visit the free museum adjoining the shop to learn more.

CHIESA D'OGNISSANTI

This 13th-century **church** (Map p103; Borgo Ognissanti; 7am-12.30pm & 4-8pm Mon-Sat, 4-8pm Sun) was much altered in the 17th century, when its baroque façade was added. Domenico Ghirlandaio's fresco, above the second altar on the right, features Madonna della Misericordia, protector of the Vespucci family. Amerigo Vespucci, the Florentine navigator who gave his name to the American continent, is supposed to be the young boy whose head peeks between the Madonna and the old man. Ghirlandaio's masterpiece, *Ultima Cena* (Last Supper), covers most of a wall in the former monastery's refectory, reached via the cloister, while his detailed portrait, *St Jerome*, is in the nave. Opposite is Botticelli's pensive *San Augustin*. All three of these works date from 1480.

LE CASCINE

About 10 minutes' walk west along Borgo Ognissanti and Via il Prato brings you to **Porta**

al Prato, part of the walls demolished in the late 19th century to make way for the ring of boulevards that still surrounds the city.

A short walk south is Florence's great green lung, **Parco delle Cascine** (Map pp98–9), a private hunting reserve of the Medici dukes, opened to the public in 1776, with boulevards, fountains, bird sanctuaries and an open-air swimming pool. Come dusk parts of it become a stomping ground for pimps and prostitutes.

Via de' Tornabuoni & Around

Renaissance mansions and classy designer fashion shops (p151) border Via de' Tornabuoni, the city's most fashionable and expensive shopping street named after a wealthy Florentine noble family (which died out in the 17th century) and often referred to as the 'Salotto di Firenze' (Florence's Drawing Room). The street follows the original course of the Mugnone tributary into the Arno.

Head east down Via della Vigna Nuova and turn into Via dei Palchetti; you'll pass the classically inspired **Palazzo Rucellai** (Map pp100–1), designed by Alberti for another of the city's wealthiest noble families whose good fortunes originated in wool and silk, and climaxed with the marriage of Bernardo Rucellai to Lorenzo the Magnificent's daughter in 1466.

Continuing south to Lungarno Corsini, you reach **Palazzo Corsini** (Map pp100–1; ☎ 055 21 28 80; www.palazzocorsini.it; Via del Parione 11b; admission free; ☼ 9am-1pm & 4-7pm Mon-Fri), residence of the Corsini family who arrived in Florence in the 13th century. The once-grandiose but now rather shabby, late-baroque edifice previously belonged to the Medici family, but they sold it in 1640, and work on the exterior wasn't completed until 1735. The most interesting feature inside is a spiral staircase known as the *lumaca* (literally 'snail').

Head east for **Ponte Santa Trinità**, a harmonious and charming bridge with statues of the seasons by Pietro Francavilla and prime views of Ponte Vecchio. Cosimo I put Vasari in charge of the project, and he in turn asked Michelangelo for advice. In the end the job was handed over to Ammannati, who finished it in 1567. The bridge was painstakingly restored after being blown up by the Nazis in 1944.

Turning inland, you arrive at the 14th-century **Chiesa della Santa Trinità** (Map pp100-1; Piazza Santa Trinità), rebuilt in Gothic style and later graced with a mannerist façade of indifferent taste. Eye-catching frescoes by Domenico Ghirlandaio depict the life of St Francis of Assisi in the south transept's Cappella Sassetti. Lorenzo Monaco, Fra Angelico's master, painted the altarpiece in the fourth chapel on the south aisle and the frescoes on the chapel walls.

Across the road looms **Palazzo Spini-Feroni** (Map pp100–1), built for Geri Spini, the pope's banker, in the 13th century and now part of the Ferragamo shoe empire. A **Salvatore Ferragamo** boutique – styled as it was in the 1940s and 1950s – languishes on the ground floor and in the basement the **Museo Salvatore Ferragamo** (Map pp100-1; ☎ 055 336 04 56; Via de' Tornabuoni 2; adult/under 10yr €5/free; ☼ 10am-6pm Wed-Mon) shows off classic Ferragamo shoes, many worn by Hollywood stars such as Marilyn Monroe, Greta Garbo and Katherine Hepburn. Money made by the museum helps fund scholarships for young shoe designers.

Sneak briefly eastwards along Borgo Santissimi Apostoli to visit the lovely **Chiesa dei Santissimi Apostoli** (Map pp100-1; Piazza del Limbo 1), a refreshingly sober church when set against Florence's Renaissance splendour. Tucked away in a sunken square that was once the cemetery for unbaptised babies, it is often overlooked by most visitors. Most of the 11th-century façade is still intact, and the rounded arches of its Romanesque interior soar heavenwards. Put €0.50 in the slot to the left of the entrance and it bursts into muted light. You will find a terracotta tabernacle by Giovanni della Robbia located at the end of the north aisle.

Most impressive of the Renaissance mansions bordering Via de' Tornabuoni is **Palazzo Strozzi** (Map pp100–1), a great colossus raised by one of the most powerful of the Medici's rival families. Although never completed, its three finished façades in heavy rusticated *pietra forte* (literally 'strong stone', a local sandstone), designed by Benedetto da Maiano, speak naked power. Inside is a grand if somewhat gloomy courtyard. The palazzo hosts art exhibitions today.

Two blocks north looms the baroque façade (1683) of **Chiesa di San Gaetano** (Map pp100–1), a church around since the 11th century. Opposite and a few strides north, **Palazzo Antinori** (Map pp100–1) was built in the 15th century by Giovanni da Maiano.

San Lorenzo Area

BASILICA DI SAN LORENZO

In 1425 the Medici commissioned Brunelleschi to rebuild what would become the family's parish church and funeral chapter – 50-odd Medici are buried here. Considered one of the most harmonious examples of Renaissance architecture, the **Basilica di San Lorenzo** (Map pp98-9; Piazza San Lorenzo; admission €2.50; 10am-5pm Mon-Sat) stands on the site of a 4th-century basilica. But it looks nothing from the outside: Michelangelo was commissioned to design the façade in 1518 but his design in white Carrara marble was never executed, hence its rough unfinished appearance.

Inside, columns of *pietra serena* (soft grey stone) crowned with Corinthian capitals separate the nave from the two aisles. Donatello, who was still sculpting the two bronze pulpits adorned with panels of the Crucifixion when he died, is buried in the chapel featuring Fra Filippo Lippi's *Annunciation*. Rosso Fiorentino's *Sposalizio della Vergine* (Marriage of the Virgin Mary; 1523) is in the second chapel on the south aisle. Left of the altar is the **Sagrestia Vecchia** (Old Sacristy), designed by Brunelleschi and decorated in the main by Donatello.

Biblioteca Laurenziana Medicea

From another entrance off Piazza San Lorenzo you enter the church's peaceful **cloisters**. Off the first cloister, a staircase leads to the **Biblioteca Laurenziana Medicea** (055 21 15 90; www .bml.firenze.sbn.it; Piazza San Lorenzo 9; by guided tour on special request only) commissioned by Guilio de' Medici (Pope Clement VII) to house the extensive Medici library and restricted today to researchers. The real attraction is Michelangelo's magnificent vestibule and a staircase, designed in walnut but subsequently executed in grey *pietra serena*. Its curvaceous steps are a sign of the master's move towards mannerism from the stricter bounds of Renaissance architecture and design.

Medicean Chapels

Nowhere is Medici conceit expressed so explicitly as in their mausoleum, the **Cappelle Medicee** (Medicean Chapels; Map pp98-9; 055 238 86 02; Piazza Madonna degli Aldobrandini; admission €6; 8.15am-1.50pm Tue-Sat, 1st & 3rd Sun & 2nd & 4th Mon of month), principal burial place of the Medici rulers, sumptuously adorned with granite, the most precious marble, semiprecious stones and some of Michelangelo's most beautiful sculptures.

In 2004 forensic scientists exhumed 49 members of the dynasty buried here as part of a research project to learn more about the Medici lifestyle, genetic make-up, diseases (syphilis and malaria were common) and – more importantly – how they died: Anna Maria Luisia (1667–1743), the last in the Medici line who bequeathed all the family art treasures to the city of Florence, died from breast cancer it was discovered. More sensational was the discovery that Francesco I and his wide Bianca Cappello, who suddenly died 11 days apart from each other in 1587, did not have malaria but rather died from acute arsenic poisoning. Francesco I lies in the **Cappella dei Principi** (Princes' Chapel) alongside Ferdinando I & II and Cosimo I, II & III. Statues of each Medici were planned for the niches, which, bar bronzes of Ferdinando I and Cosimo II, remain bare, lending the chapel a surprisingly austere air.

From the Princes' Chapel, a corridor leads to the stark but graceful **Sagrestia Nuova** (New Sacristy), Michelangelo's first architectural work and showcase for three of his most haunting sculptures. *Aurora e Crepusculo* (Dawn and Dusk) lounge on the sarcophagus of the unpopular Lorenzo Duke of Urbino (1492–1519), to whom Machiavelli dedicated *The Prince*. *Notte e Giorno* (Night and Day) mark the spot opposite where a son of Lorenzo il Magnifico is buried. Michelangelo never finished the grandiose funerary monument planned for the tomb of Lorenzo il Magnifico, simply adorned with a serene *Madonna col Bambino* (Madonna and Child).

PALAZZO MEDICI-RICCARDI

When Cosimo il Vecchio felt fairly sure of his position in Florence, he decided to move house and entrusted Michelozzo with the design in 1444. The result is this **palace** (Map pp98-9; 055 276 03 40; www.palazzo-medici.it; Via Cavour 3; adult/concession €5/3.50; 9am-7pm Thu-Tue), a blueprint that influenced the construction of Florentine family residences, such as Palazzo Pitti and Palazzo Strozzi, for years to come.

The fortress townhouses with their towers reminiscent of Gothic Florence were no longer necessary, and Cosimo's power was more or less undisputed, allowing Michelozzo to create a self-assured, stout but not inelegant pile on three storeys. The rusticated façade of the ground floor gives a rather stern aspect to the building, though the upper two storeys are less aggressive, maintaining restrained classical lines – already a feature of the emerging Renaissance canon – and topped with a heavy timber roof whose broad eaves protrude over the street below.

The Medici stayed here until 1540, making way for the Riccardi family a century later who gave the palace a comprehensive remodelling and built the sumptuously decorated **Galleria** on the 2nd floor. Luca Giordano adorned the ceiling with his complex *Allegory of Divine Wisdom* (1685), a rather overblown example of late baroque, dripping with gold leaf and bursting with colour.

Cappella dei Magi

Also known as Capella di Benozzo, this tiny Chapel of the Magi upstairs flaunts a series of wonderfully detailed serene frescoes (1459) by Benozzo Gozzoli, a pupil of Fra' Angelico. His ostensible theme of *Journey of the Magi* is but a slender pretext for portraying members of the Medici clan in their best light; try to spy Lorenzo il Magnifico, Cosimo il Vecchio and the artist's self-portrait in the crowd.

Only eight visitors are allowed in at a time for a maximum of just seven minutes; reserve your slot in advance at the palace ticket desk.

San Marco Area
GALLERIA DELL'ACCADEMIA

A lengthy queue marks the door to this **gallery** (Map pp98-9; ☎ 055 238 86 09; Via Ricasoli 60; adult/concession Dec-Aug €8/4, Sep-Nov €6.50/3.25; ⏰ 8.15am-6.50pm Tue-Sun), simply because it contains one of the greatest masterpieces of the Renaissance, Michelangelo's original *David*.

He doesn't disappoint. The subtle detail (not quite as illuminated on copies) of the real thing – the veins in his sinewy arms, the muscles in his legs, the change in expression as you move around the statue – *is* impressive. Spend time encircling it, viewing it from different angles, digesting its history and playing with Digital David, an interactive visualisation of the statue to see his locks, sling and so on in 3D on a computer screen. Carved from a single block of marble already worked on by two sculptors before him (both of whom had given up), Michelangelo's most famous work was also his most challenging – he didn't choose the marble himself, it was veined and its dimensions

were already decided. For this reason alone the resultant masterpiece (dubbed Colossus by Florentines) gained near-mythical status even before assuming its pedestal in front of Palazzo Vecchio on Piazza della Signoria in 1504. This coupled with Florentines embracing the larger-than-life nude as a symbol of power and liberty and civic pride in their Republic ensured lasting notoriety for David, depicted for the first time as a man in the prime of life rather than a young boy.

Michelangelo was also the master behind the unfinished *San Matteo* (St Matthew; 1503) in the same hall and the four *Prigioni* ('prisoners' or 'slaves'; 1530), who seem to be writhing and struggling to free themselves from the marble; they were meant for the tomb of Pope Julius II, itself never completed. A plaster model of Giambologna's *Ratto delle Sabine* (Rape of the Sabine) dominates the **Sala del Colosso**, the first room you cross before hitting *David*.

Off to the left, in the **Sala dell'Ottocento** (19th-Century Room), shelves heave with the weight of dozens of nameless, ghostly busts commissioned by wealthy Victorian 'Grand Tourists' – members of the moneyed middle and upper classes who toured Europe, especially Italy, to soak up the culture and history, and round off their classical education. Elsewhere in the museum, the works by Botticelli and Taddeo Gaddi are worth scouting out.

MUSEO DI SAN MARCO

At the heart of Florence's university area sits Chiesa di San Marco and the adjoining Dominican convent where gifted painter Fra Angelico (c 1400–55) and the sharp-tongued Savonarola piously served God. Today the **Museo di San Marco** (Map pp98-9; ☎ 055 238 86 08; Piazza San Marco 1; adult/concession €4/2; ⏰ 8.15am-1.50pm Tue-Fri, 8.15am-6.50pm Sat, 8.15am-7pm 2nd & 4th Sun & 1st, 3rd & 5th Mon of month), it is one of Florence's most fascinating museums.

Essentially a showcase for Fra Angelico's art, you enter via Michelozzo's **Chiostro di Sant'Antonio** (1440). Turn immediately right to enter the **Sala dell'Ospizio** where Fra Angelico's attention to perspective and the realistic portrayal of nature comes to life in the *Deposizione di Cristo* (Deposition of Christ; 1432), a commission taken on by the friar after the original artist, Lorenzo Monaco, died. Many critics deem the end result one of the first true paintings of the Renaissance.

FLORENCE

Giovanni Antonio Sogliani's fresco *La Providenza dei Domenicani* (The Miraculous Supper of St Domenic; 1536) dominates the former monks' refectory in the cloister; and Fra Angelico's huge *Crocifissione* (Crucifixion) fresco (1442) decorates the former Chapterhouse. But it is upstairs where the monk cells remain that is the most haunting: At the top of the stairs, Fra Angelico's most famous works, *Annunciazione* (c 1440), faced on the opposite wall by a Crucifixion featuring St Dominic, leaps off at the walls at you. A stroll around each of the 20 cells reveals snippets of many more fine religious reliefs by the Tuscan-born friar, who decorated the cells in 1440 and 1441 with deeply devotional frescoes to guide friars' meditation. Most were executed by Fra Angelico himself, others by aides under his supervision, including Benozzo Gozzoli. Among several masterpieces is the magnificent *Madonna delle Ombre* (Virgin of the Shadows; c 1450), on the external wall between cells 25 and 26.

After centuries of being known as 'Il Beato Angelico' (literally 'blessed angelic') or simply 'il Beato' (the blessed), the Renaissance's most blessed religious painter was made a saint by Pope John Paul II in 1984. See p41 and p173 for more on Fra Angelico's art.

Contrasting with such pure beauty is the cell – a three-room suite in fact – which Savonarola called home from 1489. Rising to prior at the Dominican convent, it was from here that the fanatical monk railed against luxury, greed and corruption of the clergy. Kept as a kind of shrine to the turbulent priest, it houses a portrait, a few personal items, the linen banner Savonarola carried in processions and a grand marble monument erected by admirers in 1873. Ten visitors at a time are allowed in Savonarola's cell.

CENACOLO DI SANT'APOLLONIA

Here in the **refectory** (Map pp98-9; Via XXVII Aprile 1; admission free; ⏰ 8.15am-1.50pm Tue-Sat & alternating Sun & Mon) of what was once a Benedictine convent,

---

WHO'S THAT BLOKE?

Name: David

Occupation: world's most famous sculpture

Vital Statistics: 516cm tall, 19 tonnes of mediocre-quality pearly white marble from the Fantiscritti quarries in Miseglia, Carrara

Spirit: Young biblical hero in meditative pose who, with the help of God, defeats an enemy more powerful than himself. Scarcely visible sling emphasises victory of innocence and intellect over brute force.

Commissioned: In 1501 by the Opera del Duomo for the cathedral, but subsequently placed in front of the Palazzo Vecchio on Piazza della Signoria where it stayed until 1873.

Famous journeys: It took 40 men four days to transport the statue on rails from Michelangelo's workshop behind the cathedral to Piazza della Signoria in 1504. Its journey from here, through the streets of Florence, to its current purpose-built tribune in the Galleria dell'Accademia in 1873 took seven long days.

Outstanding features: (a) His expression which, from the left profile, appears serene, Zen and boyish; from the right, concentrated, manly and highly charged in anticipation of the gargantuan Goliath he is about to slay; (b) the sense of counterbalanced weight rippling through his body, from the tension in his right hip on which he leans to his taut left arm.

Why the small dick: In classical art a large or even normal-sized packet was not deemed elegant, hence the daintier size.

And the big head and hands: *David* was designed to stand up high on a cathedral buttress in the apse, from where his head and hand would have appeared in perfect proportion.

Beauty treatments: body scrub with hydrochloric acid (1843); clay and cellulose pulp 'mud pack', bath in distilled water (2004)

Occupational hazards: Over the centuries he's been struck by lightning, attacked by rioters and had his toes bashed with a hammer. The two pale white lines visible on his lower left arm is where his arm got broken during the 1527 revolt when the Medici were kicked out Florence. Giorgio Vasari, then a child, picked up the pieces and 16 years later had them sent to Cosimo I who restored the statue, so the story goes.

restoration work revealed some remarkable frescoes, including a *L'Ultima Cena* (Last Supper) in rich shades of red, blue and purple, painted by Andrea del Castagno around 1450. Above it, another three frescoes of his portray Jesus' crucifixion (with a rare example of a beardless Christ figure), burial and resurrection.

PIAZZA DELLA SANTISSIMA ANNUNZIATA

Giambologna's equestrian statue of Grand Duke Ferdinando I de' Medici commands the scene from the centre of this square, teeming with students rather than tourists.

The church that gives the square its name, **Chiesa della Santissima Annunziata** (Map pp98–9; Piazza della Santissima Annunziata; 7.30am-12.30pm & 4-6.30pm), was established in 1250 by the founders of the Servite order, and rebuilt by Michelozzo and others in the mid-15th century. It is dedicated to the Virgin Mary, and in the ornate tabernacle, to your left as you enter the church from the atrium, is a so-called miraculous painting of the Virgin.

No longer on public view, the canvas is attributed to a 14th-century friar, and legend says it was completed by an angel. Also of note are frescoes by Andrea del Castagno in the first two chapels on the left of the church, a fresco by Perugino in the fifth chapel, and the frescoes in Michelozzo's atrium, particularly the *Nascita della Vergine* (Birth of the Virgin) by Andrea del Sarto and the *Visitazione* (Visitation) by Jacopo Pontormo. The mannerist Il Rosso Fiorentino (the Redhead from Florence) is also an important contributor to the frescoes. Above the main entrance to the church is a mosaic lunette of the *Annunciation* by Davide Ghirlandaio, Domenico's little brother. Within the church's official opening hours, you'll need to time it just right in order to squeeze yourself in between each morning's seven masses.

The **Spedale degli Innocenti** (Hospital of the Innocents, Map pp98–9) was founded on the southeastern side of the piazza in 1421 as Europe's first orphanage, hence the 'innocents' in its name. Brunelleschi designed the portico, which Andrea della Robbia (1435–1525) famously decorated with terracotta medallions of babies in swaddling clothes. At the north end of the portico, the false door surrounded by railings was once a revolving door where unwanted children were left. A good number of people in Florence with surnames such as degli Innocenti, Innocenti and Nocentini can trace their family tree only as far back as the orphanage. Undoubtedly, life inside was hard, but the Spedale's avowed aim was to care for and educate its wards until they turned 18.

Works by Florentine artists, including Domenico Ghirlandaio's striking *Adorazione dei Magi* (Adoration of the Magi; 1488), fill the **Galleria dello Spedale degli Innocenti** (055 249 17 08; www.istitutodeglinnocenti.it; Piazza della Santissima Annunziata 12; adult/concession €4/2.50; 8.30am-7pm Mon-Sat, 8.30am-2pm Sun) on the 2nd floor.

About 200m southeast of the piazza is the **Museo Archeologico** (Map pp98-9; 055 23 57 50; Via della Colonna 38; admission €4; 2-7pm Mon, 8.30am-7pm Tue & Thu, 8.30am-2pm Wed & Fri-Sun), whose rich collection of finds, including most of the Medici hoard of antiquities, plunges you deep into the past and offers an alternative to Renaissance splendour. On the 1st floor you can either head left into the ancient Egyptian collection or right for the smaller section on Etruscan and Greco-Roman art.

Santa Croce Area
PIAZZA DI SANTA CROCE

The Franciscan stands haughty watch over the piazza of the same name, today lined with restaurants and souvenir shops. The square was initially cleared in the Middle Ages, primarily to allow hordes of the faithful to gather when the church itself was full. In Savonarola's day, heretics were executed here.

Such an open space inevitably found other uses, and from the 14th century it was often the colourful scene of jousts, festivals and *calcio storico* matches. This last was like a combination of football and rugby with no rules. Look for the marble stone embedded in the wall below the gaily frescoed façade of **Palazzo dell'Antella** (Map pp100–1), on the south side of the piazza; it marks the halfway line on this, one of the oldest football pitches in the world.

Curiously enough, the Romans used to have fun in much the same area centuries before. The city's 2nd-century amphitheatre took up the area facing the western end of Piazza di Santa Croce. To this day, Piazza de' Peruzzi, Via de' Bentaccordi and Via Torta mark the oval outline of the north, west and south sides of its course.

BASILICA DI SANTA CROCE

The French writer Stendhal was so dazzled by the **Basilica di Santa Croce** (Map pp100-1; 055 246 61

05; adult/concession incl Museo dell'Opera €5/3; ⏱ 9.30am-5.30pm Mon-Sat, 1-5.30pm Sun) that he was barely able to walk for faintness. He is apparently not the only one to have felt so overwhelmed by the beauty of Florence; Florentine doctors treat a dozen cases of 'stendhalismo' each year so they say.

Designed by Arnolfo di Cambio between 1294 and 1385, the church's name stems from a splinter of the Holy Cross donated to the Franciscans by King Louis of France in 1258. The magnificent façade enlivened by the varying shades of coloured marble is a 19th-century neo-Gothic addition, as indeed is the bell tower. Inside, its massive, austere interior is divided into a nave and two aisles by solid octagonal pillars. Peer up to see a fine example of the timber, A frame–style ceiling occasionally used in Italy's Gothic churches.

It is the famous Florentines buried inside this church that draw most visitors, though. Michelangelo's tomb, designed by Vasari (1570), is along the southern wall between the first and second altars. The three muses below it represent his three principal gifts: sculpture, painting and architecture. Next along is a 19th-century cenotaph to the memory of Dante (whose remains, in fact, are in Ravenna), and Galileo Galilei's (1737), easy to spot with its bust of the great scientist clutching a telescope and gazing skywards, lies directly opposite, in the left aisle.

Otherwise, Santa Croce's artistic treasures come in the shape of frescoes, some substantially better preserved than others. Five chapels on either side of the **Cappella Maggiore** line the transept, the two nearest the right side of the chapel being decorated with fragmentary frescoes by Giotto – these are the best examples of his work in Florence. Those depicting scenes from the life of St Francis (1315–20) in the **Capella Bardi** are the best preserved, but still too poor quality to make any decent comparison with the frescoes painted by his assistant and most loyal pupil, Taddeo Gaddi (1300–66), who frescoed the neighbouring **Chapelle Majeure** and nearby **Cappella Baroncelli**; the latter features the life of the Virgin.

Taddeo's son Agnolo (1345–96), meanwhile, painted the **Cappella Castellani** (1385) with delightful frescoes depicting the life of St Nicholas (later transformed into 'Santa Claus') and was also responsible for the frescoes above the altar.

From the transept chapels a doorway designed by Michelozzo leads into a corridor, off which is the **Sagrestia**, an enchanting 14th-century room dominated on the left by Taddeo Gaddi's fresco of the *Crocifissione*. There are also a few relics of St Francis on show, including his cowl and belt. Through the next room, the church bookshop, you can access the **Scuola del Cuoio** (p150), a leather school and shop, where you can see the goods being fashioned and also buy the finished products. At the end of the corridor is a Medici chapel with a fine two-tone altarpiece in glazed terracotta by Andrea della Robbia.

Cloisters & Cappella de' Pazzi

Brunelleschi designed the serene **cloisters** just before his death in 1446. His **Cappella de' Pazzi**, at the end of the first cloister, with its harmonious lines and restrained terracotta medallions of the Apostles by Luca della Robbia, is a masterpiece of Renaissance architecture. It was built for, but never used by, the wealthy banking family destroyed in the Pazzi Conspiracy – when papal sympathisers sought to overthrow Lorenzo il Magnifico and the Medici dynasty.

The **Museo dell'Opera di Santa Croce** (Map pp100-1; admission incl basilica adult/concession €5/3; ⏱ 9.30am-5.30pm Mon-Sat, 1-5.30pm Sun), in the first cloister, features a Crucifixion by Cimabue, restored to the best degree possible after flood damage in 1966 when more than 4m of water inundated the Santa Croce area. Other highlights include Donatello's gilded bronze statue *St Louis of Toulouse* (1424), originally placed in a tabernacle on the Orsanmichele façade, a wonderful terracotta bust of St Francis receiving the stigmata by the della Robbia workshop, and frescoes by Giotto, including an *Ultima Cena* (Last Supper; 1333).

MUSEO HORNE

Herbert Percy Horne was one of those eccentric Brits living abroad with cash. He bought this house in the early 1900s, renovated it to re-create a Renaissance ambience, and installed his eclectic collection of 14th- and 15th-century Italian paintings, sculptures, ceramics, furniture and other oddments to create his own **Horne Museum** (Map pp100-1; ☎ 055 24 46 61; www.museohorne.it in Italian; Via de' Benci 6; adult/concession €5/3; ⏱ 9am-1pm Mon-Sat). There are a few works by masters such as Giotto, Filippo Lippi and Lorenzetti, though most are by minor artists. More interesting is the furniture, some exquisite.

PONTE ALLE GRAZIE

The first bridge here was built in 1237 by Messer Rubaconte da Mandella, a Milanese *podestà*. It was swept away in 1333 and chapels were built on its replacement. The bridge was called after one of them, the Madonna alle Grazie. The Germans blew up the bridge in 1944, and the present version went up in 1957.

PIAZZA SANT'AMBROGIO & AROUND

From Casa Buonarroti, walk north up Via Michelangelo Buonarroti and continue to Piazza dei Ciompi, venue for a small flea market.

The **Loggia del Pesce** (Fish Market; Map pp100-1; Via Pietrapiana) was designed by Vasari for the Mercato Vecchio (Old Market), which was at the heart of what is now Piazza della Repubblica. The loggia was moved to the Convento di San Marco when the Mercato Vecchio and the surrounding area were cleared in the 19th century, and finally re-erected here in 1955.

A block east, the plain **Chiesa di Sant'Ambrogio** (Map pp100-1; Via Pietrapiana) presents an inconspicuous 18th-century façade on the square of the same name. The first church here was raised in the 10th century, but what you see inside is a mix of 13th-century Gothic and 15th-century refurbishment. The name comes from Sant'Ambrogio (St Ambrose), the powerful 4th-century archbishop of Milan, who stayed in an earlier convent on this site when he visited Florence. The church is the last resting place of several artists, including Mino da Fiesole and Verrocchio.

Just north of Piazza Sant'Ambrogio rises the shiny copper-turned-vibrant pea-green domes of Florence's **Sinagoga** (Synagogue; Map pp100-1; ☎ 055 234 66 54; Via Luigi Carlo Farini 6; adult/concession €4/3; ⏰ 10am-6pm Sun-Thu Jun-Aug, to 3pm Apr-May & Sep-Oct, to 2pm Nov-Mar, 10am-2pm Fri year-round), a fanciful structure built between 1874 and 1882 with Moorish and neo-Byzantine elements. Inside its **Museo di Arte e Storia Ebraico,** Jewish ceremonial objects and richly embroidered vestments are displayed. A memorial in the garden lists the names of Florentine Jews who died in Nazi concentration camps.

Oltrarno

Literally 'Beyond the Arno', trendy Oltrarno takes in all of Florence south of the river.

PONTE VECCHIO

The first documentation of a stone bridge here, at the narrowest crossing point along the entire length of the Arno, dates from 972. The Arno looks placid enough, but when it gets mean, it gets very mean. Floods in 1177 and 1333 destroyed the bridge, and in 1966 it came close to being destroyed again. Many of the jewellers with shops on the bridge were convinced the floodwaters would sweep away their livelihoods, but this time the bridge held.

They're still here. Indeed, the bridge has twinkled with the glittering wares of jewellers, their trade often passed down from generation to generation, ever since the 16th century, when Ferdinando I de' Medici ordered them here to replace the often malodorous presence of the town butchers, who used to toss unwanted leftovers into the river.

The bridge as it stands was built in 1345 and was the only one saved from destruction by the retreating Germans in 1944; some say on Hitler's express orders, others that the German commander disobeyed those very orders (yet still wreaked havoc by razing the medieval quarters at either end).

At the southern end of the bridge is the medieval **Torre dei Mannelli** (Map pp100-1), which looks rather odd as the Corridoio Vasariano was built around it, not simply straight through it as the Medici would have preferred. Across Via de' Bardi as your eye follows the Corridoio, you can glimpse the **Torre degli Ubriachi** (Map pp100-1), the Drunks' Tower.

CHIESA DI SANTA FELICITÀ

The most captivating thing about the façade of this 18th-century remake of what had been Florence's oldest (4th-century) **church** (Map pp100-1; Piazza Santa Felicità; ⏰ 9am-noon & 3.30-6pm Mon-Sat, noon-1pm Sun) is the fact that the Corridoio Vasariano (p106) passes right across it; the Medici could stop by and hear Mass without being seen.

Inside, in Brunelleschi's small **Cappella Barbadori**, on the right as you enter, Jacopo Pontormo (1494–1557) left his mark with a fresco of the *Annunciazione* (Annunciation) and a *Deposizione* (Deposition), depicting the taking down of Christ from the Cross in disturbingly surreal colours.

PALAZZO PITTI

Wealthy banker Luca Pitti commissioned Brunelleschi to build this forbidding-looking palace (Map pp100-1; ☎ 055 238 86 14; Piazza de' Pitti; adult/concession €11.50/5.75; ⊗ 8.15am-6.50pm Tue-Sun) in 1457, but by the time it was completed, the family fortunes were on the wane, forcing them to sell it to arch-rivals, the Medici, in 1549 – to the joy of Eleonora de Toledo, wife of Cosimo I, who took it upon herself to oversee the extensions, which continued for centuries.

Incredibly the original design was consistently respected, making it almost impossible to distinguish the various phases of construction: the original nucleus of the palace embraced the space encompassing the seven sets of windows on the second and third storeys.

Following the demise of the Medici dynasty, the palace remained the residence of the city's rulers, the dukes of Lorraine and their Austrian and (briefly) Napoleonic successors. When Florence was made capital of the nascent Kingdom of Italy in 1865, it became a residence of the Savoy royal family, who presented it to the state in 1919.

Museums

Irrespective of how much you do – or don't – want to see, one ticket covers admission to everything: the palace's royal apartments and art galleries, silver museum and gardens with porcelain museum. Reserve at least an afternoon to take it all in.

A stroll around the ground-floor **Museo degli Argenti** (Silver Museum) reveals far more than extraordinary silverware, amber, ivory and *pietre dure* (hard stone) pieces amassed by the Medici. The first room you enter, the Sala di Giovanni da San Giovanni, stuns with its lavish head-to-toe frescoes (1635–42) celebrating the life of Lorenzo the Magnificent – spot Michelangelo giving Lorenzo a statue. 'Talk little, be brief and witty' is the curt motto above the painted staircase in the next room, the public audience chamber, where the Grand Duke received visitors in the presence of his court. Only a lucky few were granted a private audience in the smaller chamber next door.

Raphaels and Rubens vie for centre stage in the enviable collection of 16th- to 18th-century art amassed by the Medici and Lorraine dukes in the 1st-floor **Galleria Palatina**, reached by a staircase from the palace's central courtyard. The backdrop is the **Appartamenti Reali** (Royal Apartments), a series of rather sickeningly furnished and decorated rooms, many embellished with ceiling frescoes of mythological scenes, where the Medici and their successors

lived, slept and received their guests. The style and division of tasks assigned to each room is reminiscent of Spanish royal palaces, all heavily bedecked with drapes, silk and chandeliers. Each room has a colour theme, ranging from aqua green to deep-wine red.

Among Tuscan masters, you can see work by Filippo Lippi, Botticelli, Vasari and Andrea del Sarto. The collection also boasts important works by other Italian and foreign painters. Foremost among them are those by Raphael, whose *Madonna della Seggiola* (Madonna of the Chair; 1515) is particularly intriguing. Caravaggio's *Amore Dormente* (Sleeping Cupid; 1608), Guido Reni's grinning *Bacco Fanciullo* (Young Bacchus; 1620), Guercino's dramatic *San Sebastian* and Tintoretto's *Deposizione* (Deposition) are just a few of the many highlights. Other artists represented include Titian, Veronese, Velasquez, Rubens and Van Dyck. Among the lesser-known works, Dosso Dossi's *Ninfa e Satiro*, featuring a grotesque satyr snarling at a nervous-looking nymph, Lorenzo Lippi's gruesome portrait of *Santa Agata* and Orazio Rimnaldi's *Amore Artifice* (False Cupid) are worth seeking out.

Only the most dedicated make it to the 2nd-floor **Galleria d'Arte Moderna** (Modern Art Gallery) and **Galleria del Costume** (Costume Gallery), displaying 18th- to mid-20th-century Tuscan works and high fashion respectively.

Giardino di Boboli

Relax in the palace's Renaissance **Boboli Gardens** (Map p103; adult/concession €6/3; ⊗ 8.15am-7.30pm Jun-Aug, 8.15am-6.30pm Apr, May, Sep & Oct, 8.15am-5.30pm Mar, 8.15am-4.30pm Nov-Feb), laid out in the mid-16th century according to a design by architect Niccolò Pericoli, aka Il Tribolo.

A shabby shadow of its former glorious self, Boboli remains a prime example of a formal Tuscan garden nonetheless and is fun to explore: skip along the **Cypress Alley**; let the imagination rip with a gallant frolic in the walled **Giardino del Cavaliere** (Knights' Garden); dance around 170-odd statues; discover bird song and species in the garden along the signposted **nature trail**; or watch a fleshy *Venere* (Venus) by Giambologna rise from the waves in the **Grotta del Buontalenti**, a fanciful grotto designed by the eponymous artist. Other typical Renaissance garden features include a six-tier **amphitheatre**, originally embellished with 24 niches sheltering classical statues surrounded by animals; an **orangery** (*limonaia*; 1777), which stills keeps around 500 citrus trees snug in winter; **botanical garden**; and Rococo **kaffeehaus** (1775), where afternoon tea can still be supped. The 17th-century maze, a Tuscan horticultural standard, was razed in the 1830s to make way for a driveway for carriages. Don't miss the monumental 'face' sculpture (1998) by Polish sculptor Igor Mitoraj (b 1944), at home in Pietrasanta near Carrara today.

At the upper, southern limit of the gardens, fantastic views over the palace complex and Florentine countryside fan out beyond the decidedly neglected **rose garden**, overlooked by the **Museo delle Porcellane** (Porcelain Museum; Map pp100–1), home to Sèvres, Vincennes, Meissen, Wedgewood and other porcelain pieces collected by Palazzo Pitti's wealthy tenants. At the top of the hill are the rambling fortifications of the **Forte di Belvedere** (p126), built by Grand Duke Ferdinando I towards the end of the 16th century to protect the Palazzo Pitti. It was closed for renovations when we last visited.

Giardino di Bardini

Smaller, better tended and more manicured are Florence's little-known **Bardini Gardens** (Map pp100–1; ☎ 055 29 48 83; Costa San Giorgio 4-6 via Boboli Gardens & Via de' Bardi 1r; adult/concession incl Boboli & Porcelain Museum €5/2.50; ☼ 8.15am-sunset), named after art collector Stefano Bardini (1836–1922) who bought the villa and gardens in 1913, restored much of the medieval garden, created an English garden and so on. Accessible from neighbouring Boboli or down by the Arno, they have all the features of a quintessential Tuscan garden – artificial grottoes, orangery, marble statues, fountains, loggia, amphitheatre and a monumental baroque stone staircase staggering up the beautiful tiered gardens – but not the crowds. A springtime stroll is an extra-special joy when its azaleas, peonies, wisteria (all April and May) and irises (June) are all in bloom.

CASA GUIDI

Robert and Elizabeth Browning lived in Florence at **Casa Guidi** (Map p103; ☎ 055 28 43 93; www .browningsociety.org; Piazza San Felice 8; admission free; ☼ 3-6pm Mon, Wed & Fri Apr-Nov), Robert writing *Men and Women* in the apartment they called home for 14 years and poetess Elizabeth giving birth to their only child and later dying here. Britain's Eton College owns the literary-rich apartment today, which can be rented for short stays.

MUSEO ZOOLOGICO LA SPECOLA

Further down Via Romana from Piazza San Felice, this rather fusty **zoological museum** (Map p103; ☎ 055 228 82 51; Via Romana 17; admission €4; ☼ 9am-1pm Thu-Tue, until 5pm Sat) offers for your delectation, the stuffed-animal exhibit apart, a collection of wax models of bits of human anatomy in varying states of bad health. An offbeat change from all that art and history!

PORTA ROMANA

Rome-bound pilgrims headed down Via Romana as they left Florence behind them. At the end of the street is the **Porta Romana** (Map p103), an imposing city gate that was part of the outer circle of city walls knocked down in the 19th century. A strip of the wall still stretches north from the gate. If you follow the inside of this wall (the area is now a car park), you soon come across an entrance that allows you to get to the top of the gate.

VIA MAGGIO

This was a posh address in the 16th century as the line-up of fine Renaissance mansions duly attests. **Palazzo di Bianca Cappello** (Map pp100–1), at No 26, is named after Bianca Cappello, Francesco I de' Medici's lover, who eventually became his wife. Across the street, a series of mansions, more or less following the same Renaissance style, include **Palazzo Ricasoli-Firidolfi** (Map pp100–1) at No 7, **Palazzo Martellini** (Map pp100–1) at No 9, **Palazzo Michelozzi** (Map pp100–1) at No 11, **Palazzo Martelli** (Map pp100–1) at No 13 and **Palazzo di Cosimo Ridolfi** (Map pp100–1) at No 15. All were built and fiddled around with over the 14th, 15th and 16th centuries. Over the road, take a glance at the squarely imposing **Palazzo Corsini-Suarez** (Map pp100–1) at No 42.

PIAZZA SANTO SPIRITO

From Via Maggio turn into Via de' Michelozzi to reach lively Piazza Santo Spirito. At its northern end, the square is fronted by the flaking façade of the **Basilica di Santo Spirito** (Map p103; ☼ 10am-noon & 4-5.30pm Mon-Sat, 11.30-noon Sun, closed Wed afternoon), one of Brunelleschi's last commissions. Inside, the entire length of the church is lined by a series of semicircular chapels, and the colonnade of grey *pietra forte* Corinthian columns lends an air of monumental grandeur.

One of the most noteworthy works of art is Filippino Lippi's *Madonna con il Bambino e Santi* (Madonna with Child and Saints) in the Cappella Nerli in the right transept. Other highlights include Domenico di Zanobi's *Madonna del Soccorso* (Madonna of the Relief; 1485), in the Cappella Velutti, in which the Madonna wards off a little red devil with a club, and Giovanni Baratta's marble and stucco *L'Arcangelo Raffaele e Tobiolo* (The Archangel Raphael and Tobias; 1698), which illustrates an episode from the Apocrypha. The main altar, beneath the central dome, is a voluptuous baroque flourish, rather out of place in the spare setting of Brunelleschi's church. In the sacristy is a poignantly tender wooden crucifix (it's not often you see Christ with a penis) attributed to Michelangelo.

Next door to the church is the refectory, **Cenacolo di Santo Spirito** (Map p103; ☎ 055 28 70 43; Piazza Santo Spririto 29; admission €2.20; ⏱ 10.30am-1.30pm Sat Apr-Nov, 9am-5pm Sat Dec-Mar). Andrea Orcagna decorated the refectory with a grand fresco depicting the *Last Supper* and the *Crucifixion* (c 1370). Also on display is the sculpture collection bequeathed to the city in 1946 by the Neapolitan collector Salvatore Romano. Among its most intriguing pieces are rare pre-Romanesque sculptures and works by Jacopo della Quercia and Donatello.

BASILICA DI SANTA MARIA DEL CARMINE
West of Piazza Santo Spirito, Piazza del Carmine is an old square used as a car park. On its southern flank is the 13th-century **Basilica di Santa Maria del Carmine** (Map p103), all but destroyed by fire in the late 18th century. Fortunately the fire spared the magnificent frescoes in its **Cappella Brancacci** (Map p103; ☎ advance reservations 055 276 82 24, 055 76 85 58; admission €4; ⏱ 10am-5pm Wed-Sat & Mon, 1-5pm Sun), entered via a separate entrance next to the basilica on the square. A maximum of 30 visitors are allowed into the chapel at a time and visits are strictly by guided tour; places *must* be booked in advance.

This chapel is a treasure of paintings by Masolino da Panicale, Masaccio and Filippino Lippi; see p173 for an in-depth look. Masaccio's fresco cycle, illustrating the life of St Peter, is considered among his greatest works, representing a definitive break with Gothic art and a plunge into new worlds of expression in the early stages of the Renaissance. The *Cacciata dei Progenitori* (Expulsion of Adam and Eve), on the left side of the chapel, is his best-known work. His depiction of Eve's anguish in particular lends the image a human touch hitherto little

seen in European painting. Masaccio painted these frescoes in his early 20s, taking over from Masolino, and interrupted the task to go to Rome, where he died, aged only 28. The cycle was completed some 60 years later by Filippino Lippi. Masaccio himself features in his *St Peter Enthroned;* he's the one standing beside the Apostle, staring out at the viewer. The figures around him have been identified as Brunelleschi, Masolino and Alberti. Filippino Lippi also painted himself into the scene of *St Peter's Crucifixion,* along with his teacher, Botticelli.

BORGO SAN FREDIANO
Heading northwards from Piazza del Carmine, you reach Borgo San Frediano. The street and surrounding area retain something of their traditional feel – that of a working-class quarter where artisans have been beavering away for centuries.

At the western end of the street stands lonely **Porta San Frediano** (Map p103), another of the old city gates left in place when the walls were demolished in the 19th century. Before you reach the gate, you'll notice the unpolished feel of the area neatly reflected in the unadorned brick walls of **Chiesa di San Frediano in Cestello** (Map p103; ⏱ 9-11.30am & 5-6pm Mon-Fri, 5-6pm Sun), its incomplete façade hiding a restrained baroque interior.

BACK TO PONTE VECCHIO
From the front of Chiesa di San Frediano in Cestello, you can follow the river bank as far as Ponte Santa Trinità along Borgo San Jacopo. Along the way you pass several family mansions, including **Palazzo Frescobaldi** (Map pp100–1) on the square of the same name. Two 12th-century towers, the **Torre dei Marsili** and **Torre de' Belfredelli**, keep watch over the area.

PONTE VECCHIO TO FORTE DI BELVEDERE
Continuing east away from Ponte Vecchio, the first stretch of Via de' Bardi shows clear signs of its recent history. This entire area was flattened by German mines in 1944, and hastily rebuilt in questionable taste after the war.

The street spills into Piazza di Santa Maria Soprarno. Follow the narrow Via de' Bardi (the right fork) away from the square and you enter a pleasantly quieter corner of Florence. The powerful Bardi family once owned all the houses along this street, but by the time Cosimo il Vecchio wed Contessina de' Bardi in 1415, the latter's family was on the decline.

Via de' Bardi expires in Piazza de' Mozzi, surrounded by the sturdy façades of grand residences. Pope Gregory X stayed at **Palazzo de' Mozzi** (Map pp100-1; Piazza de' Mozzi 2) when brokering peace between the Guelphs and Ghibellines.

Next, turn east down Via dei Renai, past leafy Piazza Nicola Demidoff, dedicated to the 19th-century Russian philanthropist who lived nearby in Via San Niccolò. At the end of Via dei Renai, 16th-century **Palazzo Serristori** (Map pp100-1) was home to Joseph Bonaparte in the last years of his life until his death in 1844; a humble end to the man who, at the height of his career, had been appointed king of Spain by his brother Napoleon.

Turn right and you end up on Via San Niccolò; walk east along this street to emerge at the tower marking **Porta San Niccolò** (Map pp100-1), all that is left of the city walls. To get an idea of what the walls were once like, walk south from Chiesa di San Niccolò Oltrarno through **Porta San Miniato** (Map pp100-1). The wall extends a short way to the east and for a stretch further west, up a steep hill that leads you to **Forte di Belvedere** (Map pp100-1), a rambling fort designed by Bernardo Buontalenti for Grand Duke Ferdinando I at the end of the 16th century. From this massive bulwark soldiers kept watch on four fronts – as much for internal security to protect the Palazzo Pitti as against foreign attack. The views are excellent.

PIAZZALE MICHELANGELO
Turn your back on the bevy of ticky-tacky souvenir stalls flogging *David* statues and how-to-make-*limoncello* tea towels and take in the soaring city panorama from this vast **esplanade** (Map pp100-1), pierced by one of Florence's two David copies: the square is a 10-minute uphill walk along the wiggly road, paths and steps that scale the hill side from the river and Piazza Giuseppe Poggi. Should it be the right season, nip into the hill-side **Giardino delle Rose** (Rose Garden; Viale Giuseppe Poggi 2; admission free; 8am-8pm Mon-Sun May & Jun) en route where 1000 types of roses in bloom – including 350 antique varieties – make a pretty picture.

Bus 13 links Stazione di Santa Maria Novella with Piazzale Michelangelo.

CHIESA DI SAN MINIATO AL MONTE
The real point of your exertions is five minutes further uphill, at this wonderful **Romanesque church** (Map pp96-7; Via Monte alle Croce; admission free; 8am-7pm May-Oct, 8am-noon & 3-6pm Nov-Apr). The church is dedicated to St Minius, an early Christian martyr in Florence who is said to have flown to this spot after his death down in the town (or, if you care to believe an alternative version, to have walked up the hill with his head tucked underneath his arm).

The church was started in the early 11th century. Its typically Tuscan multicoloured marble façade, featuring a mosaic depicting Christ between the Virgin and St Minius, was tacked on a couple of centuries later. Inside 13th- to 15th-century frescoes adorn the south wall and intricate inlaid marble designs line the length of the nave, leading to a fine Romanesque crypt. The raised choir and presbytery have an intricate marble pulpit and screen, rich in complex geometrical designs. The **sacristy**, in the southeast corner, features marvellously bright frescoes depicting the life of St Benedict. The four figures in its cross vault represent the Evangelists.

Slap bang in the middle of the nave is the bijou **Capella del Crocefisso**, to which Michelozzo, Agnolo Gaddi and Luca della Robbia all contributed.

The **Cappella del Cardinale del Portogallo**, beside the north aisle, features a tomb by Antonio Rossellino and a tabernacle ceiling in terracotta by della Robbia.

Come around 4.30pm (in winter) or 5.30pm (in summer) and you can hear the monks' Gregorian chant wafting up from the crypt.

Bus 13 stops nearby.

North of the Old City
FORTEZZA DA BASSO
This huge defensive **fortress** (Map pp98-9) was built in 1534 on the orders of Alessandro de' Medici. It was a statement of Medici power, aimed at overawing the potentially rebellious Florentines, rather than a defence against invasion. Nowadays it's used for exhibitions, cultural events and a catwalk to Italy's annual children and menswear fashion shows (p60).

CHIESA RUSSA ORTODOSSA
A couple of blocks east, the onion-shaped domes on this Russian Orthodox **church** (Map pp98-9) colour the skyline. Built in 1902 for the resident Russian populace, it was designed in the northern-Russian style, with two interior levels decorated in part by Florentine artists but mostly by Russians who were experts in iconography.

MUSEO STIBBERT

Anglo-Italian, Florence-born Frederick Stibbert (1838–1906) was one of the grand 19th-century wheeler-dealers on the European antiquities market and amassed an intriguing personal collection, showcased in Villa di Montughi, aka the **Stibbert Museum** (Map pp96-7; ☎ 055 47 55 20; www.museostibbert.it; Via Stibbert 26; adult/child €5/2; ☼ 10am-2pm Mon-Wed, 10am-6pm Fri-Sun), north of Fortezza da Basso.

Great for kids is the **Sala della Cavalcata** (Parade Room) where life-sized figures of horses and their riders in all manner of suits of armour from Europe and the Middle East rub shoulders. Other varied exhibits include clothes, furnishings, tapestries and 16th- to 19th-century paintings.

Take bus 4 from Stazione di Santa Maria Novella to the 'Gioia' stop on Via Fabroni, from where it is a short walk.

MEDICI VILLAS

In the 15th and 16th centuries as their wealth and prosperity grew, the Medici built several villas in what was then countryside around Florence – now city suburb and industrial sprawl. Only the gardens of this trio are open to visitors.

Villa Medicea La Petraia (Map p155; ☎ 055 45 26 91; Via della Petraia 40; admission free; ☼ 8.15am-8pm Jun-Aug, to 7pm Apr, May & Sep, to 6pm Mar & Oct, to 5pm Nov-Feb, closed 2nd & 3rd Mon of the month), 3.5km north of the city in Castello, was commissioned by Cardinal Ferdinando de' Medici in 1576. Its magnificent gardens feature a fountain by Giambologna, and May, when its flowering tubs are brought out from the lemon groves and hothouses, is an exceptional time to visit. Take ATAF bus 28 or the City Sightseeing bus (p131) from Stazione di Santa Maria Novella.

Lorenzo il Magnifico's summer home, **Villa Medicea di Castello** (Map p155; ☎ 055 45 47 91; Via di Castello 47; admission free; ☼ 8.15am-8pm Jun-Aug, to 7pm Apr, May & Sep, to 6pm Mar & Oct, to 5pm Nov-Feb, closed 2nd & 3rd Mon of the month), a little further north in Castello, was a favourite of Cosimo I and is framed by sumptuous gardens with an animal-sculptured grotto, all the rage in Renaissance Florence. Same bus routes as La Petraia.

Lorenzo il Magnifico breathed his last in 1492 at **Villa Medicea di Careggi** (Map p155; ☎ 055 427 97 55; Viale Pieraccini 17; admission free; ☼ 9am-6pm Mon-Fri, 9am-noon Sat), administrative offices for the local hospital today in Careggi. The gardens here can also be visited; take the ATAF bus 14C from Stazione di Santa Maria Novella.

South of the Old City
BELLOSGUARDO

The hill of Bellosguardo (Beautiful View), southwest of the city centre, was a favourite spot for 19th-century landscape painters. A narrow, winding road leads up past a couple of villas from Piazza Torquato Tasso to Piazza Bellosguardo. You can't see anything from here, but if you wander along Via Roti Michelozzi into the grounds of **Albergo Torre di Bellosguardo** (Map p103; www.torrebellosguardo.com; Via Roti Michelozzi 2), you'll see what the fuss was about. The top-end hotel, long appreciated as a bucolic escape from the city heat, started life as a 14th-century castle.

CERTOSA DI FIRENZE

From Porta Romana located at the southern tip of the Oltrarno, follow Via Senese south for 3km to the village of Galluzzo and its remarkable 14th-century Carthusian monastery, the **Certosa di Firenze** (Map pp96-7; ☎ 055 204 92 26; Via Senese 206-208r, Galluzzo; admission free; ☼ guided tour 9am, 11.30am, 3pm & 4.30pm or 5.30pm Tue-Sun), also called Certosa del Galluzzo, where Carthusian monks make liqueur and honey between prayers. The great cloister is decorated with busts from the della Robbia workshop, and there are frescoes by Pontormo in the Gothic hall of Palazzo degli Studi. Take bus 37 from Stazione di Santa Maria Novella.

ACTIVITIES

On those torrid summer days when they pull back the roof over the Olympic-size pool, **Piscina Bellariva** (Comunale Nannini; Map pp96-7; ☎ 055 67 75 21; Lungarno Aldo Moro 6; ☼ 10am-6pm daily, 8.30-11.30pm Tue & Thu Jun-Aug) is heaven. Bus 14 from Piazza dell'Unità and the Duomo passes nearby.

Piscina Le Pavonière (Map pp96-7; ☎ 055 36 22 33; Viale della Catena 2; ☼ 10am-6pm & 8pm-2am Jun–mid-Sep) has a pizzeria and bar. Dip in the evening when admission is free.

From mid-September to June, opening times are restricted in both pools; call to check before diving in.

WALKING TOUR

This route introduces you to many of the city's brightest highlights.

Begin in Piazza di Santa Maria Novella, overlooked by **Basilica di Santa Maria Novella** (**1**; p115). Then take Via degli Avelli north, as far as busy Piazza dell'Unità Italiana, and continue east on Via del Melarancio, past Piazza Madonna degli Aldobrandini, and on to Piazza San Lorenzo, with its market stalls and **Basilica di San Lorenzo** (**2**; p118). From here, slip in a quick detour northwards up Borgo La Noce to enjoy the contemporary bustle of **Mercato Centrale** (**3**; p143), Florence's pre-

mier produce market. Back at walk south along Borgo San L you see the **Duomo** (**4**; p105) and p107). Take a spin around Piazza d then walk southwards along Via Roma, on into Piazza della Repubblica, an ideal coffee stop (p145). Just beyond the square, turn left (east) into Via Orsanmichele, where you'll find **Chiesa di Orsanmichele** (**6**; p109) with its ornate statuary.

Turn right to follow Via de' Calzaiuoli southwards as far as Piazza della Signoria with its **Loggia della Signoria** (**7**; p111) and the commanding presence of **Palazzo Vecchio** (**8**; p110), home of Florentine government since the Middle Ages. South just a few steps is the **Uffizi** (**9**; p112), housing one of the world's

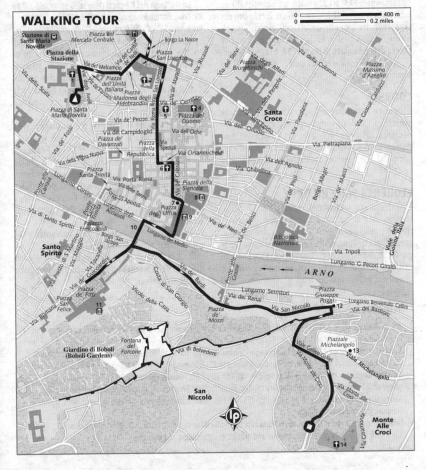

WALKING TOUR

most precious collections of primarily Renaissance art. Piazza degli Uffizi leads on to the River Arno.

Face west to see the **Ponte Vecchio** (**10**; p123). Cross this bridge, and you will be in the Oltrarno. Continue south along Via de' Guicciardini as far as the brooding hulk of **Palazzo Pitti** (**11**; p123), one-time seat of the Medici dynasty.

Returning to the river and Ponte Vecchio, head upstream along altogether quieter Via de' Bardi as far as Piazza de' Mozzi, surrounded by grand residences, and continue along Via San Niccolò as far as **Porta San Niccolò** (**12**; p126), one of Florence's few surviving city gates. Behind the gate, you'll find a steep, winding footpath leads up to **Piazzale Michelangelo** (**13**; p127) with its breathtaking panorama over the city. From here, barely five minutes more of sturdy uphill work along Viale Galileo Galilei brings you to the **Chiesa di San Miniato al Monte** (**14; p127**), a beautiful Romanesque jewel and a fitting end to your exertions.

COURSES

Florence has dozens of schools offering courses in Italian language and culture. Numerous others teach art, art history, film, dance and so on. For general information, see p402; for courses covering food and wine, see p76.

FLORENCE FOR CHILDREN

Children are welcomed pretty much anywhere, any time, in Florence, families frequently going out with young children in the evenings, strolling with a *gelato* or dining with gusto in a restaurant. That said, Florence is not the easiest city to visit with very young children; green spaces and playgrounds are scarce and, while some of the pricier hotels can provide baby-sitters, there's no organised service for tourists.

Several locally published books and games help children discover Florence – the bookshop in Palazzo Vecchio (p110) has a particularly tip-top selection. Nancy Shroyer Howard's activity-driven book *Fun in Florence* kits out kids aged six to 10 years with pencils and do-and-find sections for major sites. Ellen & Marvin Mouchawar's *Treasure Hunt Florence* sets the same age group chasing around the city looking for items or opportunities to carry out simple tasks. For older children, try *Florence, Just Add Water* by Simone Frasca and *Florence: Playing with Art* by Maria Salvia Baldini.

La Bottega dei Ragazzi (Map pp98–9; ☎ 055 247 83 86; www.istitutodeglinnocenti.it; Via dei Fibbiai 2; one/three workshops €10/20; ☷ 9am-1pm & 3-7pm Mon-Sat), an inspirational 'play and learn with art' space next to the Spedale degli Innocenti, runs workshops for children aged three years to five years and six to 11 years; book in advance or simply turn up. Any time, parents and kids can pop in to play with its many toys, books and games.

At the **Palazzo Vecchio** (p110), younger children aged three to seven years can watch a shadow theatre about a theft from Francesco's studiolo and visit the latter; while those aged eight years or more can learn about Michelangelo though a theatre sketch, meet Cosimo I and Eleonora de Toledo (actors dressed up) or take a tour of the place with Vasari.

Boys can drool over knights in shining armour at the **Museo Stibbert** (p127), and 'Galileo' talks kids through the exhibits at the **Museo di Storia della Scienza** (p110), which has a gory medical section.

TOP FIVE COURSES

Alice Atelier (Map pp100-1; ☎ 055 28 73 70; www.alicemasks.com; Via Faenza 72r) Mask-making courses with Professor Agostino Dessì and daughter, Alice.

British Institute of Florence Language Centre (Map pp100-1; ☎ 055 267 78 200; www.britishinstitute.it; Piazza degli Strozzi 2) Much-respected institution dating to 1917; language, art history, cooking and wine appreciation.

Centro Lorenzo de' Medici (Map pp98-9; ☎ 055 28 73 60; www.lorenzodemedici.it; Via Faenza 43) Language with huge variety of supplementary courses, including jewellery design, archaeology and film production.

Florence Dance Center (Map p103; ☎ 055 28 92 76; www.florencedance.org in Italian; Borgo della Stella 23r) Classical, jazz and modern dance.

Istituto per l'Arte e il Restauro Palazzo Spinelli (Map pp100-1; ☎ 055 24 60 01; www.spinelli.it; Borgo Santa Croce 10) Fresco restoration, interior and graphic design, gilding and marquetry.

Watching Giovanni Franchini make spaghetti in his old-fashioned **Laboratorio** (☎ 055 28 09 09; Via dei Rustici 6) is a fun escapade, as is racing up the bell-tower and dome of the **Duomo** (p105); playing hide-and-seek between statues in the **Giardino di Boboli** (p124) or tearing round **Parco delle Cascine** (Map pp96–7), which in summer has an open-air **swimming pool** to splash around in. The vintage **carousel** on Piazza della Repubblica never stops enchanting.

If you speak Italian, the musical activities at the **Ludoteca Musicale** (Map pp100-1; ☎ 055 263 86 00; www.musicarte.it in Italian; Via Pandolfinoi 18; admission free; 9.30am-12.30pm Mon-Sat) offer a good opportunity to mingle with Florentine parents and their children.

The best **playgrounds** for children under six years are in the Oltrarno: the river-side space along Lungarno Santa Rosa (cross the river using Ponte Amerigo Vespucci and turn right) and on Piazza Torquato Tasso (lunch before/after at **Al Tranvai**, p141).

Otherwise there's **Mondobimbo** (Map pp98-9; ☎ 055 553 29 46; Via del Ponte Rosso; admission €5; 10am-midnight May-Sep, 10am-7pm Oct-Apr), a soft-play area in a tent with bouncy castles, ball pools etc for kids aged two to 10 years.

TOURS

Bus

CAF Tours (☎ 055 21 06 12; www.caftours.com; Via Sant'Antonino 6r) Half- and full-day city coach tours (€42 to €90); designer-outlet shopping tours (€23 to €30; p151) and trips to Pisa, Lucca and other towns (€40 to €115); book online, at its office or at Consorzio ITA (Map pp98-9; p132) inside Stazione Santa Maria Novella.

City Sightseeing Firenze (Map pp98-9; ☎ 055 29 04 51; www.firenze.city-sightseeing.it) Tour Florence by open-top bus, hopping on and off as you please at bus stops sprinkled around the city; line A links Stazione di Santa Maria Novella (bus stop next to ATAF bus stops opposite the station's southeastern exit) with Piazzale Michelangelo; line B yo-yos between Porta San Frediano and Fiesole; and line C tours the Medici villas. Tickets valid 24 hours including audioguide: lines A & B adult/five to15 years/family €20/10/60, line C adult/six to 15 years €28/20. If you intend using public transport and route A or B, buy a one-day PassePartour (€22/11).

Cycling

Accidental Tourist (☎ 055 69 93 76; www.accidentaltourist.com) Become an accidental tourist (membership €10) then sign up for an activity tour – sunset strolls, natural trails, picnics, walking and snoozing tours as well as walking and one-day bike tours (€75).

> **A GARDEN TOUR**
>
> It is quite astonishing just how many exquisitely landscaped, lovingly tended gardens, many of a historical nature, hide behind high walls in Florence and around. Mostly privately owned, **Hortibus** (☎ 348 910 07 83; www.hortibus.com) holds the key. Working with the Italian Historical Homes Association, the horticultural society organises private tours of gardens in Florence and around Florence every Thursday and Saturday afternoon (€25), always with a specialist guide and invariably with the owner of the garden. Advance reservations are obligatory.

Bicycle Tuscany (☎ 055 22 25 80; www.bicycletuscany.com; Mar-Nov) One-day bike rides in the Tuscan countryside (including transport, bike and equipment, lunch and vineyard visit €60).

Florence by Bike (Map pp98-9; ☎ 055 48 89 92; www.florencebybike.it; Via San Zanobi 120-122r) Straight bike rental (per hour/five hours/day/three days including self-guided city itineraries €2.70/7.50/14/34.50) and a 32km-long day tour of Chianti (including lunch €75).

I Bike Italy (☎ 055 234 23 71; www.ibikeitaly.com) 'No museums, no churches and no annoying crowds' is the pledge of this tour company, which runs one- and two-day bike tours in the Tuscan countryside.

I Bike Tuscany (☎ 335 812 07 69; www.ibiketuscany.com; Via Belgio 4) One-day rides on the outskirts of Florence, Siena and Il Chianti led by former bike racer Marco Vignoli: 'professional, accommodating, extremely fun and easy-going', says Lonely Planet reader Katie J, USA.

Tour Bike Florence (☎ 055 234 30 48, 340 635 18 00; www.tourbikeflorence.it; Via Fiesolana 14r) Bike rental (per one/three/five/seven days including self-guiding itineraries €13/32/50/65), three-hour city tours (€35), and day trips to Fiesole and Il Chianti (both €65 including lunch).

Walking

Florence Guided Tours (☎ 055 21 03 01, 349 316 46 77; www.florapromotuscany.com; Via Pellocceria 1) Florence in a Day (€70), the Uffizi (€30), Galleria dell'Accademia (€25) and various theme tours by Florapromotuscany.

Mercurio Tours (☎ 055 21 33 55; www.mercurio-italy.org) Three-hour walking tours of the city (€42.50) and half-day Il Chianti trips (€67.50). Reserve by phone or online.

Walking Tours of Florence (Map pp100-1; ☎ 055 264 50 33, 329 613 27 30; www.italy.artviva.com; Via de'Sassetti 1) Excellent one- to three-hour walks of the

city (€25 to €39) led by historians or art history gradu-
ates, including an evening Medici murder stroll (€25, 1½
hours).

FESTIVALS & EVENTS

Carnevale in February aside, festivals abound.

Festa di Anna Maria Medici (Feast of Anna Maria
Medici) 18 February, the date of the death in 1743 of
the last Medici, Anna Maria, is marked with a costumed
parade from Palazzo Vecchio to her tomb in the Cappelle
Medicee.

Scoppio del Carro (Explosion of the Cart) A cart of
fireworks is exploded in front of the cathedral at 11am on
Easter Sunday.

Festa di San Giovanni (Feast of St John) On 24 June
Florence celebrates its patron saint with the *calcio storico*
(medieval football) matches on Piazza di Santa Croce and
fireworks over Piazzale Michelangelo.

Maggio Musicale Fiorentino A major summer music
festival (see p148).

Festa delle Rificolone (Festival of the Paper Lanterns)
A procession of children carrying lanterns, accompanied
by drummers, *sbandieratori* (flag throwers), musicians
and others in medieval dress, winds its way from Piazza di
Santa Croce to Piazza SS Annunziata to celebrate the Virgin
Mary's birthday on 7 September.

SLEEPING

The city has hundreds of hotels in all categories, some excellent hostels and a burgeoning
bed and breakfast (B&B) scene. Many places
in central Florence have rooms with a view
(across burnt-red rooftops interspersed by
at least one church spire or bell tower), while
the city's plethora of beautiful historical palaces is not reserved strictly for the top-end of
the market. Several good-value budget and
midrange sleeping options ooze that distinct
Florentine charm of hundreds of years too.

But get in quick. Florence is a hot destination for much of the year and rooms are
in constant demand, reflected by the city's
inflated prices. Places in this section have been
selected for their good value for money; plenty
more Florence options are reviewed online at
www.lonelyplanet.com.

Tourist offices don't recommend or reserve
places, but do carry lists of what is available,
including *affittacamere* (rooms in private
houses). Towns like Arezzo, Prato and Pisa
are a short train trip away and offer cheaper
accommodation.

For general information on reservations,
seasonal rates, the costly nightmare hotel
parking is etc, see p397.

Accommodation agencies

For free or a small fee, these agencies – two
of which have offices inside the main train
station – can find/reserve a hotel room for
you.

Agenzie 365 Hotel Reservation (Map pp98-9;
☎ 055 28 42 01; firenze1.gb@agenzie365.it; ⊗ 8am-
9pm Mon-Sat, 10am-7pm Sun) Platform 5, Stazione Santa
Maria Novella; reservation fee €5.50.

Consorzio ITA (signposted Informazione Turistiche
Alberghiere; Map pp98-9; ☎ 055 28 28 93; ⊗ 8am-
7.30pm) In the main hall of Stazione di Santa Maria
Novella next to the pharmacy; reservation fee €3.

Florence Promhotels (☎ 055 55 39 41, 800 86 60 22;
www.promhotels.it; ⊗ 9am-7pm Mon-Fri, 9am-1pm Sat)
Online and telephone reservations for one- to five-star
hotels in and around Florence.

Top Quark (☎ 055 33 40 41, 800 60 88 22; www
.familyhotels.com; Viale Fratelli Rossi 39r) B&Bs, apartments and hotels in Florence and Tuscany; book online or
by telephone.

Apartment Rental

Self-catering apartments can be expensive and
hard to source; see p398 for a list of spots to
look online.

Guesthouse Villino Giulia (Map pp96-7; ☎ 055
20 40 085; www.trattoriabibe.com; Via Della Bagnese 11r,
Galuzzo; s €50-70, d €60-120) Run by one of Florence's most-loved inns (p138), this 1930s
house with garden contains three beautifully
furnished apartments – unbeatable value for
money. From floor rugs to toilet-paper holder,
everything is top-notch quality and breakfast
is provided for short stays. The neighbouring road is busy but you are just 3km from
central Florence.

Palazzo Alfani (Map pp98-9; ☎ 055 29 15 74, 346 033
99 31; www.palazzoalfani.com; Via Ricasoli 49; apt for 4 people
€200-350, 6 people €350-500; ⊠ ▢) There's no reason to queue outside Galleria dell'Accademia
for guests staying in the five beautiful apartments inside this convent-turned-palace with
interior garden pierced by a medlar tree: it's
bang-slap opposite the gallery. Original prints
decorate the walls; dressing gowns, slippers
and self-pamper products add to the pleasure of the Jacuzzi showers; and father Marco
Alfani and daughter Francesca could not be
friendlier.

Camping

Campeggio Michelangelo (Map pp100-1; ☎ 055 681 19
77; www.ecvacanze.it in Italian; Viale Michelangelo 80; adult/
car & tent low season €8.90/10.70, high season €9.90/11.90;

A ROOM WITH A VIEW

Looking for the most romantic room with a view in town? Then look no further than those tucked up high on the roofed veranda atop the Renaissance palazzo on Piazza Santo Spirito (No 9), where Zeffirelli shot several scenes of *Tea with Mussolini*. Run for years as shabby, over-priced but wholly irresistible Pensione Bandini, this noble old Renaissance palazzo is now shut and awaiting a facelift. Don't miss it when it reopens.

P) The closest site to the city centre, just off Piazzale Michelangelo, south of the River Arno. Big and comparatively leafy with lovely city views, it's handy for the historic quarter, though it's a steep walk home. A backpacker with tent can pitch for €10.50 year-round. Take bus 13 from Stazione di Santa Maria Novella.

The leafy grounds of Ostello Villa Camerata (below) or Campeggio Panoramico (p156) are the other alternatives.

Hostels

Ostello Santa Monaca (Map p103; ☎ 055 26 83 38; www .ostello.it; Via Santa Monaca 6; dm €17-19; 💻) Once a convent, this large Oltrarno hostel, run by a cooperative since the 1960s, comes warmly recommended. There is a kitchen for guests' use, a laundrette, free safe deposits and two computers to surf (per hour €3). Single-sex dorms sleep four to 22 and are locked between 10am and 2pm. Curfew 2am.

Ostello Archi Rossi (Map pp98-9; ☎ 055 29 08 04; www.hostelarchirossi.com; Via Faenza 94r; dm incl breakfast & sheets €18-26; 💙 closed 2 weeks Dec; 💻) Guests' paintings and graffiti brighten up the walls at this private hostel near Stazione di Santa Maria Novella. Bright white dorms have three to 12 beds (those across the garden are quieter); there are washing machines (€3), frozen-meal dispensers (€3.50), microwaves for guests to use and free unlimited wi-fi in the five-terminal internet corner. No curfew (knock to get in after 2am).

Ostello Gallo d'Oro (Map pp98-9; ☎ 055 552 29 64; www.ostellogallodoro.com; Via Cavour 104; dm/d incl breakfast €30/75; 💻) Play happy families at this dynamic 24-bed hostel, run by bubbly young duo Florentine Silvia and Umbrian Max, who serve guests a free *aperitivo* and tablecloth

dinner (€10) each evening. Dorms max at five beds and three have a tiny balcony.

Ostello Villa Camerata (Map pp96-7; ☎ 055 60 14 51; florenceaighostel@virgilio.it; Viale Augusto Righi 2-4; dm €18, d/tr/q with bathroom €60/69/80, all incl breakfast; **P** 💻) In a converted 17th-century villa surrounded by extensive grounds a 30-minute bus ride from town, this HI-affiliated hostel is among Italy's most beautiful. Bus 17 from Stazione di Santa Maria Novella stops 400m from the hostel.

East of Stazione di Santa Maria Novella
BUDGET
Soggiorno La Pergola (Map pp100-1; ☎ 055 213 886; www.soggiornolapergola.it; Via della Pergola 23; s €45-60, d €72-103, tr €80-134) This budget place around the corner from Teatro della Pergola oozes character – that of larger-than-life host Letizia Barlozzi. A jungle of orange trees and other plastic plants greets guests in the cupboard-sized hallway and rooms (no greenery) are equally exuberant. Look for the electric buggy parked nearby.

MIDRANGE
Hotel Paris (Map pp100-1; ☎ 055 28 02 81; www .parishotel.it; Via dei Banchi 2; s €80-125, d €110-165; **P** 🍴 💻) Designed by Bernardo Buontalenti in the 15th century, this twin-set of palaces linked on the 2nd floor by a glass walkway is the place to sleep the Renaissance experience. Three-star rooms sport high ceilings, and window pelmets and bed heads are adorned with rich, embroidered drapes. The painted ceiling in the breakfast room is breathtaking.

our pick Hotel Morandi alla Crocetta (Map pp98-9; ☎ 055 234 47 47; www.hotelmorandi.it; Via Laura 50; s €80-115, d €140-180; **P** 🍴) This medieval convent-turned-hotel away from the madding crowds is a stunner. Rooms are refined, tasteful, and full of authentic period furnishings and paintings. A couple of rooms have handkerchief-sized gardens to laze in, but the *pièce de résistance* is frescoed No 29 – the room where the nuns 'attended' Mass at the chapel they weren't allowed to enter next door. Breakfast is €11 and parking is €16.

Hotel Casci (Map pp98-9; ☎ 055 21 16 86; www.hotel casci.com; Via Cavour 13; s €60-110, d €90-150, tr €120-190, q €150-230, all incl breakfast; 💙 closed 2 weeks Jan; **P** 🍴 💻) Run by a super-efficient mother-and-son team, Casci was the first hotel in Florence in 1926 to have hot-and-cold running water in its rooms. Flat-screen TVs,

FLORENCE

TIP-TOP B&BS

Bed and breakfast (B&B) is a booming business in busy old Florence where visitors are increasingly turning to the extraordinary value for money, charm and hospitality that staying in a local Florentine home offers. Unusually, the owner rarely lives in. **Associazione Bed & Breakfast Affittacamere** (AB&BA; ☎ 055 654 08 60; www.abba-firenze.it) is a great one-stop shop for B&Bs. Some favourites:

■ Alle Rampe (Map pp100-1; ☎ 055 680 01 31; www.villaallerampe.com; Piazza Ferrucci 6-7; d €60-140; 🞫 P) Step behind this mustard house across from the Arno and an olive grove staggers down the hill towards you, making this five-room B&B a lovely spot to escape the city mayhem – in the city. Virgin Mary guards the entrance, pots of flowers add a warm welcome and there's space for five cars to park on the driveway.

■ Il Salotto di Firenze (Map pp100-1; ☎ 055 21 83 47; www.ilsalottodifirenze.it; Via Roma 6r; s €70-80, d €90-130; 🞫 🖳) Nestled above Gucci, the Drawing Room of Florence is well named. Quality and stylish furnishings become incidental to the soul-stirring views from the windows of this six-room B&B overlooking the baptistry, cathedral and busy square. Every room has its own bathroom, the Giovanni Fattori room has a little terrace peeking down on Via Roma and there are plenty of books in the library to borrow.

■ Johanna & Johlea (Map pp98-9; ☎ 055 463 32 92; www.johanna.it; Via San Gallo 80; s €70-120, d €85-175, all incl breakfast; 🞫) One of the most established B&Bs in town, J&J has more than a dozen tasteful, impeccable, individually decorated rooms split between four historic residences. Those desiring total luxury can ask about its suite apartments; last-minute offers online.

■ Relais del Duomo (Map pp100-1; ☎ 055 21 01 47; www.relaisdelduomo.it in Italian; Piazza dell'Olio 2; s €50-90, d €75-130; 🞫) Location is the prime selling point of this upscale B&B, perfectly placed in a 17th-century *palazzo* on a quiet traffic-free street around the corner from the cathedral. Push open the hefty wooden door to be greeted by the lovely Maria and four elegant, pastel-coloured rooms. There is an Irish pub next door but rooms are sound proofed. Minimum stay two nights.

■ Residenza Santo Sprito (Map p103; ☎ 055 265 83 76; www.residenzasspirito.com; Piazza Santo Spirito 9; d €110-130, tr €145-170, q €180-210; 🞫) Brilliantly placed on Florence's most buzzing summertime square, this romantic trio of rooms with sky-high ceilings in Palazzo Guadagni (1505) is remarkable. The frescoed Gold Room is the first to go and the Green Room with two connecting double rooms is the family favourite.

■ In Piazza della Signoria (Map pp100-1; ☎ 055 239 95 46; www.inpiazzadellasignoria.com; Via dei Magazzini 2; s €140-210, d €200-280; 🞫) Alessandro and Sonia bought this house, a split second off Piazza delle Signoria, in 2000 and spent a year doing it up. The result: a stylish, refined *residenza d'epoca* (historical residence), with the family's portraits in the hallway, period furnishings and plenty of knick-knacks to make it feel like home.

shell-shaped corner baths as well as a feisty breakfast buffet with a bottomless cappuccino could make its twin set of stars become three soon. Free internet station and wi-fi are also available.

TOP END
Hotel Monna Lisa (Map pp100-1; ☎ 055 247 97 51; www.monnalisa.it; Borgo Pinti 27; s €116-158, d €193-308, tr €262-460, q €286-520, all incl breakfast; P 🞫) Monna Lisa is a Renaissance palazzo packed with family heirlooms. Nonchalantly adorning the old-

world palace are works by Giovanni Dupré, the 19th-century sculptor, whose descendents own the hotel. Some rooms overlook the bijou flower-bedecked garden where guests sit for breakfast in summer. Hotel parking costs €15.

Around Piazza di Santa Maria Novella
BUDGET & MIDRANGE
Hotel Pensione Ferretti (Map pp100-1 ☎ 055 238 13 28; www.pensioneferretti.it; Via delle Belle Donne 17; s €40-75, with bathroom €50-85, d €50-85, with bathroom €60-105,

extra bed €30, all incl breakfast; 💻) Roberto and Sandra will make you feel right at home in their no-frills, unpretentious hotel with 16 rooms. Those of the 3rd floor have been refurbished, making them the most white and sparkly. No air-con but ceiling fans. Free internet point.

Hotel Abaco (Map pp100-1; ☎ 055 238 19 19; www .abaco-hotel.it; Via dei Banchi 1; d €45-75, tr €65-110, q €80-135; 🔀 💻) The seven rooms in this simple establishment are each named after a Renaissance artist and furnished in high-baroque style with canopy beds; three have private bathrooms. Pay €5 extra a night to get the aircon switched on – or settle the bill in cash and get air-con and breakfast (€5) for free.

Tourist House (Map pp100-1; ☎ 055 26 86 75; www .touristhouse.com; Via delle Scala 1; s €50, d €60-85, tr €100-120, q e €100-140, all incl breakfast; 🔀) The nine basic rooms with air-con to cool things down on steamy summer days may not set hearts racing, but they represent good value for money, and breakfast on the plant-bedecked terrace between rooftops is a welcome breath of fresh air.

ourpick Hotel Scoti (Map pp100-1; ☎ 055 29 21 28; www.hotelscoti.com; Via de' Tornabuoni 7; s €50-75, d €75-115, tr €100-140, q €130-165) Wedged between Dior, Prada and McQueen, this *pensione* dating to 1875 is a splendid mix of old-fashioned charm and great value for money. Run with smiling aplomb by Australian Doreen and Italian Carmello, the hotel is enthroned in a 16th-century palazzo on Florence's smartest shopping strip. Rooms have antique pieces and contemporary private bathrooms, but the star of the show is the floor-to-ceiling frescoed living room (1780).

Hotel Consiglia (Map p103; ☎ 055 21 41 72; www .hotelconsigli.com; Lungarno Amerigo Vespucci 50; d €100-150, tr €120-170, all incl breakfast; 🅿 🔀) A short walk from town, this river-side Renaissance palace is perfect for peace-seeking guests happy to cycle to dinner. It is next door to the road-blocked US embassy, meaning motorised vehicles are kept well away ,and its flowery terrace with deck chairs is a star gazer's dream. Parking is €15.

TOP END

Grand Hotel Minerva (Map pp100-1; ☎ 055 272 30; www .grandhotelminerva.com; Piazza di Santa Maria Novella 16; d €155-440; 🅿 🔀 💻 🏊) Stand-out features of this four-star hotel with cream façade and oyster shutters include a winter garden (you could be several kilometres from the obelisk-

studded square outside) and – unusually for this city – a rooftop swimming pool. Parking is €28.

JK Place (Map pp100-1; ☎ 055 264 51 81; www.jkplace .com; Piazza di Santa Maria Novella 7; d €290-330, penthouse €610-750, all incl breakfast; 🅿 🔀 💻) With an interior designed by one of Florence's top architects, Michele Bonan, and a James-Bond penthouse with views guaranteed to make you swoon, this boutique hotel means business. Design-driven with a mix of old and new – retro 1950s lamps, Charles X fireplace and breakfast in a glass-topped courtyard – it is all very *alla moda*.

Between the Duomo & the Arno
BUDGET

Hotel Dalí (Map pp100-1; ☎ 055 234 07 06; www .hoteldali.com; Via dell'Oriuolo 17; s/d €40/65, d with bathroom €80; 🕒 closed three weeks Jan; 🅿) This spruce, simple hotel on Clock Rd is run with unrelenting energy and smiles by busy parents-of-three Marco and Samanta. Rooms overlooking the leafy inner courtyard are serene; those facing the street can be noisy. Doubles are big and easily sleep four or five (extra bed €25) and there's free parking for motoring guests – a concept as rare as icebergs in Florence. Low season rates are 10% to 15% less.

Hotel San Giovanni (Map pp100-1; ☎ 055 28 83 85; www.hotelsangiovanni.com; Via de' Cerretani 2; s €40-58, d €50-95, tr €68-98, q €80-108; 🔀) Buzz to enter and ride the rattly old cage lift (forget jumbo-sized suitcases) up to this former bishop's private residence – a 14th-century palazzo – where fresco traces still adorn room No 3. Lofty ceilings top off the other eight light and spacious rooms, just two of which have a private bathroom and four of which have air-con: Nos 6, 7 and 8 face the cathedral. Breakfast is €5.

ourpick Hotel Cestelli (Map pp100-1; ☎ 055 21 42 13; www.hotelcestelli.com; Borgo SS Apostoli 25; s €45-55, d €60-75, d with bathroom €80-110, extra bed €15-25; 🕒 closed 2 weeks Jan, 3 weeks Aug) The scent of joss sticks and flicker of night lights add a soothing Zen air to this eight-room hotel, stylish home of Florentine photographer Alessio and Japanese massage therapist Asumi. Each room is different and the couple brim with dependable dining recommendations.

Hotel Orchidea (Map pp100-1; ☎ 055 248 03 46; www .hotelorchideaflorence.it; Borgo degli Albizi 11; s €35-55, d €50-75, tr €75-100, q €80-125) This old-fashioned *pensione* in the mansion where the Donati (p109) family roosted in the 13th-century

FLORENCE

(Dante's Gemma was allegedly born in the tower) is charm itself. Its seven rooms with sink and shared bathroom are simple; Nos 5, 6 and 7 have huge windows overlooking a gorgeous garden while No 4 spills out onto a terrace. Have a cuppa and let Miranda answer all your questions. No credit cards.

MIDRANGE

Hotel Perseo (Map pp100-1; ☎ 055 21 25 04; www.hotel perseo.it; Via dei Cerretani 1; s €85-99, d €110-140, tr €135-170, q €160-200; 🌂 🖵) Don't be deceived by the grubby façade. Once out of the cage lift in this three-star hotel overhauled in 2006, décor is all sweetness, light and modern – flat-screen TVs, walk-in showers and mellow natural hues. Doubles cleverly turn into bunk-bed quads, making it a great family choice.

Hotel Hermitage (Map pp100-1; ☎ 055 28 72 16; www.hermitagehotel.com; Vicolo Marzio 1; d €160-220; 🌂) With a flowery rooftop terrace, reception and breakfast room on the 5th and 6th floors of a river-side building near the Uffizi, the Ponte Vecchio view is hard to beat. But don't expect the same panorama from your room; they're lower down. Observe how high the Arno rose in 1966 before getting in the lift.

TOP END

Borghese Palace Art Hotel (Map pp100-1; ☎ 055 28 43 63; www.borghesepalace.it; Via Ghibellina 174r; s/d €190/350; 🅿 🌂) A key address for art lovers, this stylish ode to design with glass-topped courtyard and sculptures looming up large in reception showcases original works of art from the 18th century to the present day. Décor verges on the theatrical and dinner by candlelight on the terrace is an impressionable affair.

ourpick Continentale (Map pp100-1; ☎ 055 2 72 62; continentale@lungarnohotels.com; Vicolo dell'Oro 6r; d incl breakfast €300-380; 🅿 🌂) Same designer, funkier design is the thrust of this next-door neighbour, an ugly concrete block opposite. But dip inside and be bowled over by a glamorous (very pink) celebration of Italian creativity and cinema in the 1950s. Rooms are hi-tech and the glass lift with cushioned sofa is cutting edge indeed.

Gallery Hotel Art (Map pp100-1; ☎ 055 2 72 63; www .lungarnohotels.com; Vicolo dell'Oro 5; d €350-450, ste €640-1110, all incl breakfast; 🅿 🌂 🖵) Owned by the Ferragamo fashion house and designed by Florence architect Michel Bonan, this modish gallery hotel is true 21st century. Peace reigns in its 74 minimalist, edgy and soft-

hued rooms – a night in its rooftop penthouse is unforgettable. Contemporary art dresses public areas, including its hip Japanese-style Fusion Bar (p143).

Oltrarno
BUDGET & MIDRANGE

Althea (Map p103; ☎ 055 233 53 41; www.florencealthea .it; Via delle Caldaie 25; s €40-60, d €60-90, tr €80-105, all incl breakfast; 🖵) The décor might be 1970s flower power with plenty of chintz, but the good value for money provided by these seven rooms is outstanding. Each is spotlessly clean, has its own bathroom, fridge, and computer terminal with Skype and free internet access.

Hotel La Scaletta (Map pp100-1; ☎ 055 28 30 28; www.hotellascaletta.it; Via de' Guicciardini 13; s €55-100, d €65-140, tr €85-160, q €100-180, all incl breakfast; 🌂 🖵) An austere air wafts through this maze of a hotel, hidden in a 15th-century palazzo. But rooms are spacious, and breakfast and *aperitivi* taken on the roof terrace overlooking Boboli is an inspiring experience; rooms Nos 20, 21 and 22 peep down on the gardens.

Hotel Silla (Map pp100-1; ☎ 055 234 28 88; www .hotelsilla.it; Via dei Renai 5; s €90-125, d €100-170, tr €140-220, all incl breakfast; 🅿 🌂) Briefly Allied headquarters in 1944 and a *pensione* since 1964, Silla sits in a palace well away from the crowds in one of the leafiest parts of Florence. Once the leaves fall in autumn, several rooms and the breakfast terrace enjoy beguiling views across the Arno; otherwise, the look out is green. Parking is €16.

TOP END

ourpick Palazzo Magnani Feroni (Map p103; ☎ 055 239 95 44; www.florencepalace.com; Borgo San Frediano 5; ste incl breakfast €335-800; 🅿 🌂 🖵) This extraordinary old palace is the stuff of dreams. Languishing across four floors with the family's private residence wedged in between, the 12 suites are vast and ooze elegance with authentic period furnishings, rich fabrics, Bulgari products in the bathroom and a choice of handmade Florentine soaps. The 360-degree city view from the rooftop is unforgettable. Parking costs €40 to €47.

EATING

Dining is more expensive here than elsewhere in Tuscany. Count on paying a minimum of €25 for a meal (three courses as well as house wine). Places listed in midrange command between €25 and €50 for a full meal, while

FAST-FOOD FLORENCE

When Florentines fancy a fast munch-on-the-move rather than a slow full lunch, they flit by a *trippaio* – a cart of wheels or mobile stand – for a juicy tripe burger. Think cow's stomach chopped up, boiled, sliced, bung in a bun and doused in hot chilli sauce. Yum!

Much loved by Slow Food (p21) as a bastion of good old-fashioned Florentine tradition, *trippaio* are increasingly far and few between these days. One faithful still going strong is **Tripperia Pier Paolo e Sergio** (Map pp100-1; Via de' Macci; 8.30am-7pm Mon-Sat Sep-May, 8.30am-3pm Mon-Sat Jun & Jul), a tripe cart parked in front of one of the city's busiest trattoria where old men sit propped up on bar stools in the street reading newspapers between tripe bites. Pay €2.30 for tripe *panini* (sandwich) doused in *salsa verde* (pea-green sauce of smashed parsley, garlic, capers and anchovies) or *salsa piccante* (chilli sauce), and not a lot more for a bowl of *lampredotto* (cow's fourth stomach chopped 'n simmered for hours 'n hours).

Or there's **Nerbone** (Map pp98-9; ☎ 055 21 99 49; Mercato Centrale, Piazza del Mercato Centrale; primi/secondi €3.50/6; 7am-2pm Mon-Sat), a market stall in business since 1872, where crowds queue for lunchtime platters of *trippa alla fiorentina* (tripe and tomato stew), tripe *panini* and – should tripe simply be too offal (!) for you to stomach – *panini con bollito*, a boiled beef bun infamously dipped in the cooking pot immediately before serving (no, it's not soggy, incredibly). Dine standing up or around a handful of tables. Complete the experience with a stroll around the market's many tripe stalls where the frilly offal, piled high, costs €6 per kg.

the bill in top-end places will be at least €50 a head.

For a look at traditional Florentine and Tuscan dishes to expect, see p66.

East of Stazione di Santa Maria Novella

The streets around the Mercato Centrale (p143) predictably cook up several tasty cheap options. The eastern side of Piazza del Mercato Centrale is lined with restaurant terraces, and tripe-hot Nerbone (above) is inside the market.

BUDGET & MIDRANGE

La Mescita (Map pp98-9; ☎ 347 795 16 04; Via degli Alfani 70r; meals €12; 10am-3pm Mon-Sat) No concessions are made to the swarms of *David*-bound tourists milling past this historic pearl with 16th-century wooden ceiling, bottle-lined walls and five tables. In business since 1927, this *fiaschetteria* (traditional tuscan wine bar) cooks tripe Monday, *lampredotto* (a type of tripe) Tuesday, *porchetta* (roast pork) Wednesday, *peposo* (a fiery spicy Tuscan beef stew) Thursday, *baccalà* (salted cod) Friday and whatever the chef fancies (*i'cche c'e c'e*) Saturday. *Panini* (€1.60 to €3) and pasta (€4) are daily staples.

Il Vegetariano (Map pp98-9; ☎ 055 47 50 30; Via delle Ruote 30r; meals €15; lunch & dinner Tue-Fri, dinner Sat & Sun Sep-Jul) This self-service veggie restaurant cooks up a great selection of Tuscan vegetable dishes, build-your-own salads and mains eaten around shared wooden tables. There's always a vegan option and the chalked-up menu changes daily.

our pick **Trattoria Mario** (Map pp98-9; ☎ 055 21 85 50; www.trattoriamario.com; Via Rosina 2; meals €20; noon-3.30pm Mon-Sat, closed 3 weeks Aug) It is in every guidebook but has not lost its soul or lure with locals: a 100% family affair opened by Mario's parents in 1953 and continued by his two sons and their children today, Trattoria Mario dishes up unforgettable dining. Tell Fabio you want a table and join the gaggle waiting outside for him to yell their name. Once in, lunch elbow-to-elbow on market produce expertly cooked by older brother Romeo. Monday and Thursday are tripe days, Friday fish day and the *bistecca* (€30 per kg) is Florence's best. Ingeniously, Mario's requires no forward planning: order one course, eat it and order the next. No credit cards.

Da Sergio (Map pp98-9; ☎ 055 28 19 41; Piazza San Lorenzo 8r; meals €20; lunch Mon-Sat Sep-Jul) Push your way into this Slow Food–recommended bolthole hidden behind market stalls since 1915 and be greeted by a collection of old Florentine men dining solo – the ultimate sign of a real trattoria. The choice on Sergio's handwritten menu is simple: four *primi*, 10-odd *secondi* and a solitary *dolci* (*cantuccini* dunked in *Vin Santo*).

GELATERIE

Carabè (Map pp98-9; ☎ 055 28 94 76; www.gelatocarabe .com; Via Ricasoli 60r) Run with a sizzling passion

FLORENCE

by Antonio and Loredana, whose family has been in the ice-cream making business for generations, this wholly Sicilian *gelateria* is the hot spot for traditional Sicilian *gelato*, *granita* (sorbet) and brioche (a Sicilian ice-cream sandwich).

Around Piazza di Santa Maria Novella
BUDGET & MIDRANGE

Trattoria Marione (Map pp100-1; ☎ 055 21 47 56; Via della Spada 27r; meals €20; ☾ lunch & dinner) Red-and-white checked tablecloths, legs of ham strung from the ceiling, lace curtains and a menu built solely from *cucina tipica casalinga fiorentina* (typical home-made Florentine cuisine) ensures the authentic trattoria experience seven days a week. Its price moreover will see you coming back for seconds.

Il Latini (Map pp100-1; ☎ 055 21 09 16; www.il latini.com; Via dei Palchetti 6r; meals €35; ☾ lunch & dinner Tue-Sun) Request a menu (as a tourist, you might not be offered one) at this Florentine favourite or put yourself in the hands of the exuberant waiters and feast on melt-in-your-mouth crostini, Tuscan soups and a huge hunk of finely roasted meat – rabbit, lamb or veal with white beans. The wine and water flows and if you're lucky you might get a complimentary plate of *cantuccini* and *Vin Santo* with the bill.

Also recommended:

Trattoria dei 13 Gobbi (Map p103; ☎ 055 21 32 04; Via del Porcellana 9r; meals €25-30; ☾ lunch & dinner Tue-Sun) Low-ceilinged and snug with plant-filled rear courtyard.

Trattoria Sostanza (Map p103; ☎ 055 21 26 91; Via del Porcellana 25r; meals €25-30; ☾ lunch & dinner

Mon-Fri) An authentic Tuscan eatery that simmers a mean minestrone.

TOP END

Osteria dei Centopoveri (Map p103; ☎ 055 21 88 46; Via del Palazzuolo 31r; meals €45; ☾ lunch & dinner) The 'hostel of the hundred poor people' is far from being a soup kitchen. It's a top-quality dining option serving creative variations on traditional Tuscan cuisine in a down-to-earth setting.

Trattoria Garga (Map pp100-1; ☎ 055 239 88 98; Via del Moro 48r; meals €55; ☾ 7.30-11pm Tue-Sun) With more than 25 successful years in business, Garga offers imaginative, creative fare – think veal kidneys or a veal escalope with avocado, asparagus and mustard, artichokes or simple lemon and butter – in a wildly colourful interior.

Between the Duomo & the Arno
The city's historic cafés (p145) likewise offer some fine, if wholly touristic, dining.

BUDGET
Several pizzerie are tucked away in the streets between the Duomo and the Arno, many touting a cent-saving takeaway option – anything from a full round disc to a simple slice (around €2).

ourpick I Fratellini (Map pp100-1; ☎ 055 239 60 96; Via dei Cimatori 38r; panini €2.10-2.60; ☾ 8am-8pm, closed Sat & Sun Jul & Aug, 2 weeks Mar & Aug) A legend in its own time and in business since 1875, this hole in the wall whips out imaginative *panini* (fennel sausage with goat cheese, spicy wild boar etc), freshly filled as you order, like you've

---

A BREATH OF FRESH AIR

When the city heat smothers, do what Florentines do – flee to Fiesole (p154) or one of these twin set venues:

■ **La Capponcina** (Map pp96-7; ☎ 055 69 70 37; www.capponcina.com; Via San Romano 17r, Settignano; meals €30-35; ☾ lunch & dinner Tue-Sun) This kitchen is renowned for its *tagliata di manzo*, beef fillets sliced and served on a bed of rocket – in a garden several degrees cooler than central Florence. Take bus 10 (bus 67 after 9pm) from Stazione di Santa Maria Novella to Piazza San Tommaseo, from where the bus terminates.

■ **Trattoria Bibe** (Map pp96-7; ☎ 055 20 40 085; www.trattoriabibe.com; Via Della Bagnese 11r, Galuzzo; meals €25-35; ☾ lunch & dinner Sat & Sun, dinner Mon, Tue, Thu & Fri Dec-Jan & Mar-Oct) Pigeon, frogs legs, hare and guineafowl are among the many meats roasted (count on at least 40 minutes) at this wonderful old-fashioned inn – so legendary Italian poet Eugenio Montale wrote a poem about Grandfather 'Bibe' in 1927. Dine elegantly inside or amid flowers outside. Find it 3km south of Florence, a stone's throw from the Certosa di Firenze; take bus 46.

never seen it before. Wash it down with a shot, glass or beaker of wine and Bob's your uncle – the perfect pavement lunch. Etiquette requires you leave your empty on a wooden shelf outside.

Leonardo (Map pp100–1; ☎ 055 28 44 46; Via de' Pecori 35r; meals €11; ☼ Sun–Fri) Regional dishes – *bolito misto, trippa alla Fiorentina* and *osso buco* – are cooked up alongside burgers at this self-service restaurant, a spot hard to beat if want to eat primarily to pinch pennies. Readers give it mixed reports.

Trattoria Bordino (Map pp100–1; ☎ 055 21 30 48; Via Stracciatella 9r; meals €20; ☼ lunch & dinner Mon–Sat) Get here fast to score a table at this astonishingly simple bistro, hidden on a dead-end street, seconds from the Ponte Vecchio crowds. Fare is wholly traditional Tuscan and the €6 lunch deal is a steal.

MIDRANGE

our pick La Canova di Gustavino (Map pp100–1; ☎ 055 239 98 06; Via della Condotta 29r; meals €25; ☼ noon–midnight) The bread comes in a bucket and the oil and vinegar in a wooden box at this laidback *osteria* (restaurant focussing on wine) arm of Gustavino (below) where cultured locals flock to lunch. Its cheese and cold meat platters are perfect wine companions and it hosts daily tastings. And yes, that misty blue glass box *is* the toilet.

Trattoria Coco Lezzone (Map pp100–1; ☎ 055 28 71 78; Via Parioncino 26r; meals €25; ☼ Mon–Sat) Another cheerful, homey spot with white tiled interior and photographs of famous customers. No credit cards, bizarrely no coffee, just a handwritten menu and very good food at this kitchen-style trattoria where unnecessary concessions simply don't need to be made. *Ribollita* (included in the excellent-value 'Florence nostalgia' menu, €25 including 25cL of wine and mineral water) is the house speciality and Friday is fresh-fish day.

Buca dell'Orafo (Map pp100–1; ☎ 055 21 36 19; Volta dei Girolami 28r; meals €30; ☼ Tue–Sat) There's no escaping tourists at this quaint pocket-sized eating spot whose simple *cucina fiorentina* was, for many years, a favourite haunt for Florentines. Find it charmingly tucked beneath the arches a stone's throw from the Uffizi.

TOP END

Gustavino (Map pp100–1; ☎ 055 239 98 06; Via della Condotta 37r; meals €50; ☼ lunch & dinner Fri–Sun, dinner Mon–Thu) Ricotta-stuffed artichoke cloaked in puff pastry and sprinkled with honeyed pine nuts or lard smothered in hot chestnuts and caramelised in grappa are Italian staples given an imaginative make-over at this inventive glass-, stone- and steel-dining space. Gustavino is among the city's most stylish.

Angels (Map pp100–1; ☎ 055 239 87 62; www .ristoranteangels.it; Via del Proconsolo 29–31r; meals €50; ☼ noon–2am) The city's best-dressed beauties clink champagne flutes beneath vaulted frescoes at this restaurant and American bar, a stylish minimalist dining space, drinking and DJ space with a popular Sunday brunch (p143). Food is unexpectedly Tuscan with a dash of Mediterranean.

our pick Alle Murate (Map pp100–1; ☎ 055 24 06 18; www.artenotai.org; Via del Proconsolo 16r; meals €65; ☼ dinner Tue–Sat) Feast on extraordinary art (the earliest known portraits of Dante and Boccaccio included) and raved-about contemporary Tuscan cuisine with a feisty southern Italian kick at this unique restaurant nestled beneath 14th-century frescoes. Décor is strictly modern, chefs beaver away behind glass and remnants of Roman Florence lurk in the cellar. Wine – an insatiable passion of charismatic owner Umberto Montana (p68), who says his mother 'never made one acceptable dish', hence his own passion for food – is the other big reason you should dine here.

GELATERIE

Festival del Gelato (Map pp100–1; ☎ 055 29 43 86; Via del Corso 75r) Just off Piazza della Repubblica and with more than 70 flavours on offer, this ice-cream parlour will satisfy the most demanding of children and tastes.

Perchè No? (Map pp100–1; ☎ 055 239 89 69; www .perche.firenze.it; Via dei Tavolini 19r; ☼ noon–7.30pm Wed–Sun) In business since 1939, this one-stop shop for top-notch ice in cones or tubs recommends marrying almond ice-cream with fig sorbet and ginger ice-cream with green-tea sorbet.

Santa Croce & East of the Centre
BUDGET

The 18 different types of imaginatively stuffed *panini* (€2.50 to €4.50) served to munch on the move at Antico Noè (see next section, p140) make for a cheap lunch.

our pick The Oil Shoppe (Map pp100–1; ☎ 055 200 10 92; www.oleum.it; Via Sant' Egidio 22r) Stand in line at this student favourite, an olive-oil and sandwich shop, which builds the best meal-sized sandwiches in town. Choose your fillings or let chef Alberto Scorzon take the lead with a 10-filling wonder. Queue at the back of the shop for hot subs; at the front for cold.

Kosher Market (Map pp100-1; ☎ 055 24 05 08; www .koshermarket.it; Via dei Pilastri 7r; ☿ 8.30am-1pm & 3-8pm Sun-Thu) Kosher sandwiches to take away.

Caffé Italiano Sud (Map pp100-1; ☎ 055 28 93 68; Via della Vigna Vecchia; meals €20; ☿ 12.30pm-1am Tue-Sun) This latest Umberto Montano project – an ode to southern Italy – promises great things. Loads of home-made pasta, including lasagne baked in a wood-burning oven, and other typical dishes from the south can be eaten in or taken away (pay a deposit for the terracotta dish). Wash it down with one of nine house wines displayed in 58L straw-cushioned glass flasks.

Ruth's (Map pp100-1; ☎ 055 248 08 88; www .kosheruth.com; Via Luigi Carlo Farini 2a; meals €15-25; ☿ lunch & dinner Sun-Thu, lunch Fri, dinner Sat) Dine at Ruth's for tasty dishes, at once kosher and vegetarian, served in the shade of the synagogue: think couscous, humus, felafel, filo pie, potato salad, tabouleh, moussaka and fish of the day.

MIDRANGE

Antico Noè (Map pp100-1; ☎ 055 234 08 38; Volta di San Piero 6r; meals €30; ☿ noon-midnight Mon-Sat) Don't be put off by the dank, rough-and-ready alley in which this legendary place (an old butcher's shop with white marble-clad walls and wrought-iron meat hooks) is found. The drunks loitering outside are generally harmless and the down-to-the-earth Tuscan fodder in the company of slow jazz and blues is a real joy.

Osteria de' Benci (Map pp100-1; ☎ 055 234 49 23; Via de' Benci 13r; meals €35; ☿ 8am-midnight Mon-Sat) Deep burgundy walls, a vaulted brick ceiling and a menu that makes no bones about what it cooks contribute to the relaxed, unpretentious air of this friendly place. Old favourites like honest slabs of *carbonata di chianina* (grilled Tuscan steak) – even more tender and succulent than the ubiquitous *bistecca alla fiorentina* – are (as the English-language menu so beautifully puts it) '... SERVED BLOODY!'

ourpick **Osteria del Caffé Italiano** (Map pp100-1; ☎ 055 28 93 68; www.caffeitaliano.it; Via Isola delle Stinche 11-13r; meals €35, menu €50; ☿ 12.30pm-1am Tue-Sun) *Osteria*, white-table cloth restaurant, wine cellar and pizzeria: this address – another

Umberto Montano venture (p68) listed in every Florentine's mobile phone – caters to all tastes. Be it tagliatelle with chickpeas and Parma ham, and skewered meat that turn heads or a *bistecca* (per kg €50) with beans, greens and roast spuds, discerning palates will be thrilled. A choice of three pizzas (€8) woo simplicity lovers in the **pizzeria** (☿ dinner Tue-Sun), which is an artfully simple dining space. It sticks to a strict 'no coffee, no credit cards' policy.

TOP END

La Pentola dell'Oro (Map pp100-1; ☎ 055 24 18 08; Via di Mezzo 24r; meals around €35; ☿ lunch & dinner Mon-Sat) Long a jealously guarded secret among Florentine gourmands, Florence's old-style Golden Pot doesn't need to advertise. Word of mouth draws the culinary curious here to sample Renaissance dishes reinvented for modern tastes by culinary artist Giuseppe Alessi. Dine at sub-street level or at the street-level offshoot with marble-topped tables, wooden benches and 25 place settings.

ourpick **Ora d'Aria** (Map pp100-1; ☎ 055 200 16 99; www.oradariaristorante.com; Via Ghibellina 3Cr; meals from €55; ☿ dinner Mon-Sat) Named after that precious hour in the day when inmates cooped up in the city prison opposite (shut in the 1980s) were let outside to exercise, this stylish gallery restaurant is different. Swing through the glass and steel door, past the empty dove cage and indulge in a *tradizione* or *creatività* feast in the company of contemporary art. Traditional or creative, everything oozes imagination. How about pigeon-stuffed tortelli with foie gras and a pecorino cream or warm hen and spider-crab salad with artichoke puree and vanilla-scented oil followed by baked pigeon breast in a white-corn crust with coffee and pepper sauce?

GELATERIE

Vestri (Map pp100-1; Borgo degli Albizi 11r; ☿ 7.30am-9pm Tue-Sat, 9.30am-9pm Sun) Chocolate is the flavour to be had at this sweet chocolate maker, which sells ice-cream too. Should hot chocolate be your heart's desire, top off what has to be the thickest, creamiest, most chocolately hot chocolate in Florence with a decadent dash of ginger, chilli or cream.

Gelateria Vivoli (Map pp100-1; Via Isola delle Stinche 7; ☿ 9am-1am Tue-Sat) It only has tubs (€1.60 to €9) but this pocket-sized ice-cream shop and

FABIO PICCHI

Memorable dining is guaranteed at this trio of eating spaces near the Mercato Sant'Ambrogio (food market; Map pp100–1), each dramatically different and run with a striking dose of panache by one of Tuscany's best-known chefs, Fabio Picchi. For a look at his culinary philosophy, see p69.

■ Trattoria Cibrèo (Via dei Macci 122r; meals €30; ☽ 12.50am-2.30pm & 6.50-11.15pm Tue-Sat Sep-Jul) Dine here and you'll instantly understand why a queue gathers outside each evening before it opens. Once in, revel in old-fashioned Tuscan cuisine: perhaps ricotta and potato flan with a rich meat sauce, puddle of olive oil and grated parmesan (divine!) or a simple plate of polenta, followed by home-made sausages, beans in a spicy tomato sauce and braised celery. Arrive before 7pm to snag one of the eight tables and bring cash – no advance reservations, no credit cards, no coffee and no pasta (to learn why, see p69).

■ Ristorante Cibrèo (☎ 055 234 11 00; Via dei Macci 118; meals €80; ☽ 12.50am-2.30pm & 7-11.15pm Tue-Sat Sep-Jul) Incredulously, many of the dishes on the menu at this justifiably famous Florentine restaurant are identical to those served at the trattoria next door – but cost loads more. Not that the extremely well-dressed punters who flock to the formal arm of the Picchi empire seem to care: this extremely elegant, stylish and upmarket restaurant is always full, rendering advance reservations essential.

■ Teatro del Sale (☎ 055 200 14 92; www.teatrodelsale.com; Via dei Macci 111r; breakfast/lunch/dinner €5/15/25; ☽ 9-11am, 12.30-2.30pm & 7.30-11pm Tue-Sat Sep-Jul) Extraordinary value for money and fabulous entertainment, this old Florentine theatre steals the show. Join the club (annual membership fee €5) and make yourself at home in a leather armchair between bookshelves in the cosy wood-panelled library or in a director's chair around fold-up tables in the airy theatre space. Serve yourself water and wine, then wait for the chef to yell out what's cooking through the glass hatch – a help-yourself feast of antipasti, a *primo, secondo, dolci* and coffee. Lunch is a laid-back affair, while dinner is followed by a performance (advance reservations required): clear away your table, line up your chair, and sit back for an evening of drama, music or comedy arranged by artistic director Maria Cassi (p64), famous Florentine actress and wife of Fabio Picchi.

café is much-loved nonetheless by Florentine families out on a Sunday afternoon *passegiata* (evening stroll). Notable flavours: chocolate with cinnamon, orange or pistachio.

Oltrarno

To taste a different side of Florence, cross the river and make a beeline for busy Piazza Santo Spirito, awash with outdoor terraces to eat and drink during the warmer months; Pop Café (p143) is perfect for a light lunch with students. The neighbouring quarter of San Frediano hides a couple of gems too.

BUDGET

Borgo Antico (Map p103; ☎ 055 21 04 37; Piazza Santo Spirito 6r; pizza €7-10, meals €20-30; ☽ lunch & dinner) Prince to pauper, local and tourist is indiscriminately welcomed with a grin (and complimentary glass of sparkling wine when queues form) at this packed-to-the-rafters eatery. A vege-stuffed calzone is a steal at €7, salads are jumbo and the pricier chef's specials

offer good value. Summer seating on the lively square outside.

our pick Napoleone (Map p103; ☎ 055 28 10 15; www.trattorianapoleone.it; Piazza del Carmine 24; pizza €7-12, meals €30; ☽ 7pm-12.30am) Hip Florentines are just mad about this pizzeria, despite an oh-so-cool staff that screams attitude and an outside terrace plump in a parking lot. That said, Napoleone cooks up a laid-back but super-sleek vibe – and its pizzas are excellent. Pre-empt the experience with an *aperitivo* at La Dolce Vita (p143), on the other side of the car park.

Trattoria Casalinga (Map p103; ☎ 055 21 86 24; Via de' Michelozzi 9r; meals €15; ☽ Mon-Sat) Family run and loved locally, punters hungry for a filling meal at a bargain-basement price can't go wrong at this unpretentious spot. Look for the red-and-white telephone sign flanked by a line-up of *motorini* (scooters) outside.

Trattoria da Ginone (Map p103; ☎ 055 21 87 58; Via de' Serragli 35r; meals €20; ☽ Mon-Sat) Established by Big Gino after WWII and run by his son today, this trattoria dating to 1949 serves wholesome food like hare, wild boar, a well-marketed choice of vegetarian dishes and juicy fruit tarts. Opt for the set €9 or €13.50 menus, or go à la carte.

Al Tranvai (Map p103; ☎ 055 22 51 97; Piazza Torquato Tasso 14r; meals €20; ☒ Mon-Fri) The menu could not be simpler at this rustic Tuscan eatery, known as The Tram and designed as such, where old men arrive at noon to bag their regular lunch spot. Sit nudged up with the locals, slurp house wine (€4 per 500mL) and take your pick from the day's dishes chalked on the board. Since it's so deservedly popular, reserve ahead of time your bench space.

Vico del Carmine (Map p103; ☎ 055 233 68 62; http://vicodelcarmine.fol.it; Via Pisana 40r; meals €20-30; ☒ lunch & dinner Tue-Sun) 'Vico' means alley – the inspiration behind the interior design of Carmine's Napolitan pizzeria in trendy San Frediano. Much loved, it is Florence's best address for pizza. *Pesce* (fish) is the other speciality.

All' Antico Ristoro di' Cambi (Map p103; ☎ 055 21 71 34; www.anticoristorodicambi.it; Via Sant'Onofrio 1r; meals €22; ☒ lunch & dinner Mon-Sat) Very much a family affair strung with hanging hams, cobs of corn and woven garlic garlands, Di Cambi (b 1950 in a former 16th-century convent) is the love child of Silvano and Bruno; their children run it today. The menu changes daily but feisty old-timers, including several tripe variations, are always bubbling away on the stove.

Trattoria Angiolino (Map p103 ☎ 055 239 89 76; Via Santo Spirito 36r; meals €24; ☒ lunch & dinner Mon-Sun) The open-all-hours policy at this meat-driven trattoria makes it a great bet on Sunday, especially in August when the searing heat sees many kitchens shut. If you've never seen a Real McCoy *bistecca alla Fiorentina* in the flesh before, come here.

Le Barrique (Map p103; ☎ 055 22 41 92; Via del Leone 40r; meals €25; ☒ dinner Tue-Sun) Hidden deep in the San Frediano area, this charming little spot with a dark-wood interior is much loved locally. Originally an *enoteca* (wine bar), Le Barrique's wine list is superb and its repertoire now embraces excellent food, too: under no circumstances miss the gorgonzola and pear-in-wine tart.

MIDRANGE

Osteria del Cinghiale Bianco (Map pp100-1; ☎ 055 21 57 06; www.cinghialebianco.it; Borgo San Jacopo 43r; meals €30; ☒ lunch & dinner Sat & Sun, dinner Mon, Tue, Thu & Fri)

The White Boar opens for dinner at 6.30pm, making it a popular choice with kid-laden families keen to eat early. Pappadelle in boar sauce or boar with polenta are among the meaty specialities.

Canapone (Map p103; ☎ 055 38 17 29; www.canapone.org; Via Mazzetta 5a) – A pea-green door and flower pots mark the entrance to this secretive Santo Spirito address, where diners definitely need to be in the know and a member (€5). Love child of disillusioned software designer Antonella, her creation is a mellow alternative dining room with soothing pink walls, art by local students and a fresh fusion cuisine.

Rifrullo (Map pp100-1; ☎ 055 234 26 21; Via San Niccolò 55r; meals €30; ☒ 7am-1am) East along the Arno in trendy San Niccolò sits this Florence institution – hybrid restaurant, café and lounge bar in a series of modern stylishly furnished rooms. Its Wednesday evening tasting dinners (€28) are particularly tasty, as is its patio seating beneath the beautiful cypress trees.

Olio & Convivium (Map pp100-1; ☎ 055 265 81 98; Via di Santo Spirito 4; meals €35; ☒ l0am-3pm Mon, 10am-3pm & 5.30-10.30pm Tue-Sat) A key address on any gastronomy agenda: not only will tastebuds drool over the legs of hams, conserved truffles and other delectable delicatessen products sold in its shop; its €15 lunchtime menu – a cold mixed platter, wine, water and dessert – is the best lunch deal in town. Come dusk, try veal-stuffed fresh artichokes or *taglierini* (narrower type of tagliatelle) with tiger prawns and black cabbage.

Ristorante Beccofino (Map p103; ☎ 055 29 00 76; www.beccofino.com; Piazza degli Scarlatti 1r; meals €35; ☒ Tue-Sun) Innovative restaurant and stylish *enoteca* with more than 50 wines to taste by the glass, Beccofino is decidedly nouvelle chic. Francesco Berardinelli (www.francescoberardinelli.com) is the hot name in the kitchen.

TOP END

Trattoria Cammillo (Map pp100-1; ☎ 055 21 24 27; Borgo San Jacopo 57r; meals €45; ☒ lunch & dinner Thu-Mon) Crostini topped with aphrodisiacal white-truffle shavings, deep-fried battered green tomatoes or zucchini flowers, lamb with artichokes, veal's brain and home-made walnut liqueur are seasonal highlights gracing the menu of this staunchly traditional trattoria where the quality of products used is just

---

TOP FIVE SUNDAY BRUNCHES

Our favourite spots on Sunday for...

- An egg-and-pancake American brunch – **Angels** (p139)

- A designer brunch – **Fusion Bar** (p136), the minimalist, design-driven bar of Gallery Hotel Art

- A cheap €8 student brunch served all day – **Pop Café** (right)

- A river-side brunch with the hip set – **Noir** (p144); or a brunch (€9/20) across the Arno at **Rifrullo** (opposite)

- Those in the know: **Canapone** (opposite)

---

top-notch. Service is gentlemanly, bow tied and impeccable.

Borgo San Jacopo (Map pp100-1; ☎ 055 28 16 61; Borgo San Jacopo 62r; meals €50; ⊙ dinner Wed-Mon) This *very* stylish number struts the catwalk in gleaming glass and stainless steel. Dress well to feel the part. It's just as innovative as you'd expect from an offshoot of the design-driven Gallery Hotel Art (p136) and, ultimately, the Ferragamo fashion house.

Filipepe (Map pp100-1; ☎ 055 200 13 97; www.filipepe.com; Via San Niccolò 39r; menus €55 & €75; ⊙ dinner) A theatrical, rustic and modern décor rolled into one makes a real change at this stylish dining space with street terrace at the front and romantic, three-table courtyard out the back. Dishes ooze innovation: fancy pearl barley crowned with goat's cheese, honey and a pear cooked in red wine? Octopus with polenta and cheese? Trendy moneyed couples are the prime clientele.

Self-Catering

A market stroll exposes a dramatically different face of Florence (not to mention a cornucopia of edible delights): **Mercato Centrale** (Map pp98-9; Piazza del Mercato Centrale; ⊙ 7am-2pm Mon-Fri, 7am-5pm Sat), inside an iron-and-glass structure dating to 1874, is the oldest and largest; while **Mercato Sant' Ambrogio** (food market; Map pp100-1; Piazza Sant' Ambrogio; ⊙ 7am-2pm Mon-Sat) retains a more intimate, local flavour.

Fill your water bottle with wine for as little as €1.30 per L at **Enoteca Vitae** (Map pp100-1; ☎ 055 246 65 03; vitae@email.it; Borgo La Croce 75r), near Mercato Sant'Ambrogio, or **Divino** (Map pp98-9; ☎ 055 21 41 21; Via Taddea 8r), near San Lorenzo

market, which also sells sweet *Vin Santo* (€12.50 per L).

Antico Forno Santi (Map pp98-9; ☎ 055 28 35 66; www.biscottisanti.com; Via Nazionale 121r; ⊙ 9.30am-1.30pm & 3.30-7.30pm Tue-Sat) Gorge on *cantuccini* (€14.50 per kg) studded with almonds, chocolate, figs or apricots at this artisan biscuit maker.

La Botega del Cioccolato (Map pp100-1; ☎ 055 200 16 09; www.bottegadelcioccolato.it; Via de' Macci 50; ⊙ 10am-1pm & 3-7.30pm Mon-Fri) Designer olive oil, saffron or balsamic-vinegar chocolates (€49 per kg) are the speciality of chocolate maker Andrea Bianchini, who also makes chocolate and sea-salt biscuits. Even more extraordinary are his white chocolates, which are filled with rosemary ganash and a single grain of sea salt at the centre.

DRINKING

Florence's dynamic drinking scene embraces the whole gambit of genres – historical café, cutting-edge lounge bar, grungy student-packed pub and old-fashioned *enoteca*, invariably dark and topped with traditional red brick, where sophisticates come to savour fine wines. From spring through to autumn, the scene shifts outside, drinkers spilling onto the street be there an official terrace or not.

There is no better time to savour all this than at sunset, the bewitching hour when the city seems to stop in its tracks for that all-essential *aperitivo*. From around 6.30pm to 9pm, many of the most fashionable bars whet appetites with a complimentary feast (feast being the operative word) of sumptuous *hors d'oeuvres* – don't be shy; just grab a plate and help yourself.

Firenzenotte (www.firenzenotte.it in Italian) is an indispensable online guide to Florence nightlife. In town, monthly mag **2night** (www.2night.it) with some English text can be picked up for free.

Cafés

Practically every piazza has at least one or two cafés with outdoor pavement terraces: Piazza della Signoria, Piazza della Repubblica, Piazza San Lorenzo and Piazza Santo Spirito are particularly lovely for hanging out for hours over cappuccino and cake.

Key fact to *never forget* about cafés in Florence: it is substantially cheaper to drink standing up at the bar; sit down at a table and prices instantly double or triple.

Procacci (Map pp100-1; ☎ 055 21 16 56; Via de Tornabourni 64r; ☻ 10.30am-8pm Tue-Sat) The last remaining bastion of genteel old Florence on Via de' Tornabuoni, this tiny café was born in 1885 opposite the English pharmacy as a delicatessen serving truffles in its repertoire of tasty morsels. Bite-sized *panini tartufati* (truffle pâté sandwiches) remain the thing to order.

La Terrazza (Map pp100-1; Piazza della Repubblica 1; ☻ 10am-9pm Mon-Sat, 10.30am-8pm Sun) For a bird's eye view of the square and Duomo way below, ride the escalators to the top floor of central department store Rinascente and cut through the kitchen and homeware section to this small jam-packed rooftop café.

Caffè Cibrèo (Map pp100-1; ☎ 055 234 58 53; Via Andrea del Verrochio 5r; ☻ 8-1am Tue-Sat) The perfect spot for a mid-morning stop after shopping at the neighbouring Mercato Sant'Ambrogio, this dark old café with wood-coffered ceiling, panelled walls and lace tablecloths is well known for its excellent coffee and famous chef (p141).

Cabiria (Map p103; ☎ 055 21 57 32; Piazza Santo Spirito 4r; ☻ 11am-1.30am Wed-Mon) Buzzing buzzing day and night is what this Oltrarno café, one of several on Florence's most happening bohemian squares, is all about. Come dusk it turns into a music bar.

Pop Café (Map p103; ☎ 055 21 38 52; www.popcafe .net; Piazza Santo Spirito 18r; meals €25; ☻ 8am-2am Sep-Jul) Students in the know have adopted this pocket-sized space as their own: grab a seat on the wooden bench (mind your head on the hanging metal) and tuck into a superhealthy breakfast, vegetarian lunch or all-day Sunday brunch (p143).

Enoteche

While the sign *vinaio* (wine merchant) seldom appears above doorways these days, the tradition has won new life in the past few years – meaning there are dozens and dozens of intimate *enoteche* scattered across the city, where the cheapest to finest of Tuscan and Italian wine can be savoured with a bite to eat.

Coquinarius (Map pp100-1; ☎ 055 230 21 53; www.co quinarius.com; Via delle Oche 15r; ☻ noon-10.30pm Mon-Sat) 'Try the Vermentino' says one Lonely Planet reader, 'it is like flying to the moon…'. Indeed, a heady choice of Tuscan wine in the company of an equally heady choice of crostini is reason enough to wine and dine beneath red bricks at Coquinarius.

Cantinetta Antinori (Map pp100-1; Via de' Tornabuoni 7; meals €45; ☻ lunch & dinner Mon-Fri) This *enoteca* is a 1960s creation of the city's most famous wine-making dynasty; the Antinoris had the palace built in 1502 and still live here. Titillate tastebuds with a Tignanello or Solaia accompanied by Tuscan *fettunata di cavolo nero* (toasted bread topped with black cabbage). Afterwards you can view models of the family's Tuscan, Umbrian and Californian wine-producing estates.

Baldovino (Map pp100-1; ☎ 055 234 72 20; www .baldovino.com; Via di San Giuseppe 18r; ☻ lunch & dinner Tue-Sun) The patterned tiles behind the bar add a moody touch to this large *enoteca-cum-trattoria*, which serves a wide choice of sophisticated food in the shadow of Santa Croce.

Enoteca Fuori Porta (Map pp100-1; ☎ 055 234 24 83; www.fuoriporta.it in Italian; Via Monte alle Croci 10r; meals around €25; ☻ Mon-Sat) In this fine old *enoteca* the wine list has more than 400 varieties – and an impressive roll call of Scotch whiskies and other liquors, too. Pick a plate or two from the limited list of *primi* (first courses) for a pleasant evening meal.

Enoteca Pinchiorri (Map pp100-1; ☎ 055 24 27 77; www.enotecapinchiorri.com; Via Ghibellina 87r; ☻ lunch & dinner Thu-Sat, dinner Wed) The crème de la crème of Florentine *enoteche*, this temple to fine wine and dining very well indeed in a 16th-century palace has stayed at the top since 1972. There are several hundred wines to taste and the bill will be in the hundreds. Dress well to come here.

Bars

Sharp savvy designer space to rustic taverna and traditional pub, you won't go thirsty in this bar-busy city. The most hip tend to be across the water in Oltrarno.

Fiddler's Elbow (Map pp100-1; ☎ 055 21 50 56; www .thefiddlerselbow.com; Piazza Santa Maria Novella 7; ☻ 11am-2am Mon-Fri, 11am-2.30am Sat & Sun) Not far from Stazione Santa Maria Novella, this is one of many Irish pubs popular with the expat and foreign-student set.

BETWEEN THE DUOMO & THE ARNO

Noir (Map pp100-1; Lungarno Corsini 12-14r; ☻ 11am-3am) Once upon a time it was called Capocaccia – until the peppermint-green tables on the street terrace and pretty much everything else turned a moody shade of black. Different name yes, but ex-Capocaccia lures the

TOP FIVE HISTORIC CAFÉS

The waiter might well ask if you mean espresso or cappuccino when you order coffee after a meal, and yes, the tourist-targeted menu is in five languages and stars club sandwiches alongside risotto, but few cafes have seen or heard as much as these old Florentine beauties.

■ Caffè Concerto Paszkowski (Map pp100-1; ☎ 055 21 02 36; www.paszkowski.com; Piazza della Repubblica 31-35r; ⏰ 7am-2am Tue-Sun) Born as a brewery overlooking the city's fish market in 1846, this Florentine institution with heated terrace and elegant, piano-clad interior lured a literary set a century on. Today it pulls the whole gambit of punters, mobile-touting Florentine youths, suit-clad businessmen and well-dressed old ladies sipping tea.

■ Caffè Giacosa (Map pp100-1; ☎ 055 21 16 56; Via della Spada 10r) This small café with claustrophobic plastic-covered street terrace and just a handful of tables inside (but loads of bar-standing space) is more famous for what it was – an 1815 child, Negroni inventor (p146) and hub of Anglo-Florentine sophistication during the interwar years – than what it is now (the café of local hotshot designer Roberto Cavalli, whose boutique adjoins it). The bar counter is original.

■ Caffè Gilli (Map pp100-1; ☎ 055 21 38 96; Piazza della Repubblica 3r; ⏰ 8am-1am Wed-Mon) The last of the historic trio aplomb the city's old Roman forum, Gilli has been serving formidable teas, cakes and chocolates to die for since 1733. But be warned: this elegant ode to all things sweet topped with Art Nouveau ceiling frescoes isn't cheap. A pot of Earl Grey and a slice of cake sitting down is €13.

■ Giubbe Rosse (Map pp100-1; ☎ 055 21 22 80; Piazza della Repubblica 13-14r; mains around €15; ⏰ 8am-2am) This is where die-hard members of the early-20th-century futurist artistic movement used to drink and debate. Inside, long vaulted halls lined with old photographs, sketches and artwork make a great place for coffee over a newspaper – some hang up for customers' use.

■ Rivoire (Map pp100-1; ☎ 055 21 44 12; Piazza della Signoria 4r; ⏰ 8am-11pm Tue-Sun) The golden oldie in which to refuel inside or out after a Uffizi or Palazzo Vecchio visit, this pricey little number with unbeatable people-watching terrace has produced some of the city's most exquisite chocolate (€55 per kg) since 1872. Black-jacketed barmen with navy ties set the formal tone in this classy spot.

same beautiful set with its generous *aperitivi* buffet, balmy river-side setting, theatrical chandelier-clad (black) interior and Sunday brunch.

Mayday Club (Map pp100-1; ☎ 055 238 12 90; www .maydayclub.it; Via Dante Alighieri 16r; ⏰ 8pm-2am Mon-Sat) Tagging itself as club and lounge café, this three-room drinking spot with eclectic furnishing defies description…almost: a place 'to explore, observe, to familiarise and to experience' is what its virtual bumph says. Theme nights, art exhibitions and live bands are frequent.

Colle Bereto (Map pp100-1; ☎ 055 28 31 56; Piazza degli Strozzi 5r; ⏰ 9am-3am Mon-Sat, 5pm-3am Sun) The dark oversized shades are vital at this hip bar where a fashion-conscious set sits cool on a sleek, wooden-decked terrace located opposite Palazzo Strozzi. Inside, pea-green neon and transparent Kartell chairs scream design.

Naima (Map pp100-1; ☎ 055 26 54 098; Via dell'Anguillara 54r; ⏰ 8am-2am) 'Cocktails and more' is the tag line of this chic sharp bar with industrial metalwork, pretty-in-pink lampshades and DJs spinning tunes after dark. *Aperitivi* are served 6.30pm to 9pm and the bar stool–clad place is a wi-fi hotspot.

Slowly Café (Map pp100-1; ☎ 055 45 354; www .slowlycafe.com; Via Porta Rossa 63r; ⏰ 12.30-2.30pm & 7pm-2.30am Mon-Sat, 7pm-2.30am Sun) Wednesday is party night for students at this stylish cocktail bar that otherwise lures a middle-of-the-road set with its generous early-evening buffet, moody lighting and happy hour well over an hour.

JJ Cathedral (Map pp100-1; ☎ 055 265 68 92; www .jjcathedral.com; Piazza San Giovanni 4r; ⏰ 10am-2.30am Mon-Sun) This busy pub's street terrace in the shade of the baptistry is always buzzing. But it is on the lone table for three perched on a wrought-iron balcony above where everyone

TOP FIVE APERITIVI

Our favourites for unusual *aperitivi* (aperitifs) and/or a handsome free fill alongside that all-essential early-evening drink…or buy a bottle of wine and head to the hottest seats in town – the east-facing stone bridge supports of Ponte Santa Trinità (p117) – where you can sit above the water, drink and stare out at a romantic star-lit Ponte Vecchio.

- Noir (p144) – The hottest in town; vast banquet of a buffet inside, seating outside on the street and across the traffic-busy road on the riverside wall.

- Negroni (below) – A comparable feast of a buffet and river-side à-la-traffic-fume seating on the other side of the Arno.

- Angels (p144) – Stylish finger-food buffet (€8 includes cocktail) and supersleek barman's specials, including a balsamic, mint or chocolate martini or a don't-mess-with-me dirty martini (€9); dress right (to kill preferably.)

- Gilli (p143) – No buffet, but how 'bout a sunset glass of champagne (€15) at one of Florence's most historic bars or a chocolate-inspired cocktail (€10.50; vanilla vodka with splash of white-cream chocolate and garnished with Gilli chocolates).

- Caffè La Torre (below) – The trendy XL choice; drink with jazz.

wants to sit – its cathedral views are heart-stopping.

Eby's Latin Bar (Map pp100-1; ☎ 055 24 00 27; www.ebysbar.com; Via dell'Oriuolo 5r; ⏰ 11am-3am Mon-Sat) Indulge in days of being happy at this student-loved Mexican joint where happy hour lasts two days and cocktails have never been fruitier or more exotic.

OLTRARNO & NEARBY QUARTERS

South of the river the streets buzz with bars and clubs, atmospheric Piazza Santo Spirito becoming one vast drinking space in summer.

Sei Divino (Map p103; ☎ 055 21 77 91; Via Borgo Ognissanti 42r; ⏰ 8am-2am) No, it's not a wine bar; it's not a lounge bar; it's an open bar with great wine, great music, DJs, video projections and wi-fi, no-fuss €7 lunch deal and themed *aperitivi* buffet (7pm to 10pm) – Indian charm, Mexican passion, Tuscan, sushi and so on.

Caffè La Torre (Map pp100-1; ☎ 055 68 06 43; www.cafelatorre.it; Lungarno Benvenuto Cellini 65r; ⏰ 10.30am-3.30am Mon-Sun) Loud wallpaper and legendary Aperitivo XL (above) at this river-facing jazz bar, a drop from Piazzale Michelangelo, spells hot with a capital H. Free wi-fi, jazz-driven DJ sets and a chef who cooks until 3am.

Plasma (Map pp100-1; ☎ 055 051 69 26; www.virtualplasma.it; Piazza Ferrucci 1r; ⏰ 6.30pm-1.30am Wed, Thu & Sun, to 2.30am Fri & Sat) This cutting-edge art bar and kitchen is a minimalist fiberoptic-lit drinking space where the hip set sip cocktails

on Level 0 and get lost in video art projected on eight 42-inch plasma screens or a waterfall on Level 1. DJs spin 'til late.

Negroni (Map pp100-1; ☎ 055 24 36 47; www.negronibar.com; Via dei Renai 17r; ⏰ 8am-2am Mon-Sat, 6pm-2am Sun) Negroni shakes up cocktails galore, including its namesake invented in the 1920s, so the story goes, when Florentine Count Camillo Negroni asked the barman at Caffè Giacosa (p145) to add gin to his Americano. To make it at home: shake equal parts gin, Campari and red Martini. Should you drift by Negroni around noon, its lunchtime buffet is a steal. Art exhibitions, DJs and dancing.

Zoe (Map pp100-1; ☎ 055 24 31 11; Via dei Renai 13r; ⏰ 3pm-2am Apr-Oct, 6pm-2am Tue-Sun Nov-Mar) With its innards glowing red and bedecked with changing art exhibitions, this busy San Niccolò bar heaves as its squadrons of punters – young locals – spill out onto the street across from the river.

O!O (Map p103; ☎ 055 21 29 17; Piazza Piattellina 7r; meals €20; ⏰ 9pm-3am Mon-Fri, 5pm-3am Sat) A '100% organic' motto drives this *bar con cucina* (bar with kitchen) located in San Frediano, where a right-on set slurps yoghurt smoothies and munches salad around fruit-patterned tables. Cocktails and concerts kick in around dusk. NB: the wallpaper is hardly sweet bedtime reading.

La Dolce Vita (Map p103; ☎ 055 28 45 95; Piazza del Carmine 6r; ⏰ 5pm-2am Mon-Sun) Just a piazza away from Santo Spirito, La Dolce Vita attracts a very stylish crowd, especially on weekends.

FLORENCE

Sip an *aperitivo* in the evening sun outside or enjoy the bold retro interior. Live bands and DJs.

James Joyce (Map pp100-1; ☎ 055 658 08 56; Lungarno Benvenuto Cellini 1r; ⏰ 6pm-2am Thu-Mon) What makes this Irish pub stand out from the crowd is its leafy outside seating. It might well overlook a single-pump petrol station on Piazza Ferrucci but it's the closest thing to a beer garden in central Florence.

SANTA CROCE AREA
In Santa Croce a rash of American- and British-style bars and pubs spot Via de' Benci.

Rex Café (Map pp100-1; ☎ 055 248 03 31; Via Fiesolana 23r; ⏰ 6pm-3am Sep-May) A vast *aperitivi* buffet (oysters and champagne Friday and Saturday), DJs, live bands and well-shaken cocktails ensure this American bar, styled after the interior of an Italian transatlantic liner called *Rex* that sunk, remains firmly on Florence's hip-hot drinking circuit. Décor is gaudy in-your-face and the air could be fresher at times, but the city's sassy set still love it.

Moyo (Map pp100-1; ☎ 055 247 97 38; www.moyo .it; Via de' Benci 23r; ⏰ 8am-2am Sun-Thu, until 3am Fri & Sat) Another drinking establishment held in great esteem by Florence's party-mad student crowd, this wi-fi–wired Santa Croce favourite with a minimalist interior (and free wi-fi) gets packed with laptop-wielding internet natives early on. DJs and cocktails kick in later.

ENTERTAINMENT
Bookshops sell *Firenze Spettacolo* (€1.60; www .firenzespettacolo.it in Italian), the city's definitive entertainment publication, published monthly. Otherwise, a clutch of freebies – including *Florence Concierge Information* (www.florence-concierge.it), *Informacittà Toscana 24ore* and *Florence Tuscany News* (www.informacittafirenze.it) – list what's on. The city listings in the local edition of *La Repubblica* (p398) are also useful.

Tickets for many cultural events are sold at central ticket outlet **Box Office** (Map pp98-9; ☎ 055 21 08 04; www.boxol.it in Italian; Via Luigi Alamanni 39; ⏰ 10am-7.30pm Tue-Sat, 3.30-7.30pm Mon). Otherwise you can also try **Ticket One** (www .ticketone.it in Italian).

Live Music
Open-air concerts are a regular feature on hip Piazza Santa Spirito in summer where half of Florence seemingly hangs around the stage here on hot sultry evenings. In May live jazz sets Piazza Santissima Annunziata jiving until the wee hours during the Jazz & Co festival and Piazza Poggi throbs with different sounds during Rime Rampanti.

Most venues for live music are well outside the town centre, with many closing in July and/or August. Admission depends on the line-up and is occasionally charged using a pesky drinks-card system – clock up drinks on your card and pay substantially more than anticipated when you leave.

Loonees (Map pp100-1; ☎ 055 21 22 49; Via Porta Rossa 15; admission free; ⏰ 8pm-3am Wed-Sat) Definite hot spot among the city's notable Anglophone and international set, this subterranean dance club run by a Danish-English duo is as much a drinking hole as dance-'til-dawn venue. Live bands play most nights and look out for some great drink deals.

Caruso Jazz Café (Map pp100-1; ☎ 055 28 19 40; www .carusojazzcafe.com; Via Lambertesca 15-16r; admission free) Jive to jazz a stone's throw from the Uffizi; live concerts most Thursday and Friday evenings.

Jazz Club (Map pp100-1; ☎ 055 247 97 00; Via Nuova de' Caccini 3; compulsory 12-month membership €6; ⏰ 9.30pm-1am Sun-Thu, 9.30pm-2am Fri & Sat Oct–mid-Jun) This is Florence's tip-top strictly jazz venue and it stages some quality acts, both local and from wider afield, in an atmospheric vaulted basement.

Be Bop Music Club (Map pp98-9; ☎ 055 21 97 99; www.bebopclub.com; Via dei Servi 76r; admission free-€10; ⏰ 8pm-2am Mon-Sat) Live music to suit every taste – everything from Led Zeppelin and the Beatles to vintage guitar, swing jazz, soul and 1970s funk – is the aim of this fresh little club.

Tenax (Map pp96-7; ☎ 055 30 81 60; www.tenax.org; Via Pratese 46; admission variable; ⏰ 10pm-4am Tue-Sun Oct-Apr) Florence's biggest venue for live bands since the 1980s, northwest of town, doubles as a club when there are no bands in town; download flyers online. Bus 29 or 30 from Stazione di Santa Maria Novella.

La Pavonière (☎ 055 63 233 39 79; Via della Catena 2; admission free; ⏰ 8pm-late May-Sep) DJ sessions and live bands by the pool is the thrust of this fabulous Miami-style summer project by Tenax – *aperitivo* and cocktail bar with music until late around the swimming pool in Parco delle Cascine.

Auditorium Flog (Map pp96-7; ☎ 055 49 04 37; www.flog.it in Italian; Via M Mercati 24b; admission free-€15;

FLORENCE

GAY & LESBIAN FLORENCE

Florence, with its unrivalled artistic and creative history, has a long tradition of openness and tolerance. Its gay community is one of Italy's most vibrant and well established, boasting several well-attended bars and clubs, not to mention its own week-long arts, cinema and video festival, the **Florence Queer Festival** (www.florencequeerfestival.it in Italian), held each year in late September. All said, Florence is no Amsterdam and there are no specifically 'gay areas' – what nightlife exists tends to be relatively low-key.

Key contact points for information on the scene is **Azione Gay e Lesbica** (Map p103; ☎ 055 22 02 50; www.azionegayelesbica.it in Italian; Via Pisana 32-34r; ☺ 6-8pm Mon-Thu) and **Arcilesbica Firenze** (Map p103; ☎ 338 88 74 205; www.arcilesbicafirenze.it in Italian), based inside service centre for the queer community, **IREOS** (Centro Servizi per la Cumunità Queer; ☎ 055 21 69 07; www.ireos.org in Italian; Via de' Serragli 3). Lesbian bookshop **Libreria delle Donne** (Map pp100-1; ☎ 055 24 03 84; Via Fiesolana 2/b) is also helpful.

Bars and clubs:

Piccolo Café (Map pp100-1; ☎ 055 24 17 04; Borgo Santa Croce 23r; ☺ 5pm-2am) Not strictly gay but a casual meeting spot in Santa Croce for the local gay and lesbian scene; hosts occasional art exhibitions.

Silver Stud (Map pp100-1; ☎ 055 68 84 66; www.silverstud.it in Italian; Via della Fornace 9; ☺ 9pm-4am Mon-Sat) Latest gay kid on the block: disco and club for men with strip rooms, video bar, labyrinth, and DJ Lorenzo spinning tunes Friday and Saturday.

Tabasco (Map pp100-1; ☎ 055 21 30 00; www.tabascogay.it in Italian; Piazza di Santa Cecilia 3r; admission free; ☺ 10pm-4am, disco until 6am Tue, Fri & Sat) Florence's only hardcore gay club around incredibly since 1974, with disco, cocktail bar and dark room.

Y.A.G B@r (Map pp100-1; ☎ 055 246 90 22; www.yagbar.com; Via de' Macci 8r; ☺ 5pm-2am) Hip, trendy and a retro mix of 1950s and industrial, this wholly gay bar is a relaxed vibrant venue with buzzing bar, live music, computer terminals to surf and video games.

☺ 9.30pm-4am) Major venue for bands, this is in the Rifredi area north of the city centre. Not nearly as big as Tenax but has a reasonable stage and dance area. Bus 14 from Stazione di Santa Maria Novella.

Clubbing

It's a far cry from London or Berlin. In fact, city slickers could well be disappointed by Florence's decidedly lame tame slow dance scene which – bar Central Park and Meccano, both with outdoor dance floors – grinds to a halt in summer (June to September).

Central Park (Map pp98-9; ☎ 055 35 35 05; Via Fosso Macinante 2-6; admission incl 1st drink €20; ☺ 11pm-6am Tue-Sat) Flit between five different dance floors in city park Parco delle Cascine where everything from Latin to pop, house and drum 'n bass plays – many a top Ibiza DJ has spun tunes here. From May the dance floor moves outside beneath the stars.

Meccanò Club (Map pp98-9; ☎ 055 331 33 71; Viale degli Olmi 1; admission incl 1st drink men/women €16/13; ☺ 11pm-5am Tue-Sat) Flo's other big-crowd disco, also in the city park, touts three dance spaces spinning house, funk and mainstream commercial music to a mainstream youthful set.

Ex-Ex (Map pp100-1; ☎ 055 263 85 83; www.ex-ex.it in Italian; Corso dei Tintori 4; admission €9-15; ☺ 9pm-4am Wed-Sat) Underground in mood and quite literally, this happening club attracts top DJs from Berlin, Amsterdam and other hot-sound European cities, giving it a great cutting-edge vibe. Music is predominantly house.

YAB Club (Map pp100-1; ☎ 055 21 51 60; www.yab .it in Italian; Via dei Sassetti 5r; admission incl 1st drink €20; ☺ 9pm-4am Wed-Mon) It's been around since the 1970s but it remains a hit with students (despite its cringing tag line 'glamour club – you are beautiful'). Various sounds play here and Yabsmoove on Monday is the hottest hip-hop night in town; Wednesday is student night.

Full Up (Map pp100-1; ☎ 055 29 30 06; www.fullupclub .com in Italian; Via della Vigna Vecchia 23-25; admission €15; ☺ 11pm-4am Mon-Sat) Full Up aptly describes this small club that gets packed with a hip-hop loving crowd: Wednesday is happy music; Friday cool and hip hop; and Saturday a return to the house with resident DJ Emijay.

Classical Music & Opera

Summer ushers in beautiful concerts of chamber music to churches across the city; **Orchestra**

da Camera Fiorentina (Florentine Chamber Orchestra; www
.orcafi.it in Italian) performs March to October and
is a name not to be missed.

Teatro del Maggio Musicale Fiorentino (Map pp98-9;
☎ information 055 27 793 50, tickets 055 28 72 22; www
.maggiofiorentino.com; Corso Italia 16) The curtain rises
on opera, classical concerts and ballet at this
lovely theatre, host to an international concert
festival in May and June.

Teatro Verdi (Map pp100-1; ☎ 055 21 23 20; www
.teatroverdifirenze.it in Italian; Via Ghibellina 99) Home
to the prestigious Orchestra della Toscana
(www.orchestradellatoscana.it in Italian).

Teatro della Pergola (Map pp100-1; ☎ 055 2 26 41;
www.pergola.firenze.it in Italian; Via della Pergola 18) Beautiful city theatre with stunning entrance that
hosts classical concerts organised by the Amici
della Musica (☎ 055 60 74 40; www.amicimu
sica.fi.it in Italian), October to April.

Cinema
Few cinemas in Florence screen *versione origi-
nale* (subtitled films), **Odeon Cinehall** (Map pp100-1;
☎ 055 21 40 68; Piazza Strozzi) and **Cinema Fulgor** (Map
p103; ☎ 055 238 18 81; Via Maso Finiguerra 22r) being
exceptions.

**British Institute of Florence Library & Cultural
Centre** (Map p103; ☎ 055 267 78 270; www.britishinsti
tute.it; Lungarno Guicciardini 9; membership €5, ticket €5)
Films, often with a Florence connection, in
English 6.30pm Wednesdays; full programme
online.

Mid-June to September, several outdoor
cinemas show films in Italian. Private ventures include **Chiardiluna** (Map p103; ☎ 055 233
70 42; Via Monte Uliveto 1) and **Cinema Poggetto** (Map
pp96-7; ☎ 055 48 12 85; Via M Mercati 24b), while the
municipality puts on outdoor screenings at
Palazzo dello Sport (Map pp96–7), in the
Campo di Marte, and Palazzo dei Congressi
(Map pp98–9).

Theatre & Dance
The season runs from October to April/May
when summertime festive arts events enjoy
centre billing instead. Mainstream theatre
takes to the stage in all the theatres listed
earlier in this section under Classical Music
& Opera; online see www.firenzedeiteatri.it
in Italian. Exciting stages for experimental
theatre and dance:

Ex-Stazione Leopolda (Map pp98-9; ☎ 055 247 83
32; www.stazione-leopolda.com; Viale Fratelli Rosselli 5)
Theatre, predominantly of the avant-garde
variety, is frequently the star of this industrial

performance space split between an old train
station, defunct since 1861, and a warehouse
called Alcatraz next door. Concerts, trade
fairs, exhibitions and fashion shows are also
held here.

Teatro della Limonaia (Map pp96-7; ☎ 055 44 08 52;
www.teatrodellalimonaia.it; Via Gramsci 426, Sesto Fiorentino)
One of Italy's leading avant-garde theatres,
north of Florence. Bus 28A or 28C from Stazione Santa Maria Novella.

Sport
Local Serie A side **ACF Fiorentina** (www.acffiorentina
.it) clings on tenaciously to its place in Italy's
premier football division. See the side in action at its home ground, 45,000-seater **Stadio
Comunale Artemio Franchi** (Map pp96-7; ☎ 055 262
55 37; Campo di Marte). Buy match tickets here, at
Chiosco degli Sportivi (Map pp100-1; ☎ 055 29 23 63; Via
Anselmi), or online at www.listicket.it (in Italian), Box Office or Ticket One (see p147).
Scarves, T-shirts and all the gear is sold at
Soccer Town (Via Ricasoli 27; ⏱ 3.30-7.30pm Mon, 10am-
7.30pm Tue- Sat).

SHOPPING
Flimsy Italian-flag boxers (€6) emblazoned
with David's packet where it matters most
and other mass-produced souvenirs are
rampant. But for serious shoppers, it is the
city's fine leather and extraordinary variety
of quality goods that tempts. Florence has
been synonymous with craftsmanship since
medieval times when goldsmiths, silversmiths
and shoemakers were as *alta moda* as sculptors and artists.

For the truly dedicated shoppers, bookshops sell *Firenze Nonsolo Shopping* (€14),
an annual glossy shopping guide by Dacia
Maraini.

In categories all of their own are the sweet-
smelling unguents, balms, soaps, lotions and
potions at 17th-century Officina Profumo-
Farmaceutica di Santa Maria Novella (p115);
and the cutting-edge street fashion and art
fused with happening evening entertainment
(*aperitivi*, DJs etc) at Open (☎ 055 263 82 58; www
.open-mutabileassoluto.com; Corso Tintori 43r), a 'concept
store for happy people'.

Leather
Via de' Gondi and Borgo de' Greci are lined
with leather shops selling jackets, trousers,
shoes and bags, as are the street markets
(p152).

Stefano Bemer (Map p103; ☎ 055 22 25 58; Borgo San Frediano 143r) The finest shoes that money can buy for contemporary men; made-to-measure shoes come in a beautiful wooden shoebox.

Francesco (Map p103; ☎ 055 21 24 28; Via di Santo Spirito 62r) Hand-stitched leather is the cornerstone of this tiny family business; men's and women's shoes.

Il Bisonte (Map pp100-1; ☎ 055 21 57 22; Via del Parione 31r) Accessories, such as handbags, desktop items, leather-bound notebooks, briefcases and the like.

Soft-as-silk leather gloves in every length and colour of the rainbow are the speciality of **Pusateri** (Map pp100-1; ☎ 055 21 41 92; Via de'Calzaiuoli 25r) and **Madova** (Map pp100-1; ☎ 055 239 65 26; Via de'Guicciardini 1r)

Paper

Florence is famous for its exquisite marbled paper; *carta fiorentina* is floral in design.

Il Papiro (Map pp100-1; ☎ 055 28 16 28; www.ilpapirofirenze.it in Italian; Piazza del Duomo 24r) One of five branches selling all manner of paper and stationery, including delightful old-fashioned notebooks to scribe your favourite hotels, restaurants, wines and *viaggi* (travels).

Pineider (Map pp100-1; ☎ 055 28 46 55; www.pineider.com; Piazza della Signoria 13r) Florence's most exclusive stationer opened here in 1774 and once designed calling cards for Napoleon no less.

Parione (Map pp100-1; ☎ 055 21 56 84; www.parione.it; Via del Parione 10r) Paper art comes to life with enchanting music boxes and miniature Renaissance theatres, all beautifully bound in Florentine paper still hand-crafted at the Laboratorio Palazzo Pucci (☎ 055 277 63 00; Via de Pucci).

Lory (Map pp100-1; ☎ 055 21 32 46; Piazza de' Frescobaldi 4-9r) Sketchpads, pencils, artist journals, paint and other fine art supplies for those in town to paint Florence.

San Jacobo Show (Map pp100-1; ☎ 055 239 69 12; Borgo San Jacopo 66r) Assemble-yourself, corrugated-cardboard mannequins are among the art pieces for sale at this contemporary art gallery – an ode to the torso.

Gold, Silver, Marble & Bronze

Goldsmiths have dominated Ponte Vecchio (Map pp100–1), Florence's infamous tourist-packed jewellery strip, since the 16th century: Gherardi at No 8 is the best-known name on the bridge.

TOP FIVE: SEE IT BEING MADE

In true Florentine fashion, the fine art of craftsmanship, fast disappearing as it is, is staunchly upheld in these highly refined workshops.

- Alessandro Dari (Map pp100-1; ☎ 055 24 47 47; www.alessandrodari.com; Via San Niccolò 115r) A couple of the fantastical, incredibly castellated pieces crafted by Florence's most innovative contemporary jeweller are in Palazzo Pitti; visit his Oltrarno showroom and workshop to see how he does it. The flamboyant jeweller also plays the guitar.

- Antico Setifico Fiorentino (Map p103; ☎ 055 21 38 61; www.anticosetificiofiorentino.com; Via L Bartoini 4) Precious silks, velvets and other luxuriant fabrics are woven on 18th- and 19th-century looms at this world-famous fabric house where opulent damasks, brocades and so on of Renaissance Florence have been made since 1786.

- Jamie Marie Lazzara (Map pp100-1; ☎ 055 28 05 73; www.masterviolinmaker.com; Via dei Leoni 4r) Jamie Marie lovingly crafts just four custom-made violins of professional soloist quality in her cupboard-sized workshop; Carlo Vettori at Arte Liutaria (Map p103; %055 21 98 48; www.arteliutaria.it; Via Guelfa 3) is another Florentine *maestro liutaio*.

- Scuola del Cuoio (p121) Watch leatherworkers fashioning goods and buy their finished products at this atmospheric workshop in the cloisters of Basilica di Santa Croce.

- Lorenzo Villoresi (Map pp100-1; ☎ 055 234 11 87; www.lorenzovilloresi.it; Via de' Bardi 14; ☼ 9am-1pm & 2-5pm Mon-Fri) Watch out for the new perfumery that Florence's famous perfumer is likely to open near Ponte Vecchio soon after this book's publication; features will include workshops, lessons, children's visits, a unique collection of aromatic raw materials and an aromatic garden. Contact his de' Bardi workshop for details.

Jewellers to drool over include Alessandro Dari (opposite) and **Torrini** (Map pp100–1; ☎ 055 23 02 401; Piazza del Duomo 10r), established in 1369 when Jacopus Torrini started forging armour for Florentine knights.

Florentines rate two addresses for silver: **Pampaloni** (Map pp100–1; ☎ 055 28 90 94; Borgo Santo Apostili 47r), founded in 1902 and known for its angular, radically untraditional designs; and **Paolo Pagliai** (Map pp100–1; ☎ 055 28 28 40; Borgo San Jacopo 41r).

Pietro Bazzanti & Figlio (Map pp100–1; ☎ 055 21 56 49; www.galleriabazzanti.it; Via del Parione 37-39) Founded in 1822, this is the place to shop should a Renaissance marble cherub or bronze Neoclassical nude be your heart's desire.

Designer Outlet Stores

Driving yourself or taking a day tour (p131) is the easiest way to reach these out-of-town factory outlets.

FLORENCE FASHION

It might not be Milan, Paris or London, but this *is* the city where the Italian fashion industry was born (p60) and where a clutch of world-renowned rag-trade greats still turn heads.

Legendary Via de' Tornabuoni (Map pp100–1) – a fashionably quaint street with a pharmacy, bookshop, several cafes and so on until Florence Fashion dug in her manicured claws and turned it into the glittering catwalk of designer boutiques it is today – is the spot to start a shopping spree. Naples-born, Florence-adopted designer Salvatore Ferragamo (1898–1960), fashioner of footwear for the world's most glamorous women, has strutted his shoes into Palazzo Spini Feroni at No 16r since 1927. Across the road, the swirly-whirly psychedelic prints that belong to Florence's fashion king struggle hard not to leap out the window: Napolitan marquis **Emilio Pucci** (Via de' Tornabuoni 20-22r) – creator of stylish, garish, look-at-me-or-else women's wear – opened his first shop in Florence in 1947, where he hob-knobs with Cartier (No 40), Tiffany & Co (No 25), Versace (13-15r), Dior (No 24r), Giorgio Armani (No 48) and Prada (No 53r) on the city's most fashionable street today.

Gucci (No 73r) is the indisputable icon of Florence fashion, creator as much of sensational scandal as men and women's fashion since 1921 when Guccio Gucci opened a saddlery shop selling leather goods on Via della Vigna Nuova, followed by another two years later on Via del Parione. It was not until 1967 that the Florentine empire, public since 1995, moved into the city's best-dressed street.

Zipping back to Via della Vigna Nuova (Florence's other fashion-hot street), leg-wear designs by anti-establishment Emilio Cavallini dazzle at No 52r; 'a triumph of technology and design' is how critics rate his hosiery and other seamless garments. Great women's wear is to be envied at BP Studio (No 15). Around the corner, **Elio Ferraro** (Via del Parione 47r) woos vintage lovers with her retro 1950s and 1960s couture and Italian furniture – all designer, of course, darling. **Soqquadro Living** (Borgo Pinti 13r) and **Ceri Vintage** (Via de' Serragli 26) are other vintage-clothing addresses.

The sensuality-driven, animal-print designs of another rebel-yell Florentine designer Roberto Cavalli (his use of denim at the Palazzo Pitti fashion show in 1972 caused a riot among straight-laced Florentines) shine bright as a button at Via de' Tornabuoni 42. Ever faithful to his home town, the designer lives in the Florentine hills with his ex–Miss Universe wife today. Exquisite hand-embroidered linens meanwhile are the handiwork of **Loretta Caponi** (Piazza Antinori 4r), another old family name to dress aristocracy for aeons.

Elsewhere, Via Roma (Map pp100–1) sizes up well with Luisa (No 19-21r), a one-stop shop for the best of designer fashion, not to mention a pioneer in state-of-the-art window and interior shop design. For clothing and design by Italian designers yet to make it big, head for **Plus Minus** (Map p103; Via Mazzetta 22r); everything sold in this boutique is handmade, from natural or recyclable material. Customers at **Ethic** (Borgo degli Albizi 37) can listen to the latest club mix and gem up on art trends and architecture with the latest mags as well as shop for affordable casual wear; while true romantics mad about getting hitched in a rose-petal wedding dress should visit **Le Spose di Laila** (Map pp98-9; Via Cavour 68), lovechild of extraordinary frock designer Laila Pappalardo.

Wanna know a secret? Rose-petal creations aside, most of the big labels – albeit last season's collection – can be bought for 20% to 70% less at a flurry of designer-outlet stores (above) around the city.

Barberino Designer Outlet (☎ 055 84 21 61; bar berino.mcarthurglen.it; A1 Florence-Bologna, exit Barberino di Mugello; ❀ 10am-8pm Tue-Fri, 10am-9pm Sat & Sun, 2-8pm Mon Jan, Jun-Sep & Dec) Outlet shuttle buses (return €9, three times daily) link the SITA bus station with the 95 boutiques at this outlet, 40km north in Barberino di Mugello. Regular buses to/from Barberino (€3.10, five a day Monday to Saturday) stop 1km short of it.

Dolce & Gabbana (☎ 055 833 13 00; Località Santa Maria Maddalena, Via Piana dell'Isola 49, Rignano sull'Arno) Train from Stazione Santa Maria Novella to Rignano Sull'Arno (€4), then taxi (€10, five minutes).

The Mall (☎ 055 865 77 75; Via Europa 8, Leccio; ❀ 10am-7pm Mon-Sat, 3-7pm Sun) The biggest and the best, 35km from Florence; Gucci, Ferragamo, Yves St-Laurent, Tod's, Armani, Valentino et al. Buses (€3.10, two or three daily) leave from the SITA bus station; by car, take the Incisa exit off the northbound A1 and follow signs for Leccio.

Prada (☎ 055 978 94 81; Località Levanella, Montevarchi; ❀ 9.30am-7pm Mon-Sat, 3-7pm Sun) Known as the *spaccio* (space), with Miu Miu, Helmut Lang and Jil Sander bargains as well as Prada. Get the train from Florence's Campo di Marte train station to Montevarchi (30 minutes), then a taxi (€15).

Roberto Cavalli (☎ 055 31 77 54; www.robertocav allioutlet.it; Via Volturno 3, Siesto Fiorentino; ❀ 10am-7pm Mon-Sat, until 6pm Sat summer) Ride the ATAF bus 29 to the Volturno stop in Siesto Fiorentino.

Olive Oils

For other food and wine to buy, see p143. To taste and buy olive oil from Tuscany and elsewhere shop at The Oil Shoppe (p139); oil specialist **La Bottega dell'Olio** (☎ 055 267 04 68; Piazza del Limbo 2r) or Olio & Convivium (p142).

Markets

Bargaining's on for cash buyers. For food markets, see p143.

Mercato de San Lorenzo (San Lorenzo Market; Map pp98-9; Piazza San Lorenzo; ❀ 9am-7.30pm Tue-Sun) Leather, clothing and jewellery of varying quality on and around Piazza San Lorenzo.

Mercato Nuovo (Map pp100-1; Loggia Mercato Nuovo; ❀ 8am-7pm Tue-Sat) Tourist kitsch and leather.

Mercato dei Pulci (Map pp100-1; Piazza dei Ciompi) Flea market, especially large on the last Sunday of the month.

Mercato delle Cascine (Map pp96-7; Parco delle Cascine; ❀ Tue morning) Big market in the city park.

GETTING THERE & AWAY
Air

Aeroporto di Firenze (Florence Airport; Map pp96-7; ☎ 055 30 61 300; www.aeroporto.firenze.it), 5km northwest of the city centre, caters for domestic and a handful of European flights.

Substantially larger is **Pisa International Airport Galileo Galilei** (☎ 050 84 93 00; www.pisa-airport .com), one of northern Italy's main international and domestic airports. It is closer to Pisa (p191), but well linked with Florence by public transport (opposite).

Bus

From the **SITA bus station** (Map pp98-9; ☎ 800 37 37 60; www.sitabus.it in Italian; Via Santa Caterina da Siena 17r; ❀ information office 8.30am-12.30pm & 3-6pm Mon-Fri, 8.30am-12.30pm Sat & Sun), just west of Piazza della Stazione, there are *corse rapide* (express services) to/from Siena (€6.50, 1¼ hours, at least hourly) or add 30 minutes to your journey and change in Poggibonsi (€4.30, 50 minutes, half-hourly), from where there are also connecting buses for San Gimignano (€5.90, 1¼ hours, 12 daily). Direct buses also serve Arezzo, Castellina in Chianti, Faenza, Grosseto, Greve, Redda and other smaller cities throughout Tuscany.

Lazzi (Map pp98-9; ☎ 055 21 51 55; www.lazzi.it in Italian; Piazza Stazione) forms part of the Eurolines network of international bus services and sells tickets for buses to various European cities. Locally, it runs buses to/from Prato (€2.40, 45 minutes, hourly), Pistoia (€3, 50 minutes, 10 daily), Lucca (€4.70, 1½ hours, frequent) and Pisa (€6.20, two hours, hourly). Several other bus companies, including **CAP** (Map pp98-9; ☎ 055 21 46 37; www.capautolinee.it in Italian) and **COPIT** (Map pp98-9; ☎ 800 57 05 30), share the same bus station.

Car & Motorcycle

Florence is connected by the A1 northwards to Bologna and Milan, and southwards to Rome and Naples. The Autostrada del Mare (A11) links Florence with Prato, Lucca, Pisa and the coast, but most locals use the FI-PI-LI – a *superstrada* (dual carriageway, hence no tolls); look for blue signs saying FI-PI-LI (as in Firenze–Pisa–Livorno). Another dual carriageway, the S2, links Florence with Siena.

The much more picturesque SS67 connects the city with Pisa to the west, and Forli and Ravenna to the east.

Train

Florence's central train station is **Stazione di Santa Maria Novella** (Piazza della Stazione). The **train information counter** (7am-7pm) faces the tracks in the main foyer, as does Consorzio ITA (signposted Informazioni Turistiche Alberghiere; p132), which makes hotel reservations (€3) and sells tickets for guided tours (p131) and shuttle buses to/from Pisa airport (below). During busy periods, the **train information office** (7am-10pm) on platform 5 also functions. The left-luggage department (p95) is located on platform 16.

International train tickets are sold at booth Nos 8, 9 and 10 in the **ticketing hall** (5.45am-10pm); No 19 has a ramp suitable for wheelchairs. For domestic tickets, skip the queue and buy your tickets from the touch-screen automatic ticket-vending machines next to the train information counter; machines have an English option and accept cash and credit cards.

Florence is on the Rome–Milan line. There are regular trains to/from Rome (€30, 1½ to two hours), Bologna (€14.20, one hour), Milan (€29.20, 2¾ to 3¼ hours) and Venice (€26.60, three hours). To get to Genoa (€18), change in Pisa; for Turin (€35), in Milan.

Frequent regional trains run to Prato (€1.70, 25 minutes, every 10 minutes), Pistoia (€2.70, 45 minutes, half-hourly), Pisa (€5.20, 1¼ hours, 40 daily) and Lucca (€4.80, 1½ hours, hourly).

GETTING AROUND
To/From the Airports

Buses to/from Aeroporto di Firenze (€4.50, 20 minutes, every 30 minutes between 6am and 11pm) depart from the SITA bus station. A taxi costs €20.

Terravision (www.terravision.eu; single/return €8/16; 1¼ hours, from Florence hourly 6am-7pm, from Pisa hourly 8.30am-midnight) coaches shuttle passengers between the bus stop outside Florence's Stazione di Santa Maria Novella on Via Alamanni (Map pp98–9) and Pisa International Airport Galileo Galilei. In Florence tickets are sold at the Hotel Reservations Office inside the train station and at the **Terravision desk** (Via Alamanni 9r; 6am-7pm) inside Deanna Bar opposite the Terravision bus stop; at Pisa airport, the Terravision ticket desk dominates the arrival hall.

Equally comfortable, cheaper (and more reliable in the early morning when coach timetables have been known to change at the last minute) are the regular trains that link Florence's Stazione di Santa Maria Novella with Pisa International Airport Galileo Galilei (€5.20, 1½ hours, at least hourly from 6.30am to 5pm).

Bicycle

Beat the traffic. Bike-tour operators Florence by Bike and Tour Bike Florence both rent wheels (p131), as does the open-air rental outlet **Biciclette a Noleggio** (Map pp98-9; Piazza della Stazione; per 8hr/day €1.50; 7.30am-7pm Mon-Sat, 9am-7pm Sun Apr-Sep, shorter hr Oct-Mar), in front of Stazione Santa Maria Novella.

Car & Motorcycle

Nonresident traffic is banned from the heart of Florence and the fines for transgressors are savage. Cyclopean cameras positioned at entry points to the historic centre snap your numberplate as you drive into the zone. Motorists staying in hotels within this zone are allowed to drive to their hotel, but must tell reception their car registration number and the time they were in no-cars-land (there's a two-hour window), so the hotel can inform the authority and ensure no fine is imposed.

Parking anywhere can induce apoplexy; the only practical advice is to dump your vehicle as soon as you can. The cheapest public car parks are in the Oltrarno beneath Piazzale di Porta Romana and Piazza della Calza (Map p103); both cost €1.50 per hour or €15 for a 24-hour period. Otherwise, many hotels can arrange pricey parking for guests; see p399 for details.

Should your car be towed away, call the **Ufficio Depositeria Comunale** (Car Pound Office; 055 328 36 60; Piazza Artom 13-14; 8am-12.45pm Mon-Wed & Fri, 8am-6pm Thu), 2km west of the city centre.

Major car-rental agencies:

Avis (Map p103; 199 10 01 33; Borgo Ognissanti 128r)
Europcar (Map p103; 055 29 04 38; Borgo Ognissanti 53-57r)
Hertz (Map p103; 199 11 22 11; Via Maso Finiguerra 33r)

Public Transport

Buses and electric *bussini* (minibuses) run by **ATAF** (Azienda Trasporti Area Fiorentina; Map pp98-9;

☎ 800 42 45 00; www.ataf.net in Italian) serve the city and its periphery. Most – including bus 7 to Fiesole and bus 13 to Piazza Michelangelo – start/terminate at the ATAF bus stops opposite the southeastern exit of Stazione di Santa Maria Novella.

Tickets cost €1.20 (on board €2) and are sold at kiosks, tobacconists and the **ATAF ticket & information office** (Map pp98-9; Piazza Adua; ☺ 7am-8pm), next to the bus stops opposite the station. A carnet of 10/21 tickets costs €10/20, a handy *biglietto multiplo* (four-journey ticket) is €4.50 and a one-/three-day pass is €5/12. Only one child shorter than 1m in height can travel for free per adult (additional children pay full fare) and passengers caught travelling without a time-stamped ticket (punch it on board) are fined €40.

Taxi
For a taxi you can call ☎ 055 42 42 or ☎ 055 43 90.

AROUND FLORENCE

One of the beauties of Florence is leaving it behind. Be it lunching in Fiesole, meandering around less-visited towns to the north and west, tracking down perfect wine in the hilly region of Il Chianti or titillating tastebuds with earthy white truffles in San Miniato, there is no shortage of places to go, pleasures to savour.

FIESOLE
After muggy old Florence this bijou village, perched in hills 9km northeast of Florence, revitalises. Its cooler air, olive groves, scattering of Renaissance-styled villas and spectacular views of the plain below has seduced for centuries (victims include Boccaccio, Marcel Proust, Gertrude Stein and Frank Lloyd Wright) – and still does.

Founded in the 7th century BC by the Etruscans, Fiesole was the most important city in northern Etruria and makes a delightful foray of a few hours from Florence. Motorists can take the at times nail-bitingly narrow country lane wending 6km east from Fiesole to **Settignano** (p138): the views of Florence from here rival Fiesole's.

Information
Just off central Piazza Mine da Fiesole, the **Tourist Office** (☎ 055 597 83 73; www.comune.fiesole.it;

Via Portigiani 3; ☺ 9am-6pm Mon-Sat, 10am-1pm & 2-6pm Sun Mar-Oct, 9am-5pm Mon-Sat, 10am-4pm Sun Nov-Feb) is a couple of doors down from the archaeological site.

Sights
Make the **Area Archeologica** (☎ 055 5 94 77; www.fiesolemusei.it; Via Portigiani 1; ☺ 9.30am-7pm Apr-Sep, 9.30am-6pm Oct & Mar, 10am-5pm Wed-Mon Nov-Dec, 11am-5pm Thu-Mon Jan & Feb) your first port of call where combined tickets (low season adult/concession/family €10/8/18, high season €13/10/20) covering all the main Fiesole sights are sold. Pretty spot to stroll aside, the archaeological area ensnares a small Etruscan temple, Roman baths, an archaeological museum with exhibits from the Bronze Age to the Roman period, and a 1st-century-BC Roman theatre where a fiesta of music and theatre takes to the stage during the **Estate Fiesolana** (June to August).

Opposite, the tiny **Museo Bandini** (☎ 055 5 94 77; Via Dupré; ☺ 9.30am-7pm Apr-Sep, 9.30am-6pm Oct & Mar, 10am-5pm Wed-Mon Nov-Dec, 11am-5pm Thu-Mon Jan & Feb) has an impressive collection of early Tuscan Renaissance works, including Taddeo Gaddi's *Annunciazione* (Annunciation).

In season a combined ticket also gets you a guided tour of the fabulous Renaissance-styled gardens of **Villa Peyron** (☎ 055 264 321; www.bardinipeyron.it; Via di Vincigliata 2; ☺ 10am-sunset by appointment only Mon-Fri), otherwise impossible to visit without an advance reservation. For ticket holders, **minibuses** (☺ 3-7pm Tue & Wed, 10am-1pm & 5-7pm Mon & Thu-Sun Mar-Oct) depart from in front of the Area Archeologica.

A lavish villa far in time and style from such Renaissance splendours is the **Museo Primo Conti** (☎ 055 59 70 95; www.fondazioneprimoconti.org; Via Dupré 18; admission €3; ☺ 10am-2pm Mon-Fri), about 300m north of the piazza, where the eponymous avant-garde 20th-century artist lived and worked. Inside hang more than 60 of his paintings. Ring to enter.

Rising up behind the central square, the **Cattedrale di San Romolo** (Piazza della Cattedrale 1; ☺ 7.30am-noon & 3-5pm) was begun in the 11th century but heavily renovated in the 19th. Inside, a glazed terracotta statue of San Romolo (St Romulus; 1521) by Giovanni della Robbia guards the entrance.

At the far end of the square, steep walled Via San Francesco ushers five-star view seekers up to the **Basilica di Sant' Alessandro** (1399), occasional host to art exhibitions. Florence

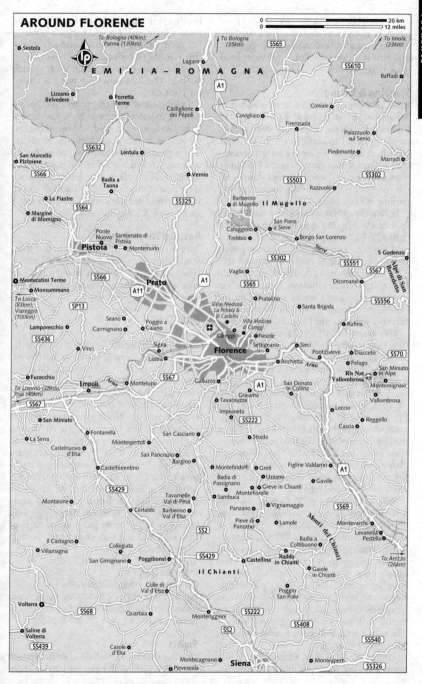

AROUND FLORENCE

0 — 20 km
0 — 12 miles

E M I L I A - R O M A G N A

To Bologna (40km);
Parma (130km)

To Bologna
(35km)

SS65

To Imola
(23km)

Sestola

Lagaro

SS610

A1

Baffadi

Lizzano
Belvedere

Porretta
Terme

Castiglione
dei Pépoli

Covigliaio

Coniale

Firenzuola

Palazzuolo
sul Senio

San Marcello
Pistoiese

SS632

Lentula

Vernio

SS503

Piedimonte

Marradi

SS302

SS66

Badia a
Taona

SS325

Razzuolo

La Piastre

SS64

Barberino
di Mugello

Il Mugello

Margine
di Momigno

Ponte
Nuovo

Santomato di
Pistoia

Cafaggiolo

San Piero
a Sieve

Pistoia

Montemurlo

Trebbio

Borgo San Lorenzo

Sieve

S Godenzo

SS302

SS551

SS567

Montecatini Terme

SS66

Prato

A11

A1

Vaglia

SS65

Dicomano

*Alpe di San
Benedetto*

SS556

Monsummano

To Lucca
(83km);
Viareggio
(100km)

SP13

Seano

Poggio a
Caiano

Pratolino

Santa Brigida

Lamporecchio

Carmignano

*Villas Medicea
La Petraia &
di Castello*

*Villa Medicea
di Careggi*

Rufina

SS436

Vinci

Signa

Lastra

Careggi

Fiesole

Settignano

Sieci

Pontassieve

Diacceto

SS70

San Miniato
in Alpe

Florence

Anchetta

Arno

Pelago

**Ris Nat
Vallombrosa**

Fucecchio

To Livorno (38km);
Pisa (40km)

Empoli

Arno

Montelupo

SS567

Galluzzo

A1

Grassina

San Donato
in Collina

Montemignaio

Vallombrosa

SS67

Tavarnuzze

Leccio

San Miniato

Fontanella

Impruneta

SS222

Cascia

Reggello

La Serra

Montespertoli

San Casciano

Strada

Castelnuovo
d'Elsa

San Pancrazio

Bargino

Montefiridolfi

Greti

Figline Valdarno

A1

Castelfiorentino

Badia di
Passignano

Uzzano

Montaione

SS429

Tavarnelle
Val di Pesa

Montefioralle

Sambuca

Greve in Chianti

Gaville

SS69

Certaldo

Barberino
Val d'Elsa

Panzano

Vignamaggio

Il Castagno

SS2

Pieve di
Panzano

Lamole

Monti del Chianti

Montevarchi

Villamagna

Collegiata

Badia a
Coltibuono

Levanella
Pestella

San Gimignano

Poggibonsi

SS429

Castellina
in Chianti

**Radda
in Chianti**

To Arezzo
(26km)

Volterra

SS68

Colle di
Val d'Elsa

Il Chianti

Gaiole
in Chianti

Quartaia

Monteriggioni

SS222

Poggio
San Polo

Saline di
Volterra

SS439

Casole
d'Elsa

SS2

SS408

SS540

Montecagnano

Pievescola

Siena

Monteaperti

SS326

views from here are staggering and there are plenty of green spots to picnic. The tourist office has a couple of brochures outlining short easy strolls – 1km to 3.5km – for those keen to carry on walking.

Sleeping & Eating

Hotel Villa Bonelli (☎ 055 5 95 13; www.hotelvil labonelli.com; Via Poeti 1; s €60-75, d €90-124; P ✗) Lacking excitement, maybe, but this friendly, family-run hotel up a little lane (off Via Gram-sci) where real people live is a solid midrange choice. Furnishings are typical of a 1964-built hotel and the sun-flooded terrace to lounge on out the front is nice. Rates include breakfast; parking is €10 a night.

Le Cannelle (☎ 055 597 83 36; www.lecannelle.com; Via Gramsci 54-56; d €80-114, tr €120-140, q €180, all incl breakfast; ✹ Mar-Jan) Stroll along Via Gramsci, past the old-fashioned single-pump petrol station by the side of the road, to reach this B&B – a townhouse with salmon-pink façade and oyster-coloured shutters. Inside, five fine rooms ensure sweet dreams, while the quaint breakfast room with dried flowers on each table is a welcome start to the day.

Villa Aurora (☎ 055 5 93 63; www.villaaurora.net; Piazza Mino da Fiesole 39; s €135-185, d €120-245, meals €50; P ✗) Built right on the main square in 1865, its four-star interior is more impressive than its paint-peeling façade suggests. Recently renovated Royal rooms offer a superb sweeping panorama of Florence. No 31 has the best view, or duck down to the pagoda-covered terrace for lunch in the company of the Florentine plain spread out grandly below. How about black and white *tagliollini* with clams and mullet fish eggs in lettuce sauce, followed by roast rabbit or pigeon? Rates include breakfast and parking.

Villa San Michele (☎ 055 56 78 200; www.villa sanmichele.orient-express.com; Via Doccia 4; d €840-1030; ✹ mid-Mar–mid-Nov; P ✗ ⬚ ⬚) This is the stuff of millionaire dreams. The 15th-century hill-side monastery with a façade designed by Michelangelo is ranked among Florence's most luxurious haunts. Guests who have signed its Golden Book include Brigitte Bardot, Naomi Campbell, Julia Roberts and a fair few royals. Lunch, afternoon tea or a candlelit dinner on the loggia overlooking Florence could well be the most romantic moment of your life.

Etrusca (☎ 055 59 94 84; Piazza Mino da Fiesole 2; pizzas €6-8) One of a line-up of tree-shaded

lunch spots on the northern side of the main square, this age-old bar-café-pizzeria has seen a thing or two – what a fabulous tree outside (it's a type of ivy)! Hang with a coffee at the bar or revel in a light lunch outside. Out of season, the place is closed on Thursday.

La Reggia degli Etruschi (☎ 055 5 93 85; www.la reggia.org; Via San Francesco; meals €35; ✹ 10am-3pm & 6-11pm) The cuisine – brandy-flavoured braised salt cod with tomatoes, home-made taglia-telle with guinea-hen sauce or *pici umbri' all agliane* (Umbrian spaghetti in a garlic and tomato sauce) – plays second fiddle to a stunning view at this five-table restaurant tucked up high in an old stone wall. Those who can't climb can ask for a lift.

Getting There & Away

Take ATAF bus 7 (€1.20, 30 minutes) from Stazione di Santa Maria Novella in Florence. If you are driving, Fiesole is signed from Florence's Piazza della Libertà, north of the cathedral.

PRATO

pop 174,600

Virtually in Florence's urban and industrial sprawl and a mere 17km to its northwest, Prato is one of Italy's main textile production centres. Tuscany's second-largest town after Florence, it has the country's biggest concentration of Chinese immigrants, many now second- or even third-generation Pratese. Founded by the Ligurians, the city fell to the Etruscans, then the Romans. As early as the 11th century it was an important centre for wool production. Continuing a tradition, textiles, together with leather working, continue to be Prato's main industries. Its compact historical heart, girdled by near-intact city walls, is worth dropping in on your way to the more picturesque cities of Pistoia, Lucca and Pisa or as a half-day trip from Florence.

Information

Post Office (Via Arcivescovo Martini 8)
Tourist Office (☎ 0574 2 41 12; www.prato.turismo .toscana.it in Italian; Piazza S Maria delle Carceri 15; ✹ 9am-1pm & 2-6.30pm Mon-Fri, 9am-1.30pm & 2-6pm Sat)

Sights

One day the impressive bulk of **Palazzo Pretorio** (Piazza del Comune), under renovation for years,

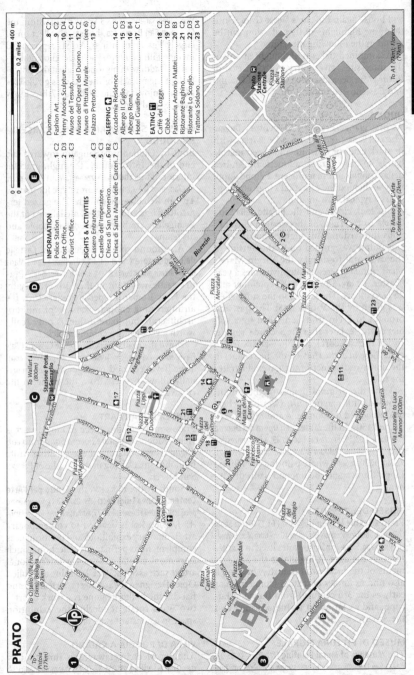

PRATO

To Pistoia
(17km)

To Ostello-Villa Fiori
(3km); Bologna
(92km)

To Wallart
(800m)

Stazione Porta
al Serraglio

To A1 (7km);
Florence
(19km)

Prato
Stazione
Centrale

To Museo per L'Arte
Contemporanea (2km)

To Luca
Mannor (200m)

0   400 m
0   0.2 miles

will house again the city's **Museo Civico**. Until then, the highlights of its collection can be found in the following museums.

A combined ticket (€6), bought at any of the three sites, gives entry to the Museo di Pittura Murale, Museo dell'Opera del Duomo and Castello dell'Imperatore.

DUOMO

At first glance Prato's 12th-century **Duomo** (Piazza del Duomo; ☒ 7.30am-noon & 3.30-7pm), with its stark exterior of white-and-green marble bands, solitary terracotta lunette by Andrea della Robbia and magnificent Filippo Lippi frescoes behind the cathedral's high altar, appears a typical Tuscan affair.

But look closer and the **Pulpito della Sacra Cintola** to the right of the western entrance pops into vision. This highly unusual exterior pulpit was grafted on to the outside of the cathedral to display the Virgin Mary's *sacra cintola* (sacred girdle) five times a year (Easter, 1 May, 15 August, 8 September and 25 December). The girdle, so the story goes, was given by the Virgin to St Thomas, and brought to Prato from Jerusalem by a soldier centuries later after the Second Crusade. Inside the cathedral, Agnolo Gaddi's fresco cycle, *Legend of the Holy Girdle,* in a chapel in the northwest corner of the nave, illustrates the tale.

View the original panels of the pulpit, adorned with playful *putti* (winsome cherubs) designed by Donatello and Michelozzo in the 1430s, in the **Museo dell'Opera del Duomo** (☎ 0574 2 93 39; Piazza del Duomo 49; adult/concession €4/2; ☒ 9.30am-12.30pm & 3-6.30pm Mon & Wed-Sat, 9.30am-12.30pm Sun), where paintings by Filippo Lippi, Caravaggio, Bellini and Santi di Tito hang.

MUSEO DEL TESSUTO

Prato's **Textile Museum** (☎ 0574 61 15 03; Via Santa Chiara 24; adult/concession €4/2; ☒ 10am-6pm Mon & Wed-Fri, 10am-2pm Sat, 4-7pm Sun) devotes itself to textiles through the ages. It highlights the achievements of the local cloth industry, but you'll also find examples of textiles (some from as early as the 3rd century) from Italy and Europe, and as far afield as India, China and the Americas.

MUSEO DI PITTURA MURALE

The **Museum of Mural Painting** (☎ 0574 44 05 01; Piazza San Domenico; adult/concession €4/2; ☒ 9am-1pm

Mon & Wed-Sat, 9am-1pm & 3-6pm Fri & Sat), within the **Chiesa di San Domenico**, houses a collection of largely Tuscan paintings. Artists represented include Filippo Lippi, Paolo Uccello and Bernardo Daddi with his touchingly naive polyptych of the miracle of the Virgin's girdle (see p105). Enjoy, too, the 14th- to 17th-century frescoes and graffiti.

CHIESA DI SANTA MARIA DELLE CARCERI & AROUND

Built by Giuliano da Sangallo towards the end of the 15th century, the high, graceful interior of this **church** (Piazza Santa Maria delle Carceri; ☒ 7am-noon & 4-7pm) was a prototype for many a Tuscan Renaissance church. The glazed terracotta frieze and, above it, medallions of the Evangelists are by Andrea della Robbia and his team.

Also found on the same piazza, **Castello dell'Imperatore** (☎ 0574 3 82 07; Piazza Santa Maria delle Carceri; admission €2; ☒ 9am-1pm Apr-Sep), Prato's castle, was built in the 13th century by the Holy Roman Emperor Frederick II. It's an interesting enough example of military architecture but, bare inside, is only really worth a visit using a combined ticket.

Down the road, sneak along the **Cassero** (Viale Piave; admission free; ☒ 10am-1pm & 4-7pm Wed-Mon), a medieval covered passageway that originally allowed access from the castle to the city walls.

CONTEMPORARY ART

Prato's most striking piece of modern art is Henry Moore's **sculpture** *Forma Squadrata con Taglio* (Cleft Square), an eye-catching white monolith smack bang in the middle of Piazza San Marco.

South of the old city, the **Centro per l'Arte Contemporanea Luigi Pecci** (☎ 0574 53 17; www.centro pecci.it; Viale della Repubblica 277; admission free-€7; ☒ variable Tue-Sat or Sun) is devoted to contemporary art. Temporary exhibitions and performances complement its permanent collection, which stars monumental creations by international artists such as Sol LeWitt, Jan Fabre and Julien Opie. Designed by architects Sarteanesi and Bacchi, the building alone is a work of art – two walls rotate rendering the exhibition space in a constant state of flux.

VILLA DI POGGIA A CAIANO

Another Medici getaway, this sumptuously decorated **villa** (☎ 055 87 70 12; Piazza de Medici 14,

Poggio a Caiano; admission free; 🕑 8am-5pm), 10km south of Prato in Poggia a Caiano, showcases a fine collection of 16th- to 18th-century still lifes in its **Museo della Natura Morta** (Still Life Museum) inside and magnificent sprawling gardens outside.

Festivals & Events

Festival delle Colline (Hills Festival) Concert series of world music, late June to late July, in various locations around Prato and 10km south in Poggio a Caiano.

Courses

Aspiring designers might want to sign up for a fashion workshop or 10-day to two-month course at **Fashion Art** (☎ 340 460 90 34; www.fashionart.it; Via Guizzelmi 6), a fashion-design school focusing on all aspects of the fashion industry, including textile technology, marketing, trend boards and so on.

Sleeping

Albergo Il Giglio (☎ 0574 3 70 49; www.albergoilgiglio.it; Piazza San Marco 14; d €55-58, with bathroom €65-70; 🕑 closed 10 days mid-August; ⚒) Squeaky clean and run with passion and pride by Alvaro Sabini since 1969, this old-style hotel with cosy could-be-home guest sitting room is a family affair. Siblings Stefania and Stefano help Papa run the show and the Tuscan welcome oozes warmth. The same family run Albergo Roma.

Albergo Roma (☎ 0574 3 17 77; www.albergoilgiglio.it; Via G Carradori 1; s €41-68, d €60-72; ⚒) Another Sabini affair close to the heart since 1974, Roma is a one-star place with 12 modest spruce rooms that offer excellent value for your euro. Ask for one at the back; the hotel overlooks a busy road.

Accademia Residence (☎ 0574 44 81 42; www.accademiaresidence.it; Via dell'Accademia 45; s €52-60, d €85-98, q €119-135; Ⓟ ⚒) Stylish fully equipped apartments with every mod-con rather than decades-old hotel, the Academy is a fantastic accommodation option. Each of the seven units is named after a famous person and peeps out onto an interior courtyard in the core of Prato's historic heart.

Wallart (☎ 0574 59 66 00; www.wallart.it; Viale della Repubblica 4-8; s €75-120, d €95-150; Ⓟ ⚒ 🖳) Those in town for Prato's art can go the whole hog and sleep, dream and eat art, too: marketed as 'a system of spaces to promote and exploit the creative synergy between business, art, history and metropolitan events', this art hotel-cum-gallery-cum-congress centre is large, striking and kitted out with the latest in interior design.

Hotel Giardino (☎ 0574 60 65 88; www.giardinohotel.com; Via Magnolfi 2-6; s €50-90, d €60-135, tr €75-160; Ⓟ ⚒) Primely placed a quick roll out of bed from Piazza del Duomo, this 28-room hotel is comfortable if not particularly exciting in décor. The place has wi-fi but it costs. Hotel parking is €11 per day.

Eating

Trattoria Soldano (☎ 0574 3 46 65; Via Pomeria 23; meals €15; 🕑 lunch & dinner Mon-Sat Sep-Jul) Prices are dirt cheap and dishes dead simple at this long-standing trattoria on a tatty street corner midway between the city walls and the train station. Mutton is the meat to try and home-made desserts conjured up by Mama and daughter in the kitchen are heaven.

Caffè delle Logge (☎ 0574 60 00 78; Piazza del Comune; meals €25; 🕑 Tue-Sun) Sprawled in the shade beneath the loggia on Prato's loveliest fountain-tinkling squares, this café-lounge and cocktail bar is perfect any time. Inside, a white moulded ceiling ensnares 1950s seating, flatscreen TV and boldly painted walls.

THE REAL MCCOY

Practically every tourist shop in Florence sells them; they are dunked in Vin Santo as sweet *dolci* worldwide and have become synonymous with Tuscany at large. Yet it is in Prato that these rock-hard, seriously crunchy rusklike biscuits studded with almonds were cooked up.

Known around the world, sure, but the Real McCoy only comes in a thick paper, cobalt-blue bag, tied with string and embossed with the mark of its maker: **Antonio Mattei** (☎ 0574 2 57 56; Via Ricasoli 20-22). Created by the artisan biscuit maker in 1858, *biscotti di Prato* or *cantucci* (as they are also known) are still baked up on the very spot where they were born.

Prato's other sweet name to know is **Luca Mannori** (☎ 0574 2 16 28; www.mannoriespace.it; Via Lazzarini 2), a world-renowned pastry, confectionery and chocolate chef whose *torta sette veli* (tart of the seven veils) will make the hardest of hearts swoon.

Cibbé (☎ 0574 60 75 09; Piazza Mercatale 49; meals €30; ☽ lunch & dinner Mon-Sat Sep-Jul) Wine bottles fill the shelves and tables are marble-topped at this no-frills *osteria* tucked behind a box-hedge terrace. Hailed by Slow Food as a gate-keeper of local culinary custom, Cibbé is the place to try *bozza di Prato* (a round unsalted bread loaf typical to Prato) and *mortadella di Prato* (smoked pork salami spiced with black pepper corns, nutmeg, coriander and garlic).

There are several more dining options on Piazza Mercatale or try:

Ristorante Baghino (☎ 0574 2 79 20; Via dell'Accademia 9; meals €30; ☽ lunch & dinner Mon-Sat) Stylishly lit with white table lamps; decent wine list.

Ristorante Lo Scoglio (☎ 0574 2 27 60; Via Verdi 42; meals €25, pizza from €7; ☽ lunch & dinner Tue-Sun) Wide-ranging menu: pizza to fresh fish.

Getting There & Away

By car, take the A1 from Florence and exit at Calenzano, or the A11 and exit at Prato Est or Ovest. The SS325 connects Prato with Bologna.

Prato is on the Florence–Bologna and Florence–Lucca train lines. Sample fares to/from its main train station (Prato Stazione Centrale) include Florence (€1.70, 25 minutes, every 10 minutes), Bologna (€9, one hour, 20 daily), Lucca (€4.30, one hour, 20 daily) and Pistoia (€1.70, 20 minutes, half-hourly).

PISTOIA

pop 84,200

Pleasant Pistoia sits snugly at the foot of the Apennines. Only 45 minutes northwest of Florence by train, it deserves more attention than it normally gets. Although it has grown well beyond its medieval ramparts – and is now a world centre for the manufacture of trains – its historic centre is well preserved. In the 16th century the city's metalworkers created the pistol, which was named after the city.

On Wednesday and Saturday mornings, the main square Piazza del Duomo and its surrounding streets become a sea of blue awnings and jostling shoppers as Pistoia hosts a lively market.

Information

Hospital (Ospedale Riuniti; ☎ 0573 35 21) Off Viale Giacomo Matteotti, behind the old Ospedale del Ceppo.

Post Office (Via Roma 5)

Tourist Office (☎ 0573 2 16 22; www.pistoia.turismo .toscana.it in Italian; Piazza del Duomo 4; ☽ 9am-1pm & 3-6pm Mon-Sat, 10am-1pm & 3-6pm Sun)

Sights

PIAZZA DEL DUOMO

Pistoia's visual wealth is concentrated on this central square – reason in itself to visit this humble city. The Pisan-Romanesque façade of the **Cattedrale di San Zeno** (Piazza del Duomo; ☽ 8am-12.30pm & 3.30-7pm Sep-Apr, 8am-7pm May-Aug) boasts a lunette of *Madonna col Bambino fra due Angeli* (Madonna and Child between two Angels) by Andrea della Robbia. The cathedral's other highlight – the silver **Dossale di San Giacomo** (Altarpiece of St James; adult/child €2/0.50) begun in 1287 and finished off by Brunelleschi two centuries later – is in the gloomy **Cappella di San Jacopo** off the north aisle. To visit, track down a church official.

Wedged between the cathedral and Via Roma is **Antico Palazzo dei Vescovi** (admission €3.60; ☽ 10am-1pm & 3.30-5pm Tue, Thu & Fri, guided tours 10am, 11.30am & 3.30pm), guardian of a wealth of artefacts that were discovered during restoration work and dating as far back as Etruscan times.

Across Via Roma is the 14th-century **baptistry** (Piazza del Duomo; admission free; ☽ 10am-1pm & 3-6pm Tue-Sat, 9am-1pm & 3-6pm Sun), elegantly banded in green-and-white marble to a design by Andrea Pisano. An ornate square marble font enlivens its otherwise bare, red-brick interior. A note on the baptistry door indicates what time guided tours of the cathedral's **bell tower** run.

The Gothic **Palazzo Comunale**, home to the **Museo Civico** (☎ 0573 37 12 96; Piazza del Duomo 1; adult/concession €3.50/2; ☽ 10am-5pm or 6pm Tue-Sat, 9.30am-12.30pm Sun) with works by Tuscan artists from the 13th to 20th centuries, dominates the square's eastern flank.

AROUND PIAZZA DEL DUOMO

The rich portico of the nearby **Ospedale del Ceppo** (Piazza Giovanni XXIII), with its detailed polychrome terracotta frieze by Giovanni della Robbia, will stop even the monument-weary in their tracks. It depicts the *Sette Opere di Misericordia* (Seven Works of Mercy), while the five medallions represent the *Virtù Teologali* (Theological Virtues), including a quite beautiful Annunciation.

A short walk westwards from the piazza along Via degli Orafi takes you past the striking Art Nouveau façade of the **Galleria Vittorio Emanuele** (Via degli Orafi 54), guarded over by a bronze statue of Mercury. Its lovely external wrought-iron balconies and internal painted ceiling above two-tiered galleries merit more than the trashy shops and booths that trade inside it today.

South of here is the **Museo Marino Marini** (☎ 0573 3 02 85; www.fondazionemarinomarini.it; Corso Silvano Fedi; admission €3; ☷ 10am-5pm or 6pm Mon-Sat), a museum-gallery devoted to Pistoia's most famous modern son, the eponymous sculptor and painter (1901–80).

Festivals & Events

Giostra dell'Orso The Joust of the Bear, a medieval equestrian and jousting festival, fills Piazza del Duomo in honour of Pistoia's patron saint, San Giacomo, on 25 July.

Pistoia Blues (www.pistoiablues.com) This Blues festival pulls in an international selection of artists for one weekend in July.

Sleeping

Canto alla Porta Vecchia (☎ 0573 2 76 92; bbanna01@virgilio.it; Via Curtatone e Montanara 2; B&B s €30, d with/without bathroom €70/60) It is impossible *not* to feel at home at this four-room *bed e breakfast*, family home to Anna and Giovanni Bresci, who give guests a warm welcome. Rooms are vast with high ceilings, old period furnishings and the odd fresco for a dash of panache. Breakfast is served around a shared table with a stunning church dome view and there is a

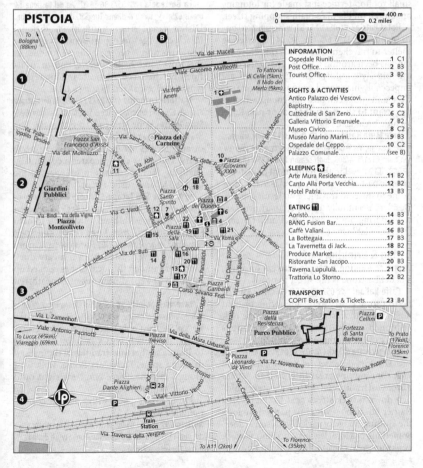

PISTOIA

INFORMATION	
Ospedale Riuniti	**1** C1
Post Office	**2** B3
Tourist Office	**3** B2

SIGHTS & ACTIVITIES	
Antico Palazzo dei Vescovi	**4** C2
Baptistry	**5** B2
Cattedrale di San Zeno	**6** C2
Galleria Vittorio Emanuele	**7** B2
Museo Civico	**8** C2
Museo Marino Marini	**9** B3
Ospedale del Ceppo	**10** C2
Palazzo Comunale	(see 8)

SLEEPING	
Arte Mura Residence	**11** B2
Canto Alla Porta Vecchia	**12** B2
Hotel Patria	**13** B3

EATING	
Aoristò	**14** B3
BANG Fusion Bar	**15** B2
Caffè Valiani	**16** B2
La Bottegaia	**17** B3
La Tavernetta di Jack	**18** B2
Produce Market	**19** B3
Ristorante San Jacopo	**20** B3
Taverna Lupululà	**21** C2
Trattoria Lo Storno	**22** B2

TRANSPORT	
COPIT Bus Station & Tickets	**23** B4

AN EXTRAORDINARY COLLECTION

A tea house, aviary and other romantic 19th-century follies mingle with cutting-edge art installations created *in situ* by the world's top contemporary artists at the **Fattoria di Celle** (☎ 0573 47 94 86, 0573 47 99 07; Via Montalese 7, Santomato di Pistoia; ☼ visits by appointment only Mon-Fri Apr-Sep), 5km from Pistoia. The extraordinary private collection and passion of local businessman Giuliano Gori, this unique sculpture park showcases comprises 67 site-specific installations sprinkled around his vast family estate. Visits – reserved for serious art lovers – require forward planning (apply in writing at least five weeks in advance) and entail a three- to four-hour guided hike around the art-rich estate.

A mere 10 minutes away is **Il Nido del Merlo** (The Yellow Beak's Nest; ☎ 0573 47 96 02, 349 806 34 68; www.nidodelmerlo.it in Italian; Via Montalese 67, Santomato di Pistoia; d/tr/qdr €70/105/140, 5-/6-person apt €175/200; ✂ P ✿), a well-regarded B&B where you can bed beneath beams and breakfast in a state-of-the-art dining room. Rooms bear Tuscan-flower and bird names and the pool proffers a dreamy Tuscan panorama.

small rooftop terrace just made for lounging on. Find it on Pistoia's main shopping street.

Hotel Patria (☎ 0573 2 51 87; www.patriahotel.com; Via Crispi 8; s €55-75, d €75-110; P ✂) Proffering shelter to travellers since 1927, this 28-room inn has been around a while, giving it a definite old-style mildly fusty air, but staff are impeccably mannered, rooms are spotlessly clean and guests can pick and choose whether they want to share a bathroom or not. Rates include breakfast.

Arte Mura Residence (☎ 0573 3725; www.artemura residence.com; Via P Bozzi 6-8; 2-/4-/6-person apt low season from €121/154/308, high season from €154/187/330; P ✂ ▣) Revel in the refinement of Pistoia's historic past at the lovely old Palazzo Desideri, home to intrepid traveller and Jesuit Ippolito Desideri. Beautifully furnished apartments are self-catering but a continental/buffet breakfast is available for €4/8.

Eating & Drinking

If you're looking for a place to eat or drink, Via del Lestrone is the street to prowl.

Caffè Valiani (☎ 0573 2 30 34; Via Cavour 55) The perfect for a pastry and cappuccino or light lunch beneath frescoed vaults; find the old-fashioned café in the former 14th-century oratory of the neighbouring church.

La Tavernetta di Jack (☎ 0573 2 04 91; Via del Presto 9; meals €20; ☼ lunch & dinner Wed-Mon) No, there's no Jack running this great little *trattoria tipica pistoiese* (traditional Pistoian eatery) hidden down a back street next to the theatre. Rather Lucciano – who just happens to look the spitting image of Jack Nicholson – does! Something of a local legend, Lucciano aka Jack cooks up great cheap filling Tuscan fare.

La Bottegaia (☎ 0573 36 56 02; Via del Lastrone 17; meals €25; ☼ lunch & dinner Tue-Sat, dinner Sun & Mon) Dishes range from staunchly traditional (black cabbage) to experimental (vegetable flan dipped in a *pecorino* cheese fondue) at this Slow Food–hailed *osteria*, known for its finely butchered cured meats and interesting wine list. Book ahead to snag a table.

Trattoria Lo Storno (☎ 0573 2 61 93; Via del Lastrone 8; meals €25; ☼ lunch Mon, Tue & Sun, lunch & dinner Wed-Sat) On the same street as La Bottegaia, The Star has a long pedigree; an *osteria* of one sort or another has existed here for the past 600 years. Today the chef prepares a continually changing array of dishes in full view of the guests. Décor is rustic-retro.

Ristorante San Jacopo (☎ 0573 2 77 86; www.ris torantesanjacopo.it; Via Crispi 15; meals €30; ☼ lunch & dinner Tue-Sun) Rabbit with black olives and tomato sauce, *zuppa di gran farro* (bean and spelt soup) or *maccheroni alla Pistoiese* (macaroni as you've never tasted it, in a meaty duck sauce) are among the local dishes cooked up at this well-kept dining room beneath red bricks.

taverna lupululà (☎ 0573 2 33 31; www.lupulula.it in Italian; Viccolo de' Bacchettoni 10; meals €30; ☼ 7pm-1am Tue-Sun) So hip it only takes lower case, design-driven lupululà brings a taste of modernity to Pistoia's otherwise traditional dining and drinking scene. From Via Roma, walk west along Via della Torre and turn right onto Viccolo de' Bacchettoni.

Other eating spaces with a definite cosmopolitan flavour:

Aoristò (☎ 0573 2 65 06; www.aoristo.it in Italian; Via de' Buti 11; ☼ lunch & dinner Tue-Sun) Stylish dining above the Globo cinema.

BANG Fusion Bar (☎ 0573 99 42 95; www.fusionbar.it in Italian; Via della Madonna 15) Eat in or take away Manhattan cheesecake, devilish brownies and other American delights at this US-styled fusion bar-café.

Produce market (☾ Mon-Sat) This market fills Piazza della Sala, west of the cathedral.

Getting There & Around

Buses connect Pistoia with Florence (€2.70, 50 minutes, hourly) and local towns in Tuscany; buy tickets, get schedules and hop aboard at the **COPIT office** (☎ 0573 363 243; Via XX Settembre 71; ☾ 6.15am-8.15pm Mon-Sat, 7am-8.10pm Sun) opposite the train station.

The city is on the A11 and the SS64 and SS66, which head northeast for Bologna and northwest for Parma respectively. Local buses 10 and 12 connect the train station with the cathedral.

Trains link Pistoia with Florence (€2.70, 45 minutes, half-hourly), Prato (€1.70, 20 minutes, half-hourly), Lucca (€3.30, 45 minutes, more than 20 per day) and Viareggio (€4.30, one hour, hourly).

Most hotels provide motoring guests with a pass ensuring free street parking between 9pm and 9am; otherwise private garage parking costs €6 per night. Those keen to free wheel around can hire a bicycle and gem up on cycling itineraries in and around Pistoia at **Panconi Cicli** (☎ 0573 2 23 95; www.panconi.it; Via Battisti 21); unfortunately the communal bikes locked up outside the train station as part of the Pistoia in Bici scheme are only for residents.

AROUND PISTOIA
Montecatini Terme

Verdi and Puccini found inspiration in graceful little Montecatini Terme, while many Hollywood stars, from Audrey Hepburn to Woody Allen, have dropped in to unwind. One of Italy's foremost spa resorts, it has a handful of *terme* (hot-spring centres), some lounging in grand *belle époque* buildings in and around a lovely central park. It offers a wide range of health and beauty treatments. Come here to relax.

The **tourist office** (☎ 0573 77 22 44; www.monte catiniturismo.it; Viale Verdi 66-68; ☾ 9am-12.30pm & 3-6pm Mon-Sat year-round, 9am-noon Sun Easter-Oct) has plenty of information on both accommodation and hot springs (which generally go hand in hand), all of which function May to October ,with the exception of **Terme Excelsior** (☎ 0572 77

85 18; Viale Verdi 61; ☾ 8am-8pm Mon-Sat, 10am-8pm Sun), open year-round.

Those who prefer the more primal could head 4km southeast to **Monsummano Terme** to detox in a cave with underground lake at the **Grotta Giusti Terme** (☎ 0572 9 07 71; www.grottagiusti spa.com; Via Grotta Giusti; ☾ 9am-1pm & 3-7pm Mon-Sat 21 Mar-8 Jan). You'll feel purer than pure after wading through paradise, purgatory and hell – three different cave zones, each hotter than the last.

From Montecatini Terme, a 19th-century **funicular** (one way/return €3/5; ☾ 10am-midnight mid-Apr-Sep, 10am-7.30pm late-Mar-mid-Apr & Oct) hauls itself uphill every half-hour to **Montecatini Alto**, Montecatini's pretty old town much fought over, besieged and battered throughout the Middle Ages. Great views of the surrounding countryside fan out and its 12th-century **Chiesa di Santa Maria a Ripa** is worth a peek; look for the bizarre, trophy-laden crucifix outside.

Should you want to stay up high, try **Hotel Villa Gaia** (☎ 0572 7 86 37; www.villagaia.it in Italian; Via Mura Grocco 11; d incl buffet breakfast €120) where some rooms come with a view. Otherwise, revel in the panorama from the terrace.

Montecatini has a couple of train stations, Montecatini Centro and Montecatini Montsummano, barely 1km apart. Trains running between Lucca (€3) and Florence (€3.60) stop at both.

IL MUGELLO

Northeast of Florence leading up to the border with Emilia–Romagna is the area known as Il Mugello, birthplace to the Medici no less, with a smattering of family castles, villas and palaces (most closed to the public) to prove it. Traditional Tuscan villages sit between elegant second homes for fortunate Florentines here, while the valley that the River Sieve winds through is one of Tuscany's premier wine areas.

In **Borgo San Lorenzo**, the **Comunità Montana del Mugello** (☎ 055 849 53 46; Via Togliatti 45), **Associazione Turismo Ambiente** (☎ 055 845 87 93; Piazza Dante 29) and **Borga Informa** (☎ 055 845 62 30; infoborgo@tin.it; Villa Pedori Giraldi) are useful sources of information about the area.

Take the SS65 north from Florence. Near Vaglia, about 5km north of Pratolino, is the **Parco di Villa Demidoff** (☎ 055 40 94 27; Via Fiorentina 176; adult/concession €3/2; ☾ 10am-8pm Thu-Sun Apr-Sep, 10am-6pm Sun Mar & Oct), a hopelessly romantic garden built around a Medici villa, long since demolished.

Follow the SS65 for another 13km and turn right for glimpses of another pair of Medici villas (both closed to the public): **Trebbio** and, further along the same road, **Cafaggiolo**, a fortress converted into a villa by Michelozzo in 1451.

Il Mugello means wonderful walking: Sorgenti Firenze Trekking (SOFT; Florence Springs Trekking) is a network of signed day or half-day trails crisscrossing the area. *Mugello, Alto Mugello, Val di Sieve,* produced by SELCA, is a decent map for hikers at 1:70,000 (its trail No 8 is an easy 3½-hour round-trip walk, starting from the villa at Cafaggiolo and passing by Trebbio).

IL CHIANTI

This *is* classic Tuscan countryside – olive groves, gentle hills, sun-baked red farmhouses and vines, lots of them, from which some of Italy's best-marketed wines are made. Post WWII, the region suffered severe economic hardship and depopulation. But in the 1960s, waves of sun-hungry foreigners started discovering these beautiful valleys enviably wedged between Florence and Siena. They snapped up holiday homes or moved in permanently to what, by 1989, had been dubbed 'Chiantishire' by playwright John Mortimer in his TV adaptation of *Summer Lease* – set in Tuscany.

Chianti Classico, a blend of red grapes with a minimum of 75% Sangiovese, sold under the Gallo Nero (Black Cockerel) symbol, is the region's oldest, most famous wine. The rest of Il Chianti embraces six more classified wine-growing regions: Colli Fiorentini, Colli Senesi, Colline Pisane, Colli Aretini, Montalbano and Rùfina, all with their distinct characteristics. The biggest wine-producing estates have shops where you can taste and

---

GET LOST

Ditch this guide and discover Il Chianti on the hoof. Your only companion: a copy of the life-savingly detailed road map *Le Strade del Gallo Nero* (The Road of the Black Cock; 1:80,000), marked up with wineries and every last back road. Buy it for €2.50 at Greve in Chianti tourist office...even if you don't want to get lost.

---

buy wine, but few vineyards – big or small – can be visited without an advance reservation; most only open their doors to tour groups.

The lovely Monti del Chianti rising into the Apennines mark the area's eastern boundary and the scenic Strada Chiantigiana (SS222) snakes from Florence to Siena. Bus hopping is feasible, but your own wheels – two or four – are the only real way to discover the region. Keen walkers can pick up a copy of *Chianti Classico: Val di Pesa-Val d'Elsa*, a map at 1:25,000 with hiking trails superimposed.

Chianti Fiorentino

This is the northern half of Il Chianti in the province of Florence. To get around by pedal or scooter power, rent wheels from **Ramuzzi** (☎ 055 85 30 37; www.ramuzzi.com; Via Italo Stecchi 23; bike/50cc scooter per day €20/30; ⊗ 9am-1pm & 3-7pm Mon-Fri, 9am-1pm Sat) in Greve in Chianti, its main town.

GREVE IN CHIANTI

This small town, 20km south of Florence on the SS222 and the only one in Chianti easily accessible from Florence by SITA bus (one hour, half-hourly), has two claims to fame. They are local *macelleria* (butcher shop) Antica Macelleria Falorni, known for its mean cuts since 1729; and Giovanni da Verrazzano (1485–1528). Local-boy-made-good and discoverer of New York harbour, Verrazzano was commemorated there by the Verrazano Narrows bridge (the good captain lost a 'z' from his name somewhere in the mid-Atlantic), linking Staten Island to Brooklyn and indelibly printed on the soles of every runner who's done the New York marathon.

Find both in the heart of Greve: at unusual triangular Piazza Matteotti, with its porticoes and a riot of wine-fuelled fun during the first or second week of September when the town celebrates its annual wine fair. The **tourist office** (☎ 055 854 62 87; Piazza Matteotti 11; ⊗ 9am-1pm & 2.30-6.30pm Mon-Sat) on the square has little documentation to browse but stocks a mine of electronic info on vineyards to visit and trails to cycle or stroll. Particularly popular is the 3km-long walk west (1½ to two hours) it suggests to **Castello di Montefioralle**, a medieval fortified hill-top village with a 10th-century Romanesque church and a couple of restaurants to lunch at.

LA STRADA DEI VINI CHIANTI RÙFINA

Forget Chianti Classico. Blaze an invisible green wine-tasting trail instead through Chianti Rùfina land, the smallest of the Chianti appellations covering a privileged pocket of 12,482 hectares east of Florence. Dry and red with hints of violets, this wine has been overshadowed by its Classico big sister for centuries.

Yet international wine critics constantly rank its best-known estates – **Fattoria Selvapiana** (☎ 055 836 98 48; www.selvapiana.it; Via Selvapiana, Rùfina) and **Castello di Nipozzano** (☎ 055 27 141; www.frescobaldi.it; Nipozzano, Pelago) tended by Florence's famous Frescobaldi family (yep, they're up there with the Antinori clan) – among Tuscany's best. The Frescobaldis also tend **Castello di Pomino**, Castello DOC infamously being recognised by Cosimo III in 1716 as one of the four best wine-making spots in Tuscany.

ourpick **Podere Castellare** (☎ 055 832 60 82, 320 407 95 92; www.poderecastellare.it; Via Casa Spasse, Diacetto Pelago; d incl breakfast €58-78 per person; P 🐾 🖳) An outstanding *agriturismo* (farm-stay accommodation) to stay within this little explored wine zone, this is an essential stop for design buffs with its funky design-driven space fashioned in an old farmhouse, olive groves and saffron cultivation. Also ideal for those wanting to flee Florence at the end of the day, it is about 7km from Pontassieve train station, from where there are frequent trains to Florence (20 mins). Arriving by car, drive past the eastern end of Diacetto village, then turn left; for images of Podere Castellare and a complete review, see p313.

For a one-stop wine-taste and shop in Il Chianti, there is no better place than **Le Cantine di Greve in Chianti** (☎ 055 854 64 04; www.lecantine.it; Piazza delle Cantine; ✆ 10am-7pm), a vast commercial *enoteca* with a small **Museo del Vino** (Wine Museum) and more than 1200 varieties of Chianti and other wines to buy. To taste some of the 140 different wines (including Super Tuscans, sweet *Vin Santo* and grappa), buy a prepaid wine card costing €10 to €25 from the central bar, stick it into one of the many taps and out trickles your tipple.

Alternatively head 3km north to the ancestral home of Greve's New York pioneer, **Castello di Verrazzano** (☎ 055 85 42 43; www.verrazzano.com; ✆ guided tours 10am & 11am Mon-Fri), a castle of an estate where the best of Tuscany – Chianti Classico, *Vin Santo*, grappa, honey, olive oil and balsamic vinegar – has been crafted for centuries. Tour its historic wine cellar and gardens then taste four different Verrazzano wines (one hour, €16) or go the whole hog and lunch on five estate-produced courses in the company of five different wines (three hours, €42).

Sleeping

Villa Vignamaggio (☎ 055 85 46 61; www.vignamaggio.it; Via Petriolo 5; d €150-200; P 🐾 🖳 🍴) Reputedly the birthplace of Mona Lisa (the daughter of the Gherardini family who owned the villa was supposedly Da Vinci's model) and a location in Kenneth Branagh's film *Much Ado About Nothing*, this exquisite 15th-century manor house is a vast complex 5km south of Greve. It makes wine and grappa; has self-catering apartments and cottages to rent; and sports an Italian garden, and a twin set of pools and tennis courts. From Greve, follow the S222 south for 2km, then turn left towards Lamole.

Greve has a couple of good hotels on its central square:

Albergo del Chianti (☎ 055 85 37 63; www.albergodelchianti.it; Piazza Matteotti 86; d incl breakfast €93-120; ✆ mid-Mar–mid-Nov; 🐾 🍴) Pretty garden and pool; minimum three-nights stay June to September.

Albergo Giovanni da Verrazzano (☎ 055 85 31 89; www.albergoverrazzano.it; Piazza Matteotti 28; s/d/tr/q incl breakfast €93/118/155/190; ✆ Mar-Jan; 🖳) Run by the same family for three generations; restaurant and cooking school.

Eating

Antica Macelleria Falorni (☎ 055 85 30 29; www.falorni.it; Piazza Matteotti 71; ✆ closed Wed pm & daily 1-4pm) The two huge chopping tables under the porticoes outside (please don't sit on them) give a clue to what is happening inside this centuries-old *macelleria* that is renowned throughout Tuscany for its prime-quality meat, including traditional *cinta senese* (a breed of pig native to Tuscany) pork and a gaggle of different salami.

Mangiando Mangiando (☎ 055 854 63 72; Piazza Matteotti 80; meals €35; ✆ Mon-Sat) Lovingly selected, quality meats (notice the gleaming

---

RECYCLED FLOORS & RENAISSANCE FRESCOES

ourpick **Fattoria di Rignana** (☎ 055 85 20 65; www.rignana.it; Val di Rignana 15, Rignana; d €95-105 incl breakfast, 8-person noble villa per week €3500; P ⊕ ⌨) This is truly a place never to forget. Dip in the infinity swimming pool with sweeping Tuscan views and pretend you're in paradise at this farmstead and noble villa, 8km west of Greve in Chianti, in Rignana. See p311 for a full review.

---

scales and slicer on the counter) ensure a permanent crowd at this intimate bistro with heavy wooden tables beneath the porticoes on the main square. Capacity is limited, so reserve.

BADIA DI PASSIGNANO

Founded in 1049 by Benedictine monks of the Vallombrosan order, this massive, towered castle-abbey encircled by cypresses sits in a magnificent setting of olive groves and vineyards about 8km west of Greve. Its church safeguards 17th-century frescoes by Passignano (so called because he was born here) and its refectory, Domenico and Davide Ghirlandaio's *Ultima Cena* (Last Supper; 1476). Given monks still live here, neither can be visited.

But the centuries-old **wine cellars** of this mighty abbey can. Used first by monks, the cellars today contain the viticulture stash of the Antinori family, one of Tuscany's oldest (think 600 years) and most prestigious wine-making families. Guided **cellar visits** (2-hr visit €25; ⊗ 3.30pm Mon-Wed, Fri & Sat) followed by a tasting of four Antinori wines must be booked in advance at the **Osteria di Passignano** (☎ 055 807 12 78; www.osteriadipassignano.com; Via Passignano 31; ⊗ wine shop 10am-11pm Mon-Sat), the Antinori wine shop and restaurant that is situated below the abbey. Wine-tasting sessions (€15, €25 and €40 depending what you taste) must also be reserved in advance, as must the short cooking courses it offers.

Sleeping & Eating

Fonte de' Medici (☎ 055 824 47 00; www.fontedemedici.it; Santa Maria a Macerata; P ⊕) A must for wine buffs, this 15th-century *borgo* (hamlet), where pilgrims en route from Florence to Siena sought refreshment from its natural spring,

is wedged between Solaia and Tignanello vineyards owned by the Antinori family. So, too, are the comfortable self-catering apartments sleeping one to six in the main farmhouse and outbuildings in Santa Maria a Macerata. Apartments in two other farmhouses on the Antinori estate are available for weekly rentals only.

ourpick **La Cantinetta di Rignana** (☎ 055 85 26 01; www.lacantinettadirignana.it; Rignana; meals €25-35; ⊗ lunch & dinner Wed-Mon) This marvellous eating spot with quintessential Tuscan views from its spectacular terrace is idyllically nestled in the old oil mill on the Rignana estate (p309) – see the old press inside. Wild boar carpaccio, truffle-stuffed ravioli, warm gooey oven-baked *tomino* (a type of cheese) with locally gathered mushrooms or a simple slab of meat grilled to perfection above an open fire are gastronomic highlights, but the icing on the cake has to be the grand finale shot of cypress- or juniper berry–flavoured grappa – a Rignana speciality. Wow.

Osteria di Passignano (fixed menus €50 & €90; ⊗ lunch & dinner Mon-Sat) Back at the abbey, the stunningly creative cuisine here is among Chianti's most expensive and exquisite.

PANZANO

There might well appear to be little to see or do in this sleepy medieval village, 7km south along the Santa Chiantigiana from Greve, but nip into the **Antica Macelleria Cecchini** (☎ 055 85 20 20; Via XX Luglio; ⊗ 9am-2pm Mon, Tue, Thu & Sun, 9am-6pm Fri & Sat), the local *macelleria*, and you'll get more than you bargained for. Very much a Tuscany celebrity, exuberant extrovert butcher Dario Cecchini has carved out a niche for himself as guardian of the infamous once-fated *bistecca* (p67) and knife-wielding performer of poetry recitals. Count on staying a good half-hour as Cecchini woos customers with wine, meat platters…and Dante.

Eating

Osteria Le Pazanelle (☎ 055 73 35 11; www.lepanzanelle.it; Lucarelli; meals €20; ⊗ lunch & dinner Tue-Sun) Perfect for a light lunch beneath trees, this road-side inn makes a great lunch stop en route to Siena (p235). Swiss-born chef Angelo cooks up a straightforward choice of around six dishes per course. Don't miss his crostini topped with *lardo di colonnata* (marinated lard from Colonnata, near Carrara) and orange peel, or his pasta dressed in a *pecorino* cheese and pear sauce. He also does a mean Tuscan-style burger, and the wine list is particularly well suited to those wanting to taste different Chianti wines. Find it 5km south of Panzano on the SP2 to Radda in Chianti.

our pick **Solociccia** (☎ 055 85 27 27; Via XX Luglio 11r; fixed menu incl wine €30; ☺ by advance reservation only 7pm & 9pm Thu-Sat, 1pm Sun Mar-Jan) If the shopping experience is not enough, share a meal with Chianti's charismatic butcher at Chez Dario aka 'Only Meat'. A chance to share his family recipes passed down between generations and show off his meat-cutting and -cooking prowess, Dario (who speaks fluent French and a spot of English) cooks up a five-course feast in his apartment restaurant near the post office.

Chianti Sienese

South of Panzano, Il Chianti dips into the province of Siena. Castellina is a great place to pick up information and hire a car if you need to.

CASTELLINA

The huge cylindrical silos at the entry to this town brim with Chianti Classico, the classic nectar that, together with tourism, brings wealth to this small community, long ago a frontier town between warring Siena and Florence.

From the southern car park, take Via Ferruccio, then turn right almost immediately to walk into town beneath the tunnel-like Via del Volte. This medieval street, originally open to the elements, then encroached upon by shops and houses, is now a long, vaulted, shady tunnel, particularly welcome in summer. Wine shops are rife here and there are plenty of places to taste and buy, among them **Antica Fattoria la Castellina** (☎ 0577 74 04 54; Via Ferruccio 26).

Nearby, the area's Etruscan roots form the focus of the modern **Museo Archeologico del Chianti Sienese** (☎ 055 74 20 90; www.museoarcheo logicochianti.it; Piazza del Comune 18; adult/child €3/2; ☺ 10am-6.30pm Tue-Mon Apr-Oct, 11am-6pm Mon-Sat Nov-Mar).

The **tourist office** (☎ 0577 74 13 92; www.essence oftuscany.it; Via Ferruccio 26; ☺ 10am-1pm & 2-6pm daily Mar-Nov, 10am-1pm & 2-4pm Mon-Sat Dec & Feb), accessible also from Via del Volte, must be Tuscany's most dynamic. It rents bikes (per day €15), has an internet station (per 30 minutes €2.50), sells books and guides

---

NO WAY

Yes way. If you really dearly desperately absolutely have to impress, pop open a fruity red Diadema IGT Supertuscan, bottle studded with Swarovski crystals, or a magnum of Diadema Diamante labelled with four carats worth of 40 diamonds embedded in white gold on silver by Torrini (p150), Florence's most famous jeweller. This strikingly contemporary Tuscan wine is the luxurious love child of **Fattoria Villa l'Olmo** (☎ 055 231 13 11; www.relaisfarmholiday.com; Via Imprunetana per Tavarnuzza 19), a wine-producing estate and *agriturismi* (farm-stay accommodation) run with a passion, 10km south of Florence in Impruneta, by the Giannotti family since 1735.

---

on Il Chianti, arranges cookery classes and sports an action-packed agenda of half- and full-day guided tours, including a one-day wine-tasting tour (€45).

Sleeping & Eating

Locanda La Capannuccia (☎ 0577 74 11 83; www.laca pannuccia.it; Borgo di Pietrafitta; d incl breakfast €90-140; ☺ Mar-Oct; **P** ☎) Tucked down a valley at the end of a 1.5km dirt road, this is a true Tuscan getaway. Its five rooms are furnished with antiques and hosts Mario and Daniela couldn't be more welcoming. Reserve in the morning for one of Daniela's very special dinners (around €25). To get there, head north along the SS222 from Castellina and turn left to Pietrafitta.

our pick **Al Gallopapa** (☎ 0577 74 29 39; www.gal lopapa.com; Via del Volte 14-16; lunch €20, dinner €40-60, Tuscan tasting menu €65; ☺ lunch & dinner Tue-Sun) A cool choice quite literally in summer, this appealing stone cellar with piano for (able) guests to tinkle on is lovely in any season. Its tables on stone-topped Via del Volte are a summer delight, as are the atmospheric dinners it serves after wine-tasting *aperitivi* at a nearby wine-producing estate as part of the innovative cultural programme Stelle in Cantina (Stars in the Cellar; www.stelleincantina .it in Italian; €80; advance reservations only ☺ 7.30pm Thu May-Aug) it runs.

RADDA IN CHIANTI

The tourist hot-spot in Il Chianti, surprisingly souvenir-shop laden Radda sits 11km east of

Castellina. Shields and escutcheons add a dash of drama to the façade of 16th-century **Palazzo del Podestà** (Piazza Ferrucci), facing the church on the main square. **Enoteca Toscana** (☎ 0577 73 88 45; Via Roma 29) is the place to taste and buy local wine and olive oil.

Or head 6km north to the gorgeous old-stone hill-top hamlet of **Castello di Volpaia** (☎ 055 73 80 66; www.volpaia.it; Piazza della Cisterna 1, Volpaia), where particularly lovely wines, olive oils and vinegars have been made for aeons. Buy some in its *enoteca*, inside the main tower of the castle, or enjoy a glass over lunch in its *osteria*. Should walking be more to your taste, pick up the booklet in the wine shop detailing 25-minute to three-hour walks around Volpaia.

Radda **tourist office** (☎ 0577 73 84 94; Piazza Castello 6; 🕙 10am-1pm & 3-7pm Mon-Sat, 10.30am-1pm Sun mid-Apr–mid-Oct, 10.30am-12.30pm & 3.30-6.30pm Mon-Sat mid-Oct–mid-Apr) has ample information on walking in the area, including several pretty half-day walks.

Sleeping & Eating

Castello di Volpaia (see above) has a handful of farmhouses and apartments to rent on its estate, as well as an inn with top-end doubles; see its website for details.

Noble *palazzo* hotels on Radda's main pedestrian street:

Palazzo San Niccolò (☎ 0577 73 56 66; www.hotel sanniccolo.com; Via Roma 16; d incl breakfast €120-180; 🕙 Feb-Dec; P ✕ 🖳 🐾) Four-star hotel.

Palazzo Leopoldo (☎ 0577 73 56 05; www.palazzo leopoldo.it; Via Roma 33; d incl breakfast €160-230; P ✕ 🖳 🐾) Great view from its restaurant terrace.

GAIOLE IN CHIANTI TO SIENA

A beautiful village with little to do, Gaiole in Chianti is a sweet spot to sleep, eat and sip some of Il Chianti's best-known wines aged in old cellars at **Castello di Meleto** (☎ 0577 74 92 17; www.castellomeleto.it; Meleto; guided tours incl bottle of wine €10; 🕙 2 or 3 times daily), 3km south of Gaiole, or at the road-side **cantine** (🕙 9am-6.30pm Mon-Fri, 11am-6.30pm Sat & Sun) of magnificent **Castello di Brolio** (☎ 0577 73 01; www.ricasoli.net; admission €5; 🕙 9am-noon & 3-6pm or 7pm summer, 9am-noon & 2.30-5pm Sat-Thu winter), Il Chianti's most quintessential castle where the famous Ricasoli family have nurtured vines since the 12th century. Walking its battlements, peeping into the burial chapel of the Ricasoli family and taking in the stun-

ning views through arrow slits is a real treat for aspiring knights and princesses.

Continuing south to Siena, take a walk on the wild art side at the **Parco Sculture del Chianti** (☎ 0577 35 71 51; www.chiantisculpturepark.it; adult/child €7.50/5; 🕙 10am-sunset Apr-Oct, by appointment Nov-Mar), a vast green wooded area studded with contemporary sculptures and art installations in Pievasciata, 20km south of Gaiole and 13km north of Siena.

Sleeping

La Fonte del Cieco (☎ 055 74 40 28; www.lafontedelcieco .it; Via Ricasoli 18, Gaiole in Chianti; s €62-82, d €100-154) Stone walls, beamed ceilings and nine pretty rooms named after Tuscan flowers (mimosa, rose, azalea and so on) make a charming combination at this age-old village inn perched over Giaole's main square.

Castello di Meleto (☎ 0577 74 91 29; www.castel lodimeleto.it; Meleto; castle s/d/tr/q €136/148/185/222, farmhouse s/d/tr €113/125/185, all incl breakfast; P 🐾) Pretend you're a princess at this fanciful part-15th-century castle, part noble villa announced by an alley of juniper and cypress. Castle rooms ooze romance (think canopied beds and the like), while those in the Casa Canonica (Priest's House), where farm workers once lived, are marginally more functional. Self-catering apartments are also available.

Florence to the Val d'Elsa

Another route south from Florence starts from the Certosa di Firenze (p128), from where you can wiggle south along the pretty SP4 to **Castelfiorentino** for wine-tasting in splendour at **Castello di Oliveto** (☎ 0571 61 508; www.castellooliveto .it; wine-tasting €13; 🕙 3.45pm Mon-Fri).

Otherwise wind along the wider Strada Chiantigiana (SS222) to **San Casciano in Val di Pesa**. An important wine centre, this town came under Florentine control in the 13th century and was later equipped with a defensive wall, parts of which remain intact. Before reaching San Casciano, you pass the **US war cemetery** (🕙 8am-6pm mid-Apr–Sep, 8am-5pm Oct–mid-Apr), where the clean rows of white crosses are a powerful reminder of the carnage of WWII.

Just before **Bargino**, take the side road east for **Montefiridolfi**, a charming little detour that takes you winding up onto a high ridge through vineyards and olive groves interspersed with the odd farmhouse or, in the case of **Castello di Bibbione** (☎ 0545 824 92 31; www. castellodibibbione.com; 2-/12- person self-catering apt per night from €120/700), owned by Niccolò Machiavelli once upon a time, picturesque stone manor houses.

Another 1.5km brings you to a large Etruscan tomb. At the crossroads turn west for **Tavarnelle Val di Pesa**, from where you can easily reach the charming little medieval *borgo* of **Barberino Val d'Elsa**, which is worth a brief stroll.

SLEEPING & EATING

This valley shelters some excellent-value accommodation.

Ostello Castelfiorentino (☎ 0571 64 002; www.ostel cast.it; Via Roosevelt 26, Castelfiorentino; dm €15.50, d/tr with private bathroom €39/55.50, all incl breakfast; ☺ reception 7.30-10am & 4pm-midnight mid-Mar–Oct; P ⏚) If Declan at Ostello del Chianti is full, try his gleaming modern red-brick and glass counterpart, a 600m walk from Castelfiorentino train station. Dorms max at four beds and advance reservations are essential November to mid-March.

Hotel Calzaiolo (☎ 055 824 90 09; Via Cassia per Siena 32, Calzaiolo; d €60) It might be dead simple and a tad short on decorative features, but this small two-star hotel with eight rooms in a road-side farmhouse 2km south of San Casciano on the SS222 is the perfect solution for those seeking clean cheap sleep.

Ostello del Chianti (☎ 055 805 02 65; www.ostello delchianti.it; Via Roma 137, Tavernelle; dm €14.50, d €31, d/tr with private bathroom €40/54; ☺ reception 8.30-11am & 4pm-midnight mid-Mar–Oct; P ⏚) One of Italy's oldest hostels going strong since the 1950s, Ostello del Chianti oozes dynamism. Spotless modern dorms max out at six beds (those in the original wing even have two bathrooms); bike hire can be arranged (per day €10 to €12); it has a great garden for *aperitivi*; and the ultracharming Italian-Irish Declan who co-manages the hostel is a mine of local information (ask him about foodie fests). Breakfast is €1.60.

our pick **Castello di Montegufoni** (☎ 0571 67 11 31; www.montegufoni.it; Via Montegufoni 18, Montagnan; 2-/4-/8- person self-catering apt per week from €620/690/1180) If it is history you're after, Montegufoni is your man. Ruined by attacking Florentines in 1135, this beauty of a fairytale castle rose from the ashes in the 13th century. It was kitted out with some wonderful works of art from 1909 onwards when eccentric British

aristocrat Sir George Sitwell, out motoring one day, stopped in front of Montegufoni and promptly decided to buy it. Tuscan home to the literary family until the 1970s, it is an amazing place to stay. You can find it located about 700m south of Montagnana on the SP4.

Mammarosa (☎ 055 82 49 454; www.trattoriamam marosa.it; Via Cassia per Siena 32, Calzaiolo; meals €30; ☺ lunch & dinner Thu-Mon) This is a Slow-Food favourite next door to Hotel Calzaiolo.

Certaldo

This pretty red-brick hill-top town, about 15km west of Barberino, is worth the detour. Its upper town (Certaldo Alto), accessible by funicular (return €1.20, every 15 minutes), has Etruscan origins, while the lower town sprang up in the valley in the 13th century. By that time both had been absorbed into the Florentine republic.

The stout figure of **Palazzo Pretorio** (☎ 0571 66 12 19; Piazzetta del Vicariato; admission €3; ☺ 9.30am-1pm & 2-7.30pm May-Sep, 10.30am-4.30pm Oct-Apr), the seat of power with richly decorated 14th-century façade, commands the upper, walled *borgo*. From here, Via Boccaccio leads past the home of Giovanni Boccaccio (p61), honoured with a bust and a marble slab on the nave floor in nearby Chiesa di SS Jacopo e Filippo. In 1783 the writer's remains were disinterred and scattered by townspeople who considered his work too scandalous.

SLEEPING & EATING

our pick **Panorama del Chianti** (☎ 0571 66 93 34; www .panoramadelchianti.it; Via Marcialla 349, Marcialla; adult/ tent & car €8/8.50; ☺ Mar-Oct; P ⏚) Wake up to a sweeping panorama of classic Tuscan landscape at this immaculate camping ground, perched on a hill in Marcialla with pool, small bar and soft grassy pitches. From Certaldo, 10km south, follow signs to Fiano.

Osteria del Vicario (☎ 0571 66 82 28; www.osteria delvicario.it; Via Rivellino 3; s €55-70, d €85-100, all incl breakfast) Four of the eight rooms here, cosy as can be and rich in antique furnishings, occupy what were once the spartan cells of a 13th-century monastery. There's a tranquil terrace and the restaurant (meals €50-70; ☺ lunch and dinner Monday to Saturday), in the cloister, is absolutely outstanding.

Upper town self-catering guesthouses:
Guesthouse Boccaccio (☎ 0571 65 24 35; www .guesthouseboccaccio.com; Via Boccaccio 32; d €65-75)

FLORENCE

THE TRUFFLE HUNT

It's the smell of the *tartufo bianco* (white truffle) that seduces. Or rather, the smell *is* the taste (think fresh mint without its smell) as my tastebuds gleefully discovered just hours after the deceptively ugly knob had been dug up fresh from the earth and brushed clean with a toothbrush (washing with water is sacrilege).

Imperio has been hunting white truffles at Barbialla Nuova, a 500-hectare estate 20km south of San Miniato, for 37 years. He might well be knocking on 80 and not quite as nimble as he was, but pair him with Toby and there's still a definite spring in his step. This season alone (the official season runs 15 September to the end of December), the pair has hunted 17kg. Their seasonal record is 24kg.

'Hunting truffles is like looking for gold or diamonds, something precious. It excites people – dogs, people and wild boar', says landowner Guido Manfredi as we walk towards the woods. Imperio marches paces ahead of us, head to toe in camouflage-green, *vanghino* (an L-shaped blade) doubling as walking stick in hand. Toby sprints ahead with canine mate Bobby, a younger more exuberant dog highly likely to wolf back every truffle he finds.

'It takes two years to train a dog, starting from when they are very small', Guido informs me, adding that a well-trained dog who has a good nose can easily be worth as much as €10,000. Unlike in neighbouring France where pigs are often used to snout out the precious truffles, Italy's prime truffle-hunter is the high-energy Lagotto Romagnolo dog breed, similar to a water dog. Ten-year-old Toby, a brown patch hiding one eye, is trained to a T and highly experienced: 'Dove? Dove?' urges his owner Imperio repeatedly in anticipation, to which Toby eventually finds the answer. He sniffs furiously at the ground, twirling his tail like a helicopter blade. His aged master throws a dusting of soil in the air, prompting Toby to rush off helter-skelter in chase while Imperio sinks his blade into the damp soil. Feeling delicately with his forefinger, he digs down further (truffles can be up to 50cm deep) until – aargh – he triumphantly prises out a grubby truffle.

Instantly it goes to every nose. Size, shape and colour don't matter; it is the aroma that is so vital. 'Garlic a bit, honey and pepper', remarks Guido, enthusiastically inhaling the excruciatingly indescribable scent. We are a party of 10 and for the rest of the hunt there is no guessing who has pocketed the 30g truffle – it can be smelled a mile off.

In season Barbialla Nuova despatches 500g of white truffles a week – wrapped in absorbent paper in an air-tight container – by DHL to the River Café in London where punters pay £69.50 for a *primi* of *taglierini* topped with 10 mouth-melting grams of shaved white truffle. True aficionados can order an additional 10g for £60. 'White truffles are very expensive. The price here is €1000 per kg and four times more in London', says Guido, adding that for a decent plate of pasta you need minimum 10g.

'White truffles are not actually white at all, but rather a creamy yellow, beige or reddish colour with a grungy-coloured veined interior that looks like the inside of a tree trunk. They are always eaten fresh, best married with plain foods and, unlike black truffles, never cooked: for me, eggs are the best, scrambled or fried, with truffles on top. But they are also very good with pasta, pheasant and steak, or a slice of bread and butter'. For this Florence-born, new-generation farmer in his 30s who inherited the organically run estate, food is as much a part of his daily life as the elegant Chianina cattle he breeds and the *agriturismi* (farm-stay accommodation) he runs at Barbialla with partners Gianluca and Marco. **Barbialla Nuova Fattoria** (☎ 0571 67 70 04; www.barbiallanuova.it; Via Casastada 49, Montaione; d/q/6 person room €70/132/186, 2-/4-/6-person apt €430/790/1035; P 🐾) stands on 500 hectares of agricultural land and is located about 20km south of San Miniato village and 20km north of San Gimignano. See the Agriturismi chapter (p314), for images and a full review.

Two hours later, reflecting on the home-made tagliatelle coated in melted butter and topped with pasta-warmed truffle shavings our hunting party has shared in the local village trattoria nearby, I can honestly say white truffle is a taste like no other.

Casa Giulia (☎ 0571 66 43 46; www.casa.giulia.it; Via Fondaccio 6; 2-/4-person apt from €80/120)

WEST OF FLORENCE

West of Florence and south of Pistoia lie several small towns of secondary interest and an extraordinary stash of white truffles from San Miniato. Here you will also find 1st-class DOCG wines, first documented in 1396, from **Carmignano**. Dash the frenzied belt down the Firenze–Pistoia *autopista* (highway), then fashion yourself a long and lazy tasting tour along this unexpectedly tempting loop of scenic countryside.

Montelupo Fiorentino

This market town, 25km west of Florence at the confluence of the Arno and Pesa Rivers, has been a well-known centre of Tuscan ceramics production since medieval times. Today it has no shortage of shops and markets ready to accept your money: a themed market (flowers, ceramics etc) fills the old-quarter streets on the third Sunday of every month and an international pottery fair rolls into town the last week of June.

Local pots from prehistoric times onwards fills the first two floors of the **Museo Archeologico e della Ceramica** (☎ 0571 5 13 52; www.museomonte lupo.it in Italian; Via Sinibaldi 43; adult/concession €3/1.50; ☺ 10am-6pm Tue-Sun), in 14th-century Palazzo del Podestà, where the **tourist office** (☎ 0571 51 89 93; ufficioturistico@museomontelupo.it; Via Sinibaldi 43; ☺ 10am-6pm Tue-Sun) is also located. Outside, a garden building explores Etruscan ceramics and contemporary work by students of Montelupo's contemporary ceramics school.

Across the Pesa stream, the imposing Medici villa known as the **Ambrogiana**, built for Ferdinando I, became a psychiatric hospital in 1888.

Frequent trains link Montelupo and Florence (€2.30, 25 minutes).

Empoli & Around

From Montelupo the road winds west to sleepy **Empoli**, an industrial town with a Romanesque **Collegiata di Sant'Andrea** (Piazza Farinata degli Uberti). The original town, documented in the 8th century, stood on the western edge of town – look for the worn profile of 12th-century **Chiesa di Santa Maria a Ripa**.

The only real reason to visit Empoli is to view fine Renaissance art in its **Museo della Collegiata** (☎ 0571 7 62 84; Piazzata San Giovanni 3; adult/concession €3/2; ☺ 9am-noon & 4-7pm Tue-Sun). From Empoli train station, turn left along Viale San Martino then right along Via Leonardo da Vinci to Piazzata San Giovanni. Trains to/from Florence (€5.20, 40 minutes) are regular.

From Empoli, motorists might meander north along the winding SP13 to **Vinci**…as in Leonardo da Vinci. A museum inside the commanding **Castello dei Conti Guidi** (☎ 0571 5 60 55; www.museoleonardiano.it in Italian; adult/child €5/2; ☺ 9.30am-6pm or 7pm), named after the feudal family that ruled the town and surrounding area until Florence took control in the 13th century, displays various nifty gadgets (a mirror-polishing machine, an underwater breathing apparatus etc) designed by the far-sighted architect and artist. The bastard child of Florentine solicitor Piero (couldn't trust lawyers, even then), Leonardo was born 3km north of Vinci at the **Casa Natale di Leonardo** (☎ 0571 5 65 19; admission free; ☺ 9.30am-6pm or 7pm), in the *borgo* of Anchiano.

For more information, visit Vinci's **tourist office** (☎ 0571 56 80 12; Via della Torre 11; ☺ 10am-7pm Mar-Oct, 10am-3pm Mon-Fri, 10am-6pm Sat & Sun Nov-Feb).

San Miniato Hills

White truffles to die for slumber elusively underground in dank sandy-soil woods around **San Miniato**, 10km west of Empoli. One of Europe's most truffle-rich villages, this is where London's River Café shops in season.

An integral part of local culture since the Middle Ages, some 400 truffle hunters in the trio of small valleys around San Miniato snout out the precious fungus, pale ochre in colour, from mid-September to December. The paths and trails they follow are a family secret, passed between generations. The truffles their dogs sniff out are worth a small fortune after all, selling for €1000 in Tuscany and four times as much in London and other European capitals.

There is no time to savour the mystique of this cloak-and-dagger truffle trade than during San Miniato's **Mostra Mercato Nazionale del Tartufo Bianco di San Miniato** (San Miniato National White Truffle Market), the last three weekends of November. The **tourist office** (☎ 0571 42 745; www.cittadisanminiato.it; Piazza del Popolo 1; ☺ 9am-1pm & 3-6.30pm Mon-Sat, 10am-1pm & 3-7.30pm Sun) has a list of truffle dealers and early morning **truffle hunts** (2hr, 1 to 6 people incl aperitif €200; late

Sep-Dec) can be arranged at Barbialla Nuovo Fattoria (see boxed text p170).

SLEEPING & EATING

Albergo Quattro Gigli (Four Lilies; ☎ 0571 46 68 78; www .quattrogigli.it; Piazza Michele da Montópoli; d incl breakfast €85 P ⌖) Grab a table on the delightful rear terrace overlooking the greener-than-green valley, or dine on imaginative Tuscan dishes (meals around €20) in a warren of small rooms and passages at this delightful family hotel-restaurant in Montópoli in Val d'Arno, run by the Puccioni family since 1930. Afterwards, pick up the *Historical Footpaths* brochure from the tourist office and explore the lovely old village.

Frescoes

Sorry, that exceeds carry-on restrictions: Piero della Francesca's *Legend of the True Cross* (p179)

BORCHI MASSIMO/4CORNERS IMAGES

'Giotto's appeal to humanity makes this fresco a clear sign of the Renaissance ahead'

Sorry, must dash: Giotto's *Noli Me Tangere* (Jesus and Mary Magdalene)

PHOTO SCALA, FLORENCE, 1990

SOCIAL COMMENTARY, RENAISSANCE STYLE

War protests, healthcare crises, prison conditions: today's newspaper coverage sounds like a Renaissance fresco. They may look like ordinary Bible stories now, but in their heyday, Renaissance frescoes provided running social commentary as well as religious inspiration. Masaccio's *The Tribute Money* spoke for Florentines whose taxes funded wars; Giotto's frescoes of St Francis among lepers touched those left orphaned and ostracised by plague; and eternal torment in Taddeo di Bartolo frescoes looked suspiciously like the late-medieval justice system.

Human adversity never looked so divine, and vice versa. Early masters mostly used the demanding *buon fresco* technique, painting pigment onto wet plaster walls. Today we can appreciate the brilliance of this technique, since many brightly coloured frescoes remain bonded to walls across Tuscany and Umbria despite centuries of exposure, earthquakes and grime. But *buon fresco* offers very little margin for error. Mistakes must be chipped out of the wall and painstakingly patched to match the rest of the image. To touch up goofs or add shimmering colour, sometimes artists would mix ground-up semiprecious stones with a binder and apply it to the dry wall. This *a secco* technique has its downsides, too: it often flakes off and fades.

But what keeps many Renaissance frescoes fresh even when they're crumbling is their remarkable empathy. They brought those haughty Byzantine saints hovering overhead on medieval mosaic domes down to eye level, where fresco details revealed awestruck eyes, quivering lips and clenched fists. Renaissance fresco artists made even dire predicaments pretty, proving that no human experience is entirely beyond understanding – or even redemption.

CIMABUE: *MAESTÀ CON SAN FRANCESCO* (MADONNA ENTHRONED WITH THE CHILD, ST FRANCIS AND FOUR ANGELS; 1278–80)
Lower Church, Basilica di San Francesco, Assisi (p334)

Of all the miracles Cimabue's Madonna is said to have performed over the centuries – restoring eyesight, delivering prescription-free fertility treatments and other feats widely advertised in spam email – perhaps the most amazing is its comeback after the 1987 earthquake that reduced much of Assisi's Basilica di San Francesco to rubble. While the dust was still clearing, thieves made off with precious fresco fragments, making the thousands of remaining pieces even harder to puzzle back together. The sleek contours that Cimabue outlined seemingly effortlessly in sludge-like drying plaster had to be laboriously pieced back together with a special computer modelling programme. Years of restoration work later, St Francis stands shyly by while the four angels fawn over an oblivious baby Jesus, who is too busy tugging his mother's robes to notice either angelic hosts or earthquakes.

GIOTTO: *NOLI ME TANGERE* (JESUS AND MARY MAGDALENE; 1307–08)
Lower Church, Basilica di San Francesco, Assisi (p334)

Hard not to feel for Mary Magdalene in this image, as she reaches out to the man who'd cast out her demons only to be told 'Don't touch me'. But Jesus had his reasons: at this point he'd already died, and had places to go and God to see. When two angelic ushers beckon on a flying red carpet, it's clearly time to go, and Giotto's gentle Jesus entrusts reformed sinner Mary Magdalene to pass the word. This is markedly different from the scenes of near-certain damnation that loomed large in many Romanesque churches, capped by stern saints who look like school principals. Even more than the perspective he applies to the rocky background landscape, it's Giotto's appeal to humanity that makes this fresco a sign of the Renaissance ahead.

AMBROGIO LORENZETTI: *ALLEGORY OF GOOD GOVERNMENT* (1338–40)
Palazzo Comunale, Siena (p237)

Makes your boss look benevolent: Tyranny in Lorenzetti's *Bad Government*
ALINARI/ THE BRIDGEMAN ART LIBRARY

Some people move to the suburbs to find a place with less crime and welcoming neighbours – but not Ambrogio Lorenzetti. In his *Good Government* frescoes for Siena's city hall, he imagined that these civic ideals might be achieved in inner-city Siena, despite the city's chequered history of elected government and gang warfare, organised charity and public stonings, booming trade and dire famines. In *The Allegory of Good Government*, his grey-bearded figure of Legitimate Authority is flanked by an entourage who'd put White House interns to shame. They've got beauty, brains and ethics too, representing key governmental

Peace plays innocent after tickling Fortitude: Lorenzetti's *Good Government*

PALAZZO PUBBLICO / THE BRIDGEMAN ART LIBRARY

virtues, from left to right: Peace unwinding with her olive branch; armed and ever-vigilant Fortitude; finger-wagging Prudence; learned Magnanimity, with book in hand; Temperance pointing at an hourglass, cautioning against hasty action; and a somewhat rough Justice bearing a head on a pike. Above them flit Faith, Hope and Charity, and to the left Concord sits confidently on her throne while the reins of justice are held taut overhead.

Next to this fresco is another showing the effects of good government: farmers bringing donkey loads of food to a spotlessly clean Siena marketplace, where all classes of citizens mingle, haggle and gleefully crash a wedding. Sadly, Lorenzetti's extraordinary vision had yet to be fully realised by 1348, when he died of the plague – and like many a glorious campaign promise, remains to be seen.

TADDEO DI BARTOLO: *FINAL JUDGMENT* (1396)
Collegiata, San Gimignano (p255)

As Renaissance painters knew, sweetness and light needs some brooding darkness to put it into perspective – and Taddeo di Bartolo more than obliged in his *Final Judgment*. Everywhere snickering are demons tormenting wayward souls: here a disembowelment, there a tongue piercing with a mallet. Tuscan wait staff may have their surly moments, but that can't compare to the treatment at the devil's table, where defrocked monks are force-fed communion wafers. Fifty years before creepmaster Hieronymus Bosch was born, di Bartolo defined grotesque with a cross-eyed, chicken-footed Lucifer, inhaling people whole and

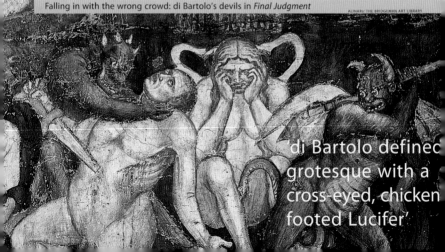

Falling in with the wrong crowd: di Bartolo's devils in *Final Judgment*

ALINARI/ THE BRIDGEMAN ART LIBRARY

'di Bartolo defined grotesque with a cross-eyed, chicken footed Lucifer' expelling them out the other end – all while gripping a human in each hand and banging their heads together like cymbals.

This may not seem like such a stretch from early Romanesque gargoyles or B-movie horror scenes, but there's a perversely gleeful gallows humour here that makes sense in its late-medieval context. Three-quarters of the city's population was wiped out in the plague by 1350, followed by bouts of war, more plague outbreaks and economic depression as the once-thriving trade centre was reduced to a Florentine vassal state. Those who did not willingly submit to Florentine authority might be convinced using the extreme methods and spiked implements today displayed in San Gimignano's Medieval Criminal Museum. By 1396, it would've taken a lot more than hellfire to shock locals who had seen worse, and the notion of brutal justice for their subjugators may have held a certain appeal, too. That this fresco still appeals today speaks volumes about Taddeo di Bartolo's skills and, perhaps, our society.

PINTURICCHIO: PICCOLOMINI LIBRARY FRESCOES (1502–07)
Cathedral, Siena (p240)

After more than 150 years of war, famine and plague followed by plague, famine and more war with Florence, Siena seemed to be running alarmingly low on people and resources, let alone inspiration. To rally the city, church elders hired Umbrian painter Pinturicchio to reassert the glory of Siena in 10 fresco panels celebrating Aeneus Sylvius Piccolomini, aka the humanist Pope Pius II of Siena, with a cameo appearance by St Catherine of Siena.

Siena briefly outlawed black attire to lift the city's spirits after the plague and Pinturrichio seems to have had a similar impulse in these frescoes. The sombre shadows and murky green tones of early Sienese painting are long gone. Pinturicchio's characters make their appearance in full party dress, in rosy hues, lush greens and an astonishing blue that appears jewel-like because it is – ultramarine was made of ground semiprecious lapis lazuli, then worth its weight in gold. To keep this lavish display of civic pride from seeming too heavy-handed, Pinturicchio covered the ceiling in frolicking grotesques: weight-lifting cherubs, griffons sticking out their tongues, banner-waving satyrs in red Superman capes, and bouncing, bat-winged babies. In the crowd scene below Pope Pius II canonising St Catherine, the artist included a self-portrait alongside his early collaborator on the Piccolomini Library: a young painter named Raphael.

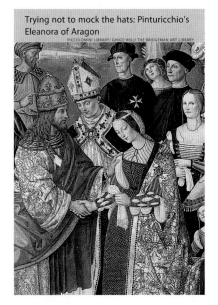

Trying not to mock the hats: Pinturicchio's Eleanora of Aragon
PICCOLOMINI LIBRARY/ GHIGO ROLI/ THE BRIDGEMAN ART LIBRARY

FRA ANGELICO:
ANNUNCIATION (1438–45)
Museo di San Marco, Florence (p119)

All those high-and-mighty religious figures on medieval cathedrals began to seem outmoded in the Renaissance with the rise of elected leadership. So instead of painting religious figures as domineering authorities, Renaissance artists painted them caught in all-too-human moments of uncertainty. Take, for example, Fra Angelico's *Annunciation*, when an angel appears to Mary to inform her she's been chosen to be the mother of God. Mary's blushing, bent-forward 'Come again?' posture and 'Who, me, a baby?' hand gesture make her instantly relatable. Anyone coming to terms with a religious calling could especially identify with Mary's predicament here, making this image ideally suited for a monastery. Fra Angelico returned to this scene several times, but the directness and poignant simplicity of the Museo di San Marco *Annunciation* makes it a masterpiece.

Home pregnancy test results circa AD 0: Fra Angelico's *Annunciation*
MUSEO DI SAN MARCO DELL'ANGELICO / THE BRIDGEMAN ART LIBRARY

'Mary's blushing, bent-forward 'Come again?' posture and 'Who, me, a baby?' hand gesture'

TOMMASSO MASACCIO: *EXPULSION FROM PARADISE* (C 1427)
Cappella Brancacci, Santa Maria del Carmine, Florence (p126)

Take a close look at Masaccio's *Expulsion from Paradise* and the adjacent *Tax Collectors* in the Brancacci Chapel and you'll appreciate not only his astounding architectural perspective but also his sly political satire. Florence had suffered five years of war at taxpayer expense by 1427, when the powerful Medici clan proposed a new tax to fund another military cam-

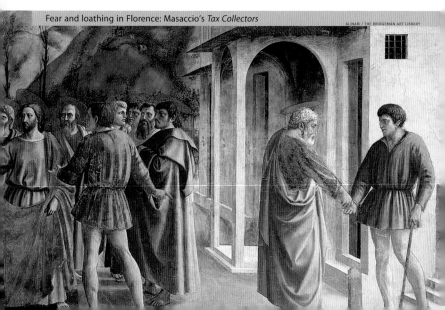

Fear and loathing in Florence: Masaccio's *Tax Collectors*
ALINARI / THE BRIDGEMAN ART LIBRARY

paign. Florentines rejected it with near unanimity, but Giovanni de' Medici pushed through the measure. Before they even had a chance to see Masaccio's finished work on their chapel, the Brancaccis were exiled from Florence for allying against the Medici. Masaccio died unexpectedly not long after this work was completed – insert conspiracy theory here – but his work stands as a brilliant rebuke to unchecked powers who wage war at taxpayer expense, and oust all opposition.

Later authorities objected not to Massacio's message but its anatomical correctness, and had Adam and Eve's bits painted over with a fig leaf in about 1680. The leaf was removed in recent restorations, so now you can see the duo as nature and Masaccio intended.

PIERO DELLA FRANCESCA: *LEGEND OF THE TRUE CROSS* (C 1452–66)
Chiesa di San Francesco, Arezzo (p296)

If the story of an inanimate object doesn't sound gripping, wait until you see what Piero della Francesca does with it. In 10 episodes he traces the story of the cross used to crucify Jesus, from when it was uprooted from the Garden of Eden and replanted as Adam's headstone *(The Death of Adam)* to its role as a holy relic fought over by kings *(The Victory of Constantine over Massentius)*. But thanks to a recent 15-year restoration effort, we can also read the cycle of frescoes as an encyclopedia of Renaissance painting tricks. Piero's realistic, directional lighting takes on nocturnal drama in *Constantine's Dream*, where light is shed from above by an angel hovering overhead like a holy streetlight. An accomplished mathematician, Piero experimented with a building shown in steep perspective in *The Discovery of the True Cross,* and a vanishing point that carefully positions Jerusalem on a distant Tuscan hill top.

LUCA SIGNORELLI: *LAST JUDGMENT* (1499–1504)
Duomo, Orvieto (p366)

Have you heard the end is near? So it must have seemed in 1499, when Signorelli picked up where Fra Angelico left off on the Orvieto cathedral and began his startling *Apocalypse* and *Last Judgment*. Green, orange and red devils stomp ruthlessly on the wayward and the weak, and winged demons raise up lost souls just to watch them fall. The chaos of this image has some basis in reality: religious crusader Savonarola had just been burned alive in Florence, the all-powerful Medici booted and France invaded Italy. The Umbrian countryside had been bedevilled by a century of earthquake and plague, and Signorelli lost a son and his assistant to the disease.

The handsome devils Signorelli painted break free of all Renaissance architectural constraints and seem ready to twist right off the wall – you'd never guess the man had worked under calm, rational Piero della Francesca. These writhing, muscular souls in torment may remind you of Michelangelo's *Last Judgment* in the Sistine Chapel, but they were done 35 years earlier. Signorelli's

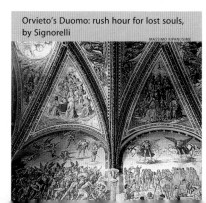

Orvieto's Duomo: rush hour for lost souls, by Signorelli

MASSIMO RIPANI/SIME

180

imagery also served as a visual reference for Sigmund Freud, the devil-child film *The Omen* and contemporary video artist Bill Viola. But when it comes to Signorelli's masterwork, the sincerest form of flattery isn't imitation, but sheer terror: as recently as 2000, doomsday predictors studied this work for signs that the end was nigh.

PERUGINO: *THE ALMIGHTY WITH PROPHETS AND SYBILS* (1503)
Collegio del Cambio, Perugia (p322)

Renaissance humanism flowered early in Perugia with a university of secular law and theology as early as 1308 and never entirely

Nice abs, but the workout regime is hell: Signorelli's *Last Judgment*
THE BRIDGEMAN ART LIBRARY

faded, thanks in part to Perugino's still-vibrant frescoes in the Collegio di Cambio (Trade Office). Old Testament prophets, classical sybils and a grey-bearded God are united here against an idyllic Umbrian landscape, under starry skies mapped with the latest Renaissance technology. For his insistence on ideals at a time when Perugia was sliding towards dictatorship and brooding mannerist imagery, Perugino's style was dismissed as outmoded and he was skipped for Vatican commissions in favour of his star pupil, Raphael. Although the Collegio was since occupied by the Church and various powerful Perugian interests, this fresco has never been dismantled or defaced. Perugino's delicate balance of faith, intellectual rigor, new technology and time-tested values remains intact, waiting for its time to come.

Perugino's Temperance pretends not to envy Fortune
ALINARI/ THE BRIDGEMAN ART LIBRARY

Northwestern Tuscany

There's mountains more on offer here than just Italy's iconic Leaning Tower. Usually hurtled through at breakneck speed en route to Florence and Siena's grand-slam queue-for-hours sights, this northwesterly chunk of Tuscany is a place to take your foot off the accelerator and go slow – on foot or by bike.

Take 'love at first sight' Lucca, a true lady of a city ageing gloriously. Ensnared by 16th-century walls made for a lazy *passeggiata* (evening stroll), butter-coloured buildings languish in a labyrinth of narrow streets, Romanesque palaces and gracious piazzas, all within a catwalk strut or wheel spin of stylish shops, cafés and boutique hotels. On the city's eastern fringe a twinset of elegant old villas stand tall, testimony to the ring of several hundred-odd villas that crowned Lucca from the 16th to 19th centuries.

Then there are those mountains – peeping down on the sea and made of marble in the case of the foothills hugging Carrara, an old town where sculptors, *David's* creator included, have flocked for aeons in search of the perfect block of *marmo bianco*. Touring a marble quarry and tasting *lardo di Colonnata* are northwestern Tuscan essentials, as is a dive deeper into the Apuane Alps. Protected as a nature park, there is little to do in this playground of soaring peaks, pine valleys, subterranean caves and chestnut groves than hike, bike and feast on the fruits of the forest over long lazy farmhouse lunches. Oh, and go slow.

HIGHLIGHTS

- Climb to the top of **Pisa's Leaning Tower** (p185) at night and take in great big gulps of Piazza dei Miracoli's natural beauty, free of crowds and vendors

- Pedal round **Lucca** (p191) to understand why Lucchese say their town was built from pure beauty

- Have a ball at Viareggio's springtime Rio-style **Carnevale** (p202)

- Delve inside **Marble Mountain**, near Carrara and taste the world's most famous marble in Colonnata, an Apuane Alp village where *lardo* lounges for months in vats of spiced oil (p207).

- Sit beneath stars and watch *Madame Butterfly*, *Tosca* or another Puccini opera at Torre del Lago's soul-stirring **Festival Puccini** (p203)

- Marvel at crystal-encrusted lakes, alabaster drapes, stalactites and stalagmites in the Garfagnana's chilly **Grotto del Vento** (p210)

- Feast on fruits of the forest in one of Tuscany's wildest, least-touched pockets, **Lunigiana** (p211)

★ Lunigiana
★ Garfagnana
★ Carrara
★ Viareggio   ★ Lucca
Pisa ★

PISA

pop 87,700

Briefly a maritime power to rival Genoa and Venice, Pisa draws its fame from an architectural project gone terribly wrong. But the Leaning Tower is just one of a trio of Romanesque splendours on the green carpet of Piazza dei Miracoli. This unforgettable square is bequeathed with one of Europe's earliest hidden collections of Oriental art, amassed by feisty Pisans that flitted from piazza to bazaar to piazza in the 11th and 12th centuries.

Pisa is an old university town and swarms with students, yet for many an off-the-coach, snap, back-on-the-coach visitor, its charms are far from apparent. On the main square, the crowds and pesky pedlars flogging knock-off bags can be mind-numbing. Throw in a four- or five-hour wait to scale the tower and you could well leave not scaling the tower and wondering what all the fuss is about. To avoid disappointment book your tower slot well in advance.

History

Possibly of Greek origin, Pisa became an important naval base under Rome and remained a significant port for centuries. The city's golden days began late in the 10th century, when it became an independent maritime republic and a rival of Genoa and Venice. A century on, the Pisan fleet was sailing far beyond the Mediterranean, successfully trading with the Orient and bringing home new ideas

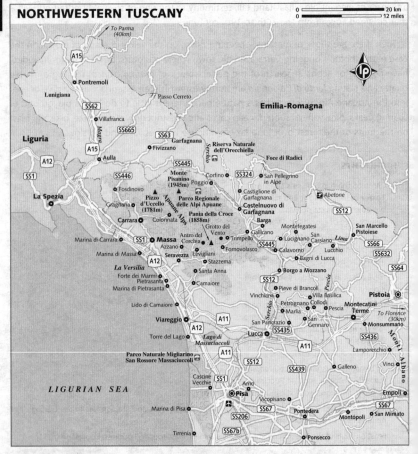

in art, architecture and science. At the peak of its glory days, which continued well into the 13th century, Pisa controlled Corsica, Sardinia and the Tuscan coast. Most of the city's finest buildings date from this period, when the distinctive Pisan-Romanesque architectural style, with its overtly Arab influence, flourished.

Pisa's support for the Ghibellines during the tussles between the Holy Roman Emperor and the pope brought the city into conflict with its mostly Guelph Tuscan neighbours, including Siena, Lucca and Florence. The real blow came when Genoa's fleet inflicted a devastating defeat on Pisa at the Battle of Meloria in 1284. After the city fell to Florence in 1406, the Medici court encouraged great artistic, literary and scientific endeavours and re-established Pisa's university. The city's most famous son, Galileo Galilei (see p35) taught at the university.

The medieval city changed under the grand dukes of Tuscany who began a process of demolition to make way for wider boulevards to ease traffic problems. During WWII about 50% of old Pisa was destroyed.

Information
INTERNET ACCESS
Internet Planet (☎ 050 83 07 02; Piazza Cavallotti 3-4; per hr €3.50; ☼ 9am-midnight Mon-Fri, 10am-10pm Sat & Sun)

Internet Surf (☎ 050 83 08 00; Via Carducci 5; per hr €2; ☼ 10am-10pm Mon-Sat, 3pm-midnight Sun) If all the machines are taken, cross the road to the internet outlet opposite.

LAUNDRY
Onda Blu (☎ 800 861 346; Via San Francesco 8a; ☼ 8am-10pm)

LEFT LUGGAGE
Train station (Piazza della Stazione; per 12/24/48hr €3/6/9; ☼ 6am-9pm) *Deposito bagagli* signposted off platform 1.

MEDICAL SERVICES
Farmacia Nuova Fantoni (Lungarno Mediceo 51; ☼ 24hr)

Hospital (☎ 050 99 21 11; Via Roma 67)

POST
Post office (Piazza Vittorio Emanuele II)

TOURIST INFORMATION
Tourist office Airport (☎ 050 50 37 00; ☼ 10.30am-4.30pm & 6-10pm); Duomo (☎ 050 56 04 64; www.pisa .turismo.toscana.it; Piazza dei Miracoli; ☼ 9am-6pm Mar-Sep, 9.30am-5pm Oct-Feb); Piazza Vittorio Emanuele II 16 (☎ 050 4 22 91; ☼ 9am-7pm Mon-Fri, to 1.30pm Sat) The Duomo branch is the main tourist office, situated near the Leaning Tower, inside Museo dell'Opera del Duomo.

Sights
No Tuscan sight is more immortalised in kitsch souvenirs than the iconic tower piercing **Piazza dei Miracoli**, also called Campo dei Miracoli (Field of Miracles) and Piazza del Duomo. One of the world's loveliest and busiest squares, with its sprawling green lawns and crowds propping up the tower for the camera, this piazza showcases one of Europe's most extraordinary concentrations of Romanesque splendour – the cathedral, baptistry and tower. Predictably, the square is protected as a Unesco World Heritage Site. Less obvious is the fact that all three monuments do, in fact, lean.

South of Piazza dei Miracoli, tourist swarms give way to the real Pisa: quiet back alleys and

---

TOP FIVE COURSES

■ Shop for antiques with an expert, learn the difference between Empire and Direttorio and discover the best dealers with **Ars Antiquaria** (www.arsantiquaria.it) at Villa Franca, 5km from Lucca.

■ Often with a spring or autumnal horticultural theme, the gardening courses at Costa d'Orsola (p211) are a true 'back to nature' experience.

■ Sculpt the world's most famous marble at sculpture studio **Arco Arte** (☎ 0585 77 70 00; www .sculturacarrar.com; Via Carriona di Colonnata 10) in Carrara; there are two-week courses for all levels.

■ Learn the ancient art of handweaving at **Castel du Gargafnana's Scuola Tessile** (☎ 339 190 47 50; www.scuolatessilegarfagnana.it; Via Vannugli 61) in the Garfagnana.

■ Tuscan garden design is what the half-day gardening courses run by passionate landscape designer Simone at **Villa Lucca** (www.frangleeson.com), 5km from Lucca, are all about.

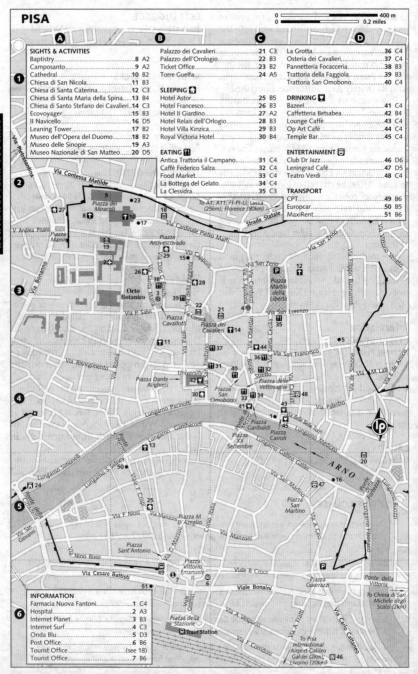

PISA

0 — 400 m
0 — 0.2 miles

SIGHTS & ACTIVITIES
Baptistry.....................................8 A2
Camposanto..............................9 A2
Cathedral.................................10 B2
Chiesa di San Nicola.................11 B3
Chiesa di Santa Caterina...........12 C3
Chiesa di Santa Maria della Spina...13 B4
Chiesa di Santo Stefano dei Cavalieri...14 C3
Ecovoyager..............................15 B3
Il Navicello...............................16 D5
Leaning Tower..........................17 B2
Museo dell'Opera del Duomo....18 B2
Museo delle Sinopie.................19 A3
Museo Nazionale di San Matteo...20 D5

Palazzo dei Cavalieri.................21 C3
Palazzo dell'Orologio................22 B3
Ticket Office.............................23 B2
Torre Guelfa.............................24 A5

SLEEPING
Hotel Astor..............................25 B5
Hotel Francesco.......................26 B3
Hotel Il Giardino......................27 A2
Hotel Relais dell'Orologio.........28 B3
Hotel Villa Kinzica....................29 B3
Royal Victoria Hotel.................30 B4

EATING
Antica Trattoria il Campano......31 C4
Caffè Federico Salza.................32 C4
Food Market.............................33 C4
La Bottega del Gelato...............34 C4
La Clessidra.............................35 C3

La Grotta.................................36 C4
Osteria dei Cavalieri.................37 C4
Pannetteria Focacceria..............38 B3
Trattoria della Faggiola.............39 B3
Trattoria San Omobono............40 C4

DRINKING
Bazeel.....................................41 C4
Caffetteria Betsabea.................42 B4
Lounge Caffè...........................43 C4
Op Art Café.............................44 C4
Temple Bar..............................45 C4

ENTERTAINMENT
Club Dr Jazz.............................46 D6
Leningrad Café.........................47 D5
Teatro Verdi.............................48 C4

TRANSPORT
CPT..49 B6
Europcar..................................50 B5
MaxiRent..................................51 B6

INFORMATION
Farmacia Nuova Fantoni..............1 C4
Hospital....................................2 A3
Internet Planet............................3 B3
Internet Surf...............................4 C3
Onda Blu....................................5 D3
Post Office..................................6 B6
Tourist Office..........................(see 18)
Tourist Office.............................7 B6

Via Petrarcamino

Via Contessa Matilde

Via Bonanno

V Andrea Pisano

Piazza Manin

Piazza dei Miracoli

Via Cardinale Pietro Maffi

Strada Statale

To A4, A11, FI-PI-LI; Lucca (25km); Florence (80km)

Piazza Arcivescovado

Via Don Bosco

Via della Faggiola

Via Santa Maria

Orto Botanico

Via P Salvi

Piazza Cavallotti

Piazza dei Cavalieri

Via Risorgimento

Via Roma

Via Corsica

Via S Apollonia

Via San Zeno

Piazza Martiri della Libertà

Via San Lorenzo

Via San Zeno

Via N Carducci

Via Oberdan

Via Santa Cecilia

Via San Francesco

Via de Simone

Via E de Amicis

Via de' Mille

Via L M Lalli

Via Palestro

University

Piazza Dante Alighieri

Via San Frediano

Via Paoli

Piazza San Omobono

Borgo Stretto

Piazza delle Vettovaglie

Via delle belle Torri

Via Filippo Buonarroti

Via Vittorio Veneto

Ponte di Mezzo

Piazza Garibaldi

Piazza Cairoli

Lungarno Mediceo

ARNO

Lungarno Pacinotti

Lungarno Gambacorti

Lungarno Galileo Galilei

Ponte Solferino

Piazza XX Settembre

Ponte della Cittadella

Lungarno Simonelli

Ponte della Fortezza

Lungarno Buozzi

Lungarno Fibonacci

Via San Giovanni

Via F Nlosi

Via Manzoni

Piazza M D'Azeglio

Corso Italia

Via San Martino

Piazza San Martino

Via A Ceci

Via G Mazzini

Via Manzoni

Piazza Sant'Antonio

Via Nino Bixio

Via Cesare Battisti

Piazza Vittorio Emanuele II

Viale B Croce

Viale Bonaini

Piazza Guerrazzi

Ponte della Vittoria

To Chiesa di San Michele degli Scalzi (2km)

Viale Gramsci

Piazza della Stazione

Train Station

Via A Vespucci

Via F Corridoni

Via A Fratti

Via Carlo Cattaneo

To Pisa International Airport Galileo Galilei (2km); Livorno (20km)

shopping streets where Pisans go about their daily business; a 14th-century **university** (1343) attended by 51,000 students; and colourful **San Martino**, the old Arab and Turkish merchant quarter of medieval Pisa on the Arno's south bank where contemporary design studios do business alongside Russian delicatessens, retro music shops and some of the city's best clubs and bars.

LEANING TOWER

No matter how many postcards you've seen, nothing prepares you for the real thing. The **Torre Pendente** (Torre Campanaria; ☎ ticket reservations 050 387 22 10; www.opapisa.it/boxoffice; admission €15, with advance reservation €17; ⏰ 8.30am-8.30pm Apr–mid-Jun & last 2 weeks Sep, 8.30am-11pm mid-Jun–mid-Sep, 9am-7pm Oct, 10am-5pm Nov-Feb, 9am-6pm or 7pm Mar) is gravity defying; see the boxed text, p186.

Admission to the tower is limited to 40 people at a time and is by guided tour (in Italian or English). If you don't want to wait for hours, book in advance (online or by telephone); otherwise run to a ticket office on Piazza dei Miracoli when you arrive to book your slot for later that day.

Visits – a breathless climb up 300 occasionally slippy steps – last 30 minutes; late-evening visits in summer proffer enchanting views of Pisa by night. All bags, including handbags, must be deposited at the free left-luggage desk next to the ticket office and children aged under eight are not allowed in.

CATHEDRAL

Pisa's **duomo** (Piazza dei Miracoli; admission Mar-Oct incl audioguide €2, free Nov-Feb; ⏰ 10am-8pm Mon-Sat Apr-Sep, 10am-7pm Mon-Sat Oct, 10am-1pm & 2-5pm Mon-Sat Nov-Feb, 10am-6pm or 7pm Mon-Sat Mar, from 1pm Sun year-round) was paid for with spoils brought home after Pisans attacked an Arab fleet entering Palermo in 1063. Begun a year later, the cathedral, with its striking cladding of alternating bands of green and cream marble, became the blueprint floor for Romanesque churches throughout Tuscany. The elliptical dome, the first of its kind in Europe at the time, was added in 1380.

The cathedral's proportions are breathtaking. Its main façade – not completed until the 13th century – has four exquisite tiers of columns diminishing skywards, while the vast interior, 96m long and 28m high, is propped up by 68 hefty granite columns in classical style. Sheer size aside, the early-14th-century

PIAZZA DEI MIRACOLI COMBINED TICKETS

Tickets to the Leaning Tower and cathedral are sold individually, but for the rest of the Piazza dei Miracoli sights cost-cutting combined tickets are available. A ticket covering one/two/three sights costs €5/6/8 and you can take your pick from the baptistry, Camposanto, Museo dell'Opera del Duomo and – for two or three sights – the cathedral. Tower aside (no under eights), children aged under 10 are free.

Tickets are sold at three **ticket offices** (www.opapisa.it) on the main square: the central ticket office behind the Leaning Tower is the busiest; those inside the Museo dell'Opera del Duomo and entrance hall of the otherwise-closed Museo delle Sinopie rarely have painfully long queues.

octagonal pulpit sculpted by Giovanni Pisano (father Nicola sculpted the pulpit in the baptistry – compare the two) from Carrara marble in the north aisle is extraordinary. His depth of detail brings a new pictorial expressionism to Gothic sculpture. A fusion of Christian (nine panelled scenes from the New Testament, including the life of John the Baptist and the betrayal, mocking and flagellation of Christ) and classical (personifications of Prudence, Fortitude and a naked Hercules which can be directly compared with Nicola's pulpit Hercules in the baptistry), it is no wonder it took Pisano 10 years to complete.

Staring down from the altar is the striking mosaic of *Christ in Majesty*. Completed by Cimabue in 1302, it is one of the few interior decorations to survive the raging fire that swept through the cathedral in 1596.

Visitors enter the cathedral through the Portale di San Ranieri – late 12th-century bronze doors of the south transept (facing the Leaning Tower) depicting the life of Christ in 20 panels and named after Pisa's patron saint Rainerius whose mummified body is inside. Palm trees, Moorish buildings and other Arab sculpted elements on the doors demonstrate just how influential the Islamic world was on Pisa at this time; the magnificent 11th-century bronze griffin that stood as a victory trophy atop the cathedral (see it in the Museo dell'Opera del Duomo) until 1828 was booty, probably Egyptian in origin.

But it is the three pairs of firmly closed, 16th-century bronze doors of the main entrance (west), designed by the school of Giambologna to replace the wooden originals destroyed (along with most of the cathedral interior) by fire in 1596, which the crowds ogle over. Quite spellbinding, hours can be spent deciphering the biblical scenes illustrating the immaculate conception of the Virgin and birth of Christ (central doors), the road to Calvary and crucifixion of Christ etc (right) and the Ministry of Christ (left). Kids can play spot the rhino.

BAPTISTRY

The unusual round **battistero** (Piazza dei Miracoli; admission incl audioguide €5; 8am-8pm Apr-Sep, 9am-6pm or 7pm Mar & Oct, 10am-5pm Nov-Feb) has one dome piled on top of another, each roofed half in lead, half in tiles, and is topped by a gilt bronze John the Baptist (1395). It was started in 1153 by Diotisalvi, notably remodelled and continued by Nicola Pisano and son Giovanni more than a century later and finally completed in the 14th century – hence its hybrid architectural style. The lower level of arcades is Pisan-Romanesque, while the pinnacled upper section and dome are Gothic.

Inside, the beautiful hexagonal pulpit (compare it with Giovanni's notably more ornate one in the cathedral) carved by Nicola Pisano in 1260 is the undisputable highlight. Inspired by Roman art, Pisano used sarcophagi from Pisa's Camposanto as models for his powerfully nude Hercules – Christian fortification personified inspiration – and other strong allegorical figures. Five panels on the pulpit illustrate Christ's life.

BRACE, BRACE, BRACE

When architect Bonanno Pisano undertook construction work on the bell tower in 1173, he was on shaky ground. Barely 2m above sea level, what lay below the deep green lawns of the Campo dei Miracoli – a treacherous sand-and-clay mix atop a series of alternate strata of clay and sand to a depth of more than 40m – was hardly ideal for one of Italy's most monumental icons.

Pisano had barely begun to build when the earth below started to give. By the time construction ground to a halt five years later, with only three storeys completed, Pisano's stump of a tower had a noticeable lean.

In 1272 a new band of artisans and masons set to work on it again, attempting to bolster the foundations but failing miserably. Yet their solution was to simply keep going, compensating for the lean by gradually building straight up from the lower storeys, creating a subtle banana curve. The bell chamber at the top was built in 1370. At some point the process came to a halt and until the 18th century the lean remained stable.

Over the following centuries, the banana solution proved no solution, as the tower leaned a further 1mm each year. By 1993 it was 4.47m out of plumb, more than five degrees from the vertical.

In addition to the problems on the ground floor, the structure – a hollow cylinder, cased on the inside and out with layers of marble – was dodgy. Between its layers was a loosely packed mix of rubble and mortar. Some observers fear that one day the stresses caused by the lean will make the casing crack and crumble.

Finally, in 1990 the tower was closed to the public. Two years later the Italian government in Rome assembled a panel of experts to debate a solution. In 1993 engineers placed 1000 tonnes of lead ingots on the northern side in a bid to counteract the subsidence on the southern side. Steel bands were wrapped around the 2nd storey to keep it all together. For a while it seemed to have worked, until in 1995 it slipped a whole 2.5mm.

In 1999 a new solution was tried that consisted of slinging steel braces around the 3rd storey of the tower. These were attached to heavy hydraulic A-frame anchors some way from the northern side. The frames were later replaced by steel cables that were attached to neighbouring buildings. The tower thus held in place, engineers began gingerly removing soil from below the northern foundations. After some 70 tonnes of earth had been extracted from the northern side, the tower sank to its 18th-century level and, in the process, rectified the lean by 43.8cm. This process was quite a success according to the experts as it guarantees the tower's future (and a fat tourist income) for the next three centuries.

TOP FIVE FACTS YOU NEVER KNEW ABOUT THE TOWER

■ In 1160 Pisa boasted 10,000-odd towers – but no bell tower for its cathedral. Loyal Pisan Berta di Bernardo righted this in 1172 when she died, leaving a legacy of 60 *soldi* (money) in her will to the city to get cracking on a *campanile* (bell tower).

■ The Leaning Tower – a whimsical folly of its inventors – was built to lean: hotly debated in the early 19th century, this theory was blown to shreds in 1838 when a clean-up job to remove muck oozing from its base revealed the true nature of its precarious foundations.

■ It is not the only tower in Pisa to lean: the octagonal bell tower of Chiesa di San Nicola (Via Santa Maria) by Nicola Pisano and that of Chiesa di San Michele degli Scalzi (Via San Michele degli Scalzi), a wonky red-brick square tower north of the centre, both lean too – as does the baptistry to a noticeably less visible degree.

■ Moscow will help restore the city of Pisa, shipping in construction workers by train from Odessa, Tashkent and Dushanbe to build skyscrapers around the cathedral and a vast car park beneath the Leaning Tower to resolve traffic congestion around one of Italy's most visited sights – the April Fools story run by *The Moscow Times* on 1 April 2004.

■ Seven bells, each sounding a different musical note and rung from the ground by 14 men, were added to the completed tower in 1370 but silenced in the 1950s for fear of a catastrophic collapse.

Pisan scientist Galileo Galilei (who, so the story goes, came up with the laws of the pendulum by watching a lamp swing in Pisa's cathedral), was baptised in the octagonal font.

Don't leave the baptistry without (a) admiring the Islamic floor, (b) climbing up to the gallery for a stunning overview and (c) risking a whisper and listening to it resound. Alternatively, the custodian demonstrates the double dome's remarkable acoustics and echo effects every half-hour.

CAMPOSANTO

Soil shipped from Calvary during the Crusades – and reputed to reduce cadavers to skeletons within days – is said to lie within the white walls of this hauntingly beautiful **cemetery** (Piazza dei Miracoli; admission incl audioguide €5; 8am-8pm Apr-Sep, 9am-6pm or 7pm Mar & Oct, 10am-5pm Nov-Feb), a beautiful final resting place for many prominent Pisans, arranged around a garden in a cloistered quadrangle. Many of the more interesting sarcophagi are of Greco-Roman origin, recycled in the Middle Ages.

During WWII, Allied artillery destroyed many of the cloisters' precious frescoes. Among the few to survive was the *Triumph of Death* – a remarkable illustration of Hell – attributed to an anonymous 14th-century painter known as 'The Master of the Triumph of Death'. Fortunately, the mirrors apparently once stuck next to the graphic, no-holds-

barred images of the damned being roasted alive on spits have since been removed – meaning a marginally less uncomfortable visit for visitors who would have once seen their own faces peering out of the cruel wall painting.

MUSEO DELL'OPERA DEL DUOMO

No museum provides a better overview of Piazza dei Miracoli's trio of architectural masterpieces than the **Museum of the Cathedral** (Piazza dei Miracoli; admission €5; 8am-8pm Apr-Sep, 9am-6pm or 7pm Mar & Oct, 10am-5pm Nov-Feb). Home to cathedral canons between the 12th and 17th centuries, it has a profusion of works of art once displayed in the tower, cathedral and baptistry. Highlights include Giovanni Pisano's ivory carving of the *Madonna and Child* (1300) carved for the cathedral's high altar and his *Madonna del Colloquio* (Madonna of the Colloquium). Legendary booty includes various pieces of Islamic art including the griffin that once topped the cathedral and a 10th-century Moorish hippogriff.

PIAZZA DEI CAVALIERI

From Piazza dei Miracoli, head south along Via Santa Maria and turn left at Piazza Cavallotti for Piazza dei Cavalieri, the city's centre of temporal power remodelled by Giorgio Vasari in the 16th century. **Palazzo dell'Orologio**, north of the piazza, occupies the site of a tower where, in 1288, Count Ugolino della Gherardesca, his sons and grandsons were starved to death on suspicion of helping the Genoese enemy at the Battle of Meloria, an incident recorded in Dante's *Inferno*.

Palazzo dei Cavalieri, on the northeastern side of the piazza, was redesigned by Vasari and features remarkable sgraffito (see the boxed text, p44) decoration. Both palace and piazza are named after the Knights of St Stephen, a religious and military order founded by Cosimo I de' Medici. Vasari designed their church, **Chiesa di Santo Stefano dei Cavalieri** (☎ 050 58 08 14; Piazza dei Cavalieri 8; admission €1.30; ۩ 9am-6pm Apr-Sep, 11am-4.30pm Mon-Sat, 11.30am-5.30pm Sun Oct-Mar).

A block east, **Chiesa di Santa Caterina** (Piazza Martiri della Libertà; ۩ 10.30am-6.30pm Mon-Sat, 1-6.30pm Sun), a fine example of Pisan-Gothic architecture, has works by Nino Pisano.

MUSEO NAZIONALE DI SAN MATTEO

Wander southwards to the area around Borgo Stretto, the city's medieval heart. East along the waterfront boulevard, Lungarno Mediceo, is the **Museo Nazionale di San Matteo** (☎ 050 54 18 65; Lungarno Mediceo; adult/concession €5/2; ۩ 8.30am-7.30pm Tue-Sat, to 1.30pm Sun), a fine gallery that journeys from the ceramics adorning the façades of medieval churches to 12th- and 13th-century Pisan painting (including on crosses) and early Renaissance sculpture. Don't miss the exquisite sculptures in wood by Valdambrino and Giovanni; paintings by Buonamico Buffalmacco who decorated Camposanto with frescoes; and Giovanni and Nicola Pisano's *Madonna del Latte* (Our Lady of Milk) sculpted for the Chiesa di Santa Maria della Spina.

CHIESA DI SANTA MARIA DELLA SPINA

Cross Ponte di Mezzo and head west to reach this gem of a church, **Chiesa di Santa Maria della Spina** (Lungarno Gambacorti; adult/concession €1.50/1; ۩ 10am-5.45pm Tue-Fri, 10am-6.45pm Sat Mar-Oct, 10am-2pm Tue-Sun Nov-Feb). A fine architectural example of Pisan-Gothic style, it was built in the early 14th century to house a thorn from Christ's crown and is refreshingly intimate after the heavyweights of Piazza dei Miracoli. Its ornately spired exterior cluttered with tabernacles and statues exudes richness but the interior is simple. Highlight: Andrea and Nino Pisano's *Madonna of the Rose*, a masterpiece of Gothic sculpture.

DO IT YOUR WAY

Pedalling Pisa using two or four wheels is the way to do it: **Ecovoyager** (☎ 050 56 18 39, 339 760 76 52; www.ecovoyager.it; Via della Faggiola 41 & Piazza dei Miracoli in front of Museo dell'Opera del Duomo; ۩ 9am-midnight Mar-Oct) rents romantic canopied *riscio* (rickshaws) made for two (€15 an hour) – or indeed up to six people (€20 an hour) – as well as conventional bicycles (€12 a day) and rollerblades (€2 an hour). Hire an English radio-guide (€1 per 30 minutes) at the same time and you are all set to explore Pisa your way.

TORRE GUELFA

Enchanting rooftop-views spill out from **Torre Guelfa** (☎ 050 2 14 41; Piazza Tersanaia; admission €2; ۩ 3-7pm Fri-Sun Mar-Oct, 2-5pm Sat & Sun, every 2nd Sun of month 10am-1pm & 3-5pm Nov-Feb), part of the old citadel a few paces west of Chiesa di Santa Maria della Spina (a combined ticket covering admission to both costs €2.50 for adults, €2 concession). Built in the 15th century, the tower was destroyed during WWII and rebuilt in 1956. Trawl up 200 steps to get to the top.

Activities

BOAT TRIPS

April to October, **Il Navicello** (☎ 050 50 31 01; www.ilnavicello.it) runs various boat cruises along the Arno; check its website for updated schedules and prices.

Tours

Great for families and tired legs is the London-style open-top double-decker red **Sightseeing Bus** (☎ 328 809 02 05; www.pisa.city-sightseeing.it; adult/child/family €15/7/44; ۩ hourly 10am-6pm Mar-Oct) that cruises around town following a circular route; stops include Viale Gramsci in front of the train station, Via Corsica (for Piazza dei Cavalieri) and Piazza Arcivescovado (for Piazza dei Miracoli). Passengers are equipped with an English-language audio commentary and can hop on/off as they please. Tickets are valid for 24 hours.

Festivals & Events

Gioco del Ponte (Game of the Bridge) Two teams in medieval costume battle it out over the Ponte di Mezzo; last Sunday in June.

Luminaria Some 50,000 candles and blazing torches light up the night sky during the Luminaria; 16 June.

Palio delle Quattro Antiche Repubbliche Marinare (Regatta of the Four Ancient Maritime Republics) The four historical maritime rivals – Pisa, Venice, Amalfi and Genoa – meet each year in June for a procession of boats and a dramatic race; the next in Pisa will be in 2010.

Regata Storica di San Ranieri The Arno comes to life with a rowing competition commemorating the city's patron saint; 17 June.

Sleeping

Hotel Astor (☎ 050 4 45 51; www.hotel-astor.com; Via Manzoni 22; d/tr/q with bathroom €80/105/13, d without bathroom €65) Something of a sore-thumb concrete block in an otherwise flowery neighbourhood, this good-value, two-star family hotel is an easy walk from the train station. Breakfast is not served but a small bar in reception sells cappuccino (€1.50) and croissants (€1.20). Night owls note Astor has a strict 'close the door at midnight' policy.

Hotel Villa Kinzica (☎ 050 56 04 19; www.hotelvil lakinzica.it; Piazza Arcivescovado 2; s €70-95, d €90-108, tr €100-124, q €110-134, all incl breakfast; P   ⊠) A tad too close to the Piazza dei Miracoli crowds for comfort, this revamped villa with sweet apricot-coloured façade and emerald-green shutters is a useful option for those seeking a restaurant in-house. Spot the tower from some rooms.

Hotel Francesco (☎ 050 55 41 09; www.hotelfrancesco .com; Via Santa Maria 129; s €75-90, d €85-100, tr €115-135; ⊠   ▢) Don't let the knight in armour next door put you off: this hotel on Pisa's main bar/restaurant drag boasts a great terrace with pretty purple wisteria and – if you sit on a far-end table – a Leaning Tower view! Rooms 201 and 202 open onto a shared balcony facing the cathedral. Breakfast costs €3 but internet access is free.

Royal Victoria Hotel (☎ 050 94 01 11; www.royalvicto ria.it; Lungarno Pacinotti 12; s/d/tr/q with bathroom €118/138/147/152, s/d without bathroom €70/80, all incl breakfast; P   ⊠) This doyen of Pisan hotels, run with love and tender care by the Piegaja family for five generations, offers old-world luxury accompanied by warm, attentive service. As part of its ecologically friendly policy, it rents bicycles to guests for €5 per day. Garage costs parking €18.

Hotel Il Giardino (☎ 050 56 21 01; www.hotelilgiardino .pisa.it; Piazza Manin 1; s/d/tr/q incl breakfast €80/100/110/120; P   ⊠) A gaggle of souvenir traders might hit you the second you walk out the door but the

Garden Hotel – an old Medici staging post the other side of the cathedral square wall – does have the advantage of a peaceful garden terrace to breakfast on while enjoying the view of the baptistry dome. Décor is contemporary and art happy.

Hotel Relais dell'Orologio (☎ 050 83 03 61; www .hotelrelaisorologio.com; Via della Faggiola 12-14; d incl breakfast €200-800; P   ⊠) Something of a wedding reception and honeymoon venue, Pisa's dreamy five-star hotel occupies a tastefully restored 14th-century fortified tower house in a quiet street. Some rooms have original frescoes and the flowery patio out back makes a welcome retreat from the crowds. Garage parking costs €20.

Eating

Being a university town, Pisa has a good range of eating places, especially around Borgo Stretto, near the university on Piazza Dante Alighieri, and south of the river in the trendy San Martino quarter. Near Piazza dei Miracoli, along Via Contessa Matilde, a multitude of places tout €12 *menu turistici* (fixed lunch menus).

La Bottega del Gelato (☎ 050 57 54 67; Piazza Garibaldi 11; 1/2/3 scoops €1.30/1.80/2.50; 🕑 Thu-Tue) Sit at Garibaldi's feet and lick a seriously creamy gelato from the most popular ice-cream parlour in town. Feeling truly decadent? Scrap the *cono* or *coppa* for a chocolate-lined *cestino* (basket).

Caffè Federico Salza (☎ 050 58 02 44; Borgo Stretto 46; salads €7, pasta €7, mains €8.50-13.50; 🕑 8am-8.30pm Apr-Oct, variable hours Tue-Sun Nov-Mar) Cakes, chocolates and sweet creations to die for are the house speciality of this long-established café and *chocolatier* popular with Pisa, sophisticates since 1898. Be it coffee and cake, a light lunch or afternoon tea, tastebuds will be seriously titillated; a cake sitting down costs €1.90 more than eaten at the bar.

Trattoria della Faggiola (☎ 050 55 61 79; Via della Faggiola 1; meals €20; 🕑 Fri & Sat, lunch Mon-Thu) An excellent-value, locally loved spot, this traditional trattoria, with brick interior and a line-up of lovingly tended potted plants outside, is delightful for lunch. The menu, chalked up on a board outside, is strictly Italian and offers a straightforward choice of three or four dishes per course.

Trattoria San Omobono (☎ 050 54 08 47; Piazza San Omobono 6/7; meals €22; 🕑 Wed-Sat, dinner Mon & Tue) A handful of tables, one Roman column and a refreshingly short 'n' sweet menu form a winning combination at this family-run bistro near the market. Main-course staples include roast beef, tripe and stockfish.

La Clessidra (☎ 050 54 01 60; Via Santa Cecilia 34; meals €25-35; ☙ dinner Mon-Sat Sep-Jul) At the upper end of Pisa's dining scale, La Clessidra cooks up a clutch of themed menus, including a *menu tipico di Pisano* (minimum two people) featuring wholly local fare, and a seafood equivalent, in a formal setting. *Dolci* (desserts) are girth-widening and the tourist-free green lawns of neighbouring Piazza Martiri della Libertà are a postlunch siesta delight.

Antica Trattoria il Campano (☎ 050 58 05 85; Via Cavalca 19; meals €30; ☙ Fri-Tue, dinner Thu) The adventurous Tuscan menu – pasta with leeks in cod sauce, octopus salad, or beef marinated with tomatoes, almonds and hazelnuts – at this long-time trattoria has the added advantage of being translated in English. Of the dining areas – under vaulted arches down or beneath bare rafters up – downstairs is the more elegant. *Tagliere del Re* (€15 per person, minimum two people) – a wonderfully rich platter of 12 kinds of Tuscan antipastos – is a meal in itself.

La Grotta (☎ 050 57 81 05; Via San Francesco 103; meals €30; ☙ Mon-Sat) As its name suggests, rustic La Grotta is a cavelike place with sackcloth curtains that serves up hearty portions of good old-fashioned Tuscan fare. The menu is simple but changes monthly to reflect the season; produce is fresher than fresh.

Osteria dei Cavalieri (☎ 050 58 08 58; Via San Frediano 16; meals €35; ☙ Mon-Fri, dinner Sat) The Slow Food recommendation for central Pisa, this *osteria* (wine bar) serves a high-speed, one-dish only – but what a dish – lunchtime special (€11) alongside an enticing array of other tasty morsels, including *carpaccio di pulpo* (octopus carpaccio). Although the size of portions may mean a siesta afterwards, the set meals (€26 to €32) are worth it and the wine list is impressive.

Panetteria Focacceria (Via Santa Maria 66) is *the* spot for well-filled *panini* (€1.50), pizza slices (€1) and pastries to picnic on. There's an open-air morning **food market** (Piazza delle Vettovaglie) off Borgo Stretto.

Drinking

Stylish bars flank Via Oberdan and Borgo Stretto. Otherwise, head south of the river where casual student hangouts abound.

Caffetteria Betsabea (Piazza Dante Alighieri 7; ☙ 7.30am-7.30pm Mon-Sat) Students from the political sciences faculty luurvvv this simple café which dishes out 20 types of well-stuffed sandwiches, meal-sized salads and loads of differently dressed pasta – all served on wicker platters – as well as drinks from dawn to dusk.

Op Art Café (www.opartcafe.it; Via San Francesco 90; ☙ 7pm-1am Wed, Thu & Sun, to 2am Fri & Sat) Art exhibitions add another dimension to this modern wine bar where a designer set meets for cocktails (€4 to €5), bruschetta (€3.50) and meal-sized salads (€5.50 to €8). It buzzes come *aperitivo* time – great buffet!

Bazeel (www.bazeel.it in Italian; Lungarno Pacinotti 1; ☙ 5pm-2am) On the corner of atmospheric Piazza Garibaldi, this music bar is a smart choice for that all-essential early-evening *aperitivo* from 6.30pm to 9pm when a feast of a buffet is rolled out. Otherwise, it serves food and bands play late.

Temple Bar (Piazza Cairoli; ☙ 6pm-1am Mon-Thu, 6pm-2am Fri & Sat) This popular Irish pub paying homage to Dublin's cultural quarter touts tables and chairs on one of Pisa's cutest squares and conveniently neighbours a fine *yoghurteria*, open pub hours, in the shape of Coppelia.

Lounge Caffè (Via delle Belle Torri 52; ☙ 4pm-1am Tue-Thu, 4pm-2am Fri, 6pm-2am Sat, 6pm-1am Sun) Directly opposite Temple Bar, this venue is worth a late-hour slug.

Entertainment

Teatro Verdi (☎ 050 94 11 11; www.teatrodipisa.pi.it in Italian; Via Palestro 40) Has opera, dance and theatre.

Club Dr Jazz (☎ 339 86 19 298; www.drjazz.it in Italian; Via A Vespucci 10; ☙ Wed-Sun) Seriously hot jazz club perfectly tuned for those keen to discover student Pisa: jam sessions Wednesday, blues and R & B Thursday and concerts at the weekend. Yes, it is that low-lying warehouse with corrugated-iron walls, entrance marked by steel gates next to the parking meter (opposite No 17).

Leningrad Café (www.leningradcafe.com in Italian; Via Silvestri 5; ☙ 8pm-late Wed-Sun) Another hip venue, this café-club down a quiet alley in the San Martino quarter of town pelts out everything from garage, punk and indie rock to rock 'n' roll, swing and soul. DJs spin during the week and Saturday sees cabaret steal the show.

VESPA TOUR

There's a certain romance to touring Tuscany on the back of a Vespa, Italy's iconic scooter that revolutionised travel when Piaggio launched it from its Pontedera factory, 25km southeast of Pisa, in 1946. The 'wasp', as the two-wheeled utility vehicle was affectionately known, has been restyled 120 times since, culminating most recently in Piaggio's vintage-inspired GTV and LXV models. Yet the essential design remains timeless.

The complete Vespa story, from the Genovese company's arrival in Tuscany in 1921 to its manufacturing of four-engine aircraft and hydroplanes, WWII destruction and rebirth as Europe's exclusive Vespa producer, is grippingly told in Pontedera's **Museo Piaggio** (☎ 0587 2 71 71; www.museopiaggio.it; Viale Rinaldo Piagio 7; admission free; ☒ 10am-6pm), in a former factory building. Ogle at custom-made Ferraris, and eco' and fantasy Vespas, alongside 1948's three-wheeler Ape (meaning 'Bee'), 1963's Vespino and other classics. In 2007 Piaggo produced a limited line of the Ape with blue bodywork, cream seats, striped tyres and wooden finishings: the 1950s cult vehicle cost €8590.

If Vespa's free-wheeling, carefree spirit bites, hook up with Chianti-based **Bella Scooter** (☎ 051 695 71 04; www.scooterbella.com; Loc Bricciano 41, Gaiole in Chianti) for your very own Hepburn-style tour of Tuscany by Vespa.

Getting There & Away

AIR

Pisa International Airport Galileo Galilei (☎ 050 84 93 00; www.pisa-airport.com), located 2km south of town, is Tuscany's main international airport and handles flights to most major European cities.

Daily destinations in the UK include London Gatwick (British Airways and Easyjet); London Stansted, Liverpool and East Midlands (all Ryanair); Bristol (Easyjet); Edinburgh, Glasgow/Prestwick, Leeds/Bradford Manchester and Newcastle (all jet2.com); and Coventry, Doncaster/Sheffield and Bournemouth (all Thomsonfly).

BUS

From its hub on Piazza Sant'Antonio, Pisan bus company **CPT** (Compagnia Pisana Trasporti; ☎ 800 012 773; www.cpt.pisa.it in Italian; Piazza Sant'Antonio) runs buses to/from Volterra (€4.80, two hours, up to 10 daily) and Livorno (€2.40, 45 minutes, half-hourly). To get to Florence, Lucca and Pistoia take the train.

CAR & MOTORCYCLE

Pisa is close to the A11 and A12. The FI-PI-LI is a toll-free alternative for Florence and Livorno, while the north–south SS1, the Via Aurelia, connects the city with La Spezia and Rome.

Car-rental agencies include the following:
Europcar (☎ 050 220 01 82; Viale F Crispi)
MaxiRent (☎ 050 220 00 53; Via Cesare Battisti 13)
Good-value car and scooter rental.

TRAIN

Pisa is connected by rail to Florence and is also on the Rome–La Spezia train line. Destinations include Florence (€5.20, 1¼ hours, 40 daily), Rome (€24, three to four hours, 20 daily), Livorno (€1.70, 15 minutes, hourly), Pistoia (€4.20, 1¼ hours, five direct daily) and Lucca (€2.20, 25 minutes, around 20 daily).

Getting Around

For Pisa airport, take a train to/from Stazione Pisa Centrale (€1.10, five minutes, 15 per day) or the LAM Rossa (red) line (€0.90, 10 minutes, every 10 minutes) run by local bus company CPT (see left) which passes through the city centre and the train station on its way to/from the airport.

Car parks (www.pisamo.it in Italian; per hour €1.50) abound around the heart of Pisa. There's a free one about 2km north of Piazza dei Miracoli, with shuttle buses to the centre. Cross fingers that the cavernous subterranean car park being gouged out beneath Piazza Vittorio Emanuele II – a building site of several years already – will be up and running by 2009.

Pick up two wheels from **MaxiRent** (☎ 050 220 00 53; Via Cesare Battisti 13; ☒ 9am-1pm & 3.30-7pm Mon-Fri, 9am-1pm Sat); bikes cost €10 a day.

For a taxi, call ☎ 050 54 16 00.

LUCCA

pop 84,000

Lovely Lucca is gorgeous, a beautiful old city that sparks love at first sight thanks to its rich history, handsome churches and smattering of excellent restaurants. Hidden behind imposing Renaissance walls, this serene city is an essential stopover on any Tuscan tour and a charming base for exploring the Apuane Alps and Garfagnana.

Founded by the Etruscans, Lucca became a Roman colony in 180 BC and a free *comune* (self-governing city) during the 12th century, when it enjoyed a period of prosperity based on the silk trade. In 1314 it briefly fell to Pisa but, under the leadership of local adventurer Castruccio Castracani degli Anterminelli, the city regained its independence and began to amass territories in western Tuscany, including marble-rich Carrara. Castruccio died in 1325 but Lucca remained an independent republic for almost 500 years.

Napoleon ended all this in 1805, when he created the principality of Lucca and placed one of the seemingly countless members of his family in need of an Italian fiefdom (this time his sister Elisa) in control of all of Tuscany. Twelve years later the city became a Bourbon duchy before being incorporated into the Kingdom of Italy.

Lucca remains a strong agricultural centre. The long periods of peace it has enjoyed explain the almost perfect preservation of the city walls, which were rarely put to the test.

Information

EMERGENCY

Police station (☎ 0583 44 27 27; Viale Cavour 38)

INTERNET ACCESS

Surfing the internet in the Piazza Santa Maria tourist office costs a pricey €3.50 for 15 minutes, €10 for 60 minutes.

Mondochiocciola (☎ 0583 44 05 10; Via del Gonfalone 12; per hr €5.50; ☒ 9.30am-1pm & 3.30-8pm Mon-Sat) Irregular hours and no sign outside.

INTERNET RESOURCES

www.in-lucca.it Practical listings guide to the city.
www.luccagrapewine.com Online version of Lucca's English-language monthly mag; buy the fuller paper version (€2) in newsagents.

LAUNDRY

Lavanderia Niagara (Via Michele Rosi 26; per wash €4; ☒ 8am-10pm)

MEDICAL SERVICES

Hospital (☎ 0583 97 01; Via dell'Ospedale) Northeast of the city walls.

POST

Post office (Via Vallisneri 2)

TOURIST INFORMATION

Tourist office Piazza Napoleone (☎ 0583 91 99 41; ☒ 10am-7pm Apr-Oct, 10am-1pm & 2-6pm Mon-Sat Nov-Mar); Piazza Santa Maria 35 (☎ 0583 91 99 31; ☒ 9am-8pm Apr-Oct, 9am-12.30pm & 3-6.30pm Mon-Sat Nov-Mar); Piazzale Verdi (☎ 0583 58 31 50; ☒ 9am-7pm Easter-Oct, to 5.30pm Nov-Easter) The Piazzale Verdi branch rents bicycles (€2.50 an hour) and excellent city audioguides in English (one/two persons €9/15), sells concert tickets, and has a left-luggage service (€1.50 an hour).

Sights & Activities

Lucca's biggest attraction is its robust city walls, built 12m high snug around the old city in the 16th and 17th centuries, defended by 126 canons and crowned with a wide silky-smooth footpath just made for a leafy **Passeggiata della Mura**. Be it strolling, cycling, running or Rollerblading, this legendary 4km-long circular footpath above the city proffers shot after shot of local Luccese life. Children's playgrounds, swings and picnic tables beneath trees add a buzz of activity to Baluardo San Regolo, Baluardo San Salvatore and Baluardo Santa Croce – three of the 11 bastions studding the way – while older kids kick balls around on the vast green lawns of Baluardo San Donato.

Down in the city, coloured *itinerario turistico* (tourist itinerary) panels map out routes for cyclists. For bike hire see p199.

CATHEDRAL

Lucca's mainly Romanesque **Cattedrale di San Martino** (☎ 0583 95 70 68; www.museocattedralelucca.it in Italian; Piazza San Martino; ☒ 9.30am-5.45pm or 6.45pm Mon-Sat, 9.30-10.45am & noon-6pm Sun Mar-Oct, 9.30am-4.45pm Mon-Sat, 9.30-10.45am & noon-5pm Sun Oct-Mar), dedicated to San Martino, dates to the 11th century. The exquisite façade was constructed in the prevailing Lucca-Pisan style and designed to accommodate the pre-existing *campanile*. Each of the multitude of columns in its upper part is different. The reliefs over the left doorway of the portico are believed to be by Nicola Pisano.

The interior was rebuilt in the 14th and 15th centuries with a Gothic flourish. Lucca-born sculptor and architect Matteo Civitali (1436–1501), who spent most of his life working on churches and villas (such as Villa Oliva,

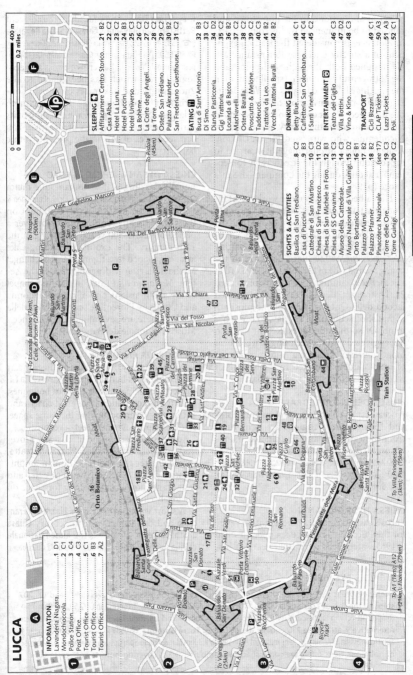

LUCCA

p199) in and around in his hometown and refused to be influenced by his counterparts in Florence, is considered the leading exponent of a strictly Lucchese Renaissance art. He designed both the cathedral pulpit and the 15th-century *tempietto* (small temple) in the north aisle that contains the **Volto Santo**. Legend has it that this simply fashioned image of a life-sized Christ on a wooden crucifix, in fact dated to the 11th century, was carved by Nicodemus, who witnessed the crucifixion. A major object of pilgrimage, it's carried in procession through the streets each 13 September at dusk during the Luminaria di Santa Croce (p196).

The cathedral's many other works of art include a magnificent *Last Supper* by Tintoretto above the third altar of the south aisle and the cool marble tomb of Ilaria del Carretto, a masterpiece of funerary sculpture, in the **sacristy** (adult/concession €2.50/1.50). Ilaria del Carretto, the young second wife of the 15th-century Lord of Lucca, Paolo Guinigi, died in childbirth aged 24. Distraught, her husband commissioned Jacopo della Quercia, perhaps the most accomplished sculptor of his day, to carve her tomb. Or so the story goes. Recent research has suggested that the reclining marble form in fact represents Caterina Antelminelli, one of four maidens engaged to Paolo – all of whom died before their wedding day.

MUSEO DELLA CATTEDRALE
A well-displayed collection of mainly 15th- and 16th-century religious art, sculptures from the cathedral and illuminated manuscripts fill the **Cathedral Museum** (☎ 0583 49 05 30; Piazza Antelminelli; adult/concession €4/2.50; ☯ 10am-6pm Apr-Oct, 10am-2pm Mon-Fri, 10am-5pm Sat & Sun Nov-Feb, 10am-5pm Mar).

CHIESA DI SS GIOVANNI
Lucca's earliest cathedral, the haunting venue for the Puccini e la sua Lucca opera festival (p196), safeguards over 1000 years of his-

tory. The 17th-century façade of the adjacent **Battistero San Giovanni & Chiesa di Santa Reparata** (☎ 0583 49 05 30; Piazza San Giovanni; adult/concession €2.50/1.50; ☯ 10am-5pm or 6pm mid-Mar–Oct, by appointment only Nov–mid-Mar) crown a vast archaeological area, which has been dated to the 2nd century and has traces of Roman construction below floor level. Today's church is largely the 12th-century remodelling of its early-Christian 5th-century predecessor. You can see traces of this in the present Gothic baptistry.

CHIESA DI SAN MICHELE IN FORO
Equally dazzling is this Romanesque **church** (☎ 0583 4 84 59; Piazza San Michele; ☯ 7.40am-noon & 3-6pm Apr-Oct, 9am-noon & 3-5pm Nov-Mar), built on the site of its 8th-century precursor over a period of nearly 300 years, beginning in the 11th century. The exquisite wedding-cake façade is topped by a figure of the Archangel Michael slaying a dragon. Inside, the serene *Madonna and Child* in the first chapel of the south aisle is one of many Madonna and Childs by Florentine sculptor Luca della Robbia (there are several more in Florence's Museo Nazionale del Bargello).

EAST OF VIA FILLUNGO
Threading its way through the medieval heart of the old city is Lucca's busiest street, **Via Fillungo**. It's a fascinating mix of smart boutiques, restaurants and buildings of great charm and antiquity – often occupying the same space; just look up, above the street-level bustle.

Just east of here is one of Tuscany's loveliest squares, oval-shaped **Piazza Anfiteatro**, so-called after the one-time Roman amphitheatre. Today houses, pavement cafés and restaurants now stand, jostling for space on the lovely ellipse.

A short walk further east is **Piazza San Francesco** and the attractive 13th-century **Chiesa di San Francesco**. Nearby is the **Museo Nazionale di Villa Guinigi** (☎ 0583 49 60 33; Via della Quarquonia;

A BIRD'S-EYE VIEW

There are great views of the city from its walls, yes, but for a sweeping overview head up 207 steps to the top of **Torre delle Ore** (☎ 0583 31 68 46; Via Fillungo; adult/concession €4/2.50; ☯ 9am-7pm, to 5pm Oct-Feb), a 13th-century clock tower hotly contested by rival families in medieval Lucca. Alternatively, attack the 230 equally steep stairs of **Torre Guinigi** (☎ 0583 31 68 46; Via Sant'Andrea 14; adult/concession €4/2.50; ☯ 9am-midnight May-Sep, to 7.30pm Mar & Apr, to 5pm Oct-Feb), where a tiny copse of holm oak trees offers welcome shade. A combined ticket covering both towers costs €6/4.

CASA DI PUCCINI

There the maestro still sits, cast in bronze, languidly lording it over Piazza Cittadella, a cigarette dangling from his slender fingers. Just north of the piazza is **Casa di Puccini** (☎ 0583 58 40 28; Corte San Lorenzo 9; adult/concession €3/2; ☺ currently closed for renovation, check with tourist office), the modest house where one of the 20th century's greatest composers was born in 1858. He lived there until studies at Milan's music conservatory beckoned him aged 22.

The day after his birth Puccini was baptised Giacomo Antonio Domenico Michele Secondo Maria in nearby Chiesa di SS Giovanni. He was a church organist during his teenage years, enjoying his first public performance as a piano accompanist at Lucca's Teatro del Giglio (p198) – the 17th-century theatre where the curtain later rose on his best-known operas: *La Bohème* (1896), *Tosca* (1900) and *Madame Butterfly* (1907). He wrote 12 in all.

Inside Casa di Puccini, everyday objects tell the tale of the composer's life. Specs and pen lay poised on the desk next to the Steinway piano on which Puccini, the last in a line of celebrated Lucca musicians, wrote much of *Turandot* (1926) while staying at his seaside villa in Viareggio in 1921. The opera, unfinished when he died, was the last before throat cancer got the better of him after last-ditch surgery in Brussels failed in 1924.

Letters, photographs and sketches in the family home portray Puccini's wife, Elvira, a sparky, savvy, hot-headed woman – already married – who eloped with Puccini to Milan in 1886 and had a son, Antonio, out of wedlock. In 1891 the couple moved to Torre del Lago (p203), where Puccini spent the bulk of his life. In 1904, following the death of Elvira's husband, the couple wed. They travelled widely, spending the summer of 1908 in Cairo for example, only to return to Torre del Lago and became embroiled in yet more scandal: Elvira accused one of their maids, Dora, of having an affair with her husband, only for Dora to poison herself, be declared a virgin and Elvira charged with defamation.

Die-hard fans can see the bed in which Puccini was conceived, situated in **Celle de Pucini**, the village 27km north of Lucca (follow the S12 north then bear east from Daecimo towards Colognora). Puccini summered as a child in his ancestral home, **Villa Puccini** (☎ 0583 35 91 54; admission €3; ☺ by appointment only).

adult/concession €4/2; ☺ 8.30am-7.30pm Tue-Sat, to 1.30pm Sun), a vast early-15th-century villa built to supplement the Guinigi family's smaller townhouse in the city. A shadow of its former self, the still-splendid villa showcases the city's works of art. Archeological remnants from Roman Lucca and various sculptures (medieval lions from Lucca's city walls included) pinprick the grounds and ground floor of the museum, while the upper floor looks at sculpture and painting from the 13th to 17th century. Domenico Beccafuma's Mannerist *The Continence of Scipio* hangs here, as does the odd Correggio, Vasari and Tintoretti. Two rooms zoom in on the work of local lads Pietro Paolini (1603–81) and Girolamo Scaglia (1620–86).

For a leafy stroll or picnic accompanied by birdsong head for Lucca's peaceful **Orto Botanico** (Botanical Garden; ☎ 0583 44 21 60; Via San Micheletto; adult/concession €3/2; ☺ 10am-5pm Apr & mid-Sep–Oct, to 6pm May & Jun, to 7pm Jul–mid-Sep, by appointment Nov-Mar), ensnared in the southeast corner of the city walls.

WEST OF VIA FILLUNGO

The façade of the **Basilica di San Frediano** (☎ 0583 49 36 27; Piazza San Frediano; ☺ 8.30am-noon & 3-5.30pm Mon-Fri, 9-11.30am & 3-5pm Sat & Sun) has a unique (and much-restored) 13th-century mosaic in a markedly Byzantine style. But that's not the only anomalous feature: unlike just about every other church this side of Jerusalem, the apse faces *west*, away from the Holy City. The main feature of the beautiful basilica's interior is the **Fontana Lustrale**, a 12th-century baptismal font decorated with sculpted reliefs, just to the right as you enter. Behind it is *Annunciation* by Andrea della Robbia. Note too the fine capitals, many of them recycled from the nearby Roman amphitheatre.

A wonderful retreat from Lucca's excess of churches and Renaissance splendour is 17th-century **Palazzo Pfanner** (☎ 340 923 30 85; Via degli Asili 33; palace or garden adult/concession €3/2.50, both €4.50/3.50; ☺ 10am-6pm Thu-Tue Mar–mid-Nov), the palace where parts of *Portrait of a Lady* (1996) with Nicole Kidman and John Malkovich was shot, not to mention a clutch of other films. A staircase leads to the sumptuously furnished living area, or you can dip into the ornate 18th-century garden, the only one of substance within the city walls, guarded by statues representing Greek and Roman deities. (Incidentally, Felix Pfanner, may God rest his soul, was an Austrian émigré who first brought beer to Italy – and brewed it in the palazzo's cellars.)

The 17th-century **Palazzo Mansi** (Via Galli Tassi 43), a wonderful piece of rococo excess (that elaborate, gilded bridal suite must have inspired such high jinks in its time), houses the smallish **Pinacoteca Nazionale** (☎ 0583 5 55 70; adult/concession €4/2; ⏱ 8.30am-7.30pm Tue-Sat, to 1.30pm Sun). It has paintings of the same period and some lively frescoes.

Festivals & Events

Puccini e la sua Lucca (www.puccinielasualucca.com) Concert series dedicated to Puccini, with opera recitals and concerts taking place in the Chiesa di San Giovanni; March to June.

Lucca Summer Festival (www.summer-festival.com) Top performers like Norah Jones, Jamiroquai, Van Morrison and Elton John have played at this pop festival in July; information and ticket office on Piazza Napoleone from early June.

Puccini festival The city that gave birth to both Puccini and Boccherini has admirably Catholic musical tastes. For more than 50 years the nearby village of Torre del Lago has been holding this annual festival, spanning July and August.

Festa di San Paolino Torch-lit procession and crossbow competition; third Sunday in July.

Luminaria di Santa Croce Solemn torch-lit procession marking the miraculous arrival in Lucca of the Volto Santo; 13 September.

Sleeping

HOSTELS

ourpick Ostello San Frediano (☎ 0583 46 99 57; www .ostellolucca.it; Via della Cavallerizza 12; dm with/without bathroom €19/17.50, d/tr/q with bathroom €48/92/115, r for 5 people €135; 🖳) Flags flutter outside as if you're entering a five-star hotel at this staggeringly historic, atmospheric and magnificent…hostel. Top notch in comfort and service, this Hostelling International–ffiliated hostel with 141 beds in voluminous rooms is serviced with a bar and grandiose dining room (breakfast/packed lunch/two-course dinner €1.60-5/7/9.50). Non HI-members can buy a €3 one-night stamp. Internet is €5 per hour.

B&BS

Those seeking the intimacy of a B&B will like **Lucca: B&B 'n Guesthouses** (www.welcomeinlucca.it), a website with links to bed and breakfasts within the walls, 1km out and in the surrounding hills; several are listed under midrange. Prices listed in this section include breakfast.

ourpick Locanda Buatino (☎ 0583 34 32 07; www .leosteriedilucca.com; Via Borgo Giannotti 508; d/tr with shared bathroom €40/60) There are few tastier places to sleep than in the trio of rooms above one of Lucca's oldest and most locally loved trattorie. Original patterned tiled floors and beamed ceilings add an authentic air.

San Frederiano Guest House (☎ 0583 46 96 30; www.sanfrediano.com; Via degli Angeli 19; s/d with bathroom €60-86/ €70-90, s/d without bathroom €35-48/€45-68; 🖳) This smartly painted salmon-pink townhouse, built in 1600, is the venue for this appealing six-room guesthouse. It has meat hooks in the beams of reception where butchers once strung their hams. Less expensive rooms – far from bare-bones – share a bathroom. If full, ask about its sister guesthouse.

Casa Alba (☎ 0583 49 53 61; www.casa-alba.com; Via Fillungo 142; s with/without bathroom €70/55, d with bathroom €80, extra bed €15; ✂) Antipodean travellers will feel at home here; the delightful owner has spent many years in Australia. Her five rooms, with fridge, are small but sunny, washed in pastel colours and decorated with arty prints. Winter prices are substantially lower.

La Bohème (☎ 0583 46 24 04; www.boheme.it; Via del Moro 2; d €90-120; ✂) A hefty dark-wood door located on a peaceful back street marks the entrance to this five-room B&B, run with charm and style by former architect Ranieri. Rooms 11 and 12 are topped by breathtakingly high, beamed wooden ceilings and are the colour of red wine. Romantics might like the four-poster bed.

Also recommended:

Affittacamere Centro Storico (☎ 0583 49 07 48; www.affittacamerecentrostorico.com; Corte Portici 16; d with bathroom €60-130, d without bathroom €30-90, tr €55-130 with bathroom) Guests get their own front-door key and rooms sport fridge and safe.

La Torre (☎ 0583 95 70 44; www.roomslatorre.com; Via del Carmine 11; s with/without bathroom €50/35, d with/without bathroom €80/50; ✂ 🖳) Overlooking a red-brick tower on Piazza del Carmine.

HOTELS

Hotel Puccini (☎ 0583 5 54 21; www.hotelpuccini.com; Via di Poggio 9; s/d €65/90) Wedged between Puccini enjoying a cigarette in style on café-clad Piazza Citadella and Piazza San Michele with its majestic church, this friendly three-star hotel with 14 modern rooms could not be better placed. No air-con – just ceiling fans.

Hotel La Luna (☎ 0583 49 36 34; www.hotellaluna .com; Corte Compagni 12; s/d €82/112; ☽ Feb-Dec; Ⓟ ☒) This is a clean, tidy hotel with a handy pizzeria across the road. Some rooms are old-style with beams and wardrobes, while others are modern but rather bland. Parking and breakfast are each €11.

Hotel Universo (☎ 0583 49 36 78; www.universolucca .com; Piazza del Giglio 1; s €75-120, d €108-190, all incl breakfast; Ⓟ ☒) Flower-power carpets scream 1960s at this venerable old inn, set aplomb a lovely people-busy, tree-lined, carousel-pierced square. All 60 rooms – a tad weary in furnishings – stare at the equally venerable Teatro del Giglio or cathedral; only some have air-con. Parking costs €26 a night.

Palazzo Alexander (☎ 0583 458 35 71; www.palazzo -alexander.com; Via Santa Giustina 48; d incl breakfast €100-170; Ⓟ ☒ ▯) Service is impeccable at this elegant boutique hotel beautifully nestled in a 12th-century palace–turned–boarding school for girls in the 1800s. Some bathrooms have whirlpools and the Tosca suite –the best in the house – has a terrace with a sublime rooftop-view of Lucca.

La Corte degli Angeli (☎ 0583 46 92 04; www.alla cortedegliangeli.com; Via degli Angeli 23; d incl breakfast €120-175; Ⓟ ☒ ▯) Occupying three floors of a 15th-century townhouse, this four-star boutique hotel oozes charm. Frescoed rooms are named after flowers: lovers in the hugely romantic Rosa room can lie beneath a pergola and swallow-filled sky.

Villa Principessa (☎ 0583 37 00 37; www.hotelprinci pessa.com; Via Nuova per Pisa 1616; d incl buffet breakfast €225-250; Ⓟ ☒ ▯ ▨) You will indeed feel like a *principessa* (princess) at this aristocratic country mansion, residence of Lucca duke Castruccio Castracani in the late 13th and early 14th century. Smothered with an abundance of foliage outside and full of fine chandeliers, period furnishings and rich wall-papers inside, it really is a stunner. Find it 3km south of Lucca.

Eating

our pick **Trattoria da Leo** (☎ 0583 49 22 36; Via Tegrimi 1; meals €15; ☽ Mon-Sat) Ask any Florentine where to lunch in Lucca and this wonderful, bustling, noisy trattoria with mixed clientele of students, workers and ladies taking a break from shopping is what they'll say. Save a corner for the *torta di fichi e noci* (fig and walnut tart). In summer the shaded outside seating comes into its own.

Machiavelli (☎ 0583 46 72 19; lucadatorre@tiscali.it; Via Cesare Battisti 28; meals €20; ☽ Mon-Sat) A much-loved Lucca favourite alongside Leo, this funky old-fashioned *osteria* has a definite retro air to it. The walls are pea-green, the bar is painted lavender-blue and the clientele is staunchly loyal, local, fun and of all ages. There is live music some nights and the cuisine – salted cod with leeks, chickpea soup and grilled pork ribs etc – oozes natural flavour.

Gigi Trattoria (☎ 0583 46 72 66; www.gigitrattoria .it; Piazza del Carmine 7; meals €20; ☽ Mon-Sat) Buzzing by noon, this 1950s cantina on the old market square – revamped by three young Lucchesi in the new millennium – is another hot address among Lucchese. Recipes are plucked straight out of grandma's cookbook, local contemporary art to buy hangs on the walls and simplicity is the predominant philosophy driving the place.

Locanda Buatino (☎ 0583 34 32 07; www.leoster iedilucca.com; Via Borgo Giannotti 508; meals €20; ☽ Mon-Sat) A Lucca legend, this age-old trattoria – it is reckoned to be Lucca's oldest – with a fun 'n' funky air of retro wafting through it, has the added advantage of being a short walk from the madding crowds, outside the city walls. Chef Angelo chalks up a different menu daily – *cionca* (veal's head) is a speciality. Live jazz sets the place jiving on Monday, October to May.

Prosciutto & Melone (☎ 0583 4 88 45; Via Anfite atro 13/17; meals €25; ☽ Wed-Mon) Next door to Osteria Baralla, it's hardly *haute cuisine* but the fine choice of pizzas and salads alongside the mainstream *primi* and *secondi* ensure an easy midday refuel. Sit within the dark-green stable doors or snag a table on the shaded street outside.

Locanda di Bacco (☎ 0583 49 31 36; Via San Giorgio 36; meals €25; ☽ Wed-Mon) It is strictly *cucina Lucchese e Toscana* – albeit of a refreshingly creative nature – at this fine specimen of a restaurant, grandly situated in an old building, with marble-topped tables. Pappardelle with hare, gnocchi with gorgonzola, honey and nuts, or a side order of cabbage cooked in red pepper wine, garlic and oil are among the many dishes with an imaginative twist.

ALL SWEETNESS & LIGHT

The icing on the cake of the all-sweetness-and-light Lucca experience is, without a doubt, a slice of *buccellato*. A cross between biscuit and bun, this typical Lucchese pastry has been made on the premises at old-fashioned *pasticceria* (pastry shop) **Taddeucci** (☎ 0583 49 49 33; www.taddeucci .com; Piazza San Michele 34; ☺ 8am-8pm) since 1881. Sample a slice of *buccellato* (€5) with coffee and cream, strawberries and wine, ricotta and rum, or a simple Vin Santo, at one of a handful of tables on the square outside, or buy a small loaf (€3.30) to take away.

Otherwise, cakes, pastries, puff-pastry apple strudels, meringues and a multitude of other killer calorie-rich sweet treats are baked at **Dianda Pasticceria** (☎ 0583 49 26 61; Via della Rosa 9), a delightful cake shop within picnic distance of Lucca's botanical gardens, and with a coffee counter to down an espresso standing up.

Vecchia Trattoria Buralli (☎ 0583 95 06 11; Piazza Sant'Agostino 9; meals €25; ☺ Thu-Tue) Once an intimate local favourite now in all the guidebooks, this busy crowd-pleaser is a great for sampling wine from the surrounding Lucchese hills. Fare is wholly traditional and a green parrot sits on the packed terrace outside.

Di Simo (☎ 0583 49 62 34; Via Fillungo 58; meals €28) This formal old-world café-cum-restaurant with much of its original furniture and the world's most subtly camouflaged toilet door was once patronised by Puccini and his coterie (the maestro would tickle the ivories of the piano at the entrance to the dining area). Then known as Antico Caffè del Caselli, contemporary Di Simo spoons out mean ice creams alongside leafy salads and mains to a well-dressed older crowd.

Buca di Sant'Antonio (☎ 0583 5 58 81; Via della Cervia 3; meals €30; ☺ Tue-Sat, lunch Sun) An outstanding spot for tasting excellent wines from Tuscany and every other wine-producing region in Italy (Champagne is the only foreigner on sommelier Cristiano Cortopassi's carefully selected wine list), this highly ranked restaurant dating to 1782 is a must-stop for visiting celebrities and politicians. The menu of deep-fried breaded lamb cutlets with artichokes, rabbit salad or roast guinea fowl with ham and grapes, and the romantic old-world setting, cannot fail to impress. Advance bookings recommended.

Osteria Baralla (☎ 0583 44 02 40; www.osteria baralla.it; Via Anfiteatro 5-9; meals €35; ☺ Mon-Sat) Dine beneath magnificent red-brick vaults against a backdrop of sotto voce piped jazz at this busy *osteria*, packed to the rafters by noon. Rich in tradition (the place dates to 1860) and local specialities, chef highlights include a hearty farro soup typical to the Garfagnana, deer chops with wild berries,

mixed boiled meat on Thursday and roast pork on Sunday.

Drinking

Festival time aside, Lucca turns in early. Piazza Cittadela has a couple of lovely cafés to drink in the company of Puccini.

Caffetteria San Colombano (☎ 0583 44 46 41; www .caffetteriasancolombano.it; Baluardo San Colombano; meals €35; ☺ Tue-Sun) Enviably nestled in one of the bastions of the city wall, this stylish café is as much a dining spot as a drinking spot. The interior is modern and a mix of styles; outside, with its wooden decking and umbrella seating, is perfect retreat-from-the-sun territory.

I Santi Vineria (☎ 0583 49 61 24; Via Anfiteatro 29a; ☺ Tue-Sun) A wine shop with a few tables and large green umbrellas in front, this is a tranquil spot to sip wine under the watchful eye of Madonna and child. Tasty morsels served are as predictable as a cheese platter and as unpredictable as stewed octopus. Wi-fi hotspot!

Betty Blue (☎ 0583 49 21 66; Via del Gonfalone 16/18; ☺ Thu-Sun) A lively spot with 1960s-style mustard plastic-coated bar stools, op art on the walls and plenty of slouching space inside and out.

Entertainment

Teatro del Giglio (☎ 0583 4 65 31; box office 0583 46 75 21; www.teatrodelgiglio.it in Italian; Piazza del Giglio 13-15) Opera and theatre.

Villa Bottini (☎ 0583 44 21 41; Via Elisa) This beautiful 16th-century villa with formal gardens is home to the city's cultural department and its prime concert, exhibition and cultural-event venue.

Vino & Kino (☎ 0583 46 76 19; www.vinoekino.it in Italian; Via della Dogana 6; admission €1; ☺ 6pm-midnight Wed-Sun, screenings 9.30pm Thu & Sun) Cult and classic movies are screened twice weekly at this cultural association where Lucca's cultured set meet for wine and aperitif nibbles.

Getting There & Away
BUS
From the bus stops around Piazzale Verdi, **CLAP** (☎ 0583 58 78 97; www.clapspa.it in Italian) runs services throughout the region, including destinations in the Garfagnana such as Castelnuovo (€3.50, 1½ hours, eight daily); and **Lazzi** (☎ 0583 58 48 76) runs buses to/from Florence (€4.70, 1½ hours, hourly), Pisa (€2.20, 45 minutes, hourly), La Spezia (€5.20, three hours, four daily) and Marina di Carrara (€3.50, two hours, six daily) via Marina di Massa.

CAR & MOTORCYCLE
The A11 runs westwards to Pisa and Viareggio and eastwards to Florence. The SS12, then the SS445 from Forno, links the city with the Garfagnana.

TRAIN
Lucca is on the Florence–Pisa–Viareggio train line and there are also services into the Garfagnana. There are frequent trains to/from Pisa (€2.20, 25 minutes) and Florence (€4.80, 1½ hours) via Pistoia (€3.30, 45 minutes) and Prato (€4.30, one hour).

Getting Around
Most cars are banned within the city walls; don't even dare to drive in. This said, most hotels will give you a permit entitling you to park in spaces reserved for residents (indicated by yellow lines) and you can generally park for free outside the city walls.

Small CLAP electric buses connect the train station, Corso Garibaldi and Piazzale Verdi but it's quicker and more pleasurable to walk – a footpath cuts across the moat and up onto Baluardo San Colombano on the city walls.

Otherwise, follow the crowd and rent a set of wheels in bike-friendly Lucca: **Poli** (☎ 0583 49 37 87; www.biciclettepoli.com; Piazza Santa Maria 42) and **Cicli Bizzarri** (☎ 0583 49 60 31; Piazza Santa Maria 32) both rent regular city bikes (€2.50 per hour) as well as tandems (€5.50 per hour), *carrellino* (covered buggies to pedal along two small kids) and *cammellino* (one-wheel kid's bike to attach on the back of an adult bike). The Piazzale Verdi tourist office also rents bikes.

For a taxi, call ☎ 0583 95 52 00.

EAST OF LUCCA
Villas
Luccan businessmen who had finally arrived built themselves opulent country residences – some 300 all told – from the 16th to the 19th centuries. Most have crumbled away, been abandoned or are inaccessible today but you will find at least a dozen fine examples of these beautiful villas still standing proud northeast of Lucca.

Much of the present appearance and meticulously planned gardens of **Villa Reale** (☎ 0583 3 01 08; Via Fraga Alta; garden tour €7; ☒ 10am-noon & 3-6pm Tue-Sun Mar-Nov), perhaps the most striking villa, 7km north of Lucca in Marlia, is owed to the tastes of Elisa Bonaparte, Napoleon's sister and short-lived ruler of Tuscany. Only the gardens can be visited, by hourly guided tour, March to November.

The neoclassical **Villa Grabau** (☎ 0583 40 60 98, 349 601 36 52; Via di Matraia 269; villa & park €6.50, park only €5.50; ☒ 10am-1pm & 3-7pm Tue-Sun Jul & Aug, 10am-1pm & 2-6pm Tue-Sun Easter-Jun, Sep & Oct), located just north in San Pancranzio, is framed by a vast 9 hectares of parkland with sweeping traditional English- and Italian-styled gardens, splashing fountains, more than 100 terracotta vases of centenary lemon trees and the Casa dei Limoni, a picture-postcard lemon house, still used to store lemons, built in 1700.

In the same village, the gardens of **Villa Oliva** (☎ 0583 40 64 62; www.villaoliva.it; garden visit €6; ☒ 9.30am-12.30pm & 2-6pm mid-Mar–mid-Nov, by appointment only rest of year), a country residence designed for the Buonvisi family by Luccan architect Matteo Civitali (see his sculptures in Lucca's cathedral, p192) and summer residence of the Oliva family today, are worth a peep. Retaining its original design, the fountain-rich park staggers across three levels and ensnares a romantic cypress alley, a pergola unusually covered in *carpini* trees (rather than vines or jasmine), lime and eucalyptus trees galore, and stables reckoned to be even more beautiful that those at Versailles.

To reach these villas, follow the eastbound SS435 towards Pescia and turn north to Marlia, signposted 7km east of Lucca.

Collodi
A further 8km east along the SS435 brings you to a turn-off north for Collodi. Carlo Lorenzini, the creator of Italy's naughtiest and best-selling fictional character Pinnochio,

THE REAL ADVENTURES OF PINOCCHIO

Pinocchio is one of the best-known children's classics. A timeless tale of a wooden puppet that turns into a boy, it is among the most widely read and internationally popular pieces of literature ever to emerge from Italy.

In the early 1880s, Carlo Collodi, a Florentine journalist, wrote a series for one of united Italy's first children's periodicals entitled *Storia di un Burattino* (Story of a Puppet). Subsequently renamed *Le Avventure di Pinocchio* (The Adventures of Pinocchio), it would have made Collodi (real name Lorenzini) a multimillionaire had he lived to exploit the film and translation rights.

Collodi did not merely intend to pen an amusing child's tale. Literary critics have been trawling the text for the past century in search of ever more evidence to show that it was as much aimed at adult readers as children.

The character of Pinocchio is a frustrating mix of the likable and the odious. At his worst he's a wilful, obnoxious, deceitful little monster who deserves just about everything he gets. Humble and blubbering when things go wrong, he has the oh-so-human tendency to resume his wayward behaviour when he thinks he's in the clear. The wooden puppet is a prime example of flesh-and-blood failings. You thought Jiminy Cricket was cute? Pinocchio thought him such a pain, he splattered him against the wall (in the real, not the sanitised, Disney, version).

Pinocchio spends a good deal of the tale playing truant and one of Collodi's central messages seems to be that only good, well-behaved, diligent schoolchildren have a hope of getting anywhere or, in this case, of turning into a fine human lad. But Collodi was not merely taking a middle-class swipe at naughty-boy behaviour. He was convinced that the recently united Italy was in urgent need of a decent education system to help the country out of its poverty and lethargy. His text can be interpreted in part as a criticism of a society that is yet incapable of meeting that need.

Indeed the story, weaving between fantasy and reality, is a mine of references, some more veiled than others, to the society of late-19th-century Italy – a troubled country with enormous socioeconomic problems compounded by the general apathy of those in power. Pinocchio waits the length of the story to become a real boy. But, while his persona may provoke laughter, his encounters with poverty, petty crime, skewed justice and just plain bad luck constitute a painful education in the machinations of the 'real' world.

---

spent time in this hilltop village as a child and took the hamlet's name as his nom de plume – prompting the ever-grateful town to repay the compliment with **Parco di Pinocchio** (☎ 0572 42 93 42; www.pinocchio.it; adult/concession €10/7; ☒ 8.30am–sunset), a theme park in a wood just outside the village. With a series of mosaics recounting the main episodes in the puppet's life, statues and tableaux, it's as much a treat for grown-ups as for kids.

Collodi's other lure is the lovely **Storico Giardino Garzoni** (☎ 0572 42 73 14; Piazza della Vittoria 1; adult/child €12/10; ☒ 9am–sunset Mar–Oct, 10am–dusk Sat Nov–Feb), a historic terraced garden with a typical Tuscan open-air theatre, elegant lily-covered water pools and butterfly house tumbling around a richly frescoed baroque villa. Only the gardens and butterfly house, aflutter with 400 butterflies, can be visited.

Few buses between Lucca and Montecatini Terme stop in Collodi; it's a lot easier by car.

Pescia
pop 18,400

Pescia, split by the course of the river of the same name, is the self-proclaimed flower capital of Tuscany, with exports worth around €130 million annually. Every other September, in even-numbered years, Pescia hosts Europe's largest flower festival, the **Biennale del Fiore**.

In season, the fields around Pescia are spectacular to drive through but the town itself

---

SLEEP DREAM EAT VILLAS

Travellers dreaming of living like a wealthy 16th-century Luccan can do so thanks to the **Associazione delle Ville e dei Palazzi Lucchesi** (☎ 0583 90 01 115; www.villelucchesi .net), an association of historic villa owners who advertise their small collection of dreamy B&Bs and *agriturismi* online. See the website for details.

has little to detain you. At the northern end of Piazza Mazzini is the 13th-century **Palazzo del Vicario**, these days the Palazzo Comunale (Town Hall). Saturday sees the square – a car park other days – abuzz with a **market**.

CLAP buses connect Pescia with Lucca (€3, 45 minutes). Lazzi services run east to Montecatini Terme (€1.50, 20 minutes, half-hourly).

LA VERSILIA

The coastal area from Viareggio northwards to the regional border with Liguria is known as La Versilia. Although popular with local holidaymakers and some foreigners (mainly Germans, French and Brits), it has been blighted by beachfront strip development and gets packed with Italy's beach-loving hoi polloi.

It is very much a gay getaway too: Grand Duke Giancarlo Leopold I was the first in Italy to decriminalise homosexuality here in 1863. Its dynamic Open Versilia marketing campaign (http://international.friendlyversilia.it) lures a large chunk of the gay community here each summer to have fun in the sun.

La Versilia makes a good gateway to the Apuane Alps (see p204), with roads from the coastal towns snaking their way deep into the heart of the mountains and connecting with small villages and walking tracks.

Trekking Bike: The Tuscan Coast details 12 walking itineraries and a 661km-long bicycle itinerary along the coast, split into 12 easy one-day legs (each three to four hours), pick it up at tourist offices. Online see www-tuscan coast.com and www.rivieratoscana.com.

VIAREGGIO
pop 61,800

This hugely popular sun and sand resort on the Versilia coastal strip is known as much for its flamboyant Mardi Gras Carnevale, second only to Venice for party spirit, as for its gorgeous line-up of old Art Nouveau façades on its seafront that recall the town's heyday in the 1920s and 1930s.

Literature lovers might like to pass by Piazza Shelley, the only tangible reference to the Romantic poet who drowned in Viareggio; his body was washed up on the beach and his comrade-in-arts, Lord Byron, had him cremated on the beach in Viareggio.

Orientation

It's a short walk from the train station to the waterfront, Via Regina Margherita, and central tourist office. The city is arranged roughly north to south on a grid pattern. South from the Canale Burlamacca, lined with pleasure boats, stretch the enticing woods of the Pineta di Levante. Another smaller wood, the Pineta di Ponente, occupies a large chunk of the northern end of town. Beyond it Viareggio merges seamlessly into the next beach resort of Lido di Camaiore.

Information

EMERGENCY
Police station (☎ 0584 4 27 41; Piazza S Antonio)

LAUNDRY
Wash & Dry (Corso Garibaldi 5)

POST
Post office (Corso Garibaldi)

TOURIST INFORMATION
Central tourist office (☎ 0584 96 22 33; www .versilia.turismo.toscana.it; Viale Carducci 10; ⊙ 9am-2pm & 3-7.30pm Mon-Sat, 9am-1pm Sun)
Tourist office kiosks Seafront (⊙ 10am-12.30pm & 4-7.30pm Tue-Sun summer); Train Station (⊙ 9.30am-12.30pm Mon-Fri, 9.30am-12.30pm & 4-6pm Sat & Sun)

Sights & Activities

The golden sandy **beach** is laden with cafés, climbing frames and other amusements for kids, and – bar the short public stretch opposite fountain-pierced Piazza Mazzini – it is divided into *stabilimenti,* individual lots where you can hire chairs, umbrellas, recliners and the like. Two recliners with umbrellas cost about €25 a day.

A good deal of the waterfront area as it appears today was built in the 1920s and '30s. Several of the buildings, such as Puccini's favourite, **Gran Caffè Margherita** (☎ 0584 96 25 53; www.ristorantemargherita.it in Italian; Viale Regina Margherita 30), wooden **Chalet Martini** (a clothes shop since 1860 with an equally fabulous interior) next door, and the old façade of the former **Bagno Balena** (public baths) a little further along, all retain something of their ornate stylishness.

When you tire of the seafront and its endless crowds and ice-cream kiosks, take a stroll along the tracks in the **Pineta di Levante**, beside the Canale Burlamacca and along Via Regina Margherita. And if you feel even the most distant call of the sea, you'll thrill to the stylish pleasure vessels, big and small, being constructed or refurbished in the town's docks and shipyards.

A couple of kilometres from the centre at **La Citadella di Carnevale** (☎ 0584 5 11 76; Via Santa Maria Goretti; admission free), 16 gargantuan hangars serve as workshop- and parking-space for the fantastic floats crafted with a passion by each highly skilled and prized *carrista* (floatbuilder) for Viareggio's annual carnival (right). The largest floats featuring a papier-mâché merry-go-round of clowns, opera divas, skeletons, kings etc; they are a staggering 20m wide and 14m tall, take five months to build and carry 200 people each during processions. Stroll around the complex and a *carrista* will inevitably invite you into his workshop. Otherwise, discover carnival history and the art of making *teste in capo* (the giant heads worn in processions) and *mascheroni a piedi* (big walking masks) in the **Museo del Carnevale** (☽ 3.30-5.30pm Sat Dec-May, plus 9.30-11.30am carnival Sundays in Feb).

Should you exhaust Viareggio, pick up a copy of the tourist office's excellent free booklet that describes in detail 14 motoring *itinerari turistici* around the coastal towns and inland mountains.

Festivals & Events

Viareggio's moment of glory lasts a good four weeks in February to early March when the city goes wild at **Carnevale** (www.viareggio.ilcarne vale.com), a festival of floats, many with giant satirical effigies of political and other topical figures, plus fireworks and a dusk-to-dawn spirit. Tickets for the Sunday processions cost €13 (under 10s free) and can be bought at the Fondazione Carnevale (Piazza Mazzini) or a ticket kiosk on the procession circuit.

Sleeping

There are half a dozen camp sites in the Pineta di Levante woods between Viareggio and Torre del Lago. Most are open April to September.

Viareggio boasts more than 120 hotels of all classes, along with *affittacamere* (rooms for rent) and villas. They jostle for space beside or a couple of blocks inland from the waterfront and are mostly modern, clean – and bland. In high summer, especially July, many charge at

least *mezza pensione* (half-board) and often *pensione completa* (full board).

Peralta (☎ 0584 95 12 30; www.peraltatuscany.com; d from €90, apartments per week from €700; ⊗ May-Oct; 🐾) High up a side valley, this wonderful abandoned hamlet resuscitated by an Anglo-Italian sculptor has stunning views. It's the perfect place to relax, though if you'd prefer a little self-improvement, there are courses in painting and cooking, plus hearty hill walking. Check the website since low-season rates can be more than 50% cheaper. Bring all you need as it's a long, vertiginous haul to the shops. Find it 10km from Viareggio, signposted from the village of Camaiore.

Eating

If you dodge full board in the hotels, there are plenty of restaurant options, although the waterfront places tend to be expensive and uninspiring.

Sergio (☎ 0584 46 12 56; Piazza del Mercato 130; meals around €12; ⊗ Sun-Fri) Beneath the arcades on the southern side of Viareggio's central market, Sergio is old kid on the block (around since 1955). More of a deli with excellent cheeses, cold meats and a few tables inside, this is the Viareggio hotspot for quick, nourishing, tasty fare to eat in or take out.

Da Giorgio (☎ 0584 4 44 93; Via G Zanardelli 71; meals around €35; ⊗ Thu-Tue) Run by the same family since 1948, this is *the* place for fish – and exclusively fish – of the freshest kind, succulently cooked. Its walls are plastered with testimonials from satisfied guests. Advance reservations essential.

Amaro (☎ 0584 96 21 83; Via San Martino 73; ⊗ Mon-Sat) Take your pick of designer chairs at this trendy contemporary restaurant-stroke-wine bar with a glassed-in kitchen for all to see and a solitary orchid on each table.

Getting There & Around

BOAT

June to September **Consorzio Marittimo Turistico** (☎ 0187 73 29 87; Via Minzoni 13, La Spezia) runs passenger boats connecting Viareggio (and also Marina de Pisa, Forte dei Marmi, Marina di Carrara and Marina di Massa) with coastal destinations in Liguria, such as the Cinque Terre villages and Portofino.

BUS

Lazzi (☎ 0584 4 62 34) and **CLAP** (☎ 0584 3 09 96) buses run from Piazza d'Azeglio, where both have offices, to destinations around Tuscany, including services running direct or via Lucca to Florence (€7, 1½ hours, seven daily).

CLAP has fairly regular buses up the coast to Pietrasanta and Forte dei Marmi, as well as up to 12 daily to Lucca (€2.70) and between three and six services a day to Massa (€2.40). It also runs the town's local buses.

From June to September long-distance buses run to such destinations as Milan (€23.50). Buy tickets at travel agencies or the Lazzi kiosk.

TAXI

Call ☎ 0584 4 70 00 or ☎ 0584 4 54 54.

TRAIN

Local trains run to Livorno (€3.20, one hour), Pisa (€2.40, 20 minutes), and La Spezia (€4, one hour) via Massa and Carrara. Regular trains run to Florence (€5.90), via Lucca (€2.10). A couple of Eurostar Italia trains bound for Rome, Genoa and Turin stop by, as do four to five fast trains, bound for Milan and Turin.

AROUND VIAREGGIO
Torre del Lago

A few kilometres south of Viareggio on the other side of the Pineta di Levante, Torre del Lago is a quiet continuation of the seaside theme, but with a key difference: Puccini had a **villa** (☎ 0584 34 14 45; adult/child €7/1.50; ⊗ 10am-12.30pm & 3-6.30pm Tue-Sun Jun-Oct, to 5.30pm Dec-Mar, to 6pm Apr & May) here by the lake where he wrote most of his operas, including *Madame Butterfly* and *Tosca*. Puccini fans can pay homage at his grave, inside a chapel in the villa; visit the villa; and watch an open-air performance of one of his operas during July and August's sensational **Festival Puccini** (www.puccinifestival.it).

From the pontoons opposite Villa Puccini, one-hour boat excursions (☎ 0584 35 02 52; €7) run across the lagoon to the **Parco Naturale Migliarino San Rossore Massaciuccoli**, one of Tuscany's rare stretches of protected coastline. Part swamp, part pine forest, the 230-sq-km park hosts particularly diverse bird life, especially during the migratory periods, when species of falcon, vulture, duck, heron, cormorant and other water birds linger or pass through. Deer, wild boar and feral goats are the biggest of the quadruped year-round residents. Its main **visitor centre** (☎ 050 53 01 01; www.parcosanrossore.it; ⊗ 9am-1pm & 2.30-6pm Jun-Sep, 9am-1pm & 2-5pm Oct-May) is in Cascine Vecchie.

CLAP bus 4 links the centre of Viareggio with Torre del Lago.

North to Liguria

Heading up the coast from Viareggio, you cross into **Lido di Camaiore**. The development becomes sparser as you press on northwards and the beaches are usually less crowded.

When you reach **Marina di Pietrasanta**, turn inland 3.5km for the town of **Pietrasanta** itself. The centre of the old town is Piazza Duomo. If it's open, pop into the Chiesa di Sant'Agostino; its rather stark, Gothic façade may be off-putting but the cloister inside is pleasant. Also here is a 13th-century cathedral and the Palazzo Moroni, with a modest archaeological museum. An elegant B&B in this area is **L'Arcadia** (☎ 0584 75 71 34; www.arcadia .lu.it; Vai di Solaio 67c; d incl breakfast €80-150), a 200-year-old family home amid olive groves in a hamlet on a hill in Vallecchia, 3km north of Pietrasanta.

Back down on the coast, **Forte dei Marmi** is the most chic resort on this stretch of coastline (post-Cannes film festival over the border, several of the stars, starlets and satellites retire here to recover). You'll find plenty of places to stay, eat and drink close to the waterfront; the **tourist office** (☎ 0584 8 00 91; www .fortedeimarmi.it in Italian; Via Franceschi 8b; ☺ 9am-1pm & 3.30-6.30pm Mon-Sat, 10am-noon Sun Jun-Sep, 9am-1pm Mon-Sat, 3-7pm Sat Oct-May) carries a list. Time your visit for the town's Wednesday **market** (replicated on Sunday in summer), when you can pick up designer label clothing for a relative snip.

Beyond Forte dei Marmi the seaside is fairly uninspiring, until you reach the border of Liguria and beyond.

APUANE ALPS

Rearing up between the coastal Versilia Riviera and, inland, the vast valley of the Garfagnana, is this mountain range protected by the **Parco Regionale delle Alpi Apuane**. Altitudes are relatively low – the highest peak, Monte Pisanino, is 1945m high – compared with the real Alps further north, but the Apuane Alps offer great walking possibilities (see p84), often with spectacular views of the coastline and Ligurian Sea. *The Alps of Tuscany* by Francesco Greco presents many more enjoyable multiday routes.

You'll find a good network of marked walking trails and *rifugi* (mountian huts). To guide your steps, pick up *Alpi Apuane Settentrionali*, published by the Massa and Carrara tourist offices with trails and *rifugi* marked up, or *Alpi Apuane*, produced by Edizione Multigraphic of Florence. Both are at 1:25,000.

Caving is the other big outdoor activity, the area riddled with 1300-plus caves. While some serve as spoil-yourself spas, others – like the Grotta del Vento (p210) or Italy's deepest (1200m) and longest (50km) cave, **Antro del Corchia** (☎ 0584 77 84 05; 2hr guided tour €12; ☺ 9am-6pm Jul & Aug, shorter hours Sat & Sun only mid-Mar–Jun & Sep–mid-Nov) near Levigliani – are truly sights to behold.

The main gateway into the Parco Regionale delle Alpi Apuane is **Seravezza**, an important centre for marble extraction since the 16th century. Here the park runs an **information centre** (☎ 0584 75 61 44; www.parcapuane.toscana.it; Via Corrado del Greco 11; ☺ 9am-1pm & 3.30-7.30pm Jun-Sep, 9.30am-12.30pm & 3-6pm Wed-Mon Oct-May) and Castelnuovo di Garfagnana (p210), which has the **Centro Visite Parco Alpi Apuane** (☎ 0583 64 42 42; www.parcapuane.it in Italian; Piazza delle Erbe 1; ☺ 9am-1pm & 3.30-5.30pm Mon-Sat, 9am-1pm & 3-7pm Sun Jun-Sep, shorter hours Oct-May). Both centres are well-stocked with maps and brochures about the Apuane Alps and have mountains of information on walking, horse-riding, *rifugi* and so on.

A recommended route from Seravessa is due southeast along the Vezza river to the picturesque hamlet of **Stazzema**, high in the hills. The village entrance is marked by the Romanesque Chiesa di Santa Maria Assunta, and it makes a great base for walks in the Apuane Alps.

CARRARA
pop 65,000

Marble Mountain is what Carrara, about 7km northwest of Massa, is synonymous with: indeed, gazing at the panorama of snowy-white mountain peaks looming large behind the town of Carrara, at the foothills of the Apuane Alps, and you could be forgiven for thinking it is snow. Nothing more than a breathtaking illusion, it is in fact marble, field upon field of it, in vast quarries that eat into the hills.

Excruciatingly mean to the environment, yes, but sculptors still flock to these scarred foothills of the Apuane Alps in search of the perfect piece. The texture and purity of

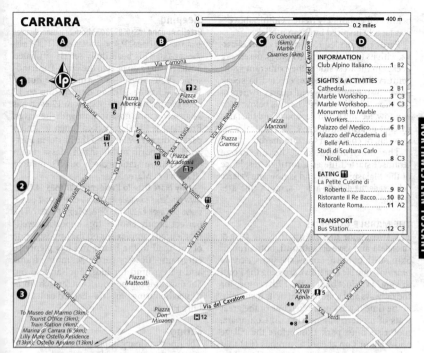

CARRARA

INFORMATION	
Club Alpino Italiano..........1	B2

SIGHTS & ACTIVITIES	
Cathedral.....................2	B1
Marble Workshop..........3	C3
Marble Workshop..........4	C3
Monument to Marble	
Workers.....................5	D3
Palazzo del Medico........6	B1
Palazzo dell'Accademia di	
Belle Arti....................7	B2
Studi di Scultura Carlo	
Nicoli.........................8	C3

EATING	
La Petite Cuisine di	
Roberto.....................9	B2
Ristorante Il Re Bacco....10	B2
Ristorante Roma............11	A2

TRANSPORT	
Bus Station....................12	C3

Carrara's white marble (derived from the Greek *marmaros,* meaning shining stone) is unrivalled and it was here that Michelangelo selected marble for some of his masterpieces, *David* (actually sculpted from a dud veined block) included. In 2006 Carrara marble exports increased by 4.43% to 3.2 million tons, worth €1.8 billion.

The marble quarries, actually 5km north of town in Colonnata and Franscritti, have been worked since Roman times. It's hard, dangerous work and on Carrara's central Piazza XXVII Aprile a monument remembers workers who lost their lives in the quarries. These tough men formed the backbone of a strong leftist and anarchist tradition in Carrara, something that won them no friends among the Fascists or, later, the occupying German forces. Nowadays, environmentalists oppose the continual massive quantity of marble that is hauled from the hillside, while quarry owners fight back in their interest and that of their 8000-odd employees.

Bar the thrill of seeing its mosaic marble pavements, marble street benches, decorative marble *putti* (winsome cherubs) and mar-

ble everything-else, the old centre of palm tree–clad Carrara is unrivetting. Its cheap and cheerful coastal counterparts, Marina di Carrara and Marina di Massa, popular with holidaying Italians, and its quarries are really what make it a fascinating place to visit.

Information

Carrara tourist office (☎ 0585 84 41 36; Viale XX Settembre; ☽ 9am-5pm Mon-Sat Apr & May, 9am-1pm & 4-8pm or 9pm Jun-Aug, 9am-1pm & 3-5pm Sep-Mar) Signposted 'Checkpoint Bus Turistic', opposite the stadium; has maps of Carrara, its marble workshops and out-of-town quarries.

Club Alpino Italiano (☎ 0585 77 67 82; caicarrara@apuanet.com; Via Loris Giorgi 1) Walking information.

Sights
TOWN CENTRE

The **cathedral** (Piazza Duomo; ☽ 7am-noon & 3.30-7pm), at the heart of the old town, is one of the earliest medieval buildings to have been constructed entirely of Apuane marble. Building began in the 11th century and dragged on for two centuries. The façade – Romanesque below and elaborately fretted Gothic above – was largely inspired by Pisan models.

Partly colonnaded 15th-century **Piazza Alberica**, with its festively painted houses, deserves a peek. On the west side is the exuberant 18th-century **Palazzo del Medico**, erected to speak power by the most powerful quarry owners of the time. Check out the cherubs below each window, leering gargoyles above and the family coat of arms sitting over the central window, all, of course, in Carrara marble.

The much-modified castle on Piazza Gramsci started life as a fortified residence of the Malaspina clan and is now the **Palazzo dell'Accademia di Belle Arti**, Carrara's fine arts school.

THE MARBLE QUARRIES

The two major marble quarries are **Cave di Colonnata** and **Cave di Fantiscritti**, both around 5km north of town. Follow the signs '*cave de marmo*' (marble quarries), crossing the Ponti di Vara, a viaduct built in the 19th century for the railways and a monument in its own right; at the time it was considered one of the great feats of modern engineering. In Colonnata, motorists must park 1km before the village and walk or hop aboard a minibus (€1) that takes you to the tiny village's central marble-paved square, Piazza Palestro.

To get an idea of the hard grind, visit the Fantiscritti *cave* (see the boxed text, opposite) or poke your nose into the dust-filled air of the workshops on Carrara's central Piazza XXVII Aprile 8. Artists frequently instruct the marble *laboratory* (workshop) on how they want a piece executed – or at least begun – thus cleverly avoiding the hard and dusty work themselves. **Studi di Scultura Carlo Nicoli** (☎ 0585 700 79; www.nicoli-sculptures.com; Piazza XXVII Aprile 8) arranges tours and sculpture courses.

Opposite the stadium, halfway between Carrara and Marina di Carrara, the well-thought-out and fascinating **Museo del Marmo** (☎ 0585 84 57 46; Viale XX Settembre; admission free; 10am-6pm Mon-Sat May, Jun & Sep, 10am-8pm Mon-Sat Jul-Aug, 9am-5pm Oct-Apr), with descriptive panels in English and a brilliant collection of modern sculpture, has more marble in more varieties than you'll ever have seen before (there are seven types of white marble alone, ranging from statuary ivory white to striped 'onion' marble) and describes extraction from chisel-and-hammer days to the 21st century's high-powered industrial quarrying.

Sleeping

Ostello Apuano (☎ 0585 78 00 34; ostelloapuano@hotmail .com; Viale delle Pinete 237, Marina di Massa; dm €11; mid-Mar–mid-Oct) This beautifully set HI–affiliated hostel is bang slap next to the sand. The handsome 1920s house – a German base during WWII – has basic clean dorms (four to 12 beds) with stunning views; room 12 even has a balcony staring nose-to-nose with the waves. Breakfast is €1.60, a packed lunch €7 and a packed dinner €9.50. Find the hostel in Partaccia, just north of Marina di Massa. From Carrara train station catch bus 53, marked Via Avenza Mare.

Lilly Mare Ostello Residence (☎ 0585 24 12 22; www.residence-lillymare.it; Marina di Massa; 2-person studio per week €230-470; Apr-Sep; P ♿) The perfect family choice, this appealing well-manicured complex sits on the opposite side of the road to the beach and has plenty to entertain – flowery garden, climbing frame and playground for kids, pool and so on. Should camping be your thing, pitch up at its neighbouring pine tree–backed camp site, Lilly Pineta.

Eating

The finest culinary opportunities are in Colonnata, where *crostoni lardo e funghi* (mushroom and lard-topped toasts) whet appetites for the chestnut-flour *tagliatelle, fresco* (fresh) and *stagionato* (mature) *pecorino* cheese and other local products.

Ristorante Roma (☎ 0585 7 06 32; Piazza Cesare Battisti 1; meals €20; Mon-Sat) Just off the square, this restaurant offers smiley, speedy service, a menu that changes according to the season and a dozen-odd grappas to shoot back. Try the seafood risotto followed by a simple yet memorable vanilla gelato.

Also recommended for local cuisine:
Ristorante Il Re Bacco (☎ 0585 77 67 78; Via Loris Giorgi 5; Mon-Sat) Excellent wine list and tastings.
La Petite Cuisine di Roberto (Via Verdi 4a; lunch menu €15; Mon-Sat) Fresh fish and seafood.

Getting There & Away

From the **bus station** (☎ 0585 8 52 11; Piazza Don Minzoni), CAT buses serve Massa to the south and, in the Lunigiana area, Fivizzano, Aulla and Pontremoli.

Trains along the coastal line (from La Spezia, Genoa, Rome, Viareggio and so on) stop nearer Marina di Carrara, from where local buses shuttle into Carrara itself.

MARBLE MOUNTAIN

'Here we are, 600m from the beginning of the tunnel, 600m from the end of it, 430m above sea level and 400m from the top. We are right in the middle of the mountain', the Cava di Fantiscritti tour guide informs us.

Zipping down a dank, wet, unlit tunnel in a dusty white minibus, grubby headlights blazing, driver incongruously dolled up in a shiny shocking-pink bomber jacket, it is all somewhat surreal. After being inside the pitch-black marble mountain for only about five minutes, we are all told to get out.

It is 16°C, foggy, damn dirty on foot (two Japanese had sensibly brought their wellies), and far from being a polished pearly white, it's grey – cold, wet, miserable grey. Rough-cut blocks, several metres long and almost as wide, are strewn about the place like toy bricks and marble columns prop up the 17m-high ceiling, above which a second gallery, another 17m high, stands tall. The place is bigger than several football pitches, yet amazingly there is still plenty of marble mountain left for the five workers employed at Miseglia's **Cava di Fantiscritti**, 5km north of Carrara, to extract 10,000 tonnes of white marble a month. The current market price: €200 to €1000 per tonne, with Carrara's very best commanding double that.

The hard graft – mechanical diamond-cutting chains, with the aid of water, slice through the rock like butter – is done in the cooler morning, leaving the afternoons free for **tour groups** (Marmo Tour; ☎ 339 765 74 70; 25min guide tour adult/child €6/3; ☼ 3.30-7pm Mon-Fri, 10.30am-7pm Sat) like us to slosh around. Marble dust is horribly fine; mix it with water and the goo is gross. Quarrying marble is definitely no holiday.

To learn how the Romans did it (the *very* hard way with chisels and axes), visit the open-air **museum** (admission free; ☼ 9am-7pm), next to the souvenir shop opposite the quarry entrance. Don't miss the B&W shots of marble blocks being precariously slid down the *lizza* (mountain pathway) to the bottom of the mountain, where 18 pairs of oxen would pull the marble to Carrara port. Indeed, these days, the bulk of marble is shipped off: see the blocks, marked in Arabic and other languages, at the port waiting to be worked elsewhere.

ourpick **Locanda Apuana** (☎ 0585 76 80 17; www.locandaapuana.com; Via Communale 1; meals €15; ☼ Tue-Sat, lunch Sun), located in Colonnata, 2km from Fantiscritti, is the place to zip to should hunger beckon. You can sate your taste for a different marble here – in the fantastic guise of *lardo di colonnata* (thinner than wafer-thin slices of local pork fat marinated in a mix of herbs and oils in shallow marble vats). Buy a vacuum-packed hunk to take home from one of the many *larderia* in the village: **Larderia il Poggio** (☎ 0585 755 80 29; Via della Fontana 52) sells lard aged for six months (€13.50 a kg) and 24 months €17 a kg), as well as *crema di lardo* (€20 a kg) and a useful pamphlet (€1) loaded with recipes using Colonnata lard. The Rolls Royce of lard (€20 a kg) is marinated, salt-coated slabs of the black-pelted Cinta Senese porker.

Then head back to Carrara for a well-spent afternoon at the Museo del Marmo (opposite) or join Mario and Caterina at **Colonnata Trekking** (☎ 0585 76 80 80) in Carrara for a hike to an abandoned village and quarry in these hollow old foothills of the Apuane Alps.

Oh, and don't wear black.

THE GARFAGNANA

At the heart of the Garfagnana is the valley formed by the Serchio river and its tributaries. Historically a region of net migration as villagers packed their bags to lead less harsh lives on the plains, it's now revitalised thanks to tourism and to the paper mills that whir outside most valley towns. (Diecimo's alone produces over 100,000 tonnes annually, including kilometre upon kilometre of Eco Lucart, the *soi-disant* environmentally friendly toilet paper.)

Prime launch pad for treks into the Apuane Alps, most visitors to this relatively undiscovered area of raw beauty are here for the active life, enjoying horse-trekking, hiking and biking. **Apians** (☎ 338 150 50 11; www.apians.com in Italian) in Castelnuova di Garfagnana organises canyoning, climbing, speleology, mountaineering and mountain-bike expeditions. An indispensable information source for independent souls keen to tour the Garfagnana and the Apuane Alps by bike is **Le Vie della Cantera** (www.panterabike.com), a truly comprehensive site

DETOUR: CARRARA TO FIVIZZANO

From Carrara take SS446 northwards, following signs to **Fosdinovo** and its formidable **Castello di Malaspina** (☎ 0187 6 88 91; guided tours adult/child €5/3; ☻ Wed-Mon). Owned by the Malaspina clan since 1340 (still today, it belongs to a branch of the family), its defensive walls and towers were gradually modified from the 16th century when the family converted it into a residence. A charming legend has it that a young princess died of a broken heart within the castle walls and at full moon her shadow can be seen drifting from window to window.

From Fosdinovo, follow the SS446 until a T-junction with the SS63. Heading right (eastwards) will bring you to **Fivizzano**, a largely modern farming centre, from where a wonderfully pretty mountain road runs northwards over the Apennines and deep into Emilia-Romagna.

with download area to pick up its 10 suggested cycling itineraries, which range from an easy 18km to a tougher 231km long.

Approaching the area along SS12, you hit **Borgo a Mozzano**, with its wacky, asymmetrical **Ponte della Maddalena** (also known as Ponte del Diavolo, or Devil's Bridge). Each of its five arches is different. Typical of the era, this medieval bridge rises to a high midpoint, then descends to the other side of the Serchio – only the 'midpoint' here is well off centre so the whole thing looks like a rearing Loch Ness monster in stone.

Bagni di Lucca
pop 6550

Small town Bagni di Lucca is small indeed. Famed in the early-19th century for its thermal waters enjoyed by the gentry of Lucca and an international set (Byron, Shelley, Heinrich Heine and Giacomo Puccini were among the celebrity guests to take to the waters), the spa town today is a pale shadow of its former splendid neoclassical self when it had its own casino, theatre and atypically ornate Anglican church (look for the stucco lion and unicorn motif above each window), now the municipal library. In the small British cemetery baroque tombs speak volumes.

There are two distinct areas: the smaller Ponte a Serraglio, clustered around a bridge that crosses the Lima river, where the **tourist office** (☎ 0583 80 57 45; Via del Casinò; ☻ 9.30am-12.30pm & 3.30-6.30pm Mon-Sat, 9.30am-12.30pm Sun mid-Mar–mid-Sep, 9.30am-12.30pm Mon & Wed-Sat mid-Sep–mid-Mar) is; and the main town, 2km north, where most shops, restaurants and hotels are.

There is just one *terme* (spa), the **Bagni di Lucca Terme** (☎ 0583 8 72 21; www.termebagnidilucca .it; Piazza San Martino 11; ☻ 8am-12.30pm Mon-Sat Apr, May, Sep & Oct, 8am-12.30pm & 2.30-6pm Mon-Sat Jun-Aug),

where the weary can be revitalised with a salt, olive oil or stone massage, and the hale and hearty can rejuvenate after a day's hiking with a session in the *grotte a vapore* (steam grottoes). Should you want to flop all night, check into **Antico Albergo Terme** (☎ 0583 8 60 34; Via del Paretaio 1; d incl breakfast €78-94; P ♨) next door. Its thermal pool, free for guests, is a toasty 30°C.

Quell hunger pangs at **Circolo dei Forestieri** (☎ 0583 8 60 38; Piazza Jean Varraud 10; meals €15-25; ☻ closed lunch Mon & Tue Easter-Oct), Bagni's *belle epoque* 'foreigners club' where a splendidly royal lunch can be tucked into beneath chandeliers at splendidly pauper prices.

Lazzi buses run here from Lucca (€2.50, 50 minutes, nine daily).

The Lima Valley & Abetone

The SS12 continues northeast from the Garfagnana into Pistoia province. If you're going to the ski slopes, it's the most picturesque route. Possible minor detours en route are to **San Cassiano**, with its 12th-century church, and **Lucchio**, spectacular for its position on the northeast slope of a wooded ridge.

Abetone (www.abetone.com in Italian) on the Emilia-Romagna border, has some 30 hotels, most of which insist on half-board in season. It's Tuscany's main ski resort and also makes a good base for a day or two of summertime striding. See p90 for more detailed skiing information.

Ostello Renzo Bizzarri (☎ 0573 6 01 17; bucaneve@abetone.com; Via Brennero 157; dm/d incl breakfast €13/40; ☻ Dec-Apr & mid-Jun–Sep), Abetone's large, secluded HI hostel with its enthusiastic staff, is very well equipped for skiers and summer walkers.

For those without their own transport, the easiest way up is to catch a bus from Pistoia (see p163).

Barga

pop 11,000

Barga is one of those irresistibly slow Tuscan hilltop towns with a disproportionately large and dynamic English-speaking community. The place is tiny yet it has its own English-language bookshop, newsletter, blog and website (www.barganews.com, which, among other things, votes on the best toilets in town) and a fair share of foreign toes tapping in its **Jazz Club** (☎ 0583 72 38 60; www.bargajazzclub.com). The village honours its patron saint on 25 July with an opera festival and throws a **Sagra del Pesce e Patate** (fish and chip festival) for 10 days of the same month. But heh! This *is* Italy's most Scottish town, as any Bargian whose ancestors emigrated to Scotland in search of a better life in the 19th century will proudly tell you.

A lovely patchwork of narrow streets, archways, ancient walls and small piazzas, the steep old town tumbles downhill at the foot of the **cathedral**, which was built between the 10th and 14th centuries. The cathedral's pulpit in particular is exquisite, carved by the idiosyncratic 13th-century sculptor Guido Bigarelli, and sits on four red marble pillars. The two front ones rest on lions that dominate a dragon and a heretic, while one of the back pillars rests on a disconsolate dwarf.

The **tourist office** (☎ 0583 72 47 45, 800 028 497; www.comune.barga.lu.it; Via di Mezzo 47; ☻ 9am-1pm Mon-Fri, 9am-1pm & 2.30-7pm Sat, 10am-12.30pm & 3-5pm Sun)

has plenty of info on Barga's multitude of cultural events and **Tuscany Walking** (☎ 0583 72 40 47; www.tuscanywalking.com; Via Al Monte 12) is a recommended English-speaking set-up which leads groups of two to 12 people on one-day guided hikes (€50 to €65 including transport if needed and lunch) from Barga into the Garfagnana and Apuane Alps.

Barga is a popular day trip from Lucca, and CLAP buses link Barga and Lucca (€3.50, 1¼ hours) up to 10 times daily, stopping in Piazzale del Fosso by Porta Mancianella, the main gate into the old town.

SLEEPING

Albergo Alpino (☎ 0583 72 33 36; www.bargaholiday.com; Via Pascoli 41; s/d €45/65; ☻ closed Nov) In the hands of the Castelvecchi family for nigh on a century, this 1920s lodge-style hotel opposite the post office has a great bar and restaurant. Rooms are tidy, clean and comfortable and the old town's a mere five minutes' walk away.

La Pergola (☎ 0583 71 12 39; www.hotel-lapergola .com; Via del Giardino; d €50-66) Don't be tricked into thinking the abandoned building on Via San Antonio is La Pergola; it moved premises a while back and remains a prettily floral place with restaurant and stunning views of the hilltop village from its 3rd-floor sun-trap terrace.

Casa Fontana (☎ 0583 72 45 24; www.casa-fontana .com; Via di Mezzo 77; d incl breakfast €98-109; ☻ mid-Mar-Oct) Six stylish en-suite doubles reside inside this 18th-century townhouse with racing-green shutters and cherry, sunflower-yellow façade. Find it clinging to the steep stagger up to the old town.

EATING

L'Osteria (☎ 0583 72 45 47; losteria@barganews.com; Piazza Angelo 13-14; meals €15; ☻ Fri-Wed) This small bistro with wood-decked terrace overlooking one of Barga's loveliest pedestrian squares, is a truly Tuscan affair. Be it sausages and beans scented with rosemary and sage. or slices of local *pecorino* cheese with pear sauce or honey and nuts, ingredients are strictly local and seasonal.

Caffè l'Altana (☎ 0583 72 31 92; Via di Mezzo 1; meals €25; ☻ Thu-Tue Mar-Jan) Another dead-simple, unpretentious eating spot where you could hang for hours: feast on the flamboyant frescoes, peppermint-blue walls and a satisfying fare courtesy of daughter Angela and mama Camilla.

DETOUR: LUCIGNANO

On the SS445 between Bagni di Lucca and Barga, take a turn right after 9.5km, past alpine meadows and just beyond Calavorno. Signposts read to the picturesque stone village of **Lucignano**, perched high above to your right. At 4.7km cross a bridge over the river and watch for the magnificent view of the medieval village of **Montefegates**i to your right. At 10km you will enter the village. Conquer the narrow ascent in first gear, squeeze your wing mirrors through the stone gateways and you'll find yourself in a world of leaning passages, cobbled squares and bent but welcoming old women. Park and ponder the magnificent view from the stone wall due north of here, before winding your way back to the main road.

Castelnuovo di Garfagnana

pop 6050

Castelnuovo, the main town in the valley, towers over the confluence of the river Serchio and its smaller tributary, the Turrite. Apart from the formidable 14th-century **Rocca**, a castle built for the Este dukes of Ferrara, there's little to see, but the town is a prime source of information on the Apuane Alps.

On the main square, the Centro Visite Parco Alpi Apuane (see p204) provides pretty much the same information as the **tourist office** (☎ 0583 64 10 07; www.garfagnanaturistica.info; Piazza delle Erbe; ☺ 9.30am-1pm & 3.30-7pm Mon-Sat, 10am-1pm & 4.30-7pm Sun Jun-Sep, closed Sun Oct-May) opposite. Both have mountains of documentation on walking, mountain biking, horse riding and other activities as well as lists of local guides, and *agriturismi* and *rifugi* off any beaten track. They also sell hiking maps, including one of the park entitled *Parco delle Alpi Apuane* (1:25,000, €6.20), and *Appennino Toscoemiliano: Reggiano, Modenese e Garfagnana* (1:25,000, €6.20), both published by Florence's Edizioni Multigraphic Firenze whose map catalogue is online at www.edizionimultigraphic.it (in Italian). At the tourist office, you can also get the coastal side of the park mapped on *Versilia: Parco delle Alpi Apuane* (1:50,000, €6.20).

Hardened walkers can meet local hardened walkers at the local branch of **Club Alpin Italiano** (☎ 0583 6 55 77; Via Vittorio Emanuelle 3; ☺ 9-10pm Thu, 6-7pm Sat).

SLEEPING & EATING

Da Carlino (☎ 0583 64 42 70; www.dacarlino.it in Italian; Via Garibaldi 15; s/d/tr/q incl breakfast €50/70/85/90, half-/full board per person €55/70) Until WWII Da Carlino operated as a tiny little restaurant on the opposite side of the street. Still run by the Anoreucci family but across the road, the flower-bedecked hotel-restaurant is a cosy spot indeed to eat and sleep. Its trout and homemade meringues are practically local legends in town.

Trattoria Marchetti (☎ 0583 63 91 57; Via Testi 10; mains from €6) This earthy, inexpensive lunch spot with tables beneath the arcades has warm wooden innards and a busy counter dishing up massive plates of delicious local dishes. For starters, dig into their *zuppa di farro*, a rich soup made from Tuscan spelt.

GETTING THERE & AROUND

There are up to 10 CLAP buses from Lucca on weekdays (€3.60, 1½ hours).

Rent a bike from **Cicli Maggi** (☎ 0583 63 91 66; Via Nicola Fabrizi 49; half-/full day €8/15).

Around Castelnuovo di Garfagnana

Several scenic roads fan out from Castelnuovo. If you've steady nerves, try the concertina of hairpin bends that lifts you, via Castiglione di Garfagnana, to the Foce di Radici pass across the Apennines and into Emilia-Romagna. The scenery in parts is quite splendid. The minor parallel road to the south leads you to **San Pellegrino in Alpe**, the site of a fine monastery.

Walkers will enjoy the small **Riserva Naturale dell'Orecchiella** on the narrow road via **Corfino**, itself a pleasant village with several hotels. Seven kilometres further north is the park's **tourist office** (☎ 0583 61 90 98; ☺ 9am-7pm Jul–mid-Sep, 10am-5pm Sat & Sun Jun & late Sep), where you can pick up information and maps for walks within the reserve. For the most scenic route to the park, turn west to Villa Collemandine along a tiny road just beyond Castiglione, then right along the road for Corfino.

The SS445 follows the Serchio Valley to the east of the Apuane Alps and bores into the Lunigiana (see p211) at Tuscany's northern limit. It's a pretty, twisting route that leads you through lush green countryside. About 8km north of Castelnuovo at Poggio, there's a turn-off to the pretty, artificial **Lago Vagli** along the Torrente Edron stream. You can do some pleasant short walks in the area, or simply a circular driving route that brings you back to Castelnuovo.

Hollowed within these hills are an astounding 1300 caves, nearly all requiring a guide and special tackle. The most accessible and spectacular is the **Grotta del Vento** (Wind Cave; ☎ 0583 72 20 24; www.grottadelvento.com), 9km west of the SS445. Here, the wonders of the underground abysses, lakes and caverns contrast with the bleak landscape above. From April to October, you can take a one-hour guided tour (adult/child €7.50/5, eight times daily), a two-hour option (adult/child €12/8.50, four times daily) or a three-hour full monty (adult/child €17/11.50, at 10am and 2pm). November to March, only the one-hour tour is on offer. Bring your woollies; it can feel chilly down there, even in high summer.

THE LUNIGIANA

Among Tuscany's wildest and least-known pockets is the Lunigiana, a landlocked enclave of territory bordered to the north and east by Emilia-Romagna, to the west by Liguria and to the south by the Apuane Alps and the Garfagnana. Pontremoli, charming in its own right, makes a great base for exploring this relatively unexplored, rugged territory.

The medieval Via Francigena, a vital route connecting northern and central Italy in Roman days and later a key access for armies and Rome-bound pilgrims alike, roughly follows the modern A15 autostrada from the Cisa pass south to Sarzana, just over into Liguria and on the coast.

VILLAFRANCA
pop 4635

A one-time waystation on the Via Francigena, Villafranca was, so local legend says, a medieval tourist trap where the difference between local tax collectors and plain old thieves was decidedly vague. At the village's northern end is a once-thriving mill turned ethnographical museum, the **Museo Etnografico della Lunigiana** (☎ 0187 49 34 17; Via dell'Antico Molino; admission €2.30; ⏰ 9am-noon & 4-7pm Tue-Sun Jun-Sep, 9.30am-12.30pm Tue-Thu, 9.30am-12.30pm & 2.30-5.30pm Sat & Sun Oct-May). Find it wedged between the church and the footbridge spanning the rocky Magra river.

Albergo Manganelli (☎ 0187 49 30 62; Piazza San Niccolò 5; d €50; P), mustard-yellow, family-run and graced with plenty of old B&W photographs of Villafranca several aeons ago, is a true bargain. Rooms are big and airy and there's a popular restaurant manned by grandma in the kitchen downstairs. Find it next to the tall finger of a ruined tower on the south side of town.

PONTREMOLI
pop 8100

An enchanting place to meander, this small town oozes charm: its cobbled piazzas are surrounded by colonnaded arches that give shade to enticing bars and cafés, and its shops are a fascinating mix of old-fashioned farm shops selling local produce, and retro boutiques showcasing 1950s Italian design.

A primary halting place along the Via Francigena, the original old town is a long sliver stretching north to south between the Magra

and Verde rivers. These watercourses served as natural defensive barriers in what was a key position for the control of traffic between northern and central Italy. In the 17th century the town enjoyed a boom and most of the fine residences date back to those times.

The **tourist office** (☎ 0187 83 37 01; www.inlunigiana.it in Italian; Piazza della Repubblica 6; ⏰ 9am-12.30pm & 3-6pm Mon-Fri, 9.30am-12.30pm Sat) operates on Saturdays from a different office within the town hall on the opposite side of the square.

From central Piazza della Repubblica and adjacent Piazza del Duomo (the latter flanked by the 17th-century **cathedral** with its neoclassical façade), walk along Via Garibaldi then bear left along Vietata l'Affissione, a pretty alley that staggers uphill to **Castello del Piagnaro** (☎ 0187 83 14 39; adult/6-16yr €4/2; ⏰ 9am-noon & 3-6pm summer, 9am-noon & 2-5pm Tue-Sun winter). Although originally raised in the 9th century, what you see today is largely the result of 14th- and 15th-century reconstruction. Views across town are enchanting and inside is a small museum showcasing several striking primitive stele found nearby.

CAT (☎ 800 22 30 10) buses run regularly south to Aulla and other destinations around the Lunigiana and you can also get to La Spezia. Pontremoli also sits on the Parma–La Spezia train line.

SLEEPING & EATING

our pick **Costa d'Orsola** (☎ 0187 83 33 32; www.costadorsola.it; Orsola; s/d incl buffet breakfast €62/99; ⏰ Mar-Oct; P 🖵 🕿) For a true taste of this beautiful untamed region, spend the night in what was a cattle shed (hard to believe) on this lovely old farmstead where three families toiled until the 1960s. Subsequently abandoned, Gianni, Daniele and Adele stepped in to breathe new life into the place in 1989, using wholly natural materials. Perfect walking terrain, consult hiking maps in the old stone or simply meander past fields and groves where 43 sheep graze (for meat) and olives slowly ripen in the sun (the farm makes its own olive oil). Lounging by the pool all day is heaven indeed and in spring and autumn, the farm runs gardening courses. Find it 3.3km from the centre of Pontremoli and 1.6km from the motorway exit, at the end of a country lane.

Da Bussè (☎ 0187 83 13 71; Piazza del Duomo 32; meals €25; ⏰ dinner Mon-Thu, lunch & dinner Sat & Sun) Literally in the shadow of the cathedral, this *osteria* – simplicity itself – has been here since the

1930s and is known far and wide for its rich picking of mushrooms in season. It opens for dinner at 7.45pm.

Caffè degli Svizzeri (Piazza della Repubblica 21-22; ☾ Tue-Sun). As a notice inside entreats at this delightful village café overlooking Pontremoli's central square, refrain from leaning your elbows on the marble-topped tables. The tables, like the café itself, which is all in panelled wood, are well over 100 years old (it dates to 1910). In winter, huddle around the ceramic stove eating *spongata degli svizzeri* (almond cake) and *biscotti della salute* (aniseed biscuits). In summer, sit beneath the arcades licking an aqua-blue ice and try to guess what flavour it is. A cappuccino costs €1.10 (€1.43 with service!).

Il Castagneto della Manganella (☎ 0187 85 07 07; Via Garibaldi 3) Dried sweetened cranberries, cranberry grappa, chestnut flour and mushroom pasta are among the many fruits of the forest sold at this delightful local produce shop just off the central cathedral square. *Porcino secco* (dried porcini mushrooms) cost €80 per kg.

Central Coast & Elba

Despite what seems an enviable setting, the Central Coast is not burdened with destinations that most people have heard of. Anonymous working cities prevail, though significant medieval towns and well-preserved Etruscan sites give the area modest pride while providing travellers with a bit of diversity from similar, over-crowded attractions further inland.

The hinterland hides eye-catching places like the ancient villages of Suvereto and Campiglia Marittima, while offering a less-sweltering alternative to the summertime coast. As in Central Tuscany, tiny roads, blind switchbacks and remote villages mean the area is best – and judiciously – explored by car.

The port city of Livorno, like the primary school girl-bully, dares you to like her. Peculiar, intimidating and well-fed, amenable camaraderie is a possibility – if she doesn't punch your lights out first. The Parco Archeologico di Baratti e Populonia, containing a wealth of Etruscan civilisation enticements, combined with nearby medieval Populonia Alta make for an absorbing diversion. Livorno and Piombino are departure points for ferries to the breezy Tuscan islands of Capraia and Gorgona and, for those going deeper into the Mediterranean, to Sardinia and Corsica too.

The Central Coast also holds a modest resort scene. Many strands are worth exploring, especially on the southern Golfo di Baratti. The region's best seaside and al fresco activities, however, are a quick ferry cruise away on Isola d'Elba. All the classic appeal of a typical Mediterranean island, including the high-season tourist frenzy, without a single high-rise fronting the beach. The rugged interior demands to be tramped. Or mountain biked. Or admired from a sea kayak.

CENTRAL COAST & ELBA

HIGHLIGHTS

- Discover the wonders of **cacciucco** (p217), a delicious and traditional seafood stew, while devouring Livorno's generous dining scene

- Combine a beach flop at **Golfo di Baratti** (p222) with an exploration of Etruscan tombs at the **Parco Archeologico di Baratti e Populonia** (p222)

- Escape to **Capraia** (p219) for some unspoiled diving, walking and sunbaking

- Conquer the tortuously steep streets of little **Suvereto** (p221)

- Alternate between the beach and copious activities on **Isola d'Elba** (p223), then indulge in a wriggling fresh seafood dinner

★ Livorno

★ Capraia

Golfo di Baratti ★
Parco Archeologico di ★
Baratti e Populonia

★ Suvereto

Isola d'Elba

LIVORNO

pop 156,000

Livorno is Tuscany's second-largest city and a quintessential port town with few apologies. Its old churches and arresting architecture may be a strangely welcome change for Tuscan-weary souls craving a little variety. Camera-free, low-impact diversions such as the seafood, reputedly the best on the Tyrrhenian coast, and the popular beaches that start south of the city make a pre/post ferry layover agreeable. Leg stretching can be done in the worthwhile, if ambitiously labelled, 'Little Venice' district.

History

The earliest references to Livorno date from 1017. The port was in the hands of Pisa and then Genoa for centuries, until Florence took control in 1421. It was still tiny – by the 1550s it boasted a grand total of 480 permanent residents. All that changed under Cosimo I de' Medici, who converted the scrawny settlement into a heavily fortified coastal bastion.

It was declared a free port in the 17th century, sparking swift development. By the end of the 18th century it was a vital, cosmopolitan city, functioning as one of the main staging posts for British and Dutch merchants who were then operating between Western Europe and the Middle East, with a permanent population of around 80,000. The 19th century again saw the city swell with injections into the economy, arts and culture.

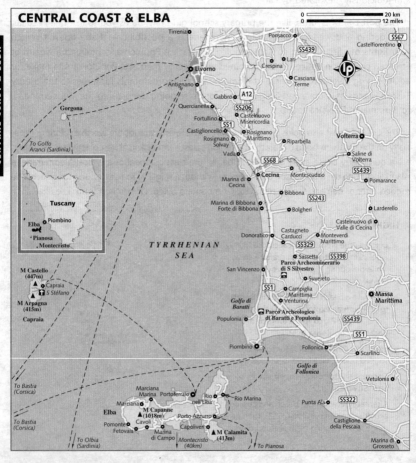

CENTRAL COAST & ELBA

Heavily bombed during WWII (it was one of Fascist Italy's main naval bases), the city was rebuilt with little regard for aesthetics, giving the centre a largely unimaginative face that only a sea captain could love. Its bizarre anglicised name, Leghorn, is rarely used – and only then by impish guidebooks.

Orientation

From the main train station on Piazza Dante walk westwards along Viale Carducci, Via de Larderel, then Via Grande into central Piazza Grande, Livorno's main square.

Information

INTERNET ACCESS

Caffè Grande (Via Grande 59; per hr €5; ☽ 7am-11pm Jun-Sep, 7am-11pm Wed-Mon Oct-May) Has four machines upstairs.

Frag Planet (Scali del Corso 9; per hr €2; ☽ 10am-1pm & 3.30-8pm, closed Sat & Mon mornings)

LAUNDRY

Niagara (Borgo dei Cappuccini 13)

MEDICAL SERVICES

Hospital (☎ 0586 22 31 11; Viale Alfieri 36)

POST

Post Office (Via Cairoli 46)

TOURIST INFORMATION

Tourist Kiosk (☎ 0586 20 46 11; www.costadegli etruschi.it; Piazza del Municipio; ☽ 10am-1pm & 3-6pm Mon-Sat Apr-Oct, 9am-5pm Mon-Sat Nov-Mar)

Tourist Office (☎ 0586 89 53 20; ☽ Jun-Sep) Near the main ferry terminal at Stazione Marittima.

Sights

The **Fortezza Nuova** (New Fort; admission free), in the area known as Piccola Venezia (Little Venice) because of its small canals, was built, using Venetian methods of reclaiming land from the sea, for the Medici court in the late 16th century. Laced with canals, what this area lacks in gondolas and tourists, it makes up for with a certain shabby charm. The waterways here are flanked by faded, peeling apartments that are brightly decorated with strings of washing hanging out to dry. The interior of the fort is now a park and little else remains except the sturdy outer walls.

Close to the waterfront is the city's other fort, the **Fortezza Vecchia** (Old Fort), constructed 60 years earlier on the site of an 11th-century building. With huge vertical cracks and bits crumbling away, it looks as though it might give up and slide into the sea at any moment.

The **Mercato Centrale** (Via Buontalenti; ☽ 6am-2pm Mon-Sat), Livorno's magnificent late-19th-century 95m-long neoclassical food market, miraculously survived Allied WWII bombing intact. For us, it's the finest site in town, both architecturally and gastronomically (see p217). Big enough to house airplanes, market stalls sell food and beverages to satisfy any self-catering need. Get there early for the full effect of the fish section, which should charge admission to view its oddities.

Livorno's friendly and hands on **Museo di Storia Naturale del Mediterraneo** (☎ 0586 26 67 11; www.provincia.livorno.it; Via Roma 234; adult/child €10/5; ☽ 9am-1pm Tue-Sat, 3-7.30pm Tue, Thu & Sun) is an exhaustive, first-rate museum experience for the natural sciences. Expanded rooms with temporary exhibits will open in 2008, while the highlight of the permanent collection is a 20m-long common whale skeleton called 'Annie'.

The **Museo Civico Giovanni Fattori** (☎ 0586 80 80 01; museofattori@comune.livorno.it; Via San Jacopo in Acquaviva 65; admission €4; ☽ 10am-1pm & 4-7pm Tue-Sun), in a pretty park, features works by the 19th-century Italian impressionist Macchiaioli school, led by Livorno-born Giovanni Fattori. The group, inspired by the Parisian Barbizon school, flouted stringent academic art conventions and worked directly from nature, emphasising immediacy and freshness through patches, or 'stains', of colour (*macchia*). Though the style was noted/criticised for its 'lack of finish', it did not go nearly as far dissolving form into light as the simultaneous work done by French Impressionists. The museum often hosts temporary exhibitions.

The city's unspectacular **cathedral**, designed by visiting British architect Inigo Jones, is just off Piazza Grande. Jones later used this piazza's layout as a model for Covent Garden.

The Etruscan Coast (Costa degli Etruschi) begins south of Livorno. The town's beaches stretch for some way southwards but they are pebbly and generally nothing special. Overlooking a few are some grand old seaside villas that merit more than a glance. Bus No 1 from the main train station heads down the coast road, passing via the town centre and Porto Mediceo.

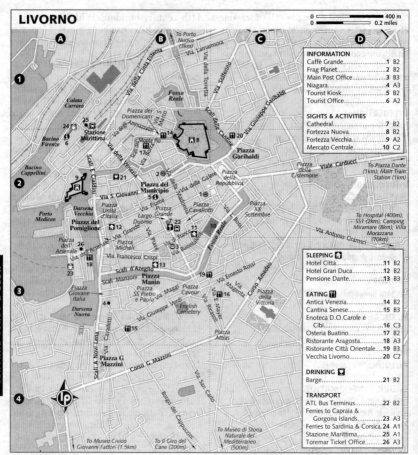

LIVORNO

Sleeping

Camping Miramare (☎ 0586 58 04 02; www.campingmira
mare.com; Via del Littorale 220; person €6-14, pitch €9-45;
year-round;) This is a shady place with
its own restaurant and pizzeria, right beside
the beach in Antignano, about 8km south of
town. There are three categories of campsites,
including some with sea-views, sun chairs
and umbrellas.

Villa Morazzana (☎ 0586 50 00 76; www.villamor
azzana.it; Via Curiel 110; hostel dm/d €16/40, hotel s/d/tr
€38/60/90, P) A HI-affiliated youth hostel
and informal hotel are housed in this attractive 18th-century villa with a huge rear garden. Its Ristorante Lavilla (dinner Thursday
to Sunday) offers gourmet cuisine and keeps
a great cellar of wines and whiskies. Bus No

3 runs hourly from Piazza Grande. Driving,
take the Montanero exit from the A12. Driving from Livorno, signage is criminally inadequate. Call ahead for directions.

Pensione Dante (☎ 0586 89 43 70; 1st fl, Scali d'Azeglio
28; s/d €35/41) Overlooking a canal and run by
a cheerful old couple, this place has eight
large, simply furnished rooms with new beds
and corridor bathrooms. It has a friendly,
rough-and-tumble family feel about it and is
not a bad option if you're euro-economising.
There's no breakfast, but the coffee-maker
is always on.

Hotel Città (☎ 0586 88 34 95; www.hotelcitta.it; Via
di Franco 32; s incl breakfast €55-89, d incl breakfast €75-120;
P) Family owned and friendly, this
is a tempting three-star option in the heart

PARCO NAZIONALE DELL'ARCIPELAGO TOSCANO

A local legend tells, when Venus rose from the waves, seven precious stones fell from her tiara, creating seven islands off the Tuscan coast. They range in size from the 530 sq km of Elba, the largest, to tiny Montecristo, at just over 1000 hectares. All except Montecristo, nowadays a closed marine biological reserve, live mainly from the income of tourism. So this national park, established in 1996, was created to protect the delicate ecosystems of the islands. But not only the land – the 60,000 hectares of sea that washes around them make up Europe's largest protected marine area. Here, typical Mediterranean fish abound and rare species, such as the wonderfully named Neptune's shaving brush seaweed, unique to the archipelago, cling on to life. And the monk-seal, driven from the other islands by human presence, still gambols in the deep underwater ravines off Montecristo.

The islands, an essential rest stop for birds migrating between Europe and Africa, are a treat for birdwatchers year-round. The shy red partridge survives on Elba and Pianosa and the archipelago supports over a third of the world's population of the equally uncommon Corsican seagull, adopted as the national park's symbol.

For more information go to www.islepark.it (in Italian) or contact Info Park Are@ (p226), the park information office on the island of Elba.

---

of town. It looks unprepossessing from the outside but rooms, though smallish, are just fine and come equipped with fridge, safe and new bathrooms. Parking will set you back €13 to €15.

Hotel Gran Duca (☎ 0586 89 10 24; www.granduca .it; Piazza Micheli 16; s/d incl breakfast €85/130; P ⚒ ☐) Built into the old protective walls of the port, the paint was still drying from renovations when we visited. Fully equipped from top to bottom, there's a jacuzzi, Turkish bath, fitness centre and wi-fi among the plunder. It's opposite the port and has a decent restaurant (meals €32 to €37). Parking is €10.

Eating

Be sure to tuck into a *cacciuco*, a remarkable mixed seafood stew and the pride of many Livorno eateries.

Ristorante Città Orientale (☎ 0586 88 82 66; Via Ginori 23; meals €12-15) For a change, this Chinese restaurant offers a wide selection of dishes without the usual migraine-inducing décor. The set menus are great value.

Antica Venezia (☎ 0586 88 73 53; Piazza dei Domenicani; meals €25-30; ☽ Mon-Sat) Attracts a smart clientele with its imaginative, orally presented menu of catch-of-the-day specials prepared with an innovative twist. The atmosphere is attractively upbeat. Book ahead.

Ristorante Aragosta (☎ 0586 89 53 95; info@argostasrl .com; Piazza dell'Arsenale 6; meals €28; ☽ Wed-Mon) Right on the waterfront, this is the place for seafood. A nondescript exterior masks inner pleasures, mainly of a fishy kind.

Vecchia Livorno (☎ 0586 88 40 48; Scali delle Cantine 34; meals €28; ☽ Wed-Mon) Facing the Fortezza Nuova, this small, intimate family restaurant has a buzzy neighbourhood feel. Expect hearty, filling food; stick with the excellent fresh fish.

our pick **Cantina Senese** (☎ 0586 89 02 39; Borgo dei Cappuccini 95; meals €30-35; ☽ Mon-Sat) Also fabulous for seafood, this popular, unpretentious local eatery is just a little inland. Squeeze onto one of the long wooden tables and, if you pass by on a Friday, try their exceptional *cacciuco di pesce*, served with garlic bread.

our pick **Il Giro del Cane** (☎ 0586 81 25 60; Borgo dei Cappuccini 314; meals €33-38; ☽ dinner only Mon-Sat, closed Aug) A Slow Food (p370) endorsed eatery, serving up classic, yet delicious Livorno seafood dishes with the occasional creative zap. It's well worth the walk to its eccentric location.

Enoteca D.O.C. Parole e Cibi (☎ 0586 88 75 83; Via Goldoni 40-44; meals €40-45; ☽ Tue-Sun) Changes its menu weekly; you can enjoy fresh pasta dishes, superb seafood and a variety of *carpaccio* served with bread that – for once – is entirely worth that vexing *coperto* (cover charge in restaurants). The wines are excellent; it styles itself as an *enoteca*, *olioteca* (oil) and whiskyteca so you can be confident of getting top quality lubricants, whatever your preference. For dessert, a sugary, chocolate pastry, with vanilla cream is only €3.60.

Though they were still painting and picking out tile at the time of writing, keep an eye out for **Osteria Buatino** (☎ 338 454 01 90; Scali del Monte

MODIGLIANI DOES PARIS

Modigliani's portraits of women with their long necks, faces like African masks and tilted oblong heads are among the most readily recognisable of all of modern art.

Born in Livorno in 1884, Amedeo Modigliani showed talent as an artist at an early age and trained under the influence of the former Macchiaioli artists who had shaken up the Florentine, and indeed Italian, art scene in the years before and after Italian unity. Livorno's own Giovanni Fattori had been a leading light among the Macchiaioli.

Modigliani was soon drawn away from his home town. His early influences were the Renaissance masters, so he headed first to Florence, then on to Venice. From Venice, he made the move to Paris in 1906, which by then was the epicentre of the art world, and where he was influenced by Cézanne, Picasso and Cocteau.

Modigliani returned to Italy briefly in 1909 but, from then until the end of his short life in 1920, continued to live in the fertile artistic environment of Montparnasse in Paris. For the next five years he turned to sculpture, rapidly accelerating the process of simplification and emphasising the contours. This period was then reflected in his subsequent paintings – the long faces typical of his later work are a result of his venture into sculpture. In 1914 and 1915 he concentrated on portraiture and then, in the last years of his life, produced the series of nudes that figure among his best-known works and display a classical and serene eroticism.

His work, like that of so many artists, only began to receive wide critical acclaim after his death, particularly in the wake of an exhibition of his paintings at the Venice Biennale in 1930. Nowadays, his canvases are prominent features of art galleries the world over.

Pio 11; (🕒 Mon-Sat) managed by the same people who run a much loved place in Lucca by the same name (p197), specialising in typical Tuscan and Livorno area cuisine.

For self-catering nirvana, visit Livorno's magnificent **Mercato Centrale** (🕒 6am-2pm Mon-Sat) to load up on all necessities, including produce, sandwich makings and seafood so fresh they think they're still swimming.

Drinking

The area around Piazza XX Settembre is the place for bars and cafés.

Barge (☎ 0586 88 83 20; Scali Delle Ancore 6; 🕒 8pm-2am Tue-Sun) Join the effortlessly hip young crowd inside this approximation of an English pub or enjoy the breeze on one of the trio of boat-shaped waterfront terraces. It also functions as a piano bar and restaurant (mains €15).

Getting There & Away

BOAT

Livorno is a major port. Regular departures for Sardinia and Corsica leave from Calata Carrara, beside the Stazione Marittima. Ferries to Capraia and Gorgona depart from Porto Mediceo, a smaller terminal near Piazza dell'Arsenale. Some services to Sardinia depart from Porto Nuovo, about 3km north of the city along Via Sant'Orlando.

Ferry companies operating from Livorno are listed below.

Porto Mediceo

Toremar (☎ 199 12 31 99; www.toremar.it in Italian) Daily services to Isola di Capraia (€10.50, 2½ hours).

Lloyd Sardegna (☎ 0565 22 23 00; www.lloydsardegna.it) Daily ferries to Sardinia (Olbia; €29, 11hours).

Stazione Marittima

Corsica Ferries/Sardinia Ferries (☎ 019 21 55 11; www.corsicaferries.com, www.sardiniaferries.com; Stazione Marittima) Offers two or three services per week (daily in summer) to Bastia, Corsica (deck-class €25 to €32, four hours), and four services per week (daily in summer) to Golfo Aranci, Sardinia (deck-class €35 to €40, six hours express, nine hours regular).

Moby (☎ 199 30 30 40; www.moby.it) Has services to Bastia, Corsica (€15 to €30, three to four hours) and Olbia, Sardinia (€24 to €50, eight to 12 hours).

BUS

ATL (☎ 0586 84 74 08) buses depart from Largo Duomo for Cecina (€2.90, one hour, half-hourly), Piombino (€6.20, 2¼ hours, six daily) and Pisa (€2.30, 45 minutes, half-hourly).

CAR & MOTORCYCLE

The A12 runs past the city and the SS1 connects Livorno with Rome. There are several car parks near the waterfront.

TRAIN

Livorno is on the Rome–La Spezia line and is also connected to Florence and Pisa. Sample destinations and fares include Rome (€17.90 to €26, three to four hours, 12 daily), Florence (€6.10, 1½ hours, 16 daily) and Pisa (€1.70, 15 minutes, hourly).

Trains are a lot less frequent to Stazione Marittima, the station for the ports, but buses to/from the main station run quite regularly.

Getting Around

ATL bus 1 runs from the main train station to Porto Mediceo. To reach Stazione Marittima, take bus 7 or electric bus PB1, PB2 or PB3. All of these bus services pass through Piazza Grande.

AROUND LIVORNO

Toremar (opposite) operates boats to the islands of Capraia and Gorgona from Livorno. Along with Elba, and four other islands further south still (Pianosa, Montecristo, Giglio and Giannutri), they form the Parco Nazionale dell'Arcipelago Toscano (p217).

The elliptical, volcanic island of **Capraia**, 8km long by 4km wide, lies 65km from Livorno. Its highest point is Monte Castello at 447m and is covered mainly in *macchia*, or scrubland. Tuscany's third-largest island after Elba and Giglio, it has changed hands several times over the course of its history, belonging to Genoa, Sardinia, the Saracens from North Africa and Napoleon.

You can join boat trips (€12) around the coastline or trek across the island. The most popular walk is to the Stagnone, a small lake in the south. There are also seven popular dive sites off the coast; contact **Capraia Diving** (☎ 0586 90 51 37; www.capraiadiving.it; Via Assunzione 72). The only beach worthy of the name is **Cala della Mortola**, a few kilometres north of Capraia town.

The tiny island of **Gorgona** is the greenest and northernmost of the islands. At just 2.23 sq km, there's not much to it. Its two towers were built respectively by the Pisans and the Medicis of Florence. Part of the island is off-limits as a low-security prison. You can effectively only visit the island on Tuesday, when the 8.30am Toremar ferry from Livorno stops there on the way to/from Capraia, giving you about five hours from the arrival time at 10am.

INFORMATION

Agenzia Viaggi e Turismo Parco (☎ 0586 90 50 71; www.isoladicapraia.it in Italian; Via Assunzione 42) Shares the same space as the tourist office in Capraia and can advise on activities, such as trekking and boat trips.

Tourist office (☎ 0586 90 51 38; Via Assunzione 42; ⊙ 9am-12.30pm & 4.30-7pm Fri-Wed Apr-Sep)

SLEEPING & EATING

Accommodation on Capraia is tight, and there are no places to stay on Gorgona.

Da Beppone (☎ 0586 90 50 01; Via della Assunzione 78; s/d €45/75) A very friendly and reliable choice. Rooms are smallish but pleasant and the bar and restaurant are a bonus.

Il Saracino (☎ 0586 90 50 18; Via Cibo 30; s incl breakfast €85-105, d incl breakfast €170-210) Down near the beach, this place has bright, modern rooms with plenty of wood and white paint. There's a snazzy rooftop bar for a nightcap under the stars.

Relais La Mandola (☎ 0586 90 51 19; www.lamandola.it; Via della Mandola 1; half-board per person €65-140; P 🛅 🐊) A seriously swish hotel with private beach (and its own beach bar). Rooms have balconies, sea views and all mod cons. Prices drop dramatically out of season.

GETTING THERE & AWAY

A daily Toremar boat to Capraia sails from Livorno (see opposite). On most days there is also a return trip but triple-check before you go. The one-way fare costs €10.50, whether you go to Capraia or Gorgona. In summer, there are excursions from Elba to Capraia.

THE ETRUSCAN COAST

The province of Livorno stretches down the coast to just beyond Piombino and the ferry to the island of Elba.

Overall, Tuscany's beaches are basic bucket-and-spade, though some have pebbles rather than sand. Watch out for the prices: you can fork out plenty for the privilege of a sun bed and brolly (around €8).

Several attractive small towns are scattered within the hilly hinterland, while the slender plain between coast and hills offers the possibility of discovering some of Tuscany's lesser-known, but often very good wines.

Livorno to Piombino

You can chug down the coast from Livorno by train or bus, but your own transport will give you greater freedom to explore.

There's a good small beach a couple of kilometres short of **Quercianella**. Heading south from Livorno, keep a watch out for a tower and castle atop a promontory. The beach is at the head of an inlet directly north of this. As you round a curve into the inlet, a small sign indicates a path down to the beach. There is limited parking.

In leafy Quercianella you'll find a couple of little grey-stone beaches. At the northern end of town, surfers gather even when an adverse wind is up. After another 5km or so, watch for the **Parco Comunale di Fortullino** sign. If you can find a place to park, walk down to the water's edge. The park is pleasant and a bar operates in summer. The beach, by contrast, is disappointing and rocky.

CASTIGLIONCELLO

This small seaside resort is agreeably unpretentious. In the late 19th century Digo Martelli, the Italian critic and patron of the arts, gave court here. He would play host to the Florentine Impressionist artists of the period, giving birth to the artistic movement known as La Scuola di Castiglioncello.

The small sandy beaches on the north side of town are the best, although sun-bed rental is expensive (from €8). At the heart of this straggling town is Piazza della Vittoria and the vast terrace of Caffè Ginori (below).

Information

Within the train station, there's a small **tourist office** (☎ 0586 75 48 90; Via Aurelia 632; ✆ 9.30am-12.30pm & 4-6pm).

Sleeping & Eating

our pick **Pensione Bartoli** (☎ 0586 75 20 51; Via Martelli 9; www.albergobartoli.com; s/d €50/60; ✆ Easter-Oct; **P**) Rich in character, this offers unbeatable value. It's an old-fashioned 'let's stay with grandma' kind of place with 18 well-dusted, large rooms, lace curtains and venerable family furniture. Rooms 19, the largest, and 21 have the best sea views.

Villa Parisi (☎ 0586 75 16 98; www.emmeti.it/Villa Parisi; Via Romolo Monti 10; s €90-224, d €128-400; ✆ Apr-Sep; **P** ✖ ✺) This is a special-occasion hotel, perched on a headland. The rooms are stylish and good-sized and most have a seamless sea view. There is a pool, new fitness and massage rooms, a sea view gazebo as well as a large sun terrace, with private access to the beach.

Caffè Ginori (☎ 0586 75 90 55; Piazza della Vittoria; ✆ daily Mar-Oct, Fri-Wed Nov-Feb) With its large, shaded terrace and redolent of the best of the 1950s, this is where locals drop by to jaw at the bar. Apart from the imprudently aged gelato, snacks here are delish. You can see why it was a favourite hangout of Italian heart-throb Marcello Mastroianni, who had a summer villa in town.

Getting There & Away

There are frequent trains to/from Livorno (€2.20, 25 minutes).

AROUND CASTIGLIONCELLO

Rosignano Marittimo perches high up a hill. Already a small settlement in Lombard times, Rosignano was one of Lorenzo il Magnifico's preferred bases for hunting. Although there has been a castle here since the 8th century, the fortifications date from the days of Cosimo I de' Medici.

Back down on the coast, **Vada** is a fairly characterless seaside spot but at least the beaches have sand. Another 8km south of Vada and you reach **Marina di Cecina**, where there is plenty of life, as well as hotels and restaurants that mainly front a beach. Children and the young at heart will enjoy splashing around **Acqua** (Via Tevere 25; ✆ Jun-Aug), a family-friendly water park.

About halfway between the sea and the modern centre of **Cecina**, the **Villa Guerrazzi**, also called La Cinquantina, houses a couple of small museums: the small **Museo Archeologico Comunale** (☎ 0586 26 08 37; adult/child €4/2.50; ✆ 4-7.30pm Tue-Sun Jul-Aug, 3.30-7pm Sat & Sun Sep-Jun) and, in the grounds, the recently established **Museo della Vita e del Lavoro**, a small folk museum with a collection of vintage agricultural machinery and bicycles from boneshakers to modern racers. It observes similar hours.

The train (€2.70, 30 minutes) and ATL buses (€3, one hour, every half-hour) both connect Cecina to Livorno.

MONTESCUDAIO

From Cecina you could follow the SS1 or minor coast roads south. Better still, head inland. The province of Livorno has developed a Strada del Vino (wine route), with a map and list of vineyards between Cecina and Montescudaio. It makes for a pretty drive, compared to the relatively drab coastal flats.

MARINA DI BIBBONA

Head south from Montescudaio to Bibbona, a medieval hill town that dominateṣ the plain running beside the coast. A little further south and on the coast is Marina di Bibbona, south of which stretches a narrow strip of sandy beach backed by *macchia* and pine woods.

There's plenty of accommodation to choose from.

Hotel Paradiso Verde (☎ 0586 60 00 22; www.hotel paridisoverde.it; Via del Forte 9; d €56-100, incl breakfast; ☼ Easter-Oct) is a small 15-room hotel located a Frisbee throw from the beach, with spick-and-span rooms and a small bar/restaurant out the front. You pay more for a balcony and sea view.

Agriturismo Le Fornacine (☎ 0586 65 30 13; www .agriturismolefornacine.com; d €65-90; ☒) was recommended to us by a delirious traveller whose glowing reports brought us to this small, modern place just outside Bibbona. Nearby activities include thermal pools, walks, beaches (7km), mountain biking and a book of tailor-made day trips meticulously researched by the affable hostess to Pisa, Florence and Volterra among others. Wine tastings can be arranged in nearby vineyards or the onsite wine cellar. There is a minimum one-week stay in August.

A short way south of Marina di Bibbona is the small but important **Rifugio Palustre di Bolgheri** (☎ reservations 0565 22 43 61; entrance just west off the SS1; adult/child €5/3; ☼ visits 9am & 2pm Sat, 9am Sun Oct-May). This nature reserve is a key stop for migratory birds, and the best time for seeing them is in December and January. Two-hour visits are severely limited and must be arranged in advance. The entrance to the park is through a narrow tunnel that passes under the *superstrada*, just south of the cypress-lined, arrow-straight road that leads eastwards to the village of Bolgheri.

BOLGHERI

In Bolgheri, the castle that takes in the city gate and Romanesque Chiesa di SS Giacomo e Cristoro was restructured towards the end of the 19th century. Although very pretty, the village has been over-heritaged, with pricey restaurants and shops. Have a quick look around, take a few photos and move on.

CASTAGNETO CARDUCCI

The next stretch of the Strada del Vino takes you through dense woodland along a minor road south of Bolgheri. The route rolls between vineyards and olive groves, then climbs up into the hills to reach Castagneto Carducci.

Behind its town walls lies a web of steep, narrow lanes crowded in by brooding houses and dominated by the castle (turned into a mansion in the 18th century) of the Gherardesca clan that once controlled the surrounding area. The 19th-century poet Giosuè Carducci spent much of his childhood here.

Traditional old recipes have been resurrected at the lovely **Ristorante Glorione** (☎ 0565 76 33 22; Via Carducci 6; meals €27-32; ☼ dinner Wed-Mon Jun-Sep, Sat & Sun Oct-May), with its tiny, but swish chandelier-lit dining room. There is a palm-shaded courtyard for atmospheric, soothing summertime dining.

Pick up some locally produced olive oil and liqueurs, distilled on the spot, at the 100-year-old **L'Elixir** (☎ 0565 76 60 17; Via Garibaldi 7).

SASSETTA

Next stop on the winding, forested hill road is the tiny hamlet of Sassetta. Approaching from Castagneto, the houses here seem to be hanging on to their perches for dear life. There is a large map at the village entrance showing the main treks in the area.

Albergo La Selva (☎ 0565 79 42 39; hotel .selva@tiscallinet.it; Via Fornaci 32; s/d incl breakfast €50/80), 1km north of Sassetta on the road to Castagneto, has squeaky-clean large rooms with a choice of bath or shower. All have balconies and there's a large terrace with positively swoony valley views. The restaurant does an excellent six-course dinner (€22).

SUVERETO

Nearby Suvereto, with its tortuous streets and steep stairways, has been a busy centre since well before the year 1000. For a while it was the seat of a bishopric, only incorporated into the Tuscan grand duchy in 1815. Today, it's a well-tended place where flowers and plants contrast with the soft tones of brick and stone.

The **tourist office** (☎ 0565 82 93 04; ☼ 10am-12.30pm & 5-10pm Mon-Sat, 5-10pm Sun Jun-Sep) is on Piazza Gramsci.

On the terrace of **Ristorante Enoliteca Ombrone** (☎ 0565 82 82 94; Piazza dei Giudici 1; meals €42-47; ☼ Tue-Sun) you can enjoy fine traditional cuisine with the attractive façade of Suvereto's mainly 13th-century Palazzo Comunale looming before you.

Enoteca dei Difficili (☎ 0565 82 80 18; Via San Le-onardo; meals €15; ☺ Tue-Sun) is an atmospheric brick-and-beam spot for a drink, snack or full meal. Alongside an array of delightful snacks, salads and main courses, you can take a pick from the blockbuster selection of wines.

Mid-August sees the traditional **Corsa delle Botte**, when townsfolk race each other, pushing huge tumbling wine barrels along the town's cobbled lanes. In December they tuck into their **Sagra del Cinghiale** (Wild Boar Festival), with plenty of eating, drinking and a show of crossbow skills.

CAMPIGLIA MARITTIMA

From Suvereto, drop down onto the plains along the SS398, signed Piombino, for about 5km, then turn off right to head back into the hills. Aim for the dun-coloured stone houses of Campiglia Marittima, another near-intact medieval town, with its roots in Etruscan times.

The one building of special interest is the **Palazzo Pretorio**, up steep Via Cavour, which is these days also a wine information centre. Long the seat of government, its main façade, plastered with an assortment of coats of arms, resembles the bulky bemedalled chest of some banana-republic general.

The **Parco Archeominerario di San Silvestro** (☎ 0565 83 86 80; admission park, Temperino & Rocca €15; ☺ 10am-7pm Tue-Sun Jun-Sep, 10am-6pm Sat & Sun Mar-May & Oct, 10am-4pm Sun Nov-Feb) is just 1.25km north-west on the road to San Vincenzo. Around 50m before the turn-off to the park entrance, a sunken lane on the right, signed *forni fusori*, leads to the remains of some Etruscan smelting ovens, once used for copper production.

The park tells the story of the area's 3000-year mining history. The highlight for most is **Rocca di San Silvestro**, a medieval mining town abandoned in the 14th century. The surrounding Temperino mines produced cop-per and lead, some used for the mints of Lucca and later Pisa.

There are two guided tours, one of Rocca di San Silvestro, the other to the Temperino mine and museum. The mine and museum (the latter is in the same building as the ticket office) are near the entrance, while Rocca di San Silvestro is accessible via a new under-ground train that ferries visitors through the mines on the way. Extreme claustrophobics can opt for the half-hour walk. Tours leave approximately every hour.

DETOUR: SAN VINCENZO TO PIOMBINO

For a low-impact day of scenery, picnick-ing and beach repose, depart from the San Vincenzo tourist office on Via B Alliata, take the coast road flanked by pine trees and dense woodland towards Piombino. Look for *tavoli* (picnic area) signs if you fancy stopping for a picnic with the luxury of ta-bles and benches. After about 11km you'll see an old water tower to your left: park by the side and cross the road to a pleasant beach backed by wild brush and poppies (in season). Continue on to more good sandy stretches at Golfo di Baratti (below) or fol-low the road to Piombino.

SAN VINCENZO

Back on the road leading away from Cam-piglia, continue westwards to the moderately attractive seaside town of San Vincenzo, pop-ular in summer with Italian visitors. There is a small **tourist office** (☎ 0565 70 15 33; Via B Al-liata) here. Yachties can park their vessels in the marina, but there's not much to do after that. Sandy beaches stretch to the north and south of town; to the south beaches are backed by *macchia* and pine plantations. Although there are quite a few hotels, getting a room in summer is challenging and so are the prices. There's only one campsite.

Ristorante La Barcaccina (☎ 0565 70 19 11; Via Tridentina; meals €35-40; ☺ Thu-Tue) serves fine seafood that matches this glassed-in restau-rant's location on a great stretch of pale golden sand. Decidedly on the smart side, it's not the kind of place where you stroll in wearing your beachwear. From the coast road (not the SS1), follow signs to the parking area near the Parco Comunale.

GOLFO DI BARATTI

Thirteen kilometres south of San Vincenzo, a minor road leads off the SP23 and heads southwest for 5km to the Golfo di Baratti. This must be one of the Tuscan coast's pret-tiest mainland beaches, although, as the weird and wonderful postures of the trees attest, it's often windy – and so a favourite with wind-surfers.

Inland from here is the **Parco Archeologico di Baratti e Populonia** (☎ 0565 2 90 02; www.parchivaldi cornia.it; Populonia; whole park adult/child/family €15/10/39,

1 sector adult/child €9/5; ⊙ 10am-6pm Jul & Aug, 10am-6pm Tue-Sun Mar-Jun & Sep-Oct, 10am-4pm Sat & Sun Nov-Feb) where several Etruscan tombs have been unearthed. Most interesting are the circular tombs in the Necropoli di San Cerbone, between the coast road and the visitors centre, which sells an excellent guidebook in English (€7.75). The Via delle Cave is a signed trail through shady woodland that passes by the quarries from which the soft ochre sandstone was extracted, and into which tombs were later cut. Allow one to two hours to see the visitors centre and the Necropoli or as much as five hours to thoroughly wander the full grounds, including the hands-on pottery exhibit in the Centre of Experimental Archaeology. Trainers and a sun hat are a must. Between March and October, there are guided tours (included within the admission fee) for each area or you can wander at will.

POPULONIA
Where the road ends, 2km beyond the park, is **Populonia Alta**, a three-street hamlet still owned by a single family. Walled in and protected by its 15th-century castle, the settlement grew up on the site of a Pisan watchtower. Its small, privately owned **Etruscan Museum** (adult/child €1.50/1) has a few local finds; opening times are sporadic. For superb views south along the coast, climb the **Torre di Populonia** (adult/child €2/1; ⊙ 9.30am-noon & 2.30-7pm), north of the museum. Among several craft workshops along the main street, the gallery at No 19 has a permanent exhibition of glass sculptures and creative lamps by artist Laura Pescae and her daughter.

Next to the car park is the **Etruscan acropolis** (⊙ 9am-7pm) of ancient Populonia. If your Italian is up to it, join a guided tour (every half-hour). The digs have revealed the foundations of an Etruscan temple dating to the 2nd century BC, along with its adjacent buildings.

Piombino
pop 34,400
A cursory tour of Piombino on your way to the Elba ferry won't significantly improve on the uncharitable coverage dispensed by those charged to write about it. A centre of steel production since the late 19th century, this Roman-era port city was heavily damaged during WWII. What precious little remains of the walled historical centre, whose focal point is the 15th-century **Torrione Rivellino**, and the fishing port are not entirely without charm.

The **Museo Archeologico del Territorio di Populonia** (☎ 0565 22 16 46; www.parchivaldicornia.it; Piazza Cittadella 8; adult/child €6/4; ⊙ 5-11pm Jul-Aug, 10am-1pm & 3-7pm Tue-Sun Jun & Sep, 10am-1pm & 3-7pm Sat & Sun Oct-May), in the western suburbs, complements and displays many of the artefacts from the Parco Archeologico di Baratti e Populonia (opposite), plus other sites in and around the Maremma.

Should you need, for whatever emergency, to stay, **Hotel Roma** (☎ 0565 3 43 41; www.htroma.it; Via San Francesco 43; s/d €40/60) is a reasonable, albeit monastically spartan, central choice two minutes' walk from the ATM bus stop.

Alternatively, **Il Garibaldi Innamorato** (☎ 0565 4 94 10; Via Guiseppe Garibaldi 5; meals €28-33; ⊙ Tue-Sun) on a tiny street near Piazza Bovio, is worth delaying your departure by an hour. Adorned with a variety of Garibaldi portraits and leftover equipment from its former butcher's shop incarnation, the menu consists of prices for a 'primo', 'secondo' and 'dolce' without further detail. The day's creative fish-centric offerings are related orally by an attentive server, testing your Italian to its limits and rewarding you with cuisine touted by both Slow Food (p370) and the Italian Celiac Association.

GETTING THERE & AWAY
Piombino-based **ATM** (☎ 0565 260 11 18) buses running between Piombino and Cecina (€4, 1½ hours) usually stop at Castagneto Carducci, Sassetta, San Vincenzo and Golfo di Baratti. Another bus line serves Suvereto (€2.30, 40 minutes) on a regular basis on its way to Monterotondo. Yet another connects Piombino with Campiglia Marittima. ATM buses also run to Massa Marittima. All leave from Via Leonardo da Vinci 13 in the centre of town.

For Livorno (2¼ hours) change at Cecina.

For coastal destinations such as San Vincenzo, the train is a better bet, but the hill towns are generally a considerable hike from the nearest train station.

Piombino is on the Rome–Genoa train line and there are fairly regular connections to Florence too.

For Elba ferry information, see p226.

ISOLA D'ELBA
pop 30,100
Napoleon would think twice about fleeing from Elba had he been exiled here today. Though it's a bit more congested now than

---

ELBA TREK

The compact size and myriad transport options of Elba means accessing worthwhile walks is a snap. The bountiful website www.elbalink.it and the tourist office provide satisfactory information for well-marked trekking options, though walkers wanting to go where no-one has gone before – on *that* particular morning, Elba is only so large – should consider picking up an absurdly detailed trekking map at Il Libraio in Portoferraio (p227).

A few of the more appealing, well-trodden walks include:

- San Lucia to San Martino – A low-impact, 90-minute walk, starting just outside Portoferraio at the church of San Lucia, traversing meadows and former farmland being repo-ed by nature for about 2.2km and terminating at Napoleon's villa in San Martino.

- Marciana to Chiessi – A 12km trek starting on high in Marciana, dribbling downhill, past ancient churches, sea vistas and granite boulders for about six hours to the seaside in Chiessi.

- La Parata to Le Panche – A short but resolve-testing two hour walk along a ridge, through an oak forrest, past the hermitage of Santa Caterina and the castle of Volterraio.

---

when he was charitably dumped here in 1814 (he managed to engineer an escape in less than a year, see the boxed text on p228), the island is an ever-glorious setting of beaches, blue waters, mountain trekking and mind-bending views, all supplemented by some very fine cuisine.

While the dismal remains of the once prevailing iron-ore mining industry groan on, the inevitable dominance of tourism has motored ahead. Over a million visitors a year take the one-hour ferry cruise out here and in Portoferraio, the primary arrival point, it sometimes feels like they've all decided to turn up on the same weekend. Elba is the largest, most visited and most heavily populated island of the Tuscan archipelago, yet this 28km-long, 19km-wide island has plenty of quiet nooks, particularly if you time a visit for April, May, September or October.

There are plenty of hotels, fine campsites and full-board resorts to satisfy any inclination, many of which offer drastically reduced prices outside of high-season.

History

Elba has been inhabited since the Iron Age and the extraction of iron ore and metallurgy were the island's principal sources of economic wellbeing until well into the second half of the 20th century. You can still fossick around to your heart's content in museums dedicated to rocks.

Ligurian tribes people were the island's first inhabitants, followed by Etruscans and Greeks from Magna Graecia. The iron business was well established by then, making the island doubly attractive to wealthier Romans, who built holiday villas here.

Centuries of peace under the Pax Romana gave way to more uncertain times during the barbarian invasions, when Elba became a refuge for those fleeing mainland marauders. By the 11th century, Pisa (and later Piombino) was in control and built fortresses to help ward off attacks by Muslim raiders and pirates operating out of North Africa.

In the 16th century, Cosimo I de' Medici grabbed territory in the north of the island, where he founded the port town of Cosmopolis (today's Portoferraio). At the same time, the Spanish took control of the southeastern strip of the island.

In the 18th century, Grand Duke Pietro Leopoldo II encouraged land reform, the drainage of swamps and greater agricultural production on the island. Nevertheless, the production of iron remained the major industry. In 1917 some 840,000 tonnes were produced, but in WWII the Allies bombed the industry to bits and by the beginning of the 1980s production was down to 100,000 tonnes. The writing was on the wall: tourism had arrived to take the place of the mining and smelting industries.

Getting There & Away

AIR

Most folk opt for the ferry but there's a small **airport** (☎ 0565 97 60 11) at La Pila, just outside Marina di Campo. **Elbafly** (☎ 0565 9 19 61; www.elbafly.it) flies to and from Pisa, Bologna, Bastia, Cuneo and Milan (Malpensa), mid-June to mid-September.

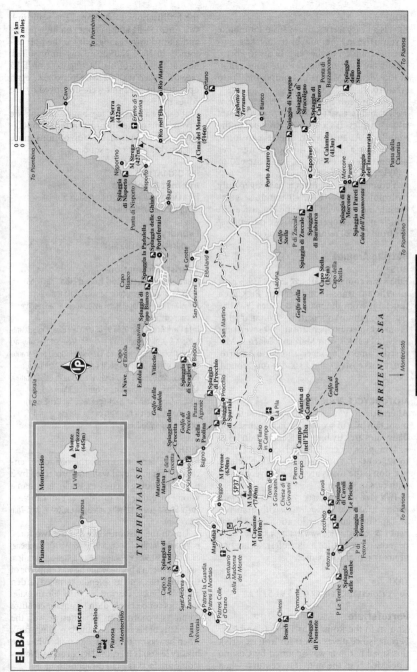

BOAT

Elba is an easy ferry journey from Piombino. If you arrive in Piombino by train, take a connecting train on to the port. Boats to Portoferraio are most frequent, while some call in at Rio Marina, Marina di Campo and Porto Azzurro.

Boats are run by **Moby** (☎ 199 30 30 40; www .moby.it) and **Toremar** (☎ 199 12 31 99; www.toremar.it in Italian). Unless it's a summer weekend or the middle of August, when queues can form, simply buy a ticket at the port. Fares (per person €6.50 to €9.50, per small car €20 to €49) vary according to season.

Toremar also operates a passenger-only hydrofoil service (€10, 40 minutes) year-round, and, between June and August, a fast vehicle and passenger service (two passengers/car from €69.20 return) to Portoferraio.

Getting Around
BUS

Elba's bus company, **ATL** (☎ 0565 91 43 92), runs an efficient trans-island service. Pick up a timetable from the main **bus station** (Viale Elba, Portoferraio), almost opposite the Toremar jetty. From Portoferraio there are at least seven runs daily (all €2) to/from Marciana Marina, Marina di Campo, Capoliveri and Porto Azzurro. A day pass costs €7 and a six-day run-around, €19.

MOTORCYCLE & BICYCLE

Alternatively, you can steam around Elba by mountain bike or scooter. Typical high season daily rates are city bikes €15, mountain bikes €24, mopeds (50cc) €28, and scooters (100cc to 125cc) €40. You can hire small vehicles – just don't; the roads are already overclogged with cars in summer.

TWN (Two Wheels Network; ☎ 0565 91 46 66; www .twn-rent.it; Viale Elba 32, Portoferraio), with branches at Capoliveri and other locations, and **Happy Rent** (☎ 0565 91 46 65; www.renthappy.it; Viale Elba 7), near the tourist office in Portoferraio, are two of many rental companies.

TAXI

In Portoferraio, call ☎ 0565 91 51 12.

Portoferraio

Known to the Romans as Fabricia and later Ferraia (since it was a port for iron exports), this small harbour was acquired by Cosimo I de' Medici in the mid-16th century, when the fortifications took shape. The walls link two forts (Stella and Falcone) on high points and a third tower (Linguella) at the port entrance. In 1814 Napoleon was 'imprisoned' here at the start of his fleeting exile on Elba (see the boxed text, p228). Steelworks began operating in 1902 but were destroyed by the Allies in 1943.

It can be a hectic place, but wandering the streets/steps of the historic centre and indulging in the exceptional eating options more than makes up for the squeeze.

INFORMATION
Internet Resources

Elba Link (www.elbalink.it) Carries lots of detailed information about the island.

Laundry

Laundrette (Viale Elba 51)

Tourist Information

Associazione Albergatori Isola d'Elba (☎ 0565 91 55 55; www.albergatorielbani.it; Calata Italia 20) The island's professional hotel association, it can reserve accommodation.

Info Park Are@ (☎ 0565 91 88 09; Viale Elba; ☒ 9.30am-1.30pm & 3.30-7.30pm daily summer, Mon-Sat rest of year) Information office of the Parco Nazionale Arcipelago Toscano.

Tourist office (Agenzia per il Turismo dell'Arcipelago Toscano; ☎ 0565 91 46 71; www.aptelba.it; Calata Italia 43; ☒ 9am-7pm Mon-Sat, 9.30am-12.30pm & 3.30-6.30pm Sun Easter-Oct, 8am-6pm Mon-Sat Oct-Easter) Near the ferry port it has a list of the island's limited internet log-on options.

SIGHTS

From the ferry terminal, the old town, enclosed by a medieval wall and protected by a pair of brooding fortresses, is a bit less than a kilometre along the foreshore. You can visit **Forte Stella** (Via della Stella; admission €1.50; ☒ 9am-7pm Easter-Sep).

Up on the bastions between the two forts, is **Villa dei Mulini** (☎ 0565 91 58 46; Piazzale Napoleone; adult/child €3/1.50; ☒ 9am-7pm Mon & Wed-Sat, 9am-1pm Sun), Napoleon's home while he was emperor of this small isle, with its splendid terraced garden and his library. During his brief Elban exile, the emperor certainly didn't want for creature comforts – contrast his Elba lifestyle with the simplicity of his camp bed and travelling trunk when he was on the campaign trail. While the history lesson is nice, the lack of actual Napoleonic artefacts is a tad disappointing.

The **Villa Napoleonica di San Martino** (☎ 0565 91 46 88; adult/child €3/1.50; ⏰ 9am-7pm Wed-Sat, 9am-1pm Sun), where Napoleon occasionally dropped in, is set in hills about 5km southwest of town. Modest by Napoleonic standards, it's dominated by the overbearing mid-19th-century gallery built to house his memorabilia. A combined ticket for both villas costs €5.

The Linguella fortifications, near the port, house the modest **Museo Civico Archeologico** (☎ 0565 91 73 38; adult/child €2/1.50; ⏰ 9am-2pm & 6pm-midnight mid-Jun–mid-Sep, 9am-8.30pm mid-Sep–Oct, 10am-1pm & 3.30-7.30pm Apr–mid-Jun), with a collection generally focussed on ancient seafarers.

ACTIVITIES
If you're here for an active time, pick up the multilingual tourist office leaflet *Lo Sport Emerge dal Mare*. It has a useful map and summarises walking and cycling trails, plus lists where to sign on for scuba diving, windsurfing and other watery activities.

The **Centro Trekking Isola d'Elba** run by Il Genio del Bosco (☎ 0565 93 08 37; www.geniodel bosco.it) leads trekking, biking and kayaking excursions around Elba, Capraia, Giglio and Pianosa.

Il Libraio (☎ 0565 91 71 35; Calata Mazzini 10), on the waterfront beside the old town, stocks a variety of walking and biking maps for the island.

You can spend a more sedentary but nonetheless enjoyable two hours out on a glass-bottom boat with **Aquavision** (☎ 328-709 54 70; Portoferraio harbour; adult/child €15/8; ⏰ Easter–mid-Oct).

SLEEPING
In the height of summer many hotels operate a compulsory half-board policy.

Albergo Ape Elbana (☎ 0565 91 42 45; www.ape -elbana.it; Salita de' Medici 2; s incl breakfast €40-70, d incl breakfast €60-100; ℗ 🏊) In the old town, overlooking Piazza della Repubblica (where guests can park for free). This butter-coloured building is the island's oldest hotel, where guests of Napoleon are reputed to have stayed. The position is its best feature as rooms, while large, are a little soulless – and occasionally malodorous. Ask for one of the larger ones looking onto the piazza.

Villa Ombrosa (☎ 0565 91 43 63; www.villaombrosa .it; Via De Gasperi 3; s incl buffet breakfast €52-126, d incl buffet breakfast €78-230; ℗) This is one of the very few hotels on the island that is open all year round. With a great location overlooking the sea and Spiaggia delle Ghiaie, it also has its own small private beach. Half-board, that is considerably more creative than many other hotels' bland buffet fare, is obligatory in summer.

THE CAMPY SIDE OF ITALY

Boy, do Italians like their outdoors. Camp sites are descended upon almost as soon as the earmuffs are packed away. Camp sites range from pitiable dirt lots overlooking the motorway to three-star, seaside facilities with bungalows, restaurants, bars and water sports centres. No tent? No problem. Many sites have permanent tents with cots – or modern cabins for those who only like their nature until shower time. The choices on Elba are dizzying. Check www.elbalink.it or www.elbaonline.com for exhaustive options. Here are a few sites that struck us:

Scaglieri Camping (☎ 0565 96 99 40; www.campingscaglieri.it; per person €7-13.60, per tent €9.50-20, 2-person chalet €60) More a resort experience than camping. Diversions include golf, swimming pool, diving, kayaking, horse rides and kid-oriented organised games, sports and even dance lessons. The onsite restaurant, pizzeria and bar eliminate the risk of charcoal stains on your sarong.

Acquaviva (☎ 0565 91 91 03; www.campingacquaviva.it; per person/tent/car €12/13/3; ⏰ mid-Mar–mid-Oct) About 4km west of town, Portoferraio's nearest campsite is a more traditional campground experience compared to many island schemes. Dirt paths encased in foliage connect pitches and modular, lego-like 'chalets' with common areas, including a tent restaurant. Modest apartments and 'mobile homes' are onsite as well. Their beach, a humble, but private 70m affair, is steps away, while other beaches are within reasonable walking distance. A great choice for simple sunsets over the sea.

Ville degli Ulivi (☎ 0565 97 60 98; www.villedegliulivi.it; per person €6.50-13, per tent €6-15, apt €67-137) Another impressive three-star, variable intensity camping experience with sleeping arrangements ranging from pup tents to condominiums. A sit-down restaurant, water park, gymnasium and wellness centre are onsite and organised parties kick off nightly.

Hotel Acquamarina (☎ 0565 91 40 57; www.hotelacqua marina.it; Località Paduella; s €52-104, d €78-180; 🞰 🅿) Just 400m away and under the same ownership as Villa Ombrosa, Acquamarina is a knockout hotel, also within strolling distance of Porto-ferraio. Rooms are sunny and bright with large balconies overlooking the naturally wild gar-dens. A path leads down to a small cove.

EATING

our pick **Cafescondido** (☎ 340 340 08 81; Via del Carmine 65; meals €25; 🕓 Mon-Sat) Way up the hill, toward Fortezza Falcone, the fronting raucous café gives no sign of the delicious food served in the back room. Servers deftly explain Elba-centric culinary permutations on the menu. The table wine is better than average and the

THE EMPEROR NAPOLEON TAKES EARLY RETIREMENT

At precisely 6pm on 3 May 1814, the English frigate *Undaunted* dropped anchor in the harbour of Portoferraio on the island of Elba. It bore an unusual cargo. Under the Treaty of Fontainebleau, the emperor Napoleon, who had held all Europe in his thrall since the turn of the century, was exiled to this seemingly safe open prison, some 15km from the Tuscan coast.

It could have been so much worse for the emperor, but the irony for someone who hailed from Corsica, just over the water, must have been bitter. Napoleon, the conqueror who had stridden across all Europe and taken Egypt, was awarded this little island as his private fiefdom, to hold until the end of his days.

His arrival was greeted with considerable pomp. The guns of Portoferraio shot off a 100-round salute, to which the English frigate replied. That, at least, is French author Alexandre Dumas' take. Other sources reckon the guns were actually firing *at* the frigate.

Whatever the case, Elba would never be quite the same again. Napoleon, ever hyperactive, threw himself into frenetic activity in his new, humbler domain. After touring the island, he prescribed a mass of public works, which included improving the operations of the island's iron-ore mines – whose revenue, it is pertinent to note, now went his way. He also went about boosting agriculture, initiating a road-building program, draining marshes and overhauling the legal and education systems. On many occasions, he would order some of the 500 members of his faithful guard to pitch in.

A great deal of ink has been spilled over the diminutive emperor's dictatorial style and seem-ingly impossible ambitions, but he can't have been all bad. To this day, they still say a Mass each May for his soul at the island's Chiesa della Misericordia.

Napoleon installed himself in the bastions of the city wall, in what became known as the Residenza dei Mulini. He'd drop into his so-called country or summer home, outside town in San Martino, for an occasional stopover on excursions but he never slept there. Some weeks after his arrival, his mother Letizia and sister Paolina rolled up. But he remained separated from his wife, Maria Luisa, and was visited for just two no doubt hectic days by his lover, Maria Walewska.

At the Congress of Vienna, the new regime in France called for Napoleon's removal to a more distant location. Austria, too, was nervous. Some participants favoured a shift to Malta, but Britain objected and suggested the remote South Atlantic islet of St Helena. The Congress broke up with no agreed decision.

Napoleon was well aware of the debate. Under no circumstances would he allow himself to be shipped off to some rocky speck in the furthest reaches of the Atlantic Ocean. A lifelong risk taker, he decided to have another roll of the dice. For months he had sent out on 'routine' trips around the Mediterranean a couple of vessels flying the flag of his little empire, Elba. When one, the *Incostante*, set sail early in the morning of 26 February 1815, no-one suspected that the conqueror of Europe was stowed away on board. Sir Neil Campbell, his English jail warden, had returned to Livorno the previous day, confident that Napoleon was, as ever, fully immersed in the business of the island.

Elba lost its emperor and Napoleon, his little gilded cage. He made his way to France, reas-sumed power and embarked on the Hundred Days, the last of his expansionist campaigns that would culminate in defeat at Waterloo – after which he got his Atlantic exile after all, dying there in 1821, from arsenic poisoning, according to the most accepted contemporary theory, probably from the hair tonic he applied to keep that famous quiff glistening.

chocolate mousse will make you wish weeping in public was socially acceptable.

our pick **La Libertaria** (☎ 0565 91 49 78; Calata Matteotti 12; meals €30; ☽ Apr-Oct) Yes, two 'our pick' restaurants in one place, we just couldn't decide. In the unlikely event that nothing on the menu turns your crank, the kitchen is open to requests! Seating capacity and backdrops are meagre ('would the gentleman like to sit in the alley or out on the sidewalk, 5cm from speeding traffic?'), but the food is divine. The *linguine sarde e finocchietto* (pasta with sardines and fennel) is an unlikely treat and the cooked-to-perfection *tonno in crosta di pistacchi* (tuna fillet with pistachio crust) may actually keep you in Portoferraio an extra night for a second helping.

Trattoria La Barca (☎ 0565 91 80 36; Via Guerrazzi 60-62; meals €32; ☽ Mon-Sat) A good place to slurp a plate of *cacciucco*. The place is popular with locals in the know, so there's not much elbow space between tables. Go for the terrace if there's room.

Stella Marina (☎ 0565 91 59 83; Banchina Alto Fondale; meals €35-40) A justifiably popular fish and seafood restaurant. Stuck in a car park beside the Toremar ferry jetty and unpromising from the exterior, its cuisine is fine and imaginative, though drinks are overpriced.

DRINKING

Sir William's Irish Bar (☎ 0565 91 92 88; Via Manganaro 28) The very name tells you the Celtic connection is tenuous, but this is the place for a wee dram o' whisky or a pint of bitter. It generally doesn't start jumping till at least midnight and pulls in all sorts, from local punters to the casually hip.

L'Inferno (☎ 0565 91 87 83; Le Foci 2) Locals pile into their cars and head to this lively bar with dancing about 5km west of town on the road to Marciana Marina.

West to Capo d'Enfola

Several modest beaches spread west from Portoferraio. Quite nice, although narrow and shelly, are **Spiaggia la Padulella** and its counterpart just west of Capo Bianco, **Spiaggia di Capo Bianco**. A couple of similar beaches dot the coast along the 7km stretch out to **Capo d'Enfola**. You can have a dip here or head south down the coast a few kilometres to **Viticcio**, with its handful of restaurants and hotels, where the road ends. From here you can walk to the beaches of the **Golfo della Biodola**.

SLEEPING & EATING

Hotel Scoglio Bianco (☎ 0565 93 90 36; www.scoglio bianco.it; Viticcio; half-board per person €39-88) This hotel has bright, spacious rooms set around a central patio decorated with deckchairs and cats. The downstairs Pizzeria da Giacomino has a terrace over the sea. The small price increase for a 'superior' room is well worth the expenditure.

Hotel Paradiso (☎ 0565 93 90 34; www.elbaturistica.it; Viticcio; B&B per person €40-85, half-board €55-120; ☽ mid-Apr–Oct; P ✕ ⊜) Owned by a British-Italian couple, Paradiso is set in the Tuscan National Park and has expansive sea views. Many rooms have good-sized balconies. Set high above the road, there is a vast outdoor bar, pool, tennis court and private beach access.

Emanuel (☎ 0565 93 90 03; Enfola; menus €19-29, meals €28; ☽ Easter-Oct) At road's end on Capo d'Enfola, Emanuel offers splendid views over the water. Enjoy a lingering dinner on its beachfront terrace, shaded by a magnificent fig tree. The cuisine is consistently good. Fish and seafood predominate but there are always a couple of inventive meat dishes and two vegetarian *degustazione* menus.

West to Marciana Marina

From Portoferraio, a provincial road heads south and then forks westwards along the coast to Marciana Marina, via Procchio.

The pick of the beaches are the sandy strands lining the **Golfo della Biodola**.

Hermitage (☎ 0565 97 40; www.hotelhermitage.it; La Biodola; half-board per person €105-295; P ✕ ⊜ ▢) is pure Beverly Hills. One of the island's truly luxurious hotels, it's a gorgeous retreat complete with infinity pool overlooking the sea and a golf course just over the fence. Amenities include a beauty centre, wi-fi and a new wretchedly excessive Jacuzzi.

PROCCHIO

In season, Procchio is a small bustling place with the added bonus of sandy beaches.

our pick **Osteria del Piano** (☎ 0565 90 72 92; Via Provinciale 24; meals €29; ☽ Apr-Oct) is an unassuming restaurant on the Procchio side of the junction where the road peels away towards Marciana Marina. The open-plan kitchen means you can watch and listen – the owner is wonderfully chatty – to the creative energy. Innovative dishes include the black-and-white spaghetti served with a crab sauce.

West from Procchio, the road hugs the cliffs, offering fine views all along the winding coast. If you can manage to park, **Spiaggia di Spartaia** and **Spiaggia della Paolina** are part of a series of beautiful little beaches, all requiring a steep clamber down.

Marciana Marina

Unlike most cookie-cutter marinas, Marciana Marina, 20km west of Portoferraio, has character and history to complement its pleasant pebble beaches. It's a fine base for attacking the island's best walking trails.

Hotel Marinella (☎ 0565 9 90 18; www.elbahotel marinella.it; Viale Margherita 38; B&B per person €40-87, half board €48-94; ☺ Easter–mid-Oct; ☒ P ☒) is a well-aged classic – waning tennis court included – beside the sea front. Rooms in the annexe overlook the garden but the best are those in the main building with balconies and sea views.

Casa Lupi (☎ /fax 0565 9 91 43; Località Ontanelli 35; s €30-42, d €45-70; ☺ closed Jan–early Mar; ☒) is about half a kilometre inland on the road to Marciana. Beside a vineyard, with a garden of peach trees and rose bushes, it's a small hotel in peaceful surroundings. Rooms are no-frills basic but comfortable and clean.

Il Ristorante Scaraboci (☎ 0565 99 68 68; Via XX Settembre 29; meals €40; ☺ Thu-Tue) is a promising fish and seafood venue where all pastas and desserts are homemade. Try, for something special, their *spaghetto al sugo d'astice* (spaghetti with lobster sauce).

Poggio & the Interior

A twisting 4km ascent into the mountains from Marciana Marina brings you to the attractive inland village of Poggio, famous for its spring water. It's an enchanting little place with steep, cobblestone alleys and stunning views of Marciana Marina and the coast.

Publius (☎ 0565 9 92 08; meals €35-40; ☺ closed Mon, Dec-Feb), at the northern entrance to the village, is the place to spill money on a great meal. The plunging views down to the coast should keep your mind off the commensurately steep prices.

From Poggio you can choose from two options: either proceed west to **Marciana** then head around the coast (see right), or opt for the narrow, spectacular SP37. Heading towards Marina di Campo, it winds through some of the highest, most densely wooded and tourist-free countryside on the island.

Following the SP37, park at the picnic site at the foot of **Monte Perone** (630m) – you can't miss it. To the left (east) you can wander up to the mountain, with spectacular views across much of the island. To the right (west) you can scramble fairly quickly to a height that affords broad vistas down to Poggio, Marciana and Marciana Marina. From there you could press on to **Monte Maolo** (749m).

The road then descends into the southern flank of the island. On the way, you pass the granite shell of the Romanesque **Chiesa di San Giovanni** and, shortly after, a ruined tower, the **Torre di San Giovanni**.

The two small hamlets here, **Sant'Ilario in Campo** and **San Piero in Campo**, are short on sights but still pleasant enough and little affected by tourism.

Hotel La Rosa (☎ 0565 98 31 91, 349 076 82 25; www .larosahotel.it; Piazza Maggore Gadani 17, San Piero; half board per person €40-65) is an old-fashioned hotel in a side street with large but rather dark rooms. The restaurant is popular, specialising in enormous plates of pasta at rock-bottom prices.

Marciana & the West Coast

From Poggio, it is possible is to continue west to Marciana, both the highest (355m) and oldest town on the island and an engaging, peaceful, tightly packed place. Puff up the town's 'pitiless' streets and stairs, past arches, flower boxes and petite balconies to drop-offs revealing views of Marciana Marina and Poggio below. Once an important defensive position under Pisan rule, Marciana subsequently passed to Piombino, the French and finally to the grand duchy of Tuscany.

The much knocked about **Fortezza Pisana** (☺ Apr-Sep), above the village, is a reminder of the old medieval days. Down a cobbled lane below it is a modest **Museo Archeologico** (☎ 0565 90 12 15; Via del Pretorio; admission €2; ☺ Wed-Mon). A 40-minute or so walk west out of town brings you to the **Santuario della Madonna del Monte**, the most important object of pilgrimage on the island. A much-altered 11th-century church houses a stone upon which a divine hand is said to have painted an image of the Virgin.

Some 750m south of Marciana, a **cable lift** (☎ 0565 90 10 20; one way/return €10/15; ☺ Easter-Nov) with open, barred cabins like parrot cages operates in summer and whisks you almost to the summit of **Monte Capanne** (1018m), the island's highest point with views as far as Corsica on a clear day.

CENTRAL COAST & ELBA

The road west out of Marciana pursues a course around the island, maintaining a prudent distance and altitude from the often precipitous coastline.

Sant'Andrea is a popular new resort with a concentration of a dozen or so hotels winding back up the hill to the main road.

Hotel Barsalini (☎ 0565 90 80 13; www.hotelbarsalini .com; Sant'Andrea; half-board per person €50-87; ☷ Easter-late Oct), just 20m from the beach, has been designed with a lot of TLC. Rooms are spacious, bright and comfortable and the aquarium-flanked restaurant has an excellent and varied menu.

Following the road round to the south side of the island, you pass several small beaches. **Chiessi** and **Pomonte** have pebbly beaches, but the water is beautiful. Sandy **Spiaggia delle Tombe** is one of the few spots on the island with a nude-bathing scene.

At **Fetovaia**, **Seccheto** and **Cavoli** you will find further protected sandy beaches, accommodation and restaurants. West of Seccheto, **Le Piscine** is another mostly nudist stretch.

Marina di Campo

Marina di Campo, on the south side of the island, is Elba's second-largest town. Curling around a picturesque bay, its small fishing harbour adds personality to what is otherwise very much a holiday-oriented town. Its beach of bright, white sand pulls in vacationers by the thousands; coves further west, though less spectacular, are more tranquil.

Camp sites abound along this stretch of coast and the place gets ridiculously packed in the height of summer. But this is where some of the island's action can be found too; several discos help keep the brat-pack happy through the hot months.

There is a seasonal **tourist office** (☎ 0565 97 79 69; Piazza dei Granatieri; ☷ Jun-Sep) in town.

Just northeast of town in the Lacona/Porto Azzurro direction, over 150 Mediterranean species swim, crawl and wave about in the **Acquario dell'Elba** (☎ 0565 97 78 85; www.acquarioelba .com; adult/child €6/3; ☷ 9am-11.30pm Jun–mid-Sep, 9am-7.30pm mid-Mar–May & mid-Sep–Nov).

Montecristo (☎ 0565 97 68 61; www.hotelmontec risto.it; Viale Nomelini; s €52-126, d €76-224; ☷ P) is a pleasantly posh hotel on the beach, with flower-framed balconies and a bar and pool overlooking the sea. The large sunny rooms have Scandinavian-style light furnishings and king-size beds.

Thomas Hotel (☎ 0565 97 77 32; www.elbathomas hotel.com; Viale degli Etruschi 32; per person €32-62, incl breakfast; ☷ mid-Mar–Oct; P), barely 100m away, is a three-star hotel, attractively set among pine trees. Popular with scuba divers, it's only a short walk from the beach and is one of the more affordable options in the town itself.

Il Tinello (☎ 0565 97 66 45; Località Casina), on the outskirts, is a heaving drinking and dancing dive, especially on summer nights.

Capoliveri & the Southeast

Up a precipitous ridgeback in the southeastern pocket of the island, this village is flirting with too-enchanting-for-its-own-good designation. The steep, narrow alleys and sandwiched houses are certainly pretty, but the tourist hoards detract. At least one Italian newspaper writer has remarked tartly that one may as well hoist the German flag at Capoliveri. Come out of season and you can discover some of the peace of this hamlet, which used to live off iron-ore mining.

EATING

Freccia Azzurra (☎ 0565 96 89 68; Via Verdi 4; meals €15-25) This is a popular budget restaurant. There's not much squeeze-by space in the dining room but its terrace on Capoliveri's main square is vast. Try the *penne gamberetti e rucola* (shrimp and rocket penne) for a real tastebud treat.

Il Chiasso (☎ 0565 96 87 09; Via Cavour 32; meals €40) One of the best restaurants in town, with a classy set menu. The décor is a savvy combination of traditional and trendy and there's an excellent wine list.

DRINKING

Fandango (☎ 0565 93 54 24; Via Cardenti 1; drinks from €4; ☷ Tue-Sun) Right beneath the main square, here you can taste fine Tuscan wines in pleasant surroundings.

Velvet Underground (Vicolo Lungo 14) This is only a short stumble from the main square. It's a pub-style bar that feels like a real local.

ENTERTAINMENT

Sugar Reef (☎ 0338 917 90 26; Località La Trappola) *The* place on the island for a little hip-swinging salsa, both live and DJ-mixed. It's about 1km south of Capoliveri on the road to Morcone.

Around Capoliveri

Directly west of Capoliveri (take the Portoferraio road and watch for signs) are the beaches of **Spiaggia di Zuccale** and **Spiaggia di Barabarca**. You end up on a dirt track – leave your vehicle in the car park and walk the final stretch.

If you take the road heading south from Capoliveri, another three charming sandy little coves – **Morcone**, **Pareti** and **Innamorata** – come in quick succession.

East of Capoliveri, you have two choices. One road takes you to the comparatively long stretch of beach at **Naregno**, fronted by a series of discreet hotels.

The more adventurous should follow signs for **Stracoligno**, one of the first in a series of beaches running down the east coast. The road at this point becomes a dirt track and, if you don't mind dusting up your vehicle, you can push on to a couple of less-frequented beaches. **Cala Nuova** is a nice enough little beach with a good restaurant.

Ristorante Calanova (☎ 0565 96 89 58; meals €35; ☻ summer only) is a table-for-two kind of place, wonderfully secluded with only the gently lapping sea for company. As you'd expect, the menu is based on seafood.

Another 4km or 5km and you reach a path down to the **Spiaggia dello Stagnone**, which even in summer should not be too crowded, if only because of the effort required to rattle down this far.

Porto Azzurro

Overlooked by its fort, built in 1603 by Philip III of Spain and now a prison, Porto Azzurro is a pleasant resort town, close to some good beaches.

Hotel Belmare (☎ 0565 9 50 12; www.elba-hotel belmare.it; Banchina IV Novembre; per person €35-65, incl breakfast; ☻ year-round; ✿) has an enviable location on the main promenade. This traditional green-shuttered hotel is nothing fancy but rooms are comfy enough, and there's a small bar and TV room for post-beach R&R. Only some rooms have air-con.

Albergo Villa Italia (☎ 0565 9 51 19; www.villaitalia hotel.it; Viale Italia 41; d/tr/q €80/90/105, incl breakfast; ☻ mid-Mar–Oct; P ✿ ▢) is a friendly, family-run place. Their 12 clean bedrooms are small but spruce and about the cheapest in town. It's on a fairly noisy road yet scarcely 200m from the beach. The wi-fi is free.

Ristorante Cutty Sark (☎ 0565 95 78 21; Piazza del Mercato 25; meals €32-37; ☻ closed Tue in winter) has a mainly fish menu with a couple of concessions to carnivores. Savour their *raviolini all'Ammiraglia*, large ravioli filled with cour-

gettes (zucchini) and shrimp meat and bathed in a shrimp and tomato sauce.

Osteria La Botte Gaia (☎ 0565 9 56 07; www.labotte gaia.com; Via Europa 5-7; meals €35-40; ☻ closed Mon in winter) is Slow Food–featured and deservedly so. Homemade pasta supplements the ever-changing daily menu that runneth over with just-caught fish options and a few veggie plates. Just 100m further up the road from Albergo Villa Italia.

The Northeast

If, on leaving Portoferraio, you swing around to the east and head for Rio nell'Elba and beyond, you will experience the least-visited part of the island, with lovely, albeit pebbly, beaches and glorious views.

The road hugs the coast on its way around to **Bagnaia**, the first worthwhile stop. En route you will scoot by **San Giovanni**, home to a rather expensive and dull mud spa, and **Le Grotte**, where a few stones still managing to stand on top of each other are all that remain of a Roman villa. At the Porto Azzurro and Bagnaia fork is **Elbaland** (☎ 335 819 46 80; www.elbaland.com; Località Fonte Murato; adult/child €7/9; ☻ 11am-sunset Jul-Aug, 10am-sunset Jun & Sep, 10am-7pm Apr-May), which is an ambitiously-priced, oversized park that has swings and minor attractions.

From Elbaland head north to Bagnaia, a lush, green part of the island with an attractive beach and some accommodation, including a camp site.

Pizzeria Sunset (☎ 0565 93 07 86; Bagnaia; pizzas from €5.50; ☻ May-Oct) offers great views across the gulf to Portoferraio, a hang-out beach-bum atmosphere, happy hour and sangria in addition to good pizza. At night, there's a head-thumping disco that spills out onto the beach.

From Bagnaia you can follow the 3km dirt road to **Nisporto** and then on to **Nisportino** with spectacular views along the way. Both have a small beach and, in summer, snack stands and one or two restaurants. From Nisportino, head back a few kilometres to the junction with the road that links Nisporto and Rio nell'Elba. About halfway along this road, stop for a short stroll to what is left of the **Eremo di Santa Caterina**, a tiny stone hermitage, and more good views.

The road plunges down to the inland bastion of **Rio nell'Elba**, the heart of the island's iron-mining operations. It's a little gloomy,

---

THE COUNT OF MONTECRISTO

This feel-good swashbuckling tale was born from author Alexandre Dumas' acquaintance with Jérome Bonaparte, Napoleon Bonaparte's brother, whom he accompanied on a trip to Elba. Dumas became aware of another island, the deserted Montecristo, deeper in the Mediterranean, and determined to write a novel in remembrance of the trip. In the person of the swashbuckling Dantes, Dumas takes a dig at the corruption of the bourgeois world. The dashing officer is imprisoned for a crime he hasn't committed and vows to get even. He escapes and, after a tip-off, searches for treasure on the island of Montecristo where, after much adventure and jolly japes, our man wins all the prizes – getting rich, becoming the Count of Montecristo and exacting a full measure of revenge on those who framed him.

Of course, it's all a tall tale (and no-one has ever found any treasure on Montecristo) but this particular yarn has made a lot of loot for a lot of people. At least 25 film and TV versions of the story have been made, with greater or lesser skill. Among the better ones are the oldies: Rowland Lee's 1935 film and the 1943 version by Robert Vernay were equally good celluloid yarns. In Italy, Andrea Giordana had women swooning at their TV sets in the 1966 series by Edmo Fenoglio. Richard Chamberlain had a go at the lead role in David Greene's 1975 *The Count of Montecristo*, as, more recently, did Gérard Depardieu in *Montecristo* (1997).

---

but the simple fact that it caters little to tourism has its appeal. The **Museo della Gente di Rio** (☎ 0565 94 34 11; Passo della Pietà; admission €2.75; 🕑 10am-1pm & 4-7.30pm Tue-Sun mid-Apr–Sep) has 200 rare mineral specimens from the east of the island and Monte Capanne.

Next, take the short run downhill to Rio nell'Elba's coastal outlet, **Rio Marina**, with yet another mineral museum. This apart, not a lot will hold you up.

Hotel Rio (☎ 0565 92 42 25; www.hotelriomarina.it; Via Palestro 31; s incl breakfast €37-48, d incl breakfast €74-156; 🕑 Apr-Oct; 🛏) is a well-worn hotel with family-size rooms, some with a sea view, plus TV room, garden, lots of paintings of dubious quality and an overall homey, retro-1970s feel. Some rooms have air-con.

Da Oreste La Strega (☎ 0565 96 22 11; Via Vittorio Emanuele 6; meals €30; 🕑 Wed-Mon) is an attractive seafood restaurant, with large windows overlooking the harbour and an excellent wine list.

The best beach hereabouts is a little further down at **Ortano**. To get there, go back a couple of kilometres towards Rio nell'Elba and swing southwards. It's a nice location

but, once again, the beach is that part-sand, part-pebble mix.

MINOR ISLANDS

Seven islands, including the island of Elba, form part of the Parco Nazionale dell'Arcipelago Toscano (see the boxed text, p217). Two out of the park's seven islands, Capraia and Gorgona (see p219), are in the central coast area and the islands of Giglio (p289) and Giannutri (p289) are further south. The remaining two are Pianosa and Montecristo.

Pianosa, 14km west of Elba, is a flat, triangular affair measuring about 5.8km by 4.6km. From 1858 until as late as the mid-1990s it was a penal colony. Day trips (return €25) to the island leave from Porto Ferraio and Marina di Campo during summer.

There are no ferry services to **Montecristo**, 40km south of Elba, which was also briefly a prison island. Since 1979 it has been a marine biological reserve and can be seen only as part of an organised visit; you need special permission from the **Ufficio Forestale in Follónica** (☎ 0566 4 06 11) on the Italian mainland.

Central Tuscany

Buildings the colour of ripe corn, hills with gentle curves and folds, scored here and there by steep ravines, as scarred and eroded as any cowboy badlands; here in the central Tuscan countryside, especially around Le Crete with its impressionist-style landscape, beats the heart of rural Tuscany. Lofty cypresses form a dramatic border to fields speckled with sheep and, if you pass by in spring, you have the additional treat of brilliant red poppy fields, sweeping to the sun-hazed green horizon. Gentle on the eye and feet, the region is ideal family walking country – and do get a first overview on the scenic Treno Natura (Nature Train), if your visit coincides with one of the summer days when it's running.

Outstanding abbeys will satisfy ecclesiastical wonder and restorative waters harnessed by a handful of spas will satisfy other things.

Some of Tuscany's most attractive towns poke up hereabouts: steep, straggling Montepulciano and the one-time defensive bulwark of Monteriggioni with its 14 defensive towers, the pilgrim-route bastion of San Gimignano, with still more medieval towers, and Volterra, the ancient brooding successor to an Etruscan settlement, standing aloof and watching over the lunar expanses to the south.

Siena's remarkable comeback after a centuries-long 'time-out' enforced by Florence is something to see. Its glorious piazza, cobbled streets and alleys counter the lamentably overtrafficked streets of Florence and its black-and-white striped cathedral is as striking as Florence's. Capitalising on the Gothic identity that once marked it as a conquered slum within the grand duchy of Tuscany is an irony that has caused Florentine cadavers to spin in their tombs.

HIGHLIGHTS

- Climb (but don't count) the 400 steps of Siena's **Torre del Mangia** (p240), then invert those glorious views from a seat in **Piazza del Campo** (p237) with a well-earned cold beverage

- Attain Gothic enlightenment in Siena's ornate **cathedral** (p240)

- Tour the striking abbeys of Sant'Antimo and Monte Oliveto Maggiore while cruising the pastureland of **Le Crete** (p250)

- Imagine the awe of your medieval predecessors as you approach the towers of **San Gimignano** (p254)

- Let the *enoteca's* Brunello wine be your guide through Montalcino's **fortezza** (p266)

- Burn off some of those carbs as you scale the steep, beautiful streets of **Montepulciano** (p273)

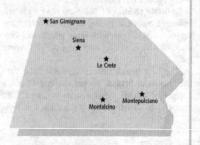

★ San Gimignano

Siena
★

★
Le Crete

★ Montepulciano
Montalcino ★

SIENA

pop 54,330

The rivalry between historic adversaries Siena and Florence continues to this day, and every traveller seems to strongly identify with one over the other. It often boils down to aesthetic preference: while Florence saw its greatest flourishing during the Renaissance, Siena's enduring artistic glories are largely Gothic. Though there is also the eternal question of who has the best patron saint (Siena, obviously).

One of Italy's most enchanting cities, Siena's medieval centre bristles with majestic buildings, such as the Palazzo Comunale on Piazza del Campo, the main square, and its stupefyingly ornamented cathedral. The profusion of churches and small museums harbour a wealth of artwork, though your day can be equally effectively filled by simply wandering the snarled lanes of the historic centre, a Unesco World Heritage Site, spending nary a euro on admission fees or untold hours standing in queues.

Budget a couple of days to digest the city's rich treasures and exceptional cuisine, then take advantage of its location and excellent bus connections to stage jaunts to nearby enticements such as San Gimignano and Volterra.

History

According to legend Siena was founded by Senius, son of Remus; the symbol of the wolf feeding the twins Romulus and Remus is as ubiquitous in Siena as it is in Rome. In reality, the city was probably of Etruscan origin, although it wasn't until the 1st century BC, when the Romans established a military colony here called Sena Julia, that it began to grow into a proper town. Even so, it remained a minor outpost until the arrival of the Lombards in the 6th century AD. Under them, Siena became a key point along the main route from northern Italy to Rome, the Via Francigena. The medieval town was an amalgamation of three areas (Città, Camollia and San Martino) that would come to be known as the *terzi* (thirds). The city was next under the control of local bishops before power passed to locally elected administrators, the *consoli* (consuls).

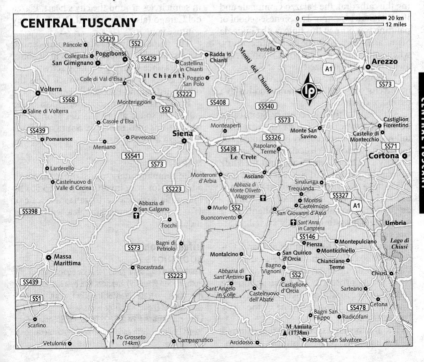

CENTRAL TUSCANY

0 — 20 km
0 — 12 miles

By the 13th century, Siena had become a wealthy trading city, producing textiles, saffron, wine, spices and wax, and its traders and bankers did deals all over Western Europe. Its rivalry with neighbouring Florence also grew proportionately, leading to numerous wars between Guelph Florence and Ghibelline Siena, each intent upon controlling ever more Tuscan territory. In 1230 Florence besieged Siena and catapulted dung and rotting donkey flesh over its walls in an inspired, medieval Mr Science attempt to spread the plague. Siena's revenge came at the Battle of Montaperti in 1260 but victory was short-lived. Nine years later the Tuscan Ghibellines were defeated by Charles of Anjou and, for almost a century, Siena was obliged to toe the Florentine line in international affairs, becoming a member of the Tuscan Guelph League (supporters of the pope).

Siena reached its peak under the republican rule of the Consiglio dei Nove (Council of Nine), an elected executive dominated by the rising mercantile class. Many of the finest buildings in the Sienese Gothic style were constructed during this period, including the cathedral, the Palazzo Comunale and the Piazza del Campo. The Sienese school of painting was born at this time, with Guido da Siena, and flowered in the early 14th century, when artists such as Duccio di Buoninsegna and Ambrogio Lorenzetti were at work.

A plague outbreak in 1348 killed two-thirds of the city's 100,000 inhabitants and led to a period of decline.

At the end of the 14th century, Siena came under the control of Milan's Visconti family, followed in the next century by the autocratic patrician Pandolfo Petrucci. Under Petrucci the city's fortunes improved, until the Holy Roman Emperor Charles V conquered it in 1555 after a two-year siege that left thousands dead. He handed the city over to Cosimo I de' Medici, who barred the inhabitants from operating banks, thus severely curtailing Siena's power.

Siena was home to St Catherine (Santa Caterina), one of Italy's most venerated saints. But saints don't make money. Siena today relies for its prosperity on tourism and the success of its Monte dei Paschi di Siena bank, founded in 1472 and now one of the city's largest employers.

Though the hapless residents that endured it may not agree, Siena's centuries-long economic downturn in the wake of the Medici takeover was a blessing that resulted in the city's present-day, matchless allure. Its predominantly Gothic surroundings have survived largely intact as no one could be bothered to undertake (or fund) demolition or new construction. Furthermore, unlike the poundings endured by neighbouring cities in WWII, the French took Siena virtually unopposed, sparing it discernible damage.

As the population began to grow again in the years after WWII (it had dropped to 16,000 in the latter half of the 18th century), Siena was the first European city to banish motor traffic from its heart (in 1966). An overt divergence from Florence's vehicle congestion and carbon monoxide fug, strolling Siena's historic centre without fear of flatten toes or side-view mirror contusions (scooters notwithstanding) is not the least of the town's pleasures.

Orientation

Historic Siena, still largely surrounded by its medieval walls, is small and easily tackled on foot, although the way in which streets swirl in semicircles around the city's heart, Piazza del Campo (also known as 'Il Campo'), may confuse you.

The names of two of Siena's main central streets, Banchi di Sopra and Banchi di Sotto, recall its once-thriving banking activity. Another artery is Via di Città, which joins the others just behind Piazza del Campo.

From Piazza Gramsci, where most buses call, walk south along Via dei Montanini, which turns into Banchi di Sopra and leads to Piazza del Campo.

MAPS

If the complimentary tourist office map isn't adequate for you, invest in *Siena* (€5.50) by Litografia Artistica Cartografia; at a scale of 1:7000, this map comes complete with a street index.

Information
BOOKSHOPS

Book Shop (☎ 0577 22 65 94; www.bookshopsiena .com; Via San Pietro 19) And how. Run by a NYC expat, restock your suitcase library of 'traveller favourites' at this emporium of English-language books.

Libreria Senese (☎ 0577 28 08 45; Via di Città 62-6) Stocks English, French and German books and international newspapers.

EMERGENCY
Police station (☎ 0577 20 11 11; Via del Castoro)

INTERNET ACCESS
Internet Train (Via di Città 121; per hr €4; ☻ 8am-8pm
Sun-Fri) A popular café with cables for laptop hook-ups.
There's another branch at Via di Pantaneto 57.
Netrunner (☎ 0577 4 49 46; www.netrunnersiena.net;
Via Pantaneto 132; per hr €6; ☻ 10am-11pm Mon-Sat,
3-9pm Sun) Has a prepaid discount card scheme for regular
customers.

LAUNDRY
Onda Blu (Via del Casato di Sotto 17; ☻ 8am-10pm)
Wash & Dry (Via di Pantaneto 38; ☻ 8am-10pm)

MEDICAL SERVICES
Hospital (☎ 0577 58 51 11; Viale Bracci) Just north of
Siena at Le Scotte.

POST
Post office (Piazza Matteotti 1)

TELEPHONE
Telecom office (Via di Città 113) The office is unstaffed,
as is the other Telecom office at Via di Pantaneto 44.

TOURIST INFORMATION
Tourist office (☎ 0577 28 05 51; www.terresiena
.it; Piazza del Campo 56; ☻ 9am-7pm) Can help reserve
accommodation.

Sights
PIAZZA DEL CAMPO
Resembling a colossal, medieval bathroom
sink, the sloping Piazza del Campo has been
Siena's civic and social centre ever since it
was staked out by the Council of Nine in the
mid-14th century.

The piazza was the site of a former Roman
marketplace, and its pie-piece paving design
is divided into nine sectors to represent the
number of members of the ruling council.
This is the city's primary gathering point –
locals sun themselves and gossip here, while
tourists parade through, awestruck, often
stopping for a good sit-down and a beverage
at a terrace table.

In 1346 water first bubbled forth from the
Fonte Gaia (Happy Fountain) in the upper part
of the square. The fountain's panels are reproductions; the severely weathered originals,
sculpted by Jacopo della Quercia in the early
15th century, are on display in the Complesso
Museale di Santa Maria della Scala (p242).

If you find the piazza irksomely congested
at lunch time on a summer day, you'll need
a powerful sedative to cope with the running
of the Palio (see the boxed text, p246), when
the astonishing crush and vigour of revellers
will alarm all but the most fearless.

PALAZZO COMUNALE
At the lowest point of the square (or the tap
of the aforementioned metaphorical sink),
stands the spare, elegant **Palazzo Comunale**,
conceived by the Council of Nine as a nerve
centre for the republican government, unit-
ing the offices and courts in one building,
thus greatly reducing the symbolic and actual
power of the feudal nobles.

Dating from 1297, the palazzo is one of
the most graceful Gothic buildings in Italy.
The ground level was constructed in stone,
the upper, crenulated levels in brick, with an
ingeniously designed concave façade to mirror the opposing convex curve formed by the
piazza. Also known as the Palazzo Pubblico,
or town hall, the palazzo was purpose-built as
the piazza's centrepiece, resulting in a wonderful amphitheatre effect.

The attached **Torre del Mangia** (1344), with
a crown designed by painter Lippo Memmi,
was designed in the veritable Sienese spirit of
the era: to be bigger and better than stupid
Florence's. An undisputed success, at 102m it

SAFE COMBINATIONS
Siena has a bewildering permutation of
combined tickets. The distribution when
we visited was as follows:

▪ Museo Civico and Torre del Mangia
(€12)

▪ Museo Civico, Santa Maria della Scala
and Palazzo delle Papesse (€11, valid for
two days)

▪ Museo dell'Opera Metropolitana, crypt,
Oratorio di San Bernardino, Museo Diocesano (€10 valid for three days)

▪ Museo Civico, Santa Maria della Scala,
Palazzo delle Papesse, Museo dell'Opera
Metropolitana, Battistero di San Giovanni, Museo Diocesano, Chiesa di
Sant'Agostino and Oratorio di San Bernardino – the bumper bundle though
not including Torre del Mangia (€17,
valid for seven days)

SIENA

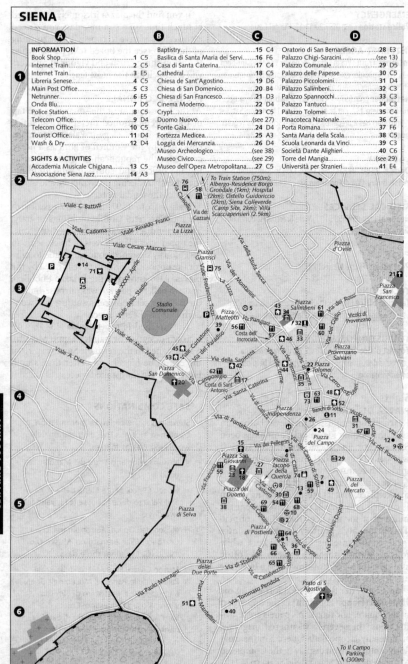

INFORMATION		
Book Shop	1	C5
Internet Train	2	C5
Internet Train	3	E5
Libreria Senese	4	C5
Main Post Office	5	C3
Netrunner	6	E5
Onda Blu	7	D5
Police Station	8	C5
Telecom Office	9	D4
Telecom Office	10	D4
Tourist Office	11	D4
Wash & Dry	12	D4

SIGHTS & ACTIVITIES		
Accademia Musicale Chigiana	13	C5
Associazione Siena Jazz	14	A3

Baptistry	15	C4
Basilica di Santa Maria dei Servi	16	F6
Casa di Santa Caterina	17	C4
Cathedral	18	C5
Chiesa de Sant'Agostino	19	D6
Chiesa di San Domenico	20	B4
Chiesa di San Francesco	21	D3
Cinema Moderno	22	D4
Crypt	23	C5
Duomo Nuovo	(see 27)	
Fonte Gaia	24	D4
Fortezza Medicea	25	A3
Loggia dei Mercanzia	26	D4
Museo Archeologico	(see 38)	
Museo Civico	(see 29)	
Museo dell'Opera Metropolitana	27	C5

Oratorio di San Bernardino	28	E3
Palazzo Chigi-Saracini	(see 13)	
Palazzo Comunale	29	D5
Palazzo delle Papesse	30	C5
Palazzo Piccolomini	31	D4
Palazzo Salimbeni	32	C3
Palazzo Spannocchi	33	C3
Palazzo Tantucci	34	C3
Palazzo Tolomei	35	C4
Pinacoteca Nazionale	36	C5
Porta Romana	37	F6
Santa Maria della Scala	38	C5
Scuola Leonarda da Vinci	39	C3
Società Dante Alighieri	40	C6
Torre del Mangia	(see 29)	
Università per Stranieri	41	E4

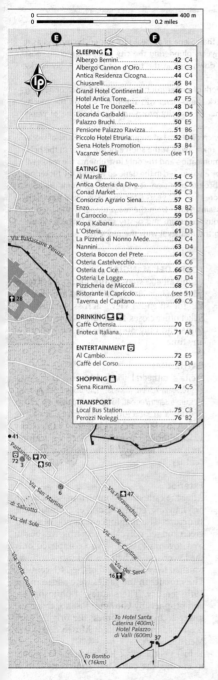

was a remarkable engineering feat and one of the tallest nonsecretarian towers in Italy.

Entry to the palazzo's ground-floor central courtyard is free. Adjacent is the entrance to the **Museo Civico** (☎ 0577 29 22 63; adult/student €7.50/4.50, museum & tower €12; ☼ 10am-6.15pm mid-Mar–Oct, 10am-5.30pm or 6.30pm Nov–mid-Mar), with a series of rooms containing frescoes by artists of the distinctive Sienese school. These frescoes are unusual in that they were commissioned by the governing body of the city, rather than the Church, and many depict secular subjects instead of the favoured religious themes of the time. As in other great buildings of Siena and elsewhere in the province (for example the Palazzo Comunale and Collegiata in San Gimignano), the decoration here tends to be rich and full, often with a foundation of deep-blue hues on the ceiling, leaving scarcely a millimetre uncovered.

Upstairs are five rather nondescript rooms filled with equally unarresting paintings, mostly by Sienese artists of the 16th to the 18th centuries. Check out the **Sala del Risorgimento** to your left with its more impressive late-19th-century frescoes serialising key events in the campaign to unite Italy.

Next is the **Sala di Balìa** (or Sala dei Priori). The 15 scenes depicted in frescoes around the walls recount episodes in the life of Pope Alexander III (the Sienese Rolando Bandinelli), including his clashes with the Holy Roman Emperor Frederick Barbarossa.

You then pass into the **Anticamera del Concistoro**, remarkable for the fresco (moved here in the 19th century) of *Santi Caterina d'Alessandria, Giovanni e Agostino* (Saints Catherine of Alexandria, John and Augustine), executed by Ambrogio Lorenzetti.

The following hall, **Sala del Concistoro**, is dominated by the allegorical ceiling frescoes of the Mannerist Domenico Beccafumi.

Back in the Anticamera del Concistoro, you pass to your right into the **Vestibolo** (Vestibule), whose star attraction is a bronze wolf, the symbol of the city. Next door in the **Anticappella** are frescoes of scenes from Greco-Roman mythology and history, while the **Cappella** (Chapel), contains a fine *Sacra Famiglia e San Leonardo* (Holy Family and St Leonardo) by Il Sodoma, and intricately carved wooden choir stalls.

The best is saved for last. From the Cappella, you emerge into the **Sala del Mappamondo** where you can admire the masterpiece of the

---

EXTREME PLUMBING

In 1556 Emperor Charles V apparently claimed that 'Siena is as beautiful under the ground as it is above it'. As he had spent the two previous years plundering the city and slaughtering most of its inhabitants, this observation did not go down well at the time. Yet his seemingly wacky observation had an element of truth.

Beneath Siena lies an incredible 24km network of underground tunnels and interconnecting passages dating back to the 13th century. Back then, Siena was the main city on the much-travelled route through northern Italy to Rome. As the city prospered, the shortage of water became critical.

The resulting underground tunnels were an incredible feat of engineering. Two teams of workers started from opposite directions: one some 16km away at the source of the water in the hills, the other underneath Siena. There was no communication and the only instruments the medieval builders had were plumb lines and pick axes. They also worked in the dark, apart from the flickering light of oil lamps. The tunnels were built with absolute precision, at a very low, constant gradient that kept the water flowing at a regular rate. More than 700 years later, the network of tunnels is still working, flowing into many of Siena's fountains. Water from the main tunnel is also used to cool the fridge of Nannini (see p248), the famous ice-cream and pastry shop; a fitting example of how Siena's history lives on, complementing the medieval with the modern.

---

entire building – Simone Martini's powerful and striking *Maestà* (Virgin Mary in Majesty) fresco, his earliest known work and one of the most important works of the Sienese school. Other large frescoes along the inside long wall depict famous Sienese victories.

The next room, the **Sala dei Nove** (or Sala della Pace), contains a three-panelled fresco series recently nominated by Francesco da Mosta as one of Italy's most interesting works of art. Painted by Ambrogio Lorenzetti, the compelling, didactic frescoes depict the *Effetti del Buon e del Cattivo Governo* (Allegories of Good and Bad Government), allegedly created as a constant reminder to those in power of the value of a committed republican government. The central Allegory fresco portrays scenes with personifications of Justice, Wisdom, Virtue and Peace, all unusually depicted as women, rendered along with scenes of criminal punishment and rewards for right-eousness. Set perpendicular from the Allegory are the frescoes *Effects of Good Government* and *Effects of Bad Government,* which hold intensely contrasting scenes set in the recog-nisable environs of Siena; the good, a sunlit, idyllic, serene city, with joyous, dancing citi-zens and a countryside filled with crops; and the bad, vices, widespread crime, disease and decimation.

Finish the visit by doing a little backtrack-ing and climbing the stairs to the **loggia**, which looks southeast over Piazza del Mercato and the countryside.

TORRE DEL MANGIA
Climb all 400 steps of this graceful **bell tower** (admission €7; ☼ 10am-7pm mid-Mar–Oct, to 4pm Nov–mid-Mar) for splendid views across the city. The ticket office closes 45 minutes before the tower shuts and only 30 people are allowed up at any time.

CATHEDRAL
Siena's **cathedral** (Piazza del Duomo; admission €3; ☼ 10.30am-7.30pm Mon-Sat, 1.30-6.30pm Sun Mar-Oct, 10.30am-6.30pm Mon-Sat, 1.30-5.30pm Sun Nov-Feb) is one of Italy's great Gothic structures. Building begun in 1196, and was largely completed by 1215, although work continued on features such as the apse and dome well into the 13th century.

Exterior
After the cathedral's completion, work began on changing, enlarging and embellishing the structure. The magnificent façade of white, green and red polychrome marble was begun by Giovanni Pisano – who completed only the lower section before his death – and was finished towards the end of the 14th century. The mosaics in the gables were added in the 19th century. The statues of philosophers and prophets by Giovanni Pisano, above the lower section, are copies; the originals are preserved in the adjacent Museo dell'Opera Metropolitana.

In 1339 the city's leaders launched a plan to enlarge the cathedral and create one of

Italy's largest places of worship. Known as the **Duomo Nuovo** (New Cathedral), the remains of this unrealised project are on Piazza Jacopo della Quercia, at the eastern side of the main cathedral. The daring plan, to build an immense new nave with the present cathedral becoming the transept, was scotched by the plague of 1348.

Interior

The cathedral's interior is truly stunning. Walls and pillars continue the black-and-white-stripe theme of the exterior, while the vaults are painted blue with gold stars. High along the walls of the nave is a long series of papal busts.

After looking up, look down…and you'll see the cathedral's most precious feature – the inlaid-marble floor, decorated with 56 glorious panels, by about 40 artists over the course of 200 years (14th to 16thcenturies), depicting historical and biblical subjects. The older, rectangular panels, including *Ruota della Fortuna* (Wheel of Fortune; 1372) and *Lupa senese e simboli delle città alleate* (The She-Wolf of Siena with the emblems of the confederate cities; 1373) are graffiti designs by unknown artists, both restored in 1864, created by chiselling into white marble and filling the holes with bitumen or mineral pitch. Domenico di Niccoló dei Cori was the first known artist to work on the cathedral, contributing several panels between 1413 and 1423, followed by renowned painter Domenico di Bartolo, who contributed *Imperatore Sigismundo in trono* (Emperor Sigismund Enthroned) in 1434. It wasn't until the tenures of director Alberto Aringhieri (1480–1504) and celebrated Sienese artist Domenico Beccafumi (1518–47) that the floor scheme saw swift, dramatic expansion. These later panels were done in more advanced multicoloured marble, inlaid with hexagon and rhombus frames. Unfortunately, all but a few are obscured by unsightly, protective covering, revealed only from 7 to 22 August each year.

Seek out the exquisite 13th-century marble and porphyry pulpit by Nicola Pisano, who was aided by his equally talented son, Giovanni. Intricately carved with vigorous, realistic crowd scenes, it's one of the masterpieces of Gothic sculpture. You can't inch as close as you might like as barriers keep you at a respectful distance. To shed a little light on the subject, stick coins into the machine

(€0.50 gets you a generous minute of illumination).

Other significant works of art include a bronze statue of St John the Baptist by Donatello, situated in a chapel off the north transept.

Libreria Piccolomini

Off the north aisle, the **Libreria Piccolomini** is another of the cathedral's great treasures. Pope Pius III built this compact hall to house the books of his uncle, Enea Silvio Piccolomini (see the boxed text, p271), who became Pope Pius II; only a series of huge choral tomes remains on display.

The walls of the hall have vividly coloured narrative frescoes by Bernardino Pinturicchio. They depict events in the life of Piccolomini, starting from his early days as a secretary to an Italian bishop on a mission to Basle, through to his ordination as pope and eventually his death in Ancona while trying to mount a crusade against the Turks.

In the centre of the hall is a group of statues known as the *Tre Grazie* (Three Graces), a 3rd-century Roman copy of an earlier Hellenistic work.

MUSEO DELL'OPERA METROPOLITANA

This **museum** (☎ 0577 28 30 48; Piazza del Duomo 8; admission €6; ⏰ 9.30am-7pm Mar-May & Sep-Nov, to 8pm Jun-Aug, 10am-5pm Dec-Feb), also known as Museo dell'Opera del Duomo, is next to the cathedral, in what would have been the southern aisle of the nave of the Duomo Nuovo. Among its great works of art, which formerly adorned the cathedral, are the 12 statues of prophets and philosophers by Giovanni Pisano that decorated the façade. Their creator designed them to be viewed from ground level, which is why they look so distorted as they crane uncomfortably forward.

On the 1st floor is Duccio di Buoninsegna's striking early-14th-century *Maestà* (Majesty), painted on both sides as a screen for the cathedral's high altar. The front and back have now been separated and the panels depicting the Story of Christ's Passion hang opposite the *Maestà*. Duccio's narrative genius is impressive. Take the lower half of the bottom big middle panel. In one 'shot', three scenes take place: Christ preaches to the Apostles in the Garden of Gethsemane; he then asks them to wait up for him; and then is portrayed while in prayer. In the half-panel above, he is kissed by Judas while Peter lops off a soldier's ear and the remaining Apostles flee.

To the right of the *Maestà*, a door leads into a back room with statues by Jacopo della Quercia, while on the left is a room with 19th-century illustrations of the entire collection of marble floor panels in the cathedral.

On the upper floors other artists represented include Ambrogio Lorenzetti, Simone Martini and Taddeo di Bartolo, and there's also a rich collection of tapestries and manuscripts.

For a great panoramic view – and a touch of physical exertion to counterbalance so much aesthetic exercise – haul yourself up the 131 steps that lead, via a very narrow, corkscrew stairway, to the **Panorama del Facciatone** (admission €6), at the top of the façade of the putative Nuovo Duomo. A combined admission ticket for the museum and panorama costs €10 and is valid for three days.

CRYPT

Just north of the cathedral and down a flight of steps is the **crypt** (admission incl audio guide €6; 9.30am-6.30pm), a room below the cathedral's pulpit discovered in 1999 during restoration work. After a period of clean-up and study – the room had been filled to the roof with debris in the 1300s and forgotten – it was opened to the public in 2003. The walls are completely covered with *pintura a secco* ('dry painting', better known as 'mural painting', as opposed to frescoes which are painted on wet plaster, making them more durable) dating from the 1200s. There's some 180 sq metre, depicting several biblical stories, including the Passion of Jesus and the Crucifixion.

BATTISTERO DI SAN GIOVANNI

Opposite the crypt is the **baptistry** (Baptistry of St John; Piazza San Giovanni; admission €3; 9.30am-7pm mid-Mar–Sep, 9am-6pm Oct, 10.30am-5pm Nov–mid-Mar). Its Gothic façade, although unfinished on the upper levels, is quite a remarkable extravagance in marble.

Inside, the ceiling and vaults are lavishly decorated with frescoes. The life of Jesus is portrayed in the apse of this oddly shaped rectangular baptistry. The one on the right showing Christ carrying the cross is of particular interest. If you look at the city from which it appears he and the crowd have come, it is hard to escape the feeling that among the imaginary buildings have been illustrated

Brunelleschi's dome and Giotto's Campanile in Florence. Could this be a nasty little anti-Florentine dig suggesting Siena's rival as the source of Christ's tribulations?

The centrepiece, literally and figuratively, is a marble font by Jacopo della Quercia, decorated with bronze panels in relief depicting the life of St John the Baptist. The panels, executed by several top-notch artists, include Lorenzo Ghiberti's *Baptism of Christ* and *St John in Prison*, and Donatello's *Herod's Feast*.

COMPLESSO MUSEALE DI SANTA MARIA DELLA SCALA

Originally a hospice for pilgrims and until quite recently a working hospital with almost a millennium of history, the **Santa Maria della Scala** (☎ 0577 22 48 11; Piazza del Duomo 2; admission €6; 10.30am-6.30pm Apr-Oct, to 4.30pm Nov-Mar) has as its main attraction the vivid, secular frescoes (quite a relief after so much spirituality all around town) by Domenico di Bartolo, lauding the good works of the hospital and its patrons.

Before entering the hospital proper, pass by the **Chiesa della Santissima Annunziata**, a 13th-century church remodelled two centuries later.

Turn right into the **Cappella del Manto**, decorated with frescoes; the most striking is by Beccafumi (1514) and portrays the *Meeting of St Joaquim and St Anna*, the supposed parents of the Virgin Mary.

You will pass into a long hall where, to the left, is the remarkable 14th-century **Sala del Pellegrinaio**, the pilgrim hall and subsequently the hospital's main ward. The bulk of its fresco series was done by di Bartolo in the 1440s. The first panel, by Il Vecchietta, depicts *gettatelli* (orphans) ascending to heaven. Taking in orphans was frequently one of the tasks of hospitals throughout Tuscany. Later panels show *balie* (wet nurses) suckling orphans and other needy children. One jolly panel depicts a doctor nodding off as his patient describes his symptoms.

Downstairs you'll find the **Fienile**, once storage space for the hospital. The original panelling of the Fonte Gaia (and a few replicas) is now housed here. Through the Fienile is the **Oratorio di Santa Caterina della Notte** (Oratory of St Catherine of the Night), a gloomy little chapel for sending up a prayer or two for the unwell upstairs.

MUSEO ARCHEOLOGICO

This **museum** (🕐 10.30am-6.30pm Apr-Oct, to 4.30pm Nov-Mar) is within Santa Maria della Scala. Most of the collection consists of pieces found near Siena, ranging from elaborate Etruscan alabaster funerary urns to gold Roman coins. In between you'll see some statuary, much of it Etruscan, a variety of household items, votive statuettes in bronze and even a pair of playing dice. The collection is well presented, and the surroundings – twisting, arched tunnels – perfectly complement it and are a cool blessing on stifling-hot summer days.

Admission to the museum is included in the price for Santa Maria della Scala.

PALAZZO DELLE PAPESSE

Change eras with a visit to this contemporary **art gallery** (🕿 0577 2 20 71; Via di Città 126; adult/child €5/free; 🕐 noon-7pm Tue-Sun) if you've had your fill of medieval religious art. The gallery houses a number of permanent pieces from the likes of Micha Ullman, Perino Vele and Antonio Catelani, mixed in with ever-changing exhibitions. The rooftop terrace has stunning views.

PALAZZO CHIGO-SARACINI

The magnificent curving Gothic façade of the **Palazzo Chigo-Saracini** (Via di Città) is in part a travesty, the result of 'restoration' in the 18th and 19th centuries to 're-create the medieval feel. From the tower, which is the genuine article apart from its brick crenellations, they say a young boy with particularly good eyesight watched the Battle of Montaperti in 1260 and shouted down details of the home side's progress against the Florentines to eager crowds in the streets below.

The palazzo is the headquarters of Accademia Musicale Chigiana (see p244).

PINACOTECA NAZIONALE

This **gallery** (🕿 0577 28 11 61; Via San Pietro 29; adult/child €4/free; 🕐 8.15am-7.15pm Tue-Sat, to 1.15pm Sun, 8.30am-1.30pm Mon), within the 14th-century Palazzo Buonsignori, displays the world's greatest concentration of Gothic masterpieces from the Sienese school. But the collection also demonstrates the subsequent gulf cleaved between artistic life in Siena and Florence in the 15th century. While the Renaissance flourished 70km to the north, Siena's masters and their patrons remained firmly rooted in the Byzantine and Gothic precepts that had stood them in such good stead from the early

13th century. Stock religious images and episodes predominate, typically pasted lavishly with gold and generally lacking any of the advances in painting, such as perspective, emotion or movement, that artists in Florence were exploring.

Start your tour on the 2nd floor where, in the first two rooms, you can see some of the earliest surviving pre-Gothic works from the Sienese school, including pieces by Guido da Siena. Rooms 3 and 4 are given over to a few works by Duccio di Buoninsegna and his followers. The most striking exhibits in Room 3 are Simone Martini's *Madonna della Misericordia* (Madonna of Mercy), in which the Virgin Mary seems to take the whole of society protectively under her wing, and his *Madonna col Bambino* (Madonna and Child).

The two brothers Pietro and Ambrogio Lorenzetti feature in Rooms 7 and 8, while the following three rooms contain works by several artists from the early 15th century.

Rooms 12 and 13 are mostly devoted to Giovanni di Paolo; a couple of his paintings show refreshing signs of a break from strict tradition. His two versions of the *Presentazione nel Tempio* (Presentation of Jesus in the Temple) have virtually no gold and introduce new architectural themes, a hint of perspective and a discernible trace of human emotion in the characters depicted.

Down on the 1st floor, the Sienese roll call continues and, although there are some exceptions, the interest starts to fade. Rooms meriting a visit include 27 to 32 and 37, which are dominated by works of the Mannerist Domenico Beccafumi and Il Sodoma. Particularly striking is Il Sodoma's *Cristo alla Colonna* (Christ Tied to the Pillar) in Room 31, where, in a particularly human touch, tears trickle down Jesus' cheeks.

CHIESA DI SANT'AGOSTINO

This 13th-century **church** (🕿 0577 38 57 86; Prato di San Agostino; admission €2.50; 🕐 11am-1.30pm & 2-5.30pm mid-Mar-Oct), a few streets south of the Pinacoteca Nazionale, was originally designed by the Dutch Vanvitelli, chief architect to the King of Naples. Its richly rococo interior dates from the 18th century, after the church had been gutted by fire. The second altar on the south aisle has a superb *Adoration of the Crucifix* by Perugino while the Piccolomini chapel's jewel is Il Sodoma's *Adoration of the Magi*.

CHIESA DI SAN DOMENICO

This imposing 13th-century Gothic **church** (Piazza San Domenico; 7.30am-1pm & 3-6.30pm) has been altered time and time again over the centuries.

The bare, barnlike interior is in keeping with the Dominican order's ascetic spirit. Near the entrance is the raised **Cappella delle Volte**, where Santa Caterina di Siena took her vows and, according to tradition, performed some of her miracles. In the chapel is a portrait of the saint painted during her lifetime.

In the **Cappella di Santa Caterina**, off the south aisle, are frescoes by Il Sodoma depicting events in Santa Caterina's life – and her head, in a 15th-century tabernacle above the altar. She died in Rome, where most of her body is preserved, but, in keeping with the bizarre practice of collecting relics of dead saints, her head was returned to Siena.

Another bit that managed to find its way here is her desiccated thumb, on grisly display in a small window box to the right of the chapel. Also on show is a nasty-looking chain whip with which she would apply a good flogging to herself every now and then for the well-being of the souls of the faithful.

CASA DI SANTA CATERINA

If you want more of Santa Caterina – figuratively speaking – visit **Casa di Santa Caterina** (☎ 0577 22 15 62; Costa di Sant'Antonio 6; admission free; 9am-6.30pm Mar-Nov, 10am-6pm Dec-Feb), where the saint was born and lived with her parents plus, says legend, 23 siblings. The rooms, converted into small chapels in the 15th century, are decorated with frescoes of her life and paintings by Sienese artists, including Il Sodoma. A crowded adjacent room contains some of St Catherine's personal effects. The lower-level bedroom, frescoed in 1893 by Alessandro Franchi, includes her untouched, nearly bare cell.

FORTEZZA MEDICEA

Northwest of the Chiesa di San Domenico, this **fortress**, also known as the Forte di Santa Barbara, is typical of those built in the early years of the grand duchy. The Sienese could not have been given a more obvious reminder of who was in charge than this Medici bastion, raised on the orders of Cosimo I de' Medici in 1560.

OTHER CHURCHES & PALAZZI

The 15th-century triple-arched balcony **Loggia dei Mercanzia**, where merchants used to plot deals, is just northwest of Il Campo. From here, strike east along Banchi di Sotto to pass **Palazzo Piccolomini**, a Renaissance palazzo housing the city's archives. Further east are the 13th-century **Basilica di Santa Maria dei Servi**, with frescoes by Pietro Lorenzetti in a chapel off the north transept, and the 14th-century **Porta Romana**.

North of Loggia dei Mercanzia on Banchi di Sopra, the 13th-century **Palazzo Tolomei** dominates Piazza Tolomei. Further north, Piazza Salimbeni is bounded by **Palazzo Tantucci**, Gothic **Palazzo Salimbeni** (prestigious head office of Monte dei Paschi di Siena bank), and the Renaissance **Palazzo Spannocchi**, from where 29 finely carved busts stare down at you from beneath the eaves.

Northeast of here, along Via dei Rossi, is **Chiesa di San Francesco**, with its vast single nave. It's suffered over the years – from a devastating 17th-century fire and use as army barracks. Beside the church is the 15th-century **Oratorio di San Bernardino** (☎ 0577 28 30 48; Piazza San Francesco 9; admission €3; 10.30am-1.30pm & 3-5.30pm mid-Mar–Oct), notable for its frescoes by Il Sodoma and Beccafumi, plus a small museum of religious art.

Courses

LANGUAGE & CULTURE

Scuola Leonardo da Vinci (☎ 0577 24 90 97; www.scuolaleonardo.com; Via del Paradiso 16) A reputable Italian-language school that offers supplementary cultural and culinary lessons.

Società Dante Alighieri (☎ 0577 4 95 33; www.dantealighieri.com; Via Tommaso Pendola 37) Offers courses in Italian language and culture.

Università per Stranieri (University for Foreigners; ☎ 0577 24 01 15; www.unistrasi.it; Via di Pantaneto 45) Offers various courses in Italian language and culture.

MUSIC

Accademia Musicale Chigiana (☎ 0577 2 20 91; www.chigiana.it; Via di Città 89) Offers classical music courses every summer as well as seminars and concerts performed by visiting musicians, teachers and students as part of the Settimana Musicale Senese (opposite).

Associazione Siena Jazz (☎ 0577 27 14 01; www.sienajazz.it; Piazza Libertà) Within the Fortezza Medicea. One of Europe's foremost institutions of its type, it offers courses in jazz.

Tours

Ecco Siena (☎ 0577 4 32 73) Runs city tours for groups and individuals. Group tours (€15; Monday to Saturday,

---

'MOM! CATHERINE'S CONSECRATING HER VIRGINITY TO JESUS AGAIN!!'

St Catherine of Siena (1347–80), copatron saint of Italy and one of only two female Doctors of the Church, was born in Siena, the 23rd child out of 25 (her twin sister died at birth). Like a true prodigy, she had a religious fixation at a very early age. She is said to have entertained plans to impersonate a man so she could be a Dominican friar and occasionally raced out to the road to kiss the place where Dominicans had walked.

At the dubious age of seven, she consecrated her virginity to Christ, much to her family's despair. At 18 she assumed the life of a Dominican Tertiary (lay affiliate) and, as wayward teens are wont to do, chose initially to live as a recluse in the family's basement, focused on devotion and spiritual ecstasy. She was noted for her ability to fast for extended periods, living only on the Blessed Sacrament, which as nutritionists might attest, probably contributed to a delirium or two. Catherine described one such episode as a 'mystical marriage' with Jesus. Feeling a surge of humanity (or possibly boredom), she emerged from her cloistered path and began caring for the sick and poor.

Another series of visions set in Hell, Purgatory and Heaven, compelled Catherine to take her work to the next level. Though it's said she didn't actually learn to write until near the end of her life, she began an ambitious and fearless letter-writing campaign – dictating up to three letters to three secretaries simultaneously – to all variety of influential people, including lengthy correspondence with Pope Gregory XI. She beseeched royalty and religious leaders for everything from peace between Italy's republics to reform within the clergy. This go-getting, early form of activism was considered highly unusual for a woman at the time and her no-holds-barred style, sometimes scolding cardinals and queens like naughty children, was gutsy by any standard. And yet, rather than being persecuted for her insolence, she was admired, her powers of persuasion often winning the day where so many others had failed.

She is said to have experienced the stigmata, but this event was suppressed as it was considered bad form at the time to associate the stigmata with anyone but St Francis.

Acting as an ambassador to Florence, she went to Avignon and was able to convince Pope Gregory XI to bring the papacy back to Rome after a seven-pope, 73-year reign in France. A few years later she was invited to Rome by newly elected Pope Urban VI to campaign on his behalf during the pope/anti-pope struggle (the Great Western Schism) where she did her best to undo the effects that his temper and shortcomings were having on Rome. This heroic, utterly exhausting effort likely contributed to her untimely death in 1380 at the age of 33.

Catherine's abundant postmortem accolades started relatively soon after her death when Pope Pius II canonised her in 1461. More recently, Pope Paul VI bestowed Catherine with the title of Doctor of the Church in 1970 and Pope John Paul II made her one of Europe's patron saints in 1999. Additionally, despite having received no formal education, her letters (over 300 have survived) are considered to be great works of Tuscan literature.

March to October) take around two hours and leave from outside the Chiesa di San Domenico at 3pm. Reserve at Siena Hotels Promotion (p246).

Hortibus (☎ 348 910 07 83; www.hortibus.com) Leads tours of private gardens and villas around Siena every Thursday and Saturday for €25 per person or €150 per group.

Treno Natura (☎ 0577 20 74 13; www.ferrovieturistiche.it; ☉ May, early Jun, Sep & Oct) A great way to see the stunning scenery of the Crete Senese, south of Siena. The line dates back to the 19th century but trains now run exclusively for tourists and are staffed by volunteers. The route loops from Siena, through Asciano, across the Val d'Orcia and Stazione di Monte Antico and back to Siena. Trains stop at Asciano and Monte Antico and connect with

the service from Florence. They only run for about 20 days a year so check the website or ask at the tourist office. Round-trip tickets cost €15 if you go by diesel, €25 if it's a steam train.

Festivals & Events

Settimana Musicale Senese Held in July and run by the Accademia Musicale Chigiana (opposite).

Il Palio The most spectacular event on the Sienese calendar, held in July and August each year. See the boxed text, p246.

Siena Jazz In July and August the city hosts this international festival promoted by the Associazione Siena Jazz (opposite) with concerts at the Fortezza Medicea and various sites throughout the city.

Estate Musicale Chigiana The Accademia Musicale Chigiana (p244) mounts this event in July, August and September. Concerts in the series are frequently held in the magnificent settings of the Abbazia di San Galgano (p252), about 20km southwest of the city, and Abbazia di Sant'Antimo (p269), near Montalcino. For information, call ☎ 0577 2 20 91.

Festa di Santa Cecilia In November a series of concerts and exhibitions takes place to honour Cecilia, patron saint of musicians.

Sleeping

Vacanze Senesi (☎ 0577 4 59 00; www.vacanzesenesi.it) has a representative in the tourist office who can arrange all forms of accommodation, or you can book on its website. Ditto **Siena Hotels Promotion** (☎ 0577 28 80 84; www.hotelsiena.com; Piazza San Domenico 5; 🕙 9am-8pm Mon-Sat). You can book online, or in person near the San Domenico church. There's an in-person €2 administration charge.

Accommodation can be difficult to find in summer – and is nearly impossible during the famous twice-yearly festival, Il Palio.

BUDGET

Siena Colleverde (☎ 0577 28 00 44; Via Scacciapensieri 47; per person/site €7.75/7.75; 🕙 mid-Apr–mid-Oct; 🚲) This camp site, 2km north of the historical centre, was going through a change of ownership

---

IL PALIO

This spectacular event, held twice yearly on 2 July and 16 August, in honour of the Virgin Mary, dates back to the Middle Ages and features a series of colourful pageants, a wild horse race around Piazza del Campo and much eating, drinking and celebrating in the streets.

Il Palio is one of very few major medieval spectacles of its type in Italy that has survived through the sheer tenacity of Sienese traditionalism. Most other displays of medieval folk tradition have in fact been brought back to life in the 20th century out of a combination of nostalgia and the urge to earn a few more tourist bucks. The Sienese place incredible demands on the national TV network, RAI, for rights to televise the event.

Ten of Siena's 17 town districts, or *contrade,* compete for the coveted *palio,* a silk banner. Each has its own traditions, symbol and colours, and its own church and *palio* museum. As you wander the streets you'll notice the various flags and plaques delineating these quarters, each with a name and symbol relating to an animal. On the downside, competition is so fierce that fist fights sometimes break out between *contrade* and Il Palio jockeys often live in fear from rival *contrade.* Scheming rivals have been known to ambush jockeys and even drug their horses.

On festival days Piazza del Campo becomes a racetrack, with a ring of packed dirt around its perimeter. From about 5pm, representatives of each *contrada* parade in historical costume, each bearing their individual banners.

The race is run at 7.45pm in July and 7pm in August. For not much more than one exhilarating minute, the 10 horses and their bareback riders tear three times around Piazza del Campo with a speed and violence that makes your hair stand on end.

Even if a horse loses its rider it is still eligible to win and, since many riders fall each year, it is the horses in the end who are the focus of the event. There is only one rule: riders mustn't interfere with the reins of other horses.

Book well in advance for a room and join the crowds in the centre of Piazza del Campo at least four hours before the start for a good view. Surrounding streets are closed off well before the race begins, except for Via Giovanni Dupré, which stays open right up until the flag drops. If you arrive late you can try your luck reaching the Piazza via this street – but don't count on it as everyone else has the same idea. If you prefer a more comfortable seat overlooking the race from one of the buildings lining the piazza, ask in the cafés and shops. They're as rare as hen's teeth but, if you do manage to find one, expect to pay around €220 for the privilege. If you can't find a good vantage point, don't despair – the race is televised live and then repeated throughout the evening on TV.

If you happen to be in town in the few days immediately preceding the race, you may get to see the jockeys and horses trying out in Piazza del Campo – almost as good as the real thing. Between May and October, **Cinema Moderno** (☎ 0577 28 92 01; Piazza Tolomei; admission €5.50; 🕙 10am-5pm) runs a mini-epic 20-minute film of Siena and Il Palio that will take your breath away.

when we passed by and was closed indefinitely. Call and confirm that they've reopened before arriving. To get there take bus 3 or 8 from Piazza Gramsci or Viale Tozzi.

Ostello Guidoriccio (☎ 0577 5 22 12; Via Fiorentina 89, Località Stellino; per person €14.30) All rooms are doubles at Siena's Hostelling International–affiliated youth hostel, about 2km northwest of the city centre. Regrettably, thin walls and the unremitting traffic on Via Fiorentina make for challenging sleeping conditions. Take bus 10, 15 or 35 from Piazza Gramsci, or bus 4 or 77 from the train station.

Hotel Le Tre Donzelle (☎ /fax 0577 28 03 58; Via delle Donzelle 5; s/d without bathroom €38/49, d with bathroom €60) Central, friendly and popular, this hotel was originally constructed as a tavern in the 13th century. Rooms are clean and simple and the shared bathrooms are spotless.

MIDRANGE

Albergo Cannon d'Oro (☎ 0577 4 43 21; www.cannondoro.com; Via dei Montanini 28; s €48-80, d €60-99, tr €77-128; P 🕮) Trim, attractive and excellent value. Don't be deterred by the golden cannon (the very one that gave the place its name) trained upon you as you debouch from a narrow alley to face the otherwise amicable reception desk. A few rooms have air-con and parking costs €15. Skip the breakfast.

Locanda Garibaldi (☎ 0577 28 42 04; Via Giovanni Dupré 18; d €75) Pro: a dozen metres from the spectacle of Piazza del Campo. Con: a dozen metres from the noise of Piazza del Campo. Rooms are big, bright, and furnished with a funky flair. The twinkly eyed, jovial host and his wife also run the well-patronised ground-floor restaurant (meals €20; closed Saturday).

Albergo Bernini (☎ 0577 28 90 47; www.albergobernini.com; Via della Sapienza 15; s with bathroom €55-78, d €75-85, d with shared bathroom €45-65; 🖳) This is a welcoming, family-run hotel (owner Mauro is a professional accordion player who often squeezes his box for guests). Its simple rooms may be a hair overpriced, but the tiny terrace has lovely views of the cathedral and the Chiesa di San Domenico. For space and views, choose room 11.

Palazzo Bruchi (☎ 0577 28 73 42; www.palazzobruchi.it; Via Pantaneto 105; s €75-90, d €85-150, all incl breakfast) Seven rooms in the 'ancient and noble' Landi-Bruchi family home in central Siena. Rooms vary in quality, but the hospitality of Maria Cristina and her daughter Camilla is warmly

consistent. There's a shared kitchen and a peaceful inner-courtyard. Breakfast is served in the rooms.

Piccolo Hotel Etruria (☎ 0577 28 80 88; www.hoteletruria.com; Via delle Donzelle 3; s/d/tr €53/86/114, s without bathroom €48) Another equally welcoming family hotel, just off Il Campo. The rooms are rather plain, with zero soundproofing, but there's a central light, airy sitting area and the location is outstanding.

our pick **Antica Residenza Cicogna** (☎ 0577 28 56 13; www.anticaresidenzacicogna.it in Italian; Via dei Termini 67; s/d €70/90, incl buffet breakfast; P 🕮 🖳) Springless beds, ornate frescoes, wi-fi and antique furniture make this central option, with a mere five rooms, justifiably popular. Class exudes from prominent elements such as the four-poster bed and the breakfast space (enormous buffet style), to subtle touches such as elaborate, thick-framed mirrors. Reception has limited core hours (8am to 1pm), so arrange your arrival in advance. Parking €15.

Hotel Antica Torre (☎ 0577 22 22 55; www.anticatorresiena.it; Via Fieravecchia 7; d €90-113; 🕮) With only eight rooms, you'll need to reserve weeks in advance. This is a snug place with exposed beams and brickwork, tucked into a 16th-century tower hidden down a side street. Haul yourself to the top floor for the best views. There's also a second property, Hotel Palazzo di Valli (see below).

Chiusarelli (☎ 0577 28 05 62; www.chiusarelli.com; Viale Curtatone 15; s €70-85, d €95-125, all incl breakfast; P 🕮 🖳) Functioning continuously since its construction in 1870, this hotel has a pleasant, spacious breakfast room and attractive, though somewhat dark, bedrooms. The rear ones are for lovers of quiet and lucky football fans – they overlook the stadium where Siena plays home matches on alternate Sundays in season. It has a popular restaurant (meals €20) where you'll be dodging elbows to find a seat among the locals.

Albergo-Residence Borgo Grondaie (☎ 0577 33 25 39; www.borgogrondaie.com; Via delle Grondaie 15; s €85-100, d €97-145, incl breakfast; 6-person apt without breakfast €185-219; P 🕮 🖳 🐾) A couple of kilometres north of the centre, is a former farm and olive oil producer. Rooms are simple and tasteful, with lots of terracotta and earthy colours. The exquisite apartments are in the former stables. There is a special-needs unit, saltwater pool and free bicycles for guests.

Hotel Palazzo di Valli (☎ 0577 22 61 02; Via Piccolomini 135; d €120-130; P) A snazzier property by the same people as Hotel Antica Torre. It's located 600m outside Porta Romana, with the added perk of free parking.

TOP END

Hotel Santa Caterina (☎ 0577 22 11 05; www.hscsiena .it; Via Piccolomini 7; s €85-115, d €98-175, all incl breakfast; **P** **X**) This renovated 18th-century elegant villa, just outside the city walls, is a stone's throw beyond the Porta Romana. It's a tranquil haven: its 22 rooms are tastefully furnished, the breakfast room is light and airy and there's a lovely garden with open views to the surrounding hills. Parking is €15.

Villa Scacciapensieri (☎ 0577 4 14 41; www.villascac ciapensieri.it; Via Scacciapensieri 10; s €85-116, d €130-245, all incl breakfast; **P** **X** **🖳** **🍴**) Around 2.5km north of Siena is a 19th-century villa with carved wooden ceilings, oil paintings, antiques, formal gardens and an old family chapel. There are tennis courts, bicycles to rent and wi-fi available.

Pensione Palazzo Ravizza (☎ 0577 28 04 62; www .palazzoravizza.com; Pian dei Mantellini 34; s/d/tr incl breakfast €140/180/260; **P** **X** **🖳**) *Pensione* is far too modest a title for this intimate, sumptuous place. Occupying a delightful Renaissance palazzo, frescoed ceilings and antique furniture coexist with flat-screen TVs and comprehensive wi-fi coverage. Service is courteous and efficient, there's a small, leafy garden and the Ristorante il Capriccio (opposite) is worth crossing town for.

Grand Hotel Continental (☎ 0577 5 60 11; www .royaldemeure.com; Banchi de Sopra 85; s/d €295/390; **🖳**) Siena's only five-star hotel has taken over the gloriously ornate, richly frescoed Palazzo Gori Pannilini. If nothing else, poke your nose into the magnificent 1st-floor reception room and reward yourself with a drink in the stylish ground-floor wine bar, open to all-comers. Wi-fi in lobby only.

Eating

According to the Sienese, most Tuscan cuisine has its origins here, though Tuscans elsewhere may well dispute such boasting. Among many traditional dishes are *ribollita* (a rich vegetable soup), *panzanella* (summer salad of soaked bread, basil, onion and tomatoes) and *pappardelle con sugo di lepre* (ribbon pasta moistened with hare ragù). *Panforte* (literally, 'strong bread') is a rich cake of almonds, honey and candied fruit, originally created as sustenance for Crusaders to the Holy Land.

BUDGET

Nannini (Banchi di Sopra 22) Always crowded, this is something of a Sienese institution, baking its finest cakes and serving good coffee with speed and panache.

Kopa Kabana (Via dei Rossi 54) Flout the places with enviable locations and be rewarded here with absurd mountains of Siena's freshest gelato, starting at €1.70 for a small.

Conad Market (Galleria Metropolitan, Piazza Matteotti; 🕙 8.30am-8.30pm Mon-Sat, 9am-1pm & 4-8pm Sun) Self-caterers can stock up on piazza picnic nosh here.

MIDRANGE

our pick **L'Osteria** (☎ 0577 28 75 92; Via dei Rossi 79/81; meals €25) We promised a local we wouldn't put this one in the book. We lied. It was just too good. Plus the place was half-filled with tourists when we visited, so it's not exactly a secret. No nonsense, but savoury dishes at prices locals will pay. Pop over to Kopa Kabana for something *dolce* afterward.

Osteria da Cice (☎ 0577 28 80 26; Via San Pietro 32; meals €25, tourist menus €12; 🕙 Tue-Sun) In the hands of a friendly team, reflecting its mainly youthful clientele, this is the place for an informal, relaxed meal. The menu has plenty of vegetarian options among its *primi piatti* (first courses).

Osteria Castelvecchio (☎ 0577 4 95 86; Via di Castelvecchio 65; meals €27; 🕙 Mon-Sat) Highly regarded by locals, this eatery has a couple of attractive bare-brick rooms. Rumbling tummies should opt for the constantly changing *menù degustazione* (€25). It's also a good spot for veggies, with at least four meatless dishes normally on offer.

Osteria Boccon del Prete (☎ 0577 28 03 88; Via San Pietro 17; meals €28) A small, reasonably priced, typical Sienese place, offering a daily changing menu. Pumpkin soup with almonds and toasted bread, chestnut gnocchi with truffle sauce, and sirloin beef slices with roasted potatoes and olive oil are on the permanent menu. The dessert menu will annihilate all self-control, particularly the white-chocolate mousse with coffee sauce.

La Pizzeria di Nonno Mede (☎ 0577 24 79 66; Camporegio 21; meals €29) Drop a coin into the well in the floor, then dive into the €7.80 buffet lunch or choose from the exhaustive pizza menu. The reasonably priced menu has a consistent spread of Tuscan favourites and the fantastic view from the terrace is also reliably Tuscan.

CENTRAL TUSCANY

Taverna del Capitano (☎ 0577 28 80 94; Via del Capitano 6-8; meals €29; ☒ Wed-Mon) A grand little spot for local food with friendly service. Specialities include *zuppa di farro* (barley soup) and *ossobuco al sienese* (marrowbone stew). The tables outdoors are pleasant in summer.

Il Carroccio (☎ 0577 4 11 65; Via del Casato di Sotto 32; meals €32; ☒ closed Tue dinner & Wed) Exceptional pasta and exceptionally busy, so arrive early for lunch and call ahead for dinner. Try the *pici*, a kind of thick spaghetti typical of Siena, followed by the *tegamate di maiale* (pork with fennel seeds) and select something a little special from the long and carefully nurtured wine list. The restaurant is a member of the Slow Food Movement (see p21) – always a good sign.

Al Marsili (☎ 0577 4 71 54; Via del Castoro 3; meals €33-38; ☒ Tue-Sun) One of the city's classiest restaurants, here you'll find white-smocked waiters dishing up traditional Sienese cuisine such as *pici all'aglione* (fresh Sienese pasta, with a garlic and tomato sauce). The restaurant also offers more innovative dishes such as stuffed *panzerotti* with truffle.

Ristorante il Capriccio (☎ 0577 28 17 57; Pian dei Mantellini 32; meals €35-40; ☒ dinner) The restaurant of Pensione Palazzo Ravizza (opposite) offers fine cuisine and the chance to eat in its wood-panelled dining room or outside in the garden.

Antica Osteria da Divo (☎ 0577 28 43 81; Via Franciosa 29; meals €37) Here you'll find background jazz that's as smooth as the walls are rough-hewn. At the lower, cellar level you're dining amid Etruscan tombs. The inventive menu includes dishes such as rolled pork, stuffed with black cabbage and truffle, followed by girth-widening goodies such as vanilla and pistachio pie with raspberry sauce.

TOP END

Enzo (☎ 0577 28 12 77; Via Camollia 49; meals €37-40, tasting menus without wine €35-55) Classic pictures of Siena decorate the walls, while classy settings decorate the tables. A variety of tasting menus relieve one from the need to choose from the lengthy menu, while curiosities like the 'deconstructed cannoli' will keep you seated for dessert. Dinner reservations a must.

Osteria Le Logge (☎ 0577 4 80 13; osterialelogge@tin.it; Via dei Porrione 33; mains €40-45; ☒ Mon-Sat) This place changes its menu of creative Tuscan cuisine almost daily. In the downstairs dining room, once a pharmacy, bottles are arranged in cases, floor to ceiling, like books in

a library (there are over 18,000 more in the cellars so you won't go thirsty); there's also a large streetside terrace.

Drinking

Enoteca Italiana (☎ 0577 28 84 97; Fortezza Medicea; ☒ noon-1am Tue-Sat, to 8pm Sun) Within the fortress walls, the former munition cellars have been artfully transformed into a classy *enoteca* that carries over 1500 labels. The Italian wine display includes some dusty *reservas,* the oldest dating back to 1944.

Caffè Ortensia (Via di Pantaneto 95) Among several pleasantly poky bars along Via di Pantaneto, this place is small, crowded and much favoured by students, both local and visiting.

Entertainment

As elsewhere in Italy, the big dance venues are generally well outside town.

Caffè del Corso (Banchi di Sopra 25) During the day, this is the place for an espresso and croissant. At night the action moves upstairs to the moody plum-coloured music bar.

Al Cambio (Via di Pantaneto 48; ☒ closed Sun) One of the few dance spots in Siena where you can indulge in a little frenetic all-night air-punching.

Shopping

Via di Città is a chic shopping street where you can buy ceramics, food items, antiques, jewellery and so on. If you're after clothes, go window-shopping along Banchi di Sopra with its stylish boutiques and designer emporia.

Pizzicheria de Miccoli (☎ 0577 28 91 64; Via di Città 93-5) Richly scented, this is a great place to stock up on picnic fodder. Its windows are festooned with sausages, piled-up cheeses and porcini mushrooms by the sackful.

Consorzio Agrario Siena (Via Pianigiani 13) A rich emporium of local food and wines.

Siena Ricama (☎ 0577 28 83 39; Via di Città 61) Promotes the crafts of Siena, in particular embroidery.

Siena's **Wednesday market** (☒ 7.30am-1pm) spreads all around Fortezza Medicea and seeps towards the Stadio Comunale. One of Tuscany's largest, it's great for foodstuffs and cheap clothing, or just aimless browsing.

Getting There & Away
BUS

The hub for buses is Piazza Gramsci. Tra-in and SITA express buses race up to Florence

(€6.50, 1¼ hours, up to 30 daily). Other regional Tra-in destinations include San Gimignano (€5.20, 1¼ hours, 10 daily either direct or changing in Poggibonsi), Montalcino (€3.20, 1½ hours, six daily), Poggibonsi (€3.60, one hour, up to 10 daily), Montepulciano (€4.50, 1¾ hours) and Colle di Val d'Elsa (€2.50, 30 minutes, hourly), with connections for Volterra. Other destinations in the Crete Senese and Chianti area include San Quirico d'Orcia (€3.20), Pienza (€3.60) and Grosseto (€6.20).

SENA buses run to/from Rome (€18, three hours, eight daily) and Milan (€25.50, 4¼ hours, three daily) and there are seven buses daily to Arezzo (€5, 1½ hours).

Both **Tra-in** (☎ 0577 20 42 46) and **Sena** (☎ 0577 28 32 03; www.sena.it) have ticket offices underneath the piazza, where there's also a left-luggage office.

CAR & MOTORCYCLE

For Florence take the SS2, the *superstrada* (expressway), or the more attractive SS222, also known as the Chiantigiana, which meanders its way through the hills of Chianti.

TRAIN

Siena isn't on a major train line and buses are generally a better alternative. By train, change at Chiusi for Rome and at Empoli for Florence. Trains arrive at Piazza F Rosselli, north of the city centre.

Getting Around
BICYCLE & SCOOTER

Perozzi Noleggi (☎ 0577 28 83 87; www.perozzi.it; Via dei Gazzani 16-18) rents mountain bikes (per day/week €10/50) and 50cc scooters (per day/week €26/150). If there's no one in the showroom, pop round the corner to Via del Romitorio 5.

BUS

Tra-in operates city bus services (€0.90). Bus 8, 9 and 10 run between the train station and Piazza Gramsci.

CAR & MOTORCYCLE

Cars are banned from the town centre, though visitors can drop off luggage at their hotel, then get out (don't forget to have reception report your licence number or risk receiving a 'souvenir' fine). Park illegally inside the city and you'll be towed away quicker than

you can yell 'Where the *&@!'s my car?' Try the large car parks at the Stadio Comunale and around the Fortezza Medicea, both just north of Piazza San Domenico, or the one at Il Campo, south of the centre, though even here locating a spot is like running the Palio.

TAXI

For a taxi, call ☎ 0577 4 92 22.

AROUND SIENA
Le Crete

Southeast of Siena, this area of rolling clay hills scored by steep ravines is a feast of classic Tuscan images – bare ridges topped by a solitary cypress tree and hills silhouetted one against another as they fade into the misty distance. The area of Le Crete changes colour according to the season – from the creamy violet of ploughed clay to the green of young wheat, which then turns to gold.

Hire a car or bike in Florence or Siena and spend a few days pottering around Le Crete, a word in the Tuscan dialect meaning clay. And should your visit coincide, book your passage on the spectacular Treno Natura (p245), which runs on certain days in summer.

ASCIANO

This pretty little hamlet has a trio of small museums dedicated to Sienese art and Etruscan finds in the area. It's most easily reached along the scenic SS438 road running southeast from Siena; the occasional slow local train from Siena also passes through. Asciano is at the heart of Le Crete, so the journey there and beyond (such as south to the Abbazia di Monte Oliveto Maggiore) is a treat in itself. There's a small **tourist office** (☎ 0577 71 88 11; Corso Matteotti 78; 🕙 10.30am-1pm & 3-6pm Tue-Sat, 10.30am-1pm Sun Apr-Oct, 10.30am-1pm & 3-6pm Fri & Sat, 10.30am-1pm Sun Nov-Mar).

ABBAZIA DI MONTE OLIVETO MAGGIORE

This 14th-century **monastery** (☎ 0577 70 76 11; admission free; 🕙 9.15am-noon & 3.15-6pm Apr-Oct, to 5pm Nov-Mar) is still a retreat for around 40 monks. Though the congregation was founded in 1313 by John Tolomei, construction didn't begin on the monastery until 1393. Visitors come here for the wonderful fresco series in the Great Cloister, painted by Luca Signorelli and Il Sodoma, illustrating events in the life of the ascetic St Benedict, founder of the Benedictine order.

Signorelli, reputed to be a widely respected, kind man, had previously done minor work on the Sistine Chapel and would later produce his masterpiece *Resurrection of the Flesh* in the Chapel of San Brizio, in Orvieto's Duomo. He started work in the monastery in 1497, producing nine frescoes. In stark contrast, Il Sodoma, born Giovanni Antonio Bazzi, was purported to have been something of a character – dressing flamboyantly, keeping a 'Noah's Ark' of unusual pets, singing original ditties of dubious taste and, according to Giorgio Vasari in the book *The Lives of the Artists*, earning the moniker 'Sodoma' 'because he always surrounded himself with boys and beardless youths whom he loved beyond measure'. He added 17 frescoes, completing the series around 1505.

The fresco series wraps around the four-sided Great Cloister, illuminated naturally by an inner courtyard. To the right of the entrance, on the west wall, the fresco cycle begins with Il Sodoma's work and continues along the south wall of the cloisters. The nine frescoes by Signorelli line the east side and Il Sodoma picks up again on the northern wall. The decorations on the pillars between some of Il Sodoma's frescoes are among the earliest examples of 'grotesque' art, copied from decorations found in the then-newly excavated Domus Aurea of Nero in Rome.

The baroque interior of the **church** adjoining the cloister is a pleasingly sober play of perspective and shape. It has further works by Il Sodoma and some wonderfully intricate marquetry choir stalls.

From the monastery, head for **San Giovanni d'Asso**, where there's an interesting 11th-century church with a Lombardic-Tuscan façade, and a picturesque hamlet with the remains of a castle. Continue on to Montisi and the pretty village of **Castelmuzio**, its entrance lined with chestnut trees, to take a look at the 16th-century **Chiesa di Santa Maria** with its Romanesque Gothic façade. Along a side road just outside Castelmuzio is the abandoned **Pieve di Santo Stefano in Cennano**, a 13th-century church.

Opened in 2001, **La Locanda della Moscadella** (☎ 0577 66 53 10; www.lamoscadella.it; Castelmuzio; d incl breakfast €120; 🖵) is a former 16th-century farmhouse that has been resurrected as a secluded hotel, restaurant and wine bar with sublime views. The venue has just unveiled a new wellness centre, with sauna, Turkish bath, 'cryomassage', sun track and sea-salt treatment.

Around 2km past Castelmuzio on the road to Pienza is the 14th-century monastery of **Sant'Anna in Camprena** (☎ 0578 74 80 37), one of the settings for the film *The English Patient*, with some lovely frescoes by Il Sodoma in the **refectory** (admission free; 🕑 9.30am-12.30pm & 3-6pm mid-Mar–Oct).

The route from Monte Oliveto Maggiore to Pienza runs almost entirely along a high ridge, offering great views of Le Crete.

MONTISI

Little more than a one-street, medieval blip capping a steep hill some 20km southeast of Asciano, Montisi has an allure that speaks to a certain disposition, particularly its expat artist community. So retiring it's almost comatose, the abundance of activities in town and the surrounding area is remarkable, ranging from English movies shown every Friday at **Cinema Hall** (🕑 Sep-May), to contemporary art exhibitions, to eight-day ballooning tours. Get a taste of the possibilities at www.montisi.com.

You can't miss **La Locanda di Montisi** (☎ 0577 84 59 06; www.lalocandadimontisi.it; Via Umberto I 39; s/d/tr incl breakfast €60/90/110; 🖵), bang in the centre of a 200m long town. All seven rooms are warm and tastefully rustic and the most searing day can't penetrate the cool cellar cantina. Not far away is **Taverna Montisi** (☎ 0577 84 51 59; www .tavernamontisi.com; Via Umberto I 3; meals €25), with a varying menu dependent on the seasons and organic farmers in the immediate area. Roberto, the force behind the food, is something of a Montisi tourism facilitator, coordinating accommodations, cheese tastings, horseback riding, wine tours and emergency dental appointments, to name a few.

BUONCONVENTO

On first approaching Buonconvento down the SS2 highway, you could be forgiven for thinking it a large roadside rest stop. Lying perfectly flat in a rare stretch of plain, the low-slung fortified walls of this farming centre hide a quiet little town of medieval origins. One of its historical moments came when the Holy Roman Emperor Henry VII, having shortly before captured the town, died here in August 1313 and so put an end to any hopes the Empire might have had of reasserting direct control over Tuscany.

The **Museo della Mezzadria Senese** (☎ 0577 80 90 75; Via Tinaia del Taja; admission €2; 🕑 10am-6pm Tue-Sun), with its lifesize figures and antique farm tools and machinery, offers a multimedia presentation of what life was like living off the land until quite recently.

You might want to slip into the local **Museo d'Arte Sacra** (☎ 0577 80 71 90; Via Soccini 18; adult/child €3.50/free; ☾ 10am-1pm & 3-6pm Tue-Sun Apr-Sep, 10am-1pm & 3-5pm Sat & Sun Oct-Mar). It contains religious art collected in the town and from neighbouring churches and hamlets.

Abbazia di San Galgano & Around

About 20km southwest of Siena on the SS73 is the ruined 13th-century **San Galgano abbey** (☎ 0577 75 67 00; admission free; ☾ 8am-7.30pm), one of the country's finest Gothic buildings in its day and now a ruin that still speaks strongly of its past. The monks of this former Cistercian abbey were among Tuscany's most powerful, forming the judiciary and acting as accountants for the *comuni* (municipalities) of Volterra and Siena. They presided over disputes between the cities, played a significant role in the construction of the cathedral in Siena and built themselves an opulent church.

As early as the 14th century, Sir John Hawkwood, the feared English mercenary, sacked the abbey on at least two occasions. By the 16th century the monks' wealth and importance had declined and the church had deteriorated to the point of ruin, and in 1786 the bell tower simply collapsed, as did the ceiling vaults a few years later.

The great, roofless, stone and brick monolith stands silent in the fields. Come on a rainy winter's day and you feel more like you are in France or England, surrounded by glistening green fields and confronted by this grey ruin, its style strongly reminiscent of French Gothic architecture.

Next door to the church are what remain of the monastery buildings, as well as a brief stretch of cloister housing a small **tourist office** (☎ 0577 75 67 38; ☾ 10.30am-7pm Easter-Oct).

The Accademia Musicale Chigiana in Siena sponsors concerts at the abbey during summer (see p246).

On a hill overlooking the abbey is the tiny, round Romanesque **Cappella di Monte Siepi**. This is the site of the original Cistercian settlement – from it came the impulse to build the great abbey below. Inside the chapel are badly preserved frescoes by Ambrogio Lorenzetti depicting the life of local soldier and saint, San Galgano, who had a vision of St Michael on this site and lived his last years here as a

hermit. A real-life 'sword in the stone' is under glass in the floor of the chapel, plunged there, legend has it, by San Galgano to indicate his renunciation of worldly life.

The bus service between Siena and Massa Marittima passes nearby.

BAGNI DI PETRIOLO

About halfway along the SS223 highway between Siena and Grosseto, a side road leads down to the hot sulphur springs of **Bagni di Petriolo**. Steaming spring water cascades into a few small natural basins. Anyone can come and sit in them, and there's usually a motley assortment of permanent campers making use of the natural shower.

Val d'Elsa
MONTERIGGIONI

This famous walled medieval stronghold is just off the SS2, about 12km north of Siena.

First raised in 1203 as a forward defensive position against Florence, the walls and towers today are the most complete example of such a fortified bastion in Tuscany. Seven of the 14 towers were reconstructed in the 20th century but you have to peer pretty closely to make out which ones. According to descriptions by Dante – a writer not averse to a little hyperbole – they were considerably higher when the Florentines had reason to fear them and their Sienese defenders.

Monteriggioni has real charm but it's in danger of being overheritaged to appeal to the tsunami of tourists that flows in each summer's day.

Hotel Monteriggioni (☎ 0577 30 50 09; www.hotel monteriggioni.net; Via Primo Maggio 4; s/d incl breakfast €120/230; P ✗ ☐ ☒) was originally two stone houses, now fused together. The interior is lavishly decorated with antiques, apart from the sparkling-new bathrooms, and all rooms have picture-postcard views. There's the added perk of a small pool within the lovely gardens, bordered by the original city walls. The hotel is open between March and December.

our pick Borgo Stomennano (☎ 0577 30 40 33; www.stomennano.it; q per week €900-1000; ☐ ☒), is a sprawling unforgettable property 2km outside Monteriggioni. This historic collection of farmhouses dating from the 1600s has been converted into apartments, furnished and decorated with an amazing collection of heirlooms dating back hundreds of years –

children under 14 are not permitted due to the delicate nature of these items. Though geared for large groups (six to 32 people) and events, couples are welcome during select periods. Self-cater or request full board. Special touches include an infinity pool, welcome bottles of wine with personalised labels and a private trail from the property through undulating fields to Monteriggioni.

Ristorante Il Pozzo (☎ 0577 30 41 27; Piazza Roma 2; meals €40; ☘ closed Sun dinner & Mon) is on the main square and passed daily by invading hordes but 'The Well' retains its individuality and character, offering delicious food, including homemade desserts such as the *dulce di ricotta* (sweet ricotta cheese) and *zuppa Inglese* (trifle with holy wine, fresh cream and melted chocolate). There's a pleasant patio for dining alfresco.

COLLE DI VAL D'ELSA
pop 20,230

All that most visitors do here is change buses for Volterra. That's a shame because Colle has long been Italy's major centre for fine glass and crystal production and, unburdened by any notable church, museum or work of art, the place has kept its character as a rural market town. The old one-street town up on its hill is fun for its own sake and for the views. Down below, the **Friday market** in and around Piazza Arnolfo is a vast bustling affair selling everything from great wheels of cheese to frilly knickers.

A **tourist office** (☎ 0577 92 13 34; Piazza Arnolfo 9; ☘ 11am-7.45pm, closed Sun afternoon) is in the main square of **Colle Bassa**, the lower town, sharing space with the bus station ticket office. Between March and October, it offers a **crystal tour** (€20) with visits to glass-blowing, shaping, cutting and engraving workshops and crystal showrooms.

The most engaging part of town is historic **Colle Alta**, perched up on a ridge. An elevator deep in the hillside eases the journey between the lower to upper sections of the city. Its **tourist office** (☎ 0577 92 27 91; proloco.colle@tin.it; Via Campana 43; ☘ 10am-1pm & 2-6pm Mon-Sat, 10am-1pm & 3-6pm Sun) is run by amiable people determined to answer any question. Park in the free lot near Porta Nova at the western end of town.

At the eastern end of Via del Castello, there's a medieval *casa torre* (tower house; No 63), birthplace of Arnolfo di Cambio, architect of Florence's Palazzo Vecchio. Piazza del Duomo, overshadowed by the cathedral's bell tower with its giant clock, is about halfway along.

Nearby are three small museums. Admission to each costs €3 or you can buy a combined ticket for €6. The **Museo Archeologico** (☎ 0577 92 29 54; Piazza Duomo 42; ☘ 10.30am-12.30pm & 4.30-7.30pm Tue-Sun May-Oct, 3.30-5.30pm Tue-Fri, 10.30am-12.30pm Sat & Sun Nov-Apr) is on the square. The **Museo Civico** and **Museo d'Arte Sacra** (☎ 0577 92 38 88; Via del Castello 31; ☘ 10am-noon & 4-7pm Tue-Sun May-Oct, 3.30-6.30pm Tue-Sun, 10am-noon Sat & Sun Nov-Apr) share premises. Most interesting is the Museo d'Arte Sacra, with some worthwhile paintings by Sienese masters.

In Colle Bassa you'll find the **Museo del Cristallo** (☎ 0577 92 41 35; www.cristallo.org; Via dei Fossi 8a; admission €3; ☘ 10am-noon & 4-7.30pm Tue-Sun Apr-Oct, 3-7pm Tue-Fri, 10am-noon & 3-7pm Sat & Sun Nov-Mar), which illustrates the history and production of crystal and displays some stunning pieces (leave your toddler at home). All descriptions are in Italian.

La Vecchia Cartiera (☎ 0577 92 11 07; cartiera@ chintiturismo.it; Via Oberdan 5-9; s €60-81, d €75-121, all incl buffet breakfast; [P] [☒]) was once just that. But The Old Papermill has been so comprehensively overhauled that you'd scarcely guess it. This hotel has all the extras and is well situated

---

NAILING THE NAIL

There are some 30 reputedly authentic nails from the one true cross around Tuscany. But Colle di Val d'Elsa's has a special distinction. Brought back from the Holy Land during the Crusades, so the story goes, it was given to a local priest, who placed it in the town's otherwise quite unremarkable cathedral. It disappeared or was stolen several times (on one occasion washed downstream by spring floods) but always made its independent way back.

Nowadays it undergoes a degree of protection worthy of Fort Knox. Under lock and key – actually four locks with four differing keys held by four different citizens – it's only allowed out of the cathedral once a year, on the second Sunday of September, when it's taken in procession around Colle Alta in, appropriately, a finely wrought crystal vessel.

for an overview of the town's Friday market. The multilingual owner is a charmer and the breakfast buffet more lavish than most. Parking costs €7.

Hotel Arnolfo (☎ 0577 92 20 20; www.hotelarnolfo .it; Via Campana 8; s/d incl breakfast €56/80) The only hotel in Colle Alta has 32 comfortable, sizable rooms. A buffet breakfast is served in the warmly decorated cellar, with coffee *barista* at the ready. The hotel is closed in February.

our pick **Il Frantoio** (☎ 0577 92 36 52; www.risorante-ilfrantoio.com; Via Castello 40; meals €38) There's cheaper places in town, but this is the only place where you'll be pampered, from the complimentary champagne and small tasting appetizer to the main events of liver-filled ravioli with walnut sauce and duck (very rare) with fruit sauce, roasted potatoes and a spinach tartlet. Tears of joy have been known to accompany the chocolate cake. Set in a multiroom cellar and equipped with an original grain grinder and grape press. A fixed-price lunch menu is available.

Hourly buses run to/from Siena (€2.50, 30 minutes) and Florence (€4.70, 1¼ hours). Up to four **Compagnia Pisana Trasporti** (CPT; ☎ 800 570 530) connecting buses head west to Volterra daily, except Sunday.

CASOLE D'ELSA & AROUND

Casole d'Elsa, a quiet fortified backwater, was a key part of Siena's western defences against Volterra and Florence during the Middle Ages. Little remains to detain you but those with romantic tastes and a Swiss bank account could stick to the tiny road that winds south out of town, call by pretty hilltop **Mensano**, then swing east to **Pievescola**.

Relais La Suvera (☎ 0577 96 03 00; www.lasuvera .it; Pievescola; d incl breakfast €385-560; ☾ mid-Apr–Oct; ⓟ ⌘) is a 12th-century former fortress and palace, still run by the Marchese Ricci family. The décor is heavily brocaded opulence with tapestries, dark and enormous oil paintings, rococo mirrors and four-poster beds. There is a health centre with a Jacuzzi bubbling out of the palace's original well.

Il Colombaio (☎ 0577 94 90 02; Località Il Colombaio; meals €50-55; ☾ closed Tue lunch & Mon), opposite vineyards with a distant view of Casole, is an elegant Michelin-starred place with stained glass, paintings and a canopy of chandeliers. Set menus range from €30 to €49. It takes wine seriously – 1400 varieties at last count, including Japanese, Israeli and a Bodegas Vega Sicilia

'90 for €500. The menu includes such goodies as quail salad and *pecorino* cheese soufflé with pear slices in chestnut honey sauce. They also have apartments to rent (doubles €80).

POGGIBONSI
pop 28,700

WWII managed to take care of what little was interesting about Poggibonsi, which takes line honours as one of the ugliest places in central Tuscany. It has a distinct port town feel, minus the port – lots of people passing through, and doing so quickly. If you're travelling by bus between Florence (€4.30, 50 minutes, half-hourly) or Siena (€3.60, one hour, up to 10 daily), heading for San Gimignano or Volterra, you can't avoid the place.

There's a **tourist office** (☎ 0577 93 51 13; ☾ 9am-1pm & 3-6.30pm) outside the train station that will do an admirable job of selling the area's meagre attractions, including what's left of the village and castle of Staggia Senese, the Fortezza Medicea and some walking/biking routes.

Albergo Italia (☎ 0577 93 61 42; www.albergo-italia .it; Via Trento 36; s 35-40, d €50-60, all incl breakfast; ⓟ ⌘), across the piazza from the train station, has simple, bright rooms – some with noisy terraces – with hostel-quality beds and tiny all-in-one toilet/showers. The staff are very pleasant, there's an attached café and you'll likely be allowed access to the reception computer for quick emailing.

SAN GIMIGNANO
pop 7400

As you crest the hill coming from the east, the 14 towers of this walled town look like a medieval Manhattan. And when you arrive you might well feel that half of Manhattan's population has moved in. Within easy reach of both Siena and Florence, San Gimignano is a tourist magnet. Come in winter or early spring to indulge your imagination a little; in summer you'll spend your time dodging fellow visitors. Even then though, you'll discover a different, almost peaceful San Gimignano, once the last bus has pulled out.

There's good reason for such popularity. The towers, which once numbered 72, were symbols of the power and wealth of the city's medieval families. San Gimignano delle Belle Torri (meaning 'of the Fine Towers' – though they're actually almost devoid of design and rather dull unless sheer height impresses you) is surrounded by lush, productive land and the setting is altogether enchanting. The area around San Gimignano is famous for the cultivation of saffron; see p69.

History

Originally an Etruscan village, the town was named after the bishop of Modena, San Gimignano, who is said to have saved the city from Attila the Hun. It became a *comune* in 1199, but fought frequently with neighbouring Volterra. Internal battles between Ardinghelli (Guelph) and Salvucci (Ghibelline) families over the next two centuries caused deep divisions. Most towers were built during this period – in the 13th century, one *podestà* (town chief) forbade the building of towers higher than his own 51m pile.

In 1348 plague wiped out much of the population and weakened the nobles' power, leading to the town's submission to Florence in 1353. Today, not even the plague would deter the summer swarms.

Orientation

Piazzale dei Martiri di Montemaggio, at the southern end of the town, lies just outside the medieval wall and next to the main gate, Porta San Giovanni. Via San Giovanni heads northwards to central Piazza della Cisterna and the connecting Piazza del Duomo. From here the other major thoroughfare, Via San Matteo, extends to the principal northern gate, Porta San Matteo.

Information

Lo Spuntino (☎ 0577 90 72 99; Via XX Settembre 4b; per hr €4.50; ⊙ 10am-8pm Apr-Oct, 2-7pm Nov-Feb) Has a few internet points.
Post office (Piazza delle Erbe 8)
Tourist office (☎ 0577 94 00 08; www.sangimignano .com; Piazza del Duomo 1; ⊙ 9am-1pm & 3-7pm Mar-Oct, 9am-1pm & 2-6pm Nov-Feb) Hires out audio guides of town (€5).

Sights

Start in triangular Piazza della Cisterna, named after the 13th-century cistern at its centre. The square is lined with houses and towers from the 13th and 14th centuries. In the Piazza del Duomo, the Collegiata (basilica) looks across to the late-13th-century **Palazzo del Podestà** and its tower, the **Torre della Rognosa**. The Palazzo Comunale, right of the basilica, is the town hall.

COLLEGIATA

Access to the town's Romanesque **basilica** (adult/child €3.50/1.50; ⊙ 9.30am-7.30pm Mon-Sat, 12.30-5pm Sun Apr-Oct, 9.30am-5pm Mon-Sat, 12.30-5pm Sun Nov–mid-Jan & Mar) is up a flight of steps from Piazza del Duomo. Its bare façade belies the remarkable 14th-century frescoes that stripe the interior walls like some vast medieval comic strip, stretching amid the black-and-white striped arches and columns that separate the three naves.

A fresco by Taddeo di Bartolo covers the upper half of the rear wall and depicts the Last Judgment, while the lower half is dominated by Benozzo Gozzoli's rendering of the martyrdom of St Sebastian. Still facing the rear wall, on the upper-left side is a fresco depicting *Paradiso* (Heaven) and on the upper-right *Inferno* (Hell). Both are by Taddeo di Bartolo, who seems to have taken particular delight in presenting the horrors of the underworld. Remember that many of the faithful in those times would have taken such images pretty much at face value.

Facing the altar, along the left (north) wall, are scenes from Genesis and the Old Testament by Bartolo di Fredi, dating from around 1367. The top row runs from the creation of the world through to the forbidden fruit scene. This in turn leads to the next level and fresco, the expulsion of Adam and Eve from the Garden of Eden, which has sustained some war damage. Further scenes include Cain killing Abel, the story of Noah's ark and Joseph's coat. The last level picks up this story with the tale of Moses leading the Jews out of Egypt, and the story of Job.

On the right (south) wall are scenes from the New Testament by the school of Simone Martini, completed in 1336. Again, the frescoes are spread over three levels, starting in the six lunettes at the top. Commencing with the Annunciation, the panels proceed through episodes such as the Epiphany, the presentation of Christ in the temple and the massacre of the innocents on Herod's orders. The subsequent panels on the lower levels summarise the life and death of Christ, the Resurrection and so on. Again, some have sustained damage, but most are in good condition.

The **Cappella di Santa Fina**, off to the right, has a pair of naive and touching frescoes by Domenico Ghirlandaio depicting events in the life of the saint and a quite superb alabaster and marble altar picked out in gold.

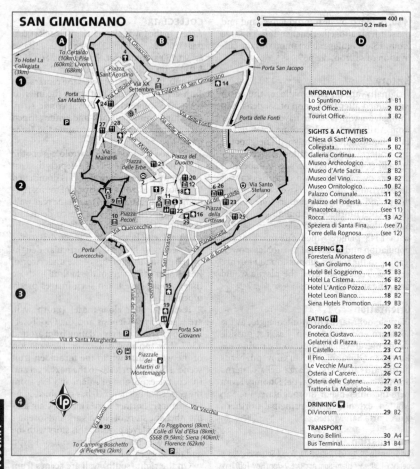

SAN GIMIGNANO

INFORMATION	
Lo Spuntino	1 B1
Post Office	2 B2
Tourist Office	3 B2

SIGHTS & ACTIVITIES	
Chiesa di Sant'Agostino	4 B1
Collegiata	5 B2
Galleria Continua	6 C2
Museo Archeologico	7 B1
Museo d'Arte Sacra	8 B2
Museo del Vino	9 B2
Museo Ornitologico	10 B2
Palazzo Comunale	11 B2
Palazzo del Podestà	12 B2
Pinacoteca	(see 11)
Rocca	13 A2
Speziera di Santa Fina	(see 7)
Torre della Rognosa	(see 12)

SLEEPING	
Foresteria Monastero di San Girolamo	14 C1
Hotel Bel Soggiorno	15 B3
Hotel La Cisterna	16 B2
Hotel L'Antico Pozzo	17 B2
Hotel Leon Bianco	18 B2
Siena Hotels Promotion	19 B3

EATING	
Dorando	20 B2
Enoteca Gustavo	21 B2
Gelateria di Piazza	22 B2
Il Castello	23 C2
Il Pino	24 A1
Le Vecchie Mura	25 C2
Osteria al Carcere	26 C2
Osteria delle Catene	27 A1
Trattoria La Mangiatoia	28 B1

DRINKING	
DiVinorum	29 B2

TRANSPORT	
Bruno Bellini	30 A4
Bus Terminal	31 B4

MUSEO D'ARTE SACRA

Across the square, the **Museo d'Arte Sacra** (☎ 0577 94 03 16; Piazza Pecori 1; adult/child €3/1.50; ☺ 9.30am-7.30pm Mon-Fri, 9.30am-5pm Sat, 12.30-5pm Sun Apr-Oct, 9.30am-5pm Mon-Sat, 12.30-5pm Sun Nov–mid-Jan & Mar) has some fine works of religious art, including a collection of medieval painted wooden statues, vestments, hangings, crosses and finely illuminated manuscripts culled, in the main, from the town's churches. Those who specialise in medieval religious objects will appreciate the items made from precious metals, including beautifully crafted chalices and thuribles (censers), as well as some exquisitely embroidered textiles. One curiosity is Sebastiano Mainardi's *Il Volto Santo Adorato* on the ground floor, where two hooded fig-

ures, looking suspiciously like KKK members, kneel at the feet of a smartly dressed Jesus on the cross.

PALAZZO COMUNALE

San Gimignano's other principal sight is this seat of secular power, which was founded in 1288, expanded in the 14th century and with a neogothic façade tacked on in the late 19th century.

From the internal courtyard climb the stairs to the **Pinacoteca** (☎ 0577 99 03 12; Piazza del Duomo; adult/child museum & tower €5/4; ☺ 9.30am-7pm Mar-Oct, 10am-5.30pm Nov-Feb).

In the main room, the **Sala di Dante**, the great poet addressed the town's council, imploring it to join a Florentine-led Guelph League. You can't miss the *Maestà*, a masterful 1317 fresco by Lippo Memmi depicting the enthroned Virgin Mary and Christ child with angels and saints. Other frescoes portray jousts, hunting scenes, castles and other medieval goings-on.

Upstairs, the collection of medieval religious works includes a crucifix by Coppo di Marcovaldo, notable for its age (c 1261) and quality, said to be superior to those of Giotto, and a pair of remarkable *tondi* (circular paintings) by Filippino Lippi.

Also on this level, there's a small frescoed room. Opinion is divided on what these frescoes, showing wedding scenes, are all about. It all looks like great fun, with the newlyweds taking a bath together and then hopping into the sack.

Climb up the palazzo's **Torre Grossa** for a spectacular view of the town and surrounding countryside.

MUSEO DEL VINO

In an unmarked gallery just outside the town's fortress is San Gimignano's **wine museum** (☎ 0577 94 12 67; Parco della Rocca; admission free; 🕙 11.30am-6.30pm Thu-Mon, 3-6.30pm Wed Mar-Oct). A sommelier is on hand to lead an informed – and paying – tasting of some of the choice local white wines. This is a one-man show – when the sommelier is sick or on holiday, the place unceremoniously shuts.

MUSEO ARCHEOLOGICO & SPEZIERA DI SANTA FINA

There are actually two **museums** (☎ 0577 94 03 48; Via Folgore da San Gimignano 11; adult/child both museums €3.50/2.50; 🕙 11am-5.30pm mid-Mar–Dec) and a gallery in this complex. The Speziera section includes ceramic and glass storage vessels from the 16th-century Speziera di Santa Fina, a reconstructed 16th-century pharmacy and herb garden. Many are beautifully painted and still contain curative concoctions. Follow your nose to the side room in Gallery 7, called 'the kitchen', which is filled with herbs and spices used for elixirs. All descriptions are in Italian.

Beyond is a small archaeological museum divided into Etruscan/Roman and medieval sections with exhibits found locally.

The museum also houses a good modern art gallery that in itself merits a visit. Permanent works include the distinctive swirly abstracts of Renato Guttuso and some excellent oils on canvas by Raffaele de Grada.

OTHER SIGHTS

Just west of the Piazza del Duomo, the **Rocca** is the crumbling shell of the town's fortress with great views across the valley, a small playground – and not much else.

Due south of the fort is the **Museo Ornitologico** (☎ 0577 94 13 88; Via Quercecchio; adult/child €1.50/1; 🕙 11am-5.30pm Apr-Sep). Its mournful collection of stuffed birds dates back to 1886 and certainly looks it.

At the northern end of the town is the **Chiesa di Sant'Agostino** (Piazza Sant'Agostino; 🕙 7am-noon & 3-7pm Apr-Oct, 7am-noon & 3-6pm Nov-Mar), which has a Benozzo Gozzoli fresco cycle in the apse depicting the life of St Augustine.

Housed in the city's old theatre, **Galleria Continua** (☎ 0577 94 31 34; www.galleriacontinua.com; Via del Castello 11; admission free; 🕙 2-7pm Tue-Sat) shows its collection of contemporary art by famous artists at virtually every major international art fair. It rarely represents Italian artists, so why they've kept this peculiar location in San Gimignano is something of a mystery. Or maybe it's a trend. The new gallery is in Beijing. Exhibitions change approximately every two months.

Tours

If you'd prefer to sip your Vernaccia di San Gimignano on the spot, the tourist office organises vineyard visits (€26). Two-hour tours leave at 11am on Tuesday and 5pm on Thursday from June to October. Advance reservations are essential.

Sleeping

In high summer San Gimignano can be as unpromising for accommodation as Christmas Eve in Bethlehem. But a couple of organisations will help to find you a roof.

Siena Hotels Promotion (☎ 0577 94 08 09; www .hotelsiena.com; Via San Giovanni 125; 🕙 closed Tue & Thu mornings & Sun) will book hotels and some very affordable *affittacamere* (rooms for rent) via its website or for callers-in (€2 surcharge for the latter). The tourist office, for its part, will reserve a wider range of *affittacamere* and also *agriturismi* (tourism accommodation on farms) if you call by in person.

BUDGET

Camping Boschetto di Piemma (☎ 0577 94 03 52; www .boschettodipiemma.it; per car/tent/person €3.30/7.30/9.30; ☺ Easter-Oct) Located at Santa Lucia, 2km south of town, this is the nearest camp site. Buses stop right outside.

   Foresteria Monastero di San Girolamo (☎ 0577 94 05 73; monasterosangimignano@gmail.com; Via Folgore da San Gimignano 26-32; per person €25; Ⓟ) Run by friendly Benedictine nuns, this is an excel-lent budget choice with basic but spacious, comfortable rooms with bathrooms, sleeping two to five people. Breakfast is €3. Ring ahead as it is perpetually booked. If you don't have a reservation, arrive between 9am and 12.30pm or between 3pm and 5.45pm and ring the monastery bell (not the Foresteria one, which is never answered).

MIDRANGE

Two highly recommended hotels flank Piazza della Cisterna, the main square. In both, you pay a little more for superb views.

   Hotel La Cisterna (☎ 0577 94 03 28; www.hotel cisterna.it; Piazza della Cisterna 24; s €60-78, d €85-95, tr €110-128, all incl breakfast; ✖ 🖳) Located in a splendid 14th-century building with vaulted

---

CHEAPER THAN WATER

It's true, a glass of house wine in an Italian restaurant will usually undercut the price of a bot-tle of water. You really have no choice but to imbibe. Since you're saving all that money, you'll be able to splash out and order a special glass now and again. Save those occasions for the following top drops.

'It kisses, licks, bites, thrusts and stings.' That's how Michelangelo, clearly drawing upon the purple end of his palate, described **San Gimignano's Vernaccia** white wine. Smooth and aro-matic with a slightly bitter aftertaste and pale golden yellow in colour, it was Italy's first DOC wine and the second white to be awarded DOCG (see p74). But these are only its most recent accolades. It's been around, though scarcely unsung, for centuries. Dante in his *Divine Comedy* banished Pope Martin IV to purgatory because of it, Boccaccio fantasised about flowing streams of cool Vernaccia, Pope Paul III reputedly bathed in it and the ever-demure St Catherine of Siena used it as medicine.

Vino Nobile di Montepulciano dates back to 1350, and is noted in documents illustrating the terms and conditions governing trade and the exportation of area wines in the Politian Archives. Pope Paul III – presumably after towelling off from a good soak in Vernaccia – gushed about this red in his late 16th-century poem 'Bacchus in Tuscany', and Francesco Redi described it as the 'king of all wines' in his 1685 poem 'Bacco in Toscana'. It was granted the description of 'noble' in the second half of the 18th century, about the same time that Voltaire was dropping the name in his 1759 novel *Candide*. More recent admirers have included the American presidents Martin Van Buren and Thomas Jefferson. Currently some 250,000 cases of Vino Nobile di Montepulciano are produced each year, more than might be deemed 'noble', but still few enough to make a bottle a special occasion.

Brunello di Montalcino ranks among the world's top wines. Collectors pay hundreds of dol-lars for a respectable bottle at auction. The price tag skyrockets into the thousands for select bottles from the 1940s and a bottle of the Biondi-Santi 1955 Brunello, voted as one of the top dozen wines of the century, could put a small nation's budget into a deficit. 'Brunello' is the name used for a handful of mutations of the sangiovese grape found around Montalcino, the result of horticultural tinkering by Clemente Santi and his grandson, Ferruccio Biondi-Santi, in the mid-19th century. Brunello almost immediately developed an exalted reputation, its grapes coming from select boutique vineyards, creating a product known for its borderline outlandish exclusivity and price as much as for its extraordinary quality. It was the first wine appellation in Italy to be granted the coveted DOCG ranking in 1970. Total annual Brunello production, grown from grapes almost entirely within a 26-sq-km radius around Montalcino, is about 350,000 cases – not even equal to a medium-sized winery.

ceilings and modest chandeliers. Be sure to request a room with a view of the square or the valley or risk getting one facing a dull courtyard. Nearly 100 years in business, it offers truly 21st-century comfort in quiet, spacious rooms.

Hotel Leon Bianco (☎ 0577 94 12 94; www.leonbianco.com; Piazza della Cisterna 13; s €65-80, d €85-140, tr €110-150, all incl breakfast; ▨ ▣) Faces Hotel La Cisterna across the square and also occupies a 14th-century mansion. This smoothly run hotel is equally welcoming and friendly with a ground-floor abundance of plants, pretty inner courtyard, breakfast patio, billiard table and fitness room. Wi-fi (extra charge) is available in common spaces.

Hotel Bel Soggiorno (☎ 0577 94 03 75; www.hotelbelsoggiorno.it; Via San Giovanni 91; d incl breakfast €90-130; ▨ ▣) With an upbeat décor, every room here is different, but each has lots of colour. Try to go for one with a countryside view. The restaurant (meals €40, set menus €38) has received rave reviews from readers. The hotel is closed in January and February.

Hotel L'Antico Pozzo (☎ 0577 94 20 14; www.anticopozzo.com; Via San Matteo 87; s €80-100, d €110-135, tr €145-160, all incl breakfast; ▨ ▣) Named after the old, softly illuminated *pozzo* (well), just off the lobby. Each room has its own personality, with thick stone walls, high ceilings, wrought-iron beds, frescoes, antique prints and peach-coloured walls. Room 20 has a magnificent domed ceiling. The hotel is closed the first two weeks of November and all of January. Wi-fi is €3 per hour.

TOP END

Hotel La Collegiata (☎ 0577 94 32 01; www.lacollegiata.it; Località Strada 27; s €120-180, d €210-345; ℗ ▨ ☒) A serious money-no-object place, you'll need a car to get here as it's outside town. A former Franciscan convent, its formal gardens are magnificent and are surrounded by parkland, while the rooms are conservative yet elegant.

Eating
BUDGET

Enoteca Gustavo (☎ 0577 94 00 57; Via San Matteo 29; snacks & wine from €2.50) There isn't much elbow space inside, so go for one of the outside tables if you can. Snacks include bruschetta and a plate of cheese with honey to go with your choice from the impressive selection of wines.

Gelateria di Piazza (☎ 0577 94 22 44; Piazza della Cisterna 4; ☽ Mar–mid-Nov) As the pictures around the wall attest, many celebrities have closed their lips around one of Gelateria di Piazza's rich ice creams ('all the family thought the ice cream was delicious' attested one Tony Blair). Master Sergio uses only the choicest ingredients: pistachios from Sicily and cocoa from Venezuela. There's a variant based on Vernaccia, the local wine, and, if you want to be more adventurous, saffron cream.

Each Thursday morning there's a **produce market** (Piazza della Cisterna & Piazza del Duomo).

MIDRANGE

Le Vecchie Mura (☎ 0577 94 02 70; www.vecchiemura.it; Via Piandornella 15; meals €30; ☽ dinner Wed-Mon) This is a wonderful spot, especially if you snap up a terrace table on a warm summer's night. The food competes with the phenomenal view of rolling green hills and the wine list has more than a dozen varieties of Vernaccia di San Gimignano. Choose from a delicious selection of *primi piatti*, such as *gnocchi con tartufo e formaggio* (gnocchi with truffles and cheese), and you can't go wrong with the perfectly prepared beef options. Book ahead to guarantee that panorama.

Osteria al Carcere (☎ 0577 94 19 05; Via del Castello 5; soups €8, meals €30-35; ☽ closed Thu lunch & Wed) A fine *osteria* that offers great food at moderate prices. The reassuringly brief menu has a half-dozen soups, including *zuppa di farro e fagioli* (local grain and white bean soup) and creative flashes like *tacchina al pistacchi e arance* (turkey with pistachios and orange sauce).

Osteria delle Catene (☎ 0577 94 19 66; osteriadellecatene.oster@tin.it; Via Mainardi 18; menù degustazione €13-31, meals €33-38; ☽ closed Wed & mid-Dec–Feb) The windows are plastered with the guidebook accolades it has justifiably received. The brick-barrelled interior is softly lit while the menu is heavy on strong meats – hare, boar, duck and rabbit. Alongside many Tuscan stalwarts and saffron experimentation such as the *zuppa medievale*, there's the *spaghetti dell'Ostria* (spaghetti with zucchini, sausages and chilli pepper in puréed sauce) and a small, but sublime carrot and leek soufflé.

Il Castello (☎ 0577 94 08 78; enotecailcastello@iol.it; Via del Castello 20; meals €35; ☽ Mar–mid-Jan) Both wine bar and restaurant, this place has a delightful patio with views and an all-brick, glass-domed courtyard. Most dishes are macho-meaty, like the frighteningly large *bistecca alla fiorentina* (grilled T-bone steak) and *cinghiale alla sangimignanese con polenta* (wild boar with polenta and tomato salad), though there's less macho fallbacks like the *pennette* with broccoli, wild mushrooms and saffron.

Trattoria La Mangiatoia (☎ 0577 94 15 28; Via Mainardi 5; meals €36-40; ☖ Wed-Mon Feb-Oct) A highly regarded trattoria serving tempting, regional fare like the small, but tasty *saccottini di pecorino al tartufo* (ravioli filled with potatoes and *pecorino* cheese with truffle sauce). With candles flickering and classical music in the background, share it with that special someone. Or hold hands after dark on the delightful summer patio.

our pick **Il Pino** (☎ 0577 94 04 15; Via Cellolese 8-10; meals €37-42; ☖ Fri-Wed) The atmosphere here is spruce, vaulted and airy. Service is friendly and attentive and the menu, which includes several truffle-based specialities, is a winner. The *raviolone di pecorino delle crete con lingua stufata e carote e porri all'aneto* (sheep's milk cheese ravioli with stewed meat, carrots and leeks) may be the most singular pasta adventure in Tuscany. The desserts, all confectioned on the premises, are dinner's final temptation.

Dorando (☎ 0577 94 18 62; www.ristorantedorando.it; Vicolo dell'Oro 2; mains €55-60; ☖ daily Easter-Oct, Tue-Sun Oct-Easter) Recognised by the Slow Food Movement, Dorando runs a classic five-course menu with dishes based on authentic Etruscan recipes such as carrot dumplings with zucchini, and *pecorino* blue cheese with a purée of shallots. The atmosphere is swanky yet cool, with intimate corners and works of art.

Drinking

DiVinorum (Piazza della Cisterna 30; ☖ 11am-midnight daily Mar-Oct, Fri-Sun Nov-Feb) Housed in cavernous former stables is this cool wine bar run by local lads. In summer, sip your drink on the tiny outdoor terrace with stunning valley views.

Getting There & Around
BUS

Buses arrive in Piazzale dei Martiri di Montemaggio, beside Porta San Giovanni. Services run to/from Florence (€5.90, 1¼ hours, 12 daily) and Siena (€5.20, one to 1½ hours, 10

ROSSELLA BRACALI

Rossella Bracali works at Galleria Continua (p257).

Since most of your artists are non-Italian you could be located anywhere, so why San Gimignano? Why not in San Gimignano? Why not in a town with such a long tradition of art? Galleria Continua was founded in 1990 by Mario Cristiani, Lorenzo Fiaschi and Maurizio Rigillo with the intention – evident in the name – to give continuity to contemporary art in a landscape rich with the signs of ancient art. The gallery seeks to act as a bridge between past and present, looking for connections between current Italian research and the language of the international circuit, by bringing important but lesser known artists into Italy and by helping and promoting young Italian artists abroad.

On the subject of 'eccentric' locations, what made you choose Beijing as the location for your new gallery? Our first contact with Chinese culture was during the solo exhibition Field of Synergy (2000) by Chen Zhen, a Chinese artist living in Paris since 1986. Subsequently, we decided to open a gallery in China because we were completely fascinated by what we saw and experienced during our first visit to Beijing in April 2004, when we participated in the first international contemporary art fair and visited the incredible 798 Art Zone. We felt the desire to be there while many things are happening in the art scene. Many galleries opened in Beijing because they were working with Chinese artists, but what we want to do is exactly the opposite: show Western artists in China. In this way we would like to open an exchange that will let the West get closer to China.

We know Giovanni Ozzola is from Florence, do you represent any other Tuscan artists? We have had other Italian artists that have a relationship with Tuscany: Luca Pancrazi was born at Figline Valdarno near Florence, Loris Cecchini lives and works from Prato and Beijing.

Considering that you represent a number of major artists ranging from high-concept to formal works, other than fame, is there a relationship to the variety of artists that you represent? The high quality of their research and work but primarily the passion of artists such as Daniel Buren, Anish Kapoor, Ilya Kabakov, Mona Hatoum to exhibit in such 'eccentric' galleries!

DETOUR: SAN GIMIGNANO TO VOLTERRA

Instead of driving the heavily trafficked SS68 between San Gimignano and Volterra, choose this back route that passes through some stunning countryside and potential picnic areas. Turn left out of the San Gimignano car park (just outside Porta San Giovanni). At 2.3km, just past Hotel San Michele, turn left again at the signposted roundabout heading for Montaione and Gambassi. Carry on along this road through green rolling valleys, wooded areas and vineyards. At 6.8km, beyond the turn, take a left (signed 'Volterra 15km', though it's actually 22km, but who's counting?). After around 10km – 10 *actual* kilometres – turn right onto the SS68 for the final stretch into town.

daily). A few are direct but most require a change at Poggibonsi. The tourist office carries timetables.

For Volterra (€4.30, 1½ hours, four daily except Sunday), you need to change in Colle di Val d'Elsa, and maybe also in Poggibonsi, which has the closest train station.

CAR & MOTORCYCLE
From Florence or Siena, take the SS2 to Poggibonsi, then the SS68 via Colle di Val d'Elsa. From Volterra, take the SS68 east and follow the turn-off signs north to San Gimignano.

There are car parks (per hour €2 or per day €5 to €15) outside the city walls, and beside and below Porta San Giovanni. There's free parking in the new parts of town, just northwest of the old centre, but this is quite a hike and competition is fierce.

Bruno Bellini (☎ 0577 94 02 01; www.bellinibruno.com; Via Roma 41) rents mountain bikes (per day €15) and scooters (per day from €31).

VOLTERRA
pop 11,400

A nippy 29km drive from San Gimignano, Volterra's well-preserved medieval ramparts give the windswept town a proud, forbidding air – particularly if you're trying to drive up to your hotel to drop off your luggage (forget it). Where San Gimignano has its towers, Volterra has its modest archaeological sites,

more-extensive network of mysterious alleys to explore and higher calf-blasting stone stairways to scale – all that and slightly more elbowroom. The surrounding gentle Tuscan countryside provides the perfect contrast.

People looking for that perfect alabaster figurine for their garden, or simply wanting to see alabaster artists in action, will have plenty of shops to choose from and the local collection of Etruscan artefacts is arguably unmatched.

History
The Etruscan settlement of Velathri was an important trading centre and senior partner of the Dodecapolis. It is believed that as many as 25,000 people lived here in its Etruscan heyday. Partly because of the surrounding inhospitable terrain, the city was among the last to succumb to Rome – it was absorbed into the Roman confederation around 260 BC and renamed Volaterrae.

The bulk of the old city was raised in the 12th and 13th centuries under a fiercely independent free *comune*. The city first entered into Florence's orbit in 1361, but it was some time before Florence took full control. When this domination was first threatened, Lorenzo Il Magnifico made one of his few big mistakes and created lasting enemies in the people of Volterra; in 1472 he marched in and ruthlessly snuffed out every vestige of potential opposition to direct Florentine rule.

Since Etruscan times, Volterra has been a centre of alabaster extraction and workmanship. During the Middle Ages, its quarries lay fallow for several centuries until their soft, semitransparent, easily worked stone again became a popular material for sculpture during the Renaissance.

Orientation
Whichever of the four main gates you use to enter Volterra, the road will lead you to central Piazza dei Priori.

Information
Web & Wine (p265) also has web access.

Enjoy Café (Piazza Martiri della Libertá 3; per hr €3) Has wi-fi and a loaner laptop for those not packing wi-fi-capable devices.

Post office (Piazza dei Priori)

Tourist office (☎ 0588 8 72 57; www.volterratur.it; Piazza dei Priori 19-20; ☼ 10am-1pm & 2-6pm) Offers a free hotel-booking service and rents out a good town audio guide (€5).

Sights

PIAZZA DEI PRIORI & AROUND

Piazza dei Priori is ringed by austere medieval mansions. The 13th-century **Palazzo dei Priori** (Piazza dei Priori; admission €1; 10.30am-5.30pm mid-Mar–Oct, 10am-5pm Sat & Sun Nov–mid-Mar), the oldest seat of local government in Tuscany, is believed to have been a model for Florence's Palazzo Vecchio. Highlights are a fresco of the Crucifixion by Piero Francesco Fiorentino on the staircase, the magnificent cross-vaulted council hall and a small antechamber on the 1st floor giving a bird's-eye view of the piazza below.

The **Palazzo Pretorio** is from the same era. From it thrusts the **Torre del Porcellino** (Piglet's Tower), so named because of the wild boar protruding from its upper section.

The **cathedral** (Piazza San Giovanni; 8am-12.30pm & 3-6pm) was built in the 12th and 13th centuries. Highlights include a small fresco, the *Procession of the Magi* by Benozzo Gozzoli, behind a terracotta nativity group tucked away in the oratory at the beginning of the north aisle. An exquisite 15th-century alabaster tabernacle by Mino da Fiesole rises above the high altar. Laterally and overhead, the black-and-white marble banding and Renaissance coffered ceiling, gilded and gleaming, both make their mark.

Just west of the cathedral is the 13th-century **baptistry** with a small marble font by Andrea Sansovino. On the west side of Piazza San Giovanni, the porticoed **Ospedale di Santa Maria Maddalena** was once a foundlings hospital. Nearby, the **Museo Diocesano d'Arte Sacra** (0588 8 62 90; Via Roma 1; 9am-1pm & 3-6pm mid-Mar–Oct, 9am-1pm Nov–mid-Mar) merits a peek

> **COMBINED TICKETS**
>
> An €8 ticket covers visits to the Museo Etrusco Guarnacci, the Pinacoteca Comunale and the Museo Diocesano d'Arte Sacra. A similar €2 ticket allows entry to both the Roman theatre and the seriously dilapidated Etruscan necropolis within the Parco Archeologico.

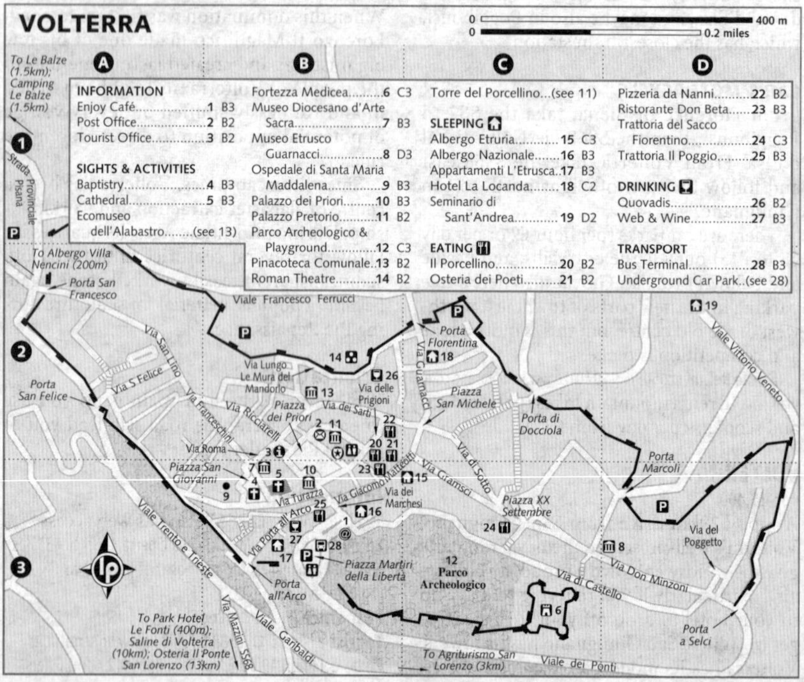

for its collection of ecclesiastical vestments, gold reliquaries and works by Andrea della Robbia and Rosso Fiorentino.

The **Pinacoteca Comunale** (☎ 0588 8 75 80; Via dei Sarti 1; ☻ 9am-7pm mid-Mar–Oct, 8.30am-1.45pm Nov–mid-Mar), in the Palazzo Minucci Solaini, houses a modest collection of local, Sienese and Florentine art. A scholarly highlight is Rosso Fiorentino's *Deposition*, due to its emotional content and similarities with the works of Goya. It is considered Fiorentino's masterpiece, straddling late-Renaissance and Mannerism.

ECOMUSEO DELL'ALABASTRO
As befits a town that has hewn the precious rock from nearby quarries since Etruscan times, Volterra has its own **alabaster museum** (☎ 0588 8 75 80; Via dei Sarti 1; admission €3; ☻ 11am-5pm mid-Mar–Oct, 9am-1.30pm Sat & Sun Nov–mid-Mar), which shares the same building as the Pinacoteca. On the ground floor are contemporary creations, including a finely chiselled mandolin and a bizarre fried egg, while on the two upper floors are choice examples from Etruscan times onwards and a re-created artisan's workshop. From the top-floor windows, there are gorgeous views of the surrounding countryside.

MUSEO ETRUSCO GUARNACCI
In terms of content, this **museum** (☎ 0588 8 63 47; Via Don Minzoni 15; adult/student €8/5; ☻ 9am-7pm mid-Mar–Oct, 8.30am-1.45pm Nov–mid-Mar) is one of Italy's finest Etruscan museums. Much of the collection is displayed in the old-style didactic manner – badly labelled, mostly in Italian, and stuffy – though some exhibits on the upper levels have been artfully enriched. The multilingual audio guide (€3) is worth the investment for much-needed descriptions and to boost the overall pep factor.

All exhibits were unearthed locally. They include a vast collection of some 600 funerary urns carved mainly from alabaster and tufa and displayed according to subject and period. The tiny casket-shaped urns typically have human figures lying in repose on the top with a scene captured on the front, often military in theme. Be selective; they all start to look the same after a while. The best examples (those dating from later periods) are on the 2nd and 3rd floors.

Original touches are the Ombra della Sera bronze *ex voto*, a strange, elongated nude

figure that would fit harmoniously in any museum of modern art, and the urn of the Sposi, a terracotta rendering of an elderly couple, their wrinkled features depicted in portrait fashion rather than the usual stylised manner.

FORTEZZA MEDICEA & PARCO ARCHEOLOGICO
The 14th-century **Fortezza Medicea**, later altered by Lorenzo Il Magnifico, is nowadays a prison (admission one felony).

To its west is the pleasant **Parco Archeologico** (☻ 8.30am-8pm May-Sep, to-5pm Oct-Apr), site of the ancient Acropolis (open 10.30am to 5.30pm mid-March to October). Little of archaeological interest has survived, apart from a few battered Etruscan tombs, but the park has swings and things for kids, and it's a good place for a picnic.

OTHER SIGHTS
On the city's northern edge is a **Roman theatre** (☻ 10.30am-5.30pm mid-Mar–Oct, 10am-4pm Sat & Sun Nov–mid-Mar), a well-preserved complex, complete with a Roman bath house.

Le Balze, a deep, eroded limestone ravine about 2km northwest of the city centre, has claimed several churches since the Middle Ages as the buildings tumbled into its deep gullies. A 14th-century **monastery**, perched near the precipice, seems perilously close to continuing the tradition. To get there, head out through Porta San Francesco, the city's northwestern gate, along Via San Lino and follow its continuation, Borgo Santo Stefano, then Borgo San Giusto.

Festivals & Events
On the third and fourth Sundays of August, the citizens of Volterra roll back the calendar some 600 years, take to the streets in period costume and celebrate **Volterra A.D. 1398** with gusto and all the fun of a medieval fayre.

Sleeping
Camping Le Balze (☎ 0588 8 78 80; Via di Mandringa 15; per car/tent/person €3/7/8; ☻ Easter-Oct; ☻) The closest camp site to town, has a pool, new bathrooms and sits right on Le Balze. Buses depart for Piazza Martiri every hour.

Seminario di Sant'Andrea (☎ 0588 8 60 28; semv escovile@diocesivolterra.it; Viale Vittorio Veneto 2; d €36, d with shared bathroom €28; P) Still an active church retreat, this is a peaceful, if a mite dilapidated,

CENTRAL TUSCANY

VOLTERRA BY DAY, FROGS & SALAMANDERS BY NIGHT

our pick **Agriturismi San Lorenzo** (☎ 0588 3 90 80; www.agriturismosanlorenzo.it; B&B d €85, apt without breakfast €90-110; ☻) This giddy-ing fusion of sustainable tourism, country-side vistas, mod cons and wonderful food is an easy 3km outside Volterra on the road to Siena. See our special agriturismi section for more detail (p316).

---

place with vaulted ceilings and 20 large, clean rooms. Open to all comers, it's a mere 600m or so from Piazza dei Priori, has free park-ing and makes an excellent budget choice. Breakfast is €3.

Albergo Villa Nencini (☎ 0588 8 63 86; www.villa nencini.it; Borgo Santo Stefano 55; s €60, d €68-83, all incl breakfast; P ☻) This is a tranquil family hotel, a mere 200m beyond Porta San Francesco yet a world away from the town's summer bustle. Choose the original 17th-century mansion or the recently constructed new wing. The grounds are shady, the views across the valley are magnificent and, with access to its restau-rant and impressive collection of wines, you're fully self-sufficient.

Appartamenti L'Etrusca (☎ 0588 8 40 73; letrusca@libero.it; Via Porta all'Arco 37-41; apt for 1/2/3 persons €40/70/80) Unlike most such rental companies, this place is happy to take you in for even a single night. The exterior of this late Renais-sance building gives no hint of all the mod cons within.

Albergo Nazionale (☎ 0588 8 62 84; www.hotelna zionale-volterra.com; Via dei Marchesi 11; s €59, d €78-83, tr €94-98, all incl buffet breakfast) DH Lawrence once stayed in this late-19th-century hotel. Rooms vary in size and style and some have balconies; Room 403, with a pair of them, is your best option. Meals in its summertime restaurant are simple, solid and uncomplicated; the re-ception desk betrays the same qualities.

our pick **Albergo Etruria** (☎ 0588 8 73 77; www .albergoetruria.it; Via Giacomo Matteotti 32; s €60-75, d €80-90, all incl breakfast; ☐) This is a good value, cosy hotel, realised by two friendly English-speak-ing ladies. There's a self-catering kitchen and, of all things, an ice machine! Look for the remains of an Etruscan wall upstairs and sa-vour the fine views from the roof garden – a genuine garden with lawns and bushes. The hotel is closed in January.

Hotel La Locanda (☎ 0588 8 15 47; www.hotel-lalocanda.com; Via Guarnacci 24-28; s €70-92, d €85-115; ☻) This is well worth flexing your credit card for. In a former nunnery, there is nothing austere about its classy rooms, most with a choice of massage shower or whirlpool. A suite with sauna will cost you a cool €250 and a handi-capped-equipped double is €80 to €105.

Park Hotel Le Fonti (☎ 0588 8 52 19; www.park hotellefonti.com; Via Fontecorrenti 8; s €85-125, d €110-165; P ☐ ☻) Abundant mod cons punctuate this four-star option, about 15 minutes' walk from the centre. Money that might have gone to making the rooms a bit fancier has been lavished all over the public areas, with classy furniture, plants, art, wi-fi and diversions such as the alabaster chessboard. The onsite restaurant (meals €45) is an all-swank affair with 200 types of wine.

Eating

Pizzeria da Nanni (☎ 0588 8 40 47; Via delle Pregioni 40; pizzas €5.80-7.50; ☯ Mon-Sat) This is a hole-in-the-wall-plus – the plus being the excellent piz-zas that Nanni spatulas from his oven, while sustaining a vivid line of backchat, notably with his long-suffering wife.

Il Porcellino (☎ 0588 8 63 92; Via delle Prigioni 10; meals €22-26; ☯ Wed-Mon) Despite its dangerous proximity to Piazza dei Priori and its tourist beacon, postersized menu, this place dishes out decent meals at very reasonable prices. The menu includes game dishes, seafood and some surprises, like boar with olives. A variety of set menus go for €13 to €23.

Osteria Il Ponte San Lorenzo (☎ 0588 4 41 60; Via Massetana, San Lorenzo; pizzas from €4.50, meals €24; ☯ Wed-Mon) Around 15km out of town, you can get superb, home-style cooking and am-bitious set menus (€25 to €40) at this rustic restaurant. Take the SS439 road south, head-ing towards Pomarance. About 3km beyond Saline di Volterra you enter San Lorenzo; the *osteria* is the highlight of this tiny, blink-and-you'll-miss-it village. They have a few rooms (singles/doubles €35/60, includes breakfast) if you're too bloated to drive back to Volterra.

Trattoria il Poggio (☎ 0588 8 52 57; Via Porta all'Arco 7; meals €28; ☯ Wed-Mon) A popular restaurant where the cheery waitresses bustle around and find time to chat with the regulars between dashes to the electric dumbwaiter raising food from the subterranean kitchen. There's a good set menu, an outdoor terrace and rich dishes such as scampi and rocket, or ravioli with asparagus and ham in a parmesan cream sauce.

Trattoria del Sacco Fiorentino (☎ 0588 8 85 37; Piazza XX Settembre 18; meals €28-32, menù degustazione €23-30; ☺ Thu-Tue) A great little vaulted trattoria that serves up imaginative dishes with a happy selection of local wines. Try the *piccione al vino santo e radicchio rosso* (pigeon baked with red radicchio and holy wine) or the mouthwatering gnocchi with baby veg.

Osteria dei Poeti (☎ 0588 8 60 29; Via Giacomo Matteotti 55; meals €30, tourist menus €12; ☺ Fri-Wed) Get here right at midday, before the business lunchers fill the last seat. Equally hectic at dinner, typical Tuscan fare is served to a backdrop of pleasing mellow brickwork and golden arches. The *antipasto del poeta*, a rich assortment of canapés, cheeses and cold cuts, is an unexpected delight, and the veal is a juicy good value. Wine pours are generous, possibly to dull the sting of the frosty service.

our pick **Ristorante Don Beta** (☎ 0588 8 67 30; Via Giacomo Matteotti 39; meals €30-35, menus €13-18; ☺ closed Mon Oct-Apr) With four truffle-based *primi piatti*, and five *secondi* enhanced by their fragrance, this is the place to sample the prized fungus, which abounds – in so far as it abounds anywhere – in the woods around Volterra. Do check on the prices first, though they are generally reasonable. Alternatively, choose the local *ciandoli alle noci*, little, spring-shaped whorls of curly pasta in a walnut sauce.

Drinking

Web & Wine (☎ 0588 8 15 31; Via Porta all'Arco 11-13; ☺ 8.30am-1am Mar-Jan, closed Thu) This is one of those splendid places that defy guidebook characterisation. It's at once internet point (web access per hour €4), a stylish *enoteca* (with a good selection of tipples), a snack stop and a hip designer café (it's not every day you step across a glass floor, revealing under-lit Etruscan remains and a 5m-deep Renaissance grain silo). Surf your way through a creamy cappuccino while checking your in-box.

Quovadis (☎ 0588 8 00 33; Via Lungo Le Mura del Mandorlo 18) If you can't survive without a shot of the dark nectar, this is the only place for miles around where you can get draught Guinness (pint €5). The garden is pleasant on hot summer nights and rumour has it there's even an Irish owner somewhere in the background.

Getting There & Away

The tourist office carries bus and train timetables.

BUS

The bus terminal is on Piazza Martiri della Libertà. **CPT** (☎ 0588 8 61 86) buses connect the town with Saline (€1.70, 20 minutes, frequent) and its train station. From Saline, 9km southwest, there are bus connections for Pisa (direct €4.80, two hours, or change at Pontedera €3.35) and Cecina (€3.35), to where there's also a train link. Buy tickets in the *tabacchi* shops, as buying on the bus is more expensive.

For San Gimignano (€4.35, 1½ hours), Siena (€4.50, 1½ hours) and Florence (€7, two hours), change at Colle di Val d'Elsa (€2.40, 50 minutes), to where there are four runs daily from Volterra, except on Sunday. The rare, direct run to Florence from Volterra is €7.10.

Other buses head south in the direction of Massa Marittima but only go as far as Pomarance (€2.30, 12 daily) and Castelnuovo di Valle di Cecina (€3.40, 10 daily).

CAR & MOTORCYCLE

By car, take the SS68, which runs between Cecina and Colle di Val d'Elsa. A couple of back routes to San Gimignano are signposted north off the SS68.

Driving and parking inside the walled town are more or less prohibited. Park in one of the designated parking areas around the circumference, most of which are free. There's a four-level paying underground car park beneath Piazza Martiri della Libertà.

TRAIN

From the small train station in Saline, you can catch a train to Cecina on the coast and change to the Rome–Pisa line.

SOUTH OF VOLTERRA

If you have a car and want to head for Massa Marittima (a worthwhile objective – see p282), the ride south from Volterra is very scenic.

The SS68 drops away to the southwest from Volterra towards Cecina. At Saline di Volterra, the SS439 intersects the SS68 on its way from Lucca, south towards Massa Marittima. **Saline di Volterra** takes its name from the nearby salt mines; a source of wealth in the 19th century.

CENTRAL TUSCANY

The lunar-landscape ride south passes through **Pomarance**, an industrial town. To the south, take the hilly road for **Larderello**, Italy's most important boric acid producer. The road out of here winds its way south to Massa.

SOUTH OF SIENA

You may already have had a taste of the gentle, seductively undulating countryside of Le Crete. For a while, similar countryside persists as you roam south amid the classic Tuscan landscape of rolling hills of hay topped with a huddle of cypress trees. Gradually the landscape gives way to more unruly territory. This part of the province offers everything: the haughty hilltop medieval wine centres of Montalcino and Montepulciano; hot sulphurous baths in spa towns such as Bagno Vignoni; the Romanesque splendour of the Abbazia di Sant'Antimo; and the Renaissance grace of Pienza, an early example of idealised town planning.

Montalcino

pop 5100

Formerly known as 'the Republic of Siena in Montalcino', the last wily holdout against Florence, even after Siena had fallen, these days Montalcino is a retiring hill town overlooking the Orcia valley. While this is a perfectly nice place to wander and bulk up your calf muscles while climbing inhumanly steep 'streets', the real attraction is its internationally coveted wine, Brunello (see the boxed text, p258). You can also savour unpedigreed, more modest but very palatable local reds such as Rosso di Montalcino.

Plenty of *enoteche* around town allow you to taste and buy Brunello (a bottle costs a minimum of €20; we did say it was special!) and restaurant servers will impetuously assume you mean Brunello when you ask for a 'glass of red', because why else would you be in Montalcino? Glasses start at €5, while a bottle from an excellent year comes with a price tag of well over the €105 mark. Beware rash, dismissive ordering of any Brunello; a bottle from the 1940s (€5000) will double the price of your month in Tuscany with the pop of a cork. There's no need to labour over prices however, as all Brunello is made to strict standards and any bottle will invariably be memorable.

INFORMATION

Essepi Informatica (☎ 0577 84 61 05; Via Mazzini 30; per hr €6) Head here for internet access.

Tourist office (☎ 0577 84 93 31; www.prolocomon talcino.it in Italian; Costa del Municipio 1; ☯ 10am-1pm & 2-5.40pm)

SIGHTS & ACTIVITIES

If you purchase a combined ticket (€6), it will give you entry to Montalcino's principal sights, the *fortezza* and the Museo Civico e Diocesano d'Arte Sacra.

The **fortezza** (☎ 0577 84 92 11; Piazzale Fortezza; courtyard free, ramparts adult/child €3.50/1.50; ☯ 9am-8pm Apr-Oct, 10am-6pm Nov-Mar), an imposing 14th-century fortress that was later expanded under the Medici dukes, dominates the town from a high point at its southern end. You can sample and buy local wines in the *enoteca* (p268) inside and also climb up to the fort's ramparts (though the view is almost as magnificent from the courtyard). Buy a ticket at the bar.

The **Museo Civico e Diocesano d'Arte Sacra** (☎ 0577 84 60 14; Via Ricasoli 31; adult/child €4.50/3; ☯ 10am-1pm & 2-5.50pm Tue-Sun), in the former convent of the neighbouring **Chiesa di Sant'Agostino**, contains an important collection of religious art from the town and surrounding region. Jewels include a triptych by Duccio di Buoninsegna and a *Madonna with Child* by Simone Martini. Other artists represented include the Lorenzetti brothers, Giovanni di Paolo and Sano di Pietro and the museum has a fine collection of painted wooden sculptures by the Sienese school.

The **cathedral**, alas, is an ugly 19th-century neoclassical travesty of what was once a fine Romanesque church.

If you want to visit **vineyards** in the Montalcino area, the tourist office can provide you with a list of 183 producers (many smaller ones have little more than a hectare or two of land). It can also advise on which vineyards are open to the public and those that have an English speaker to help you.

If you're a jazz-loving oenophile, you'll savour the annual **Jazz & Wine festival**, held in the second and third weeks of July and attracting national and international acts.

There's a vigorous **Friday market** on and around Via della Libertà.

SLEEPING

Both Il Giardino and Il Giglio have restaurants that are well worth a visit.

Il Giardino (☎ /fax 0577 84 82 57; Piazza Cavour 4; s €40-53, d €53) An excellent-value, family-run,

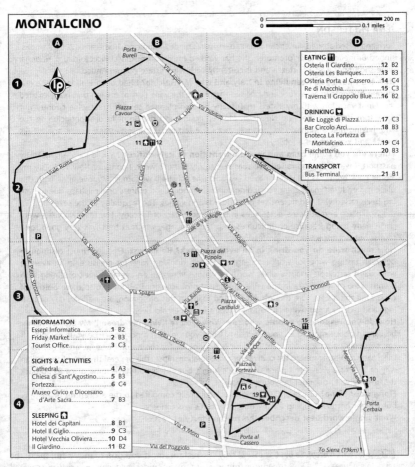

MONTALCINO

0 — 200 m
0 — 0.1 miles

To Siena (19km)

friendly, two-star hotel overlooking Piazza Cavour.

Hotel Il Giglio (☎ 0577 84 81 67; www.gigliohotel .com; Via Soccorso Saloni 5; s/d/tr €70/100/115, annexe s/d €50/70, apt 2-4 people €90-110; 🅿) Montalcino's oldest hotel, recently and substantially renovated, is another family concern. Rooms have comfortable wrought-iron beds – each gilded with a painted *giglio* (lily) – and all doubles have panoramic views. Il Giglio also has a small annexe just up the street and a couple of apartments. Room 1 has an enormous terrace that comes at no extra cost.

Hotel dei Capitani (☎ 0577 84 72 27; www.deicapitani .it; Via Lapini 6; s/d incl breakfast €100/115; 🟐 🖳 🔌) Set in a 15th-century building, rooms vary greatly, ranging from superspacious to small with a

view, so take a look first. There's a pretty terrace with a pool to splash around in.

Hotel Vecchia Oliviera (☎ 0577 84 60 28; www.vec chiaoliviera.com; Angolo Via Landi 1; d incl breakfast €150-175; 🅿 🟐 🖳 🔌) Just beside the Porta Cerbaia, this is a former olive mill, tastefully restored with earthy colours and terracotta tiles. Tranquil – it's at the very limit of the town – each of its rooms is individually decorated. The back patio has stunning views. Wi-fi costs extra.

EATING
Osteria Porta al Cassero (☎ 0577 84 71 96; Via Ricasoli 32; meals €24; ⏱ Thu-Tue) A simple place selling hearty peasant-style fare such as bean and vegetable soup, and Tuscan pork sausage with white beans.

JENA PATTERSON

Born and raised abroad, American Jena Patterson has made Montalcino, home since 2001. A impassioned Brunello educator/promoter, she has worked for producer Ciacci Piccolomini d'Aragona, wine shop Enoteca La Fortezza and is currently with wine estate Poggio Antico.

How long have you been living in Italy and why Montalcino? I had been working in the restaurant business in New York and realised that it was the wine part of my job that really excited me. On a vacation with my sisters to Tuscany we had planned to visit great wine country but were torn between the Vino Nobile of Montepulciano and the Brunello of Montalcino. In the end, having met a Montalcino producer at a wine tasting at the restaurant, I came to visit his estate and was offered a job.

Where did you come from and was the transition to Italy difficult? While I am American by passport, I was born and raised overseas due to my father's work. I consider New York City my 'home back home' as it's where I lived last and where I still have family. My love affair with this place has endured many things including cultural blunders and professional mishaps due to having been raised with a different set of standards and values. The inequality of the sexes both in the workplace and at home perseveres in this remote part of Tuscany. The first two years were particularly trying because of difficulties with the language, which at best was very good for a tourist but not for a working professional.

How much wine do you drink in an average week? Be honest. First, we must distinguish between tasting wine for work (spitting it out) and drinking wine for pleasure. In an average work day I taste/spit about a glass worth of various wines. In an average week of dining with friends, 90% of whom are in the wine business, I probably drink about two to three bottles of wine. One thing's for sure though, for me and many in this profession, after a long day of tastings and talking about wine all you really want is a nice cold beer.

How do you respond to people who say 'Wow, you're living my dream!' My answer is this: be careful about moving to your paradise. Once you do, it will no longer be your paradise. It can certainly be an improvement on your quality of life for the natural beauty, art, food, wine, the space and atmosphere for cultivating close relationships…the general rhythm of the Italian way of life. It's a wonderful place to live, it's home, but unless you have some place to go back to, Tuscany will no longer be your getaway.

Florence or Siena? *Grosseto!* OK, it might lack culturally compared to the art centres of Tuscany but it's got better shopping for my budget and it's less touristy.

What single word best describes the Tuscan lifestyle? Passion.

---

our pick **Taverna Il Grappolo Blu** (☎ 0577 84 71 50; Scale di Via Moglio 1; meals €28) Does ingenious things with local ingredients – try the juicy *coniglio al Brunello* (rabbit cooked in Brunello wine). We did. And we still remember that evening fondly. Non-Brunello-enriched options are scant – which may be local law – so save your server the disquiet and just stick with the theme.

Osteria Il Giardino (☎ 0577 84 90 76; Piazza Cavour 1; meals €30; ✆ closed Wed) All light wood and arches, this place has a good selection of traditional dishes, including *risotto al radicchio rosso*, *Brunello e pecorino* (risotto with red chicory, Brunello wine and *pecorino* cheese) and wild boar.

Osteria Les Barriques (☎ 0577 84 84 11; Piazza del Popolo 20-22; meals €30-34) Beyond the impulse-buy *enoteca*, lined floor to ceiling with a dizzying selection of bottles, is a newly minted, full restaurant. If you don't fancy a full meal, the menu includes bruschetta, *crostini* (toasted bread brushed with olive oil) and at least five different salads.

Re di Macchia (☎ 0577 84 61 16; Via Soccorso Saloni 21; meals €32, menus €19; ✆ Fri-Wed) This is a very agreeable small restaurant run by an enterprising young couple. Roberta selects the freshest of ingredients and the wine cellar is impressive; to sample a variety, try Antonio's personal selection of four wines (€15), each to accompany a course.

DRINKING

We make no apologies for the disproportionate number of recommended drinking dens in this very wine-oriented town!

Enoteca La Fortezza di Montalcino (☎ 0577 84 92 11; Piazzale Fortezza; wine by the glass from €4) Within the fort itself, this *enoteca* is perfect for trying out one of countless varieties of Brunello, buying a bottle and/or climbing up onto the ramparts. It also puts on informal tastings, accompanied by delectable nibbles.

Fiaschetteria (Piazza del Popolo 6) A fine tiled old café full of crusty locals, this is the perfect place for putting the world to rights over a bottle of wine.

Alle Logge di Piazza (Piazza del Popolo 1; ☾ closed Wed Sep-Mar & all Jan) Across the square, this is brighter and more consciously modern. Wine selection changes constantly, while the light menu doesn't. Staff shake cocktails something fierce; the choice is almost as long as the wine list. Happy hour is 7pm to 9pm.

Bar Circolo Arci (Via Ricasoli 2) Defying the local *enoteche* trend, this is a run-of-the-mill bar, complete with pool table, where local pensioners play cards and shamelessly flirt with the lovely staff. Housed within 16th-century Palazzo Pieri, it has a lovely cobbled courtyard.

GETTING THERE & AWAY

The **bus terminal** is on Piazza Cavour. Regular Tra-in buses run to/from Siena (€3.20, 1½ hours, six daily).

Abbazia di Sant'Antimo

This beautiful isolated Romanesque **church** (☎ 0577 83 56 59; admission free; ☾ 10.30am-12.30pm & 3-6.30pm Mon-Sat, 9am-10.30am & 3-6pm Sun) is best visited in the morning, when the sun, streaming through the east windows, creates an almost surreal atmosphere. At night too, it's impressive, lit up like a beacon. Set in a broad valley, just below the village of **Castelnuovo dell'Abate**, its architecture is clearly influenced by northern European versions of Romanesque architecture, especially that of the Cistercians.

Tradition tells that Charlemagne founded the original monastery here in 781. In subsequent centuries, the Benedictine monks became among the most powerful feudal landlords in southern Tuscany, until they came into conflict with Siena in the 13th century. Until the mid-1990s, the church and abbey lay pretty much abandoned. Then a body of monks moved in and supervised restoration work. There are regular daily prayers and Mass in the church, which are open to the public. This is a worthwhile exercise as the monks sing Gregorian chants. If you can't make it, they can sell you the CD.

The exterior, built in pale travertine stone, is simple but for the stone carvings, which include various fantastical animals, set in the bell tower and apsidal chapels. Inside study the capitals of the columns lining the nave, especially the one representing Daniel in the lion's den (second on the right as you enter). Below it is a particularly intense polychrome 13th-century Madonna and Child and there's a haunting 12th-century Christ on the Cross above the main altar.

Concerts are sometimes held here as part of Siena's Estate Musicale Chigiana (see p246).

Locanda Sant'Antimo (☎ 0577 83 56 15; www.locandasantantimo.it; Via Bassomondo 8; meals €14-18), less than 1km away at Castelnuovo dell'Abate, serves solid traditional cooking. A three-course, fixed menu with wine and coffee is a mere €15. Should you wish to catch the early morning light over the abbey, there are four rooms (single/double €50/70).

Agriturismo Aiole (☎ 0577 88 74 54; www.agriturismo-aiole.com; Strada Provinciale 22 della Grossola; d/tr incl breakfast €70/90; ☒), 8km southeast of the abbey and 900m down a signed dirt road, is a fabulous place to stop for one day – or five. Family-friendly, it's in a restored 19th-century farmhouse with knockout views, a pool and a children's playground. There's a kitchen available for groups or save yourself the bother and enjoy your hostess's dinner (€25, reserve in advance).

Three buses a day run from Montalcino (€1.20) to Castelnuovo dell'Abate, from where it's a short walk to the church.

You may want to consider an alternative lunch or dinner excursion west from Castelnuovo dell'Abate along a dirt road to **Sant'Angelo in Colle**. The views from the village are wonderful. You can eat excellent home-cooked food at **Trattoria Il Pozzo** (☎ 0577 84 40 15; meals €22), in the middle of Sant'Angelo, just off the square.

San Quirico d'Orcia

Fortified. Compact. Medieval. San Quirico has the usual Tuscan adjectives and few singular attractions, unless a tranquil, good-value stopover sounds attractive, in which case you've got yourself a winner. A one-time pilgrim pitstop on the Via Francigena, it's now an atypical stopover, just off the SS2 at a crossroads between Montalcino and Pienza. Its Romanesque **Collegiata** is notable for its unusual three doorways, decorated with lonelyplanet.com

bizarre stone carvings. Inside is a triptych by Sano di Pietro.

Just off Piazza della Libertà, the main square, the **Horti Leononi** are lovely formal Italian Renaissance gardens with clipped and cropped geometrical boxwood hedges.

The **tourist office** (☎ 0577 89 72 11; www.comune sanquirico.it in Italian; Via Dante Alighieri 33a; ☑ 10am-1pm & 3-6pm Mon-Fri, 10am-1pm & 2-5pm Sat & Sun Easter-Dec) also acts as the information office for the Parco Artistico Naturale e Culturale della Val d'Orcia.

The harmonious Val d'Orcia, a land of flat, chalky plains and gentle conical hills, is the latest Italian area to be declared a Unesco World Heritage Site. The equally recent **Parco Artistico Naturale e Culturale della Val d'Orcia** (www.parcodellavaldorcia.com), with its headquarters located in San Quirico d'Orcia, protects this legacy.

Affittacamere L'Orcia (☎ 0577 89 76 77; Via Dante Alighieri 49; s/d €30/50), right in the centre of town, has a pleasantly old-fashioned Spartan feel about it, complete with drapes and religious pictures. In this case, no-frills also means no one in reception. Call ahead to arrange your arrival.

Alternatively, you can do all-frills for a comparative bargain at **Palazzo del Capitano** (☎ 0577 89 90 28; www.palazzodelcapitano.com; Via Poliziano 18; d incl breakfast €120-230; P 🖳), in a beautifully restored army captain's home, dating from 1400. All rooms are classically and individually decorated and the huge garden invites sustained repose.

Trattoria Al Vecchio Forno (☎ 0577 89 73 80; Via Piazzola 8; meals €30; ☑ Thu-Tue) is a sister venture of Palazzo del Capitano, with equal attention to quality. Enjoy the intimate dining room with its mellow brick arches or savour the lovely mature garden. Famed for its roasts and grills, it also simmers a mean *pollo al Brunello* (chicken in a Brunello wine sauce). Just order the bottle, their glass pours are light.

REMOTENESS HAS ITS PRIVILEGES

ourpick Le Case (☎ 0577 88 89 83; www.agri turismolecase.com; Strada Provinciale 323; s/d/tr incl breakfast €40/70/80) Just 1km south of Castiglione d'Orcia, this is one the best-value *agriturismi* we've seen. See our special *agriturismi* section for more detail (p311).

Inside **Bar Centrale** (Piazza della Libertà 6) the local menfolk play cards and knock back grappa, while the outside terrace is more popular with the younger ice-cream-and-cola set.

There's a magnificent small **cheese shop** (Via Dante Alighieri 113b), an outlet for the Fattoria Pianporcino cheesemakers, where you can pick up the renowned *pecorino di Pienza* and other richly aromaed delights.

Bagno Vignoni

About 5km from San Quirico along the SS2 towards Rome, this tiny spa town dates back to Roman times and was later a popular overnight stop for pilgrims eager to soothe weary limbs. The hot sulphurous water bubbles up into a picturesque pool, built by the Medicis and surrounded by mellow stone buildings. Some 36 springs cook at up to 51°C and collect in the pool, although in winter the water is considerably cooler.

You can't dunk yourself in the pool. To take to the waters, dive into nearby Hotel Posta Marcucci's open-air **Piscina Val di Sole** (day ticket adult/child €12/8).

You can dip your fingers into the hot-water streams trickling through **Il Parco dei Mulini di Bagno Vignoni**, just above the entrance to the hotel, and read at length about how the two vast cubes hewn into the rock were once holding tanks for water-driven windmills below.

Albergo Le Terme (☎ 0577 88 71 50; www.albergo leterme.it; s/d €68/116; ☑ closed Dec; P 🐾 🖳) is sumptuous, with lots of shiny wood and plush fabrics. This 15th-century building (the top floors were added in the mid-20th century) was built by Rossellino for Pope Pius II, who used it as a summerhouse. Ask for a room at the front with views of the pool. Meals at their new restaurant are €25.

Osteria del Leone (☎ 0577 88 73 00; Piazza del Moretto 28; meals €29; ☑ Tue-Sun) is a pleasantly lit rustic building with a heavy-beamed ceiling, back a block from the pool. You can eat solid Tuscan country fare, such as *coniglio con pere e mandorle tostate* (rabbit cooked with pears and almonds).

Bagni San Filippo

Those who prefer free hot-water frolics could press on about 15km south along the SS2 to Bagni San Filippo. Just uphill from Hotel le Terme, the village's only hotel, follow a sign, 'Fosso Bianco', down a lane for about 150m

---

THE NOTORIOUS P-I-U-S

Let's be honest, there's been a lot of popes over time and not all of them have been news-worthy, or even popeworthy for that matter. Pope Pius II (1405–64) was both. Born Enea Silvio Piccolomini, the man was everywhere, evidenced by how many times we drop his name in this chapter alone. He was a tireless traveller, writer of erotic and comic stories, poet laureate, diplo-mat, bishop, exhaustive autobiographer (13 volumes!) and medieval urban-planning trend-setter. And most of that occurred before he was even pope! His early 'faults' in life being no secret, that he redressed his motivations and developed into such a distinguished and likable leader is particularly estimable. Noted above all for being 'human', an elusive papacy trait apparently, he's also remembered for his tireless diplomacy, even in the face of uncooperative leaders and insurmountable odds.

---

to a bridge and a set of hot tumbling **cascades** where you can enjoy a relaxing soak. It's a pleasant if slightly whiffy spot for a picnic – and best in winter, when the hotel's closed and the water pressure greater.

Pienza
pop 2230

If the primary road to Montepulciano didn't pass right through town, little Pienza might not inspire people to take their foot off the accelerator. Fortunately it does, so pull over and take a few hours to absorb its few, but compelling attractions. Or stay longer and benefit from its great-value food and accom-modation. Self-caterers will love (or loathe) that virtually all shops here are geared towards connoisseurs – cheese, meats and preserves are top choice and top price.

Urban-planning geeks will get a wicked buzz from Pienza's Renaissance town blue-print, instigated by Pope Pius II in an effort to jazz up his birthplace. He secured the services of architect Bernardo Rossellino, who applied the principles of his mentor, Leon Battista Alberti. The result was the superb Piazza Pio II and the surrounding buildings.

INFORMATION

Internet Café (Via della Balzello 2; per hr €5; 9am-12.30pm & 2.30-7pm) Has internet points and wi-fi.
Tourist office (0578 74 99 05; Corso Il Rossellino; 10am-1pm & 3-7pm) Within the Museo Diocesano.

SIGHTS

Stand in Piazza Pio II and spin 360 degrees. You have just taken in Pienza's major monu-ments. Gems of the Renaissance and all con-structed in a mere three years between 1459 and 1462, they're all grouped around Piazza Pio II.

The square was designed by Bernardo Ros-sellino, who left nothing to chance. The space available to him was limited so, to increase the sense of perspective and dignity of the great edifices that would grace the square, he set the Palazzo Borgia and Palazzo Piccolomini off at angles to the cathedral.

The **cathedral** (8.30am-1pm & 2.15-7pm) was built on the site of the Romanesque Chiesa di Santa Maria, of which little remains. The Renaissance façade, in travertine stone, is of clear Albertian inspiration.

The interior of the building, a strange mix of Gothic and Renaissance, contains a col-lection of five altarpieces painted by Sienese artists of the period, as well as a superb marble tabernacle by Rossellino. The papal bull of 1462 forbade any changes to the church, so revel in the thought that views are virtually the same now as they were for visitors in the Middle Ages.

Perhaps the most bizarre aspect of the building is the state of collapse of the transept and apse. Built on dodgy ground, the top end of the church seems to be breaking off. The huge cracks in the wall and floor are matched by the crazy downwards slant of this part of the church floor. Various attempts to prop it all up have failed to solve the problem, as is quite clear from the major cracking in the walls and floor.

The **Palazzo Piccolomini** (0578 74 85 03; adult/child 30-min guided tour €7/5; 10am-12.30pm & 3-6pm Tue-Sun), to your right as you face the cathe-dral, was the pope's residence and is consid-ered Rossellino's masterpiece. Built on the site of former Piccolomini family houses, the building demonstrates some indebtedness on Rossellino's part to Alberti, whose Pal-azzo Rucellai in Florence it appears in part to emulate.

CENTRAL TUSCANY

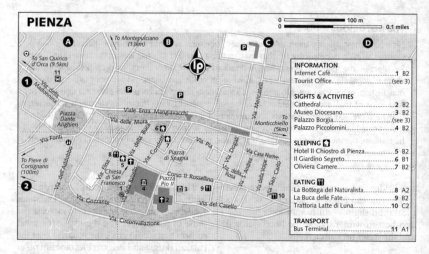

PIENZA

INFORMATION
Internet Café..............................**1** B2
Tourist Office.............................(see 3)

SIGHTS & ACTIVITIES
Cathedral...................................**2** B2
Museo Diocesano.......................**3** B2
Palazzo Borgia..........................(see 3)
Palazzo Piccolomini...................**4** B2

SLEEPING
Hotel Il Chiostro di Pienza..........**5** B2
Il Giardino Segreto.....................**6** B1
Oliviera Camere.........................**7** B2

EATING
La Bottega del Naturalista............**8** A2
La Buca delle Fate......................**9** B2
Trattoria Latte di Luna.................**10** C2

TRANSPORT
Bus Terminal.............................**11** A1

Inside is a fine courtyard, from where stairs lead you up into the papal apartments, now filled with an assortment of period furnishings, minor art and the like. To the rear, a three-level loggia offers a spectacular panorama over the Val d'Orcia below.

To the left of the cathedral is the **Palazzo Borgia** (also known as Palazzo Vescovile), built by Cardinal Borgia, later Pope Alexander VI, and containing the **Museo Diocesano** (☎ 0578 74 99 05; Corso Il Rossellino 30; adult/child €4.10/2.60; ☺ 10am-1pm & 3-7pm Wed-Mon mid-Mar–Oct, Sat & Sun only Nov–mid-Mar), which has an intriguing miscellany of artworks, illuminated manuscripts, tapestries and miniatures.

Make time to visit the Romanesque **Pieve di Corsignano**, leaving Pienza by taking Via Fonti from Piazza Dante Alighieri. This church dates from the 10th century and boasts a strange circular bell tower. There are no fixed visiting times but it is usually open between Easter and November.

SLEEPING & EATING

Oliviera Camere (☎ 0578 74 82 74, 338 952 04 59; www .nautilus-mp.com/oliviera; Via Condotti 4b; s/d incl breakfast €30/50, apt without breakfast d/q €60/70) Once an olive oil mill and squeezed into a side street, this place represents excellent value. Its four rooms are simple, but fresh and attractive. There are also three larger studio apartments.

Il Giardino Segreto (☎ 0578 60 44 52; www.ilgiardi nosegreto.toscana.nu; Via Condotti 13; d €62, apt €67-115, all incl breakfast) Across the road and a slight step up in quality, the collection of quiet doubles

and apartments here have the added perk of a lovely, enclosed garden.

Hotel Il Chiostro di Pienza (☎ 0578 74 84 00; www .relaisilchiostrodipienza.com; Corso il Rossellino 26; r incl breakfast €160-290; ☺ closed Jan–mid-Mar; ☒ ☐) Come here to wallow in luxury – and history; it occupies the former convent and cloister of the adjacent Chiesa di San Francesco. The décor is refreshingly unfussy and the manicured gardens have views and definite romantic appeal. Access to internet points and wi-fi (common areas only) included.

La Buca delle Fate (☎ 0578 74 82 72; Corso Il Rossellino 38a; meals €20; ☺ closed Mon & 15-30 Jun) Despite its dress-for-dinner appearance, this eatery is one for euro-economisers. There are no surprises on the tiny menu but the standard is high for the price. Save room for the dessert trolley.

Trattoria Latte di Luna (☎ 0578 74 86 06; Via San Carlo 6; meals €25; ☺ Wed-Mon) On a kind of squarette where the street splits off from Corso Il Rossellino, this trattoria has a lovely terrace with plenty of shady umbrellas and a flirtatious, talking bird providing comic relief. Try the *anatra arrosto alle olive* (roast duck with olives) topped off with homemade hazelnut ice cream.

Bottega del Naturalista (Corso Il Rossellino 16) Almost a monument in its own right, this pungent *bottega* has a truly mouthwatering choice of cheeses, from fresh to well-aged and smelly, from the classic *pecorino di Pienza* to ones lightly infused with peppers or truffles.

GETTING THERE & AWAY

Up to six buses run on weekdays between Siena and Pienza (€3.50, 1¼ hours) and nine to/from Montepulciano. The bus terminal is just off Piazza Dante Alighieri. Buy tickets at the nearby bar.

Montepulciano

pop 14,100

After a day of walking through Montepulciano, you'll acquire a newfound appreciation for the term 'hotel restaurant', as any other option will mean climbing another hill. This reclaimed narrow ridge of volcanic rock will push your quadriceps to the failure-point. When it happens, collapse against a centuries-old stone wall, drink in the views over the Valdichiana countryside, then fall into the nearest cantina and treat yourself to a generous pour of the highly reputed Vino Nobile.

A late-Etruscan fort was the first in a series of settlements here. During the Middle Ages, it was a constant bone of contention between Florence and Siena, until in 1404 Florence won the day. And so the Marzocco, or lion of Florence, came to replace the she-wolf of Siena as the city's symbol, atop a column just off Piazza Savonarola. The new administration introduced a fresh architectural style as Michelozzo, Sangallo il Vecchio and others were invited in to do some innovative spring cleaning, imparting a fresh wind of Renaissance vigour to this Gothic stronghold. That intriguing mix alone makes this town worth the sustained leg cramps.

ORIENTATION

The town sheers off to left and right from the main street, which rises equally steeply southwards from Porta al Prato to the Piazza Grande and fortress beyond. The 750m walk may leave you breathless but, bordered by the town's finest buildings, it's well worth the exercise.

INFORMATION

Strada del Vino Nobile di Montepulciano Information Office (☎ 0578 71 74 84; www.stradavinonobile .it; Piazza Grande 7; ✆ 10am-1pm & 3-7pm Mon-Sat) Can book accommodation. Among other activities, it arranges cooking courses, slow food tours, wine tastings, bike rentals and unstrenuous country walks, culminating in lunch.
Tourist office (☎ 0578 75 73 41; www.prolocomonte pulciano.it; Piazza Don Minzoni; ✆ 9.30am-12.30pm & 3-7pm Easter-Jul, Sep & Oct, 9.30am-8pm Aug, 9.30am-12.30pm Mon-Sat & 3-6pm Sun Nov-Easter) This large and friendly resource can reserve accommodation without charge. It has internet points (per hour €3.50), sells local bus and train tickets, and rents bikes and scooters.

SIGHTS & ACTIVITIES

Most of the main sights are clustered around Piazza Grande, although the town's streets harbour a wealth of palazzi, fine buildings and churches.

The **Chiesa di Sant'Agnese**, with its beelike banding around the façade, lies just outside the city walls. The original church was built in the early 14th century but this version was the result of a remake by Antonio da Sangallo il Vecchio in 1511. He may also have restructured the medieval gate leading into the city proper, the **Porta al Prato**.

From the gate, walk southwards along Via di Gracciano nel Corso. At the upper end of Piazza Savonarola is the **Colonna del Marzocca**, erected in 1511 to confirm Montepulciano's allegiance to Florence. The splendid stone

---

DETOUR: MONTICCHIELLO

From Pienza main junction (northern gate) take the minor road south out of town signposted to San Lorenzo Nuovo and Monticchiello. Follow this road as it wiggles through green valleys and farmland. At 6.2km, just after you cross a small bridge, take the left turn signposted to Monticchiello. At the 11km junction, turn right and continue for 500m until you reach the car park.

Don the best arch-support at your disposal and take an hour to wander around this pretty medieval village, stopping for an ice cream at Bar La Guardiola just outside the main gate or, better yet, a memorable meal at **Ristorante La Porta** (☎ 0578 75 51 63; www.osterialaporta.it; Via del Piano 3; meals €30) on its terrace with unspeakable views of Val d'Orcia.

Monticchiello is home to the internationally celebrated **Teatro Povero** (Poor Theatre; www .teatropovero.it), staging plays spotlighting the area's peasant, sharecropping history. It also has a wonderfully sophisticated interactive theatre museum.

When you leave, turn left and follow the signs to Montepulciano.

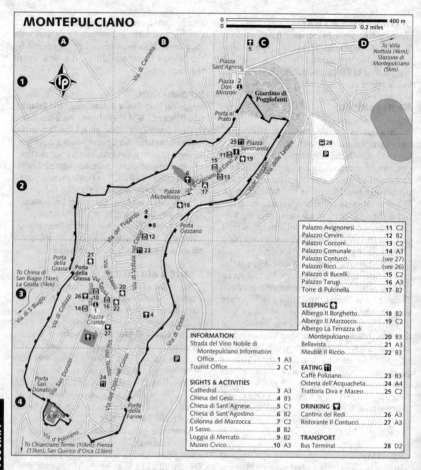

MONTEPULCIANO

Palazzo Avignonesi	11 C2
Palazzo Cervini	12 B2
Palazzo Cocconi	13 C2
Palazzo Comunale	14 A3
Palazzo Contucci	(see 27)
Palazzo Ricci	(see 26)
Palazzo di Bucelli	15 C2
Palazzo Tarugi	16 A3
Torre di Pulcinella	17 B2

SLEEPING
Albergo Il Borghetto	18 B2
Albergo Il Marzocco	19 C2
Albergo La Terrazza di Montepulciano	20 B3
Bellavista	21 A3
Meublé Il Riccio	22 B3

EATING
Caffè Poliziano	23 B3
Osteria dell'Acquacheta	24 A4
Trattoria Diva e Maceo	25 C2

DRINKING
Cantina del Redi	26 A3
Ristorante Il Contucci	27 A3

TRANSPORT
Bus Terminal	28 D2

INFORMATION
Strada del Vino Nobile di Montepulciano Information Office	1 A3
Tourist Office	2 C1

SIGHTS & ACTIVITIES
Cathedral	3 A3
Chiesa del Gesù	4 B3
Chiesa di Sant'Agnese	5 C1
Chiesa di Sant'Agostino	6 B2
Colonna del Marzocca	7 C2
Il Sasso	8 B2
Loggia di Mercato	9 B2
Museo Civico	10 A3

lion, squat as a pussycat atop this column is, in fact, a copy; the original is in the town's Museo Civico.

The late-Renaissance **Palazzo Avignonesi** by Giacomo da Vignola is at No 91. Several mansions line Via di Gracciano nel Corso, including the **Palazzo di Bucelli** at No 73, the lower courses of whose façade are recycled Etruscan and Latin inscriptions and reliefs. Sangallo also designed **Palazzo Cocconi** at No 70.

Continuing up Via di Gracciano nel Corso, you'll find Michelozzo's **Chiesa di Sant'Agostino** (Piazza Michelozzo; 9am-noon & 3-6pm) with its lunette above the entrance holding a terracotta Madonna and Child, John the Baptist and St Augustine. Opposite, **Torre di Pulcinella**, a medieval tower house, is topped by the town clock

and the hunched figure of Pulcinella (Punch of Punch and Judy fame), which strikes the hours.

Keep ascending the hill and turn right at the **Loggia di Mercato**, first left into Via del Poggiolo, then left again into Via Ricci. In the Renaissance **Palazzo Ricci** is Cantina del Redi (p276), a cavernous warren of ancient wine cellars that you can wander through, ending up at the wine-tasting room and shop.

The town's **Museo Civico** (☎ 0578 71 73 00; Via Ricci 10; adult/child €4.15/2.60; 10am-7pm Tue-Sun Aug, 10am-1pm & 3-6pm Tue-Sun Sep-Jul) is opposite in the Gothic Palazzo Neri-Orselli. The small collection features terracotta reliefs by the della Robbia family and some Gothic and Renaissance paintings.

CENTRAL TUSCANY

Overlooking Piazza Grande, the town's highest point, is the **Palazzo Comunale** (admission free; ☼ 9am-1.30pm Mon-Sat). Built in the 13th-century Gothic style and remodelled in the 15th century by Michelozzo, it still functions as the town hall. From the top of its **tower** (entry on 2nd fl; admission €1.60; ☼ Apr-Oct) on a clear day, you can see as far as the Monti Sibillini to the east and the Gran Sasso to the southeast.

Opposite is the **Palazzo Contucci**, and its extensive wine cellar, Ristorante Il Contucci, open for visiting and sampling (see p276).

Palazzo Tarugi, attributed to Giacomo da Vignola, is beside a well, surmounted by a particularly genial pair of lions.

The beautiful16th-century **cathedral** (Piazza Grande; ☼ 9am-noon & 4-6pm) has an unfinished façade. Above the high altar is a lovely triptych by Taddeo da Bartolo depicting the Assumption.

If you take the low road from Piazza Michelozzi and follow Via di Voltaia nel Corso, you pass first, on your left at No 21, the Renaissance **Palazzo Cervini**, built for Cardinal Marcello Cervini, the future Pope Marcellus II. The unusual U-shape at the front – most palazzi have austere, straight fronts – also incorporates a courtyard into the façade design and appears to have been another Sangallo creation. A few blocks further along on the left, is the **Chiesa del Gesù**, bleak brick outside and elaborately Baroque within.

To the west and prominent in the valley below is domed **Chiesa di San Biagio** (Via di San Biagio; ☼ 9am-12.30pm & 3-7pm, to 6pm winter), a fine Renaissance church built by Antonio da Sangallo the Elder which was undergoing major restoration when we last passed. Its highlight is an impressive marble altarpiece.

COURSES
Il Sasso (☎ 0578 75 83 11; www.ilsasso.com; Via di Gracciano nel Corso 2) Italian language courses for non-native speakers.

FESTIVALS & EVENTS
Bravio delle Botti takes place on the last Sunday in August, when Montepulciano's eight rival *contrade* (districts) continue a centuries-long spirit of fervent neighbourhood competition – like Siena's Palio, this is a key component of local social life – by racing unwieldy giant barrels in two-person teams up the steep streets to Piazza Grande. The Bravio was contested as a frenzied horse race until the 17th century.

The less perilous barrel challenge began in 1974. There's copious ancillary flag waving, Medieval dress-up and general merriment.

SLEEPING
our pick **Bellavista** (☎ 347 823 23 14; bellavista@bccmp .com; Via Ricci 25; d €56-70; P) At the budget end, this is an excellent choice, where nearly all of its 10 high-ceiling, double rooms have fantastic views – room 6 has a private terrace. Some rooms have refrigerators and all have great beds. No-one lives here so phone ahead in order to be met and given a key (if you've omitted this stage, there's a phone in the entrance lobby from where you can call).

Villa Nottola (☎ 0578 70 78 13; www.villanottola .com; Loc Notola 15; d €75-110, ste €110-130; P ☒ ☒) Four kilometres east of Montepulciano, this massive complex has standard rooms, apartments, wine-tasting room, cellar and a giant pool. The buffet breakfast is generous and the onsite Tuscan restaurant (meals €30 to €35; open Wednesday to Monday) cooks up handmade pasta. Follow the signs for 'ospital' out of Montepulciano, turn left after the hospital and the entrance is on the right.

Albergo Il Marzocco (☎ 0578 75 72 62; www.albergo ilmarzocco.it; Piazza Savonarola 18; s/d incl breakfast €60/95; P) Run as a hotel by the same family for over a century, the rooms in this fabulous 16th-century building are large, comfortable and well furnished. Those with a balcony and views come at no extra cost.

Albergo La Terrazza di Montepulciano (☎ 0578 75 74 40; Via Pié al Sasso 16; s/d/tr €72/95/118, all incl breakfast; P) Exuberant and talkative, you'll be charmed by the owner before you even see one of his 10 large rooms or his pride-and-joy breakfast terrace. A self-catering kitchen is available.

Meublé Il Riccio (☎ 0578 75 77 13; www.ilriccio.net; Via Talosa 21; s/d €80/100; P ☒ ☐) This gorgeous tiny hotel, with only six bedrooms, occupies a Renaissance palazzo just off Piazza Grande. It has large rooms, antiques, a solarium, a porticoed courtyard and a terrace bar for your glass of *vino* with a view.

Albergo Il Borghetto (☎ 0578 75 75 35; www.il borghetto.it; Via Borgo Buio 7; s/d €93/105; P) It may look like every other 15th-century building on this street but once inside, this place is a gem, packed with antiques – including Napoleonic-era beds. There's even a tunnel, leading to the house across the street. The hotel is normally closed from mid-January to February.

EATING

Osteria dell'Acquacheta (☎ 0578 75 84 43; Via del Teatro 22; meals €15-20; ☺ Wed-Mon) This is a small eatery with the look and feel of a country trattoria. The food is excellent and mainly meaty, ranging from *misto di salami Toscani* (a variety of Tuscan sausages and salamis) to huge steaks.

Trattoria Diva e Maceo (☎ 0578 71 69 51; Via di Gracciano nel Corso 90; meals €24-28; ☺ Wed-Mon) An uncomplicated place, Trattoria Diva e Maceo is popular with the locals and carries a good selection of local wines. You can feast on Tuscan cuisine like *taglatelle al tartufo* (tagliatelle with truffles) in simple surroundings.

Caffè Poliziano (☎ 0578 75 86 15; Via di Voltaia nel Corso 27; meals €24) Established as a café in 1868, Poliziano has had a chequered past – at times café-cabaret, minicinema, grocery store and, once again since 1990, an elegant café, lovingly restored to its original form by the current owners. Plan carefully to win a seat on one of the tiny, precipitous balcony tables with expansive views.

La Grotta (☎ 0578 75 74 79; ristorante.lagrotta@tiscali.it; Via di San Biagio 2; meals €45-55; ☺ Thu-Tue) Opposite the church of San Biagio, La Grotta is Montepulciano's finest restaurant. Inside this 15th-century building the dining is appropriately elegant while the tables in the garden are tempting for a summer lunch.

DRINKING

There are plenty of places, including several long-established cantinas, where you can whet your palate on the local red, Vino Nobile.

Cantina del Redi (Via Ricci 19; ☺ 10.30am-1pm & 3-7pm) 'No smoking, No microphones, Do not shout out, No dogs, No trash, Do not touch the casks' is the notice that welcomes you. This place doubles as a cool wine cellar that is free to tour.

Ristorante Il Contucci (☎ 0578 75 70 06; www.ristoranteilcantuccio.com; Palazzo Contucci, Piazza Grande; ☺ 8am-12.30pm & 2.30-6.30pm) Vintners since Renaissance times, this is another active cellar where you can sample a drop of the local wine. The owner is a great character and will give you a personal tour, tasting and photo session. The restaurant (meals €30 to €35; open Tuesday to Sunday) is also cellar-fabulous.

GETTING THERE & AROUND

Tra-in runs eight buses daily between Montepulciano and Siena (€4.50, 1¾ hours) via Pienza. Regular LFI buses connect with Chiusi (€2.20, 50 minutes, half-hourly) and continue to Chiusi-Chianciano Terme train station.

There are three services daily to/from Florence (€8) and two to/from Arezzo (€3.70; change at Bettolle). Buses leave from the terminal shared with car park No 5, outside the Porta al Prato at the northern end of town.

Chiusi-Chianciano Terme, 18km southeast and on the main Rome–Florence line, is the most convenient train station (rather than Stazione di Montepulciano, which has very infrequent services).

By car, take the Chianciano Terme exit from the A1 and follow the SS146. Cars are banned from the town centre, but many hotels can issue on-the-spot parking permits, valid for their immediate vicinities, saving guests the death march up the hill with their bags. There are car parks near the Porta al Prato, from where minibuses weave their way to Piazza Grande.

Chianciano Terme

pop 7230

You could skip Chianciano Terme, a short trip south from Montepulciano, unless you think a local spa-water treatment for your liver is in order. The town has a small medieval core, which seems to recoil at all the surrounding development. Given its proximity to Montepulciano, however, it could make a good base with its some 250 hotels catering to spa guests. Most are fairly bland and modern, yet reasonable. However, be prepared for half or full board as, strangely, there are precious few bars and restaurants in town.

Chiusi

pop 8800

One of the most important of the 12 cities of the Etruscan League, Chiusi was once powerful enough to attack Rome, under the leadership of the Etruscan king Porsenna. These days it's a fairly sleepy country town but well worth dropping into. The **tourist office** (☎ 0578 22 76 67; prolocochiusi@bcc.tin.it; ☺ 10am-noon & 3-6pm Jun-Aug, 10am-noon Sep-May) is on central Piazza Carlo Baldini.

SIGHTS

Chiusi's main attractions are the **Etruscan tombs** dotted around the surrounding countryside. Unfortunately, almost all are in such a serious state of disrepair that they are closed. Guided visits (€2, 11am and 4pm March to October, 11am and 2.30pm November to February) to the two accessible tombs, Tomba della Scimmia (the best) and Tomba del Leone, about 3km from town, leave from the **Museo Archeologico Nazionale** (☎ 0578 2 01 77; Via Porsenna 93; adult/child €4/free; ♥ 9am-8pm). You'll need your own transport. The museum itself has a fair collection of artefacts from local tombs that are well displayed and documented in English.

The Romanesque **cathedral**, reworked in the 19th century, holds little interest, although the adjacent **Museo della Cattedrale** (☎ 0578 22 64 90; Piazza Duomo; adult/child €2/€0.50; ♥ 9.30am-12.45pm & 4.30-7pm Jun–mid-Oct, 9.30am-12.45pm Mon-Sat, 10am-12.45pm & 4.30-7pm Sun mid-Oct–May) has an important collection of psalm books.

Beneath the Piazza del Duomo is the **Labirinto di Porsenna**, a series of tunnels dating back to Etruscan times that formed part of the town's water-supply system. A section can be visited with a guide (€3; buy your ticket at the Museo della Cattedrale).

A combined ticket giving entry to both the cathedral and Labirinto di Porsenna costs €4 and there are guide sheets in English.

You can also visit several Christian **catacombs** (admission €5; ♥ guided tours 11am & 5pm Jun–mid-Oct, 11am Mon-Sat, 11am & 4pm Sun mid-Oct–May), 2km from Chiusi. Tours leave from the Museo della Cattedrale, where you buy your ticket.

SLEEPING & EATING

Albergo La Sfinge (☎ 0578 2 01 57; www.albergolasfinge.com; Via Marconi 2; s/d €52/77; ♥ closed Feb; ⊠ ⊒) Just within the confines of Chiusi's historical centre, the clean, attractive rooms here have wrought-iron bedsteads. Some rooms come with a balcony and a few have great views. Room 12 manages both.

La Solita Zuppa (☎ 0578 2 10 06; Via Porsenna 21; meals €30-34; ♥ Wed-Mon) A predominantly Tuscan-based menu with a wide range of soup options is this restaurant's forte. The food is wholesome and cooked to perfection, and the owners make you feel like a long-lost friend.

GETTING THERE & AWAY

Chiusi is just off the A1. Its train station, in the valley below the town, is on the main Rome–Florence line.

Sarteano & Cetona

Heading into this quiet rural territory, you sense that you have left the last of the tour buses well and truly behind. Sarteano and Cetona, delightful little medieval towns amid gentle countryside, are well worth a wander, perhaps extending to a hike up Monte Cetona (1145m), which overlooks Cetona. Pick up Touring Club Italiano's detailed walking map *Cetona* (€1) at 1:15,000 from the town's **tourist office** (☎ 0578 23 91 43; www.cetona.org; ♥ 10am-noon & 5-7pm mid-Jun–mid-Sep, 9am-12.30pm Sat mid-Sep–mid-Jun) on Cetona's Piazza Garibaldi.

Four buses a day go to both towns from Montepulciano and seven from Chiusi.

SARTEANO

Sarteano, topped by a brooding castle, made international headlines not too long ago (see the boxed text, below). Its **tourist office** (☎ 0578 26 92 04; turismo@comune.sarteano.siena.it; ♥ 9.30am-12.30pm & 3.30-7.30pm Aug–mid-Sep, 10am-noon Wed-Mon Jun-Jul, 10am-noon Sat & Sun mid-Sep–May) is at Corso Garibaldi 9. The **Archaeological Civic Museum** (☎ 0578 26 92 61; Via Roma 24; admission adult/child €2.50/2) is a few steps away on the ground floor of Palazzo Gabrielli, displaying a modest collection of local artefacts ranging from the Bronze Age to late-Roman.

THE TOMB OF THE INFERNAL CHARIOT

In 2003 archaeologists excavating an intact 4th-century-BC tomb in the necropolis of Pianacce, just outside Sarteano on the road to Cetona (signposted 'tombe etrusche delle Pianacce'), discovered a unique fresco, its colours still as bright as the day they were applied. On the walls surrounding the alabaster sarcophagus, a demonic figure with wild flowing russet hair drives a chariot pulled by a pair of lions and two griffins. Fabulous monsters – a three-headed snake and a huge seahorse – rear up and two male figures, 'perhaps a father and son as their distinct age difference shows', have an affectionate moment.

The deceased had chosen his last resting place well, with its commanding views over the Val di Chiana, and it's worth the short diversion for the panorama alone. Tours cost €5 and are only possible on Saturdays. Reserve through the Archaeological Civic Museum in Sarteano.

YOU'LL NEVER LOOK AT A SIENESE PIG THE SAME WAY AGAIN

our pick **Agriturismo La Silva** (☎ 0564 95 06 03; www.agriturismolasilva.it; per person incl breakfast €42-60; 🖳 🐖) Situated 3km outside of Seggiano (near Castiglione d'Orcia), is this transformed farmhouse with a celebrated fixation with *suino cinto senese* (a black and white pig native to central Tuscany). See our special agriturismi section for more detail (p315).

At the well-equipped camp site of **Parco Campeggio delle Piscine** (☎ 0578 2 69 71; www.parco dellepiscine.it; Via Campo dei Fiori 30; per person/tent/car €14/14/6.50; 🕘 Apr-Sep; 🖳 🐖) guests can luxuriate in the warm mineral waters of three pools including the large Piscina Bagno Santo, which is also open to noncampers (€12 to €15).

CETONA

Just off Piazza Garibaldi, the main square, cavelike **Cantina la Frasca** (Via Roma 13; 🕘 Thu-Tue) sells its own oil, wine and *pecorino* cheese, straight from the farm, and is a pleasant spot for a snack.

La Frateria di Padre Eligio (☎ 0578 23 82 61; www .lafrateria.it; Via di San Francesco; s €140-160, d €220-240, both incl breakfast) is for those seeking a special retreat. Up a signed lane ('Mondox la Frateria Conv S Francesco') 1km from Cetona on the road to Sarteano, this former convent dating from 1212 has been lovingly restored and converted into a top-class seven-room hotel and gourmet restaurant (meals €88, open Monday to Wednesday, closed january to mid-February), where you can expect an eight-course dining experience of world-class standing.

More modestly, you'll sleep like a top after a day's walking at **La Cocciara** (☎ 0578 23 79 31; www.ostellocetona.it in Italian; Via San Sebastiano 18; dm/d €12/26; 🕘 year-round), Cetona's smart new HI-affiliated youth hostel, and eat well on one of the two floors of **Osteria Vecchia** (☎ 0578 23 90 40; Via Cherubini 11; meals €30; 🕘 Wed-Mon), just off Piazza Garibaldi. The *spaghetti dell'osteria* is a spicy little number and the meat dishes, such as roast pork and Chianina steak, are cooked to perfection.

Abbadia San Salvatore & Around

On your travels in this part of Tuscany you'd have to be short-sighted not to notice the village of **Radicófani**, 17km southwest of Sarteano on the SS478 – or, more precisely, its **rocca** (fortezza; adult/child €3/2; 🕘 10am-7pm May-Oct, 10am-6pm Fri-Sun Nov-Apr). Built high on a blancmange-shaped hill, it's an impressive sight from any approach, and the views from its ramparts are stunning. It now houses a small **museum** devoted to medieval times.

La Torre (☎ 0578 5 59 43; Via G Matteotti 7; d incl breakfast €60) is the only place to stay in town. Don't be put off by the bland red-brick exterior. The rooms, with balconies, are good value and the restaurant is always full of locals here for the appetising wild boar and other homemade fare.

Eighteen kilometres further southwest is **Abbadia San Salvatore**, a largely ugly mining town that grew rapidly and tastelessly from the late 19th century. It does have a couple of saving graces, however. The old town, a sombre stone affair entered off Piazzale XX Settembre, is curious enough, although perhaps not really worth an excursion on its own. Its small **tourist office** (☎ 0577 77 58 11; 🕘 9am-1pm & 4-7pm Mon-Sat) operates from Via Adua 25.

The **Abbazia di San Salvatore** (☎ 0577 77 80 83; abb aziasansalvatore@virgilio.it; Piazzale Michelangelo 8; 🕘 7am-5pm Mon-Sat, 10.30am-6pm Sun Apr-Oct, 7am-5pm Mon-Sat, to 5pm Sun Nov-Mar) was founded in 743 by the Lombard Erfo. It eventually passed into the hands of Cistercian monks, who still occupy it today. Little remains of the monastery, but the church more than compensates. Built in the 11th century and Romanesque in style, it was reconstructed in the late 16th century, when the whole area from the transept to the apse was raised and adorned with broad, frescoed arches that give the impression of walking into a tunnel. Best of all, however, is the 8th-century Lombard crypt, a remarkable stone forest of 36 columns.

The town lies in the shadow of **Monte Amiata** (1738m) and serves as a base for local holidaymakers getting in a little skiing, snow permitting, in winter or some walking in summer. You can, for instance, walk right around the mountain following a 30km-trail known as the **Anello della Montagna**. The path is signposted and the tourist office has maps that also cover other walks in the surrounding area.

There are many hotels in Abbadia San Salvatore and others in towns dotted about the broad expanse of the mountain, so you shouldn't have too much trouble finding a place to stay.

From Siena, two RAMA buses (€4.60, 1¾ hours) call by the abbey daily.

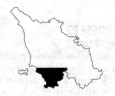

Southern Tuscany

The south of Tuscany, bordering the neighbouring region of Lazio, is a land of lush rumpled hills, distant smoky mountains and ancient hill-top villages. Inland are several of Tuscany's most important Etruscan sites, including the enigmatic *vie cave*, or sunken roads, over whose significance archaeologists still puzzle. For pure drama, the medieval town of Pitigliano is inimitable, looming above a mountainous cliff face pitted with the caves of former Etruscan tombs. Sovana too, just along the road, is rich in Etruscan remains. When you've had your fill, you can dunk yourself in the hot natural pools of Saturnia, only a short drive away.

Grosseto's old town provides an atmospheric setting for the *passeggiata* (traditional evening stroll), while Massa Marittima, the only other inland town of any size, has an equally small, equally charming old quarter and a couple of worthwhile mining museums.

Back on the coast, the Monte Argentario peninsula has smart marinas, good beaches, shady pine groves ideal for a picnic, and a craggy interior, beckoning cyclists and walkers to enjoy a strenuous day out. To its north, the quiet Parco Regionale della Maremma embraces the most varied and attractive stretch of the Tuscan coastline, protected at its rear by the Monti dell'Uccellina range. The park is threaded with signed walking trails or you can hire a mountain bike. You can even join a guided canoe trip along its quiet backwaters. Then again, you could just flop on one of its long, sandy beaches.

Tuscany's southern tip has a couple of delights. The saltwater Lago di Burano teems with bird life, especially in winter. Nearby, and all the more extraordinary for being implanted in such a natural setting, the Giardino dei Tarocchi (Tarot Garden) is an astounding sculpture park on a grand scale, created over the years by Franco-American artist Niki de Saint Phalle.

HIGHLIGHTS

- Try to take a bad picture of breathtaking **Pitigliano** (p290), then delve into its tiny Jewish quarter

- March through the extraordinary *vie cave* (sunken roads) used since Etruscan times in the necropolises around **Sovana** (p292)

- Bathe in the natural hot springs of **Saturnia** (p290)

- Tramp through the diverse, unspoiled surroundings of the sprawling **Parco Regionale della Maremma** (p285)

- Dine on top-value seafood then join the *passeggiata* on the picturesque waterfront in **Porto Santo Stefano** (p287)

GROSSETO

pop 75,100

With the notable exceptions of Bastardo and Schito, Grosseto has the most uninviting, Anglicised ring to its name in all of Italy. On a possibly related note, its public relations efforts have failed to excite significant visitor interest. Yet it's these shortcomings that have contributed to the city's obscure charm. The old walls, raised in 1559, form a near-perfect hexagon. Within, where refreshingly few tourists penetrate, the historic old town has unpretentious enticements and genuinely friendly, good-value eating and sleeping options. It's also one of the rare places in Tuscany where the oft-proclaimed 'no car zone' means almost that. *Passeggiata* anyone?

Grosseto was one of the last Siena-dominated towns to fall into Medici hands in 1559. Once in control, Florence had the walls, bastions and fortress raised in order to protect what was then an important grain and salt depot for the grand duchy.

Information

Caffè Ricasoli (☎ 0564 2 62 20; Via Ricasoli 20; per hr €4; ⏰ 7am-9.30pm Mon-Sat) Internet access.

Seasonal tourist office (☎ 0564 42 78 58; Via Gramschi; ⏰ 9.30am-noon & 4-6pm Mon-Sat Apr-Oct) At the entrance to the old town.

Tourist office (☎ 0564 46 26 11; www.lamaremma.info; Via Monte Rosa 206; ⏰ 9.30am-noon & 4-6pm Mon-Sat) Outside the old quarter, it's well informed about the town and region, including the Parco Regionale della Maremma.

SOUTHERN TUSCANY

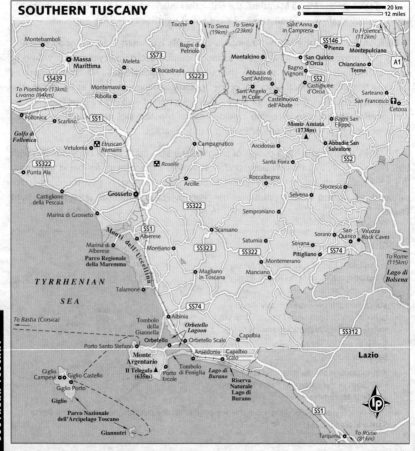

Sights

Within the city walls, Grosseto's **cathedral** (☉ 7.30am-noon & 3.30-7pm), started in the late 13th century, has a distinctive Sienese air. It has been added to and much of the façade was renewed along neo-Romanesque lines during the 19th century. Once inside, the choc-ice painted white-and-brown bands can be an assault on your eyes, but to make up for it there is a lovely tabernacle altar and an elaborate sculpted font. Next door, on Piazza Dante, the **Palazzo della Provincia** seems to be Sienese Gothic, which is exactly what its early-20th-century architects hoped you might think.

Sharing common premises, **Museo Archeologico e d'Arte della Maremma** and smaller **Museo d'Arte Della Diocesi di Grosseto** (☎ 0564 48 87 50; Piazza Baccarini 3; adult/child €5/2.50; ☉ 10am-1pm & 5-8pm Tue-Sat, 9.30am-1pm & 4.30-7pm Sun) are well worth a visit. On the ground floor are Etruscan and Roman artefacts unearthed from Roselle. Room 11 in particular has some imposing statues and fragments, ingeniously jigsawed together. The next floor displays items recovered from Vetulonia and other Maremma sites, while the top storey is mainly devoted to Grosseto's rich ecclesiastical heritage. Ask for the guide sheet in English. Opening hours change frequently (and whimsically).

Sleeping & Eating

Hotel Mulinacci (☎ 0564 2 84 19; Via Mazzini 78; s/d incl breakfast €45/70; **P**) This is a well-priced choice, right in the heart of the old town. With traditional green shutters and a friendly welcome, it has small but comfy rooms like you'd find at your auntie's. Its ground-floor Ristorante l'Italiana is popular with locals – always a good sign.

Bastiani Grand Hotel (☎ 0564 2 00 47; www.hotelbastiani.com; Piazza Gioberti 64; s/d incl breakfast €84/146; **P** ✻) A smart hotel within a grand old building, complete with a *Gone with the Wind*–type, dance-me-down staircase. Rooms are woody and elegant, with bathrooms – most with a bathtub – that are tiled, gold-fixtured and gleaming. The buffet breakfast is vast. Parking is €18.

Danubio Blu (☎ 0564 2 22 16; Via Cavour 6; meals €25) This is a hugely popular, noisy restaurant with cheery, frazzled staff and a dizzying choice of dishes, including the traditional polenta and risotto – and occasional surprises like chichen (sic) curry.

Ristorante il Canto del Gallo (☎ 0564 41 45 89; Via Mazzini 29; meals €32; ☉ dinner Mon-Sat, lunch bookings only) This is a long, thin tunnel of a place. The Cock Crow is decorated with every possible variant upon the cockerel (rooster) theme, even down to the stoppers used on the rich choice of grappas. The genial, beaming chef emerges from her kitchen, clucks an order or two, greets her guests, then retires to prepare another delicious platter, while the sole waiter darts up and down like an Olympic sprint finalist.

Getting There & Around

Rama (☎ 0564 2 52 15; www.griforama.it in Italian; Piazza Marconi) buses cover destinations throughout the province of Grosseto. Most services leave from the train station. Buses for Siena, where you can connect with either Tra-in or SITA buses to Florence, run roughly every hour. Alternatively, there are three direct services.

There is only one direct bus a day to Massa Marittima (€3.40). Other destinations include Piombino (€5, 1¼ hours, three daily), Magliano in Toscana (€2, 60 minutes, two to five daily), Follonica (€3.40, one hour, three daily), Castiglione della Pescaia (€4.40, 50 minutes, 15 daily), Porto Santo Stefano (€3.40, one hour, three daily) and Pitigliano (€6, two hours, five daily).

Grosseto is on the main coastal train line between Rome (€14.80, two hours) and Livorno (€10, 1½ hours). For places such as Pisa (€8.20, two hours), Florence (€11.70, three hours) or Siena (€6.10, 1½ hours), the train is probably a smarter bet.

There's plenty of parking, albeit paying, beneath the exterior of the city walls.

AROUND GROSSETO
Roselle

Populated as early as the 7th century BC, Roselle was a middle-ranking Etruscan town that came under Roman control in the 3rd century BC.

Although there are no great monuments left standing, the extensive **historic site** (☎ 0564 40 30 67; admission €4; ☉ 9am-sunset) retains its Roman defensive walls, an oddly elliptical amphitheatre, traces of houses, the forum and streets. You will also find remains of an abandoned medieval village. There are wonderful views down to the plains and out to the sea.

SOUTHERN TUSCANY

Vetulonia

This windswept mountain village seems to rise out of nothing from the surrounding plains. It retains elements of the ancient surrounding wall and has a small **Museo Archeologico** (☎ 0564 94 80 58; Piazza de Vetulonia; adult/child €4.50/2.50; ☻ core hours 10am-1pm & 3-6pm Tue-Sat, to 8pm Jun-Sep) that contains a rich display of artefacts revealed by excavations at the two nearby **Etruscan sites** (☎ 0564 94 95 87; admission free; ☻ 10am-7pm Apr-Sep). The more extensive area, known as **Scavi Città** (Town Excavations), is just below the village as you leave by the only road.

More interesting are four unearthed **Etruscan tombs** (Via dei Sepolcri; ☻ 10am-7pm), a couple of kilometres further downhill and along a turn-off to the right. Best is the last, about 1km down a rough dirt track.

Taverna Etrusca (☎ 0564 94 98 02; www.tavernaen trusca.it; Piazza Stefani 12; s €50-60, d €55-70; ☻ Easter-Oct; ☒ ⧉) has 10 large rooms with fantastic panoramic views, some with terraces. The views will successfully distract from the Spartan furnishings – that money was shrewdly put into the new beds. There is an onsite restaurant that serves satisfying meals for about €24.

A daily bus runs to/from both Grosseto and Castiglione della Pescaia.

MASSA MARITTIMA

pop 8840

Massa is a compelling place with a pristine and comparatively serene medieval centre by Tuscan standards. Briefly under Pisan domination, it thrived on the local metal mining industry, even becoming an independent *comune* (municipality) in 1225, only to be swallowed up by Siena a century later. The plague in 1348, and the end of mining 50 years later, reduced the city almost to extinction. Not until the 18th century, with the draining of marshes and re-establishment of mining, did Massa Marittima finally come back to life.

Orientation

The centre is split in two; the twisted and scenic old quarter and – up a steep hill, through the massive Arco Senese – the curiously grid-pattered new part, where attractive photo-ops are in short supply.

MASSA MARITTIMA

INFORMATION	
Tourist Office	1 A2

SIGHTS & ACTIVITIES	
Arco Senese	2 B2
Cathedral	3 A3

Museo Archeologico	4 A2
Museo degli Organi Santa Cecilia	5 C2
Museo della Miniera	6 A3
Museo di Arte e Storia delle Miniere	7 B2
Museo di Arte Sacra	8 C2
Palazzo Comunale	9 A2
Palazzo del Podestà	(see 4)
Torre del Candeliere	(see 2)

SLEEPING	
La Fenice Park Hotel	10 C2
Ostello Santa Anna	11 C3

EATING	
L'Antica Osteria	12 A2
Osteria da Tronca	13 A2
Trattoria Vecchio Borgo	14 A3

DRINKING	
Pub dei Fantasmi	15 A3

TRANSPORT	
Bus Stop	16 C2
Massa Veternensis	17 A2

Information

Tourist office (☎ 0566 90 27 56; www.altamarem maturismo.it; Via Todini 3/5; ✆ 9.30am-12.30pm & 3.30-7.30pm Mon-Sat, 10am-1pm & 4-7pm Sun Jun-Sep, 9.30am-12.30pm & 3.30-6.30pm Mon-Sat, 10am-1pm Sun Apr, May & Oct, 9.30am-12.30pm & 3-6pm Mon-Sat Nov-Mar) Down a side street, beneath the Museo Archeologico.

Sights

The heart of medieval Massa is Piazza Garibaldi, watched over by the imposing bulk of the **cathedral** (St Cerbone's Cathedral; ✆ 8am-noon & 3-5pm) and the several dozen loiterers sitting on its steps at any given moment. Cleverly set asymmetrical to the square to better show off its splendour, the cathedral is a commendably assembled, snap-on conglomeration of enlargements and renovations supplementing its first, pre-Romanesque incarnation from the 12th century. The Pisan-Romanesque façade includes a central door flanked by two lion heads and topped by five panels depicting scenes from the life of St Cerbone. Blind arcades of 13th-century Pisan design line the sides and the roof was crowned with a polygonal dome in the 15th century. The lower half of the attached Gothic *campanile* (bell tower) dates from around 1400, while the upper part was redone at the beginning of the 20th century.

The cathedral's interior is a standard basilica-plan layout with rib vaults in both the aisles (17th century) and nave (15th century), highlighted by the *Arca di San Cerbone* (St Cerbone's Ark; 1324) carved by Goro di Gregorio and adorned with bas-relief episodes of the saint's life. A wooden crucifix (early-14th century) by Giovanni Pisano hangs over the huge marble altar by Flaminio del Turco (1626). The remainder of the interior is graced with an assortment of sculpted panels from the 12th and 13th centuries, substantial remnants of frescoes and several paintings, including an ailing *Madonna delle Grazie* attributed to Siena's Duccio di Buoninsegna. There's also a fine 14th-century total immersion baptismal font.

Opposite is the **Palazzo Comunale**, the city's historic seat of government. The coat of arms of Florence's Medicis is less aesthetically moving than the symbol of rival Siena's one-time ascendancy here – the wolf with Romulus and Remus.

The 13th-century **Palazzo del Podestà** houses the **Museo Archeologico** (☎ 0566 90 22 89; www.coop collinemetallifere.it/musei; Piazza Garibaldi 1; adult/child

€3/1.50; ✆ 10am-12.30pm & 3.30-7pm Tue-Sun Apr-Oct, 10am-12.30pm & 3-5pm Nov-Mar). A monkey fossil from the Miocene era and a simple, but compelling stele dating from the 3rd millennium BC are the hands-down highlights of the ground floor's archaeological collection. The upper levels have a modest collection of ancient Roman and Etruscan artefacts recovered from around town.

Up in the Città Nuova (New Town) is the **Torre del Candeliere** (Piazza Matteotti; adult/child €2.50/1.50; ✆ 10am-1pm & 3-6pm Tue-Sun Apr-Oct, 11am-1pm & 2.30-4.30pm Tue-Sun Nov-Mar). The tower is linked to defensive bastions in the wall by the vast sweep of the so-called **Arco Senese** (Sienese Arch). You can enter the tower and walk across the arch for stupendous views over the Città Vecchia (Old Town).

Music-lovers will enjoy the **Museo degli Organi Santa Cecilia** (☎ 0566 94 02 82; www.museodeglior gani.it; Corso Diaz 28; adult/child €4/2; ✆ 10am-1pm & 4-8pm Apr-Oct, 10.30am-12.30pm & 3-6pm Tue-Sun Nov-Mar) with its collection of antique organs, harpsichords and clavichords, which, if you strike it lucky, the curator will play for you.

Museo della Miniera (☎ 0566 90 22 89; Via Corridoni; adult/child €5/3; ✆ guided visits 10am-12.30pm & 3-5.30pm Apr-Sep, 10am-noon & 3-4.30pm Tue-Sun Oct-Mar) relates the city's long mining history. The display includes a replica of a length of mine. Guided tours in Italian and optional English last around 45 minutes.

The smaller **Museo di Arte e Storia delle Miniere** (☎ 0566 90 22 89; Piazza Matteotti 4; adult/child €1.50/1; ✆ 3-5.30pm Tue-Sun Apr-Oct) has more mining material and a strong photographic collection.

At the far end of Corso Diaz is the **Museo di Arte Sacra** (☎ 0566 90 19 54; Corso Diaz 36; adult/child €5/3; ✆ 10am-1pm & 3-6pm Apr-Sep, 11am-1pm & 3-5pm Oct-Mar), the new home for Ambrogio Lorenzetti's magnificent *Maestà* (Majesty) as well as a collection of alabaster bas-reliefs, sculptures, a wooden crucifix by Pisano, paintings by Sano di Pietro and Stefano di Giovanni, and other items collected from local churches.

Festivals & Events

Balestro del Girifalco This medieval festival, punctuated by a crossbow competition, takes place in Piazza Garibaldi. Held on the fourth Sunday in May and the second Sunday in August.

Toscana Foto Festival (www.toscanafotofestival.com in Italian) Held in the first two weeks of July, the festival attracts international professional photographers, whose works are displayed all over town until mid-August.

Sleeping & Eating

Many hotels and restaurants in Massa take a long winter break between January and March.

Albergo Il Girifalco (☎ 0566 90 21 77; Via Massetana Nord 25; s €50-70, d €55-75, all incl breakfast) This low-key place is just outside the walls. It's family friendly, with a playground and picnic area. Rooms are clean and bright, and many have sweeping views.

Ostello Santa Anna (☎ 0566 90 26 65, 339 278 62 72; Via Gramsci 3; per person €15; ☺ reception 9am-12pm & 5-7.30pm; P) A quiet, budget option, a 1km up-hill walk from the centre, with six-bed dorms each with bathrooms. Breakfast is €1.50.

Duca del Mare (☎ 0566 90 22 84; www.ducadelmare.it; Piazza Dante Alighieri 1/2; s €50-60, d €85-100, all incl buffet breakfast; P ☒ ☒) Duca del Mare is about 10 minutes' walk from the historic centre. This modern, sunny hotel has a Scandinavian air with lots of shiny light wood and Ikea-style furnishings. All rooms have terraces, some party-sized, with tree-obscured views of the countryside.

La Fenice Park Hotel (☎ 0566 90 39 41; www .lafeniceparkhotel.it; Corso Diaz 63; s €90-110, d €150-200, all incl breakfast; ☒ ☐ ☒) This is a seductive marble-clad hotel (bathrooms are a gleaming, sensual delight) where all rooms have a minikitchen. The junior suites (€170 to €225) are essentially roomy, fully equipped apartments, and there's a croquet-quality lawn and raised pool. Wi-fi in lobby. The hotel has wheelchair access.

Osteria da Tronca (☎ 0566 90 19 91; Vicolo Porte 5; meals €23-28; ☺ Tue-Sun) Squeezed into a side street, da Tronca is an intimate stone-walled restaurant. There's lots of antipasto (€3) to choose from. For mains, try anything with *cinghiale* (wild boar).

L'Antica Osteria (☎ 0566 90 26 44; Via Norma Parenti 19; meals €25; ☺ Thu-Tue) This *osteria* (restaurant focussing on wine) is great value, offering several lip-smacking vegetarian options, including cheese-filled ravioli with mushrooms, and it also has an inexpensive pizza menu.

Trattoria Vecchio Borgo (☎ 0566 90 39 50; taverna .vecchioborgo@libero.it; Via Norma Parenti 12; meals €30-40; ☺ Tue-Sun) A brick-clad restaurant with a cavernous barrel-vaulted interior where a welcoming fire roars away in winter. There's a set menu and a good variety of dishes, and its *gnocchi al pomodoro* (gnocchi in a tomato sauce) is hard to beat.

Drinking

Pub dei Fantasmi (☎ 0566 94 02 75; Via Norma Parenti 2/4; ☺ 9.30pm-2am or 3am Thu-Tue) This is the place to head if you're feeling frisky after dinner; it's about the only place in town big enough to hold a crowd. There's occasional live jazz.

Getting There & Away

There are two daily buses to Siena (€4.40) at 7.05am and 4.40pm, and around four to Volterra (changing at Monterotondo). The nearest train station is Massa-Follonica, served by a regular shuttle bus (€2). All buses call at the stop on Piazza XXIV Maggio. **Massa Veternensis** (☎ 0566 902 20 62; Piazza Garibaldi 18) sells both bus and train tickets.

THE COAST

There are no great swaths of sand as you cruise the coast south from Piombino, where occasional stretches of pine-backed beach are pleasant without being breathtaking. What does deserve a detour along this southern stretch of mainland Tuscan coast is the Parco Regionale della Maremma.

Golfo di Follonica

Maintaining an industrial tradition that dates back to Etruscan times, the gulf these days is mostly chimney stacks and factories – all necessary, to be sure, but no reason to hang about. Heading south, the first town you will reach is **Follonica**, with its cheap and scruffy high-rises. The outlook improves a few kilometres further around the gulf with a pleasant pinewood backdrop to the beaches; look for the turn-off signs inland for **Scarlino**.

Some sadistic committee in **Punta Ala** succeeded in devising the most Kafkaesque road system for this leafy but rather fake getaway for the seriously moneyed. On the plus side, the promontory is green and sparingly brutalised by building development, and, along the northern flank, there is a pleasant pine-backed sandy beach.

Castiglione della Pescaia

pop 7300

The modern sprawl around the foot of the hill on which this medieval stone village sits lives harmoniously enough with its more venerable antecedent.

The walled old town has no monuments of interest, but is pleasant to stroll through – and views out to sea are majestic.

The **tourist office** (☎ 0564 93 36 78; www.castigli onepescaia.com; Piazza Garibaldi 6; ☎ 9am-1pm & 3-7pm Mon-Sat) is in the main square of the lower town.

SLEEPING & EATING

Hotel Bologna (☎ /fax 0564 93 37 46; Piazza Garibaldi 8; s with/without bathroom €36/29, d with/without bathroom €68/53; ✱) This is a no-frills small hotel whose rooms have surprisingly comfortable beds, while the remaining furniture's dated and retro-plastic. Doubles with bathrooms are worth the upgrade. The location, however, is five-star superb – across from the harbour, with great views from the corner breakfast room and some bedrooms.

Hotel Lucerna (☎ 0564 93 36 20; www.hotellucerna. it; Via IV Novembre 27; s €46-65, d €78-100, all incl breakfast; P ✱) An attractive traditional hotel that's been run by the same family for three generations. Rooms are cheerful and large, and have balconies with sea or old-town views. The adjacent restaurant and pizzeria is handy for staving off hunger pangs. Parking is free, but limited.

L'Andana (☎ 0564 94 43 21; www.andanahotel.com; d incl breakfast €332-460; P ▢ ✱) To sum this place up – *mamma mia*! Down a gated, kilometre-long, tree-lined dirt track flanked by vineyards, olive trees and 50 sq km of rolling hills, is this once summer abode of Duke Leopold. Opened in 2004 and designed with the help of French, three-star Michelin chef Alain Ducasse, this 16th-century property is the last hotel you'll ever want to stay in. And you can bet your tongue that the onsite Trattoria Toscana (open dinner only, Tuesday to Sunday) won't disappoint. Avail yourself of the indoor and outdoor swimming pools, spa with signature treatments, tennis court, 18-hole golf course, lobby wi-fi and the largest showers in Tuscany – maybe Europe.

Ristorante La Fortezza (☎ 0564 93 61 00; Via del Recinto 1/3; meals €33; ☎ daily Mar-Oct, Tue-Sun Nov-Feb) La Fortezza is just beyond the massive gate leading to the old town. You can dine outside or within the cavelike interior and savour typical dishes of the Maremma, including pasta with lobster.

GETTING THERE & AWAY
Rama buses run to/from Grosseto (€4.40, 50 minutes, 15 daily) and connect with other places on the coast, such as Marina di Grosseto (€2.50).

Marina di Grosseto
The beach is broad and sandy, but the resort is modern, with slapped-together housing and an anonymous gridlike street system. At least it's predominantly low-rise and well camouflaged by the umbrella pines typical of the Maremma coast. It's a favoured spot for locals to come and splash in the sea, but there are more interesting places close by.

Parco Regionale della Maremma
The Maremma extends along the Tuscan coast from just north of Grosseto to the southern border with Lazio, embracing the Parco Regionale della Maremma and Monte Argentario. Fronting the coast, it's an area of long, sandy beaches and reclaimed marshland, crisscrossed by dykes and drainage ditches. This **nature park** (admission €6-9) protects its most spectacular parts and incorporates the **Monti dell'Uccellina**, which drop to a magnificent stretch of unspoiled coastline. Native wild boar, wild cats and porcupines share the area with cowboy-supervised herds of oxen and horses, all spread out over a string of adjacent ecosystems: agricultural, forest, humid, rocky and dune landscapes.

The park's main **visitor centre** (☎ 0564 40 70 98; www.parcomaremma.it; ☼ 8am-5pm mid-Mar–Sep, 8.30am-1.30pm Oct–mid-Mar) is in Alberese, at the park's northern edge. It has shelves of information on the park and activities, including guided horse tours. There's a small **seasonal centre** (☎ 0564 88 71 73; ☼ 8am-noon & 5-8pm Jul & Aug, 8am-1pm Sep-Jun) at the park's southern extremity, 400m up a dirt lane about 1km before Talamone. Talamone itself is a little coastal village, surmounted by a plain, functional blockhouse of a fortress, from whose base there's a great sea view.

Entry to the park is limited and cars must be left in designated areas. Walking is the best way to explore its riches on 11 unique, signed walking trails, varying from 2.5km to 12km long. Within surprisingly shorts distances, walks lead through thick pine forests into beaches, past caves, around bays, through marshes and bushland, skirting ponds and along coastline. There's also a guided night tour. Entry (by ticket bought at one of the visitor centres) varies according to whether a minibus transports you to your chosen route. Depending upon your trail, you stand a chance of spotting deer, wild boar, foxes and hawks.

The **Centro Turismo Il Rialto** (☎ 0564 40 71 02), 600m north of the main visitors centre, offers guided canoe outings (adult/child €16/8; two hours) and rents mountain bikes (per hour/day €3/8). It doesn't have set core hours, so call ahead or risk finding the place abandoned.

Between July and September, when the park gets very crowded, a couple of routes are closed and two others can only be undertaken in a guided group because of the high risk of forest fire. There are no shelters within the park, so make sure you wear sun block and carry water.

To restore your energy after a walk, there are a couple of simple, good-value eating options. Situated beside the Centro Turismo Il Rialto is **Il Mangiapane** (☎ 0564 40 72 63; meals €15), but the service can be patchy here. The better option is **Trattoria e Pizzeria Mancini e Caduro** (☎ 0564 40 71 37; Via del Fante 24; meals €19; ☯ Tue-Sun Apr-Sep), located in nearby Alberese. It has a short, affordable menu of homemade Tuscan standards – *tortelli ricortta espinace* (pasta with cheese and spinach), *aquacotta* (soup with bread, onion, tomatoes, celery

and egg) – and pizzas served on the small terrace.

Osteria la Nuova Dispensa (☎ 0564 40 73 21; Via Aurelia Vecchia 11; meals €28-32; ☯ Thu-Tue) occupies the old village store and also offers local specialities. If you like your food spicy, fire up on the *peposo*, a peppery stewed beef dish with vegetables and Tuscany's answer to a vindaloo. The restaurant's 4.5km south of Alberese, just before the junction with the SS1.

MONTE ARGENTARIO
pop 13,000

Once an island, this rugged promontory came to be linked to the mainland by an accumulation of sand that is now the isthmus of Orbetello. Further sandy bulwarks form the Tombolo della Giannella and the Tombolo di Feniglia to the north and south. They enclose a lagoon that is now a protected nature reserve.

Intense building, poor urban planning and stunning mobs of people have spoiled the northern side of the promontory (Porto Santo Stefano and around), but the south and centre have been left in peace (forest fires

---

COWBOY CULTURE

The fascination Europe held for the cowboy culture of the American West was never more apparent than in the late 1800s when Colonel William Cody (alias Buffalo Bill) took his fabulously successful Wild West show on two grand European tours.

Buffalo Bill brought the show to Italy, complete with the sharp-shooting Annie Oakley and bands of real Sioux warriors, many the very same braves who had fought Custer at the Battle of Little Big Horn. The troupe was invited to the Vatican to attend the celebration of the 10th anniversary of the coronation of Pope Leo XIII. Then, in Verona, Cody fulfilled his ambition of exhibiting his Wild West in the ancient Roman amphitheatre, where the high point was a bronco-busting challenge match between Buffalo Bill's cowboys and the *butteri*. These were Tuscany's legendary cowboys, who survived the harsh conditions of the Maremma, its swampland a breeding ground for malarial mosquitoes. The Maremma was divided among landowners of vast estates where the *butteri* tended herds of Cajetan horses, one of the most unmanageable and wild breeds in Europe. In front of a crowd of some 20,000 spectators, the *butteri* challenged the American cowboys to break the Cajetans. The Rome correspondent of the *New York Herald* wrote: 'The brutes made springs into the air, darted hither and thither in all directions, and bent themselves into all sorts of shapes, but all in vain. In five minutes the cowboys [*butteri*] had caught the wild horses with the lasso, saddled, subdued and bestrode them. Then the cowboys rode them around the arena while the dense crowds applauded with delight.'

Today, longhorn cattle and horses still graze free in the Maremma, the swamps have all been drained, the grass is lush, and malaria a menace of the past. On the first Sunday in August, the *butteri* gather and brand the cattle. The **Equinus Association** (☎ 0564 2 49 88; www.cavallomaremmano.it) organises *butteri* shows and equestrian tourism, and even provides information on buying – presumably tamed – Maremma horses. There is also an official organisation, **Butteri di Alta Maremma** (www.butteri-altamaremma.com), which protects and promotes the remaining *butteri* and also arranges rodeo-style events.

aside). The area is generally up-market-leaning and a favourite summer weekend getaway for Romans, when it gets packed to the gunwales. Ambitious hotel prices make this poor value in high season and parking, particularly in Porto Santo Stefano, is cut-throat. Late April to early May and late September to early October are optimum times to visit, when warm days, cool nights, reduced crowds and lower prices dramatically improve the atmosphere.

GETTING THERE & AROUND

Frequent **Rama** (☎ 0564 86 79 29) buses connect most towns on Monte Argentario with downtown Orbetello (€1.50, 20 minutes) and continue to the train station. They also run to Grosseto (€3.40, one hour, up to four daily).

By car, follow signs for Monte Argentario from the SS1, which connects Grosseto with Rome.

Orbetello

pop 15,000

Set on a balance-beam isthmus running through the lagoon, Orbetello is an easily digestible, less-raucous regional destination. Its modest, main attraction is the **cathedral** (Piazza della Repubblica; ☿ 9am-noon & 3-6pm), which has retained its 14th-century Gothic façade despite being remodelled in the Spanish style during the 16th century. Other reminders of the Spanish garrison that was stationed in the city for nearly 150 years include the Viceroy's residence located on Piazza Eroe dei Due Mondi, the fort and the city walls, parts of which are the original Etruscan fortification.

The **tourist office** (☎ 0564 86 04 47; ☿ 9.30am-12.30pm & 4-7pm Apr-Sep, to 8pm Jul & Aug, 9am-12.30pm & 4-7pm Oct-Mar) is opposite the cathedral.

The best place for observing bird life (as many as 140 species have been identified) on Orbetello's lagoon is out along the Tombolo di Feniglia, the southern strip of land linking Monte Argentario to the mainland. It is blocked to traffic, but you can park your car near the camp site and continue on foot or bicycle. The beach on the seaward side is one of the best on the peninsula.

SLEEPING & EATING

Hotel I Presidi (☎ 0564 86 76 01; Via Mura di Levante 34; s €100-110, d €130-160, all incl breakfast; P ☒ ▢) This is an airy, thoroughly modern hotel, wedged between the lagoon-side road and the old quarter. The striped wallpaper in the rooms is offset by a floral frieze and flowery coverlets. Those on the 4th floor have a small balcony, and there's a peaceful interior patio. Off-street parking is €10 per day.

Osteria il Nocchino (☎ 0564 86 03 29; Via Furio Lenzi 64; meals €30; ☿ Wed-Mon Mar-Oct, Fri-Sun Nov-Feb) Another excellent choice, albeit with about as much seating capacity as a glorified matchbox (supplemented in summer by outdoor seating). Prices are moderate and the food is like *mamma* used to make.

Osteria del Lupacante (☎ 0564 86 76 18; Corso Italia 103; meals €35, tourist menus €21; ☿ Thu-Tue) This *osteria* is run by a Sicilian family. You really must begin with one of the splendid soups, which is almost a meal in itself. The *spaghetti alla messinese* (Messina style, with swordfish, tomato, peppers, sunflower seeds and spices) is only one of the imaginative creations.

Porto Santo Stefano

Porto Santo Stefano's linked, crescent waterfront layout divides the objectionable port from the fashionable harbour. Both sides are equally chaotic, though the Ferraris, yachts and scantly clad bodies on the harbour side are significantly more enthralling. From the waterline, the city shoots up the mountainside on ultrathin streets, devoid of parking and sidewalks, where one lingering vehicle can back up traffic all the way down to the port in an instant.

The harbour, however, is a *passeggiata* dream: spacious and lined with restaurants, cafes, *gelatarie*, and plenty of places to sit and observe this endearing social phenomenon.

INFORMATION

Il Galeone (Lungomare dei Navigatori 40; per hr €6; ☿ 8am-midnight) A bar with a couple of internet points.

Tourist office (☎ 0564 81 42 08; www.lamaremma .info; Piazzale Sant'Andrea; ☿ 9am-1pm & 3.30-7.30pm Mon-Sat Apr-Sep, 9am-1pm & 2-4pm Mon-Sat Oct-Mar) Is appallingly located at the eastern end of the port.

SIGHTS & ACTIVITIES

Fortezza Spagnola (☎ 0564 81 06 81; Piazza del Governatore; adult/child €3/2; ☿ 6pm-midnight Jun-Sep, 10.30am-12.30pm & 3-7pm Sat & Sun Oct-May), several uneven streets and stairways above the harbour, houses a small collection of underwater archaeological finds and an exhibition of wooden boat-making. It affords breathtaking views of Porto Santo Stefano – if you've any breath left after the steep ascent.

If you've wheels, follow signs for the narrow and sometimes dangerously overcrowded **Via Panoramica**, a circular route offering great coastal views over the water to the hazy whaleback of the Isola de Giglio. For another spectacular drive, take a right turn 6km east of Porto Santo Stefano, up the signed road leading to **Convento dei Frati Passionisti**, a convent with sensational views across to the mainland.

There are several good **beaches**, mainly of the pebbly variety.

SLEEPING

ourpick Pensione Weekend (☎ 0564 81 25 80; www .pensioneweekend.it; Via Martiri d'Ungheria 3; d €50-80; **P**) This *pensione* is a true gem and the only pseudo-budget option in town. Rooms are small and scrubbed, with eccentric components like the intercom surviving from an upgrade done in the '60s. New bathrooms have been recently shoehorned into every room. The friendly, polyglot owner can give you a parking permit for the tiny lot across the road.

Hotel La Caletta (☎ 0564 81 29 39; www.hotelcaletta .it; Via del Fortino 51; s €50-120, d €60-164; **P** **X**) This is a three-star hotel whose prices seasonally swing from good value to dubious value. The floral and white décor may be a bit girly for some, but the private beach is a nice perk. Half-board is compulsory in August, when prices peak.

Albergo Belvedere (☎ 0564 81 26 34; Via del Fortino 51; s €60-70, d €90-100, all incl breakfast; **X** Apr-Oct; **P** **X**) Just 1km east of the harbour, overlooking the water, this is a nondescript, but peaceful option with a private beach. Some rooms have balconies with sea views.

Hotel Torre di Cala Piccola (☎ 0564 82 51 11; www .torredicalapiccola.com; Cala Piccola; s €170-310, d €200-370, tr €270-500, all incl breakfast; **X** Mar-Oct; **P** **X** **□** **R**) This hotel is a self-contained complex in splendid isolation, built around an old Spanish watchtower, 8km southwest along the Via Panoramica. There are spectacular seascapes from the balcony of the luxury rooms, and the dining setting in the garden is particularly glorious. A minibus transports you down the hillside to the hotel's private beach. The onsite restaurant (meals €45 to €50) has a celebrated chef with a seafood fixation.

EATING

Il Moletto (☎ 0564 81 36 36; www.moletto.it; Via del Molo 52; meals €28-32; **X** Thu-Tue) Among several enticing quayside seafood restaurants, this place wins for its location. At this wooden cabin, set apart from the rest at the end of a mole, you can dine beside a picture window or on the jetty as the evening breeze cools your pasta.

Lo Sfizio (☎ 0564 81 25 92; Lungomare dei Navigatori 26; pizzas from €6, meals €30-35; **X** daily May-Oct, Tue-Sun Nov-Apr) Its corny fish-theme décor and bar of blinking lights looks unpromising, but what draws in diners is the very reasonably priced fish and seafood dishes and the friendly informality of its youthful staff.

Trattoria Da Siro (☎ 0564 81 25 38; Corso Umberto 100; meals €32-37; **X** Tue-Sun) Overlooking the waterfront, this trattoria also manages a good mix of well-prepared fish and seafood, spiced with an impressive seascape.

ourpick Il Veliero (☎ 0564 81 22 26; Via Panoramica 149-151; meals €35-40; **X** Tue-Sun Feb-Dec) An excellent restaurant, high above the port, that serves the freshest of fare from the sea – the owner's father runs a fish shop in town. It's a steep climb (head up the steps, guarded by a terracotta lion, just above Pensione Weekend) but well worth the exertion. The *pasta fresca alla chitarra* (guitar-string pasta with a light tomato-lobster sauce) is heavenly.

For a great view without paying panoramic prices, grab a pizza from **Pizzeria da Gigetto** (☎ 0564 81 44 95; Via del Molo 9) and munch it on the waterfront terrace, then finish off with an ice cream from Bar Gelateria Chioda, right next door.

Porto Ercole

Situated in a picturesque position between two Spanish forts, Porto Ercole still manages to retain some of its fishing village character. Far less hectic than the north side of the island, you can wander the hillside historic centre, past the sandwiched Chiesa di Sant'Erasmo – final resting place of painter/hellion Caravaggio (1571–1610) – and sometimes wonder if you're the only person in town. The climb to the ho-hum fortress is a steep one. Down by the water, the beach is serviced, so it's clean but cluttered with deck chairs and umbrellas. Further away, it becomes less crowded but, as with most public beaches in Italy, also dirtier.

You can camp at **Camping Feniglia** (☎ 0564 83 10 90; www.campingfeniglia.it; per person/site €9/13, bungalow per week d €220-700; year-round) In Feniglia, about 1.5km north of Porto Ercole, and just 50m from the sea. Trouble is, most of it is occupied by permanently planted caravans and family tents. It also has bungalows at weekly rates.

Gatto e la Volpe (0564 83 52 05; Via dei Cannoni 3; meals €38; Tue-Sun) is the last stop on the right as you sweep down the road to the far end of the harbour. The views are wonderful. Try the speciality *linguine all'astice* (lobster linguine), leaving room for the homemade desserts.

THE ISLANDS

More than a few locals skip Monte Argentario altogether and choose to head off on excursions to one of two islands off the coast. The islands of Giglio and Giannutri are both part of the Parco Nazionale dell'Arcipelago Toscano.

Giannutri

This tiny island, just 5km long, has a grand old ruin of a Roman villa (1st century AD) but not much else, aside from a pleasant shady bay, Cala Spalmatoio, on the eastern side. In summer you can get there by a ferry service run by **Maregiglio** (www.maregiglio.it).

Giglio

The hilly island of Giglio is Tuscany's second largest after Elba. Some 14km off Monte Argentario, its pristine waters are increasingly popular with divers. Regular boat services from Porto Santo Stefano make getting to this pretty little spot easy. You arrive at colourful **Giglio Porto**, once a Roman port and now the best spot to find accommodation. A local bus service will take you 6km to the inland fastness of **Giglio Castello**, dominated by a Pisan castle.

Aside from a couple of patches of sand the size of a beach towel, the only beaches are on the western side of the island, in and around the modern resort of Giglio Campese, built around the old watchtower.

Toremar (0564 81 08 03) and **Maregiglio** (0564 81 29 20; www.maregiglio.it) run several daily ferries (adult/child return €10/5) between Porto Santo Stefano and the island.

LAGO DI BURANO & AROUND

Little more than 10km further east along the coast from Monte Argentario, this saltwater flat is a nature reserve, **Riserva Naturale Lago**

di Burano (0564 89 88 29; Capalbio Scalo; admission €5.25; guided visits 10am & 2.30pm Sun Sep-Apr), run by the World Wide Fund for Nature (WWF). Covering 410 hectares and stopping about 5km short of the regional frontier with Lazio, it is typical of the Maremma in its flora, but interesting above all for its migratory bird life. Tens of thousands of birds of many species winter here, including several kinds of duck and even falcons. Among the animals, the most precious is the beaver. A path with seven observation points winds its way through the park.

About 8km south of the lake turn-off, you can see the terraces of **Il Giardino dei Tarocchi** (0564 89 51 22; www.nikidesaintphalle.com; Località Garavicchio-Capalbio; adult/child €10.50/6; 2.30-7.30pm May–mid-Oct), a fantastic collection of oversized Antoni Gaudí–influenced sculptures tumbling down a hillside. This theme park–scale profusion of dreamy, mosaic-covered sculptures skilfully merges with surrounding nature. The colossal effort, by Franco-American artist Niki de Saint Phalle (1930–2002), depicts the main players from the tarot card pack, such as the Moon, the Fool, the High Priest of Feminine Intuitive Power – and the Empress, within whose innards the artist lived for months during construction. Your interest in divination notwithstanding, these pleasing exhibits transcend age and aesthetic leanings and are the kind of roadside fun that Midwestern American tourists drive 20 miles out of their way to see.

For both, take the Capalbio Scalo exit from the SS1.

INLAND & ETRUSCAN SITES

The deep south of Tuscany is home to thermal springs, medieval hill towns and Etruscan archaeological finds.

Magliano & Scansano

From **Albinia**, at the northern tip of the Orbetello Lagoon, take the SS74 in the direction of Manciano and make a detour left (north) up the SS323.

The first stop is **Magliano in Toscana**, impressive above all for its largely intact city walls. Some date from the 14th century, while most were raised by Siena in the 16th century. The town is a little scrappy on the inside.

Lunch at **Antica Trattoria Aurora** (0564 59 20 30; Via Chiasso Lavagnini 12/14; meals €40; Thu-Tue) is a good idea, and there's a pretty sheltered garden, open for dinner. Cutting-edge menu concepts include *cinghiale al finocchio selvatico* (wild boar tortellini with wild fennel).

Next, continue up to **Scansano**. Although there are no monuments of great importance, the old centre, all narrow lanes and archways, is a pleasure to wander around and offers some great views over the surrounding countryside.

Montemerano, Saturnia & Manciano

Continuing from Scansano towards Manciano along the SS322, you first hit the small, walled medieval town of **Montemerano**. Pick up a bottle of the excellent local Morellino di Scansano wine at **La Vecchia Dispensa** (Via Italia 31), a richly scented delicatessen that presses its own olive oil, then drop into **Chiesa di San Giorgio**, decorated with 15th-century frescoes of the Sienese school. Finally, stroll up to harmonious, oh-so-photogenic Piazza del Castello.

Claiming to be among the first farmhouse stays in Tuscany, **Agriturismo Le Fontanelle** (☎ 0564 60 27 62; www.lefontanelle.net; s/d incl breakfast €47/78; 💻) is a wonderfully rustic place 1.2km down a turn-off 2.5km south of Montemerano. A large variety of cabin and chalet accommodation allows you to choose your optimum level of exposed wood and/or modern bathrooms. The massive, zoolike property has a duck pond, plenty of shady trees, geese, mallards, herons, goats and deer. Daughter Daniella is a sparkling hostess for dinner (€20), taken alfresco with other guests around a large communal table.

From here it's 6km to **Saturnia**, with its Etruscan remains, including part of the town wall. A tomb at **Sede di Carlo**, just northeast of the town, is one of the area's best preserved.

The sulphurous spring and thermal baths at **Terme di Saturnia** (☎ 0564 60 01 11; www.termedisaturnia.it; day admission €22, after 3pm €17; 🕘 9.30am-7.30pm Apr-Sep, to 5.30pm Oct-Mar; 🅿) are 2.5km south of the village. You can happily spend a whole day dunking yourself in the hot pools and signing on for some of the ancillary activities such as the alluring 'four-hand massage shower' or, for that light-as-air feeling, the 'infiltration of gaseous oxygen to reduce excess fat'. Parking here costs €4.

Econo-bathers can avail themselves of the waters running parallel to the road for several hundred metres, starting just south of the Terme di Saturnia turn-off. Look for the telltale sign of other bathers' cars parked on the road, then forage down the dirt path until you find a suitable spot of gratis cascading water, with temperatures at a constant 37.5°C.

Manciano is another former Sienese fortress. Apart from the much-interfered with *rocca* (fortress), there is not much else to keep you here.

Pitigliano
pop 4100

Check your mirrors before screeching to a halt outside Pitigliano. This hill-top fastness, organically sprouting from a high volcanic rocky outcrop towering over the surrounding country, is photo-op fodder that will make your blog visitors swoon. The gorges that surround the town on three sides constitute a natural bastion, completed to the east by the manmade fort.

Originally built by the Etruscans, Pitigliano remained beyond the orbit of the great Tuscan city-states, such as Florence and Siena, until it was finally absorbed into the grand duchy under Cosimo I de' Medici.

DETOUR: MONTE ARGENTARIO TO MANCIANO

Travelling from Monte Argentario to Manciano, turn right after 18.8km at the Vallerana sign (if driving the opposite direction, take the *second* signed turn for Vallerana or you'll regret it deeply). Turn left after 1.4km, in the direction of Pitardi. You'll pass vineyards on your left as the road continues through seamless rolling countryside, with the town of Manciano straddled on a hill top in the distance. After 3.2km, turn into the farm on your left (look for the *vendita vino-olio* sign) and ask for Rinaldo, the farmer, who has excellent olive oil, and red and white wine for sale. Rinaldo has commenced his retirement, but his son and family are carrying on the wine/oil business while he greets visitors and enjoys a well-earned sit down.

After you've made your purchases, turn left out of the gate, turn left again 700m later and continue on until you rejoin the Monte Argentario–Manciano main road happily weighed down with *vino*.

In the course of the 15th century, a Jewish community settled here, increasing notably when Pope Pius IV banned Jews from Rome in 1569. They moved into a tiny ghetto, where they remained until 1772. From then until well into the following century, the local community of 400 flourished and Pitigliano was dubbed Little Jerusalem. By the time the Fascists introduced the race laws in 1938, most Jews had moved away (only 80 or so were left and precious few survived the war).

INFORMATION
Tourist office (☎ 0564 61 71 11; Piazza Garibaldi; ◷ 10.20am-1pm & 3-7pm Tue-Sun Apr-Oct, 10.20am-1pm & 2-6pm Tue-Sun Nov-Mar)

SIGHTS & ACTIVITIES
The first glimpse of Pitigliano from the Manciano approach road (arrive at night and you see it lit up) is breathtaking. Within the town, twisting stairways disappear around corners, cobbled alleys bend tantalisingly out of sight beneath arches and the stone houses seem to have been piled up higgledy-piggledy by some giant child playing with building blocks.

The main sights are within a stone's throw of Piazza Garibaldi. Just off the square is an imposing 16th-century **viaduct** and, keeping watch over interlinked Piazza Garibaldi and Piazza Petruccioli, the 13th-century **Palazzo Orsini** (☎ 0564 61 44 19; adult/child €2.50/1.50; ◷ 10am-1pm & 3-7pm Tue-Sun Apr-Sep, to 6pm Oct-Mar). Eighteen of its rooms are open to the public and decked out with a cluttered collection of ecclesiastical objects, assembled, you get the feeling, as much to fill the vast empty space as for any aesthetic merit.

Opposite is the altogether more organised **Museo Archeologico** (☎ 0564 61 40 67; Piazza della Fortezza; adult/child €2.50/1.50; ◷ 10am-1pm & 3-7pm Tue-Sun Apr-Sep, 10am-1pm & 3-6pm Tue-Sun Oct-Mar), which has a rich display of finds from local Etruscan sites. They're well displayed, but descriptive panels are in Italian only.

Only the tall bell tower remains as a reminder of the Romanesque original of Pitigliano's **cathedral**, with its baroque façade and unexceptional interior.

The town's medieval lanes and steep alleys are a delight to wander, particularly around the small **Ghetto** quarter. Head down Via Zuccarelli and turn left at a sign indicating **La Piccola Gerusalemme** (☎ 0564 61 60 06; Vicolo Manin 30; adult/child €2.50/1.50; ◷ 10am-12.30pm &

4-7pm Sun-Fri May-Oct, 10am-12.30pm & 3-5.30pm Sun-Fri Nov-Apr). The area fell into disrepair with the demise of Pitigliano's Jewish community at the end of WWII, and was practically rebuilt from scratch in 1995. A visit includes the tiny, richly adorned synagogue and a small museum of Jewish culture, including the old bakery, kosher butcher and dyeing workshops.

There are some spectacular **walks** around Pitigliano. The base of the rocky outcrop is stippled with Etruscan tomb caves carved into the soft tufa, many of them recycled as storage cellars. From there, you can follow a signed trail (about 6km) to Sovana.

SLEEPING & EATING
Albergo Guastini (☎ 0564 61 60 65; www.albergoguastini.it; Piazza Petruccioli 16; s/d/tr €37/62/90; ◷ closed mid-Jan–mid-Feb) Pitigliano's only hotel is friendly and welcoming. Perched on the edge of the cliff face, many of its rooms have side views of the bastion that rank among the best hotel-room vistas in Tuscany. Its highly regarded restaurant (meals around €25) also merits a visit. The neighbouring bar has a mournful internet point (per hour €5).

Hotel Valle Orientina (☎ 0564 61 66 11; www.valleorientina.it; Località Valle Orientina; s €50-80, d €90-150; P ☺) In lovely pastoral surroundings about 3km from town, this is a relaxing spot with its very own 7th-century thermal baths and the potential for gentle or more strenuous walking in the surrounding countryside.

Osteria Il Tufo Allegro (☎ 0564 61 61 92; Vico della Costituzione 2; meals €27; ◷ closed Wed lunch & all Tue) This *osteria* is just off Via Zuccarelli. The aromas emanating from its kitchen should be enough to draw you into the cavernous chamber, carved out of the tufa foundations. The excruciatingly small-portioned lamb is admittedly succulent and the *taglialini* with asparagus is a good vegetarian option.

Pick up a stick or two of *sfratto*, a gorgeously sticky local confection of honey and walnuts, from **Il Forno** (Via Roma 16). Counterbalance the sweetness with a glass of the town's lively dryish Bianco di Pitigliano wine from one of the shops lining Via San Chiara, off Piazza Petruccioli.

DRINKING
Jerry Lee Bar (☎ 0564 61 40 99; Via Roma 28; ◷ Tue-Sun; ▯) This place has an entertaining range of patrons from certified drunks to young

hipsters and occasional live music. Internet access is €5 per hour.

Il Ghetto (Via Zuccarelli 47) A smart flagstone-and-brick wine bar, Il Ghetto has cheese and salami snacks to accompany that favourite tipple.

GETTING THERE & AWAY

Rama (☎ 0564 61 60 40) buses leave from the train station at Grosseto for Pitigliano (€5, two hours, four daily). They also connect Pitigliano with Sorano (€1.10, 15 minutes, seven daily) and Sovana (€1.10, 20 minutes, one daily). For Saturnia, change at Manciano.

Sovana

Sovana is really little more than a one-street village of butterscotch-coloured sandstone – but, gosh, it's pretty and has some fine Etruscan sites nearby.

INFORMATION

The **tourist office** (☎ 0564 61 40 74; ⏰ 10am-1pm & 3-7pm Tue-Sun Mar-Dec, 10am-1pm Fri-Sun Jan-Feb) is in the Palazzo Pretorio.

If you plan to visit most of the archaeological sites in and around Sovana and Sorano, invest in a €7 combined ticket. It gives entry to Tomba della Sirena, Tomba di Ildebranda, Fortezza Orsini in Sorano, Necropoli di San Rocco, and the Vitozza rock caves outside San Quirico. Buy a ticket at any of the sites.

SIGHTS

The **Chiesa di Santa Maria** (Piazza del Pretorio; ⏰ 9am-6pm), opposite the tourist office, is a starkly simple Romanesque church (although it was interfered with in parts in later centuries) with some rich Renaissance frescoes and, over the altar, a magnificent 9th-century ciborium, or canopy, in white marble, one of the last remaining pre-Romanesque works left in Tuscany.

Walk west along Via del Duomo to reach the imposing Gothic-Romanesque **cathedral** (⏰ 10am-1pm & 3-7pm Mar-Nov, 10am-1pm & 3-6pm Dec-Feb). Although largely rebuilt in the 12th and 13th centuries, the original construction dates back to the 9th century. The striking portal on the north wall is pieced together from fragments of this earlier building – or, as some would maintain, from a pagan temple.

Sovana was the birthplace of Pope Gregory VII; at the eastern end of the village are a cluster of medieval mansions and the remains of a fortress that belonged to his family.

Within the **Necropoli di Sovana** (admission €5; ⏰ 9am-7pm Mar-Nov, 10am-5pm Fri-Sun Dec-Feb), 1.5km south of the village, are Tuscany's most significant Etruscan tombs. Look for the yellow sign on the left for the **Tomba della Sirena**, where you follow a trail running alongside a rank of tomb façades cut from the rock face, as well as walk along a *via cava*.

VIE CAVE

There are at least 15 rock-sculpted passages spreading out in every direction from the valleys below Pitigliano. These sunken roads *(vie cave)* are enormous, up to 20m deep and 3m wide, and are believed to be sacred routes linking the necropolises and other sites associated with the Etruscan religious cult. A less popular, more mundane explanation is that these strange megalithic corridors were used to move livestock or as some kind of defence, allowing people to move from village to village unseen. Whatever the reason, every spring on the night of the equinox (19 March) there is a torch-lit procession down the Via Cava di Giuseppe, which culminates in a huge bonfire in Pitigliano's Piazza Garibaldi. It serves as a symbol of purification and renewal marking the end of winter.

The countryside around Pitigliano, Sovana and Sorano is riddled with *vie cave*. Two particularly good examples, 500m west of Pitigliano on the road to Sovana, are Via Cava di Fratenuti, with its high vertical walls and Etruscan graffiti, and Via Cava di San Giuseppe, which passes the Fontana dell'Olmo, carved out of solid rock. From this fountain stares the sculpted head of Bacchus, the mythological god of fruitfulness, as the water flows from his mouth. Via Cava San Rocco, near Sorano, is another fine example. It winds its way through the hills for 2km between the town and the Necropoli di San Rocco.

There's a fine **walk** from Pitigliano to Sovana (8km, three hours) that incorporates parts of the *vie cave*. Inquire at the tourist office in Pitigliano for routes and the all-important return transport.

CAN YOU CANTER?

`our pick` **Il Cornacchino** (☎ 0564 95 15 82; www.cornacchino.it; full board per person €63) is about 10km north of Sorano, 3km off the SS2. This horse-fixated *agriturismo* cum 'village' offers a dizzying variety of all-inclusive riding courses and trekking trips. See our special *agriturismi* section for more detail (p316).

About 300m beyond is the **Tomba di Ildebranda**, by far the grandest of Etruscan mausoleums and the only surviving temple-style tomb, which still preserves traces of its columns and stairs.

Due east of the village, just outside the tiny hamlet of San Quirico and signposted from the main square, are the **Vitozza rock caves** (☎ 0564 61 40 74; admission €2; ☉ 10am-6pm Tue-Sun Mar-Oct, by appointment Nov-Feb), more than 200 of them, peppering a high rock ridge. One of the largest troglodyte dwellings in Italy, the complex was first inhabited in prehistoric times.

SLEEPING & EATING

The local hotels have banded together under the same **management** (www.sovana.eu), including a new four-star 'Romantik' hotel and resort. When booking, specify which property you want.

Taverna Etrusca (☎ 0564 61 65 31; Piazza Pretorio 9; s/d incl breakfast €70/90; P ⚽ 🖳) This is a three-star hotel whose simple but attractive rooms have stripped wooden floors. Its restaurant (meals €40; closed Wednesdays), in the hands of a vastly experienced cook, serves mainly 'creative Tuscan' specialities and always has at least one vegetarian option.

Albergo Scilla (☎ 0564 61 65 31; Via R Siviero 1-3; d incl breakfast €90; P ⚽) Scilla has eight terracotta-and-white rooms with marshmallow-soft pillows and attractive wrought-iron beds, mosaic bathrooms and a quiet garden. Across the road you can enjoy fine fare at its glassed-in restaurant, Ristorante dei Merli (meals €30; closed Tuesday), which has vegetarian options.

Sorano
pop 3810

Retrace your route from Sovana, pass the turn-off for Pitigliano and continue northeast to Sorano. Two kilometres before the village are the **Necropoli di San Rocco** (admission €2; ☉ 11am-6pm Tue-Sun Mar-Oct, Fri-Sun Nov-Feb), another Etruscan burial site. From here it's possible to walk to Sorano along a *via cava*.

Sorano is something of a poor relation of the three hill towns. High on a rocky spur, its houses, many unoccupied and forlorn, seem to huddle together in an effort not to shove one another off the precarious perch.

There's a small **tourist office** (☎ 0546 63 30 99) on Piazza Busati.

The town's main attraction is the partly renovated **Fortezza Orsini** (☎ 0564 63 37 67; Piazza Cairoli; admission €2; ☉ 10am-1pm & 3-7pm mid-Mar–Oct Tue-Sun), with its medieval museum and underground passageways, visited by separate guided tour (€3; every hour).

You could also climb up **Masso Leopoldino** (admission €2; ☉ 10am-1pm & 3-7pm Apr-Nov), a large platform at the top of the village, for spectacular views of the surrounding countryside.

SLEEPING & EATING

Hotel della Fortezza (☎ 0564 63 20 10; Piazza Cairoli 5; s €90, d €130-150; ☉ Mar-Dec) The long walk through the *fortezza* before you even hit the door amplifies the profound historic feel of this 14-room hotel and restaurant. Wood-beamed ceilings, tapestries, antique furnishings and fantastic views complete the sensation.

Talismano (☎ 0564 63 32 81; Via San Marco 29; meals €20; ☉ Wed-Mon) This is a cavernous place highly popular with locals. The menu has an excellent selection of pizzas and Tuscan dishes, so you'll be hard-pressed not to find something to your liking.

Locanda dell'Arco (☎ 0564 63 36 08; Via Roma 22; meals €23) Deep in the historic centre, from inside it looks like someone started to build a church here, then switched to a cellar part way through, then said 'to hell with it' and opened a restaurant. Family owned, with friendly service and a basic menu of filling Tuscan standards. It has rooms too (single/double €20/40).

Eastern Tuscany

Don't let the brevity of this chapter fool you. Eastern Tuscany holds some cinematic oh-wow moments (both aesthetically and celluloid-ally), and with relatively few people bothering to venture beyond Arezzo's historic centre, you'll be wowed with plenty of elbowroom. With most destinations being within pasta-flinging range of the Rome–Florence rail line, access is largely uncomplicated.

The curiously sloping Piazza Grande in Arezzo's Etruscan centre – the heart of both the city and the region – and the Pieve di Santa Maria, a key example of Tuscan Romanesque construction, are just a taste of Arezzo's enticements. The city is also the perfect staging area for forays into the countryside. Nearby Cortona wrote the parchment on spectacular, hill-top eyries, offering mind-bending views over the Tuscan and Umbrian plains and beyond to Lago di Trasimeno.

Film location scouts have twice deemed the area a Tuscan superlative recently. Roberto Benigni filmed scenes of his Oscar-winning film *Life Is Beautiful* in Arezzo and Cortona, while Audrey Wells chose Cortona for some scenes from *Under the Tuscan Sun*.

The Piero della Francesca art trail arguably peaks with his fresco cycle of the *Legend of the True Cross* in Arezzo's Chiesa di San Francesco, but a definitive and enormously worthwhile build-up requires stops in the quietly satisfying towns of Sansepolcro and Monterchi.

The undeservedly obscure hill country of the Casentino is a lush forested landscape, making for a low-key drive with copious photo-ops, in between its assortment of minor castles and noteworthy monasteries, including the vast St Francis Sanctuary in Verna.

HIGHLIGHTS

- Submit to a transcendental and/or wine-induced medieval reverie at the Giostra del Saracino in Arezzo's **Piazza Grande** (p297)

- Contemplate the idealised mathematical depiction of (or just look at) the subjects in Piero della Francesca's outstanding fresco cycle in the **Chiesa di San Francesco** (p296) in Arezzo

- Explore the back roads of the little-visited **Casentino region** (p303), including the massive **St Francis Sanctuary** (p304)

- Take the **Piero della Francesca** multicity tour (p301) from Arezzo through Monterchi to Sansepolcro

- Soak in the Etruscan heritage of **Cortona** (p305), ascending its storybook streets and enjoying the superb countryside views

★ Casentino

★ Sansepolcro

Arezzo
★ ★ Monterchi

★ Cortona

AREZZO

pop 94,700

Bombed back to the Renaissance Age during WWII, Arezzo may not be a Tuscan centre-fold, but the surviving parts of the historic centre and its ancillary attractions are worthy competition for any destination in the region. Though a day trip from Florence or Perugia is easily achieved, with both accommodations and eating value here being superior, why would you? A fine meal in one of its restaurants and an early evening wander through the charming, if architecturally scattered, centre is worth shifting your bags for a night. Furthermore, the city serves as an ideal staging area for a day trip to Sansepolcro or sallying forth to destinations in the Casentino region.

The lopsided, architectural jumble of Piazza Grande is riveting, particularly from the many restaurants and *enotecas* (wine bars) on the perimeter offering choice people watching vantage points. The renowned five-star fresco cycle by Piero della Francesca in the Chiesa di San Francesco will beguile, whether you adore art or just endure it, as will the Romanesque epitome of Pieve di Santa Maria.

Long a vital Etruscan trading post, Arezzo later prospered immensely while part of the Roman Empire. The staunch Ghibelline city was a free republic by the 10th century and maintained a firm screw-the-Pope platform during lengthy, bloody clashes between the emperor and the papacy. The city went into a centuries-long period of decline after being swallowed whole by the swell of Guelph Florence in 1384. It was not to experience significant prosperity again until after the unification of Italy and the arrival of the railroad in 1866.

It's the birthplace of the Renaissance poet Petrarch, who popularised the sonnet format, penning his verses in both Latin and Italian, and Giorgio Vasari (p46), the prolific painter and architect whose contributions to Renaissance Florence included the Uffizi Gallery, the Palazzo dei Cavalieri and the tomb of Michelangelo in San Croce.

Another illustrious son, born in a nearby village, is comic actor and director Roberto Benigni, who created and starred in the Oscar-winning film, *Life Is Beautiful*. Locations used in the film are marked throughout Arezzo by signs featuring stills and dialogue in Italian and English.

Orientation

From the train station on the southern edge of the city, pedestrianised, shop-lined Corso Italia, the town's main promenade, leads to the Piazza Grande, Arezzo's nucleus.

Information

Centro di Accoglienza Turistico (☎ 0575 40 35 74; Via Ricasoli; ☽ 9.30am-6.30pm Jun-Oct, 10am-6pm Nov-May) An alternative tourist office. Hires out audioguides to Arezzo (adult/child per day €2.50/2) with an accompanying map.

Eutelia (Via Guido Monaco 61; per hr €1.50; ☽ 9am-9pm) Offers internet access & cheap international phone calls.

Nuovo Ospedale San Donato (☎ 0575 25 50 01; Via A de Gasperi) Hospital outside the city walls.

Police station (☎ 0575 31 81; Via Fra Guittone 3)

Post office (Via Guido Monaco 34)

Tourist office (☎ 0575 2 08 39; www.apt.arezzo.it; Piazza della Repubblica 28; ☽ 9am-1pm & 3-7pm Apr-Sep, 10am-1pm & 3-6pm Mon-Sat, 9am-1pm Sun Oct-Mar) Has a representative from tour operator Colori Toscani onsite who can arrange accommodation and tours free of charge.

EASTERN TUSCANY

0 — 20 km
0 — 12 miles

To Forlì (27km)
SS310
Emilia-Romagna
E45
Alpe di San Benedetto
Parco Nazionale delle Foreste Casentinesi, Monte Falterona e Campigna
M Falterona (1654m)
Papiano
Stia
Camaldoli
Le Marche
Pratovecchio
Badia
SS71
Pratáglia
Casentino
Poppi
Verna
Bibbiena
SS208
Pieve di Santo Stefano
Chiusi della Verna
SS258
Caprese Michelangelo
Alpe della Luna
Loro Ciuffenna
SS3b
Sansepolcro
Anghiari
Umbria
Monterchi
A1
Arezzo
SS73
Castiglion Fiorentino
SS73
Castello di Montecchio
E45
Monte San Savino
SS71
Cortona

Sights

CHIESA DI SAN FRANCESCO

Gracing the apse of this 14th-century **church** (Piazza San Francesco; ☽ 9am-6.30pm Mon-Fri, 9am-5.30pm Sat, 1-5.30pm Sun) is one of the greatest works of Italian art, Piero della Francesca's fresco cycle of the *Legend of the True Cross*. Painted between 1452 and 1466, it relates in 10 episodes the story of the cross on which Christ was crucified.

The illustration of this medieval legend, as entertaining as it is inconceivable, begins in the top right-hand corner and follows the story of the tree that Seth plants on the grave of his father, Adam, and from which, eventually, the True Cross is made. A scene on the opposite wall shows the long-lost cross

being rediscovered by Helena, mother of the emperor Constantine; behind her, the city of Jerusalem is represented by a medieval view of Arezzo. Even Khosrow, the Persian emperor accused of making off with the cross, features, ignominiously. Rarely will you get a better sense of medieval frescoes as strip cartoon, telling a tale with such vigour and sheer beauty. Likewise, art buffs will be struck by Piero's innovations with perspective and geometric perfection and the stillness he created by his lack of naturalism.

As is often the case, the mere survival of these frescos has been part extraordinary luck, part back-breaking restoration. Damage endured/eluded from fires, earthquakes and allied bombs notwithstanding, time and

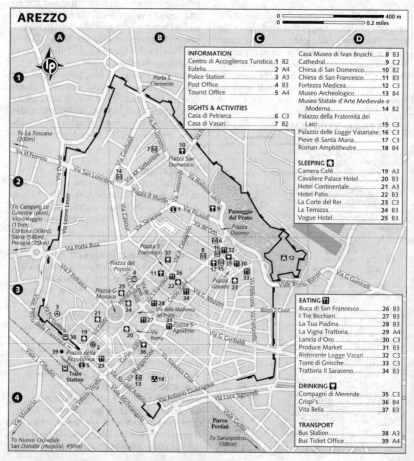

AREZZO

INFORMATION	
Centro di Accoglienza Turistico..**1** B2	
Eutelia..............................**2** A4	
Police Station.....................**3** A3	
Post Office........................**4** B3	
Tourist Office.....................**5** A4	
SIGHTS & ACTIVITIES	
Casa di Petrarca...................**6** C3	
Casa di Vasari.....................**7** B2	

Casa Museo di Ivan Bruschi.......**8** B3	
Cathedral..........................**9** C2	
Chiesa di San Domenico..........**10** B2	
Chiesa di San Francesco.........**11** B3	
Fortezza Medicea..................**12** C3	
Museo Archeologico..............**13** B4	
Museo Statale d'Arte Medievale e	
Moderna.........................**14** B2	
Palazzo della Fraternità dei	
Laici.............................**15** C3	
Palazzo delle Logge Vasariane..**16** C3	
Pieve di Santa Maria.............**17** C3	
Roman Amphitheatre.............**18** B4	
SLEEPING	
Camera Café.......................**19** A3	
Cavaliere Palace Hotel...........**20** B3	
Hotel Continentale................**21** A3	
Hotel Patio.........................**22** B3	
La Corte del Rei...................**23** C3	
La Terrazza........................**24** B3	
Vogue Hotel.......................**25** B3	

EATING	
Buca di San Francesco...........**26** B3	
I Tre Bicchieri....................**27** B3	
La Tua Piadina...................**28** B3	
La Vigna Trattoria...............**29** A4	
Lancia d'Oro......................**30** C3	
Produce Market...................**31** B3	
Ristorante Logge Vasari.........**32** C3	
Torre di Gnicche.................**33** C3	
Trattoria Il Saraceno............**34** C3	
DRINKING	
Compagni di Merende..........**35** C3	
Crispi's............................**36** B4	
Vita Bella.........................**37** B3	
TRANSPORT	
Bus Station........................**38** A3	
Bus Ticket Office.................**39** A4	

COMBINED TICKET

You can buy a combined ticket (€12) giving entry to the Piero della Francesca frescoes in the Chiesa di San Francesco, plus Museo Archeologico, Museo Statale d'Arte Medievale e Moderna and Museo di Casa Vasari, at any of the four venues.

---

the elements were also conspiring to sully the work. When Piero's *Dream of Constantine* was cleaned up during major restoration, the piece that was formerly thought to be 'the first realistic nocturnal scene in Italian art' turned out to be set at dawn. It was just dirty.

You can get some sense of the frescoes from beyond the cordon in front of the altar, but to really appreciate them up close you need to plan ahead for a **visit with audio guide** (☎ 0575 35 27 27; www.pierodellafrancesca.it; admission €6; ♥ 9am-6.30pm Mon-Sat, 1-5pm Sun Apr-Oct, 9am-5.30pm Mon-Sat, 1-5pm Sun Nov-Mar). Since only 25 people are allowed in every half-hour, it's essential to pre-book, either by phone or at any of the sights that participate in the combined ticket scheme. The ticket office is at Piazza San Francesco 4, to the right of the church's main entrance.

PIEVE DI SANTA MARIA & AROUND

This 12th-century **church** (Corso Italia 7; ♥ 8am-1pm & 3-7pm May-Sep, 8am-noon & 3-6pm Oct-Apr) has a magnificent Romanesque arcaded façade – reminiscent of the cathedral at Pisa writ small, yet without the glorious marble facing – where each column is different. Over the central doorway are carved reliefs representing the months of the year. The 14th-century bell tower with its 40 apertures is something of an emblem for the city. The monochrome of the interior's warm stone is relieved by Pietro Lorenzetti's fine polyptych *Madonna and Saints*, beneath the semidome of the apse.

Below the altar is a 14th-century silver bust reliquary of the city's patron saint, San Donato. Other treasures on display include a 13th-century crucifix by Margherito di Arezzo and a carved marble bas-relief of the *Adoration of the Magi*.

Opposite the church is the **Casa Museo di Ivan Bruschi** (☎ 0575 35 41 26; Corso Italia 14; admission €3; ♥ 10am-1pm & 3-7pm Tue-Sun Apr-Sep, 10am-1pm & 2-6pm Tue-Sun Oct-Mar), where you can cast an eye over the varied collection of art and antiques

amassed by the man who founded the Arezzo antiques fair.

PIAZZA GRANDE & AROUND

This cobbled piazza, the venue for the Giostra del Saracino (p298), is overlooked at its upper end by the porticoes of the **Palazzo delle Logge Vasariane**, completed in 1573. The **Palazzo della Fraternità dei Laici** with its churchlike façade, in the northwest corner, was started in 1375 in the Gothic style and finished after the onset of the Renaissance. A frenzied antiques fair (p298) is held here on the first weekend of each month.

Via dei Pileati leads to **Casa di Petrarca**, the poet's former home, which contains a small museum and the Accademia Petrarca, a library and research institute devoted primarily to Petrarch. Visits are by appointment and really only for serious Petrarch fans. Enquire at the tourist office for more details.

CATHEDRAL & AROUND

Arezzo's **cathedral** (Piazza Duomo; ♥ 6.30am-12.30pm & 3-6.30pm), at the top of the hill, was started in the 13th century, yet was not completed until well into the 15th century. In the northeast corner, to the left of the bulky, intricately carved main altar, there's an exquisite fresco of *Mary Magdalene* by Piero della Francesca, itself dwarfed in size but not beauty by the multitiered, rich marble reliefs of the adjoining tomb of Bishop Guido Tarlati, featuring a frieze of priests and an acolyte chanting while holding a censer, a prayer book and candles.

Off the north aisle, the Capella della Madonna del Conforto has a pair of fine glazed terracotta images from the della Robbia workshop. On the right as you enter is the tomb of Pope Gregory X, who died in Arezzo in 1276.

Up high to the southeast of the cathedral, across the peaceful gardens of the **Passeggio del Prato**, rears the **Fortezza Medicea** (admission free; ♥ 7am-8pm Apr-Oct, 7.30am-6pm Nov-Mar), completed in 1560 and offering grand views of the town and surrounding countryside.

CHIESA DI SAN DOMENICO & AROUND

The short detour to the **Chiesa di San Domenico** (Piazza San Domenico 7; ♥ 8.30am-7pm), with its unusual, asymmetrical façade, is a must. Above the main altar rears a haunting *Crucifixion*, one of Cimabue's earliest works, painted around

1265. Note too the pair of well-preserved frescoes by Spinello Aretino (1350–1410) at the western end, and, in the south aisle, a statue by the della Robbia school of San Pietro Martire with a sword cleaving his skull.

To the west, the **Casa di Vasari** (☎ 0575 40 90 40; Via XX Settembre 55; admission €2; ☑ 8.30am-7.30pm Mon & Wed-Sat, 8.30am-1.30pm Sun) was built and sumptuously decorated (overwhelmingly so in the case of the Sala del Camino, the Fireplace Room) by the architect himself – ring the bell if the door's closed.

Further west again, the **Museo Statale d'Arte Medievale e Moderna** (☎ 0575 40 90 50; Via San Lorentino 8; adult/student €10/7; ☑ 9am-7pm Tue-Sun) primarily houses works by local artists. The two small rooms on the ground floor mostly contain sculptures from local churches, while on the next floor is a display of medieval paintings, including works by Bartolomeo della Gatta and Domenico Pecori, a collection of glazed terracotta pieces by the della Robbia family, and colourful majolica plates. Upstairs, in addition to works by Luca Signorelli and several canvases on the grand scale by Vasari, the chronology continues into the 19th century.

MUSEO ARCHEOLOGICO & ROMAN AMPHITHEATRE

The **Museo Archeologico** (☎ 0575 2 08 82; Via Margaritone 10; admission €4; ☑ 8.30am-7pm) is in a former convent overlooking the remains of the **Roman amphitheatre** (admission free; ☑ 8.30am-7pm Apr-Oct, to 6pm Nov-Mar), which once seated up to 10,000 spectators. Inside, there's a sizable collection of Etruscan and Roman artefacts, including locally produced ceramics and bronzes. Among the highlights is the Cratere di Euphronios, a large 6th-century-BC Etruscan vase, decorated with vivid scenes showing Hercules in battle, and, upstairs, an exquisite tiny portrait of a bearded man executed on glass in the 3rd century AD.

Activities

Alessandro Madiai (☎ 338 6491481; torrequebrada@virgilio.it) A passionate cyclist, Alessandro runs two five-hour bicycle tours, plus overnighters, around the enchanting southern Tuscany countryside within reach of Arezzo.

Centro di Accoglienza Turistico (p295) Their 'Room 180' shows a 30-minute film about Arezzo (adult/child €2.50/2) in six languages on a 180-degree screen.

Festivals & Events

Antiques Fair Arezzo stages a huge and highly reputed antiques fair that pulls in over 500 exhibitors and spreads over the Piazza Grande and surrounding streets on the first Saturday and Sunday of every month.

Arezzo Wave (www.arezzowave.com in Italian) Over six days in July, the town hosts this music festival featuring artists and bands from Italy and abroad. It occasionally includes some top international acts (bill-toppers have included the likes of Motorhead in 2005 and Sinead O'Connor in 2006).

GIOSTRA DEL SARACINO

With its origins back in the time of the Crusades, the 'Joust of the Saracen' is one of those grand, noisy affairs involving extravagant fancy dress and neighbourhood rivalry that Italians delight in. Like many such Tuscan folk spectacles, the tournament was revived in its present form in 1931 after long neglect. The day begins with a herald reading a proclamation, followed by a procession of precisely 311 people in 14th-century dress and 31 horses. The jousters are then blessed on the steps of the cathedral by the Bishop of Arezzo. It's the highlight of the year for the city's four Quartieri (Quarters), each of which puts forward a team of 'knights' armed with lances. In the Piazza Grande, the knights try their hand jousting at a wooden effigy, known as the 'Buratto', representing a Saracen warrior. In one hand the Buratto holds a shield, etched with various point-scores, which the knights aim for while trying to avoid being belted with the *mazzafrustro* – basically three heavy leather balls on ropes – which dangle from the Buratto's other hand. The winning team takes home the coveted Golden Lance, bringing glory to their Quartiere.

Arezzo's division into Quartieri dates back to at least the 11th century, and there's still a strong sense of neighbourhood pride and loyalty, with heraldic flags fluttering from shops and homes, and communal events taking place throughout the year. The Quartieri are named after the four gates of the city, and each has its own distinctive colours. They are the centre of social and cultural life for their inhabitants, throwing dinners, running excursions and generally fostering community spirit.

Giostra del Saracino (opposite) Held on the second-last Sunday of June, and on the first Sunday of September.

Sleeping

Camping Le Ginestre (☎ 0575 36 35 66; www.camping leginestre.it; Via Ruscello 100; per person €8, pitch €6-13; ☺ year-round) This is the nearest camp site. From Arezzo train station, take LFI bus to Ruscello and request the camping stop.

La Toscana (☎ /fax 0575 2 16 92; Via M Perennio 56; s/d €35/49; P) A little away from the action, La Toscana is a good budget choice. Its 20 rooms are clean as a new pin. There's a small garden at the rear and free off-street parking.

La Terrazza (☎ 0575 2 83 87; laterrazza@lycos.it; 5th fl, Via Guido Monaco 25; d with bathroom €60, s/d without bathroom €40/50) Comprised of apartments on two floors, with right large, bright rooms and a kitchen for guest use, this place is good value. and welcoming. Alas, acoustically transparent walls mean an early morning. The complimentary breakfast features tasty homemade cakes. Go down the passage beside Blockbuster. Cash only.

our pick Camera Café (☎ 347 032 44 05; nicolette .borgogni@fastwebnet.it; Via Guido Monaco 92; s/d incl breakfast €40/55; ☒) Across the street from the train station, the dorm room décor here is supplemented by cushy beds, fat duvets and terraces with city views. The huge, self-serve kitchen has a gorgeous dining terrace. Some rooms have air-con.

Hotel Continentale (☎ 0575 2 02 51; www.hotel continentale.com; Piazza Guido Monaco 7; s/d €74/108; P ☒ ☐) A modern, central, three-star hotel, with comfy, spotless rooms. There's individual internet access in every room, a bar that tempts you to linger and a roof terrace with fine views. Valet parking is €15.

Cavaliere Palace Hotel (☎ 0575 2 68 36; www .cavalierehotels.com; Via della Madonna del Prato 83; s/d incl breakfast €93/135; P ☒) This is a reliable four-star choice, barely 200m from the station, that offers a friendly welcome. Rooms, while unexciting, are snug, well soundproofed and more than adequate. Hotel parking is €13.

La Corte Del Re (☎ 0575 29 67 20; www.lacortedelre .com; Via Borgunto 5; s/d €100/130; ☒) A collection of six apartments, centimetres from Piazza Grande, harmoniously blending contemporary design into elements of the historic building. The Pietro Aretino Suite has an ultra-modern bathroom that bleeds right into an Etruscan wall. Some apartments have kitchenettes and views of the square.

Vogue Hotel (☎ 0575 2 43 61; www.voguehotel .it; Via Guido Monaco 54; s incl breakfast €108-132, d incl breakfast €138-162; ☐ ☒) Themed rooms, improbably placed showers, classic wood furniture, wall-mounted plasma TVs, ceiling frescos and the occasional wall o' Roman rock peeking through to remind you where you really are.

Hotel Patio (☎ 0575 40 19 62; www.hotelpatio.it; Via Cavour 23; s/d/ste €130/176/224; P ☒) This is Arezzo's most characterful hotel, with 10 themed rooms, each dedicated to one of Bruce Chatwin's travel books. Each has original furnishings from the various countries represented, including Australia, Morocco and China. Valet parking is €18.

Eating

La Tua Piadina (☎ 0575 2 32 40; Via de' Cenci 18; snacks €3.50) A justifiably popular takeaway place hidden away down a side street, where you can get a range of hot, tasty *piadine*, the Emilia version of the wrap.

Buca di San Francesco (☎ 0575 2 32 71; www.bucadi sanfrancesco.it; Via San Francesco 1; meals €23; ☺ closed Mon dinner & Tue) The walls of this arched and vaulted cellar are decorated with frescoes and copious religious art in deference to neighbouring Chiesa di San Francesco. It does three church-themed – 'friar', 'abbot' and 'prior' – and church-priced menus (€13 to €19). The congenial owner takes indecisiveness as an invitation to usurp control and design a menu for you.

Torre di Gnicche (☎ 0575 35 20 35; Piaggia San Martino 8; meals €25; ☺ Thu-Tue) Just off the Piazza Grande, this is a fine old traditional restaurant that offers a rich variety of antipasti. Choose from the ample range of local *pecorino* cheeses, accompanied by a choice red from its extensive wine list.

Trattoria Il Saraceno (☎ 0575 2 76 44; www.ilsara ceno.com; Via G Mazzini 3a; meals €25-30; ☺ Thu-Tue) With 60 years in business, this trattoria serves quality, varied Tuscan fare attracting a lunch crowd that keeps the swarm of servers dashing. The impressive wine collection is hard to miss, as it conspicuously lines the walls. Pizzas start at €5.

our pick Ristorante Logge Vasari (☎ 0575 30 03 33; www.cittadiarezzo.com/loggevasari; Via Vasari 19; meals €30-35; ☺ Wed-Mon) This restaurant has a terrace fronting Piazza Grande, two pleasant interior rooms and class that defies stereotypically dire 'piazza cuisine'. The *menu degustazione* (€40, including wine) is a parade of flavours and interesting flourishes to local dishes. Let your server choose the wine – he'll be right.

La Vigna Trattoria (☎ 0575 35 19 94; Via Spinello 27; meals €30-35; Thu-Tue) Choose your meat, then watch it sizzle on the giant, open fireplace. Apart from possibly the bread, vegetarians will have little choice here. Less zealous carnivores are able to choose from the short pizza menu and a selection of homemade desserts.

Lancia d'Oro (☎ 0575 2 10 33; Piazza Grande 18-19; meals €45; closed Sun evening & Mon) A sophisticated place with fresh flowers on the tables where your order is supplemented by excellent snacks and titbits that arrive unannounced. There's a jolly, waggish waiter, while the interior, painted with swags and green-and-white stripes, is like dining in a marquee. It is run by two brothers who also run Logge Vasari (p299), and has a terrace under the loggia that looks down over Piazza Grande.

I Tre Bicchieri (☎ 0575 2 65 57; Piazzetta Sopra I Ponti 3-5; meals €50-55; Tue-Thu) An upscale restaurant in a little square off Corso Italia, serving, among a range of innovative options, dishes such as roast quail in Chianti and creative fresh pasta options.

A veritable produce melee erupts at **Piazza Sant'Agostino's market** each Tuesday, Thursday and Saturday.

Drinking

Compagni di Merende (☎ 0575 182 23 68; Logge Vasari 16) A friendly, unassuming little wine bar with an unparalleled position, tucked under the loggia overlooking Piazza Grande. Enjoy a plate of cheese or cold cuts, or simply a restorative glass of wine.

Vita Bella (Piazza San Francesco 22) Opposite the Chiesa di San Francesco, Vita Bella is an agreeable place with wrought-iron chairs where you can sip a Negroni and watch the world go by.

Crispi's (☎ 0575 2 28 73; Via Francesco Crispi 10/12) This is a restaurant (pizzas from around €5.50) that, from 10.30pm, converts into a pub, where you can have an evening tipple among a primarily young crowd.

Getting There & Away

Services from the bus station at Piazza della Repubblica include Cortona (€2.80, one hour, more than 10 daily), Sansepolcro (€3.30, one hour, seven daily) and Siena (€5, 1½ hours,

seven daily). For Florence, you're better off hopping on the train.

Arezzo is on the Florence–Rome train line, with frequent services to Rome (€20.50, two hours) and Florence (€10.10, 1½ hours). Trains call by Cortona (€2.20, 20 minutes, hourly).

Arezzo is a few kilometres east of the A1, and the SS73 heads east to Sansepolcro.

NORTHEAST OF AREZZO

In addition to being low-key, agreeable walled cities, Monterchi and Sansepolcro are irresistible enticements for Piero della Francesca enthusiasts. Both are easy day trips from Arezzo.

Monterchi & Anghiari

Visit tiny Monterchi to see Piero della Francesca's renowned fresco **Madonna del Parto** (☎ 0575 7 07 13; Via della Reglia 1; adult/child €3.10/free; 9am-1pm & 2-7pm Tue-Fri, 9am-7pm Sat & Sun Apr-Sep, to 5pm Oct-Mar). Painted in just seven days, the Pregnant Madonna is considered one of the key works of 15th-century Italian art and the only known representation from the period. The fresco depicts two angels pulling back tabernacle flaps, presenting the Pregnant Madonna to a group of believers, thus associating her (a mortal) with God, a sacred no-no in the 15th-century. As such, the church routinely destroyed such images, this being one of the few to survive. To the untrained eye, the gloomy look on her face suggests profound ninth-month misery, but experts assert that this is a pensive moment, as the Madonna, regarding her stomach, reflects on looming motherhood and the impact her child will have on the world.

A sensitive touch: pregnant women get free admission. There are also free medieval music recitals at 9pm on Wednesdays from June to August. Parking can be a problem since there's no special provision.

A few kilometres north of Monterchi and the SS73 lies the pretty medieval village of Anghiari, which is worth a brief stop-off to meander along its narrow twisting lanes.

Some 17km north of Anghiari is **Caprese Michelangelo**, birthplace of the great artist. Within the town's castle is the **Museo Michelangelo** (☎ 0575 79 37 76; Via Capuluogo 1; adult/child €4/3; 11am-6pm, Sat & Sun Jun-Sep, 10am-6pm Mon-Fri Oct-May), a rather lifeless affair devoted to the man and his works.

DETOUR: PIERO DELLA FRANCESCA TRAIL

The so-called 'Piero della Francesca trail' makes for a pleasant day trip, taking in the Valtiberina (High Tiber Valley) during the easy, if somewhat lacklustre, drive from Arezzo to Sansepolcro and Monterchi.

Though many details about his life are hazy, it is believed that della Francesca was born around 1420 in Sansepolcro to a privileged family, his father being a successful tanner and shoe-maker, allowing him to receive a good education and indulge in the study of painting with Sienese-trained artists in the area. He spent the bulk of his productive life in Arezzo, though he also worked in Rimini, Ferrara and Rome, returning to Sansepolcro in his twilight years where he died on 12 October 1492, the same day that Columbus arrived in the New World.

By 1439 he was already in Florence where he worked with Domenico Veneziano on frescoes for the hospital of Santa Maria Nuova, while establishing valuable contacts and exposing himself to the influential works of Donatello, Brunelleschi, Masaccio and Fra Angelico.

Considering his frequent movements, it is believed that he never belonged to any one workshop, choosing to work and evolve on his own, making no effort to conform to contemporary trends or styles. Piero's growing distinction revolved around his use of perspective and his skill with backgrounds, creating an overall, salient 'serene humanism'. He cultivated his methods of applied geometry and mathematical foreshortening for all objects on the canvas at a level previously unknown, never mind unachievable, to most painters. He eventually ditched painting altogether to write several treatises on the subject, most notably *De Prospectiva Pingendi* (On Perspective in Painting). Though it has never been confirmed, it is believed that della Francesca lost his sight near the end of his life.

His most celebrated works include *Flagellazione di Cristo* (The Flagellation) on display in the Galleria Nazionale della Marche in Urbino, dubbed 'the greatest small painting in the world', the *Madonna del Parto* in Monterchi, *Resurrezione* (The Resurrection) in Sansepolcro, and the renowned *Legend of the True Cross* in Arezzo's Chiesa di San Francesco (p296).

John Pope-Hennessy's book *The Piero della Francesca Trail* (1993) is an interesting source of information on the painter and the region.

Sansepolcro

pop 16,000

A prototypical Tuscan walled town dating from AD 1000, traversable on foot in three hasty minutes if necessary, Sansepolcro is best known as the probable birthplace of Piero della Francesca (see boxed text above). While the surrounding industrial sprawl won't dislodge many jaws, the town's medieval heart, a Roman settlement designed like a *castrum* (military defensive position), is pleasing.

Reaching its current size in the 15th century and walled in the 16th century, the historic centre is tightly packed with stone structures abutting somewhat less historic structures in a pleasant jumble, with delightfully anorexic streets where one guidebook writer's carelessly parked car can cause a traffic jam in seconds.

Sansepolcro's light tourist scene is largely attributed to its thin public transport connections – only accessible by bus from Arezzo or the agonisingly slow train from Perugia – meaning an overnight will tickle your Tuscan escapism.

ORIENTATION

Via Matteotti connects Piazza Torre di Berta and Piazza Fra Luca Pacioli, with the Duomo, Civic Museum and the Palazzo delle Laudi.

INFORMATION

The newly enlarged **tourist office** (☎ 0575 74 05 36; infosansepolcro@apt.arezzo.it; Via Matteotti 8; 🕑 9.30am-1pm & 3-6pm Apr-Sep, 9.30am-12.30pm & 3.30-5.30pm Mon-Sat, 9.30am-12.30pm Sun Oct-Mar) is packed with multilingual information.

SIGHTS

The **Museo Civico** (☎ 0575 73 22 18; www.sansepolcro.net in Italian; Via Aggiunti 65; adult/child €6/3; 🕑 9.30am-1.30pm & 2.30-7pm Jun-Sep, 9.30am-1pm & 2.30-6pm Oct-May) features a couple of Piero della Francesca's masterpieces. In the *Resurrezione* (Resurrection), the newly risen Christ stares out at the viewer, banner in hand like a triumphant warrior, while his guards slumber. In the splendid *Madonna della Misericordia* polyptych, the Virgin spreads her protective cloak over the painting's benefactors.

There are also works by distinguished Piero protégées Luca Signorelli, Pontormo, Raffaellino dal Colle and Santi di Tito, whose *Riposo Durante la Fuga in Egitto* (Rest During the Flight into Egypt) portrays the Holy Family in a tender and humanistic light.

Upstairs there's a display of 14th- and 15th-century frescoes, including a haunting portrait of St Sebastian, while the basement holds a small gathering of archaeological finds and ecclesiastical knick-knackery.

About 150m eastwards is the **Aboca museum** (☎ 0575 73 35 89; Via Aggiunti 75; adult/child €8/4; 🕙 10am-1pm & 3-7pm Tue-Sun Apr-Sep, 10am-1pm & 2.30-6pm Oct-Mar), dedicated to the history of pharmacy and herbal medicine, with a re-creation of a 17th-century laboratory. Given the high ticket price, it's likely to appeal only to those with a specialist interest in things alternative and pharmaceutical.

Just south of the tourist office is the newly renovated **cathedral**. Its most celebrated treasure is the *Volto Santo* (Holy Visage), a striking wooden crucifix with a wide-eyed Christ, dating back to AD 950 and one of only three in the world. Also gawk-worthy are frescoes by Bartolomeo della Gatta and a polyptych by Matteo di Giovanni.

The **Museo della Vetrata Antica** (☎ 0575 74 07 82; Via Giovanni Buitoni 9; adult/child €1.50/1), in San Giovanni church (1126), holds several modest stained-glass exhibits wholly eclipsed by a gigantic *Last Supper*, composed of 25 stained-glass panels, measuring 8.48m long by 4.58m high in total, fashioned by Cecilia Caselli-Moretti.

Step into any church with open doors, as they're all lovely, but make a point of calling at **San Antonio church** (cnr Via San Antonio and Via del Campaccio) which has a magnificent processional banner with paintings on two sides by Luca Signorelli.

On the second Sunday in September, the **Palio della Balestra**, a crossbow contest, pits costumed archers from Gubbio against Sansepolcro's best.

SLEEPING & EATING

Orfeo (☎ 0575 74 22 87; fax 0575 74 22 87; Viale Armando Diaz 12; s/d/tr incl breakfast €35/60/75) An unremarkable, but decent budget option just outside the old town's western gate.

our pick **Locanda Giglio** (☎ 0575 74 20 33; Via L Pacioli 60; s/d/tr incl buffet breakfast €50/75/100,; P ❲❳) and **Ristorante Fiorentino** (meals €25-30) This exceptionally friendly place has been in the same family for four generations. The four hotel rooms, with their oak floors, underfloor lighting and period furniture recovered from the family loft, have been imaginatively renovated by daughter Alessia, an architect/sommelier (see interview below). Request 'La Torre', with a lovely low bed and the best view. Dad, Alessio, still runs the restaurant with panache. The pasta's homemade, and the imaginative menu changes with the seasons (Alessio tells you with pride that there'll never be a freezer in *his* kitchen).

Also consider **Albergo da Ventura** (☎ 0575 74 25 60; www.albergodaventura.it; Via Niccolo Aggiunti 30; s/d incl breakfast €40/60) with five modern, cream-coloured rooms and a restaurant downstairs

---

THE FAMILY BUSINESS

Name? Alessia Uccellini

Where are you from? Sansepolcro, Tuscany, Italy

How do you earn your crust? I work in my family's restaurant (above) in Sansepolcro.

You are an architect, sommelier and Master in tourism? What keeps you in Sansepolcro? After a pilgrimage all over Italy – Florence, Verona, Rome and Bologna – my family restaurant keeps me in Sansepolcro. There was a time in which the family's 200-year-old restaurant and hotel had to be divided between my father's relatives and so we had to decide whether to sell the business or to keep it going. So I decided to save the family business and leave my work as an architect. But the two jobs are not so far apart. Next year I am taking a university course about the space of the kitchen from the campfire right up to the modern open space and food design.

Where do you see yourself in 20 years? All over Italy and the world writing books about the history of kitchens, food design and working for my restaurant.

What is your favourite place in Tuscany and why? First and foremost is Sansepolcro, of course, the reason that keeps me home. My second choice is Florence because I lived there when I was at university. Third is Isola d'Elba because I like the sea.

(meals €29) or **Casa Mila** (☎ 0575 73 34 77; www
.casamila.it; Via della Firenzuola 49; s/d €55/70) with both
apartments and B&B rooms and a three-day
minimum stay during high-season.

GETTING THERE & AWAY
SITA buses link Sansepolcro with Arezzo
(€3.30, one hour, 20 daily) and several trains
leave daily to Perugia (€3.95, 1¾ hours) where
you can change to Rome (2¾ hours).

THE CASENTINO REGION
A tour through the remote forest and farming
region of Casentino takes you through a little-
visited area that boasts a couple of still active
monasteries and some wonderful walking in
the Parco Nazionale delle Foreste Casentinesi,
Monte Falterona e Campigna.

    La Ferroviaria Italiana (LFI; ☎ 0575 3 98 81; www.lfi.it
in Italian), a private train line, runs from Arezzo,
following the upper reaches of the River Arno,
and serves towns and villages as far as Stia.
The rest of the region is only practicably accessible with your own transport, for which
we describe a one-day circuit.

Parco Nazionale delle Foreste Casenti-nesi, Monte Falterona e Campigna
This **national park** (www.parcoforestecasentinesi.it)
goes over both sides of the Tuscany–Emilia-
Romagna border, taking in some of the most
scenic stretches of the Apennines. The Tuscan
part is gentler than the Emilian side.

    One of the highest peaks, **Monte Falterona**
(1654m), marks the source of the Arno. Apart
from the human population, including the
inhabitants of two monasteries, the park is
also home to a rich assortment of wildlife,
including foxes, wolves, deer and wild boar,
plus nearly 100 bird species. The dense forests
are a cool summer refuge, ideal for walking
and also escaping the maddening crowds. The
Grande Escursione Appenninica (GEA) trekking trail passes through here, and myriad
walking paths crisscross the park.

    From Arezzo take the SS71 northwards
through Bibbiena and on up to **Badia Prataglia**, a pleasant little mountain village in the
Alpe di Serra, near the border with Emilia-
Romagna. Its **visitors centre** (☎ 0575 55 94 77; www
.badiaprataglia.com in Italian; ☉ 9am-12.30pm & 3.30-6pm
Tue-Sun Jun-Sep, 9am-12.30pm Tue-Sat, 9am-12.30pm & 3.30-
6pm Sun Oct-May) carries a wealth of information
about the park, including two useful titles in
English: The National Park of the Casentine

Forests: Where the Trees Touch the Sky (€12)
and The National Park of the Forests of Casen-
tin, Monte Falterona and Campigna (€7.50).
There's a free leaflet in Italian detailing nine
short, signed nature walks within the park.
For more strenuous hiking, pick up the Carta
Excursionista, Parco Nazionale delle Foreste
Casentinesi, Monte Falterona e Campigna map
(€8.25) at 1:25,000, which features more than
800km of trails.

Camaldoli
From Badia Prataglia, go back along the SS71,
then turn right after 3.5km to head for Camaldoli and its **monastery** (☎ 0575 55 60 12; www
.camaldoli.it; ☉ 8.30am-12.30pm & 2.30-6.30pm). The
monks managed the forests that still stand
around the monastery, and developed all sorts
of medicinal and herbal products. You're free
to wander about the place and visit the **Antica
Farmacia** (☉ 9am-12.30pm & 2.30-6pm). The monks
still make all manner of products, including
liqueurs, honey, perfumes and chocolate. If
the monastery's closed, the bar of the Albergo
Camaldoli opposite sells some of its products,
which are also available in other towns in the
region, including Arezzo.

    Continue for a further 1.5km, then turn
right and follow signs to the more interesting
Eremo di Camaldoli. Apparantly, Conte Maldolo
gave the land for this isolated retreat to St
Romualdo in 1012. From the name of the
count came that of the location, and around
1023 Romualdo set about building the monastery that became home to the Camaldolesi,
an ascetic branch of the Benedictines and a
powerful force in medieval Tuscany. You can
visit his wood-panelled cell, the model for 20
small, tiled houses that are the cells of today's
resident Benedictine monks.

    Retrace your route for 600m, then turn
right at the point signed Pratovecchio, which
is reached after 16km. The drive itself is a
delight, the lush forest and superb views easily
compensating for the energy exerted coping
with the bends.

Pratovecchio & Around
Pratovecchio itself is of little interest apart
from its porticoed Piazza Garibaldi. The LFI
private train line runs through here, with
regular trains connecting Arezzo (via Bibbiena and Poppi) with Stia.

    Just west of town you can make a detour to fol-
low signs to the attractively sited Romanesque

Pieve di Romena, then on between the fields to **Castello di Romena**. This crumbling, mainly 13th-century castle, closed indefinitely for safety reasons, has known better days. Erected around AD 1000 on the site of an Etruscan settlement, it was in its heyday an enormous complex surrounded by three sets of defensive walls. Dante, says legend, got his inspiration for the Circles of Hell from observing the castle's prison tower at the heart of its concentric defensive walls. An unfriendly overabundance of 'private property' signs discourages exploration around the castle, but leg-stretching can be done on the hiking trail leading from the car park down into the valley.

Take the SS310 down the valley to Poppi, then on to Bibbiena.

Poppi & Bibbiena

The most striking town of the Casentino region is Poppi, perched on a hill in the Arno plain. It's topped by the gaunt, commanding presence of the **Castello dei Conti Guidi** (☎ 0575 52 05 16; www.buonconte.com in Italian; Piazza Repubblica 1; adult/child incl audioguide €6/5; ☉ 10am-6.30pm Jul-Oct), built by the same counts who raised the Castello di Romena.

Interior attractions include a small 'ancient prison', a fairytale courtyard, stone staircase and balcony, the Sala della Feste with its restored medieval frescoes and the internationally acclaimed library, containing hundreds of medieval texts and manuscripts. The main attraction, however, is the chapel on the 2nd floor, with frescoes by Taddeo Gaddi. The scene of *Herod's Feast* shows Salome apparently clicking her fingers as she dances, accompanied by a lute player, while John the Baptist's headless corpse lies slumped in the corner.

Poppi is home to **Casa Ombuto** (www.italiancookerycourse.com), which hosts week-long, highly reputed (and highly priced), all-inclusive cooking courses.

Bibbiena has reasonable transport links to the national park. Buses depart from the train station to both Camaldoli (€1.70, seven daily Monday to Saturday) and Verna (€2.30, four daily), each taking around 45 minutes.

Santuario di San Francesco (Verna)

This Franciscan monastic complex is 23km east of Bibbiena in Verna. Of more interest than the Camaldoli monastery to many modern pilgrims, it's where St Francis of Assisi is said to have received the stigmata, and, in a sense, it's closer to the essence of the saint than Assisi itself.

By car, follow signs just outside Verna for the **sanctuary** (☎ 0575 53 41; www.santuariodellaverna .com; ☉ 6.30am-8.30pm) or take the mildly taxing, but agreeable 30-minute uphill hike from the visitor centre in the city. The Chiesa Maggiore (also known as the Basilica) has some remarkable glazed ceramics by Andrea della Robbia. Here, you will also discover reliquaries containing items associated with the saint, including his clothing that is stained with blood from stigmatic wounds and the whip with which he used to impose a little self-discipline.

Beside the Basilica entrance is the **Cappella della Pietà**. From it, the **Corridoio delle Stimmate**, painted with frescoes recounting the saint's life, leads to a cluster of chapels, with a short detour to the cave and the unforgiving slab of rock that St Francis called a 'bed'. At the core of the sanctuary, is the **Cappella delle Stimmate**, beautifully decorated with terracotta works by Luca and Andrea della Robbia. Allow at least an hour to lose yourself in the sanctuary's seemingly endless series of halls, courtyards, frescoes, nooks and lengthy, unsigned dead ends.

SOUTH OF AREZZO
Castiglion Fiorentino

This commanding hillside village merits a quick stop off on the route between Arezzo and Cortona. Fought over throughout the Middle Ages for its strategic position, it finally fell to Florentine rule in 1384.

Above the main Piazza del Municipio and at the highest point of the old town, is the **Pinacoteca** (☎ 0575 65 74 66; Via del Cassero; adult/child €3/2; ☉ 10am-12.30pm & 4-6.30pm Tue-Sun), whose paintings include works by Taddeo Gaddi. Nearby, the **Museo Archeologico** (☎ 0575 65 94 57; Via del Tribunale 8; www.icec-cf.it; admission €3; ☉ 10am-12.30pm & 4-6.30pm Tue-Sun Apr-Oct, 10am-12.30pm & 3.30-6pm Tue-Sun Nov-Mar) has a small collection of local finds. A combined ticket giving access to both costs €5/3 per adult/child.

A few kilometres further south along the road to Cortona, you can't miss the **Castello di Montecchio**, a formidable redoubt that Florence gave to the English mercenary Sir John Hawkwood (c1320–94) in return for his military services. You can see the knight's portrait in the Duomo (see p105) in Florence. The

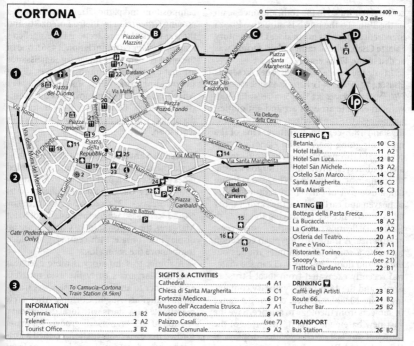

CORTONA

SLEEPING	
Betania	10 C3
Hotel Italia	11 A2
Hotel San Luca	12 B2
Hotel San Michele	13 A2
Ostello San Marco	14 C2
Santa Margherita	15 C2
Villa Marsili	16 C3

EATING	
Bottega della Pasta Fresca	17 B1
La Bucaccia	18 A2
La Grotta	19 A2
Osteria del Teatro	20 A1
Pane e Vino	21 A1
Ristorante Tonino	(see 12)
Snoopy's	(see 21)
Trattoria Dardano	22 B1

DRINKING	
Caffè degli Artisti	23 B2
Route 66	24 B2
Tuscher Bar	25 B2

TRANSPORT	
Bus Station	26 B2

SIGHTS & ACTIVITIES	
Cathedral	4 A1
Chiesa di Santa Margherita	5 C1
Fortezza Medicea	6 D1
Museo dell'Accademia Etrusca	7 A1
Museo Diocesano	8 A1
Palazzo Casali	(see 7)
Palazzo Comunale	9 A2

INFORMATION	
Polymnia	1 B2
Telenet	2 A2
Tourist Office	3 B2

privately owned castle is presently closed to visitors.

Cortona
pop 22,600

With a layout indicative of someone spilling a bucket of 'Etruscan town' down a hillside, rooms with a view are the rule, not the exception in Cortona. A small settlement when the Etruscans moved in during the 8th century BC, it later became a Roman town. In the late 14th century Fra Angelico lived and worked here, and fellow artists Luca Signorelli (1450–1523) and Pietro da Cortona (1596–1669) were both born within its walls.

Avid fans of the film *Under the Tuscan Sun*, adapted from the book by Frances Mayes, will know that Cortona served as a location for shooting. Though don't go looking to re-enact the *Dolce Vita* homage, fountain frolicking bit…The fountain, built especially for shooting, flowed only for the scene and is now dry.

The town, with its steep captivating streets, twisting off at mirthfully impossible angles, can be easily seen in a few hours, though over-

nighters will be treated to sensational dusk and dawn views over Val de Chiana, as far as Lago di Trasimeno.

ORIENTATION

Piazza Garibaldi, on the southern edge of the walled city, is where buses arrive. From it, there are sensational views across the plain to Lago di Trasimeno. From the piazzale, walk straight up Via Nazionale – about the only flat street in the whole town – to Piazza della Repubblica, the main square.

INFORMATION

Telenet (☎ 0575 60 10 96; Via Guelfa 25; internet per hr €3.50; ⏰ 9am-10pm May-Sep, 9am-8pm Mon-Sat Oct-Apr) A phone/internet shop.

Tourist office (☎ 0575 63 03 52; Via Nazionale 42; ⏰ 9am-1pm & 3-7pm Mon-Sat, 9am-1pm Sun May-Sep, 9am-1pm & 3-6pm Mon-Fri, 9am-1pm Sat Oct-Apr)

SIGHTS
Piazza della Republica & Piazza Signorelli

Brooding over lopsided Piazza della Repubblica is the **Palazzo Comunale**, built in the 13th century, renovated in the 16th, and once again in the 19th. To the north is attractive Piazza Signorelli and, on its north side, 13th-century **Palazzo Casali**, whose rather plain façade was added in the 17th century.

Inside the palace is the **Museo dell'Accademia Etrusca** (☎ 0575 63 04 15; Piazza Signorelli 9; adult/child €7/4; ☸ 10am-7pm Apr-Oct, 10am-5pm Tue-Sun Nov-Mar), with an eclectic array of art and antiquities, including Etruscan bronzes, medieval paintings and 18th-century furniture. One of the most intriguing pieces is an elaborate 2nd-century-BC bronze Etruscan oil lamp, decorated with satyrs, sirens and a Gorgon's head, weighing in at a hefty 55kg. The Medici Room contains a pair of early-18th-century globes of heaven and earth, where the cartographer takes artistic licence portraying the 'Isola di California' floating free from the western coast of America. A transitory Egyptian collection featuring a couple of mummies rounds out the ground floor. Upstairs you can see material recently excavated from local Etruscan tombs and the 18th-century library containing some 10,000 volumes, covering a range of subjects from theology to science. Save the vast new basement exhibit, the pride of the museum, for last. Well-executed displays of Etruscan and Roman ruins, archaeological models, jewellery, bronze accoutrements, pottery and mosaics are enriched by multimedia presentations describing all. Book in advance for a guided tour of the museum in English (€5, minimum six people) and three Etruscan tombs (adult/child with guide €10.50/7.75) in the surrounding countryside. Combined tours of both cost €15/9.50.

Piazza del Duomo

Little is left of the original Romanesque character of the **cathedral** (Piazza del Duomo), northwest of Piazza Signorelli. It was completely rebuilt late in the Renaissance and again, indifferently, in the 18th century. Its true wealth lies in the riches within the **Museo Diocesano** (☎ 0575 6 28 30; Piazza del Duomo 1; adult/child €5/3; ☸ 10am-7pm Apr-Oct, 10am-5pm Nov-Mar) in the former church of Gesù.

Room 1 has a remarkable Roman sarcophagus decorated with a frenzied battle scene between Dionysus and the Amazons. Here and continuing into the adjoining Room 4 are paintings by Luca Signorelli, including his *Compianto sul Cristo Morto* (Grief over the Dead Christ; 1502), a masterpiece of colour,

composition and pathos. In Room 3 there's a moving *Crucifixion* by Pietro Lorenzetti, and the star work of the collection: Fra Angelico's *Annunciazione* (Annunciation; 1436), one of the most recognisable images of Renaissance art that by its sheer luminosity leaves all the surrounding works in the shade. Also by Fra Angelico and almost as moving is his exquisite *Madonna*. Downstairs the Oratorio is decorated with biblical frescoes by Vasari's workshop.

Chiesa di Santa Margherita & Fortezza

Scale the steep, quiet labyrinth of cobbled lanes in the eastern part of town to the largely 19th-century **Chiesa di Santa Margherita** (Piazza Santa Margherita; ☸ 7.30am-noon & 3-7pm Apr-Oct, 8.30am-noon & 3-6pm Oct-Apr) where the remains of Saint Margaret, the patron saint of Cortona, are on display in an ornate, 14th-century, glass-sided tomb above the main altar.

A sinner-to-saint story if there ever was one, St Margaret's early life as a mistress and mother to an illegitimate son was transformed after arriving in Cortona. After a few regrettable false-starts with local dreamboats, she found her Franciscan groove. Margaret formed her own congregation, opened a hospital, received ecstasy-charged messages from heaven, prophesised the date of her death and surrounded herself with the poor, ill, reformed, pious and penitent. She was canonized in 1728 by Pope Benedict XIII.

It's a stiff climb, but it's worth pushing even further uphill to the forbidding **Fortezza Medicea** (☎ 0575 63 04 15; adult/child €3/1.50; ☸ 10am-1.30pm & 2.30-6pm Apr-Oct). This is Cortona's highest point, with stupendous views over the surrounding countryside.

ACTIVITIES

The tourist office can provide a comprehensive list of nearby excursions, bicycle hire and walks, including those led by **Cortona Wellness** (☎ 0575 60 31 36; www.cortonawellness.com in Italian) who organise guided four- to five-hour hikes (per group €30) for groups of two or more in the spectacular countryside around Cortona.

Films are shown at **Giardino del Parterre** in English every Wednesday night.

COURSES

Polymnia (☎ 0575 61 25 82; www.polymnia.net; Vicolo Boni 18), A.K.A. Koine, offers group as well a one-on-one Italian language courses and related cultural and social activities for non-native speakers.

FESTIVALS & EVENTS

Giostra dell'Archidado A full week of merriment in May or June (the date varies to coincide with Ascension day), with trumpeting, parading and neighbourhood rivalry, culminating in a crossbow competition first held in the Middle Ages. Among other festivities, contestants from the city's traditional neighbourhoods dress up in medieval garb to compete for the *verretta d'oro* (golden arrow).

Mostra Antiquaria Every year for about a week from late August into the first days of September, Cortona hosts one of Italy's main antique fairs.

Sagra del Fungo Porcino Held in mid-August this is a similar celebration to the Steak Festival, honouring this delectable variety of mushroom.

Sagra della Bistecca (Steak Festival) Held on 14 and 15 August this is a gastronomic celebration, when Giardino del Parterre becomes one vast open-air grill.

SLEEPING

Ostello San Marco (☎ 0575 60 13 92; ostellocortona@libero. it; Via Maffei 57; dm/d €13/34, incl breakfast) An HI-affiliated youth hostel a short, steep walk east of Piazza Garibaldi, this budget option is a run-down, ill-cared-for place, despite its impressive premises.

Santa Margherita (☎ 0575 63 03 36; comunita cortona@smr.it; Via Cesare Battisti 15; s/d/tr/q €32/46/56/76) Run by sweet, obliging nuns from the religious institute, the cloister-quality rooms here are clean, though it's hard to be sure with the 40-watt light bulbs used throughout. This is a popular place, so call ahead (with Italian phrasebook at the ready).

Betania (☎ 0575 63 04 23; www.casaperferiebetania .com; Via Severini 50; s with/without bathroom €38/32, d with/without bathroom €48/44) Across the road and in the same religious spirit of Santa Margherita. A gated, beautiful, tree-lined entrance, large garden, great views and onsite church give the area a distinct monastic feel. They do dinner for €14. Off-street parking is €25 per day, though the street is just fine.

Hotel Italia (☎ 0575 63 02 54; www.planhotel.com /hitalia; Via Ghibellina 5/7; s/d/tr €79/105/135, incl breakfast; ☒ 🖳) Italia is in a 17th-century palazzo just off Piazza della Repubblica. Standard rooms have traditional cross-beamed ceilings and are decorated in warm orange tones, while each of the unique superior rooms features giant bathtubs. Views are breathtaking from the roof-level breakfast room. Oriental mas-

sages, wi-fi and mountain bike hire are also available.

Hotel San Luca (☎ 0575 63 04 60; www.sanlucacortona .com; Piazza Garibaldi 2; s/d incl breakfast €85/120; ☒ 🖳) Handy for the bus stop and its proximity to free parking, San Luca also has an upscale restaurant, Tonino. Rooms are generally satisfactory, some with magnificent panoramic views, though lightly peppered with minor maintenance issues.

Hotel San Michele (☎ 0575 60 43 48; www.hotelsan michele.net; Via Guelfa 15; s €99, d €109-120, incl breakfast; 🕑 closed Jan–mid-Mar; 🅿 ☒) This is Cortona's finest hotel. Primarily Renaissance, but with elements dating from the 12th century and modifications over subsequent centuries, it's like a little history of Cortona in stone. Rooms are airy, spacious and exquisitely furnished. Parking is €20.

Villa Marsili (☎ 0575 605 252; www.villamarsili.net; Via Cesare Battisti 13; s/d incl breakfast €110/180; 🕑 closed Nov-Feb; 🅿 🖳) Complimentary drinks each evening, frescoes on the walls and ceiling, sparingly, but elegantly antique-furnished rooms with all mod cons and wi-fi in case you want to email your friends to crow. The walk into town is a 15-minute uphill puff. Parking is €12 per night.

EATING

Pane e Vino (☎ 0575 63 10 10; Piazza Signorelli 27; snacks €6; 🕑 dinner only Tue-Sun) This is a hugely popular dining hall in the centre of town. For a quick snack of regional specialities, go for the *piatto del cacciatore*, the hunter's platter of wild boar, deer, goose and turkey. There are more than 500 wines to choose from and most of the pasta is homemade.

La Grotta (☎ 0575 63 02 71; Piazzetta Baldly 3; meals €18-25; 🕑 Wed-Mon) At the end of a blind alley just off Piazza della Repubblica, this is a rock-reliable choice, though the service (and opening hours) can be a little haphazard. Twin-roomed and intimate, it has all the virtues of a traditional trattoria. If you go for strong flavours, begin with the melted *scrota* smoked cheese with either porcini mushrooms or black truffles.

Trattoria Dardano (☎ 0575 60 19 44; Via Dardano 24; meals €24; 🕑 Thu-Tue) Dardano is just one of half a dozen reliable, no-nonsense trattorie that line Via Dardano.

Ristorante Tonino (☎ 0575 63 05 00; Piazza Garibaldi 1; meals €30-35; 🕑 closed Mon dinner & Tue) Tonino has magnificent views as far as Lago di Trasimeno from its summer terrace, and specialises in antipasti. Try the *ravioli al tartufo e pecorino* (ravioli with truffles and *pecorino* cheese).

La Bucaccia (☎ 0575 606 039; www.labucaccia.it; Via Ghibellina 17; meals €33) Etruscan cellar ambiance with appropriate ornamentation: wine racks, grape press, tiny wine barrels, cheese wheels and an Etruscan cistern displayed under floor glass. The service is indisputably warm, but agonising slow, even for Italy.

Osteria del Teatro (☎ 0575 63 05 56; www.osteria-del-teatro.it; Via Maffei 2; meals €40; ⏰ Thu-Tue) Friendly service, fresh flowers on every table and a liberal meting of truffle shavings awaits diners here. Featured in nearly every Italian gastronomic guide, its walls are clad with photos of actors who have dined here. In summer try the *ravioli ai fiori di zucca* (pumpkin-flower ravioli). Watch your head when the unwieldy phallus of a pepperpot is heaved out for random seasoning.

Self-caterers should stock up at **Bottega della Pasta Fresca** (Via Dardano 29), a glorious little hole-in-the-wall shop that makes its own pasta. There's a Saturday market, including farmers' products, in Piazza Signorelli.

GELATERIE

Snoopy's (Piazza Signorelli 29) Gelato is served in generous portions here, starting at €1.50 for a small.

DRINKING

Tuscher Bar (☎ 0575 6 20 53; Via Nazionale 43; ⏰ closed Mon) This is a stylish place where you can enjoy a coffee or cocktail, and it also does good light lunches.

Caffè degli Artisti (☎ 0575 60 12 37; Via Nazionale 18) Across the road and in the same vein, this place also has a long menu of typical Italian food and pours a decent pint of Guinness.

Route 66 (☎ 0575 6 27 27; Via Nationale 78) Just off Piazza Garibaldi, offering ultra-modern décor, lung-vibrating music, hypnotic lights and fru-fru drinks.

GETTING THERE & AROUND

From the bus station at Piazza Garibaldi, LFI buses connect the town with Arezzo (€2.60, one hour, more than 10 daily), via Castiglion Fiorentino.

Shuttle buses (€1, 15 minutes) run at least hourly to Camucia–Cortona train station, on the main Rome–Florence line. Destinations include Arezzo (€2.20, 20 minutes, hourly), Florence (€6.70, 1½ hours, hourly), Rome (€9.40, 2¼ hours, every two hours) and Perugia (€2.80, 40 minutes, over 12 daily).

The tourist office has timetables and sells both bus and train tickets.

By car, the city is on the north–south SS71 that runs to Arezzo. It's also close to the SS75 that connects Perugia to the A1.

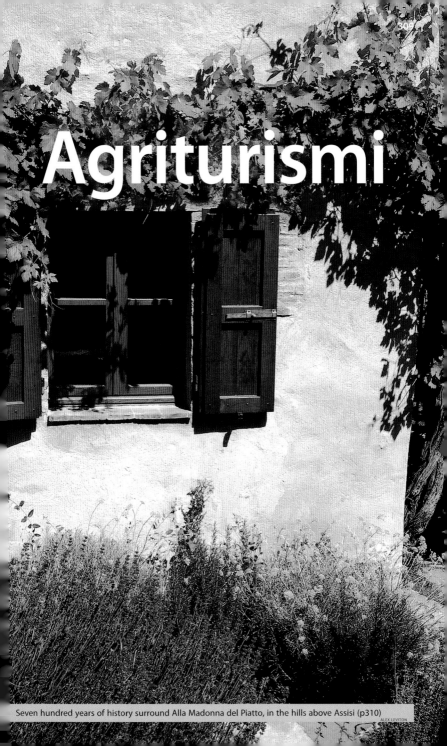

Agriturismi

Seven hundred years of history surround Alla Madonna del Piatto, in the hills above Assisi (p310)

ESCAPE TO THE COUNTRY

Trade museums and Manolos for barns and bunnies at what has proven to be one of Central Italy's most unique and ubiquitous accommodation options – the *agriturismo*. Quickly gaining in popularity in the rural (and not so rural) areas of Tuscany and Umbria, *agriturismi* are working farms and country houses that offer rooms to visitors on holiday. The legal definition requires *agriturismi* to grow at least one product. While many make olive oil or wine, others are expansive farming complexes that produce anything from wheat or jam to cattle or lentils. The majority of *agriturismi* are located in historic buildings – old farmhouses, former stables or even castles. Guests might stay in basic rooms with shared bathrooms, or at some locations rooms might look more like villa suites. But most of them share one thing in common – a respect for the beautiful landscape and 'slow' lifestyle, which makes Central Italy so special.

If you want a hands-on experience, go through www.wwoof.org. The list of Italian WWOOF farms is on www.wwoof.it/gb/list.html. Potential participants need to join World Wide Opportunities on Organic Farms (WWOOF) Italia before contacting farms.

We've listed a dozen *agriturismi* here and another dozen within the chapters, but there are hundreds of *agriturismi* in Tuscany and Umbria alone. They're not easy to find, so it takes a bit of pre-planning to arrange a stay. Many close in winter, require a two-night or one-week minimum stay and almost all of them are in rural areas, well signposted but often down a windy or dirt road. You can buy books from www.touringclub.com, including its excellent *Italian Farm Vacation: The Guide to Countryside Hospitality* (€16.95); and check websites for listings (see Top 10 Web Resources boxed text, opposite). Once in the region, pick up *Osterie & Locande d'Italia: A Guide to Traditional Places to Eat & Stay in Italy* (Slow Food Editore; €22).

ASSISI, NORTHERN UMBRIA (p340)

Up a road as beautiful as it is isolated, it would be virtually impossible to realise you're less than 15 minutes from civilisation if you couldn't see the Basilica di St Francesco in Assisi glistening through the surrounding oaks. Owned by a charming multilingual Italian-Dutch couple, **Alla Madonna del Piatto** (☎ 075 819 90 50; www.incampagna.com; Pieve San Nicolo 18; d incl breakfast €85-120; ☷ Mar–mid-Nov;

A noble night's sleep in the 17th-century villa at Rignana

NICOLA WILLIAMS

Breathtaking surrounds at Todi Castle (p316)
ALEX LEVITON

TOP 10 WEB RESOURCES

Agriturismi aren't always easy to find, so it may take a bit of pre-planning to arrange a stay. Here are some useful websites and books to get you started:

- www.agriguida.com
- www.agritour.net
- www.agriturismo.it
- www.agriturismo.regione.toscana.it
- www.agritursimi-toscana.com
- www.agriturist.it
- www.bellaumbria.net
- www.holidayfarm.net
- www.italyfarmholidays.com
- www.tuscanydreamers.com

P) is understandably popular with English-speaking Slow Foodies. Each of the six Moroccan- or Indian-designed guest chambers is truly a room with a view, with windows that sweep open onto views of Assisi and the surrounding hills. But the real reason to stay here is the intimate cooking classes Letizia runs (in Italian or English) from her professional kitchen. Students start the day in local markets shopping for local ingredients, then learn how to roll pasta dough or create the perfect tiramisu, and finish it off with a feast or tasting of their own creation.

BADIA DI PASSIGNANO, FLORENCE (p166)

Divine, divine, divine…**Rignana** (☎ 055 85 20 65; www.rignana.it; Val di Rignana 15, Rignana; d incl breakfast €95-105, noble villa for 8 per week €3500; **P** **R** **□**)
is truly a place never to forget, as this old farmstead and noble villa 3.8km from Badia di Passignano oozes panache. Every last detail – from the recycled wine-barrel flooring in the 17th-century noble villa with two frescoed apartments to the more rustic *fattoria* rooms, once used to store vinegar, *Vin Santo* and so on – has been thoughtfully renovated using original materials from the estate that Italian-German owner Cosimo Gericke inherited from his father in the 1990s. Potted citrus fruit trees adorn the interior courtyard where breakfast is served; guests can serve themselves to chilled soft drinks and wine as they fancy; and grappa-fuelled lunches and dinners can be had in the former oil mill on the estate. Dip into the infinity swimming pool with sweeping Tuscan views and pretend you're in paradise.

> 'Dip into the infinity swimming pool with sweeping Tuscan views and pretend you're in paradise'

CASTIGLIONE D'ORCIA, CENTRAL TUSCANY (p270)

Just 1km south of Castiglione d'Orcia, **Le Case** (☎ 0577 88 89 83; www.agriturismolecase.com; Strada Provinciale 323; s/d/tr incl breakfast €40/70/80) occupies a gorgeous, 18th-century stone farmhouse and is one of the

A tranquil stay at Le Case
LEIF PETTERSEN

best value *agriturismi* we've seen. Run by a warm Italian couple, all five rooms are tastefully decorated and charming in their simplicity. Still a working farm, an elderly farmer can be regularly spotted around the property, resolutely continuing his daily chores. Somewhat remote and fittingly peaceful, nearby diversions include guided horseback riding, hiking, wine-tasting, and the spas in Bagni San Filipo and Bangi Vignoni, with a variety of abbeys and hill towns within an hour's drive. Discounts available for long stays.

CITTA DI CASTELLO, NORTHERN UMBRIA (p355)

Potential farmhands and travelling softies alike can find their bliss at 'the turtle doves' organic farm, **Agriturismo/B&B Le Tortorelle** (☎ 075 941 09 49, 347 975 44 67 for English speakers; www.letortorelle.it; Loc. Molino Vitelli 180, Umbertide; 2 nights minimum per person incl breakfast €35; P 🐾). Aldo and Teresa left big-city life in Milan to raise their family in the hills of northern Umbria, growing organic wheat, aloe and herbs, and eating only natural, organic fare. The farm is one of 234 in Italy's WWOOF programme, and offers those willing to get their hands dirty the chance to learn organic farming. Or, take a course in making natural cosmetics and salves. Those on holiday are

Dine on home-grown lentils and spelt at Casale nel Parco
ALEX LEVITON

Escape to an island eco-hostel at Fattoria Il Poggio in Lake Trasimeno
ALEX LEVITON

very welcome to stay as guests in a handful of comfortable rooms and share delicious home-made meals with the family. In summer, cross your fingers you'll arrive on a night when the family cooks pizza in the 200-year-old outdoor brick oven.

LAKE TRASIMENO, NORTHERN UMBRIA (p360)

Enjoy an entire island to yourself at **Fattoria Il Poggio** (☎ 075 965 95 50; www.fattoriaisolapolvese.com; Isola Polvese; dm/f incl breakfast €15/17, meals €10; 🕙 Mar-30 Oct, reception closed 3-7pm; 🖳), a farmhouse-turned-youth hostel that is more like an *agriturismo* than most *agriturismi*. The mini eco-resort is in Umbria's Lake Trasimeno, as close to Tuscany as it is nearby Perugia. An array of solar panels powers a bio pool (not for swimming) filled with an ecological aquatic garden that naturally filters the island's grey-water system. Home-made dinners might include wild cherries or fava beans grown on the island, or the hostel's

Go olive picking at Rignana (p311)
NICOLA WILLIAMS

own production of olive oil. The farmhouse's only neighbours are an environmental education lab and a soon-to-be-restored monastery and fortress, where concerts and events are held in summer.

NORCIA, SOUTHERN UMBRIA (p385)

Casale nel Parco (☎ /fax 0743 81 64 81; www.casale nelparco.com; Loc. Fontevena 8; s incl breakfast €50-60, d incl breakfast €100-120, half-board s €70-80, d €130-150, full board d €170-190, extra person €30-35; **P** 🐎) is close enough to the town centre of Norcia – gateway to the raw landscape of the Valnerina and Monti Sibillini, and the Umbrian headquarters for pork – to admire the ancient city walls as you slowly meander to town. The organic lentils, spelt and vegetables grown on the property are on the dinner menu in its restaurant, along with local truffles, cheese, *salume* (cold cuts), pork and wild boar. Guests often gather in the library to peruse information about the local area, as many have arranged activities through the *agriturismo* – horseback riding, spelunking, parachuting or mule trekking. The ambience in the 14 guest rooms is rustic farmhouse mixed with modern Italian fixtures, with a dash of old-world romance.

RÙFINA CHIANTI, FLORENCE (p165)

'*Agriturismo* boutique' is how the funky 14-room **Podere Castellare** (☎ 055 832 60 82, 320 407 95 92; www.poderecastellare.it; Via Casa Spasse, Diacetto Pelago; d incl breakfast per person €58-78; 🕙 Easter-early Nov;

MEET YOUR SOUL

Aldo and Teresa and their daughters Alessia and Alessandra left the big city of Milan for the simpler life on an organic, vegetarian farm in Umbertide, about an hour north of Perugia. 'In a big city like Milan,' says Aldo, 'everything can be polluted. In some way, we felt polluted, as well.' On Le Tortorelle, Teresa says, 'We have a better quality of food, health, time and relationships. We've had to learn how to take care of animals and plants and prepare the garden and the wood for the winter. It's been possible to start a strong internal dialogue and be conscious of who we are inside and what's possible to do with our own hands – to make bread and cheese, to chop wood, to harvest our own food.' They decided to open their farm to guests like they would open their home to extended family. Daughter Alessia says, 'We hope visitors can take away a new awareness of themselves and start to meet their soul when they are here. There's no better way to meditate than by doing with our hands and feeling the new sensations on our skin!'

Aldo and Teresa Alessi are the owners of Agriturismo/B&B Le Tortorelle (opposite)

Prized Chianina bulls graze the lush Tuscan hillsides

NICOLA WILLIAMS

'Oak woods where creamy Chianina cows graze and wild boars ferret for truffles'

Modern waxed-concrete bathrooms at Podere Castellare

NICOLA WILLIAMS

P **㊇** **🖳**) labels itself. A smart hop east of Florence in the heart of the Rùfina Chianti wine region, it was the grandparent's farm of siblings Elizabeth and Patrizio Pandolfi, who breezed through the heirloom with the help of well-known Florence architect studio MBLR. They turned it into a bold ode to Kartell, Luceplan and other Italian design houses. The farm still makes its own oil and grows saffron, while rooms are named after local flora (no guessing what colour Poppy is). Waxed-concrete bathrooms sport unusual handmade soaps made from the previous season's remaining olive oil; and the veranda screams candyfloss pink. Come dusk, guests mingle over complimentary aperitifs in the Corbusier-styled salon, followed by dinner around a shared table. Lazing around the Jacuzzi and pool with view is a big day-time temptation.

SAN MINIATO HILLS, FLORENCE (p170)

The Zen creation of trained economists Guido and Gianluca and lawyer Marco, **Barbialla Nuova Fattoria** (☎ 0571 67 70 04; www .barbiallanuova.it; Via Casastada 49, Montaione; d/q/6

WHAT AN EXPERIENCE

Every *agriturismi* offers a slightly different experience. Some are full-service compounds with dozens of guest rooms, English- or French-speaking staff, horseback-riding facilities, and spa or restaurant (or all three). Others are intimate farmhouses growing just one or two crops, run by the same family for generations. Here is a sampling of what you might experience at an *agriturismo*:

- Hike for hours in the peaceful surrounding area
- Swim, relax with a wellness package, visit a spa
- Tie on an apron and learn a few new recipes (often using the *agriturismo's* home-grown ingredients)
- Taste wines or olive oils
- Go truffle-hunting
- Eat at the *agriturismo's* restaurant, usually serving home-grown, local or organic fare
- Go medieval with archery
- Take horseback-riding trips or lessons
- Contribute to the farm as a working guest
- Learn new skills – ceramics, painting, even yoga

Imperio truffle-hunting at Barbialla Nuova Fattoria
NICOLA WILLIAMS

Cooking at Todi Castle (p316)
ALEX LEVITON

people incl breakfast €70/132/186, 2-/4-/6-people self-catering apt €430/790/1035; P ⚡) stands on 500 hectares of agricultural land (the farm is certified 100% organic) and oak woods, where creamy Chianina cows graze and wild boars ferret for truffles between tree roots when Imperio and his dog Toby aren't looking. Farmhouse apartments are a hip mix of rustic old and minimalist new: think stainless-steel fridges, antique wooden dressers and the fabulously satisfying smell of wood-fuelled heating throughout. Should you like eggs for breakfast, search out Imperio at the hen house. Barbialla Nuova is in Montaione, 20km south of San Miniato (p171) and 20km north of San Gimignano (p254).

SEGGIANO, CENTRAL TUSCANY (p278)

Three kilometres outside of Seggiano (near Castiglion d'Orcia), you'll find **Agriturismo La Silva** (☎ 0564 95 06 03; www.agriturismolasilva.it; per person incl breakfast €42-60; ⚡ 💻). This cleanly transformed farmhouse is run by a disarmingly friendly team of young go-getters. Apart from their celebrated fixation with *suino cinto senese* (a black and white pig native to central Tuscany, known for its particularly savoury meat and often seasoned with salt, pepper or spices like cinnamon, fennel or chilli), the attractions here include guided horseback-riding tours, pool, sauna, massage and staring in awe at the expansive view. Some 400m down the hill from 'Il Cacciatore' restaurant, go down the precipitous dirt road signed 'Poggio Ferro' to get here.

Agriturismo San Lorenzo: 15th-century stone outside, farmhouse chic inside

LEIF PETTERSEN

SORANO, SOUTHERN TUSCANY (p293)

About 10km north of Sorano, 3km off the SS2, is the *agriturismo*-cum-village, **Il Cornacchino** (☎ 0564 95 15 82; www.cornacchino.it; full board per person €63), which offers a great selection of trekking trips and horseback-riding courses. Choose from a three-day, on-site class (all ages) or one of its week-long themed horseback-riding treks, like 'Mountain–Sea', 'Etruscan' and 'Maremma Park'. It has 54 horses, including 12 Haflingers, six Appaloosas, two Paints, six Maremmans, six part-Arabs and four Arab-Haflingers. While horse enthusiasts gallop around, nonequestrian companions can engage in standard *agriturismo* diversions, like wandering the countryside or partaking in a cooking class (by advanced request).

TODI, SOUTHERN UMBRIA (p373)

For those looking to rent an entire villa or an honest-to-goodness castle with an *agriturismo* twist look no further than **Todi Castle** (☎ 0744 95 20 04; www.todicastle.com; Vocabolo Capecchio, Morre; weekly villa/castle for up to 10 people incl breakfast from €1500/4500; ☼ Mar-Oct; **P** ☲). The sprawling compound is located in one of the most stunning spots in Umbria, not far from Lago di Corbara, Todi or Orvieto. The grounds provide visitors with fresh eggs, olive oil and wine, and nearby farms produce just about everything else you'll need for the cooking class the owners will set up for you. Be sure to stop by your private swimming pool or the deer park on your walk.

VOLTERRA, CENTRAL TUSCANY (p264)

Just 3km outside Volterra on the road to Siena, **Agriturismo San Lorenzo** (☎ 0588 3 90 80; www.agriturismosanlorenzo.it; B&B d €85; apt without breakfast €90-110; ☲) is a giddying fusion of sustainable tourism, countryside vistas, mod cons and wonderful food. The mountain spring-fed biological swimming pool, complete with frogs and salamanders, fronts the converted farmhouse circa 1400s. Rooms are 'farmhouse chic', individually decorated and colourful with modern kitchens and bathrooms. Walking, biking, horseback riding and hands-on, seasonal olive-oil production are immediately available, as are cooking classes with meals served in the 12th-century Franciscan chapel. Curse or blessing, some mobile-phone services don't work out here.

Northern Umbria

Small towns with atmosphere seeping out of medieval, Roman and Etruscan walls. Generations of families who have been living in the same stone farmhouse for 200 years. Fields of vineyards, wildflowers, sunflowers and olive trees.

There are endless reasons to visit Umbria. It hosts more festivals, medieval tournaments, outdoor movies, concerts, parades, antique fairs and organic markets than any other place in Italy. Plus, the outdoor activities and walking trails can't be beaten. Tuscany's turn on the overcrowded tourist radar has little to fear from Umbria, which is most content to stay wholly off the beaten path.

Umbria is Italy's most rural region, and the only province that borders neither the sea nor another country. Yes, it has the rolling hills, ancient stone villas and expanses of vineyards you'd find in Tuscany, but Umbria is a less manicured place, its untamed geography scattered with jagged rock formations and snow-capped peaks.

In paintings of Umbria, you'll notice that not much has changed in the past, oh, 400 years or so. Northern Umbria's most popular draw – Assisi – still offers ample paths that wind through ancient pink-stone buildings, looking much the same as it did in the days of St Francis of Assisi in the 13th century.

Perugia's range of restaurants, cultural events, museums and churches gives it a historic yet cosmopolitan air. The hill town of Gubbio – famous for its Corsa dei Ceri on 15 May – feels otherworldly any time of year. But the heart of northern Umbria can be found in the smaller towns and countless tiny villages where one could get lost for days.

NORTHERN UMBRIA

HIGHLIGHTS

- Take the human-birdcage **Funivia Colle Eletto** (p348) to Sant'Ubaldo church, perched on top of Monte Ingino above Gubbio
- Spend an hour reflecting on the life of St Francis in the crypt of Assisi's **Basilica di San Francesco** (p334)
- Sip on the famous Sagrantino or Montefalco Rosso at the vineyard of **Arnaldo Caprai** (p344) in Montefalco
- Stay on your own semi-private island in a youth hostel/*agriturismo* (farm stay accommodation) on **Isola Polvese** (p360) in the middle of Lake Trasimeno
- Try your hand at spinning ceramics on the wheel at **Maioliche Nulli** (p333) in Deruta

★ Gubbio

★ Lake Trasimeno

★ Assisi

Deruta ★

★ Montefalco

PERUGIA

pop 161, 390

One of Italy's best-preserved hill towns replete with museums and churches, Perugia is also a hip student town with a never-ending stream of cultural events and concerts. Within the city walls, little has changed architecturally for over several hundred years, and a few hotels and restaurants are in triple-digit ages. Culturally, however, Perugia is on the edge. Two major universities, a steady stream of foreigners and a thriving art scene ensure that Perugia melds the modern in with its past.

History

Although the Umbri tribe once inhabited the surrounding area and controlled land stretching from present-day Tuscany into Le Marche, it was the Etruscans who founded the city, leading to its zenith in the 6th century BC. It fell to the Romans in 310 BC and was given the name Perusia.

During the Middle Ages the city was racked by the internal feuding of the Baglioni and Oddi families. In 1538 the city was incorporated into the Papal States under Pope Paul III, remaining under papal control for almost three centuries.

Perugia has a strong artistic tradition. In the 15th century it was home to fresco painters Bernardino Pinturicchio and his master Pietro Vannucci (known as Perugino), who would later teach the famous painter Raphael. Its cultural tradition continues to this day with

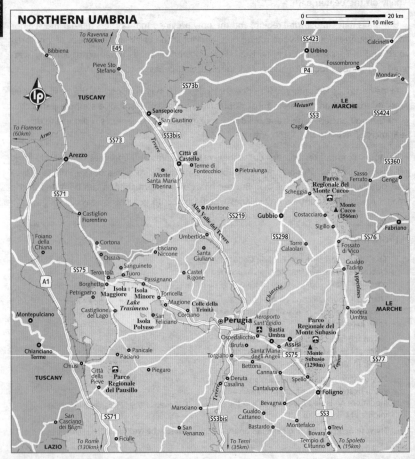

NORTHERN UMBRIA

both the University of Perugia and several universities, including the famous Università per Stranieri (University for Foreigners), which teach Italian, art and culture to thousands of students from around the world.

Orientation
Old Perugia's main strip, Corso Vannucci (named after home-town artist Pietro Vannucci, aka Perugino), runs north from the top of Rocca Paolina, through Piazza Italia and into the heart of the city, Piazza IV Novembre, where you'll find the Fontana Maggiore and the cathedral. Almost every listing in this chapter is within a kilometre of here. *Urbano* (city) buses originate from Piazza Italia, while *extraurbano* (intercity) buses drop you off at Piazza Partigiani. From here, take a few sets of *scale mobili* (elevators) through the Rocca Paolina to reach Piazza Italia. If you have heavy luggage, watch out: *scale mobili* interchange with staircases up the steep hillside. From the train station it's an enormous hike, especially with that luggage, or a quick €1 bus ride, 1.5km up the hill to Piazza Italia.

Information
BOOKSHOPS
La Libreria (☎ 075 573 50 57; Via Oberdan 52; ◷ 9am-8pm Mon-Sat, 9am-1pm & 4.30-8pm Sun) Stocks a selection of English-language books, as well as maps and Lonely Planet guidebooks in Italian and English.
Libreria Betti (☎ 075 573 16 67; Corso Vannucci 107; ◷ 9am-8pm Mon-Sat) A good selection of English-language books, cookbooks, guidebooks and dictionaries.

EMERGENCY
Police station (☎ 075 572 32 32; Palazzo dei Priori)

INTERNET ACCESS
Over a dozen internet cafés have popped up recently, most charging around €1.50 per hour. If you're sticking around, ask for an *abbonamento* discount card from the café you frequent the most, which will save you about 15% on 10 hours. Many cafés now have Skype, with accompanying headphones and cameras.
Coffee Break (☎ 075 571 63 22; Via Danzetta 22; per hr €1, wi-fi free; ◷ 9am-11pm Mon-Sat, 10am-11pm Sun) Buy anything from the café downstairs and use its (slow) wi-fi as long as you like.
Tempo Reale (☎ 075 573 55 33; Via del Forno 17; ◷ 10am-11.30pm) Central and friendly, with high-speed connection, ample opening hours and cheap long-distance telephone service.

INTERNET RESOURCES
Perugia Online (www.perugiaonline.com) Offers info on accommodation, restaurants, history, activities and sights. The main site, www.umbriaonline.com, lists information for every tourist town in Umbria in Italian or English.

LAUNDRY
67 Laundry (Via Fabretti; ◷ 8am-10pm) Wash €3, dry €3, single-serve detergents €1.

LEFT LUGGAGE
Stazione Fontivegge (◷ 6.30am-7.30pm) Costs €3 per bag for the first 12 hours, then €2 every 12 hours thereafter.

MEDIA
Little Blue What-to-Do This free English-language booklet is a must-have for students or anyone staying longer than a few hours. Known as the 'little blue book', it's available at the Teatro del Pavone, the tourist office and newsstands. Find restaurants, housing suggestions, side trips and a description of local characters.
Viva Perugia – What, Where, When The *comune di Perugia's* monthly publication (€0.80 from newsstands) lists events and public-transport schedules.

MEDICAL SERVICES
Emergency doctor (☎ 075 34 024; ◷ Sat & Sun & nights)
Farmacia San Martino (Piazza Matteotti 26) This pharmacy has a list of all the pharmacies that are open 24 hours.
Ospedale Silvestrini (☎ 075 57 81; S Andrea delle Frate) Hospital.

MONEY
Banks line Corso Vannucci. All have ATMs, known as *bancomats*. Cashing travellers cheques inside banks usually garners at least a 2% to 5% service charge, and establishments that accept them are becoming quite rare.

POST
Mail Boxes etc (☎ 075 50 17 98; Via D'Andreotto 71) Uphill along a one-way street from the train station, or take bus no 7 and it's just past the Agip petrol station on the left. Ship packages home by FedEx, UPS or DHL here (make sure you're not shipping any perishables like meat or cheese; they'll most likely get confiscated). Staff will also wrap and box purchases for a small fee.
Main post office (Piazza Matteotti; ◷ 8am-6.30pm Mon-Sat)

TOILETS
A growing drug problem in Perugia means it is probably safer to use the *bagni* (toilet)

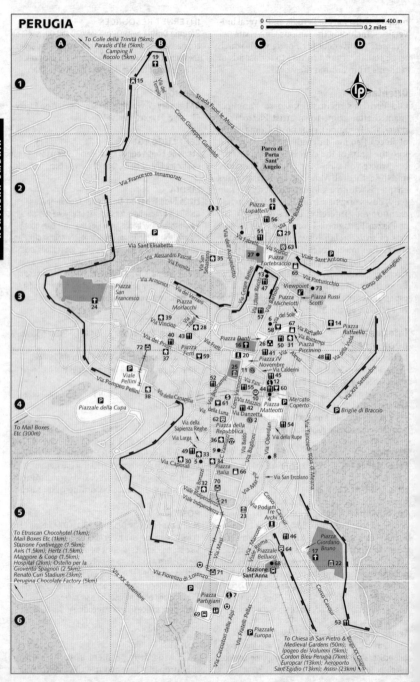

PERUGIA

To Colle della Trinità (5km);
Paradis d'Été (5km);
Camping Il
Rocolo (5km)

Strada Fuori le-Mura

Corso Giuseppe Garibaldi

Via del Tempio

Via Francesco Innamorati

Parco di
Porta
Sant'
Angelo

Via Sant'Elisabetta

Via Alessandro Pascoli

Via San Sebastiano

Via dell'Acquedotto

Via dell'Eremita

Piazza
Lupattelli

Via del Bulagaio

Viale Sant'Antonio

Corso dei Bersaglieri

Piazza
San
Francesco

Via Armonica

Via del Verzaro

Via Cesare Battisti

Piazza
Morlacchi

Piazza
Fortebraccio

Viewpoint

Via Pinturicchio

Piazza Russi
Scotti

Piazza
Michelotti

Piazza
Raffaello

Via Vincioli

Via Fratti

Via Italia

Via del Sole

Piazza Danti

Via Raffaello

Piazza
Piccinino

Via dei Priori

Piazza
Ferri

Piazza IV
Novembre

Viale
Pellini

Via Bontempi

Via Pompeo Pellini

Via della Canapina

Via Calderini

Via Bonazzi

Via Comunale

Via della Luna

Via Mazzini

Piazza
Matteotti

Mercato
Coperto

Briglie di Braccio

Piazzale della Cupa

Via XIV Settembre

To Mail Boxes
Etc (300m)

Via della Sapienza Reghe

Via della Rupe

Via Danzetta

Piazza della
Repubblica

Via Larga

Via Baldo

Via Oberdan

Via Baglioni

Via Caporali

Via Mari

Via San Ercolano

Piazza
Italia

Via Bovaro

Via Indipendenza

Corso Cavour

Via Podiani
Tre
Archi

Viale Indipendenza

Via Narconi

Viale Roma

Corso Cavour

Piazza
Giordano
Bruno

Piazzale
Bellucci

Stazione
Sant'Anna

Via XX Settembre

Via Fiorenzo di Lorenzo

Piazza
Partigiani

Via Fratelli Pellas

Via Cacciatori delle Alpi

Piazzale
Europa

0   400 m
0   0.2 miles

inside a bar or restaurant and to steer clear of public toilets, where you might come across syringes.

TOURIST INFORMATION

eGeneration (☎ 075 585 23 87; www.egeneration.pg.it; Via Fabretti 48; ⊙ 10am-1pm & 3.30-6pm) Website and office have up-to-date information on concerts, arts and student events. Organises cheap trips to various Italian cities.

InfoUmbria (☎ 075 57 57; www.infoumbria.com in Italian; Piazza Partigiani Intercity bus station, Largo Cacciatori delle Alpi 3; ⊙ 9am-1pm & 2.30-6.30pm Mon-Fri, 9am-1pm Sat) Private InfoUmbria, also known as InfoTourist, offers information on all of Umbria, and is a fantastic resource for *agriturismi* (farm-stay accommodation), festivals, sights, hotels and general information.

Tourist office (☎ 075 573 64 58; info@iat.perugia.it; Piazza Matteotti 18; ⊙ 8.30am-1.30pm & 3.30-6.30pm Mon-Sat, 9am-1pm Sun) Famously unhelpful, the office nevertheless offers scads of tourist pamphlets (behind the desk) for hotels, activities, events etc. Also has the most up-to-date bus and train timetables.

TRAVEL AGENCIES

Grifo Viagge (☎ 075 572 48 41; www.grifoviagge.it; Via Bonazzi 31/33; ⊙ 9am-1pm & 3.30-7.30pm Mon-Fri, 10am-12.30pm Sat) Basic full-service travel agency.

Il Periscopio (☎ 075 573 08 08; Via del Sole 6) Arranges excursions, escorted tours and trips within Italy or abroad. The owner speaks fluent English and French.

A WALK BACK IN TIME

For a thorough self-guided archaeological tour from Etruscan to Renaissance Perugia, pick up the *Archaeological Itineraries* booklet at the Perugia tourist office. Plan on it taking about three or four hours, and wear comfortable shoes.

Sights
CORSO VANNUCCI

The centre of Perugia – and therefore the centre of Umbria – is Piazza IV Novembre. For thousands of years, it was the meeting point for the ancient Etruscan and Roman civilisations. In the medieval period, it was the political centre of Perugia. Now students and tourists gather here to eat gelato.

On the north end of the piazza is the **Cathedral of San Lorenzo** (☎ 075 572 38 32; Piazza IV Novembre; ⊙ 10am-1pm & 2.30-5.30pm Tue-Sun). Although a church has been on this land since the 900s, the version you see was begun in 1345 from designs created by Fra Bevignate in 1300. Building of the cathedral continued until 1587, and the doorway was built in the late 1700s; however, the main façade was never completed. Inside you'll find dramatic Gothic architecture, an altarpiece by Signorelli and sculptures by Duccio. The steps in front of the pink façade are where seemingly all of Perugia congregates.

NORTHERN UMBRIA

In the very centre of the piazza stands the **Fontana Maggiore** (Great Fountain). It was designed by Fra Bevignate, and father-son team Nicola and Giovanni Pisano built the fountain between 1275 and 1278. Along the edge are bas-relief statues representing scenes from the Old Testament, the founding of Rome, the 'liberal arts', and a griffin and lion. Look for the griffin all over Perugia – it's the city's symbol. The lion is the symbol for the Guelphs, the Middle Ages faction that favoured rule by the papacy over rule by the Holy Roman Empire.

PALAZZO DEI PRIORI

The Palazzo dei Priori houses some of the best museums in Perugia. The foremost art gallery in Umbria is the stunning **Galleria Nazionale dell'Umbria** (National Gallery of Umbria; ☎/fax 800 69 76 16; Palazzo dei Priori, Corso Vannucci 19; adult/concession €6.50/3.25; ☑ 8.30am-7.30pm), entered from Corso Vannucci. It's an art historian's dream, with 30 rooms of artwork dating back to Byzantine-like art from the 13th century, as well as rooms dedicated to works from home-town heroes Pinturicchio and Perugino.

Also in the same building is what some consider the most beautiful bank in the world, the **Nobile Collegio del Cambio** (Exchange Hall; ☎ 075 572 85 99; Corso Vannucci 25; admission €2.60; ☑ 9am-12.30pm & 3-7pm Mon-Sat summer, 2.30-5.30pm winter), which has three rooms: the Sala dei Legisti (Legist Chamber), with wooden stalls carved by Giampiero Zuccari in the 17th century; the Sala dell'Udienza (Audience Chamber), with frescoes by Perugino; and the Chapel of San Giovanni Battista, painted by a student of Perugino's, Giannicola di Paolo. The **Nobile Collegio della Mercanzia** (Merchant's Hall; ☎ 075 573 03 66; Corso Vannucci 15; admission incl Collegio del Cambio €3.10; ☑ 9am-12.30pm & 2.30-5.50pm Tue-Sun summer, often closed afternoon winter) highlights an older audience chamber

from the 13th century, which is covered in wood panelling by northern craftsmen.

The **Sala dei Notari** (Notaries' Hall; ☎ 075 577 23 39; Piazza IV Novembre, Palazzo dei Priori; admission free; ☑ 9am-1pm & 3-7pm Tue-Sun) was built from 1293 to 1297 and is where the nobility met. The arches supporting the vaults are Romanesque, covered with frescoes depicting biblical scenes and Aesop's fables. To reach the hall, walk up the steps from the Piazza IV Novembre.

SOUTH OF CORSO VANNUCCI

At the southern end of Corso Vannucci is the tiny **Giardini Carducci**, which has lovely views of the countryside and hosts the antiques market. The gardens stand atop a once-massive 16th-century fortress, now known as the **Rocca Paolina** (main entrance Piazza Italia, entrances on Via Marzia, Via Masi & Viale Indipendenza; admission free; ☑ 8am-7pm). Pope Paolo III Farnese built the monstrosity in the 1540s, wiping out entire sections of what had been a wealthy neighbourhood. Now used as the throughway for the *scale mobili*, you can still see former homes of Perugia's powerful medieval families, capped with the bricked-over roof of the Papal fortress. Its nooks and crannies are now used for art exhibits throughout the year, and the last weekend of the month sees the antiques market.

PERUGIA CITY MUSEUM CIRCUIT

You can buy a combined ticket called the Perugia City Museum Circuit (adult/child/senior €2.50/1/2) at any of the three following sights; the ticket is valid for one week. First, you can venture down into the 3rd-century-BC **Pozzo Etrusco** (Etruscan Well; ☎ 075 573 36 69; Piazza Danti 18; ☑ 10am-1.30pm & 2.30-6.30pm Apr-Oct, 10.30am-1.30pm & 2.30-5pm Nov-Mar, Wed-Mon except in Apr & Aug when open daily). The 36m-deep well was the main water reservoir of the Etruscan town, and,

---

THE PASSEGGIATA

One of the very best things to take advantage of in Umbria is the *passeggiata* (traditional evening stroll). No matter how big or small a town, locals and visitors of all ages take to the streets with friends or family, by themselves or, these days, attached to a mobile phone. Most towns in Umbria are built concentrically around a main square that might have started out as a Roman forum or medieval gathering place. Best of all, *'un passeggio'* is free, doesn't require any preplanning and practically forces you to eat a double gelato. Think of it as improvised urban street theatre. In Perugia, watch as the students preen and flirt, jostling their way towards adulthood. In Orvieto, sit around the cathedral with older locals, who come to deliver Italian lessons to unsuspecting visitors. In Castelluccio, your *passeggiata* will most likely be shared with the town's herd of goats.

more recently, the source of water during WWII bombing raids. The second stop is the **Cappella di San Severo** (☎ 075 573 38 64; Piazza Raffaello, Porta Sole; 🕑 10am-1.30pm & 2.30-6.30pm Apr-Oct, 10.30am-1.30pm & 2.30-5pm Nov-Mar, Wed-Mon except in Apr & Aug when open daily), decorated with Raphael's *Trinity with Saints* (thought by many to be his first fresco) during the artist's residence in Perugia (1505–08) and frescoes by his pupil, Perugino dating to 1521. The third museum included is the **Cassero di Porta Sant'Angelo** (Scenic Tower; ☎ 075 41 67 0; Porta Sant'Angelo, Corso Garibaldi; 🕑 11am-1.30pm & 3-6.30pm Apr-Oct, 11am-1.30pm & 3-5pm Nov-Mar, Wed-Mon except in Apr & Aug when open daily). The panoramic view facing back on to Perugia is the main reason to come out here, plus it offers a historical briefing of the three city walls.

CORSO GIUSEPPE GARIBALDI

At the end of Via Ulisse Rocchi facing Piazza Fortebraccio and the Università per Stranieri are the ancient city gates, the **Arco Etrusco** (Etruscan Arch) dating from the 3rd century BC. The upper part is Roman and bears the inscription 'Augusta Perusia'. The loggia on top dates from the Renaissance.

North along Corso Giuseppe Garibaldi is the **Chiesa di Sant'Agostino** (Piazza Lupattelli; 🕑 8am-noon & 4pm-sunset), a church that boasts a beautiful 16th-century choir by sculptor and architect Baccio d'Agnolo. Small signs forlornly mark the places where artworks once hung before they were carried off to France by Napoleon and his men. Further north along the same thoroughfare, Via del Tempio branches off to the Romanesque **Chiesa di Sant'Angelo** (☎ 075 57 22 64; Via Sant'Angelo; 🕑 10am-noon & 4-6pm), one of Italy's oldest churches, dating back to the 5th and 6th centuries. The remnants are even older, however; it's said to stand on the site of a pagan temple, and several of its inside columns were taken from Roman structures.

ORATORIO DI SAN BERNARDINO

After the canonisation in 1450 of St Bernardino of Siena, who visited Perugia many times to preach, the local Franciscan order built a church to commemorate the saint. Designed by the Tuscan Agostino di Duccio in 1461, the **Oratorio di San Bernardino** (☎ 075 573 39 57; Piazza San Francesco; admission free; 🕑 9am-1pm & 3.30-5.30pm winter, to 6pm summer; mass 5.30pm Mon-Sat, 12pm & 5.30pm Sun) is one of the best examples of Perugia's early Renaissance masterpieces.

The bas-relief is layered with multicoloured marble, limestone, and terracotta angels and musicians. Do check out the exterior polychrome façade.

CORSO CAVOUR

The city's largest church is the **Chiesa di San Domenico** (☎ 075 573 15 68; Piazza Giordano Bruno; 🕑 8am-noon & 4pm-sunset), originally built in 1304, unfinished until 1458, and then rebuilt in the 17th century. Part of its interior cloisters date back to a former Romanesque church, but its enormous stained-glass windows arrived in the Gothic period. Legend has it that Pope Benedict XI, who lies buried here, died suddenly in Perugia in 1304 after eating figs poisoned by his nemesis.

The adjoining convent is home to the **Museo Archeologico Nazionale dell'Umbria** (☎ 075 572 71 41; Piazza Giordano Bruno 10; adult/concession €4/2; 🕑 8.30am-7.30pm Tue-Sun, 10am-7.30pm Mon), which will boggle the mind with its collection of Etruscan and prehistoric artefacts – carved funerary urns, coins, Bronze Age statuary – dating back to the 16th century BC. The Cippo Perugino (Perugian Memorial Stone) has the longest Etruscan-language engraving ever found, offering a new window into the language.

Just west of Corso Cavour is the modern art museum **Museo di Palazzo della Penna** (☎ 075 577 24 16; Via Podiani 11; adult/concession €3/2; 🕑 10am-1pm & 4-7pm Tue-Sun Mar-Oct, 10.30am-1pm & 4-6pm Tue-Sun Nov-Mar), as stunning for its palatial surroundings as for its artwork. Frescoes from the 18th and 19th centuries share space with 20th-century futurist Gerardo Dottori and German painter and sculptor Joseph Beuys, a radical ideologist whose artwork transcends social boundaries.

Just past the Porta di San Pietro is the 10th-century **Chiesa di San Pietro** (☎ 075 3 47 70; Borgo XX Giugno; 🕑 8am-noon & 4pm-sunset), entered through a frescoed doorway in the first courtyard. The interior is an incredible mix of gilt and marble and contains a pietà (a sculpture, drawing or painting of the dead Christ supported by the Madonna) by Perugino. Many of the paintings in this church feature depictions of biblical women.

Take a stroll or picnic at the **Medieval Gardens** (☎ 075 585 64 32; Borgo XX Giugno 74; admission free; 🕑 8am-6.30pm Mon-Fri), entered behind the Chiesa di San Pietro. During the medieval period, monasteries often created gardens reminiscent of the Garden of Eden and biblical stories, with plants that symbolised myths and sacred stories.

Numbered locations through this garden include the following:

3 The Cosmic Tree, symbolising the forefather of all trees;
6 The Tree of Light and Knowledge;
7 The Tree of Good and Evil;
11 & 12 Medicinal and edible plants used for centuries;
16 Remnants from an ancient fish pond;
20 The Cosmogonic Ovulation Spring (a lily-pad pond)
24 The exit of the Medieval Gardens, symbolising the elevation of man from the natural plane.

Be sure to check out the groovy alchemist's studio tucked into the corner near no 20, the Yggdrasil Incline.

OUT OF TOWN
About 5km southeast of the city is the **Ipogeo dei Volumni** (☎ 075 39 33 29; Via Assisana 53; adult/concession €3/1.50; ☼ 9am-1pm & 3.30-6.30pm Sep-Jun, 9am-12.30pm & 4.30-7pm Jul & Aug), a 2nd-century-BC Etruscan burial site. An underground chamber contains a series of recesses holding the funerary urns of the Volumnio family. The surrounding grounds are a massive expanse of partially unearthed burial chambers with several buildings housing artefacts that haven't been stolen over the years. Take a train or APM bus 3 from Piazza Italia to Ponte San Giovanni and walk west from there. By car, take the Bonanzano exit heading south on the E45.

The trick for independent travellers visiting the **Perugina chocolate factory** (☎ 075 527 67 96; Van San Sisto; admission free; ☼ 9am-1pm & 2-5.30pm Mon-Fri year-round, 9am-1pm Sat Oct-Jan & Mar-May) is to either call ahead to arrange a guided tour, or simply latch on to a tour group (conducted in either Italian or English). After visiting the simple museum, you'll wend your way through an enclosed sky bridge, watching as the white-outfitted Oomp-, er, factory workers go about their god-granted talent for creating chocolate. Drive through the gates of the humourously nondescript factory entrance marked Nestlé, or take bus 7 to San Sisto.

Courses
Check with the tourist office for lists of all current classes in and around Perugia.
Comitato Linguistico (☎ 075 572 14 71; www .comitatolinguistico.com; 3rd fl Largo Cacciatori delle Alpi 5) Catering to a more serious crowd, the lessons here are slightly more rigorous than at Università per Stranieri.

Two- and four-week courses start throughout the year, starting at €130 per week. The school can arrange private or family accommodation.
Cordon Bleu Perugia (☎ in Italian 075 592 50 12, in English 075 692 02 49; www.cordonbleuperugia.com; Via dei Lilla 3, Casaglia) Come for a three-hour beginners class or a week-long professional chef course on Italian cuisine. Day courses teach newbies how to make bread, pasta and Umbrian appetisers; and there's even a singles cooking course. Week-long courses cost €350 to €600.
Università per Stranieri (☎ 075 5 74 61; www .unistrapg.it; Palazzo Gallenga, Piazza Fortebraccio 4) This is Italy's foremost academic institution for foreigners, offering courses in language, literature, history, art, music, opera and architecture, to name a few. A series of degree courses is available, as well as one-, two- and three-month intensive language courses starting at €300 a month and semester-long accredited programmes for students.

Tours
Marco Bellanca (☎ 075 573 68 53, 347 600 22 09; bellsista@yahoo.com; 3/6hr for up to 16 people €100/200) Will meet guests in any town in Umbria, but specialises in art and history in Perugia and Assisi. Umbrian-born, fluent in German and English.

Festivals & Events
Perugia – and Umbria in general – has no less than 80 gazillion events, festivals, concerts, summer outdoor movies and *sagre* (traditional festivals). Check www.bellaumbria.net or www.umbria2000.it for details.
Umbria Jazz (☎ 800 46 23 11, 075 500 11 07; www .umbriajazz.com in Italian) This attracts top-notch international performers for 10 days each July, usually around the middle of the month. In the past, the festival has featured performances by hundreds of jazz greats, including Pat Metheny, the Buena Vista Social Club, Chick Corea and Al Jarreau. Single tickets cost €10 to €100, and week-long or weekend passes are also available. Be sure to check out Giardini Carducci during the day or any number of restaurants or nightspots for impromptu concerts.
Sagra Musicale Umbra (Holy Music Festival; ☎ 075 572 22 71; www.perugiamusicaclassica.com in Italian; ticket office Via Danzetti 7; tickets €7-50) One of the oldest music festivals in Europe. Begun in 1937, it's held in Perugia from mid- to late September and features world-renowned conductors and musicians.
Eurochocolate (☎ 075 502 58 80; www.eurochocolate .com) Most Perugini (Perugians) know to run, run far away from this most over-hyped of festivals, which often sees up to one million visitors. Held around the third week of October, hundreds of booths sell every known concoction of cacao, cocoa and chocolate. If you must, plan your hotel stay months in advance and don't even think of driving.

Sleeping

Perugia has a decent array of hotels and *pensioni* (small hotels), and is a good place to stay if you're visiting Umbria by train or bus, as many towns can be visited on day trips from Perugia. There's no reason to stay outside the historic centre: it's noisier, less charming and not much cheaper.

RENTAL ACCOMMODATION

Be warned that some apartment services in Perugia have a reputation for ripping off students looking for short-term accommodation, especially inventing problems caused by the renter that requires the landlord to withhold part or all of the deposit. A good way to deal with this is to carefully walk through the property beforehand with the landlord and take date-stamped photos.

Atena Service (☎ 075 573 29 92; www.atenaservice .com; Via del Bulagaio 38) can arrange accommodation from €200 per month for a shared room in an apartment, and from €550 per month for a one-bedroom apartment.

Il Periscopio (see p321) arranges accommodation for students, business travellers and long-term visitors.

There are also several ways to investigate rental accommodation yourself:

- ask at the tourist office, which can help with pricier weekly accommodation;
- check any newsstand on Wednesday and Saturday for *Cerco e Trovo* (I search and I find; €1.50) for apartment listings. Be sure to call before noon, as rooms go quickly;
- check posted flyers at the Università per Stranieri (opposite) or at eGeneration (p321);
- through word of mouth from other students, teachers or staff at the universities, or at *caffès* (cafés) or pubs.

BUDGET

Camping & Hostels

The city has two camping grounds, both in Colle della Trinità, 5km northwest of the city, which can be reached by taking bus 9 from Piazza Italia. Ask the driver to drop you off at the Superal supermarket, from where it's a 300m walk to the camp sites.

Camping Il Rocolo (☎ /fax 075 517 85 50; www.il rocolo.it; Str Fontana 1/n, Loc. Colle della Trinità; per person €5-6.50, car/tent €3/5.50; ☼ Easter-Sep & during Euro-chocolate; ☐) International newspapers, Skype

telephone connection, 24-hour hot showers and 100 shaded sites make this a safe choice, but there's also an on-site restaurant, friendly multilingual staff and plenty of extras (barbecue pit, TV area, bocce party, small market and proximity to a bus into Perugia).

Paradis d'Été (☎ 075 517 31 21; www.wel.it/cparadis; Strada Fontana Trinità 29/h, Colle della Trinità; per person €5.50-7, car/tent €3/5; ☼ Mar-Oct; ☎) This camping ground has 46 well-shaded sites in a park-like setting with a swimming pool. Facilities include hot showers, laundry sinks, bar and children's playground.

Centro Internazionale per la Gioventù (☎ 075 572 28 80; www.ostello.perugia.it; Via Bontempi 13; dm €15, sheets €2; ☼ mid-Jan–mid-Dec; ☐) If the 9.30am to 4pm lockout and the midnight curfew (no exceptions) don't scare you off, then you'll appreciate the sweeping countryside view and wafting sounds of church bells from the hostel's terrace, where guests often gather after making dinner in the well-stocked kitchen. Enjoy the 16th-century frescoed ceilings and tidy four- to six-person rooms.

Ostello per la Gioventù Spagnoli (☎ 075 501 13 66; www.ostellionline.org; Via Cortonese 4; dm/s/d/tr incl breakfast & sheets €15/22/34/51, towels €1, laundry €3) A few kilometres from the city centre is Perugia's main Hostelling International (HI) hostel. It's large (80 beds) and doesn't have the romance of the city-centre hostel, but it's clean, there's no curfew and the lockout is only 10am to 2pm. Take bus 9 and 10.

B&Bs & Hotels

Pensione Paola (☎ 075 572 38 16; Via della Canapina 5; s/d €33/52) It's a great bet if you want use of your own kitchen but don't want the lockout of the hostel. It has eight simply furnished rooms. Take bus 6 or 7 heading towards Piazza Italia and get off at the Pellini car park. Signs will guide you up the steps to the right. From the city centre, walk down Via dei Priori.

Hotel San Sebastiano (☎ 075 573 78 65; www.hotel sansebastiano.it; Via San Sebastiano 4; s €40-50, d €50-70, s with shared bathroom €25-40, all incl breakfast) Near Perugia's university is an old-school family-style *pensione*. Its side-street location guarantees a good night's sleep in its sparse rooms.

Casa Spagnoli B&B (☎ 075 573 51 27, 340 350 38 93; www.perugiaonline.com/bbspagnoli; Via Cesare Caporali 17; s €30-38, d €50-58, tr €60-75, all with shared bathroom) The motto is *semplice*: simple. Although the slightly cantankerous Spanish-speaking grandmother now runs daily operations, this private-home B&B is still great value, and perfectly located near Piazza Italia.

Pensione Anna (☎ /fax 075 573 63 04; www.alber goanna.it; Via dei Priori 48; s €35-45, d €50-70, tr €54-80, with shared bathroom s €25-35, d €45-56; **P**) On the 4th floor with no elevator, this eclectic place is great if you want a central location that is quiet, but don't have a lot of heavy luggage.

MIDRANGE

Albergo Morlacchi (☎ 075 572 03 19; www.hotelmorlacchi .it; Via Tiberi 2; s €38-62, d €60-82; **P**) In a great location near the Università per Stranieri but quiet enough for visiting parents, this family-run two-star hotel is a popular choice. Rooms are furnished with simple but comfortable antique furnishings, and a few even have fireplaces.

Primavera Mini Hotel (☎ 075 572 16 57; www .primaveraminihotel.it; Via Vincioli 8; s €42-48, d €60-70, tr €84-90; ❉ 💻) This central and quiet hotel run by a dedicated English- and French-speaking mother-daughter team is a fabulous find, quietly tucked away in a corner. The magnificent views complement the bright and airy rooms and common areas. All rooms come with private bathroom, telephone and TV, and breakfast is available (€3 to €6). Great value.

Etruscan Chocohotel (☎ 075 583 73 14; www .chocohotel.it; Via Campo di Marte 134; s €42-65, d €64-124; **P** ❉ 💻 🏊) The first hotel in the world dedicated to chocolate. Try items from the restaurant's 'chocomenu', shop at the 'chocostore' or swim in the rooftop pool (sadly, filled with water). Free on-site parking, lobby wi-fi and triple-paned windows make up for the location (on a busy street near the main train station).

Hotel Fortuna (☎ 075 572 28 45; www.umbriahotels .com; Via Bonazzi 9; s €69-98, d €99-128, tr €147; ❉ 💻) In a location both quiet and central, this spotless hotel is partially housed in a building dating back to the 1300s. Ancient stone, frescoes and Venetian plaster walls accompany comfortable new furnishings, new parquet floors and (thankfully) modern bathrooms. Eschew the lower-priced doubles, as they're located in a musty reconverted one-star hotel with no air-con.

Hotel la Rosetta (☎ /fax 075 572 08 41; www.perugia online.com/larosetta; Piazza Italia 19; s/d/tr incl breakfast €85/130/174; **P** ❉ 💻) You'll be so close to the centre of Perugia that you can practically crawl to most sights. Although the building is hundreds of years old, the décor is from the

19th century and 1920s. Updated with computer outlets, Sky TV and modern showers, and offering conference space and meeting rooms, the Rosetta is a business hotel where leisure travellers are just as comfortable. The hotel has a few free parking spaces; otherwise it'll cost you €20 in a nearby parking garage.

TOP END

Locanda della Posta (☎ 075 572 89 25; novelber@tin.it; Corso Vannucci 97; s €90-108, d €134-170; ❉) The service on our visit was less than friendly and the amenities scarce, but the location and heavy advertising keeps it full most of the year. You could save money by staying at the almost-as-centrally located Hotel la Rosetta or Hotel Fortuna, or upgrade for an experience of a lifetime at the Hotel Brufani Palace.

Hotel Brufani Palace (☎ 075 573 25 41; www.sina hotels.com; Piazza Italia 12; s €215, d €320, ste €440-850; **P** ❉ 🏊) One of Umbria's two five-star hotels, and a truly spectacular experience. Special touches include frescoed main rooms, impeccably decorated bedrooms and suites, a garden terrace in which to dine during summer, and helpful trilingual staff. Swim over Etruscan ruins in the subterranean fitness centre. It also has a 24-hour concierge, high-end Umbrian restaurant, wi-fi (€3 per hour) and is wheelchair accessible.

Eating

Because of the great number of students and tourists, the amount of places to dine in Perugia is staggering. The first days of spring when the mercury rises above 15°C or so (usually in March) sees dozens of open-air locales spring up along Corso Vannucci (the best two – Ristorante Il Bacio and Caffe di Perugia – are listed on p327).

BUDGET

Il Cedro (Via Ulisse Rocchi; meals €3; ⏱ 11.30am-3.30pm & 5pm-2am Tue-Sun) Those in need of a food product besides pasta should drop in for a quick kebab at what is reputedly the best in the city. The tiny tiled takeaway is run by a family from Lebanon, who serves up good, cheap and filling shawermas and kebabs to students, tourists and passers-by.

Tuttotesto (☎ 075 573 66 66; Corso Garibaldi 15; meals €9; ⏱ Tue-Sun) Beyond Perugia's pasta and meat focus is this casual university spot where professors and students debate Nietzsche over sweet and savoury crepes, salads and *torta al testo* (Umbrian flatbread sandwiches).

Ristorante Il Bacio (☎ 075 572 09 09; Via Boncampi 6; meals €11; ☽ to 12.30am Thu-Tue) This rather cavernous *ristorante* and pizzeria sells good, cheap meals and also sets up a decent outdoor café on Corso Vannucci, but its selling point is that it's one of the only late-night restaurants in the historic centre.

Pizzeria Mediterranea (☎ 075 572 13 22; Piazza Piccinino 11/12; meals €11; ☽ Wed-Mon) Perugini know to come here for the best pizza in town. A spaceship-sized wood-fired brick oven heats up pizzas from the simplest margherita to the 12-topping 'his and hers'. Add delectable *mozzarella di bufala* (fresh buffalo-milk mozzarella) to any pizza for an additional €1.60. It gets busy enough to queue, especially Thursday and Saturday nights.

Ristorante dal Mi'Cocco (☎ 075 573 25 11; Corso Garibaldi 12; set meals €14; ☽ Tue-Sun) Don't ask for a menu because there isn't one at this most traditional Perugian restaurant. Diners receive a set menu of a starter, main course, side dish and dessert. You may receive asparagus risotto in May, or tagliatelle (long, ribbon-shaped pasta) with peas and ham in November. Extremely popular with students, it's best to call ahead.

Il Segreto di Pulcinella (☎ 075 573 62 84; Via Larga 8; meals €18; ☽ Tue-Sun) Come here for the only 'real' Neapolitan pizza in Perugia, as well as a beautiful selection of salads and pasta dishes.

MIDRANGE

Ristorante Nanà (☎ 075 573 35 71; Corso Cavour 206; meals €23.50; ☽ Mon-Sat) It's a good sign when approximately 47 members of the same family run a 15-table restaurant. Simply furnished with a small menu, the food is *nuovo italiano*: paté with Sardinian flatbread (€7) or *gnochetti* in a pepper and radicchio cream sauce (€6.50). The wine list is equally impressive and affordable.

Enone (☎ 075 572 19 50; www.enone.it; Corso Cavour 61; meals €26; ☽ 7pm-1am Wed-Mon) The new trendy hotspot on the Perugian dining and drinking scene. A mix between an *enoteca* (wine bar), restaurant and club, the vaulted brick walls hide all sorts of goings-on, such as live music (usually on Monday) and sushi made by a Japanese chef (usually Thursday). The regular menu features funky dishes like carrot and black truffle gnocchi in a parmesan basket.

Il Gufo (☎ 075 573 41 26; Via della Viola 18; meals €26; ☽ 8pm-1am Tue-Sat) The owner-chef gathers ingredients from local markets and cooks up whatever is fresh and in season. Try dishes such as *cinghiale* (wild boar) with fennel (€9) or *riso nero* (black rice) with grilled vegetables and brie (€9). There are great salads for €5.

Ristorante Sole (☎ 075 573 50 31; Via della Rupe 1; meals €31;) Sure, there are better-quality restaurants in Perugia, but you're here for the view. The pasta's not bad, and the duck *carpaccio* with truffles and *grana* (granular cheese) might just trick you into thinking you came here for the food.

Wine Bartolo Hosteria (☎ 075 571 60 27; Via Bartolo 30; meals €32; ☽ Thu-Tue) Descend a staircase into a low-ceilinged hobbitlike burrow that's lined with walls of wine bottles set around a handful of cosy tables. The chef does beautiful things with Chianina beef – stewed with Sangiovese or as a *carpaccio* with lemon over radicchio.

CAFÉS

Many of the restaurants that line Corso Vannucci open up pavement cafés in the warmer months. Don't expect the food to be top-notch, as you're paying for atmosphere.

Sandri (☎ 075 572 41 12; Corso Vannucci 32; ☽ 10am-8pm Tue-Sun) When you enter into your third century of business, something must be right. Known for delectable chocolate cakes, candied fruit, espresso and pastries, the staff wrap all take-home purchases (picked up at the counter but paid for at the till), no matter how small, in beautiful red paper with a ribbon bow.

Caffè Morlacchi (☎ 075 572 17 60; Piazza Morlacchi 6/8; ☽ 8am-1am Mon-Sat) Bring your bongo drums and leftist rhetoric to this most hip of establishments. Students, professors and expats nosh on international fare, sipping tea or hot chocolate during the day and cocktails at night.

Caffè di Perugia (☎ 075 573 18 63; Via Mazzini 10; meals €29; ☽ noon-3pm & 7pm-midnight Wed-Mon) The fanciest sit-down café in town, its desserts are worth the high prices. It also serves a fine choice of basic pasta and meat dishes, and offers outdoor seating in summer and a smoking room indoors. Combine dessert and dinner with the *tagiolini al caco con ragù di cervo* (pasta in chocolate sauce with deer).

Bar Centrale (Piazza IV Novembre 35; ☽ 7am-11pm) A popular meeting place for students with an indoor salon and outdoor tables where you can munch a *panini* (sandwich) and watch the students on the cathedral steps.

SELF-CATERING

Coop (Piazza Matteotti; 9am-8pm Mon-Sat) The largest grocery store in the historic centre, Coop sells all the staples, fruits and vegetables, and has a deli counter with fresh pasta and cheeses.

Covered market (Piazza Matteotti; 7am-1.30pm Mon-Sat) Found below Coop, you can buy fresh produce, bread, cheese and meat from this market. From Piazza Matteotti, head down the stairs of the arched doorway labelled 18A.

Coop (075 501 65 04; Piazza Vittorio Veneto; 9am-7.45pm Mon-Sat) This supersized supermarket has its own parking garage directly across from the main train station (two hours' free parking with validation).

Bangladeshi Alimentari (075 572 36 41; Via dei Priori 71; 11am-10pm) Just the basics, but check out those opening hours.

Drinking

Lunabar (075 572 29 66; Via Scura 1/6 at Corso Vannucci; 8am-2am Tue-Sun) Atmospherically equidistant between New York and Umbria, the city-centre lounge spins together frescoed, Venetian plaster walls with a grey and onyx bar and space-age restrooms. Smokers enjoy their own room and the hungry will appreciate the *apertivo* (aperitif) selection.

Cinastik (075 572 09 99; Via dei Priori 36; 6.30pm-2.30am Mon-Sat) Feel very much like you're on the Continent in this swanky hot spot. Downstairs is pumping with sultry music and the mixed drinks are flowing. Upstairs is a little quieter (make sure you check out the coolest bathrooms in Perugia).

Bottega del Vino (/fax 075 571 61 81; Via del Sole 1; 7pm-1am Mon-Sat) A fire or candles burn atmospherically on the terrace. Inside, live jazz and hundreds of bottles of wine lining the walls add to the romance of the setting. You can taste dozens of Umbrian wines, which you can purchase with the help of sommelier-like experts.

La Terrazza (Piazza Matteotti 18a; summer) Should you sit in the park and enjoy the view of the sun setting over the Umbrian hillside, or head into a darkened pub for a drink? Well, you can come here for both. On the back terrace of the building that houses the Coop and covered markets is this open-air bar, perfect for an evening *aperitivo*.

Entertainment

Much of Perugia's nightlife parades outside the cathedral and around Fontana Maggiore. Hundreds of local and foreign students congregate here practically every night, playing guitars and drums and chatting with friends. Tourists mix in easily, slurping gelati and enjoying this fascinating version of outdoor theatre. When the student population grows, some of the clubs on the outskirts of town run a bus to Palazzo Gallenga, starting around 11pm. Students get paid to hand out flyers on Corso Vannucci, so check with them or ask at the steps. Most clubs get going around midnight, so be warned on your way back into town: the *scale mobili* stop running at about 1am.

Cinema Teatro del Pavone (075 572 49 11; www .cinegatti.it; Corso Vannucci 67) A grand theatre now showing films – on Mondays in their original language (usually English) for €4. Come early to grab a box seat. During the summer, the owners run outdoor movies; check at the cinema for schedules and directions.

Contrappunto (075 573 36 67; Via Scortici 4/a; evenings until late Tue-Sun) What was a jazz club now opens its doors to all sorts of music. Jazz jams are just on Wednesday, but try live rock on Thursday, disco on Friday and world-famous DJs on Saturdays (until 5am). Food is available; try the huge antipasto plate for two to four people for €16.

Velvet (075 572 13 21; Viale Roma 20; Tue-Sun) Come to where the beautiful people play. It opens around 10pm, but the well-dressed party here until the wee hours.

Perugia football team (075 500 66 41; www.perugia calcio.it; Renato Curi Stadium, Via Piccolpasso 48; tickets €2-40) Perugia Calcio has been knocking back and forth between Serie A, B and C, and ticket availability goes up (or down) with the tide, as does the gossip, a favourite discussion topic for Perugia's residents. Take bus 9, 11 or 13 to the Renato Curi stadium.

Shopping

Augusta Perusia Cioccolato e Gelateria (075 573 45 77; www.cioccolatoaugustaperusia.it in Italian; Via Pinturicchio 2; 10.30am-8pm Mon-Sat) Giordano worked for Perugino for 25 years. In 2000, he opened his own shop, creating delectables from the old tradition, including *baci* (hazelnut 'kisses' covered in chocolate) from the original Perugian recipe. Handmade chocolate bars come in boxes with old paintings of Perugia – great

OFF THE EATEN PATH

Many of the best Umbrian restaurants are outside of town, or in towns most visitors skip. These five restaurants are a bit far afield – from a truffle-lover's paradise in the hills above the Valnerina to a neighbourhood trattoria in often-missed Foligno.

I Quattro Sensi (p333) Although it's no more than 30 minutes from Perugia, Torgiano or Montefalco and Bevagna, the Relais Borgo Brufa's restaurant isn't terribly near anything but is a beautiful drive from just about everywhere. The wine list knows no boundaries, and never has shrimp tasted this tender.

Il Bacco Felice (p347) Well known by foodies from around the world, Salvatore's neighbourhood *osteria* (restaurant focussing on wine) in the often-overlooked town of Foligno attracts international food critics and casual friends alike.

Ristorante Country House L'Antico Forziere (p334) A few kilometres south of Deruta is a lovely enough country house with a restaurant that deserves all the praise it's garnered and more. After dishes like blueberry *cinghiale* (wild boar) or turnip pasta, be sure to partake in a dessert worthy of a photograph.

Ristorante Piermarini (p389) Signore Piermarini knows a thing or two (or three) about how to put together Umbrian ingredients. He is also a truffle hunter, olive farmer and cookery teacher, and his family has worked the land for generations. Ristorante Piermarini is well, well off the beaten path, located a few kilometres off the SS209 in the Valnerina town of Ferentillo, but it is well worth a day trip solely for the fresh *tartufi nero* (black truffles) with soft-boiled egg.

Vissani (p372) One of Umbria's only Michelin-starred restaurants, master chef Gianfranco Vissani cooks up meals as passionate as his mood. Judge for yourself whether Umbrians are right when they say he's overrated. Equidistant between Todi and Orvieto along Lago di Corbara down a private gated drive.

for gifts – or pick up some of the city's best gelato for yourself.

Mercato Mensile Antiquariato (Antiques Market; Giardini Carducci; 9am-6pm or 7pm) If you're lucky enough to be in Perugia on the fourth weekend of the month, spend a few hours wandering through this market around the Piazza Italia and in the Giardini Carducci. It's a great place to pick up old prints, frames, furniture, jewellery, postcards and stamps.

Umbria Terraviva (Organic Market; 075 835 50 62; Piazza Piccinino) On the first Sunday of the month, check out this market located along the side of the Duomo heading towards Via Bonanzi. You'll find all sorts of organic fruits, vegetables, and fabulous canned or packaged items to take home as gifts.

For the best boutique shopping in town, head down Via Oberdan from Piazza Matteotti (towards Corso Cavour). Above the windy pedestrian street hangs a banner announcing 'Via Oberdan – Shopping Street' and the thoroughfare offers jewellery, shoes, music shops, a bookshop and clothing both chic and thrifty.

Getting There & Away
AIR
Aeroporto Sant'Egidio (PEG; 075 59 21 41; www .airport.umbria.it), 13km east of the city, offers at least three daily Alitalia flights to Milan, plus

a new Ryanair service to London Stansted thrice weekly. A one-way or round-trip taxi to Sant'Egidio costs €25 from the city centre, or there's an extremely convenient bus line **Sulga** (800 09 96 61; www.sulga.it) that coincides with all arrivals and departures. The white shuttle buses (€3.50) leave from Piazza Italia about an hour and 10 minutes before a scheduled departure, stopping at the train station 15 minutes into the journey. From the airport, buses leave once everyone is off the planes with their luggage.

BUS
Several towns in Umbria have no train station, but several buses pick up the slack, except on Sunday, when it's impossible to get just about anywhere by bus.

Intercity buses leave from Piazza Partigiani (take the *scale mobili* from Piazza Italia). Sulga also offers a Perugia–Florence service (€10.50, 2½ hours) that runs once daily, except Sunday, leaving Perugia at 7.30am and Florence at 6pm (from Piazza Adua at Santa Maria Novella). Most routes within Umbria are operated by **APM Perugia** (800 51 21 41, mobile 0755731707; www.apmperugia.com) in the north and **SSIT** (074 267 07 46; www.spoletina.com) or **ATC Terni** (0744 40 94 57; www.atcterni.it) in the south. APM Perugia has recently upgraded its fleet with two-dozen ecologically friendly buses.

Buses head to Deruta (€2.60, 25 minutes, 13 daily), Torgiano (€1.30, 25 minutes, nine daily) by *extraurbano* or by city bus 5A, Assisi (€3, 50 minutes, nine daily), Todi (€4.30, one hour and 10 minutes, seven daily), Gubbio (€4.30, one hour and 10 minutes, 10 daily), Gualdo Tadino (€5.20, one hour and 20 minutes, five daily) and Lake Trasimeno towns (€3 to €4.70, 50 minutes to one hour and 10 minutes, six to 10 daily). To get to Narni or Amelia, take an ATC Terni bus from Piazza Partigiani or preferably the FCU train to Terni and switch there. Check the TV monitors above the terminals. To get to Spello, Foligno, Spoleto or Orvieto, it's best to take the train.

Current train and bus routes, company details and timetables are listed in the monthly booklet *Viva Perugia* (€1), available at the tourist office, hotels and some newsstands.

CAR & MOTORCYCLE

From Rome, leave the A1 at the Orte exit and follow the signs for Terni. Once there, take the SS3bis/E45 for Perugia. From the north, exit the A1 at Valdichiana and take dual carriageway SS75 for Perugia. The SS75 to the east connects the city with Assisi.

You'll find three car-rental companies at the main train station, Stazione Fontivegge. All are open from 8.30am to 1pm and 3.30pm to 7pm Monday to Friday, and from 8.30am to 1pm Saturday.

Avis (☎ /fax 075 500 03 95; alvalrent@hotmail.com)
Hertz (☎ 075 500 24 39; hertzperugia@tiscali.it)
Maggiore (☎ 075 500 74 99; www.maggiore.it in Italian)

Airport Sant'Egidio also offers the following:
Europcar (☎ 075 692 06 15; www.europcar; 🕑 8.30am-1pm & 3-7pm Mon-Fri, 8.30am-12.30pm Sat, by request Sun)

ARRIVING FROM FIUMICINO?

It's quite easy to take a direct bus from Rome's Fiumicino (FCO) airport to Perugia. Pick up a blue **Sulga** (☎ 800 09 96 61; www .sulga.it) bus across the street from international terminal C. From Monday to Saturday, there are four daily buses to Perugia (€15, 3½ to four hours) departing at 9am, 12.30pm, 2.30pm and 5pm, and two buses on Sundays and holidays at 12.30pm and 4.30pm. Heading back to Fiumicino, buses leave Piazza Partigiani at 6am, 8am and 9am Monday to Saturday, and 7.30am and 8.30am on Sundays and holidays. Several buses stop in Assisi. Check the website for details.

TRAIN

Although Perugia's main train station is named 'Stazione Fontivegge', the sign at the station simply reads 'Perugia'. It is on Piazza Vittorio Veneto, a few kilometres west of the city centre and easily accessible by frequent buses from Piazza Italia. The ticket office is open from 6.30am to 8.10pm (closed for lunch 12.50pm to 1.20pm), but you can buy tickets at the automated machines at any time of day with a credit card or cash. For train information, call **Tren Italia** (☎ 89 20 21). Most travellers won't make use of Perugia's other train stations – which are located in the suburbs – except for those visiting the Etruscan necropolis Ipogeo dei Volumni, walking distance from the Ponte San Giovanni station.

Perugia is on a spur line, so there's almost always a change in Foligno to the southeast or Terontola to the northwest. Regular trains

---

TOP FIVE PLACES IN UMBRIA TO VISIT BY CAR

Castelluccio (p387) There are only two buses to this town: Thursday morning and Thursday afternoon, so driving is your best bet. It shouldn't be missed, especially in May and June when the Piano Grande is abloom with wildflowers.

La Scarzuola (p372) A hike from just about anywhere listed in this book, the beautiful drive here will set you in the mood to appreciate the stunning mystery of this combination garden-architectural monument-Franciscan monastery-concert theatre.

Lake Trasimeno (p356) It's possible to get here and around using the train and bus, but a car will allow you to meander through fields of sunflowers and olive trees.

Monte Castello di Vibio (p377) Many establishments will pick up guests at the Fratta Todina train station, but a car will get you out to Fattoria di Vibio *agriturismo* (p377) for a lunch that makes it worth renting wheels.

Wine region (p344) Vineyards are just starting to open tasting rooms to the public in the rolling hills surrounding Bevagna and Montefalco. Just make sure you have a designated driver!

run to Rome (€10.10 to €18.45, 2¼ to three hours), Florence (€7.90 to €12.50, two hours) and Arezzo (€4.50, one hour and 10 minutes, every two hours). Within Umbria, it's easy to reach Assisi (€1.65, 25 minutes, hourly), Gubbio (€4.30, 1½ hours, seven daily, change in Foligno), Spello (€2.05, 30 minutes, hourly) and Orvieto (€6.10 to €6.80, 1¼ hours, at least every other hour).

About half of the tourist destinations in Umbria require a ride on the **Ferrovia Central Umbra** (FCU; ☎ 075 57 54 01; www.fcu.it in Italian; Stazione Sant'Anna, Piazzale Bellucci). These adorable graffitied 'Thomas the Tank Engine' trains also head to Rome (switch in Terni). You must validate your ticket on board, not before boarding as with all other Italian trains.

Take the FCU south to Fratta Todina for Monte Castello di Vibio (€2.05, 40 minutes, 18 daily), Todi (€2.55, 50 minutes, 18 daily) or Terni (€4.40, 1½ hours, 17 daily). The Sansepolcro line heads north to Umbertide (€2.05, 45 minutes, 19 daily) and Città di Castello (€3.05, one hour and 10 minutes, 16 daily).

Getting Around

It's a steep 1.5km climb uphill from Perugia's train station, so a bus is highly recommended, essential for those with luggage. The city bus costs €1 and takes you as far as Piazza Italia in the historic centre. Be sure to validate your ticket upon boarding or you will be fined on the spot. If you haven't bought a ticket, you can buy one on the bus for €1.50. Buses 6, 7, 9, 11 and 15 run between the train station and Piazza Italia. Buy your bus ticket from the small green bus kiosk in front of the train station, in Piazza Italia, or at *tabacchi* (tobacconists) throughout the city. If you're going to stick around for a while, buy a 10-ticket pass for €8.60. The 'mini-metro' light rail system was supposed to have been finished by 2003, so expect it to be running by 2012 or so.

Give **Scootyrent** (☎ 075 572 07 10, 333 102 65 05; www.scootyrent.com; Via Pinturicchio 76) a call for scooter rental. For about €20 a day, you can feel like a real Italian, transporting yourself and taking your life in your hands, all at the same time.

CAR & MOTORCYCLE

Perugia is humourously difficult to navigate and most of the city centre is only open to residential or commercial traffic (although tourists may drive to their hotels to drop off luggage). Rumour has it that parking police are more lenient on rental cars, but if you park illegally for too long you run the risk of getting towed.

Parking

Perugia has six fee-charging car parks: Piazza Partigiani and the Mercato Coperto are the most central and convenient, plus Viale Sant'Antonio, Viale Pellini, Briglie di Braccio and Piazzale Europa. The free car park is located at Piazza Cupa. *Scale mobili* or *ascensori* (lifts) lead from each car park towards the city centre, but take note: they don't operate 24 hours a day, and they usually stop between about midnight or 1am and 6am or 7am.

Parking fees cost €0.80 to €1.20 per hour, 24 hours a day, in the city centre lots. If you intend to use a car park frequently, buy a tourist *abbonamento* (unlimited parking ticket pass) from the ticket office at the car park. If you're just parking for a while, try the Coop (see p328) on Piazza Vittorio Veneto by the train station, where you can park free for two hours with any purchase. Also, many of the spaces near the train station charge only from 9am to 1pm and 4pm to 7pm Monday to Friday, including a car park just north of the station.

Call the **information line** (☎ 075 577 53 75) if your car has been towed or for general parking information.

Your best bet is simply to rent a car on your way out of Perugia.

TAXI

Taxi services are available from 6am to 2am (24 hours a day in July and August) – call ☎ 075 500 48 88 to arrange pick-up.

A ride from the city centre to the main train station, Stazione Fontivegge, will cost about €12. Tack on €1 for each suitcase.

TORGIANO

pop 5862

Fans of wine and olive oil will appreciate this town, a monument to these two most important Umbrian, and indeed Italian, products. Torgiano, just a 25-minute bus ride from Perugia's Piazza Partigiani, is famous throughout the world for its fine wines, and the Lungarotti family, the closest thing Umbria has to a ruling noble family these days, owns many of the local vineyards, the excellent wine museum and the second of Umbria's two five-star hotels.

THE LUNGAROTTI FAMILY

Founded in the 1960s by winemaker and patriarch Giorgio Lungarotti, the Lungarotti vineyard has become one of Umbria's most famous exports. After Giorgio's passing in 1999, daughters Chiara Lungarotti and Teresa Severini took over the family business and have become two of the most well-known women in Italian wine. With a lifetime spent in the vineyards around Torgiano and degrees in agronomy from Perugia's university, Chiara and Teresa have each taken on a sector of the family business. Teresa focuses on marketing and communications for the Lungarotti empire, while Chiara's knowledge of oenology and travel earned her the presidency of Italy's **Movimento Turismo del Vino** (www.movimentoturismovino.it), the Wine Tourism Movement. The Lungarottis own more land in Umbria than any other entity, but still maintain that Umbrian sense of community and family (in fact, the daughter of Giorgio's head carpenter is now Chiara's secretary).

Information

Tourist office (☎ 075 988 60 37; Piazza Baglioni; ☉ 9am-12pm & 2.30-5pm Tue-Sun) Pick up information on wine-tasting, the Strada dei Vini del Cantico (below) or the Brufa sculpture garden here.

Sights & Activities

The most important wine museum in Europe, Torgiano's **Museo del Vino** (☎ 075 988 02 00; Corso Vittorio Emanuele 31; adult/concession €4.50/2.50, incl Museo dell'Olivo e dell'Olio €7, audio guide €2; ☉ 9am-1pm & 3-7pm summer, to 6pm winter) was started in 1974 by the Lungarotti matriarch, Maria Grazie. The 20-room former palace traces the history of the production of wine in the region back to Etruscan times. Displays of utensils, graphic art, wine containers and production techniques sit alongside a personal collection of photos from the 1950s.

With support from research institutes in Italy and abroad, the Lungarotti family helped organise the **Museo dell'Olivo e dell'Olio** (☎ 075 988 03 00; Via Garibaldi 10; adult/concession €4.50/2.50; ☉ 10am-

---

LA STRADA DEI VINI DEL CANTICO

La Strada dei Vini del Cantico (www.strada deivinidelcantico.it) is one of Umbria's four wine routes, encompassing the tourist route of Torgiano, Perugia, Bettona, Cannara, Spello, Assisi, Todi and Marsciano. Tourist offices in all eight towns carry maps and brochures listing the vineyards, hotels, *agriturismi* and restaurants of particular interest to wine lovers. Follow the map by car (or, for the brave, by bicycle) to find ancient archaeology, stone farmhouses, stunningly beautiful landscapes and plenty of spots to quench the thirst of anyone who comes to Italy to eat, drink and enjoy the view.

1pm & 3-7pm summer, to 6pm winter), which opened in 2000. Contained in a series of medieval houses, the museum traces the production cycle of the olive, displays olive-oil accoutrements, and documents the culture and use of olives and how they relate to the economy, the landscape, religion, medicine, diet, sport, crafts and traditions.

Festivals & Events

In the second half of November, the **Banco d'Assaggio dei Vini** (www.bavi.it in Italian) – a dedicated wine-tasting demonstration – is an important event on the international calendar.

Sleeping & Eating

Al Grappolo d'Oro (☎ 075 98 22 53; www.algrappolodoro .net; Via Principe Umberto 22/24; s €50, d €90-105, all incl breakfast; P ✕ ✎) One of the best hotel deals in Umbria, this is worth a stay just for the vineyard view from the pool. Smartly furnished 19th-century rooms have been upgraded with DSL, satellite TV, DVD, hairdryers and towel warmers.

Le Tre Vaselle (☎ 075 988 04 47; www.3vaselle.it; Via Garibaldi 48; rooms s €170, d €205-230, ste €270; P ✕ ✎) One of Umbria's most exclusive restaurants is found in Torgiano: Le Melograne, housed in this luxury hotel (both owned by the Lungarotti family – are you starting to see a theme here?). The restaurant serves deluxe Umbrian cuisine (meals €90) amid luxurious furnishings and beautiful brick floors. Dishes include veal *carpaccio* topped with black truffles, and risotto cooked with Rubesco red wine produced by, of course, the Lungarottis. The fabulous features of the hotel, Umbria's second five star (Hotel Brufani Palace in Perugia is the first), including indoor and outdoor swimming pools and 300-year-old oak-beamed ceilings, are sadly met with several unimpressive ones, including poor sound-proofing and three star–quality beds.

Ristorante Siro (☎ 075 98 20 10; Via Giordano Bruno 16; meals €24.50; ☺ lunch & dinner) This old-school eatery is one of those spots where waiters and customers all know each other by name. The *antipastone al tagliere* (a huge board of anti-pasti; €15 for two) starter would feed a hungry family and *gnochetti al rubesco e radicchio* (little gnocchi with rubesco wine and radicchio) takes advantage of the local wine. Home-made tiramisu to die for.

AROUND TORGIANO

Between Torgiano and Perugia Ponte San Giovanni is the hamlet of **Brufa**, formerly a *frazione* (defense town) of Torgiano. The countryside drive alone is worth a detour, but the added bonus is the 20-piece public sculptures that pop up along the drive into Brufa and at various points around town. On the **Strada del Vino e dell'Arte**, you'll see a series of sculptures, some over 6m high while others are a fraction of that. They were created each year by some of Italy's top sculptors starting in 1987. When in Torgiano, the tourist office's *In Viaggi* map of Torgiano carries an inset map of Brufa's sculptures.

For a truly magnificent experience, stay in sumptuous luxury at the newly refurbished **Relais Borgo Brufa** (☎ 075 98 52 67; www.borgobrufa .it; Via del Colle 38; s €95-130, d €125-180, ste €185-355; **P** ✖ ☐ ☎). Formerly a quiet, out-of-the-way country estate, the relais is now a homage to opulence. If the outdoor salt-water pool (more delicate on tanned skin) and archi-tecturally designed suites seamlessly blend-ing old and new aren't enough, its **Wellness Centre** (☎ 075 988 78 50; ☺ 10am-1pm & 2.30-8pm; treatments €30-75) is a quiet secret, but it is open to the public. The six treatment rooms have warm lighting, a mosaic Turkish bath with twinkling lights and a hydromassage pool. And there is the restaurant, **I Quattro Sensi** (meals €40), which is destined for greatness. In ad-dition to elegant surroundings, food here is tastefully and ingeniously presented: porcini mushroom tempura, pumpkin soup with cav-iar, and shrimp softer than butter. The relais is less than a 15-minute drive to Perugia's Sant'Egidio airport.

For a lighter dinner, stop in at **I Birbi Osteria** (☎ 075 988 90 41; Loc. Le Casacce, Miralduoro di Torgiano; meals €30; ☺ dinner Tue-Sun, lunch Sat & Sun, closed 2 weeks Nov, 3 weeks Jan) on a beautiful hill just east

of Brufa. A Tuscan/Umbrian couple hosts their extended family and friends in front of a great hearth. Sure, there's technically a menu, but go with the menu of the day, much of it local meats grilled over the wood-fired hearth.

DERUTA
pop 8687

Just south of Perugia is an ancient 'company' town known for one thing: majolica ceramic technique. The Etruscans and Romans worked the clay around Deruta, but it was not until the bright blue and yellow metallic-oxide ma-jolica glazing technique was imported from Majorca in the 15th century that the ceramics industry took off.

Contact the local **tourist office** (☎ 075 971 00 43; Piazza dei Consoli; ☺ 9am-12pm & 2.30-5pm Tue-Sun) for general information or details about ad-ditional accommodation.

Prices for ceramics in Deruta can be lower or higher than towns like Gubbio or Assisi, but realise what you're getting (ie either pricier quality handmade items at boutique outlets or cheaper, mass-produced factory knockoffs at the larger operations). For the best quality, head to a smaller shop that fol-lows the centuries-old Deruta traditions.

Try **Maioliche Nulli** (☎ /fax 075 97 23 84; Via Tiberina 142; ☺ 9am-1pm & 4-7pm), where Rolando Nulli creates each item by hand, while his brother Goffredo, wife Tiziana or son Luca finishes them with intricate paintings, specialising in classic medieval designs. If they're not busy and you ask nicely in Italian, they might even bring you downstairs and teach you to throw a bowl on the wheel. They'll even package and ship your purchases anywhere in the world. Parking's available. Bring your camera!

You can get a taste for the genuine article at the **Museo Regionale della Ceramica** (☎ /fax 075 971 10 00; Largo San Francesco; adult/concession/child under 6yr €3/2/free; ☺ 10am-1pm & 3-6pm or 7pm, Wed-Mon only winter), in the former Franciscan convent. The history of the production of pottery in Deruta from the 14th century until the beginning of the 20th century is presented here, along with an explanation of the development of the special glaze, including some splendid examples.

Maioliche CAMA Deruta (☎ 075 971 11 82; www .camaderuta.com; Via Tiberina 112) is one of the biggest operations in town, but is also one of the most respected in Deruta. It sells wine and food, as well, and offers almost everything online, which it also packs and ships.

At **Scuola d'Arte Ceramica** (☎ 075 97 23 83; www .scuoladarteceramica.com in Italian; Via Tiberina Sud 330), intermediate and expert ceramicists will get a thorough lesson in Derutan techniques over several days or even weeks. Courses are usually taught in Italian but some popular summer courses have an English translator.

For a great and cheap meal, try **Hotel Ristorante Asso di Coppe** (☎ 075 971 02 05; SS3bis/E45, Km 73,400; meals €22), a place populated by locals and serving basic but delicious Umbrian cuisine.

Just south of Deruta in the village of Casalina is **Ristorante Country House L'Antico Forziere** (☎ 075 972 43 14; www.anticoforziere.com; Via della Rocca 2, Loc. Casalina di Deruta; r €85-100, ste €125-150; P ⊠ ⊠), a charming country house with several well-decorated rooms in an enviable position to reach most of northern Umbria (although a tad close to the highway). However, the restaurant (meals €32) is what brings travellers (and food critics) in the know out here. Three brothers perform magic with dishes such as turnip pasta with leek and poppy seeds and saffron risotto with cinnamon pork. Don't even think of leaving before trying (and photographing) the dessert sampler. Closed on Mondays.

APM buses connect the town with Perugia (€2.60, 25 minutes, 13 daily).

ASSISI
pop 26,452

The spiritual capital of Umbria is Assisi, a town more tied to its most famous son than anywhere else. St Francis of Assisi was born here in 1182 and preached his message throughout Umbria until his death in 1224.

To visit Assisi now is to see it almost as Francis himself saw it. Except, of course, for the millions of pilgrims and tourists now attempting to share in the same tranquillity as you.

History

Assisian history dates back to 1000 BC, when Umbrians built small settlements in the hospitable countryside. It has bounced around between almost a dozen ruling factions since, including Roman rule as far back as 295 BC and Ostrogoth invaders in the 6th century. In the 13th century when Assisi was a free commune, the Ghibelline (pro-Empire) residents often fought against its Guelph (pro-Papacy)

neighbour, Perugia. One such soldier was the future St Francis of Assisi.

Orientation

Piazza del Comune is the centre of Assisi. At the northwestern edge of this square, Via San Paolo and Via Portica both eventually lead to the Basilica di San Francesco. Via Portica also leads to the Porta San Pietro and the Piazzale dell'Unità d'Italia, where most intercity buses stop, although APM buses from smaller towns in the area terminate at Piazza Matteotti. Train riders arrive at Piazza Matteotti by shuttle bus (€1) from Santa Maria degli Angeli.

Information

EMERGENCY
Police station (☎ 075 81 28 20; Piazza del Comune)

INTERNET ACCESS
Bar Sabatini (☎ 075 81 62 46; Via Portica 29b; per 30min €3; ☺ 8am-8pm) Internet facilities.

LAUNDRY
Acquazzura (☎ 075 804 09 27; Via San Bernardino Siena 6, Santa Maria degli Angeli) A self-service laundromat between the train station and basilica in Santa Maria degli Angeli.

MEDICAL SERVICES
Hospital (Ospedale di Assisi; ☎ 075 81 39 1; Via Fuori Porta Nuova) Hospital about 1km southeast of Porta Nuova in Fuori Porta.

POST
Post office Porta Nuova (☺ 8am-1.30pm Mon-Fri, 8am-12.30pm Sat); Porta San Pietro (☺ 8.10am-6.25pm Mon-Fri, 8.10am-1pm Sat & Sun)

TOURIST INFORMATION
Tourist office (☎ 075 81 25 34; info@iat.assisi.pg.it; Piazza del Comune 22; ☺ 8am-2pm & 3-6pm Mon-Sat, 10am-1pm & 2-5pm Sun summer, 9am-1pm Sun winter) Also a branch office outside Porta Nuova from Easter through October.

Sights
BASILICA DI SAN FRANCESCO
The **Basilica di San Francesco** (☎ 075 81 90 01; Piazza di San Francesco) has a separate **information office** (☎ 075 819 00 84; www.sanfrancescoassisi.org; ☺ 9am-noon & 2-5pm Mon-Sat) opposite the entrance to the lower church.

The basilica saw heavy damage and four deaths during a series of earthquakes on 26

ASSISI

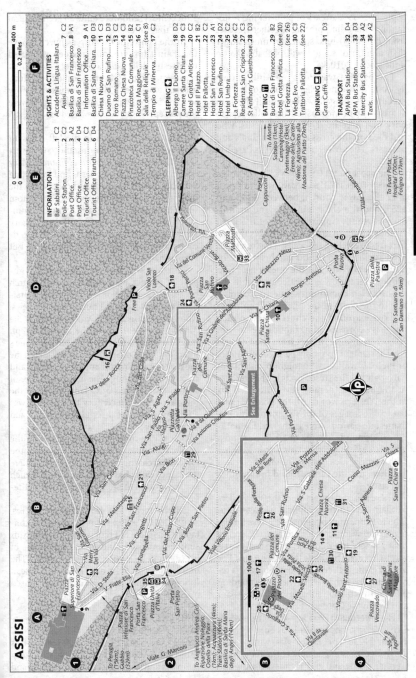

NORTHERN UMBRIA

September 1997. Years of painstaking restoration – including piecing together frescoes from crumbled bits, some not much larger than a grain of sand – will probably go on until at least 2010.

The basilica was built on a hill known as Colle d'Inferno (Hell Hill). People were executed at the gallows here until the 13th century. St Francis asked his followers to bury him here in keeping with Jesus, who had died on the cross among criminals and outcasts. The area is now known as Paradise Hill.

The **upper church** (☉ 8.30am-6.50pm Easter-Nov, to 6pm Nov-Easter, to 7.15pm holidays) was built just after the lower church, between 1230 and 1253, and the change in style and grandiosity is readily apparent. One of the most famous pieces of art in the world is the 28-part fresco circling the walls. The fresco has been attributed to Giotto and his pupils for hundreds of years, but the question of who produced it is now under debate within the art-historian community. The fresco starts just to the right of the altar and continues clockwise around the church. Above each image is a corresponding biblical fresco with 28 corresponding images from the Old and New Testament (possibly painted by Giotto, or Pietro Cavallini, who might or might not have painted the fresco cycle). The frescoes in the basilica literally revolutionised art in the Western world. All the gold leaf and flat iconic images of the Byzantine and Romanesque periods were eschewed for natural backgrounds, people of all classes and a human, suffering Jesus. This was in keeping with Francis' idea that the human body was 'brother' and the earth around him mother and sister.

These fresco painters were the storytellers of their day, turning biblical passages into Bibliae Pauperum: open public Bibles for the poor, who were mostly illiterate. The scenes in St Francis' life were tied to the scenes as a way to translate the Bible through images. For instance, the fifth fresco shows St Francis renouncing his father, while the corresponding biblical fresco shows the disobedient Adam and Eve in the Garden of Eden.

The **lower church** (☉ 6.30am-6.50pm Easter-Nov, to 6pm Nov-Easter, to 7.15pm holidays) was built between 1228 and 1230. The stained-glass windows are the work of master craftsmen brought in from Germany, England and Flanders during the

13th century, and were quite an architectural feat at that time.

In the centre of the lower church, above the main altar, are four frescoes attributed to Maestro delle Vele, a pupil of Giotto, that represent what St Francis called 'the four greatest allegories'. The first was the victory of Francis over evil, and the other three were the precepts his order was based on: poverty, obedience and chastity.

Lorenzetti's triptych in the left transept ends with his most famous and controversial, *Madonna Who Celebrates Francis*. Mary is seen holding the baby Jesus and indicating with her thumb towards St Francis. On the other side of Mary is the apostle John, whom we're assuming is being unfavourably compared with Francis. In 1234 Pope Gregory IX decided that the image was not heretical because John had written the gospel, but Francis had lived it.

Cimabue was the most historically important painter who worked in this church because he was the only artist to get a first-hand account from St Francis' two nephews, who had personally known the saint. In the *Madonna in Majesty*, in the right transept, much has been tampered with, but Cimabue's intact depiction of St Francis is considered the most accurate. Francis appears peaceful and calm in this painting. The first biographer of St Francis, Thomas of Celano, wrote in the middle of the 13th century that Francis was an eloquent man, of cheerful countenance and of a kindly aspect.

One of the most moving locations in the basilica complex is downstairs from the lower church: the crypt of St Francis, where the saint's body has been laid to rest. Bench seating around the tomb allows for quiet reflection.

The basilica's **Sala delle Reliquie** (Relics Hall; ☎ 075 81 90 01; ☉ 9am-6pm, 1-4.30pm holidays) contains items from St Francis' life, including his simple tunic and sandals and fragments of his celebrated *Canticle of the Creatures*. The most important relic here is the Franciscan Rule parchment, the *Book of Life* composed by Francis.

CHURCHES & MUSEUMS
Basilica di Santa Chiara (☎ 075 81 22 82; Piazza Santa Chiara; ☉ 6am-noon & 2-7pm summer, to 6pm winter) is 13th-century Romanesque church, with steep ramparts and a striking façade. The white and

pink stone that makes up the exterior here (the same stone that makes many buildings in Assisi look like they glow in the sunlight) came from nearby Subasio. The daughter of an Assisian nobleman, St Clare was a spiritual contemporary of St Francis and founded the Sorelle Povere di Santa Chiara (Order of the Poor Ladies), now known as the Poor Clares. She is buried in the church's crypt. The Byzantine cross that is said to have spoken to St Francis is also housed here.

From the basilica, take Via S Chiara back to Piazza del Comune, once the site of a partially excavated **Foro Romano** (Roman Forum; ☎ 075 81 30 53; Via Portica; adult/child incl Pinacoteca €3/2; ☽ 10.30am-1.30pm & 2-6pm summer, to 5pm winter). Some of the shops on the piazza open their basements to reveal Roman ruins. The **Chiesa Nuova** (☎ 075 81 23 39; Piazza Chiesa Nuova; ☽ 6.30am-noon & 2.30-6pm summer, 6.30am-noon & 2-6pm winter) was built by King Philip III of Spain in the 1600s on the spot reputed to be the house of St Francis' family. Mass is said daily at 7am, with an extra service on holidays at 10am.

The **Tempio di Minerva**, facing Piazza del Comune and Palazzo dei Priori, is now a church but retains its impressive pillared façade with six fluted columns dating back to Roman times. The turn-of-the-millennium pagan temple, dedicated to the goddess of peace, is featured as the backdrop to the *Homage to the Simple Man* fresco in the Basilica's upper church. Heading northwestwards up Via San Francesco, the city's **Pinacoteca Comunale** (☎ 075 81 20 33; Palazzo Vallemani, Via San Francesco 10; adult/child incl Foro Romano €3/2; ☽ 10am-1pm & 3-6pm 16 Mar-15 Oct, 10am-1pm & 3-5pm 16 Oct-15 Mar) displays Umbrian Renaissance art and frescoes from Giotto's school.

Dominating the city, with an equally dominant view of the valley, is the massive 14th-century **Rocca Maggiore** (☎ 075 81 52 92; Via della Rocca; admission €2; ☽ 10am-sunset), an oft expanded, pillaged and rebuilt hill fortress offering 360-degree views of Perugia. Walk up windy staircases and claustrophobic passageways to reach the archer slots that served Assisians as they went medieval on Perugia.

The 13th-century Romanesque **Duomo di San Rufino** (☎ 075 81 60 16; Piazza San Rufino; ☽ 7am-noon & 2.30-7pm, to 6pm winter), remodelled by Galeazzo Alessi in the 16th century, contains the fountain where St Francis and St Clare were baptised. The façade is festooned with grotesque figures and fantastic animals.

FRANCISCAN SITES

Around 1.5km south of the Porta Nuova, the **Santuario di San Damiano** (☎ 075 81 22 73; admission free; ☽ 10am-noon & 2-6pm summer, 10am-noon & 2-4.30pm winter, vespers 7pm summer & 5pm winter) was built on the spot where St Francis first heard the voice of Jesus and where he wrote his *Canticle of the Creatures*. You can visit the original convent founded by St Clare in 1212 here, as well as its cloisters and refectory.

About 4km east of the city is **Eremo delle Carceri** (☎ 075 81 23 01; admission free; ☽ 6.30am-7.15pm Easter-Nov, to sunset Nov-Easter), the hermitage that St Francis retreated to after hearing the word of God. The *carceri* (prisons) are the caves that functioned as hermits' retreats for St Francis and his followers. Apart from a few fences and tourist paths, everything remains as it was in St Francis' time. Eremo delle Carceri is a great jumping-off point for walks through Monte Subasio or picnics under the oaks.

A quick walk from the train station is the imposing **Basilica di Santa Maria degli Angeli** (☎ 075 8 05 11; Santa Maria degli Angeli; ☽ 6.45am-1pm & 2.30-8pm summer, 6.15am-1pm & 2.30-7.30pm winter), built between 1565 and 1685 around the first Franciscan monastery and tiny Porziuncola Chapel. Perugino fans will appreciate his intact Crucifixion, painted on the rear wall. St Francis died at the site of the Cappella del Transito on 3 October 1226.

Activities

St Francis buffs and nature lovers will appreciate the plethora of strolls, day hikes and overnight pilgrimage walks leading into and out of Assisi. Many make the trek to Eremo delle Carceri or Sanctuario di San Damiano on foot. The tourist office has maps for those on such a peregrination, including a route that follows in St Francis' footsteps to Gubbio (18km).

A popular spot for hikers is nearby Monte Subasio. Local bookshops sell all sorts of walking and mountain-biking guides and maps for the area, and the tourist office can help with brochures and maps as well.

Bicycle rentals are available at **Angelucci Andrea Cicli Riparazione Noleggio** (☎ 075 804 25 50; www.angeluccicicli.it; VG Becchetti 31) in Santa Maria degli Angeli and at Ostello della Pace (p338).

Courses

Accademia della Lingua Italiana Corsi di Lingua e Cultura Italiana (☎ /fax 075 81 52 81; www.aliassisi.it; Via San Paolo 36) runs a variety of courses, including

---

POOR MR POPULAR: ST FRANCIS OF ASSISI

How did a small-town guy become the most beloved saint of Catholics? It's your classic riches to rags tale. Young Francis of Assisi had charm, wit, a place in his father's booming textile business, and a flair for fashion that impressed even his fellow Italians. But all that didn't save him from a year in jail for joining an attack on rival city Perugia c 1201. He emerged spoiling for a fight, and signed on to fight a war in Naples. But when he had a dream in Spoleto telling him to turn back, he returned to Assisi a changed man. He began giving away money to lepers, and took cloth from his dad's warehouse to raise funds for his church. Outraged, his dad threatened to cut him off – but Francis shocked everyone by embracing poverty. The former fashionista threw off his clothes, donned an Umbrian peasant robe and moved into a hut.

Others soon followed his example, including a local teenage heiress named Clare, who hacked off her hair, devoted herself to Francis' rule of charity and poverty, and soon led the first Franciscan convent. Francis set off on a gruelling trip that sounds like *The Mediterranean on a Shoestring* gone horribly wrong, with mixed success winning converts – the French were unimpressed, and the bemused Sultan approached by Francis in the midst of a Crusade in Egypt set him firmly on his way. Meanwhile, his following was growing back home. His care of the terminally ill started several hospices; his legendary kindness to animals inspired some of Europe's first known animal hospitals; and his love of nature led to organised conservation efforts. Francis was canonised soon after his death in 1226, and named the patron saint of ecologists, merchants, lepers, animals and pretty much everyone else.

Italian language, culture, singing, painting and cooking. It also offers free preparation for the CILS (Italian teacher abroad) course. There's a maximum of 12 students per class and costs start at about €300 for two weeks of instruction.

Festivals & Events

Settimana Santa (Easter Week) Celebrated with processions and performances.

Festa di Calendimaggio (starts 1st Thursday after 1 May) Colourful festival which celebrates spring in medieval fashion.

Festa di San Francesco (3 and 4 October) The main religious event in the city.

Marcia della Pace (1st week in October) This is Europe's largest peace march. It began in 1961 and attracts more than 150,000 pilgrims who walk the 24km route between Perugia and Assisi.

Sleeping

Assisi has a phenomenal amount of rooms, which ensures the best prices in any Umbrian town popular with tourists. Keep in mind that in peak periods such as Easter, August and September, and during the Festa di San Francesco, you will need to book accommodation well in advance.

The tourist office has a complete list of private rooms, religious institutions (of which there are 17), flats and *agriturismi* options in and around Assisi and can assist with bookings in a pinch. Otherwise, keep an eye out for *camere* (rooms for rent) signs as you wander the streets.

BUDGET

Camping/Hotel Fontemaggio (☎ 075 81 23 17; www.fontemaggio.it; Via Eremo delle Carceri 8; per person/tent/car €6/5/3, dm/s/d/tr/q €20/35/52/72.50/96, 4- to 6-person bungalow with kitchen €32-110) The sort of place St Francis himself probably would have stayed. A full complement of bungalows, camp sites and hotel rooms offer up a bed for just about any taste. On the way to Eremo delle Carceri, it's a beautiful walk into town, but the restaurant might just keep you for the evening.

Ostello della Pace (☎ 075 81 67 67; www.assisihostel.com; Via Valecchie 177; dm incl breakfast €15-17; ☺ 2 Mar -9 Jan; ℗ 🖳) Assisi's HI youth hostel is lovingly family run, in a beautiful and quiet location, and has great pillows. It's on the shuttle-bus route between Santa Maria degli Angeli and Assisi. There's a laundry room for guests. Full and half-board are available or, if you prefer, just packed lunch (€6.50) or dinner (€9.50).

Albergo Il Duomo (☎ 075 81 27 42; www.hotelsanrufino.it; Vicolo San Lorenzo; s/d €36/47) Owned by the same folks who run the two-star San Rufino, this is a lovely one-star choice on a quiet alleyway just a stone's throw from the Piazza del Comune. For this price there aren't too many extras, but the nine rooms are understandably popular, so book ahead.

Hotel Grotta Antica (☎ 075 81 34 67; www.bellaum bria.net/hotel-grottaantica; Via Macelli Vecchi 1; s/d €35/50) The price is not a mistake. Perfectly located on a tiny side street less than 30m from the Palazzo del Comune, it's a wonder these rooms are also clean and hospitable. Abele speaks fluent English and Spanish, and takes care of the seven simple rooms and the restaurant of the same name (see p340).

Hotel San Rufino (☎ 075 81 28 03; www.hotelsan rufino.it; Via Porta Perlici 7; s €44, d €54-60, tr €68) A small hotel owned by the same family as Il Duomo, this is around the corner and just as quiet. Sweetly decorated rooms all come with direct-dial phone and TV. It also offers cradles for babies, plus breakfast is available (€5).

St Anthony's Guesthouse (☎ 075 81 25 42; atoneassisi@tiscali.it; Via Galeazzo Alessi 10; s/d/tr incl breakfast €35/55/75; P) Look for the iron statue of St Francis feeding the birds and you've found your Assisian oasis. Rooms are austere but welcoming and six have balconies with take-your-breath-away views. Gardens, ample parking, an 800-year-old breakfast salon and an ancient Door of Death make this a heavenly choice. Like most religious accommodation, it has a two-night minimum and 11pm curfew.

ourpick Camere Santa Chiara (☎ 075 81 34 67; camere.santachiara@yahoo.it; Vicolo Sant'Antonio 1; s/d/tr/q incl breakfast €35/55/65/75) Depending on which of the eight rooms in this brand-new hotel you choose, you might sleep on top of a glass-covered Roman ruin, watch a TV propped up on a medieval wall or enjoy breakfast on your private patio. Curl up with a book, head phones or DVD in the video library or, if you're feeling social, have a drink at the piano bar. Bring your car here first, and staff will show you where to park nearby for free.

MIDRANGE

La Fortezza Hotel (☎ 075 81 24 18; www.lafortezzahotel .com; Vicolo della Fortezza 2b; r with/without breakfast €65/52) Seven simply outfitted rooms offer guests a comfortable respite at this charming and intimate hotel run by the well-known Assisian Chiocchetti family, popular restaurateurs and hoteliers for decades. The stone building is up a stone staircase, quietly tucked above the Piazza del Comune and the hotel's extremely popular restaurant (see p340).

Hotel Pallotta (☎ 075 81 26 49; www.pallottaassisi.it; Vicolo della Volta Pinta; s/d/tr incl breakfast €40/65/75) Yet another great-value hotel right in the heart of Assisi. Rooms are as modern as they are ancient; medieval walls and shuttered windows coexist with tile showers and wall-mounted TVs. Be sure to check out the view from the top floor.

Hotel San Francesco (☎ 075 81 22 81; www.hotelsanfranc escoassisi.it; Via San Francesco 48; s €52-100, d €70-130, all incl breakfast; 🖳) For travellers who are looking for a serious view of the basilica, you need only look out most windows for a postcard shot. If your view isn't perfect enough, head to the rooftop deck with a view of the basilica with Monte Subasio as its backdrop. Amenities include satellite TV (with BBC, CNN, France 2), mini-bar, elevator, hairdryer, double-pane windows and a hotel shuttle service that will come and collect you at any of the car parks (you can also drive in and drop off your luggage first). Fill up for a hearty day of sightseeing at the enormous breakfast buffet. There are also discounts in the low season and for children.

Hotel Umbra (☎ 075 81 22 40; www.hotelumbra.it; Via Degli Archi 6; s €72-85, d €96-125, all incl breakfast; 🖳) It's physically impossible to spend the night here without imagining what life would have been like in these buildings over the last few centuries. The 25-room hotel has been in the same family since the turn of the last century, when it was cobbled together from almost a dozen medieval buildings. Antique furnishings complement a cosy fireplace inside, while the grapevine-shaded terrace is there for your after-dinner grappa.

Hotel Il Palazzo (☎ 075 81 68 41; www.hotelilpalazzo .it; Via San Francesco 8; s €90-105, d €125-160, all incl breakfast; 🕑 closed Nov, Jan & Feb) The rooms in this lovely 15th-century palazzo, half of which is occupied by the owners (descendants of the original occupants), have been restored in the simple elegance that Italians are famous for: white walls, terracotta floors, a few pieces of fine old furniture in splendidly carved wood, and beautiful carpets. Despite its central position, the hotel is also very quiet and filled with light. The only disadvantage is that there are a lot of stairs to negotiate.

TOP END

Residenza San Crispino (☎ 075 815 51 24; www.sanc rispinoresidence.com; Via Sant' Agnese 11; ste €130-200; P) Assisi's happiest guests seem to stay at this peaceful historic residence, which receives a constant stream of raves, and for good reason. Rooms are medieval old but have been upgraded with kitchenettes to blissful apartment suites named after St Francis' *Canticle of the Creatures* – Brother Sun, Sister Water etc. If the short stroll to the Basilica di Santa Chiara or monastic-quiet garden hasn't calmed you down quite enough, jump on one of the shuttles to the 'beauty farm', where relaxing massage treatments await.

Eating

RESTAURANTS

While we normally recommend staying away from hotel restaurants, most of Assisi's better restaurants (even the more inexpensive ones) are part of hotels.

Grotta Antica (☎ 075 81 34 67; Vicolo Buscatti 6; meals €16) Abele – hotel proprietor, lawyer and chef – is from Liguria, so you can rest assured that although there are only a handful of menu items, you needn't look past the pesto dishes for a cheap and filling main course. His wine prices can't be beaten anywhere in Assisi.

La Fortezza (☎ 075 81 24 18; Via della Fortezza 2b; meals €22; ☉ Fri-Wed) This family-run restaurant off Piazza del Comune serves traditional Umbrian dishes and flame-roasted meats, as well as those from Trentino, and a good selection of local wines. Credit cards are accepted.

Trattoria Pallotta (☎ 075 81 26 49; Vicolo della Volta Pinta; meals €23; ☉ Wed-Mon) Head through the Volta Pinta (Painted Vault) off Piazza del Comune, careful not to bump into someone as you gaze at the 16th-century frescoes above you, into this gorgeous setting of vaulted brick walls and wood-beamed ceilings. All the Umbrian classics are cooked here: rabbit, homemade *strangozzi* (round stringlike spaghetti), even pigeon. Readers have assured us its selection for vegetarians is excellent.

Medio Evo (☎ 075 81 30 68; Via Arco dei Priori 4; meals €28; ☉ Thu-Tue) Traditional Umbrian dishes are served in fabulous vaulted 13th-century surroundings, including rabbit stew (€12) and truffle omelettes (€10). The early 6.45pm opening time is geared for, and highly appreciated by, non-Italian tourists.

Buca di San Francesco (☎ 075 81 22 04; Via Brizi 1; meals €29; ☉ Tue-Sun) Sample traditional Umbrian dishes and specialities of the house in an elegant medieval setting. Choose from bruschetta, local sausage, *spaghetti alla buca* (house-speciality spaghetti made with roasted mushrooms), gnocchi and home-made desserts, and from the extensive wine list with the help of one of Assisi's only sommeliers.

SLEEPING (AND COOKING) ABOVE THE FRAY

our pick **Agriturismo alla Madonna del Piatto** (☎ 075 819 90 50; www.incampagna.com; Pieve San Nicolo 18; d €80-115; ☉ Mar–mid-Nov; **P**) This B&B/*agriturismo* has seen many upgrades since its inception as a shepherd's outpost some 700 years ago. It's now a refurbished stone farmhouse with heated terracotta-tile floors, six double rooms, an open fireplace, and a working farm and olive orchard. Set in verdant hills, it's not unusual to see wild boar or pheasants stroll on by. The multilingual Letizia runs the most magnificent cooking classes out of her small kitchen for guests or visitors (in Italian or English); see p310.

CAFÉS

Gran Caffè (☎ 075 815 51 44; Corso Mazzini 16; ☉ 8am-midnight) This elegant place has the most fabulous gelati, mouth-watering pastries and cakes, and a great selection of drinks. Try the *tè freddo alla pesca* (iced tea with peach) on a hot day, or choose from a selection of delicious hot chocolates and coffee when the weather is cool. Remember it costs much more to sit.

Shopping

Assisi is a good town for shopping as many shops stay open during siesta. The closer you get to the Basilica, the tackier the souvenirs – Franciscan friar shot glasses and nuns playing poker – but meander off the beaten path for leather, ceramics and clothing. Open-air markets take place in Piazza Matteotti on Saturday and Santa Maria degli Angeli on Monday.

Getting There & Away

Assisi is extremely easy to reach, by bus or train. Although Assisi's train station is 4km west in Santa Maria degli Angeli, shuttle bus C (€0.80) runs between the train station and the APM bus station on Piazza Matteotti every half-hour. Tickets are available in the *tabacchi* at the station and in town. Assisi is on the Foligno–Terontola line with regular services to Perugia (€1.80, 25 minutes, hourly). You can change at Terontola for Florence (€9.40 to €15.20, 1¾ to 2¾ hours, 10 daily) and at Foligno for Rome (€9.40 to €16, two to 2½ hours, hourly).

APM Perugia (☎ 800 51 21 41; www.apmperugia.it) runs to Perugia (€3, 50 minutes, nine daily) and Gubbio (€5.20, one hour 10 minutes, 11 daily) from Piazza Matteotti. The buses all start at Piazza Matteotti and a few stop at Porta Nuova on the way to Perugia. **Sulga** (☎ 800 09 96 61; www.sulga.it) buses leave from the intercity bus station at Porta San Pietro for Florence (€11, 2½ hours, one daily at 7am) and Rome's Stazione Tiburtina (€16.50, 3¼ hours, three daily).

To reach Assisi from Perugia by road, take the SS75, exit at Ospedalicchio and follow the signs.

Getting Around
A shuttle bus (€0.80) operates every half-hour between Piazza Matteotti and the train station. Normal traffic is subject to restrictions in the city centre and daytime parking is all but banned. Six car parks dot the city walls (they are connected to the centre by orange shuttle buses), or head for Via della Rocca where, for the price of a short but fairly steep walk, you should be able to find free parking.

For a taxi, dial ☎ 075 81 31 00, or head to Piazza Unità d'Italia's taxi stand.

SPELLO
pop 8580
Sometimes it seems like it's just not possible for the next Umbrian town to be any prettier than the last. And then you visit Spello. It's often passed by as tourists head to nearby Assisi or Perugia, but the proliferation of arched stone walkways and hanging flowerpots make it well worth a visit, especially in spring when the whole bloomin' town smells of flowers.

Information
EMERGENCY
Police station (☎ 0742 65 11 15; Piazza della Repubblica)

INTERNET RESOURCES
Bella Umbria (www.bellaumbria.net/spello) A private tourist website with information on accommodation, history and events.
www.comune.spello.pg.it The city website

MEDICAL SERVICES
Doctor (☎ 0742 30 20 16) Can locate a local doctor.
Farmacia Bartoli (☎ 0742 30 14 88; Via Cavour 63; ☺ closed Sat morning)

POST
Post office (☎ 0742 3 00 81; Piazza della Repubblica; ☺ 8am-6.30pm Mon-Fri, 8am-12.30pm Sat)

TOURIST INFORMATION
Pro Loco (tourist office; ☎ /fax 0742 30 10 09; prospello@libero.it, Piazza Matteotti 3; ☺ 9.30am-12.30pm & 3.30-5.30pm) It can provide you with a list of accommodation and has maps of walks in the surrounding area, including an 8km walk across the hills to Assisi. Purchase a city map here for €0.50.

Sights
Perhaps the best sight in all of Spello is to head up to the **Arco Romano**. From here you can get the best view of the **Anfiteatro Romano** (closed to the public) – the amphitheatre used for spectacles thousands of years ago in Roman 'Hispellum' (the Roman name for modern-day Spello) – and the surrounding countryside. Nearby is the **Chiesa di San Severino**, an active Cappuccin monastery with a Romanesque façade.

As you enter Spello, you'll come across Piazza Kennedy, the main entrance to the town, with a partially Roman gate, **Porta Consolare**. Further into town, Piazza Matteotti features two enormous churches: the austere **Chiesa di Sant'Andrea** (☺ 8am-7pm), where you can admire *Madonna with Child and Saints* by Bernardino Pinturicchio, and a few doors down, the 12th-century **Chiesa di Santa Maria Maggiore** (☺ 8.30am-12pm & 2-7pm Mar-Oct, until 6pm Nov-Mar). You'll also find the town's real treat, Pinturicchio's beautiful frescoes, in the Cappella Baglioni. The fresco is in the right-hand corner as you enter, behind glass, but be aware that you need to pay to illuminate the fresco. This is done not just to make money; constant light damages the paint. Also of note is the Cappella's exquisite floor (dating from 1566) made of tiles from Deruta. The **Pinacoteca Civica** (☎ 0742 30 14 97; Palazzo dei Cannonica, Piazza Matteotti; adult/concession €4/3; ☺ 10.30am-1pm & 3-6.30pm Tue-Sun Apr-Sep, 10.30am-12.30pm & 3-5pm Tue-Sun Oct-Mar) shows off Spello's artistic, religious and architectural past.

Continuing through to town, you'll reach **Piazza della Repubblica**. Further along, in the same piazza as the Palazzo Comunale, is the **Chiesa di San Lorenzo** (☺ 8.30am-12.30pm & 3-7pm summer, to 6pm winter), with a collection of sacred works. At the far north of town is yet another imposing church, **Santa Maria di Vallegloria**, built in the 1320s in Gothic style with frescoes by

Spacca. The **Torre di Properzio** (Porta Venere) stands guard over the western Roman walls. Named after the Roman poet Propertius, the gate and its towers are a hodgepodge of Roman, medieval and 20th-century reconstructionist architecture.

Activities

The Pro Loco (and the tourist office in Assisi) has a badly drawn map called the *Passeggiata Tra Gli Ulivi*, a walking route between Spello and Assisi down the Via degli Ulivi (Road of Olives). It's not a long walk (8km) and passes through scenery of flower fields and ancient gnarled olive trees, but you will be walking on a lightly trafficked asphalt road for a spell. Stop in (by foot or car) at the **Azienda Agricola**

Ragani (☎ 0742 30 11 56; www.olioragani.com; Via degli Ulivi 8), which is open sporadically to the public, but a lucky few passers-by will have a chance to taste its renowned olive oils.

Festivals & Events

Spello, like nearby towns, has no shortage of festivals:

L'Infiorata del Corpus Domini (usually in June) The most beautiful and best smelling festival in Spello. Takes place on Corpus Domini, the Sunday 60 days after Easter. Those familiar with Semana Santa in Guatemala and other Latin American countries will recognise the similar *alfombras* (flower carpets) that decorate the streets presented in colourful artistic displays. If you want to enjoy it, come on the Saturday evening before to see the floral fantasies being laid out (from about 8.30pm) and participate in the

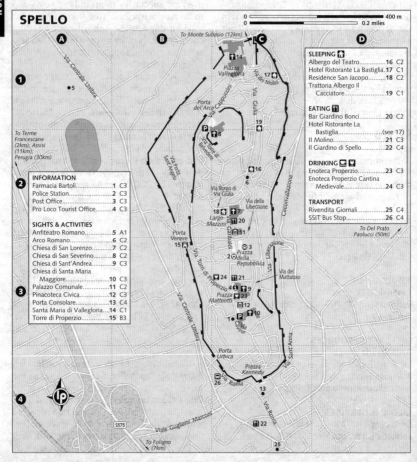

SPELLO

0	400 m
0	0.2 miles

To Monte Subasio (12km)

To Terme
Francescane
(2km); Assisi
(11km);
Perugia (30km)

Piazza
Vallegloria

Porta
del'Arce

Porta
Vertere

Porta
Consolare

Porta
Urbica

Piazza
Kennedy

To Del Prato
Paolucci (50m)

To Foligno
(7km)

INFORMATION
Farmacia Bartoli..................1 C3
Police Station......................2 C3
Post Office..........................3 C3
Pro Loco Tourist Office.........4 C3

SIGHTS & ACTIVITIES
Anfiteatro Romano...............5 A1
Arco Romano.......................6 C2
Chiesa di San Lorenzo...........7 C2
Chiesa di San Severino..........8 C2
Chiesa di Sant'Andrea...........9 C3
Chiesa di Santa Maria
Maggiore.........................10 C3
Palazzo Comunale................11 C2
Pinacoteca Civica.................12 C3
Porta Consolare....................13 C4
Santa Maria di Vallegloria.....14 C1
Torre di Properzio.................15 B3

SLEEPING
Albergo del Teatro...............16 C2
Hotel Ristorante La Bastiglia..17 C1
Residence San Jacopo..........18 C2
Trattoria Albergo Il
Cacciatore....................19 C1

EATING
Bar Giardino Bonci..............20 C2
Hotel Ristorante La
Bastiglia.....................(see 17)
Il Molino...........................21 C3
Il Giardino di Spello............22 C4

DRINKING
Enoteca Properzio...............23 C3
Enoteca Properzio Cantina
Medievale.....................24 C3

TRANSPORT
Rivendita Giornali...............25 C4
SSIT Bus Stop.....................26 C4

festive atmosphere. On the day of the festival, the Corpus procession commences at 11am, but beware – it can become extremely crowded. Make sure you have already made hotel reservations well in advance, or alternatively, just travel in from Assisi or Perugia and visit for the day's celebrations.

Sleeping

Del Prato Paolucci (☎ 0742 30 10 18; Via Brodolini 4; s €35-45, d €50-62; P) Located just outside the city walls, these are the least expensive rooms in town. However, you'll have a perfectly acceptable bathroom, TV and phone, and a few rooms have views. Call ahead and the gregarious owners will pick you up at the train station.

Residence San Jacopo (☎ 0742 30 12 60, 333 223 28 99; www.residencesanjacopo.it in Italian; Via Borgo di Via Giulia 1; mini-apts for 2/3 people €62/93) This vacation house saw its first incarnation in 1296 as the hospice of San Jacopo, a way station for pilgrims heading to Compostella in Galicia. Much has been rebuilt over the last eight centuries and San Jacopo is as comfortable as it is charming. Seven mini-apartments feature a kitchenette, bathroom and TV, and are furnished with rustic antiques. Vanya, the owner, also runs a nearby *enoteca*, and knows everything about local wine and delicacies.

Trattoria Albergo Il Cacciatore (☎ 0742 65 11 41; www.ilcacciatorehotel.com; Via Giulia 42; s €50-60, d €75-90, tr €95-115) This place has 21 rooms that are spread over three floors that are large and modern, and plainly furnished in 'business casual', some with a small sitting area. Ask for a room with a view. There's also a great restaurant (closed Monday) with a large terrace that's perfect for a summer lunch amid a panoramic view.

Albergo del Teatro (☎ 0742 30 11 40; www.hotel delteatro.it; Via Giulia 24; s €60-85, d €90-110, ste €200-220, all incl breakfast) This 18th-century building is enviably located in the middle of Spello and pleasantly outfitted with a sitting room and fireplace, terraces with hill-top views and up-dated guest rooms.

Hotel Ristorante La Bastiglia (☎ 0742 65 12 77; www.labastiglia.com; Via dei Molini 7; s €70-105, d €80-155, tr €110-185, ste €210-300; P ✖ ✖) This place has been welcoming well-heeled pilgrims, bicyclists and tour participants for decades. Three classes of rooms open the stunning grounds to a larger swathe of the travelling public, all of whom enjoy seasonal breakfast (Italian style, so quite small) on the terrace.

Eating

Il Giardino di Spello (☎ 0742 30 14 45; Via Centrale Umbra 36; tapas €4.50; ✔ 7am-midnight Tue-Sun) Near the train station and main bus stop is a one-stop quick meal stop. For just a few euros, diners on the cheap can load up on tapas. Tack on two more euros for Spello's best home-made gelato.

Bar Giardino Bonci (Via Garibaldi 10; mains €6; ✔ 7am-10pm Fri-Wed, to midnight summer) This simple bar has decent light meals and gelati, but the best thing is the back veranda, where you could while away hours admiring the view.

Il Molino (☎ 0742 65 13 05; Piazza Matteotti 6/7; meals €29; ✔ Wed-Mon) Owned by the Hotel Palazzo Bocci, the Molino is set in a 700-year-old building. It specialises in truffles, legumes, winter game meats, wild asparagus and cooking with local mountain-grown herbs.

Hotel Ristorante La Bastiglia (☎ 0742 65 12 77; Via dei Molini 17; meals €55; ✔ Fri-Tue & dinner Thu) Connoisseurs come from all over the world to dine here. The food is beyond outstanding and a rare example of Umbrian nouvelle cuisine. Who would have thought blood and gnocchi would go together, or pigeon and puff pastry? But they do, and artfully so.

Drinking

Enoteca Properzio (☎ 0742 30 15 21; www.enoteche.it; Palazzo dei Canonici, Piazza Matteotti 8/10; ✔ 9am-11pm Apr-Oct, 9am-8pm Nov-Mar) Umbrian vineyards aren't usually open to the public, so one of the only chances visitors have of tasting several wines at once without breaking the bank (or getting sloshed) is to stop off at an *enoteca* in town. And there's no better place in Umbria to do so than here, where for €30, you can try a half-dozen Umbrian wines while snacking on cheese, prosciutto and bruschetta. For €144, you can have a dozen bottles shipped abroad.

Enoteca Properzio Cantina Medievale (☎ 0742 30 16 88; Via Torri di Properzio 8a) This is a more intimate bar around the corner, is set in a medieval vault and sells many edibles.

Getting There & Away

Spello is directly on the train line between Perugia and Foligno, so trains run at least hourly to Perugia (€2.30, 30 minutes) and Assisi (€1.30, 10 minutes). Spello is on the SS75 between Perugia and Foligno. The station is often unstaffed, so buy your tickets at either the self-service ticket machine or at the news-stand **Rivendita Giornali** (Piazza della Pace 1).

LA STRADA DI SAGRANTINO

Wine connoisseurs are not the only ones who would enjoy the tourist-friendly 'route of Sagrantino wine'. It is one of four Umbrian driving (or, for the brave, bicycling) wine routes that follow signposted roads through stunningly beautiful landscape filled with vineyards, castles, sunflower fields and five charming villages. The two main towns in the area are the postcard-perfect burgs of Montefalco and Bevagna, but meandering countryside through Gualdo Cattaneo, Giano dell'Umbria and Castel Ritaldi are equally charming. All tourist offices near the region carry Strada del Sagrantino brochures with detailed driving maps, vineyards and *enoteche* (restaurants that offer wine tasting), or find information on accommodation (including *agriturismi* and B&Bs), restaurants, public transport and history at the region's tourism website www.stradadelsagrantino.com (in Italian, English and German).

Montefalco
pop 5693
The ancient town of Montefalco looks as if it grew, along with the local vines, out of the

ground organically. Known as the *ringhiera dell'Umbria* (the balcony of Umbria), the perfectly perched village sits atop a hill with a view so lyrically beautiful, it practically begs for an ode. As if that wasn't enough, Montefalco is the headquarters for the distinctly Umbrian red, Sagrantino di Montefalco. Imbibe in the main square, Piazza del Comune, in no less than four *enoteche* (Enoteca L'Alchimista has a good reputation).

The most important building in Montefalco is the **Museo Civico San Francesco** (☎ 0742 37 95 98; Via Ringhiera Umbra 6; adult/concession €5/2; ⏰ 10.30am-1pm year-round & 2.30-5pm Nov-Feb, 2-6pm Mar-May, Sep & Oct, 3-7pm Jun & Jul, 3-7.30pm Aug, closed Mon Nov-Feb). The museum is housed next to the deconsecrated St Francis Church, with a 'narrated' fresco cycle by the painter Benozzo Gozzoli, who was the first Umbrian painter of the 1400s to use perspective to paint human form. There's also a decent *pinacoteca* (picture gallery), plus tools from a medieval monastic vineyard. Ask for the well-written guides in Italian, English and French.

If you are looking for somewhere special to stay in the area, try **Villa Zuccari** (☎ 0742 39 94 02; www.villazuccari.com; San Luca di Montefalco; s €95-170, d €110-240, ste €190-320; 🅿 ⌧ 🐾 ⌧). The most recent Zuccari family lineage (the first ones inhabited this house in the 16th century)

MY KINGDOM FOR A GLASS OF WINE

Oenophiles might want to plan an Umbrian trip to coincide with 'Cantina Aperte', the last Sunday in May when all vineyards are open to the public. Unlike neighbouring Tuscany or wine routes in Australia or the US, most Umbrian vintners are not normally open to the public. Cantina Aperte is the only chance for those buying less than, say, 10 cases to descend upon smaller vineyards. Check with the **Centro Agro Alimentare** (www.umbriadoc.com) for information. The rest of the year, the best place to try wine is at an *enoteca* (wine bar; try Spello's Enoteca Properzio; p343) or by the glass at a restaurant.

Next to Torgiano's Lungarotti (see p331), the second most famous vineyard in Umbria is **Arnaldo Caprai** (☎ 742 37 88 02; www.arnaldocaprai.it; Loc. Torre di Montefalco; ⏰ 9am-1pm & 3-7pm Mon-Fri, 9am-1pm Sat), the wine-makers who single-handedly brought the now-famous Denominazione d'Origine Controllata e Garantita (DOCG) Sagrantino back from obscurity. The Caprai vineyard has just built a beautiful new tasting room and is one of the few vintners in Umbria open to the public on a regular basis. Plus, if you love the wine (we suggest the white fruity Greccheto and the earthy Sagrantino), you're in luck; Caprai is one of the largest Umbrian wine exporters and distributes its goods in about two-dozen countries, from Australia to Brazil and Korea to the US. To reach the winery, follow the signs on the road towards Bevagna to Località Torre or Torre di Montefalco

On the road out of Bevagna heading towards Spoleto, stop by **Paolo Bea** (☎ 0742 37 81 28; www.paolobea.com; Loc. Cerrete 8; ⏰ Sun summer) for a true tasting experience. The family creates four special wines, which you can taste for €18 along with home-made bruschetta and crostini. It also sells its own olive oil and Parmesan. During the summer, a harp player entertains visitors on Sunday. The vineyard is also open when the owners are home and not busy.

turned this ancestral home into a hotel, as it felt a tad large. Now, guests in 34 unique guest rooms and suites can know what it feels like to sip champagne on one's own private balcony or bathe in an in-suite Jacuzzi tub under a frescoed ceiling. But it's the welcoming service that gains praise from guests the world over. Exit the SS3bis at Trevi/Montefalco and follow signs for Madonna della Stella, towards Montefalco.

Thirty metres from Montefalco's main entrance, **Villa Pambuffetti** (☎ 0742 37 94 17; www.villa pambuffetti.com; Viale della Vittoria 20; s €88-150, d €140-260, ste €160-200, all incl breakfast; ☒ Feb-Dec; **P** ✗ ✿) is another unique place for an overnight stop. Hippie nobility reigns over this country house. She, a chef; he, a sommelier – together, they run the 'shabby chic' noble villa. Each of the 15 rooms is decorated with antiques, used by the family before they turned the estate into a hotel in 1992. Alessandra's cooking courses are reason enough to stay, as all recipes are from her own cookbook.

The basic **Hotel Ristorante Ringhiera Umbra** (☎ 0742 37 91 66; www.ringhieraumbra.com; verziere@tiscali .it; Via Mameli 20; d €75, q €150, all incl breakfast) has a fantastic, inexpensive restaurant located in a cosy stone-and-brick cave, and serves excellent *strangozzi* with truffles and Sagrantino sauce.

SSIT buses (☎ 0742 67 07 47; www.spoletina.com) travel from Montefalco to Foligno (€3.20, 30 minutes, eight daily) and Perugia (€4.40, one hour, three daily). Buses go between Bevagna and Montefalco (€2.20 to €3.40, 20 to 40 minutes, five daily), some direct and others through Foligno.

Bevagna
pop 5023

If a visitor had only one day to spend in Umbria, Bevagna wouldn't be a bad choice. The town was once named the most beautiful village in Italy, and the townsfolk do seem a little happier here. Ancient city walls ring the main drag, Corso Matteotti, and everything listed is within about a 10-minute walk of the square, Piazza Silvestri. Bevagna began first as an Umbrian settlement, then became Etruscan and eventually a Roman municipium on the Via Flaminia. For visitors, Romanesque churches, *enoteche* and a dearth of tourists add to the charm.

The **Pro Loco tourist office** (☎ 0742 36 16 67; pbevagna@bcsnet.it; Piazza Silvestri 1; ☒ 9.30am-1pm &

2.30-7pm) can help with accommodation and wine-tasting. The **post office** (☎ 0742 36 15 68; Piazza Matteotti; ☒ 8.10am-1.25pm Mon-Sat) is on the next square. Parking just outside the city centre is free.

The **Pinacoteca Comunale** (☎ 0742 36 00 31; Corso Matteotti 70; adult/concession €5/2; ☒ 10.30am-1pm & 3-7pm summer, 10.30am-1pm & 3-5.30pm or 6pm Tue-Sun winter) features a rudimentary exhibit on local archaeology and ceramics.

The ticket price for the *pinacoteca* also includes entrance into the **Roman Mosaic Museum of Antiquities** (☎ 075 572 71 41; Via di Porta Guelfa; ☒ 10.30am-1pm & 3-4.30pm Tue-Sun), featuring a well-preserved tile floor from ancient Roman baths. There are also the remains of an old Roman theatre, and a Roman and medieval wall, plus a monastic winery.

At the end of June, Bevagna goes medieval with the **Festival of the Gaite**. For two days, the town goes back in time a few hundred years. Artisans give demonstrations on the crafts of the day – glass-blowing, candle-making, ironworks – dressed in period attire.

If you happen upon the area during the last third of August and fancy eating a mollusc or three, the little town of Cantalupo di Bevagna celebrates its **Sagra della Lumaca** (Festival of the Snail), with snail dishes cooked in every way imaginable (snail pasta, bruschetta with snail sauce, roasted snails, snail antipasti etc), as well as exhibits, dancing and general slug-related merriment. Accordingly, you'll find *lumache* (snails) on the menu at many restaurants (including Coccorone in Bevagna; see p346).

SLEEPING & EATING
Agriturismo/Camping Pian di Boccio (☎ 0742 36 01 64; www.piandiboccio.com; per person/car/child/tent €6.50/2.50/3.25/6, 2-/6-person apt €57/140; **P** ✿) This multifaceted camping ground has archery, a swimming pool and a pizzeria, and nine rustic but comfortable apartments that come with firewood, fully equipped kitchen and TV. Kids will love summer evenings, where they can dance, bowl or gather at special events with new international friends. The *agriturismo* produces its own olive oil, jam and tinned goods, and raises barnyard animals. You'll find it 4km southeast of Bevagna.

Enoteca and Locanda Piazza Onofri (☎ 0742 36 19 20, 335 718 89 03; www.enotecaonofri.it; Piazza Onofri 2; mini-apt €80-130; ☒ enoteca Thu-Tue) For one-stop shopping, the always cheerful Assù runs this delicious restaurant and good-value hotel in addition to their wine shop, La Bottega di Piazza Onofri. You only have to stumble upstairs after dinner to relax under arched stone windows, or feel free to cook up a light meal in your own kitchenette.

Ristorante Hotel L'Orto Degli Angeli (☎ 0742 36 09 67; www.ortoangeli.it; Via Dante Alighieri 1; r, ste & apt €220-350; P ⛶ 🖳) Try to peek at the hanging gardens of this prestigious residence and not want to spend a week. The hotel has had one of the most stunning historical renovations. The higher the room price, the more lavish the details: antique-laden sitting rooms, gold-trimmed canopies, stone or marble fireplaces, grotesque frescoed ceilings. The restaurant menu changes weekly, but you're guaranteed it will be Umbrian dishes made with local produce. The home-made *strangozzi* is truly excellent. The restaurant's closed on Wednesdays.

La Bottega di Piazza Onofri (☎ 339 374 57 05; 102 Corso Matteotti 102; meals €4-8; ⛤ 10.30-3.30pm & 6-9pm Thu-Tue Mar–mid-Jan) Head to this central location to enjoy a selection of home-made small meals served up by Assú of Enoteca and Locanda Piazza Onofri fame. She pours about a half-dozen tasting wines each day (purchased by the glass).

Coccorone (☎ 0742 37 95 35; Largo Tempestivi; €29; ⛤ Thu-Tue) Secretly hidden along a quiet side street, Coccorone has tables outside where you can enjoy the stone walkway. Bring out your adventurous side for the menu, heavy on game and unusual meats, such as *rabbit alla cacciatori* (Italian sauce with green peppers), pigeon and snails.

La Farfalla (Piazza Garibaldi 13a; ⛤ 8.30am-1pm & 3pm-midnight, Wed-Mon) Head here for your chance to try Sagrantino wine–flavoured gelato. You can also sample *cacio e pera* (sheep's milk cheese and pear) and *cannoli* (a type of pastry), which are all home-made by a jovial Sicilian family.

Getting There and Away

SSIT buses (☎ 0742 67 07 47; www.spoletina.com) head from Bevagna to near the train station in Foligno (€2.60, 20 minutes, six daily), where you can continue on to the north towards Perugia or to the south towards Spoleto. Buses travel between Bevagna and Montefalco (€2.20 to €3.40, 20 to 40 minutes, five daily), some are direct and others go through Foligno.

TREVI
pop 8125

Trevi has miraculously avoided any sort of bowing to Umbria's burgeoning tourist industry, and would feel downright foreign to anyone just coming from San Gimignano or Siena. Trevi allied itself with Perugia against Spoleto during the papal rule – it was a papal state until the Unification of Italy. It witnessed several exciting firsts: the first press association and the first pawn shop. Nowadays, you can actually hear the z-z-z-zip as it rolls itself up for siesta, and nary a local soul ventures out between 1pm and 4pm. The town calls itself a 'Slow City' (see the boxed text, p370), and residents pride themselves on its utter mellowness. Greenish-grey olive trees swathe every inch of hill-side around Trevi, and the olive oil here is reputedly some of the best in Italy.

The **Pro Loco** (☎ /fax 0742 78 11 50; www.protrevi .com; Piazza Mazzini 5; ⛤ 9am-1pm & 3.30-7pm) is run entirely by volunteers, so be warned you might find it closed sporadically.

Trevi was a theatre town, all the way back to Roman times. The **Teatro Clitunno** (☎ 0742 38 17 68; Piazza del Teatro) remains the town's most important gathering point. Remnants of concentric rings of a Mura Romana (Roman Wall) and a Mura Medievali (Medieval Wall) still encircle the historic centre of the town. The **Museo della Civiltá dell' Ulivo** (Olive Museum; ☎ 0742 33 22 22; ⛤ 10.30am-1pm & 3-6pm Tue-Sun summer, closed Tue-Thu winter) is a must-see while in the area, as it details the history of olive-oil production in Umbria for millennia. For something a little more contemporary, the **Flash Art Museum** (☎ 0742 38 19 78; Palazzo Luncarini; free admission; ⛤ 4-7pm Tue-Fri) has a funky collection of multimedia modern art.

Antica Dimora alla Rocca (☎ 0742 38 54 01; www .hotelallarocca.it; Piazza della Rocca 1; s €70-122, d €85-174, ste €176-251, all incl breakfast; P ⛶ 🖳) is a breathtakingly decorated hotel, with palatial furnishings and frescoed hallways. It feels palatial for a reason: the hotel was actually built in the 1500s as a prince's palace. Check the website to get a 20% (or more) midweek discount.

Albergo Ristorante Il Terziere (☎ 0742 78 359; www.ilterziere.com; Via Coste 1; s €50-65, d €70-100, all incl breakfast; P 🖳), a beautiful hotel and restaurant outside the city centre, is just behind the parking area in Piazza Garibaldi. An impressive upgrade makes four of the 12 rooms feel modern rather than austere, with DSL and Sky TV in each room. At the restaurant (open Thursday to Tuesday), be sure to try the gnocchi in Sagrantino sauce and its signature home-made *tagliate* pasta.

Named after its location as the old post office, **La Vecchia Posta** (☎ 0742 38 54 01, rooms 333 392 47 37; www.lavecchiaposta.net; Piazza Mazzini 14; s €35-50, d €50-70, ste €70-90) is a charming restaurant (meals €27, open Friday to Wednesday) with a few rooms to let. The *strangozzi* and truffles or chicken in porcini cream should satisfy just about any taste. The candied pear dessert with mint and chocolate sauce is legendary.

Maggiolini (☎ 0742 38 15 34; Via San Francesco 20; meals €26), a beautiful restaurant, is best in summer when you can dine alfresco on several reasonably priced truffle dishes and home-made pasta.

Bus services to Trevi are spotty, so take the train, as it is conveniently located along the main line to Perugia (€3.05, one hour, hourly), Assisi (€1.80, 30 minutes, hourly) and Spoleto (€1.55, 15 minutes, hourly).

FOLIGNO
pop 54,381

If you've come to Foligno, you've landed in the centre of the universe…especially if you decide to play billiards. Although Foligno is a commercial city now and has lost some of its charm and history to industry (and, in 1997, to a devastating earthquake), it is a transport hub with good shopping, an excellent youth hostel and a restaurant that requires a visit.

At the **tourist office** (☎ 0742 35 44 59; www.comune .foligno.pg.it/cultura/servizioturistico in Italian; Corso Cavour 126; ☯ 9am-1pm & 4-7pm Mon-Sat, 9am-1pm Sun), no-one speaks English, but there's information behind the desk for Foligno, as well as for the surrounding towns of Bevagna, Gualdo Cattaneo, Montefalco, Spello and Trevi. It's located near the Porta Romana.

The cathedral is in Piazza della Repubblica, in which St Feliciano is buried. The building dates from the 12th century and is a hodgepodge of many architectural styles, from Roman-Gothic to 16th-century Renaissance additions. There are some stunning 16th-century Vespasiano Strada frescoes. In the same square is the worthwhile **Palazzo Trinci** (☎ 0742 35 07 34; admission free; ☯ 10am-7pm Tue-Sun), which has some paintings and frescoes from the 15th century.

The Trinci family was part of the *seigniories* (feudal lordships), which ruled over much of

papal-controlled Umbria in the later medieval period. (You'll notice buildings all over Umbria named after these families: the Baglionis in Perugia or the Vitellis in Città di Castello.) The Trincis paid Ottaviano Nelli to decorate their palace – although they didn't score like the Vitellis in Città di Castello, with Raphael and Giorgio Vasari. There's a small museum (descriptions in Italian only) in the palazzo, which features some of the historic costumes you'd find at the Quintana festival.

If you're in the area during the beginning of June or in September, the main festival is **La Giostra della Quintana** (☎ 0742 35 40 00; www.quintana it), a medieval equestrian tournament reinvented from the 1400s. Ten neighbourhoods vie against each other in a friendly jousting competition complete with elaborate velvet-and-lace traditional costumes, and dishes from the 15th century.

Ostello Pierantoni (☎ 0742 34 25 66; www.ostel lionline.com in Italian; Via Pierantoni 23; dm/f/s incl breakfast €15/17/22; ☯ reception 7am-noon & 2pm-midnight), only 500m from the train station, is a full-service hostel with 199 beds, washer/dryer, internet facilities, an outdoor garden, bike rental, access for people with disabilities and a restaurant. It feels like a palace with its frescoed, echo-high ceilings, but it was actually a monastery for some extremely comfortable monks.

ourpick Il Bacco Felice (☎ 0742 34 10 19; Via Garibaldi 73; meals €0-60; ☯ Tue-Sun) The walls are held up by graffiti, books and bottles, but this neighbourhood joint has reached a mythic level fitting for a town that calls itself 'the centre of the universe'. The godhead figure, then, is Salvatore Denaro (p72), the chef and owner who will turn away anyone on a mobile phone or to whom he takes a disliking. Tourists Salvatore dislikes often subsidise the meals of those he does, so check your bill at the end to find out how you measured up. Don't worry for lack of a menu; diners might find fava beans from his garden and organic locally grown pork one day and Chianina beef the next.

Il Barbablu (☎ 0742 35 46 97; Via Umberto I 46; pizza slice €1) On the way to the hostel is this fantastic cheap pizza place. Try the corn or zucchini.

Getting There & Away

Many public transport users will go through Foligno at some point. If you arrive by train and are switching to a bus, head out of the train station down Viale Mezzetti. The main bus terminal is about 50m to your left. To get to Trevi, head about 40m further to the grandiose Porta Romana. You can buy tickets for either location at the Blu Bar, next to the petrol station at the bus terminal. There are hourly trains to Perugia (€2.55, 40 minutes) and Assisi (€1.55, 15 minutes).

GUBBIO

pop 32,622

While most of Umbria feels soft and rounded by the millennia, Gubbio is angular, sober and imposing. Perched along the steep slopes of Monte Ingino, the Gothic buildings wend their way up the hill towards Umbria's closest thing to an amusement park ride, its open-air funicular. During Christmas time, the side of the mountain becomes the world's largest Christmas tree.

Gubbio is famous for its Eugubine Tablets, which date from 300 to 100 BC and constitute the best existing example of ancient Umbrian script. An important ally of the Roman Empire and a key stop on the Via Flaminia, the town declined during the Saracen invasions. In the 14th century it fell into the hands of the Montefeltro family of Urbino and was later incorporated into the Papal States.

Orientation

The city is small and easy to explore. The immense traffic circle known as the Piazza Quaranta Martiri, at the base of the hill, is where buses to the city terminate, and it also has a large car park. The square was named in honour of 40 local people who were killed by the Nazis in 1944 in reprisal for partisan activities. From here it is a short, if somewhat steep, walk up Via della Repubblica to the main square, Piazza Grande, also known as the Piazza della Signoria. Or, you can take the lift from the Piazza del Podestà to the Palazzo Ducale and the cathedral. Corso Garibaldi and Piazza Oderisi are to your right as you head up the hill.

Information

Hospital (Ospedale Civile; ☎ 0 75 923 91; Piazza Quaranta Martiri) Will move in 2009 but the phone number will remain the same.

Internet Point (☎ 075 927 74 30; Via Perugina 32; per hr €3; ☼ 9am-1.30pm & 3.30-7.30pm Tue-Sat, 3.30-8pm Sun) Phone also available for €0.15 to US, UK and most of Europe; €0.30 to Australia.

Police station (☎ 075 927 37 70; Via Mazzatinti)

Post office (☎ 075 927 39 25; Via Cairoli 11; ☼ 8am-6.30pm Mon-Fri, 8am-12.30pm Sat)

Tourist office (☎ 075 922 06 93; info@iat.gubbio.pg.it; www.gubbio-altochiascio.umbria2000.it; Via della Repubblica 2; ☼ 8am-2pm & 3-6pm Mon-Fri, 9am-1pm & 3-6pm Sat, 9.30am-12.30pm & 3-6pm Sun & holidays)

Sights

Gubbio's most impressive buildings look out over Piazza Grande, where the heart of the Corsa dei Ceri event takes place.

PIAZZA GRANDE

The piazza is dominated above all by the 14th-century **Palazzo dei Consoli**, attributed to Gattapone. The crenellated façade and tower can be seen from all over the town. The building houses the **Museo Civico** (☎ 075 927 42 98; Piazza Grande; adult/concession incl gallery €4/2.50; ☼ 10am-1pm & 3-6pm Apr-Oct, 10am-1pm & 2-5pm Nov-Mar), which displays the Eugubian Tablets, discovered in 1444. The seven bronze tablets are the main source for research into the ancient Umbrian language. Upstairs is a picture gallery featuring works from the Gubbian school. Across the square is the **Palazzo del Podestà**, also known as the Palazzo Pretorio, built along similar lines to its grander counterpart. Now the city's active town hall, the impressive vaulted ceilings might be peeked at if you ask nicely.

FUNIVIA COLLE ELETTO

Although the **Basilica di Sant'Ubaldo** – where you'll find the body of St Ubaldo, the 12th-century bishop of Gubbio – is a perfectly lovely church, the adventure is in the getting there. Take the **Funivia Colle Eletto** (☎ 075 922 11 99; adult/child return €5/4; ☼ 9am-8pm Jul-Aug, 9.30am or 10am-1.15pm & 2.30-5.30pm or 7pm Mar-Jun, Sep & Oct, 10am-1.15pm & 2.30-5pm Thu-Tue Nov-Feb), where your first rule is to believe the man when he tells you to stand on the dot. He will then throw you into a moving metal contraption that looks frighteningly like an open-topped human birdcage. You're whisked instantly away on a cable car that looks more like a precarious ski lift, dangling dozens of metres above a rocky hill (bring a camera, but hold tight). The ride up is as frightening as it is utterly beautiful. There's a restaurant on top of the hill and the aforementioned church, but the nicest way to spend the day is to bring a picnic and have a wander.

Just below the Funivia Colle Eletto is the **Museo della Ceramica a Lustro e Torre Medioevale**

di Porta Romana (☎ 075 922 11 99; Via Dante 24; admission €2.50; ☺ 10.30am-1pm & 3.30-7pm). The a lustro ceramic style has its origins in 11th-century Muslim Spain. On the 2nd floor, ceramics from prehistoric times share space with medieval and Renaissance pieces. There's also a collection of crossbows from the 18th century, some of which have a target range as far as 50m. Check out the really un-fun-looking chastity belt on the 4th floor and appreciate the fact that you are alive today instead of 300 years ago.

VIA FEDERICO DA MONTEFELTRO

Walk up Via Federico da Montefeltro (also called Via Ducale or Via della Cattedrale) to a triumvirate of ancientness. The 13th-century

pink **cathedral** (Via Federico da Montefeltro; donations welcome; ☺ 10am-5pm), with a fine 12th-century stained-glass window and a fresco attributed to Bernardino Pinturicchio. Opposite, the 15th-century **Palazzo Ducale** (☎ 075 927 58 72; Via Federico da Montefeltro; adult/concession €2/1; ☺ 9am-7.30pm Tue-Fri & Sun, 9am-10.30pm Sat) was built by the Duke of Montefeltro family as a scaled-down version of their grand palazzo in Urbino; its walls hide an impressive Renaissance courtyard. Next door is the **Museo Diocesano** (☎ 075 922 09 04; Via Federico da Montefeltro; adult/concession €5/2.50; ☺ 10am-7pm Mon-Sat summer, 10am-6pm Mon-Sat winter, 10am-6pm Sun & holidays year-round), a winding homage to Gubbio's medieval history.

Perugia's Fra Bevignate is said to have designed the **Chiesa di San Francesco** (Piazza Quaranta

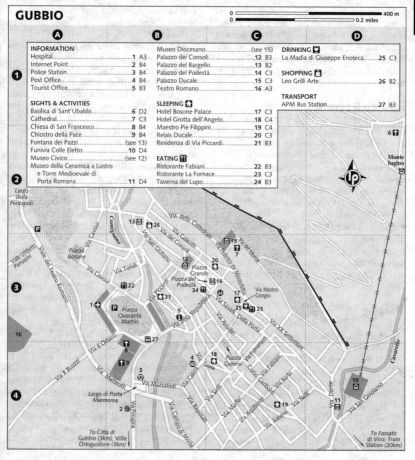

GUBBIO

0 — 400 m
0 — 0.2 miles

INFORMATION
Hospital.................................**1** A3
Internet Point.......................**2** B4
Police Station.......................**3** B4
Post Office............................**4** B4
Tourist Office.......................**5** B3

SIGHTS & ACTIVITIES
Basilica di Sant'Ubaldo.........**6** D2
Cathedral..............................**7** C3
Chiesa di San Francesco.......**8** B4
Chiostro della Pace...............**9** B4
Fontana dei Pazzi...........(see 13)
Funivia Colle Eletto.............**10** D4
Museo Civico.................(see 12)
Museo della Ceramica a Lustro
    e Torre Medioevale di
    Porta Romana...............**11** D4

Museo Diocesano...........(see 15)
Palazzo dei Consoli.............**12** B3
Palazzo del Bargello............**13** B2
Palazzo del Podestà............**14** C3
Palazzo Ducale....................**15** C3
Teatro Romano....................**16** A3

SLEEPING 🛏
Hotel Bosone Palace............**17** C3
Hotel Grotta dell'Angelo......**18** C4
Maestro Pie Filippini...........**19** C4
Relais Ducale.......................**20** C3
Residenza di Via Piccardi.....**21** B3

EATING 🍴
Ristorante Fabiani...............**22** B3
Ristorante La Fornace.........**23** C3
Taverna del Lupo................**24** B3

DRINKING 🍷
La Madia di Giuseppe Enoteca.......**25** C3

SHOPPING 🛍
Leo Grilli Arte.....................**26** B2

TRANSPORT
APM Bus Station..................**27** B3

Martiri; 7.15am-noon & 3.30-7.30pm). It features impressive frescoes by local artist Ottaviano Nelli. Built in a simple Gothic style in the 13th century, it has an impressive rose window. Wander into the **Chiostro della Pace** (Cloister of Peace) in the adjoining convent to view some ancient mosaics and stroll around the peaceful garden.

In the western end of the medieval section is the 13th-century **Palazzo del Bargello**, the city's medieval police station and prison. In front of it is the **Fontana dei Pazzi** (Fountain of Lunatics), so-named because of a belief that if you walk around it three times, you will go mad. On summer weekends the number of tourists actually carrying out this bizarre ritual is indeed cause for concern about their collective sanity.

Southwest of Piazza Quaranta Martiri, off Viale del Teatro Romano, are the overgrown remains of a 1st-century-AD **Teatro Romano** (075 922 09 22; admission free; 8.30am-7.30pm Apr-Sep, 8am-1.30pm Oct-Mar). In the summer, check with the tourist office about outdoor concerts held here.

Festivals & Events

Gubbio is host to many colourful festivals:
Corsa dei Ceri (Candles Race) A centuries-old event held each year on 15 May to commemorate the city's patron saint, Sant'Ubaldo. It starts at 5.30am and involves three teams, each carrying a *cero* (these 'candles' are massive wooden pillars weighing about 400kg, each bearing a statue of a 'rival' saint) and racing through the city's streets. This is one of Italy's liveliest festivals and has put Gubbio on the map.
Palio della Balestra Held on the last Sunday in May, this annual an archery competition involves medieval crossbows, in which Gubbio competes with its neighbour San Sepolcro. The festival carries over all through the year in tourist shops, which are alive with crossbow parapher-nalia.

Sleeping

The tourist office has an extremely thorough list of all accommodation options that are available throughout the area.

Città di Gubbio & Villa Ortoguidone (075 927 20 37; www.gubbiocamping.com; Loc. Ortoguidone 49; per person €5.50-9, tent €7-9, car €2.50, 2-/4-person apt €30-100; Easter-Sep;) In addition to the full-service four-star camping ground, there are also stunning apartments in an old stone manor house with TV, beautiful wooden furnishings and private bathroom. July and August vis-

its require a one-week stay. From the SS298, follow the signs for 3km to 'Agriclub Villa Ortoguidone'.

Maestro Pie Filippini (075 927 37 68; Corso Garibaldi 100; per person €20) Six basic rooms serve up to 16 guests in this religious accommodation. A few have bathtubs, and there's an open salon for reading. There's a minimum two-night stay and 10.30pm curfew, and advance reservations are required.

Residenza di Via Piccardi (075 927 61 08; e.biagiotto@tiscali.it; Via Piccardi 12; s/d/mini-apt incl breakfast €30/55/60; closed 2 weeks in Feb) Step through the arched gate into the romantic garden of this period residence. Share an amorous breakfast for two in the garden or cook up a simple dinner in the mini-apartment's kitchenette. Family owned, the characteristically medieval stone building has cosy rooms decorated in cheery florals with all the basic comforts. Great value.

Ristorante Hotel Grotta dell'Angelo (075 927 17 47; www.grottadellangelo.it; Via Gioia 47; s €38-42, d €55-60; closed 2 weeks in Jan) While it is mostly a popular restaurant with all sorts of truffle dishes and a beautiful garden, the Grotta dell'Angelo also serves up a few basic rooms for rent. Spotlessly clean and pin-drop quiet at night, the hotel is owned by a multigenerational family, so it openly welcomes guests with small children.

Hotel Bosone Palace (075 922 06 88; www.men carelligroup.com; Via XX Settembre 22; s €80-90, d €110-140, f €160-190, ste €184-230, all incl breakfast;) Fancy a fresco with your breakfast? How about staying in a room once frequented by Dante Alighieri? The patrician Bosone family enjoyed Dante as a guest several times. The place went through a complete renovation in 2005 to move from three-star to four-star category, deservedly so. All rooms have minibar, satellite TV and phone in the bathroom, and many have gorgeous views of the surrounding valley. For the experience of a lifetime, think about getting an upgrade to a Renaissance Suite.

Relais Ducale (075 922 01 57; www.mencarelligroup .com; Via Galeotti 19; s €110-130, d €155-178, ste €230-265, all incl breakfast;) Owned by the same savvy group that runs the Bosone Palace, the Relais is a step up – literally, as it's several storeys straight up from the Piazza Grande – and lavishly, as it's a fully outfitted, grand four-star hotel. Smallish rooms are detailed with the finest additions – satellite TV and towel warmers, and sheets so warm and snugly that you'd better set an alarm, as you're liable to sleep through the decked-out buffet breakfast. The junior suite dates back to the 15th century, with a balcony that may drive one to look for boiling oil to pour over. Near this suite is where you'll find the secret stone passageway that was used by guests of the Duke of Montefeltro – it helped them avoid the above-ground riffraff as they made their way to the palace.

Eating

Ristorante Fabiani (☎ 075 927 46 39; Piazza Quaranta Martiri 26; meals €27; Wed-Mon) A fabulous spot to sit on the back patio and enjoy the garden for a few hours. The selection here is vast, and it offers a rotating €15 tourist menu or a €20 *menù gastronomico* of whatever is in season. Stop in on Thursday or Friday for its fish specials.

our pick **Ristorante La Fornace di Mastro Giorgio** (☎ 075 922 18 36; Via Mastro Giorgio 2; meals €40; Wed-Mon) Named after Gubbio's most famous medieval ceramicist (whose oven still graces one of the restaurant's ancient walls), Mastro Giorgio is our favourite place for a special occasion (not just for the 500-item wine list, either). The seasonal menu includes modern takes on traditional dishes: venison *carpaccio* wrapped with salt, olive oil and asparagus, and its signature dish, a *stinco* (veal shank) stewed to falling-off-the-bone perfection.

Taverna del Lupo (☎ 075 927 43 68; Via Ansidei 21; meals €40; Tue-Sun) Il Lupo was the wolf that St Francis domesticated, a wolf that supposedly came back to this restaurant to dine. He made an excellent choice. The atmosphere is sophisticated, if a bit stiff, and diners will feel more comfortable smartly dressed. Most ingredients are locally produced in the surrounding Apennines, including its cheese, truffles and olive oil. Set aside at least two hours for a meal.

Drinking

La Madia di Giuseppe Enoteca (☎ 075 922 18 36; Via Mastro Giorgio 2; 10am-midnight Thu-Mon, Wed dinner) Fairly new on the scene in Gubbio is this stone-walled *enoteca*, one of the rare locations in Umbria where guests can sample several different glasses of wine. But it is not just for drinking – beautiful plates of nibbles (€5 to €14) such as prosciutto and cheeses, bruschette and sweets grace the café tables. What's more: they sell a selection of local goods for you to take away and enjoy, too.

Shopping

Leo Grilli Arte (☎ 075 922 22 72; Via dei Consoli 78; 9.30am-1pm & 3-7pm Tue-Sun) In the Middle Ages, ceramics were one of Gubbio's main sources of income and there are some fabulous contemporary samples on sale in this crumbly 15th-century mansion.

Getting There & Around

APM (☎ 800 51 21 41) buses run to Perugia (€4.30, one hour and 10 minutes, 10 daily), Gualdo Tadino (€2.60, 50 minutes, 10 daily) and Umbertide (€3, 50 minutes, three daily). Buses depart from Piazza Quaranta Martiri.

The closest train station is at Fossato di Vico, about 18km southeast of the city. Hourly APM buses connect the station with Gubbio (€2.60, 30 minutes). From Fossato di Vico, hourly trains take about 30 minutes to Foligno (€2.55), where you can switch for other cities, including Perugia (€4.50, 1½ hours, hourly).

By car or motorcycle, take the SS298 from Perugia or the SS76 from Ancona, and follow the signs. Parking in the large car park in Piazza Quaranta Martiri costs €0.80 per hour.

Walking is the best way to get around, but APM buses connect Piazza Quaranta Martiri with the funicular station and most main sights.

AROUND GUBBIO

South on the SS3, on the way from Parco Regionale del Monte Cucco, **Gualdo Tadino** is a fairly industrial town. Although it doesn't offer much in the way of tourist attractions, it does have the best-named site: the 13th-century **Rocca Flea**, a former fortress that now houses art exhibits. One of the town's major industrial outputs is ceramics; in August it celebrates a month-long exhibition of ceramics. Slightly more enticing than its neighbour Gualdo Tadino, **Nocera Umbra** is mostly known for its spring water, and still has a few vestiges from the past. Its most notable monument is the prominent **Torre dei Trinci**, a medieval tower that was built by the *seigniory* Trinci family.

PARCO REGIONALE DEL MONTE CUCCO

East of Gubbio, this park is a haven for outdoor activities and is dotted with caves, many of which can be explored. It is well set up for walkers, rock climbers and horse riders, and has many hotels and *rifugi* (mountain huts).

Costacciaro, accessible by bus from Gubbio (€1.95, 30 minutes) via Scheggia or Fossato di Vico, is a good base for exploring the area and is the starting point for a walk to the summit of **Monte Cucco** (1566m).

Monte Cucco is a fantastic place to go caving or spelunking. The Monte Cucco karst system is the largest in Italy and the fifth-deepest in the world (922m). Sinkholes, wells and dolines create unique geological formations and lush habitats for various species of birds and plants.

Club Alpino Italiano (CAI) produces a walking map *Carta dei Sentieri Massiccio del Monte Cucco* (€12), for sale in local bookshops and newsagents. The free *Monte Cucco Park: Country Walks through History* booklet is available in English at *rifugi* and tourist offices throughout Umbria. Use this as a guide to the best of Umbria's nature and history. The booklet describes in detail 11 walks in the area that take you through some of Umbria's most picturesque terrain, more alpinelike than the typical rolling hillside. The guides detail the estimated time needed while walking at a good pace, the presence of water sources on the trail and a thorough map of each route (most take at least four hours and are far from civilisation, so take lots of water and emergency supplies). If you don't have your walking gear, Tour 6 is a 62km driving route through ancient abbeys and monasteries in the region.

The **Centro Escursionistico Naturalistico Speleologico** (☎ 075 917 04 00; www.cens.it in Italian; Via Calcinaro 7A, Costacciaro) can help with information about exploring local caves, walking and mountain-bike routes. You can also get information at the **park office** (☎ 075 917 73 26; parco .montecucco@libero.it; Via Matteotti 52, Villa Anita, Sigillo). Online, look for information at www.parks .it/parco.monte.cucco.

The **Camping Rio Verde** (☎ 075 917 01 38; www.camp ingrioverde.it in Italian; per adult/car/child/tent €5/2.50/3/4.50) camping ground, 3km west of Costacciaro, offers horse riding (€13 per hour, in summer), rock climbing and caving. Many *agriturismo* establishments in the area can also arrange horse riding. Be warned that if you come here on a weekend in August, the rates sometimes more than quintuple. A good mountain inn is the **Rifugio Escursionistico Dal Lepre** (☎ /fax 075 917 77 33; Pian del Monte, Sigillo, Montecucco; per person incl breakfast €15), which also features a decent restaurant.

It is possible to hire mountain bikes at the **Coop Arte e Natura** (☎ 075 917 07 40; Via Stazione 2)

in the village of Fossato di Vico, about 8km southeast of Costacciaro.

CITTÀ DI CASTELLO
pop 38,476

Most travellers to Umbria don't make it terribly far north of Perugia, but those who do will be rewarded with the area known as Museum Valley for its extraordinary collection of art and history. The area surrounds the Tiber River, so is known as the Alta Valle di Tevere, and the history is laid on thick, especially in the largest and most central town: Città di Castello.

The town is surrounded by some pretty awful suburbs, but if you can look past this, it has a beautiful historic centre, many grand buildings and the second-most important art museum in Umbria after the Galleria Nazionale dell'Umbria (p322) in Perugia.

Note: don't come to Città di Castello on a Monday. Most museums are closed, as are many restaurants.

History

Known as Tifernum Tiberium in the Roman era, Castrum Felicitatis (Town of Happiness) in the medieval period and Città di Castello today, it actually has neither a castle nor is a city. The town was economically depressed until the 1960s, but is now known for its thriving paper, book, ironworks and furniture industries. The town's favourite son is Alberto Burri, and two galleries proudly display much of his lifetime's work. (The town's current favourite daughter is actress Monica Bellucci.)

Orientation

The entire town, including its historic centre, is within a valley, so it's almost all on flat ground and easily walkable (a rarity in Umbrian towns). Apart from the cobblestones, people using wheelchairs should have few problems getting around here.

From the train station, walk straight ahead for 200m. Turn right under Porta Santa Maria Maggiore and take Corso Vittorio Emanuele to Piazza Matteotti. Driving is mostly forbidden in the walled city, but there's plenty of free parking just outside the walls, mostly around Porta San Giacomo and Piazza Garibaldi.

Information
BOOKSHOPS

Libreria Paci (☎ 075 855 43 41; Piazza Matteotti 2; ☷ 9am-1pm & 4.30-8pm, Tue-Sat) Has English- and

German-language books, as well as a growing collection of maps and Lonely Planet titles.

EMERGENCY
Police station (☎ 075 852 92 22; Piazza Garibaldi)

INTERNET ACCESS
Internet Point (☎ 348 398 55 753; Via Mazzini 8;

per hr €1.50; 🕑 8am-11pm) Phone calls to the US, UK or Australia cost €0.15 per minute, €0.25 to mobile phones.

INTERNET RESOURCES
cdcnet (www.cdcnet.net) This is the official *comune* (city-state) site. It contains English-language sections on history and art.

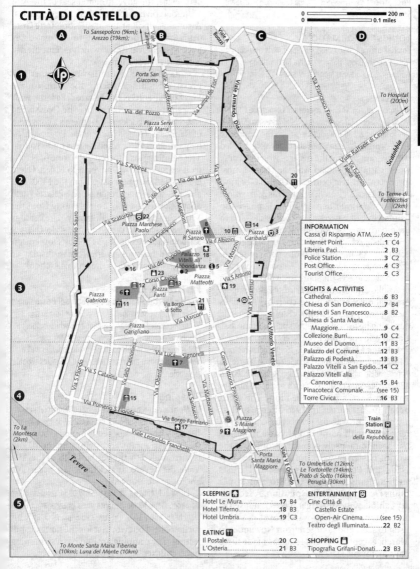

CITTÀ DI CASTELLO

INFORMATION
Cassa di Risparmio ATM	(see 5)
Internet Point	**1** C4
Libreria Paci	**2** B3
Police Station	**3** C2
Post Office	**4** C3
Tourist Office	**5** C3

SIGHTS & ACTIVITIES
Cathedral	**6** B3
Chiesa di San Domenico	**7** B4
Chiesa di San Francesco	**8** B2
Chiesa di Santa Maria Maggiore	**9** C4
Collezione Burri	**10** C2
Museo del Duomo	**11** B3
Palazzo del Comune	**12** B3
Palazzo di Podestà	**13** B3
Palazzo Vitelli a San Egidio	**14** C2
Palazzo Vitelli alla Cannoniera	**15** B4
Pinacoteca Comunale	(see 15)
Torre Civica	**16** B3

SLEEPING
Hotel Le Mura	**17** B4
Hotel Tiferno	**18** B3
Hotel Umbria	**19** C3

EATING
Il Postale	**20** C2
L'Osteria	**21** B3

ENTERTAINMENT
Cine Città di Castello Open-Air Cinema	(see 15)
Teatro degli Illuminata	**22** B2

SHOPPING
Tipografia Grifani-Donati	**23** B3

NORTHERN UMBRIA

MEDICAL SERVICES
Hospital (☎ 075 8 50 91; Via Angelini)

MONEY
Cassa di Risparmio (Piazza Matteotti 3a) This bank's ATM is the most convenient, to the left of the tourist office.

POST
Post office (☎ 075 855 3529; Via Gramsci; ⊗ 8.15am-5pm)

TOURIST INFORMATION
Tourist office (☎ 075 855 49 22; info@iat.citta-di-castello.pg.it; Logge Bufalini, Piazza Matteotti; ⊗ 9am-1.30pm & 3.30-6.30pm Mon-Sat, 9.30am-12.30pm Sun)

Sights

The collection at the **Pinacoteca Comunale** (☎ 075 855 42 02; Via della Cannoniera; adult/child/concession €5/1.50/3; ⊗ 10am-1pm & 2.30-6.30pm, Mon-Sat), in the imposing 15th-century **Palazzo Vitelli alla Cannoniera**, is filled with paintings from the masters who lived here when Città di Castello was the second most important artistic centre in Umbria, behind Perugia. Luca Signorelli painted his *Martyrdom of Saint Sebastian* here in 1498. Raphael also painted in Città; two of his works still stand in the *pinacoteca*. Ask for the information booklet in English, which will guide you through the paintings, giving explanations and context to the more prominent works. A cool astrological fresco cycle graces the staircase, with depictions of Apollo and the muses, erudites and emperors, seahorses and winged cherubs. The halls include wall frescoes from Cristoforo Gherardi, depicting historical subjects, such as Hannibal, Caesar and Alexander the Great.

Collezione Burri (☎ 075 855 46 49; Palazzo Albizzini, Via Albizzini 1, secondary exhibit at Ex Seccatoi del Tabacco, Via Pierucci; adult/child/concession €5/2/3; ⊗ 9am-12.30pm & 2.30-6pm Tue-Sat, 10.30am-12.30pm & 3-6pm Sun) houses Alberto Burri's main collection. The artist began his art career in 1946 after a stint as a prisoner of war in Texas. His contemporary work with paint and physical materials has been immensely popular throughout the world. His early work influenced the New Dada and Pop Art movements, and artists such as Rauschenberg, Christo and Jasper Johns credit him as an inspiration. A secondary exhibit of mostly larger pieces is housed in an old tobacco-drying warehouse – a site in itself to see – and is closed from November to March, except by special requests made three days in advance.

Not much remains of the original Romanesque **cathedral**, but the building houses some treasures. **Museo del Duomo** (Museo Capitolare; ☎ 075 855 47 05; Piazza Gabriotti 3\a; adult/child/concession €5/2/3; ⊗ 9.30am-1pm & 2.30-7pm Tue-Sun summer, 10am-1pm & 2.30-6.30pm Tue-Sun winter) holds the most impressive collection of sacred artefacts in all of Umbria. In the same building is the **Palazzo del Comune**, the governmental seat of the Alte Valle del Tevere for the past few centuries. Also take a look at the statuesque **Torre Civica** (Piazza Gabriotti), the city's bell tower that dates back to medieval times, which is temporarily closed for renovation.

Città di Castello also has many other impressive buildings. Facing the main square Piazza Matteotti is the **Palazzo di Podestà**, with a façade by Nicola Barbioni. The **Chiesa di San Francesco** dates back to 1291; there's a copy here of Raphael's *The Marriage of the Virgin*, which he painted in Città when he was quite young. The painting was a forced gift to one of Napoleon's generals, who moved it to Milan. **Chiesa di Santa Maria Maggiore** dates from the 1400s and also has some fine frescoes. The **Palazzo Vitelli a San Egidio** is a stately home, dating from the 1500s, built by the Vitelli family. The ceilings feature frescoes in the grotesque style. **Chiesa di San Domenico** was built in 1271 by Domenican friars and features an impressive display of frescoes by painters in the Umbria school.

Festivals & Events

Mostra Mercato Tartufo e Prodotti del Bosco During the first week in November, the town plays host to this festival dedicated to the area's ubiquitous white truffle. Farmers and growers bring every type of truffle product that is imaginable to this epicurean trade show, as well as honey, mushrooms and many other local delicacies avaiable to sample.

Sleeping

La Montesca (☎ 075 855 85 66; Loc. Montesca; per person €6.50-8, per tent €6-6.50, per car €2.50-3; ⊗ May-Sep; P ⊠) This fully stocked camping ground has its own restaurant and swimming pool, and is surrounded by the verdant hills of the Alta Valle del Tevere. It is wheelchair accessible and dogs are allowed.

Luna del Monte (☎ /fax 075 857 00 54; camping@tline.net; Voc S Pietro 10, Monte Santa Maria Tiberina; adult/child/car/tent €6/4.50/2.50/6; ⊗ Jun–mid-Sep; P ⊠) A bit further afield but worth it for the fantastic hill setting. The camping ground has a swimming pool, children's playground and bocce.

WHERE MOTHER EARTH WOULD STAY

ourpick **Agriturismo/B&B Le Tortorelle** (☎ 075 941 09 49, in English 347 975 4467; www.letortorelle
.it in Italian; Loc. Molino Vitelli 180, Umbertide; per person incl breakfast €40; P ⓧ) It means 'the turtle
doves', and you will most certainly find peace here. The iron gates lead you to this small family-
run farm specialising in the production of wheat, aloe, herbs and organic salves. You can either
volunteer in exchange for room and board as part of the World-wide Opportunities on Organic
Farms (WWOOF – see www.wwoof.org) programme or chill out as a guest. Learn to make organic
pasta, wine or cheese, or luck out by arriving in time for a pizza from the outdoor wood-fired
brick oven. Teresa and Aldo will pick you up at the train station in Umbertide, on the Sansepolcro
line between Perugia and Città di Castello. See also p312.

Hotel Umbria (☎ 075 855 49 25; www.hotelumbria
.net in Italian; Via S Antonio 6; s/d incl breakfast €35/55) The
least expensive hotel within the city walls,
Hotel Umbria is a fairly charming place to
spend the night and is well located. All rooms
have bathrooms with showers, satellite TV
and IDD telephone. Phone ahead, as it sometimes hosts raucous school groups.

Hotel Le Mura (☎ 075 852 10 70; www.hotel lemura
.it; Via Borgo Farinario 24; s/d incl breakfast €48/80; ⓧ ▢)
Located along the ancient city walls, this mod-
ernist hotel isn't the most charming, as it caters to both business and leisure travellers. It
does offer an array of comforts – satellite TV,
internet access (€0.50 per 30 minutes), minibar, hairdryer, king-sized bed and a rather
good restaurant.

Terme di Fontecchio (☎ 075 852 06 14; www.ter
medifontecchio.it; Loc. Fontecchio 4; hotel s €52-60, d €74-90,
hermitage s incl breakfast €150-170, d €175-200; P ⓧ ⓧ)
This spa resort has a well-priced hotel on its
expansive park grounds, two restaurants, a
pizzeria and a seven-room hermitage-cum-
hotel, all within a few kilometres of Città di
Castello. The hotel has 90 modern rooms with
internet access, Sky TV, minibars and firm
mattresses. The hermitage feels a world way,
as ancient stone walls coexist with elegant
antiques and low oak-beamed ceilings. The
'well-being centre' offers single-session treatments or day- or week-long curative retreats
filled with shiatsu massage, therapeutic mud
baths and thermal pool gymnastics. There's
a two-night minimum booking, with a one-
week minimum in August.

Hotel Tiferno (☎ 075 855 03 31; www.hoteltiferno.it
in Italian; Piazza R Sanzio 13; s €95, d €156, all incl breakfast;
P ⓧ ▢) Opened in 1985, this is one of Città
di Castello's top hotels. The building was a
monastery for the nearby Chiesa di San Francesco, then became a palace in the 17th century and is now a four-star hotel. Rooms still
include period details of the building's past
lives but have been modernised with artwork
by Burri. Each room has a hairdryer, minibar
and satellite TV, and has been soundproofed.
Room service is offered.

Eating

L'Osteria (☎ 075 855 69 95; Via Borgo di Sotto; mains
€5.50-13.50) Nothing fancy, but good typical
Umbrian food. Friday features fish specialities. Try the asparagus when it's in season (late
spring to early summer).

Il Postale (☎ 075 852 13 56; Via Raffaele di Cesare 8; 3-
course menu €30-40; ☿ Tue-Fri, Sat night, Sun) If there's
such a thing as *nouvelle* Umbrian cuisine, this
is the place to try it. The husband and wife
team at Il Postale serves dishes such as duck
with fennel compote, or carp with hazelnuts.
Specialities include its lentil dishes and, of
course, truffles.

Entertainment

Teatro degli Illuminata (☎ 075 855 50 91; Via dei Fucci)
This civic theatre features musicals and all
kinds of live-arts performances.

Cine Città di Castello Estate (☎ 075 852 92 49; adult/
child €5/4) During the summer, the *pinacoteca*'s
lawn is the perfect place to take in an open-air
film. All genres of movies are shown – from
Harry Potter to art-house Italian films. Movies
are usually screened on Friday and Saturday at
9.15pm from July to the end of August.

Shopping

Retro Antiques & Old Things Market On the third
weekend of every month the town hosts this
market in Piazza Matteotti. It's not as big as
the one in Perugia, but it's still a great place to
get a hands-on history lesson (and to purchase
unique gifts not found anywhere else).

Tipografia Grifani-Donati (☎ 075 855 43 49; Corso
Cavour 4; ☿ 8.30am-12.30pm & 3-7pm Mon-Sat) Sells

paper and artwork using the same printing techniques as when it opened in 1799. It has a small museum on the 2nd floor.

Getting There & Away

Città di Castello is just east of the E45. The Ferrovia Centrale Umbra railway connects Città di Castello with Perugia (€3.05, one hour and 10 minutes, 16 daily) and onto Todi (€4, 1¾ hours, 10 daily).

LAGO DI TRASIMENO (LAKE TRASIMENO)

It would have been easy for drop-dead gorgeous Lake Trasimeno to become a holiday haven for busloads of Northern European sunseekers, à la the coast of Le Marche. Granted, you'll find plenty of such folks during the summer months, but the majority of the area – outside Passignano and a strip leaving San Feliciano – has thankfully eschewed the Stalinist high-rise mono-architecture of such Adriatic holiday villages. *Agriturismi* cover the hills like the omnipresent sunflower, historic Castiglione del Lago folds travellers in gently to allow room for all and everyone respects the delicate ecology of the precious lake.

Outside of overcrowded August, relaxed visitors enjoy the water sports, local cuisine, never-ending walking trails and Umbria's best hostel, located on its own practically private island.

The region known as Lake Trasimeno is made up of eight different *comuni* (municipalities): Castiglione del Lago, Città della Pieve, Magione, Paciano, Panicale, Passignano, Piegaro and Tuoro. Castiglione del Lago and Panicale are the most pleasant places in which to spend a day or two, while Città della Pieve is a further drive but chock-full of artwork for the connoisseur.

Orientation

Two major highways skirt the lake, the SS71 heads from Chiusi to Arezzo on the west side (in Tuscany) and SS75bis crosses the north end of the lake, heading from the A1 in Tuscany to Perugia. Public-transport users can arrive easily by train into Magione, Torricella and Castiglione del Lago, and by bus from Perugia.

Tourist offices can provide you with fold-out maps, such as *Le Mappe di Airone per il Trekking* or *Le Mappe di Airone per il Cicloturismo*. The walking guide has 13 maps and the *cicloturismo* (cycle tourism) guide has six maps. The *Kompas Lake Trasimeno* map (€6.95) is extremely thorough for both sightseers and walkers.

Information

INTERNET RESOURCES

Trasimeno 2005 (www.lagoTrasimeno.net) The area's best website, with restaurants, hotels, itineraries and history.

MEDICAL SERVICES

Emergency First-aid Castiglione del Lago (☎ 075 9 52 61); Passignano & Tuoro (☎ 075 829 87 51)

POST

Post office (⊙ 8.10am-1.20pm Mon-Fri, 8.10am-12.30pm Sat) Castiglione del Lago (**Via F lli Rosselli**); Città della Pieve (**Via Veneto 6**); Passignano (**Via Rinascita 2**); Tuoro (**Via Baroncino 1**)

TOURIST INFORMATION

Città della Pieve tourist office (☎ 0578 29 93 75; www.cittadellapieve.org; Piazza del Plebiscito; ⊙ 10.30am-12.30pm & 3.30-6pm summer, 10am-2.30pm & 3.30-6pm winter)

Panicale tourist office (☎ 075 837 80 17; www .lagodarte.com; Piazza Umberto I; ⊙ 10am-12.30pm & 3.30-7.30pm Easter-Oct, closed Sun winter) Offers tours of the town's major sites at 10.10am, 11.30am, 3.40pm, 5pm and 6.10pm in summer.

Pro Loco Passignano (☎ 075 829 62 11; Piazza Trento e Trieste 6, Passignano; ⊙ 10.30am-12.30pm & 4-7pm Mon-Sat, 10.30am-12.30pm Sun)

Trasimeno Area/Castiglione del Lago Tourist office (☎ 075 965 24 84; www.castiglionedellago.it; Piazza Mazzini 10, Castiglione del Lago; ⊙ 8.30am-1pm & 3.30-7pm Mon-Sat & 9am-1pm Sun) The most comprehensive tourist office in the region, it will help make hotel and *agriturismi* reservations, and offers a host of maps and advice on walking and biking trails and water sports.

Sights

PANICALE

Perched on a hill with an expansive view of the lake, the entire town of Panicale is one giant fortress. In the **La Chiesa di San Sebastiano** is Perugino's *Martyrdom of St Sebastian*, painted by the master in 1505. In the background of the painting is a landscape of the lake as it looked in Perugino's day. If you look closely, especially at the bottom of the painting, you'll see what's known as the *tratteggio* restoration technique, where artists create tiny vertical

---

SOLDIERS OF FORTUNE

In the 13th century, Italy's burgeoning *comuni* (city-states) were in a bit of a bind: they had active governments and prosperous citizens, but not much in the way of armies. So, they outsourced to the medieval Italian cross between a cocaine cartel warlord and a rock star: independent contractors known as the *capitani di ventura* (captains of fortune or luck) or *condottieri* (leaders of mercenary soldiers). These fickle mercenaries' allegiances were so easy to gain with promises of riches and fame that they were known to switch sides *during* battle. Umbria gave birth to many *condottieri*: Erasmo di Narni (1370–1443, known as Gattamelata), who served Florence, Venice and the pope before becoming dictator of Padua; Boldrino da Panicale (1331–91), who fought for Florence against Pisa, for Pisa against Florence and was sometimes paid a salary to make him stay away from a city; and Bartolomeo d'Alviano (1455–1515), whose adventures you can follow at the Museo Storico Multimediale Bartolomeo d'Alviano e i Capitani di Ventura (see p396), which is located outside of Amelia and find out how he led his troops into battle even after his death.

---

brushstrokes to fill in damaged artwork. The result is seamless from far away but art historians can tell what is original and what has been restored. In 2005, art historians discovered another fresco in the church, *Madonna in Trono con Angeli Musicanti*, which they have attributed to Raphael.

Craft fans will appreciate the **Museo del Tulle** (Lace Museum; ☎ 075 83 78 07; Chiesa Sant'Agostino; ☒ 10am-12.30pm & 4.30-7pm Jun-Sep, Fri-Sun winter & by appt), with examples of traditional lace and tulle from the area, housed in a deconsecrated frescoed church. If you want to buy lace, head to San Michael Sq No 2 and ring the doorbell. If she's home, Fede Boldrino, who jokes she is the wife of Boldrino da Panicale (see above) and is nearly the right age, still creates lacework by hand.

The **Museo della Chiesa della Sbarra** (admission €2; ☒ 9am-12.30pm & 3-5.30pm), in the church of the same name, offers an up-close view of church vestments, statues and altar regalia from the past five centuries. Of particularly creepy note are the relic boxes filled with the bones of saints. Entry here is payable at the lace museum.

The **Teatro Cesare Caporali** is an 18th-century theatre, beautifully designed, which has concerts all year long. During the summer, the Musica Insieme Panicale runs a series of concerts from July until September, in addition to the Mosaico Sonoro free concert every Thursday in the main square at 9pm.

CASTIGLIONE DEL LAGO

Castiglione del Lago's history dates back to an Etruscan settlement and is now a popular (but not overwhelmingly so) tourist destina-

tion. In the 7th century, the town became an important defensive promontory for the Byzantine Perugia. It was fought over and traded between the papacy, the emperor and various territories for about 1000 years.

An ancient ducal palace, **Palazzo della Corgna** (☎ 075 965 82 10; Piazza Gramsci; admission incl Rocca del Leone adult/concession €3/2; ☒ 10am-1pm & 4-7.30pm Mar-Oct, 9.30am-4.30pm Sat & Sun Nov-Mar) houses an important series of 16th-century frescoes by Giovanni Antonio Pandolfi and Salvio Savini. It was built in the 16th century by Jacopo Barozzi, who incorporated parts of ancient houses once owned by the feudal Baglioni family from Perugia.

A covered passageway connects the palace with the 13th-century **Rocca del Leone** (Fortress of the Lion), a pentagon-shaped fortress built in 1247 and an excellent example of medieval military architecture. Seen from the lake, rearing up on a rocky promontory, it cuts a striking pose.

ISOLA POLVESE

There's not much to do in Isola Polvese, which, to those who seek out its tranquillity, is its charm. The main attraction is that the entire island is a scientific and educational park. Many school groups come here to use the environmental labs that are devoted to teaching preservation of biodiversity and sustainable technologies. Make sure you visit the **Garden of Aquatic Plants**, to see biodiversity at work. Also of interest are the **Monastery of San Secondo** and the **Church of St Julian**. There are also remains of a 14th-century castle. The only inhabited building is the **Fattoria Il Poggio** hostel (see p360).

CITTÀ DELLA PIEVE

Città della Pieve is culturally and geographically considered part of Lake Trasimeno, but it's about 20km to the south. Although he became known as 'Il Perugino' (the Perugian), the famous Renaissance painter Pietro Vannucci was born here in 1445 and his paintings are all over the town. Buy a 'museum circuit' ticket at the tourist office or one of the museums listed below for €4.

The **Cattedrale di San Gervasio e Protasio** houses Perugino works and was developed from the ancient baptismal church (known as a *pieve*). Perhaps Perugino's most famous work in his home-town is *Adoration of the Magi*, on view at the **Oratory of Santa Maria dei Bianchi** (admission €2; ☺ 9.30am-12.30pm & 4-7.30pm Mar-Oct, 10am-12.30pm & 3.30-6pm Nov-Mar).

The head of the della Corgna family was appointed as governor of the town by his uncle, Pope Julius III, and subsequently commissioned artists to paint works for the town, known then as Castel della Pieve (it was elevated to a city in 1600). The frescoes located in the statuesque **Palazzo della Corgna** (☎ 0578 29 81 85; Piazza Antonio Gramsci 1; admission €2) include ones by Il Pomarancio and Salvio Savini. It is now a library that is open to the public, so feel free to step inside and have a wander around.

ISOLA MAGGIORE

The lake's main inhabited island, Isola Maggiore, near Passignano, was reputedly a favourite with St Francis. The hill-top **Chiesa di San Michele Arcangelo** contains a Crucifixion by master painter Bartolomeo Caporali. The island is famed for its lace and embroidery production and you can see examples in the **Museo del Merlotto** (Lace Museum; ☎ 075 825 42 33; Via Gugliemi, Isola Maggiore; admission €3; ☺ 10am-1pm & 2.30-6pm), near the port.

SAN FELICIANO

This working town still sees fishermen leave to trawl for fish in the morning (see opposite to join them). Although primarily a strip of hotels catering to northern Europeans on a sunny holiday, San Feliciano's main draw is the **Fishing Museum** (☎ 075 847 92 61; www.museodellapesca.it in Italian; Via Lungolago della Pace e del Lavoro 20; adult/child/concession €3/1/2; ☺ 10.30am-1pm & 3.30-7pm summer, 9-11pm Jul & Aug), which showcases fishing techniques from ancient times to modern day.

PASSIGNANO

Passignano is the most holiday-ish of the Trasimeno towns, with many restaurants, hotels, gelato joints and souvenir shops. The medieval castle on the top of the hill is closed to visitors, but the view from in front of it is as good as it gets. Check out the 16th-century **Chiesa della Madonna dell'Uliveto** (☎ 075 82 71 24; ☺ 5-7pm Wed & Thu, 4-8pm Fri & Sat, 10am-noon & 5-7pm Sun) on the road to Tuoro. Inside, the sanctuary features a *Madonna* by Bartolomeo Caporali and a decorated holy water trough. A must-see for anyone stopping here on the last Sunday of July is the **Palio delle Barche** (Boat Race), when groups of neighbourhood men carry a heavy boat to the castle on the top of the hill.

TUORO

The only reason to visit Tuoro, otherwise a rather sleepy residential area with a handful of decent hidden *agriturismi* in the surrounding hills, is to take a drive through the grounds of the Battle of Trasimeno (see the boxed text, opposite). Stop off at the **Tuoro tourist office** (City Library ☎ 075 82 52 20; ☺ 9am-12pm & 4-7pm Mon-Fri, 9am-12pm Sat 12 Jun-12 Sep) to check out the permanent exhibition before heading out around town. There is an archaeological connect-the-dots walking or driving tour of the battlefield, signposted by 12 numbered stops, describing the events that took place 2300 years ago.

Also visit **Field of the Sun** (Campo del Sole), a group of 27 contemporary sand sculptures made by celebrated artists and looking like a modern-day Stonehenge. You will find it near Loc. Navaccia Lido, close to the lake's edge.

MAGIONE

You may end up here if you suddenly realise that you need a heap of groceries or a mosaic table. It's the commercial centre of the lake and, as such, not terribly interesting. However, the train stops here and it does have a fascinating castle. Originally constructed between 1160 and 1170, the Templars used Magione's fortified abbey as a hospital for crusaders going back and forth to fight in the crusades in Jerusalem. The Knights of Malta took the abbey from the Templars and, to this day, still own it. You can drive up to the **Castle of the Knights of Malta** (☎ 075 84 38 59; admission free), which is open in summer only.

HANNIBAL V ROMANS

During the second Punic War between Rome and Carthage, Lake Trasimeno was the site of one of the deadliest battles in all of Roman history. Roman troops led by Consul Caius Flaminius were set up around the area that is now Tuoro. Quite the wartime strategist, Carthaginian general Hannibal made it look as though he was just passing by on his way to Rome, as nonchalantly as one can with 50,000 troops, 9000 horses and 37 elephants. Hannibal's men even lit a series of torches far from the lake, leading Flaminius' forces to believe the Carthaginians were too far away to be a threat. Under the cover of the lake's typical misty morning, Hannibal ambushed so expediently that the Romans hardly had time to suit up, killing over three-fifths of Flaminius' 25,000-strong army. A local stream ran with the blood of Flaminius and his soldiers for three straight days, earning the new name Sanguineto (the bloody).

Festivals & Events

As with the rest of festival-happy Umbria, Lake Trasimeno hosts countless events throughout the year:

Art & Culture festival In Città della Pieve over the first weekend in June.

Palio delle Barche Held on the last Sunday in July. Passignano's annual boat race of a different sort; see opposite.

Palio dei Terzieri This showcases the town's Renaissance past with some serious revelry, including acrobatics, fire-eating and archery. Held in mid-August.

Activities

Popular activities at the lake include hiking, wine-tasting, camping, water sports and *dolce far niente* (the sweet enjoyment of doing nothing). Many also go for the culinary delights. The locals are very proud of their excellent produce, most notably their high-quality DOC (Denominazione di Origine Controllata) wines (see p74) and DOP (Denominazione d'Origine Protetta, or Protected Denomination of Origin) olive oils. If you are interested in following the Strada del Vino (Wine Route; see p75) of the Colli del Trasimeno (Trasimeno Hill district), the **Associazione Strada del Vino Colli del Trasimeno** (☎ 075 58 29 41; www.montiTrasimeno.umbria.it in Italian) produces a brochure with suggested itineraries. It lists open cellars, which means you can stop by and try wine, but you almost always need to call ahead. You can also pick up this brochure at the tourist office in Castiglione del Lago. Look out, too, for the guide to local restaurants, *Trasimeno a Tavola*, which includes sample menus and price guides, also available from the tourist office.

Do as the locals do, with a day of **fishing** (☎ 075 847 60 05; www.albaTrasimeno.it in Italian; Via Alicata 19, San Feliciano; fishing per person €55), for eel, trout, perch, tench and carp, out on the lake. Two

people at a time can join locals for a four-hour angling or early morning fishing trip. After reeling in your catches at dawn, the fisherman can guide you to restaurants that will cook up your fish using traditional recipes. Book at least one day in advance. Nature trips (for up to 10 people €90) are also available.

For a fun cultural and gastronomic experience, don't miss the **weekly markets**, which have all sorts of fresh local produce and basic goods. They take place from 8.30am to 1pm at the following locations: Castiglione del Lago (Wednesday), Magione (Thursday), Tuoro (Friday) and Passignano (Saturday). Ask at each town's tourist office for more information.

Ask at one of the tourist offices for a booklet of walking and horse-riding tracks. Horse-riding centres include the **Maneggio Oasi** (☎ 0337 65 37 95; Loc. Orto, Castiglione del Lago) and **Poggio del Belveduto** (☎ 075 82 90 76; www.poggiodelbelveduto .it; Via San Donato 65, Loc. Campori di Sopra, Passignano), which also offers archery courses if you're feeling particularly medieval.

Canoe, windsurfing and sailboat rentals can be found in Castiglione del Lago at **La Merangola** (☎ 075 965 24 45; Loc. Lido Arezzo) or in Tuoro at **Belneazione Tuoro** (☎ 328 454 97 66; Loc. Punta Navaccia). La Merangola also has a small beach and restaurant, and turns into a *discoteca* (disco) at night.

Sleeping

The Lake Trasimeno area is filled with every type of lodging imaginable, including no less than 151 *agriturismi*.

For a full list of places to stay in this area, pick up a brochure from the local tourist office, check www.umbria2000.it or consult the Umbria Infotourist Map. The map is available from **InfoUmbria** (Map p320; ☎ 075 57 57;

HOSTEL? AGRITURISMO? HOW ABOUT BOTH?

our pick **Fattoria Il Poggio** (☎ 075 965 95 50; www.fattoriaisolapolvese.com; Isola Polvese; dm/f incl breakfast €15/17; ☺ Mar-30 Oct, reception closed 3-7pm; ☐) Besides being impeccably run, you would hardly ever know you're staying in an HI youth hostel. This former barn has dorm, doubles and family rooms all with views of the surrounding lake. Kayaks, private beaches, games, TV with DVDs, and laundry room are all on offer. Groups can book in the low season by appointment only. Meals are also available (€10). Last ferry to Isola Polvese leaves San Feliciano around 7pm. See also p312.

---

www.infoumbria.com in Italian; Piazza Partigiani Intercity bus station, Largo Cacciatori delle Alpi 3, Perugia; ☺ 9am-1.30pm & 2.30-6.30pm Mon-Fri, 9am-1pm Sat), where staff will also help you make reservations.

BUDGET

Camping Badiaccia (☎ 075 965 90 97; www.badiaccia .com; Via Trasimeno I 91, Bivia Borghetto; per person €5.50-7, tent €5.50-6.50, car €2-2.50, 3-/6-person bungalows €35-93; ☐ ☐ ☐) Practise your Dutch while playing tennis, table tennis or *bocce*, eating at the surprisingly good *ristorante*/pizzeria, or swimming in one of three pools (one hydromassage and just for adults). The camping ground is paradise for families, but the childless can enjoy renting a kayak, bicycle or paddleboat, exercising in the fitness room, and the excellent beachfront location. For a small fee, staff will pick you up at the Terontola train station; the camping ground is located just south of the SS75 on the SS71.

Paola's B&B (☎ 075 573 08 08, 335 624 72 40; Città della Pieve; per person €30-50) For an authentic Italian experience, stay in Paola's home. She rents out two rooms in her 17th-century apartment (be sure to ask for a peek at the frescoes in her daughter's bedroom). Paola also offers cooking and Italian lessons (usually at the same time). During winter, she cooks in her open-hearth fireplace. Paolo speaks French and a bit of English.

La Casa sul Lago (☎ 075 840 00 42; Via del Lavoro, Torricella; dm €18, s €25-30, d €50-60, all incl breakfast; ☐) Comfortable enough to want to spend a few nights, or a few weeks. The private rooms could be in a three-star hotel, and all rooms have access to every amenity known to hostelkind: laundry, bicycle rental, wi-fi, internet access, home-cooked meals, bar and private garden… all within 50m from the lake. A short walk from the Torricella train station but not near much else.

Il Torrione (☎ 075 95 32 36; www.trasinet.com/iltor rione; Via delle Mura 4, Castiglione del Lago; r incl breakfast €65-70; ☺ 1 Mar-10 Nov) Romance abounds at this artistically minded tranquil retreat. Each room is decorated with artwork painted by the owner and a private flower-filled garden overlooks the lake, complete with chaises longues from which to watch the sunset. Rent the 'tower' mini-apartment, complete with kitchenette, for an amorous hideaway.

MIDRANGE

La Torre (☎ 075 95 16 66; www.trasinet.com/latorre; Via Emanuele 50, Castiglione del Lago; s €50, d €60-80; ☒) The price is right at this central three-star hotel, a renovated palace. The rooms are a tad sterile but fully outfitted with TV, minibar and telephone, and the owners run the yummy bakery below.

Hotel Da Sauro (☎ 075 82 61 68; fax 075 82 51 30; Via Guglielmi 1, Isola Maggiore; r €80) This family-run establishment has just 10 rooms in a rustic stone building. It's found at the northern end of the main village on the island, not far from a private beach. The restaurant downstairs is very popular, so expect a lot of noise at meal times. This is a great place to try local fish.

Hotel Miralago (☎ 075 95 11 57; www.hotelmiralago .com; Piazza Mazzini 6, Castiglione del Lago; s €68-76, d €88-93, tr €108-113; ☺ closed mid-Jan–mid-Mar; ☒) The Miralago is central, and top-floor rooms have magnificent lake views. It's rather austere (besides the plush fabrics), but it has amenities such as satellite TV and room service. There's also a good restaurant downstairs – La Fontana (a perennial favourite).

Agriturismo Madonna delle Grazie (☎ 057 829 98 22; www.madonnadellegrazie.it; Voc Madonna delle Grazie 6, Città della Pieve; d B&B €90-120, half-board €130-180; ☐ ☒ ☒) The largest and most commercial of Umbria's organic *agriturismi*. Very popular with Italian families on holidays, the establishment is truly a working, family-run farm producing wine, olive oil, honey, meats and jams, all used in its meals. Rooms can be a tad 'rustic' (translation: sparse) and it's not cheap, but it does come with horse riding, archery, bicycle rentals and a stunning location.

TOP END

ourpick Relais Alla Corte del Sole (☎ 075 968 90 08; www.cortedelsole.com; Loc. I Giorgi, Petrignano; d €166-230, ste €225-340; P ⊠ ⊠) You'd swear you must have seen this astonishing hotel as the backdrop of a period drama – a soulful chat in front of a private in-room fireplace, chess and brandy in the fabric-draped *orangerie* (with its 360-degree countryside view), or a lovers spat in the floral garden behind the olive-tree thicket.

Casa San Martino (☎ 075 84 42 88; www.tuscanyvacation.com, San Martino 19, Lisciano Niccone; d with 3-night minimum €100-160, per week for up to 8 people €2000-3000; P ⊠) Come with one or seven of your best friends to this farmhouse in the hills north of the lake. The main building is impeccably decorated with terracotta-tile floors, woodbeamed ceilings and an open-hearth fireplace, and comes with a completely stocked kitchen, washer and dryer, and four bedrooms (three with bathrooms). Outside is a pool facing an expansive countryside view (with a few castles

thrown in) and a stone barbecue grill. The building is often rented out weekly during the summer (a three-night minimum booking applies otherwise), but in the low season it opens as a B&B offering cooking and fresco painting classes.

Eating

The main specialties of the Trasimeno area are *fagiolina* (little white beans), olive oil and wine. In addition, you'll find many fish dishes, such as carp *in porchetta* (cooked in a wood oven with garlic, fennel and herbs) and *tegamaccio*, a kind of soupy stew of the best varieties of local fish, cooked in olive oil, white wine and herbs.

La Cantina (☎ 075 965 24 32; Via Emanuele 93, Castiglione del Lago; mains €6.60-13.20; ☼ Tue-Sun) Not only is this well-priced restaurant fabulous – a stately interior with a lovely outdoor terrace for summer dining – but there's also an adjacent *magazzino* (shop) where you can sample and buy the area's best wine, olive oil

---

HONEYMOONING IN UMBRIA (ON ANY BUDGET)

Whether you are travelling on a shoestring or with platinum purse strings, Umbria offers a vast array of romantic getaways to suit any price point, especially in the areas surrounding Lake Trasimeno.

Fattoria Il Poggio (opposite) You don't need to spend a lot of *soldi* (money) to have a romantic tryst. For less than the cost of most bridal bouquets, you can spend a few nights in your own room on this private island's hostel in Lake Trasimeno, kayaking, dining with your fellow hostel mates and wandering through the abandoned castle. Romantically placed benches allow for quiet moments alone.

Il Torrione (opposite) Climb up a set of pirate-ship steps to your personal honeymoon tower cottage, where you just might be tempted to skip going sightseeing to sleep in until noon, cook lunch in your kitchenette and dine outside in the sunshine on your private terrace. This superb artist-designed bed and breakfast is located just a stone's throw away from the main square of the eminently wanderable Castiglione del Lago – the most congenial town on Lake Trasimeno.

Relais Alla Corte del Sole (above) The only worry that honeymooners might have at this wonderful spot, is why they didn't get married here as well. Walking distance from the Tuscan border in the Lake Trasimeno *borgo* (hamlet) of Petrignano, this beautiful former monastic village offers every romantic amenity available in one picture-perfect package – sweetly scented gardens, romantic in-room fireplaces, a glass enclosed circular *orangerie* from which to write your thank-you notes and, for exhausted newlyweds, organised excursions that leave the planning to someone else.

Relais Borgo Brufa (p333) Even if you don't stay in the Imperial Suite with its gold-plated bed and in-room swimming pool, the candlelit Turkish sauna, scrumptious restaurant and quintessential countryside views are just as sumptuously decadent. Staff even pick guests up at Perugia's Sant'Egidio airport, which is located about 15 minutes away.

Villa Zuccari (p344) After spending a year or more planning your nuptials, wouldn't it be nice to have someone take care of you for a while? The noble family that runs Villa Zuccari are expert hosts, excelling in taking care of all their clients' needs, which honeymooning couples will especially appreciate at this most romantic of hotels. The palatial rooms (some with in-room Jacuzzi tubs or stone balconies), excellent restaurant and private garden with heated swimming pool might just tempt you to stick around. If you do decide to venture out, Montefalco's restaurants and *enotecas* (wine bars) are just minutes away.

and treats. Try the delicious trout with local *fagiolina* (€8.20).

L'Acquario (☎ 075 965 24 32; Via Vittoria Emanuele 69, Castiglione del Lago; set menu €25; Thu-Tue) This rather refined restaurant is a great place to try out the local carp *in porchetta* fresh from the lake or have an appetiser of eel in *tegamaccio*.

La Locanda di Gulliver (☎ 075 952 82 28; Voc. I Cucchi, Petrignano; meals €27) Even if the food wasn't absolutely fantastic (which it is), the drive out here would be reason enough to stop in. Housed in an old brick farmhouse near sunflower-draped fields of yellow, the inventive menu features gems like *cinghiale* (wild boar) bruschetta with local olive oil, eel and yellow pumpkin risotto, and tagliatelle with local smoked lake fish. Did we mention the homemade pizzas, hot out of the brick oven?

Le Grotte di Boldrini (☎ 075 83 71 61; Via Virgilio Ceppari 30, Panicale; meals €28; 7.30-10pm) Umbrian-style comfort food abounds at this hill-top trattoria in Panicale, above the lake. Meats are grilled on an open fire, perfect for a chilly day, and fresh fish is served on Fridays. Try the decadent macaroni in *norcina* (from Norcia) cream sauce with spicy sausages (€7).

Da Settimio (☎ 075 847 60 00; Via Lungolago Alicata, San Feliciano; meals €28; Fri-Wed Jan-Oct) If you stay on Isola Polvese, you'll most likely pass by this restaurant near the ferry terminal in San Feliciano. It doesn't look like much, but lo-cals know it as the best fish restaurant in the area, handed down from father to son for four generations. Try the *risotto alla pescatora* (fisherman's risotto) or the appetiser of 'fried little fishies'.

Getting There & Around

APM buses connect Perugia with Passignano (€3, one hour and 10 minutes, nine daily) and Castiglione del Lago (€4.60, one hour and 15 minutes, nine daily). Trains head from Perugia around hourly to Torricella (€1.80, 25 minutes), Passignano (€2.30, 30 minutes) and Castiglione del Lago (€3.30, one hour, nine daily).

APM (☎ 800 51 21 41) also operates ferry services. The company has offices on the waterfront at each town, where you can pick up a timetable. From approximately Easter until the end of September, hourly ferries head from Passignano to Castiglione del Lago (€4, 40 minutes), San Feliciano to Isola Polvese (€3.10, 10 minutes) and Castiglione del Lago to Isola Maggiore (€3.70, 30 minutes). Ferries stop running at 7pm.

You can rent bicycles at most camping grounds, Fattoria Il Poggio (p360) or La Casa sul Lago (p360) or at these outlets:

Cicli Valentini (☎ /fax 075 95 16 63; Via Firenze 68b, Castiglione del Lago)

Marinelli Ferrettini Fabio (☎ /fax 075 95 31 26; Via B Buozzi 26, Castiglione del Lago)

Southern Umbria

While Northern Umbria is easily categorised as a 'slow' destination, Southern Umbria is slower still. The landscape is at once languid and striking, mystical and unmanicured. Sunbeams twist through ancient glass windows, mothers in sensible shoes urge their grown sons to 'Eat! Eat!' and stray cats curl up in front of old barns, content to let the world be.

Like its northern counterpart, Southern Umbria closes shop for three to four hours in the middle of each day to take *pranzo* (lunch) and visitors will undoubtedly adapt quickly. One of Italy's most famous restaurants Vissani, on the bank of Lago di Corbara, is packed with visitors from around the world, but even its website is closed on Wednesdays.

Towns here feel like home after just a few days. Todi has been described as one of the world's most perfect small towns. In Narni, you can visit lions, saints and castles, usually unencumbered by other tourists. Orvieto's magnificent cathedral, built by generations of artists, lures visitors like a gilded gem. Spoleto offers enough sights and activities to keep visitors occupied for a week, but all you'd probably want to do is wander up and down the ancient cobbled streets. You'll just want to give the entire town of Amelia one big hug.

Embrace your inner adrenaline junkie in Southern Umbria. Outdoor enthusiasts can indulge in just about any sport they desire. Fancy hang-gliding? Try Castelluccio, near the Piano Grande. Rafting? Several places along the Nera and Corno Rivers offer white-water rafting, kayaking and canoeing. You can rent bikes outside of Orvieto, rock climb in Ferentillo or go spelunking (caving) in the Valnerina.

SOUTHERN UMBRIA

HIGHLIGHTS

- Picnic in fields of blooming lentil flowers flanked by snow-capped peaks in the **Piano Grande** (p386)
- After walking through two thousand years of history in the **Museo Claudio Faina e Civico**, step into the Piazza Duomo at sunset to watch the sun reflect off the exterior mosaic of Orvieto's **cathedral** (p366)
- Take in a concert or performance at the **Spoleto Festival** (p381)
- Road trip through the **Valnerina** (p387) to raft, rock climb, dine in an ancient abbey, walk under a Roman-engineered waterfall or to see desiccated corpses
- In Narni, savour the view from the top of the fortress **La Rocca Albornoz** (p391) or below at the inquisition prison **Narni Sotteranea** (p391) or on stage at the Narni Opera's **Open Air Theatre** (p394)

SOUTHERN UMBRIA

ORVIETO
pop 20,909

The entire town is placed precariously on a cliff made of the area's tufaceous stone, a craggy porous limestone that seems imminently ready to crumble under the weight of Orvieto's magnificent Gothic cathedral (or, at least under all the tourists who are now drawn to see it). Just off a main autostrada, Orvieto can get a bit crowded with summer bus tours, but they're all here for good reason.

History

Orvieto has held a lofty position as one of Umbria's most influential towns for almost 3000 years running. The Etruscan settlement started as far back as the 8th or 9th century BC, and thrived as a centre for bronze and ceramics. The ancient evidence is still on display at several of Orvieto's museums, including the Museo Claudio Faina e Civico and the Museo Archeologico Nazionale. The second zenith in Orvieto's history was the late Middle Ages when it reigned as a leader in the papal states, a position that led to the construction of the stunning cathedral and the stately civic and religious buildings that now create a leisurely way to stroll back in time.

Orientation

Trains pull in at Orvieto Scalo and from here you can catch bus 1 up to the old town or board the cable car (funicular) to take you up the steep hill to Piazza Cahen.

Those with cars should head to a free car park behind the train station (at the roundabout in front of the station head in the direction of 'Arezzo' and turn left into the large parking lot). There's plenty of parking space in Piazza Cahen and in several designated areas outside the old city walls. The Orvieto Unica Card will buy you five hours of free parking at the former Campo della Fiera and a ride on the *ascensore* (lift) into the city centre.

Information

BOOKSHOPS

Libreria dei Sette (☎ 0763 34 44 36; Corso Cavour 85; ⏱ 9am-11pm Mon-Fri, 10am-8pm Sat & Sun) Stock up on a collection of maps, English-language books or Lonely Planet guidebooks.

CAR RENTAL

Avis (☎ 0763 39 00 30, 389 567 89 10; orvieto.pk1@avisautonoleggio.it; Via I Maggio 57; ⏱ 9am-1pm & 3-7pm Mon-Fri, 9am-1pm Sat) Located 100m from the train station.

EMERGENCY

Police station (☎ 0763 3 92 11; Piazza Cahen)

INTERNET ACCESS

Caffè Montanucci (☎ 0763 34 12 61; Corso Cavour 21; 🖵 per 30min €3.10; ⏱ 6.30am-midnight Mon-Fri, until 1am Sat & Sun) Pick up a supply of chocolate or a *panini* (sandwich) at this café (see p370), while you surf the internet.

MEDICAL SERVICES

After-hours doctor (☎ 0763 30 18 84) Call here for the hospital at night and on the weekend.

ORVIETO

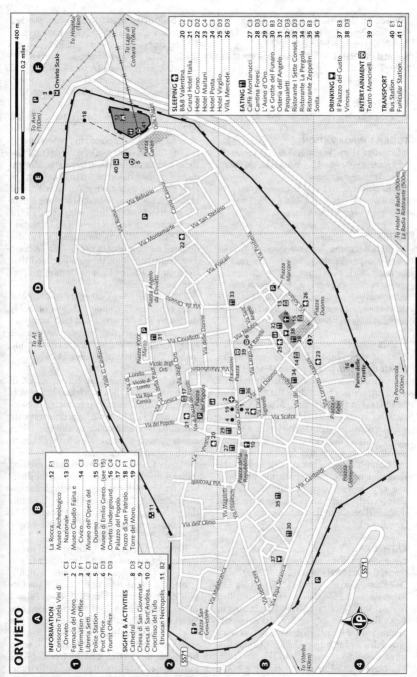

INFORMATION
Consorzio Tutela Vini di
  Orvieto.....................................**1** C3
Farmacia del Moro.....................**2** C3
Information Office.......................**3** F1
Libreria Setti..............................**4** C3
Police Station............................**5** E2
Post Office.................................**6** D3
Tourist Office.............................**7** D3

SIGHTS & ACTIVITIES
Cathedral..................................**8** D3
Chiesa di San Giovenale............**9** A2
Chiesa di Sant'Andrea..............**10** C3
Crocifisso del Tufo...................
Etruscan Necropolis...................**11** B2

La Rocca...................................**12** F1
Museo Archeologico
  Nazionale..............................**13** D3
Museo Claudio Faina e
  Civico....................................**14** C3
Museo dell'Opera del
  Duomo...................................**15** D3
Museo di Emilio Greco...........(see **15**)
Orvieto Underground...............**16** C4
Palazzo del Popolo...................**17** C2
Pozzo di San Patrizio...............**18** F1
Torre del Moro..........................**19** C3

SLEEPING
B&B Valentina..........................**20** C2
Grand Hotel Italia.....................**21** C2
Hotel Corso..............................**22** D2
Hotel Maitani............................**23** C4
Hotel Posta...............................**24** C3
Hotel Virgilio............................**25** D3
Villa Mercede...........................**26** D3

EATING
Caffè Montanucci......................**27** C3
Cantina Foresi...........................**28** D3
L'Asino d'Oro............................**29** C3
Le Grotte del Funaro.................**30** B3
Osteria dell'Angelo...................**31** D2
Pasqualetti...............................**32** D3
Ristorante I Sette Consoli..........**33** D3
Ristorante La Pergola................**34** C3
Ristorante Zeppelin...................**35** B3
Sosta.......................................**36** C3

DRINKING
Il Palazzo del Gusto..................**37** B3
Vinosus....................................**38** D3

ENTERTAINMENT
Teatro Mancinelli......................**39** C3

TRANSPORT
Bus Station...............................**40** E1
Funicular Station.......................**41** E2

SOUTHERN UMBRIA

Farmacia del Moro (Pharmacy; ☎ 0763 34 41 00; Corso Cavour 89; ☺ 9am-1pm & 4.30-7.45pm Mon-Sat) Posts 24-hour pharmacy information.
Hospital (☎ 0763 30 71) In the Ciconia area, east of the railway station.

POST
Post office (☎ 0763 39 83 1; Via Largo M Ravelli; ☺ 8.10am-6pm Mon-Fri, 8.10am-12.30pm Sat)

TOURIST INFORMATION
Information office (ATC; ☎ 0763 30 23 78; bottom of the funicular; ☺ 9am-4pm) Buy funicular, bus and Carta Unica tickets here.
Tourist office (☎ 0763 34 17 72; info@iat.orvieto.tr.it; Piazza Duomo 24; ☺ 8.15am-1.50pm & 4-7pm Mon-Fri, 10am-1pm & 3-6pm Sat, Sun & holidays)

TOURS
Leo Pretelli (Chauffeur, Tour Guide, Concierge; ☎ 335 155 89 49; leopretelli@mac.com; full-day tours of up to four people from €240) An English-speaking local expert who has an infectious *joie de vivre*, Leo is like your long-lost Umbrian uncle who knows every tiny off-the-beaten-path restaurant and viewpoint. Leo is a perfect choice for a designated driver at Umbria's 40-plus wineries.

Sights
For one-stop visitor shopping, pick up an **Orvieto Unico Card** (adult/concession valid 1 yr €18/15). It entitles its owner to entrance to the nine main attractions (including the Cappella di San Brizio in the cathedral, Museo Claudio Faina e Civico, Orvieto Underground, Torre del Moro, Museo dell'Opera del Duomo and the Crocifisso del Tufo Etruscan Necropolis) and either five hours' free car parking at the Campo della Fiera car park next to the funicular or a round trip on the funicular and city buses. It can be purchased at the Campo della Fiera car park, the attractions listed earlier, the tourist office or the funicular car park.

CATHEDRAL
Little can prepare you for the visual feast that is the **cathedral** (☎ 0763 34 11 67; Piazza Duomo; ☺ 7.30am-12.45pm year-round, 2.30-7.15pm Apr-Sep, 2.30-6.15pm Mar, Oct & 2.30-5.15pm Nov-Feb), often called the 'golden lily' of cathedrals. Originating in 1290, this remarkable edifice was originally planned in the Romanesque style but, as work proceeded and architects changed, Gothic features were incorporated into the structure. The black-and-white marble banding of the

main body of the church, reminiscent of other great churches you may already have seen in Tuscan cities such as Siena and Pisa, is over-shadowed by the rich rainbow colours of the façade. A harmonious blend of mosaic and sculpture, plain stone and dazzling colour, it has been likened to a giant outdoor altar screen.

Pope Urban IV ordered that the cathedral be built following the so-called Miracle of Bolsena in 1263. A Bohemian priest who was passing through the town of Bolsena (near Orvieto) had his doubts about transubstantiation dispelled when blood began to drip from the Host onto the altar linen while he celebrated Mass. The linen was presented to Pope Urban IV, in Orvieto at the time, who declared the event a miracle and set the wheels in motion for the construction of the cathedral. He also declared the new feast day of Corpus Domini. The reliquary holding the blood-stained altar cloth now leads the Corpus Domini procession, held in June.

The building took 30 years to plan and three centuries to complete. It was probably started by Fra Bevignate and later additions were made by Lorenzo Maitani (responsible for Florence's cathedral), Andrea Pisano and his son Nino Pisano, Andrea Orcagna and Michele Sanicheli.

The façade appears almost unrelated to the main body of the church and has greatly benefited from meticulous restoration, completed in 1995. The three huge doorways are separated by fluted columns and the gables are decorated with mosaics that, although mostly reproductions, seem to come to life in the light of the setting sun and in the evening under spotlights. The areas between the doorways feature 14th-century bas-reliefs of scriptural scenes by Maitani and his pupils, while the rose window is by Andrea Orcagna. The great bronze doors, the work of Emilio Greco, were added in the 1960s.

Reopened in late 1996 after years of painstaking restoration, Luca Signorelli's fresco cycle *The Last Judgement* shimmers with life. Look for it to the right of the altar in the **Cappella di San Brizio** (admission €3; ☺ 10am-12.45pm & 2.30-7.15pm Apr-Sep, to 6.15pm Mar & Oct, to 5.15pm Mon-Sat, to 5.45pm public holidays Nov-Feb). Signorelli began work on the series in 1499, and Michelangelo is said to have taken inspiration from it when he began the Sistine Chapel fresco of the same subject 40 years later. Indeed, to some,

Michelangelo's masterpiece runs a close second to Signorelli's work. Not to be ignored in the chapel are ceiling frescoes by Fra Angelico. The chapel is closed during Mass.

The **Cappella del Corporale** (admission free; 7.30am-12.45pm & 2.30-7.15pm summer, varies winter, closed during Mass) houses the blood-stained altar linen of the miracle, preserved in a silver reliquary decorated by artists of the Sienese school. The walls feature frescoes depicting the miracle, painted by Ugolino di Prete Ilario. Mass is celebrated here daily at 9am (in Italian). Tickets for the Cappella di San Brizio are available from the tourist office; both capella are closed during Mass.

MUSEO CLAUDIO FAINA E CIVICO

An absolutely fantastic museum for ancient history is the **Museo Claudio Faina e Civico** (☎ 0763 34 15 11; www.museofaina.it; Piazza Duomo 29; adult/concession €4.50/3; 9.30am-6pm Apr-Sep, 10am-5pm Tue-Sun Oct-Mar), opposite the cathedral. Much of the display here comes from the Etruscan Necropolis found on the outskirts of town. There are examples of Gorgons, an incredibly thorough collection of numismatics (coins, many with the likeness of famous Roman emperors) and bronze figures from the 2nd and 3rd centuries BC. Kids will enjoy following the questions (in Italian and English) for developing little historians to ponder along the way. There are guided tours at 11am and 4pm (3pm October to March).

AROUND THE CATHEDRAL

Next to the cathedral is the **Museo dell'Opera del Duomo** (☎ 0763 34 24 77; Palazzo Soliano, Piazza Duomo; adult/concession €5/4; 10am-1pm & 3-7pm Jul & Aug, 10-6pm Apr-Jun & Sep-Oct, 10am-5pm Nov-Mar, closed Tue in winter), which houses a clutter of religious relics from the cathedral, as well as Etruscan antiquities and works by artists such as Simone Martini and the three Pisanos: Andrea, Nino and Giovanni.

Around the corner in the Palazzo Papale you can view Etruscan antiquities in the **Museo Archeologico Nazionale** (☎/fax 0763 34 10 39; Palazzo Papale, Piazza Duomo; adult/concession €3/1.50; 8.30am-7.30pm). It doesn't have information in English, so visit the Museo Claudio Faina e Civico first to get your bearings.

Museo di Emilio Greco (☎ 0763 34 46 05; Palazzo Soliano, Piazza del Duomo; adult/concession €2.50/1.50; 10.30am-1pm & 2.30-6pm Apr-Sep, 10.30am-1pm & 2-5.30pm Tue-Sun Oct-Mar) displays a collection of modern pieces donated by the creator of the cathedral's bronze doors. You can get a combined ticket (adult/child €5.50/4) which will give you admission to the Pozzo di San Patrizio.

NORTH OF THE CATHEDRAL

Near the end of the main drag is the **Torre del Moro** (Moor's Tower; ☎ 0763 34 45 67; Corso Cavour 87; adult/concession €2.80/2; 10am-8pm May-Aug, 10am-7pm Mar, Apr, Sep & Oct, 10.30am-1pm & 2.30-5pm Nov-Feb). Climb all 250 steps (or take an elevator part of the way) for a sweeping pigeon's-eye views of the entire city.

To see a bit of striated history, head to the 12th-century **Chiesa di Sant'Andrea** (Piazza della Repubblica; 8.30am-12.30pm & 3.30-7.30pm), where its curious decagonal bell tower is a good choice. As with many Italian churches, it was built over a Roman structure, which itself incorporated an earlier Etruscan building. You can see the ancient foundations in the crypt. The piazza, once Orvieto's Roman forum, is at the heart of what remains of the medieval city.

North of Corso Cavour, the 12th-century Romanesque-Gothic **Palazzo del Popolo** presides over the piazza of the same name. At the northwest end of town is the 11th-century **Chiesa di San Giovenale** (Piazza Giovenale; 8am-12.30pm & 3.30-6pm), a church constructed in the year 1000, its interior brightened by 13th- and 14th-century frescoes. Its Romanesque-Gothic art from the medieval Orvieto school is an astounding contrast.

ORVIETO UNDERGROUND

The coolest place in Orvieto – literally – is the **Orvieto Underground** (☎ 0763 34 06 88, 339 733 27 64; Parco delle Grotte; adult/concession €5.50/3.30; tours 11am, 12.15pm, 4pm & 5.15pm daily Mar-Jan, Sat & Sun Feb), a series of 440 caves used for millennia by locals for various purposes. The caves were initially used as wells by the Etruscans, who needed water but with the Romans about couldn't risk leaving the hill. During the Middle Ages, locals experiencing a high volume of sieges used the caves for protected sustenance, this time they trapped pigeons in dovecotes for food (pigeon is still found on Umbrian menus to this day – look for *palomba* or *piccione*). During WWII, the caves were turned into bomb shelters, but luckily they never had to be used, as the tufaceous volcanic rock that makes up the hill crumbles easily. Tours leave from in front of the tourist office.

Hint: during summer, take the 12.15pm tour, as you'll enjoy the year-round temperature of around 15°C while most sights and shops are closed.

EAST OF PIAZZA DEL DUOMO

Standing watch at the town's eastern most tip is the 14th-century **La Rocca**, part of which is now a public garden. To the north of the fortress, the **Pozzo di San Patrizio** (St Patrick's Well; ☎ 0763 34 37 68; Viale Sangallo; adult/concession €4.50/3.50; ☼ 10am-6.45pm Apr-Sep, to 5.45pm Oct-Mar) is a testament to the hardy disposition of the townsfolk. More than 60m deep, it is lined by two staircases for water-bearing mules and a Latin inscription reading: 'What nature denied for defence, in this case water, was added by the work of man'. It was sunk in 1527 on the orders of Pope Clement VII. If you're planning on visiting the Museo di Emilio Greco, buy a combined ticket.

CROCIFISSO DEL TUFO ETRUSCAN NECROPOLIS

Besides the Hypogea di Volumni outside of Perugia, the **Crocifisso del Tufo Etruscan Necropolis** (☎ 0763 34 36 11; Loc. Le Conce, SS71, Km 1.6; adult/concession €3/1.50; ☼ 8am-7pm) is one of only two Etruscan necropolises that travellers can visit in Umbria. It dates back to the mid-6th century BC. Several series of burial chambers feature the etched names of their deceased residents. The manner in which the graves are laid out shows the preciseness of good ancient urban planning, albeit one whose residents couldn't quite appreciate it. Many of the furnishings from the Necropolis can be found at the Louvre, British Museum and various other museums, though some of the collection hasn't left: the Museo Claudio Faina e Civico still holds onto a good chunk.

Festivals & Events

Orvieto's most famous festival is the **Palombella**, held every year on Pentecost Sunday. Unusually, it is world famous for its highlight event rather than the parades and crafts fairs. For traditionalists, the sacred rite has been celebrating the Holy Spirit and good luck since 1404. For animal rights activists, the main event celebrates nothing more than scaring the living crap out of a bewildered dove.

For six centuries, the ritual has gone like this: take one bewildered dove, cage it, surround the cage with a wheel of exploding fireworks, and hurtle the cage 300m down a wire towards the cathedral steps. If the dove lives (which it usually does), the couple most recently married in the cathedral become its caretakers (and, presumedly, the ones who pay for post-traumatic dove-stress disorder counselling). It's not likely you'll see a fake dove in the cage, but if so, you'll know who has won.

Umbria Jazz Winter takes place from the end of December to early January, with a great feast and party on New Year's Eve. Ask at the tourist office for a programme of events. See p324 for details of the summer jazz festival.

Sleeping

Orvieto does not lack for hotels, and visitors will benefit from the highly competitive pricing. It's always a good idea to book ahead in summer or on the weekend or if you're planning to visit during New Year when the Umbria Jazz Winter festival is in full swing.

BUDGET

Porziuncola (☎ 0763 34 13 87; Loc. Cappuccini 8; dm €10-15; Ⓟ) With only eight beds in two separate single-sex rooms, you'd do best to call ahead. Take bus 5 from Piazza Cahen to the Cappuccini neighbourhood, just a few kilometres away.

Hotel Posta (☎ 0763 34 19 09; www.orvietohotels.it; Via Luca Signorelli 18; s with/without bathroom €37/31, d €56/43; breakfast €6) Sometimes 'palatial' isn't an adjective one might use to describe a palace. Although the building was a bit musty and ramshackle, the hotel was undergoing a full renovation at the time of writing that included new mattresses and some much needed TLC, so expect the quality to increase.

Villa Mercede (☎ 0763 34 17 66; www.argoweb.it/casareligiosa_villamercede; Via Soliana 2; s/d/tr incl breakfast 50/60/70; Ⓟ) Heavenly close to the Duomo, at 76 rooms, there's space for a gaggle of pilgrims. The building dates back to the 1500's, so the requisite frescoes adorn several rooms. High ceilings, a quiet garden and free parking seal the deal. Vacate rooms each morning by 9.30am or you'll earn the housekeepers' wrath.

B&B Valentina (☎ 393 970 58 68; valentina.z@tiscali net.it; Via Vivaria 7; s/d/tr incl breakfast €50/70/90, apt €160) As if being set back on a quiet street wasn't enough, the rooms are also soundproof, casually elegant and spacious. Valentina lives downstairs with two friendly dogs. All rooms

---

TOP FIVE GREAT-VALUE PLACES TO SLEEP IN UMBRIA

For the top bang for your buck, try these hotels:

Al Grappolo d'Oro (p332) With an outdoor pool, inclusive breakfast, in-room DSL connection and breathtaking vista, you'll feel like you should be paying double.

La Casa sul Lago (p359) With every amenity known to hostelkind – including laundry, free internet access, bicycle rentals, a bar, comforting home-cooked meals, etc, etc, etc – Mom will trust you're in good hands.

Residenza di Via Piccardi (p350) Start your day off with breakfast in the quiet garden in this sweet and romantic home-away-from-home.

Residenza d'Epoca Vecchio Molino (p378) Not inexpensive, but the weeping willows, sacred river and 600 years of history feel like they should be in a five-star resort.

Hotel dei Priori (p393) Perfectly central with an excellent restaurant and a mix of modern and historic rooms, most with a view, is reason enough to venture into the undiscovered hamlet of Narni.

---

have private bathroom, TV and hairdryer, and laundry service is available.

MIDRANGE

Hotel Corso (☎ /fax 0763 34 20 20; www.hotelcorso.net; Corso Cavour 343; s €50-64, d €80-87, tr €100-115; ✗ ▢) Set a bit further away from the cathedral than most other hotels, this is nevertheless an excellent choice. Several rooms are enveloped with wood-beamed ceilings, terracotta bricks or antique cherry furniture, allowing one to describe them as snug rather than tiny. The breakfast buffet is an extra €6.50 but it's worth it to sit on the outdoor terrace. There's a 10% discount for stays of more than two nights.

Hotel Virgilio (☎ 0763 34 18 82; www.hotelvirgilio.com; Piazza Duomo 5) This three-star hotel on the Piazza Duomo was undergoing a full renovation when we visited, so check the website for the most recent prices.

Hotel Maitani (☎ 0763 34 20 11; www.hotelmaitani.com; Via Lorenzo Maitani 5; s/d/ste €77/126/170, breakfast €10; ℗) Every detail is covered, from a travel-sized toothbrush and toothpaste in each room to chocolates (Perugino, of course) on your pillow. Several rooms have cathedral or countryside views. Rooms are pin-drop quiet, as they come with not one but two double-paned windows.

TOP END

Grand Hotel Italia (☎ 076 334 32 75; www.grandhotelitalia.it; Via di Piazza del Popolo 13; s €90, d €150-200, all incl breakfast; ℗) The rooms reflect the elegance of the 19th-century building, many with superb views and a few with balconies. An elegant garden, fireplaces in the salon and a sumptuous breakfast buffet are just a few of the extras

at this city-centre hotel. Its private parking costs €8.

Hotel La Badia (☎ 0763 30 19 59; www.labadiahotel.it; Loc. La Badia 8; d/ste €221/270; ℗ ✗ ☜) Occupied 1200 years ago by Benedictine monks, this hotel – claimed to be the oldest in Italy – was once known as the Abbey of St Severo and Martirio. It's been a holiday retreat since the 15th century, with guests such as Pope Paul II, Borghese and Barberini. For the past century it's been under the ownership of a noble family who turned it into the hotel it is today. Twenty-one rooms and seven suites consist of modern comforts along with attractive antiques and furnishings, a swimming pool and tennis court. The hotel is closed early January to early March.

Eating

RESTAURANTS

Sosta (☎ 0763 34 30 25; Corso Cavour 100a; mains €5) This extremely simple self-service restaurant actually serves up some very good pizza and pasta. It's cafeteria style so you order as much or as little as you like, including meat and vegetable dishes. Students get a discount.

Le Grotte del Funaro (☎ 0763 34 32 76; Via Ripa Serancia 41; mains around €10; ☻ Tue-Sun) Eating here, you'll think you have died and gone to…well, a funerary cave. This restaurant was created out of a cavern and drips with atmosphere. There's an amazing view through the narrow windows, as well as antique agricultural objects and a piano bar.

Osteria dell'Angelo (☎ 0763 34 18 05; Piazza XXIX Marzo 8a; mains €22; ☻ Tue-Sun) Judged by local food writers to be one of the best restaurants in Umbria, this is certainly an elegant place.

SOUTHERN UMBRIA

SLOW FOOD, SLOW CITY

In 1986 McDonald's was about to open a restaurant at the famed Spanish Steps in Rome. Carlo Petrini, a wine writer, was so appalled that he started a movement that has grown to include around 80,000 members on five continents. Called 'Slow Food' (see p21), about half of the members are based in Italy, but conviviums are opening around the world at a rapid pace as people are adopting the Italian and, more so than any other province, Umbrian way of cooking and eating.

From the Slow Food Movement grew the Slow City Movement. Its members are concerned that globalisation is wiping out differences in traditions and culture and replacing them with a watered-down homogeneity.

To become a Slow City (or *Città Lenta* as they're known in Italy, where most of the Slow Cities are located), towns have to pass a rigid set of standards, including having a visible and distinct culture. The towns must follow principles such as relying heavily on autochthonous (from within) resources instead of mass-produced food and culture, cutting down on air and noise pollution, and relying more and more on sustainable development, like organic farming and public transport. Umbria boasts six Slow Cities: Trevi (p346), Todi (p373), San Gemini, Orvieto (p364), Città di Castello (p352) and Castiglione del Lago (p357).

As you travel through these towns, you will never hear a car alarm, you can be assured you'll find plenty of public space and there will never, ever be a McDonald's.

Your meal is being cooked by the winner of the 2000 'Chef to Watch' competition. The banana soufflé with a rum-and-cream sauce is recommended and the wine list is extensive.

Ristorante La Pergola (☎ 0763 34 30 65; Via dei Magoni 9b; meals €26; ☉ Thu-Tue) The food at this restaurant is typically Umbrian – good and filling – but the real draw here is dining in the flower-filled garden in the back. Try the *cinghiale* (wild boar).

ourpick L'Asino d'Oro (☎ 0763 34 44 06; Vicolo del Popolo 9; meals €28; ☉ Tue-Sun) The 'Golden Ass' has gained fame as one of Umbria's best simple trattorie. And for good reason. The menu changes daily, but a dedicated chef cooks inventive dishes such as a smoked 'streaky' bacon with radicchio appetizer (€9) and golden raisins or *cinghiale* in *agridolce* (sweet and sour) sauce sprinkled with cocoa (€14).

Ristorante Zeppelin (☎ 0763 34 14 47; Via Garibaldi 28; meals €32; ☉ Mon-Sat, lunch Sun) This natty place has a cool 1920s atmosphere, jazz on the stereo and a long wooden bar where Ingrid Bergman would have felt right at home. It serves creative Umbrian food, including well-priced tasting menus for vegetarians (€25), children (€20), truffle lovers (€40) and traditionalists (€25). Ask about its day-long cooking courses.

La Badia Ristorante (☎ 0763 30 19 59; Loc. La Badia 8; meals €45; ☉ Thu-Tue) The restaurant at La Badia is as refined as its hotel (p369). The

chef's speciality is suckling pig and tagliolini pasta with truffles. If you enjoy the Orvieto Classico here, tell the owner, Count Fiumi, as it comes from his vineyards. Even if you don't stay or eat here, you can still see it; when you're in the Orvieto Underground, look for the 8th-century abbey in the fields below.

ourpick Ristorante I Sette Consoli (☎ /fax 0763 34 39 11; www.isetteconsoli.it; Piazza Sant'Angelo 1/a; meals €45; ☉ Thu-Tue) Foodies have been known to flock here from Rome or Milan just for lunch, as it is quickly gaining fame as one of Umbria's top restaurants. With dishes like pan-fried pigeon with caramelised grapes or tagliolini pasta with zucchini blossoms and baby squid, it's no wonder it's considered a leader in nouvelle cuisine. In summer, dine under the gauzy tent out in the private garden. Reservations highly recommended for dinner.

CAFÉS

Caffè Montanucci (☎ 0763 34 12 61; Corso Cavour 21; 6.30am-midnight Mon-Fri, 7am-midnight Sat & Sun) An affable one-stop shop for cocktails, espresso, gelato, *panini*, internet access (per 30 minutes €3.10) and the best part: the wall o' chocolate. Hundreds of bars from all over the world congregate around a few tables, causing plenty of passing mouths to water.

Cantina Foresi (☎ /fax 0763 34 16 11; Piazza Duomo 2; snacks from €4.50) A family-run *enoteca* (wine bar) and café serving up *panini* and sausages, washed down with dozens of local wines from the ancient cellar.

GELATERIE
Pasqualetti (☎ 0763 34 10 34; Piazza Duomo 14) This *gelateria* serves mouth-watering gelato, plus there are plenty of tables on the piazza for you to gaze at the magnificence of the cathedral while you gobble.

Drinking
Il Palazzo del Gusto (☎ 0763 39 35 29; www.orvietowine .info; Via Ripa Serancia I 16; wine-tastings €5-11; ⊙ 11am-1pm & 3-5pm Mon-Fri winter, 11am-1pm & 5-7pm Mon-Fri summer) This Etruscan subterranean wine cellar is as infused with atmosphere as it is with yeast. Several tunnels have been redecorated for wine-tastings and parties. Peek behind the glass doors for a look at ancient Etruscan tunnels. Check with the tourist office if one of its many weekend events are open to the public.

Vinosus (☎ 0763 34 19 07; Piazza Duomo 15; tapas €6-10; ⊙ Tue-Sun) In photo-op range of the cathedral's northwest wall is this wine bar and eatery. The smattering of cheese plates makes this an elegant spot for a wine and cheese break. It is open until the wee hours for wine-tasting.

Entertainment
Teatro Mancinelli (☎ 0763 34 04 22; Corso Cavour 122; adult/concession €2/1, with guide €5/4; ⊙ 10am-1pm & 3-6pm) Plays host to Umbria Jazz Winter but offers ballet, concerts and tours all year in a stunning 19th-century theatre lined with elegant boxed seats and frescoes.

Shopping
Despite being a tourist town, Orvieto still has plenty of shops selling decent ceramics, lace, and delicious sample packs of local wines, sausage, olive oil, cheeses and *funghi* (mushroom) products. Via Garibaldi is a pedestrian shopping street with as many clothiers as ceramicists.

Getting There & Away
Orvieto is on the main Rome to Florence train line, so is ridiculously easy to reach. Main connections include Rome (€7.10, 1¼ hours, hourly), Florence (€10.40 to €18.50, 1½ to 2½ hours, hourly), and Perugia (€6.10 to €6.80, 1¼ hours, at least every other hour). Buses depart from the bus station on Piazza Cahen, stopping at the train station. **Bargagli** (☎ 057778 62 23) runs a daily bus service to Rome (€8, one hour 20 minutes, 8.10am and 7.10pm). The city is on the A1, and the SS71 heads north to Lake Trasimeno.

SOUTHERN UMBRIA

LE STRADE DEL VINO

The Etruscans produced wine in the district, the Romans continued the tradition and today several regions around Umbria embrace their viticulture heritage.

However, although Umbria is a major wine-growing region, it is just starting to adopt the concept of wine-tasting. Most visitors have simply tasted their wines one bottle or glass at a time with lunch and dinner, or in town at an *enoteca* (wine bar) or a shop that offers *degustazione* (tasting). But Umbria is starting to offer the driving wine routes many seasoned wine lovers would recognise.

If you do want to venture out to the countryside, pick up a brochure of one of these guided itineraries at any nearby tourist office. Umbria is divided into four wine routes known as the *strada dei vini* (wine trails). Each route is based not only on wine, but the history, culture, art, tradition and archaeology of a region. The routes are quite lengthy and seem to cover at least 80% of Umbrian secondary roads, but you can do just a section of the route. Check the website www.umbriadoc.com (in Italian) for more information on the routes and links to the wineries themselves.

La Strada dei Vini del Cantico The most sprawling route, it criss-crosses a triangle between Perugia, Todi and Spello, stopping in Torgiano, Assisi and Marsciano.

La Strada dei Vini Etrusco Romana Connects Orvieto with Amelia and many points in between.

La Strada del Sagrantino The area surrounding Bevagna and Montefalco, the fastest-growing wine area in the region.

La Strada del Vino Colli del Trasimeno Starts at Corciano near Perugia and circles through the *colli* (hills) around the lake.

DETOUR: LA SCARZUOLA

Fans of architecture, theatre, philosophy, religion, history, horticulture or conspiracy theory should head out to the country to **La Scarzuola** (☎ 0763 83 74 63; http://grandigiardini.it/2005/eng /giardini/umbria/scarzuola.htm; Montegabbione; admission €10; ☻ year-round). Famous Milanese architect Tommaso Buzzi (1900–81) bought this property, the site of a 1218 Franciscan monastery, in 1956. Francis was said to have planted a bush here that developed into a spring, growing the *la scarza* (marsh plants) he and his followers used to build themselves shelter. Buzzi added onto the monastery – itself a treasure-trove of relics – in a labyrinthine stone structure he called 'The Ideal City'. It symbolises the dance between the sacred and the profane, surrealism and simplicity, life without death. Ancient Greek architecture, monsters and a mysterious Egyptian third eye (his nephew, who runs La Scarzuola now, confirms Buzzi was a Mason) intertwine into the most curious of edifices. Starting in 2006, La Scarzuola will hold a series of evening concerts open to the public (check the website). To visit during the day, call ahead, as it requires at least 10 visitors a day to open.

To arrive, head to the far central western part of Umbria, between Orvieto and Città della Pieve. On the road from Pornello to Montegiove, keep your eyes out for a tiny sign on the left for La Scarzuola. Head down a dirt road that's much longer than you'd expect and you'll see the expansive gates.

Getting Around

A century-old cable car connects Piazza Cahen with the train station, with carriages leaving every 10 minutes from 7.20am to 8.30pm Monday to Friday and every 15 minutes from 8am to 8pm Saturday and Sunday (€1.80 round trip, including the bus from Piazza Cahen to Piazza Duomo). Bus 1 also runs up to the old town from the train station (€0.90). Once in Orvieto, the easiest way to see the city is on foot, although ATC bus A connects Piazza Cahen with Piazza Duomo and bus B runs to Piazza della Repubblica.

For a taxi, dial ☎ 0763 30 19 03 for the train station or ☎ 0763 34 26 13 for Piazza Repubblica.

LAGO DI CORBARA

Running along the SS448 road that connects Orvieto and Todi is a meandering lake with several excellent restaurants and a fantastic *agriturismo* (farm-stay accommodation).

Scacco Matto Bar/Ristorante Camping/Hotel Lamincia (☎ 0744 95 01 63; www.scaccomatto.net; SS448, Lago di Corbara; camping per person €5-5.50, per tent €5-5.50, per car €3; hotel s €44-49, d €67-75; ☻ camp sites Mar-Oct; **P** ⚡) A full-service stop closer to Orvieto than Todi on the SS448 just alongside the lake, hotel rooms, camp sites, a restaurant (meals €28; open Thursday to Tuesday) and a bar. The one-star camp site has a few dozen basic spots (no hot showers), but it's practically on the lake.

Agriturismo Castello Titignano (☎ 0763 30 80 00; www.titignano.it; Loc. Titignano di Orvieto; r per person incl breakfast €45, per person half-/full board €60/75; **P** ⚡) Titignano has been turned into somewhat of a holiday complex for guests looking for a bit of history, relaxation and gastronomic adventure. The castle was built in the astonishingly old date (even for Umbrian standards) of 937 AD. As you see it now, the attached village was built as its court in the 16th and 17th centuries. In it, you'll find a shop for buying its wine and olive oil. The castle's later addition, the palace is now used for the stunning restaurant (meals €35), with a stone balcony romantically overlooking Lago di Corbara

Trippini (☎ 0744 95 03 16; www.trippini.net; Civitella del Lago; meals €30; ☻ Tue-Sun) Although Vissani and Trippini went to school together, Trippini opened a simple restaurant while Vissani opened an empire. Adolfo Trippini's restaurant is within the town centre, where one could describe it in contrast as elegant but not cloyingly so, and creative without the overkill. He does beautiful things to shrimp and seafood, and even teaches cookery courses (call the number listed above for information).

Vissani (☎ 0744 95 02 06; www.vissani.net; meals €145; ☻ closed Mon lunch, Wed all day, Thu lunch, Sun dinner, holidays in late Jul, late Aug & Christmas) The hype surrounding Gianfranco Vissani's eponymous restaurant has hit astronomical levels of name recognition, even for Italian standards. While the rest of Italy and the world flock to Umbria just to eat at the famed restaurateur's lake-side abode (located down a locked private drive), and Gambero Rosso (the source of all food knowledge in Italy) has rated Vissani as Italy's top restaurant – Umbrians are not yet convinced.

Sit near the kitchen, as you can watch the chefs' artistry – up to 17 at a time, as apprentices from all over the world pay for the privilege of cooking at Vissani's – through the gilded framed windows. Dishes change seasonally, but the tuxedoed service remains the same. After dinner, guests are invited to move to the dessert room, where an after-dinner drink apothecary serves espresso and tea while diners sup gorgeously designed sweets.

TODI

pop 17,041

Todi embodies all that is good about a central Italian hill town. Ancient structures line even more ancient roads, and the pace of life inches along, keeping time with the fields of wildflowers that languidly grow with the seasons. Foreign artists share Todi's cobblestone streets with local families who have lived amid Todi's enclosed Roman and Etruscan walls for generations.

Like rings around a tree, Todi's history can be read in layers: the interior walls show Todi's Etruscan and even Umbrian influence, the middle walls are an enduring example of Roman know-how, and the 'new' medieval walls boast of Todi's economic stability and prominence during the Middle Ages.

History

Todi has been thriving for millennia. Three thousand years ago, the Umbri tribe developed the area, sharing it for a spell with the Etruscans. Rome conquered Todi around the 2nd century BC. In Roman days, Todi was known as Tuder and was the home to temples of Jupiter and Minerva and Roman baths. The Dark Ages weren't terribly kind to Todi, but in 1213 the city cemented its reputation as an area powerhouse.

Information

EMERGENCY
Police station (☎ 075 895 62 43; Piazza Jacopone)

BUS TICKETS
Rosso Pomodoro (Piazza Jacopone 7; ☼ 7.30am-8pm Mon-Sat, 10am-8pm Sun) Also sells decent slices of pizza for under €2.

ONE WEEK IN THE UMBRIAN COUNTRYSIDE

our pick **Todi Castle** (☎ 0744 95 20 04; www.todicastle.com; Vocabolo Capecchio, Morre; weekly villa/castle for up to 10 people from €1500/4500; p) Here's your chance to live in an honest-to-goodness castle for a week, or an equally perfect (and much more affordable) private villa, set not far from Lago di Corbara. The best part about staying here is the incredible attention to detail the staff provides – help setting up visiting itineraries, freshly squeezed orange juice and cakes for breakfast, even a fabulous driver for hire. See p316

INTERNET ACCESS
Biblioteca Comunale Lorenzo Leonj (☎ 075 895 67 10; ☼ 8.30am-2pm Mon-Fri, 3-6pm Tue & Thu) Two free high-speed internet terminals. Requires passport for first-time registration.

INTERNET RESOURCES
Todi (www.todi.net)
Todi Comune (www.comune.todi.pg.it) The official governmental tourist site.

MEDICAL SERVICES
Hospital (☎ 075 8 85 81; Via Giacomo Matteotti)

POST
Post office (☎ 075 894 24 26; Piazza Garibaldi; ☼ 8am-6.30pm Mon-Fri, 8am-12.30pm Sat)

TOURIST INFORMATION
Tourist office (☎ 075 894 54 18; Piazza del Popolo 37; ☼ 9.30am-1pm & 3.30-6.30pm Mon-Sat, 10am-1.30pm Sun & holidays Mar-Oct, 9.30am-1pm & 3-6pm Mon-Sat, 10am-1pm Sun & holidays Nov-Mar)

Sights

Just try to walk through the **Piazza del Popolo** (Piazza of the People) without feeling compelled to sit on medieval building steps and write a postcard home. Todi's town centre, the Piazza del Popolo, is one of the most renowned squares in all of Italy. Its lugubrious medieval cathedral and buildings cradle the interior piazza, enclosed with four gates during the medieval years but now filled with bustling shops, cappuccino-sipping residents and travellers gazing in wonderment at living history. The Lombard-style 13th-century

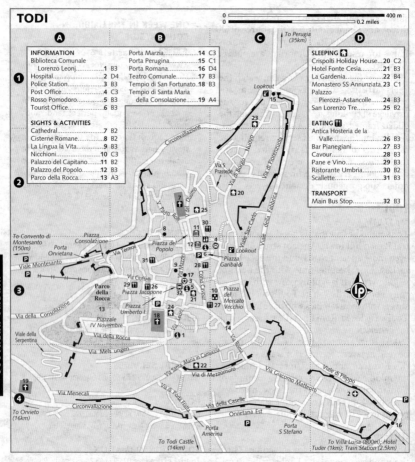

TODI

0 ————— 400 m
0 ———— 0.2 miles

INFORMATION
Biblioteca Comunale
  Lorenzo Leonj...............1 B3
Hospital............................2 D4
Police Station....................3 B3
Post Office........................4 C3
Rosso Pomodoro................5 B3
Tourist Office....................6 B3

SIGHTS & ACTIVITIES
Cathedral.........................7 B2
Cisterne Romane...............8 B2
La Lingua la Vita...............9 B3
Nicchioni........................10 C3
Palazzo del Capitano........11 B2
Palazzo del Popolo...........12 B3
Parco della Rocca.............13 A3

Porta Marzia.....................14 C3
Porta Perugina..................15 C1
Porta Romana..................16 D4
Teatro Comunale..............17 B3
Tempio di San Fortunato..18 B3
Tempio di Santa Maria
  della Consolazione......19 A4

SLEEPING
Crispolti Holiday House....20 C2
Hotel Fonte Cesia............21 B3
La Gardenia.....................22 B4
Monastero SS Annunziata.23 C1
Palazzo
  Pierozzi-Astancolle......24 B3
San Lorenzo Tre...............25 B2

EATING
Antica Hosteria de la
  Valle............................26 B3
Bar Pianegiani.................27 B3
Cavour............................28 B3
Pane e Vino.....................29 B3
Ristorante Umbria............30 B2
Scallette.........................31 B3

TRANSPORT
Main Bus Stop.................32 B3

To Perugia (35km)

Lookout

Circonvallazione

Via S Prassede

Via del Duomo

Via del Borgo Nuovo

Via di Fiorenzuola

Via Paolo Rolli

Via della Fabbrica

To Convento di
Montesanto (150m)

Piazza Consolazione

Porta Orvietana

Via Termoli

Piazza del Popolo

Via Mazzini

Lookout

Piazza Garibaldi

Via San Carlo

Viale della

Viale Montesanto

Via Ciuffelli

Piazza Jacopone

Parco della Rocca

Via della Consolazione

Piazzale IV Novembre

Via della Rocca

Piazza Umberto I

Corso Cavour

Piazza del Mercato Vecchio

Via Leonj

Viale della Serpentina

Via Mels ungen

Via Santa Maria in Camuccia

Via di Mezzomuro

Via della Caselle

Via di Porta Fratta

Via Giacomo Matteotti

Viale di Filippo

To Orvieto (16km)

Circonvallazione

Orvietana Est

Via Menecali

Porta Amerina

Porta S Stefano

To Todi Castle (14km)

To Villa Luisa (800m); Hotel Tuder (1km); Train Station (2.5km)

SOUTHERN UMBRIA

Palazzo del Capitano links to the **Palazzo del Popolo** to create what is now the **Museo Pinacoteca di Todi** (☎ 075 895 62 16; Piazza del Popolo; admission €3.10; ☺ 10am-1.30pm & 3-6pm Tue-Sun Mar-Oct, 10.30am-1pm & 2.30-5pm Tue-Sun Nov-Feb), which features an elegant triple window and houses the city's recently restored *pinacoteca* (picture gallery) and an expansive archaeological museum housing exhibits on archaeology, numismatics (coins), weaving and ceramics, in addition to the impressive frescoed rooms of the *pinacoteca*. Artwork includes paintings by Giovanni di Pietro (Lo Spagna) and a copy of an Etruscan statue of the Roman god Mars (the original bronze is at the Vatican).

Check out the **Cisterne Romane** (Roman Cisterns; ☎ 075 894 41 48; adult/concession €2/1.50; ☺ 10.30am-

1pm & 2.30-5pm daily Mar-Oct, open Sat, Sun & holidays only Nov-Mar), a Roman architectural feat that would impress the most demanding modern engineer (or any other history nerds). Not only did the two systems in 12 rooms serve as the water supply for Todi until medieval times, it was built in the tiny valley that was the Piazza del Popolo and still stands as the support structure for the square.

The **cathedral** (☎ 075 894 30 41; Piazza del Popolo; ☺ 8.30am-12.30pm & 2.30-6.30pm), at the northwest end of the square, has a magnificent rose window and intricately decorated doorway. However, there are two much more impressive churches which no visit to Todi should go without. The lofty **Tempio di San Fortunato** (Piazza Umberto 1; admission free; ☺ 9am-1pm & 3-7pm

Wed-Mon Mar-Oct, 10am-1pm & 2.30-5pm Wed-Mon Nov-Mar), contains frescoes by Masolino da Panicale and the tomb of Beato Jacopone. Inside, make it a point to climb the **Campanile di San Fortunato** (adult/concession €1.50/1; ☾ 10am-1pm & 3-6.30pm Mar-Oct, 10.30am-1pm & 2.30-5pm Nov-Mar, closed Mon), where you can gaze across the hills and castles surrounding Todi. Just across from the temple you'll find the **Teatro Comunale**, the municipal theatre inaugurated with a Verdi opera in 1876, that is still used today (check with the tourist office for a schedule).

The postcard home you've just written from the Piazza del Popolo (see above)? Most likely it's of Todi's famed church, the early Renaissance masterpiece **Chiesa di Santa Maria della Consolazione** (no phone; Via della Consolazione at Via della Circonvallazione; ☾ 9.30am-12.30pm & 2.30-6.30pm Mar-Oct, 9.30am-12.30pm & 2.30-5pm Nov-Mar, Wed-Mon), considered one of the top architectural masterpieces of the 16th century, is just outside the city walls. Possibly designed by Donato Bramante in 1508 but not completed until 99 years later, the construction was a veritable modern feat in Renaissance architecture. Inside, fans can admire its geometrically perfect Greek cross design. Outside, its soaring cupola-topped dome is visible from 10km away.

The **Parco della Rocca** is at the highest point in Todi and contains the ruins of the old *rocca* (fort). From here you can see part of the old Roman wall, called the Nicchioni. These mysterious 'little niches' are a bit of a misnomer, as the loggia-like arches embedded in the Roman walls are up to 7m high. No-one quite knows their origin or use, but historians have hazarded a few guesses – possibly recesses used for the civic forum, or an engineering device used to help hold up the above road.

Todi features a staggering amount of old city walls, some of them medieval, some Roman and some pre-Roman. The gates are a magnificent example of ancient architecture, especially the Porta Romana (Roman Gate), Porta Perugina (Perugia Gate) and Porta Marzia (Gate of Mars).

Just outside the main town walls you can see the Convento di Montesanto, now a working convent but built as a fortress in 1325 to guard against Orvieto.

Courses

Sign up for some courses at **La Lingua La Vita** (☎ 075 894 83 64; www.lalingualavita.com; Via Mazzini 18).

COMBINED TICKET

If you'll be spending a day or two in Todi, it's a good idea to buy a **biglietto cumulativo** (adult/concession/child €6/5/4), which will allow you to gain entry into the Museo Pinacoteca, Cisterno Romano and the Tempio di San Fortunato. The ticket can be purchased at any of the museums or at the tourist office.

While many students and younger folk head to Perugia to learn and party, the more mature student (meaning 25 plus) might enjoy studying Italian in Todi. You can sign up for group or individual lessons, but both options involve participation in a handful of activities including cooking classes, Italian films and field trips in and around Todi. Costs start at €400 per week for accommodation and classes.

Festivals & Events

The **Todi Festival** (www.todiartefestival.it), held for 10 days each July/August, is a mixture of classical and jazz concerts, theatre, ballet and cinema.

Sleeping

Todi has only six hotels (all but one are three-star or higher) so you might need to be a bit creative in your sleeping options.

BUDGET

Monastero SS Annunziata (☎ 075 894 22 68; www.monasterosmr.it; Via San Biagio 2; s/d/tr incl breakfast €35/70/105) Get away to this tranquil retreat within the city walls. Set around a lovely garden, all rooms come with private bathroom and bed linens, and some with furnishings from the 1400s. Try to catch a meal with your hosts, nuns from the Mary's Servant of Repair order.

MIDRANGE

Villa Luisa (☎ 075 894 85 71; www.villaluisa.it; Via Cortesi 147; s €45-60, d €70-135, incl breakfast; P ⊠ ⊜) Once a grand villa, the statuesque hotel is still set in parklike grounds worthy of a visit even if you're not staying here. The pool and terrace mean you can spend hours enjoying the view, and the full-service staff will help arrange baby-sitting, laundry or sightseeing itineraries. It's just outside the city walls, along the bus line coming in from the train station, with an on-site restaurant.

Crispolti Holiday House (☎ 075 894 48 27; www .crispoltiholidayhouse.com; Via S Prassede 36; s €50, d €80-90, tr €90-120, q €120-160, incl breakfast) What a coat of paint will do to turn an institutionally functional religious hotel into a 'holiday house' for tourists. Although it still retains that 'Little Orphan Annie' vibe from its first incarnations as a convent and orphanage, the stunning view from the terrace and period details throughout bump up its modern comfort.

San Lorenzo Tre (☎ 075 894 45 55; www.sanlorenzo3 .it; Via San Lorenzo 3; s/d incl breakfast with bathroom €73/110, s/d without bathroom €68/78; ☺ Mar-Dec) Five generations of the same family have lived at this proper historic residence, and the current owner, Marzia, keeps the B&B's décor an honest a representation as you'll find anywhere in Umbria. Filling, home-cooked breakfasts, a library dating back a century and a stunning rooftop view of the surrounding valley add to the romance.

Hotel Tuder (☎ 075 894 21 84; www.hoteltuder.com; Via Maesta dei Lombardi 13; s €50-60, d €100-125, incl breakfast; P X) This three-star hotel is about 1km outside the city centre on the bus route from the train station. The 40 rooms are divided into 'standard' and 'comfort', and you'll get posher furniture, better showers, more space and higher prices in the comfort category. All rooms come with TV and direct-dial phones.

Palazzo Pierozzi-Astancolle (☎ 320 273 1035; Piazza Umberto 1; www.palatodi.it; 2-8 guests per day €90-200, per week €450-1000) Years of restoration went into creating this masterpiece of 16th-century Italian history and 21st-century Scandinavian minimalist design. The English-speaking Danish/Italian couple who oversee the apartments are charming and erudite hosts, armed with a wealth of knowledge of the area and Italy. Five apartments can be rented separately or together, but each is outfitted with a modern kitchen and various exquisite touches: balconies, fireplaces, antique tapestries, frescoes, plush living rooms and washing machines.

La Gardenia (☎ 347 611 52 20; www.lagardeniatodi.com; Via Santa Maria in Camuccia 45; up to 5 guests per week €450-550) A fruit basket greets you at your new home in Todi. This central apartment has everything to make you feel like Todi is home, including two double beds, one single bed, a washing machine, dining room, TV, stereo and iron. The view of Santa Maria delle Consolazione,

the hills and the campanile will bring anyone to tears. Trade English and Italian lessons with your sweetheart of a host, Carlo.

Hotel Fonte Cesia (☎ 075 894 37 37; www.fonte cesia.it; Via Leoni 3; s €112-116, d €140-164, ste €192-208, incl breakfast; P X) The top hotel in Todi, the exquisitely decorated rooms have all the amenities: satellite TV, hairdryer, minibar etc. You can upgrade to a junior suite, some of which have private balconies and claw-foot bathtubs.

Eating

Cavour (☎ 075 894 37 30; Corso Cavour 21; pizzas from €4.50; ☺ until 2am Thu-Tue) A casual place populated with locals, this is where to come to get a light meal or pizza. Serves several different traditional soups (€4 to €5), a nice addition on a rainy day.

Antica Hosteria de la Valle (☎ 075 894 48 48; Via Ciuffelli 17/19/21; meals €23; ☺ Tue-Sun) Most of the time you will be dining here with the locals. The pasta is homemade and delicious, but the traditional *farro* (spelt) soup (€7) should not be missed.

Scallette (☎ 075 894 44 22; Via delle Scallette 1; meals €24; ☺ Tue-Sun) Wander off the main road down this ancient stairway for a reasonably priced feast in a hobbit-like abode. This ancient farmhouse feels like it's practically in Middle Earth and, with its stone walls, roasted meat dishes and decadent desserts, is a precious spot for a mini-medieval banquet.

Pane e Vino (☎ 075 894 54 48; Via Ciuffelli 33; meals €26; ☺ Tue-Thu) Now you're definitely in Italy. Dine on dishes such as risotto with yellow pumpkin (€8) or just nibble on the antipasto plate (€11) while tasting from the extensive wine list that includes wines from all over Italy. Relax on the outdoor patio or at candlelit tables under the curved brick ceiling in this narrow, atmospheric *enoteca*.

Ristorante Umbria (☎ 075 894 27 37; Via Santa Bonaventura 13; meals €29; ☺ Thu-Tue) What's more enjoyable: the food or the outdoor patio with a view back in time? Look in the display case to salivate over which goodies you'd like for your meal, perhaps some prosciutto or *salumi* (cured pork)? Try the *palombaccio* (€13), a type of pigeon, a risotto dish or its speciality (truffles, of course).

Bar Pianegiani (☎ 075 894 23 76; Corso Cavour 40; ☺ 6am-midnight Tue-Sun) Just like Clark Kent, this nondescript neighbourhood bar puts on an innocent front to conceal the magic that lies beneath, but 50 years of tradition has created the world's most perfect gelato. Try the black cherry or hazelnut.

Getting There & Away

APM (☎ 800 51 21 41) buses leave from Perugia's Piazza Partigiani (€5.20, one hour) every hour or so, but only four reach Piazza Jacapone in the city centre. The rest stop at Piazza Consolazione, where it's possible to take city bus A or B or walk uphill 2km. Heading back to Perugia from Piazza Jacapone are five buses a day at 6.35am, 12.40pm, 1.30pm, 3.38pm and 4.58pm (Monday to Saturday). There is one daily service to Spoleto (€5.20, 1½ hours, 6.50am).

Todi is on the **FCU** (☎ 075 57 54 01; www.fcu.it in Italian) train line, which runs through Deruta to Perugia (€2.55, 50 minutes, 18 daily). Although the train station is 3km away, city bus C (€0.90, eight minutes) coincides with arriving trains, every other hour on Sundays. By road, Todi is easily reached on the SS3B–E45, which runs between Perugia and Terni, or take the Orvieto turn-off from A1 (the Milan–Rome–Naples route).

MONTE CASTELLO DI VIBIO

pop 1657

The real draw in this tiny speck of a town about 20km from Todi is its even tinier speck of a theatre. Throw in sleeping (or dining) in a castle, gorgeous views and a working *agriturismo* and you're set for one or two days.

Monte Castello di Vibio feels like it's in the middle of nowhere, but it's just a few kilometres from the SS3B–E45 that links Perugia and Terni (just north of Todi). Tourist information can be found at the Associazione Culturale (Via Roma 1), just behind the theatre. The post office next door sells stamps with the image of the theatre.

In keeping with the proportions of the tiny town, **Teatro della Concordia** (Teatro Piccolo; ☎ 075 878 07 37, 328 918 88 92; www.teatropiccolo.it; admission free but donations accepted; ☼ 10am-12.30pm & 3.30-7.30pm Apr-Aug, 10am-12pm & 3-6pm Sat, Sun & holidays, closed Sat morning Nov-Feb) is billed as the smallest theatre in the world. It seats 99 people, 32 on the main floor and 67 in the stalls. The theatre was built in 1808, when nine Monte Castello di Vibio families decided that their town needed a theatre. In 1850 residents added frescoes to the ceiling and stalls. Along with red velvet seats, the theatre gained a sophisticated look to rival any larger, grander theatre. Gina Lol-

labrigida acted in her very first play here. In 1951 the theatre was almost shut down for lack of revenue, but the community voted to pay extra taxes to keep the theatre going. In 1993 the theatre teamed up with the theatre in Parma – one of the world's largest – to put on a series of events. Performances are staged for much of the year, especially on Saturday nights. The theatre is also open by appointment and an English audio guide is available. It also does fantastic destination weddings.

A brilliant marketing campaign (and honestly, a really fun way to spend a day and a half) is to take advantage of the **Weekend in Umbria** (%075 89 42 161; weekend@teatropiccolo.it) package (for one/two people €90/150). Available only on Saturday night, you arrive in Monte Castello di Vibio and are provided with accommodation at Relais Il Castello or one of the local *agriturismi*, as well as dinner, a show at the theatre and breakfast on Sunday morning. You can even arrange to be picked up at the closest train station, in Fossato di Vico.

ourpick **Agriturismo/Ristorante Fattoria di Vibio** (☎ 075 874 96 07; www.fattoriadivibio.com; Località Buchella 9, Doglio; per day €80-105, per week €455-735, 3-bdrm cottages per week €800-1900; P ⊠ ⚊) The view from the spa's pool – out a plate glass window, overlooking an enormous expanse of perfectly rolling, stone villa-capped hills – is reason enough to make the haul here. In the middle of nowhere but with absolutely every amenity a world-class *agriturismo* might need, the *fattoria* offers enough activities to keep guests busy for a week of dining, getting massaged, wine-tasting, horseback riding…or, just relaxing and staring at the view.

Relais Il Castello (☎ 075 878 06 60; www.relaisil castello.it; Piazza Marconi 5, Monte Castello di Vibio; B&B per person €45-57, half-board per person €57-77, full board per person €68-87, P ⊠ ⚊) A suit of armour greets visitors at the door in this honest-to-goodness castle. While the former Hotel Il Castello may have taken the relais concept a tad far (a relais usually refers to a very high-end establishment), the Il Castello has nevertheless upgraded significantly since undergoing renovation in 2006. Rooms that felt historical (but not necessarily in a good way) now feature slightly more comfortable furnishings and several upper-end amenities such as room service, private balconies and satellite TV. Fans of King Arthur will want to dine in the downstairs restaurant, every inch covered in medieval stone walls with an enormous wrought-iron chandelier. The menu is huge for Umbrian standards and features an array of risotto, soup and pasta dishes (meals €27).

Take the SS3–E45 from Todi to Perugia. Exit at the Monte Vibio sign and continue for about 4km (at the roundabout that doesn't tell you where to turn, veer left). It's on the S397 between Todi and Marsciano.

CAMPELLO SUL CLITUNNO
pop 2407

If you're heading between Foligno and Spoleto, a pleasant place for a stroll is the Campello sul Clitunno, where you'll find the **Fonti del Clitunno** (☎ 0743 52 11 41; Loc. Pissignano; admission €2; 10am-12.30pm & 2.30-5.30pm winter, 9am-8pm summer), the source for the Clitunno river. This Zen-like garden proffers crystal clear springs, a tranquil lake and exquisitely lush foliage. In ancient times, it was a popular site for religious pilgrimages. Caligula was known to come here to consult the god of the Clitunno River and it was also used for theatre performances, feasts and gladiator matches. While you can't witness gladiator matches, you can stroll the lovely grounds.

In the same area is the **Tempietto del Clitunno** (☎ 0743 27 50 85; Via Flaminia, Km 139; 9am-8pm Apr-Oct, 8am-6pm Nov-Mar). This Paleo-Christian building was first thought to be an ancient Roman ruin, but artefacts have shown that it was built sometime between the 5th and 8th centuries AD. It has many of the classic Roman features, such as Corinthian columns and neo-Augustan inscriptions (in big block lettering).

Residenza d'Epoca Vecchio Molino (☎ 0743 52 11 22; www.vecchio-molino.it; Via del Tempio 34, Loc. Pissignano, Campello sul Clitunno; s/d/ste incl breakfast 73/115/135; Easter-Oct; P) We have a reader's letter to thank for alerting us to this sacredly soothing historical residence, and Umbrians backed up the recommendation wholeheartedly. The former 15th-century mill sits on the languid banks of the Clitunno River, where, according to local myths, the Italian people were born. Every centimetre of the hotel is covered in medieval history, from the vaulted oak-beamed ceilings to the stone bridge over the river.

SPOLETO
pop 38,717

Spoleto was one of those sleepy Umbrian hill towns until, in 1957, Italian-American composer Gian Carlo Menotti changed everything. For a while, Spoleto saw its tourist season peak for only 10 days from the end of June to the beginning of July during its immensely popular Spoleto Festival (p381). During the festival this quiet town takes centre stage for an international parade of drama, music, opera and dance.

Now so many people have discovered the town via the festival that it's become a popular destination for most of the year (although as in the rest of Umbria, you'll have the town mostly to yourself in winter). Even outside the festival season, Spoleto has enough museums, Roman ruins, wanderable streets and vistas to keep you busy for a day or two.

If you plan to visit during the Spoleto Festival, book accommodation and the most popular performances at least two or three months in advance. Or, stay in one of the adjacent towns along the train route (Trevi, Spello, Assisi or Perugia are good choices) and ride in for performances.

History

Umbria was first divided in half between the Etruscans and Umbrians. After Rome fell, it was divided again: Byzantines on the east of the Tiber River, Lombards to the west. Spoleto, which was just to the west of the Tiber, became the capital of the Lombardy duchy and in 890 AD, the title of Holy Roman Emperor went to a duke from Spoleto. Although much of its pre-Lombard artwork has been lost, you'll see many of the signature religious buildings and hermitages in the area.

The surrounding Umbra Valley is a masterpiece of well over 2000 years of agricultural practice. From the original Umbrian tribes to the Romans and farmers in the medieval period, the Vale di Spoleto, as it was known then, has been drained using an intricate system of hydraulics and agricultural techniques.

Orientation

The old part of the city is about 1km south of the main train station; every 20 minutes, an orange shuttle bus (€0.80) marked A, B or C heads to Piazza della Libertà in the centre, where you'll find the tourist office city and the Roman-era theatre. Piazza del Mercato, a short walk northeast of Piazza della Libertà, marks the engaging heart of old Spoleto. Between here and Piazza Duomo you'll find the bulk of the city's monuments and some fine shops.

Information
BOOKSHOPS
Il Libro (☎ 0743 46 678; Corso Mazzini 63) A wide selection of maps, cookbooks, guidebooks and novels in English.

EMERGENCY
Police (Polizia Municipale; ☎ 0743 23 241; 191 Via la Marconi)

INTERNET ACCESS
A Tutta Birra (☎ 348 241 18 40; Via di Fontesecca 7; ☯ noon-11pm Wed-Mon)
Pizzeria Zeppelin (p382; per hr €3)

MEDICAL SERVICES
Ospedale di Madonna di Loreto (Hospital; ☎ 0743 21 01; Via Madonna di Loreto)

POST
Post office (☎ 0743 20 15 20; Piazza della Libertà 12; ☯ 8am-6.30pm Mon-Fri, 8am-12.30pm Sat) The entrance is off Viale Giacomo Matteotti.

TOURIST INFORMATION
Con Spoleto (☎ 0743 22 07 73; www.conspoleto.com; Piazza della Libertà 7) A privately owned service that can book accommodation.
Tourist office (☎ 0743 23 89 20/1; info@iat.spoleto .pg.it; Piazza della Libertà 7; ☯ 9am-1pm & 4-7pm Mon-Fri, 10am-1pm & 4-7pm Sat & Sun Apr-Oct, 10am-1pm & 3.30-6.30pm Mon-Sat, 10am-1pm Sun Nov-Mar)

Sights
ROMAN SPOLETO
Make your first stop the **Museo Archeologico** (☎ 0743 22 32 77; Via S Agata; adult/concession/child €4/2/free; ☯ 8.30am-7.30pm), located on the western edge of Piazza della Libertà. Since 1985, this former Benedictine monastery and prison has been used as a museum. It holds a well-displayed collection of Roman and Etruscan bits and bobs from the area, including two marble statues of Augustus and possibly Caesar. Then step outside to view the mostly intact 1st-century **Teatro Romano** (Roman Theatre), which often hosts live performances during the summer (check with the museum or the tourist office) and is an understandably popular venue during the Spoleto Festival.

East of Piazza della Libertà, around the Piazza Fontana, are more Roman remains, including the Arco di Druso e Germanico (Arch of Drusus and Germanicus; sons of the Emperor Tiberius), which marked the grandiose entrance to the Roman forum. The

excavated **Casa Romana** (Roman House; ☎ /fax 0743 23 42 50; Via di Visiale; adult/child €2.50/2; ☯ 10am-6pm daily) isn't Pompeii, but it gives visitors a peek into what a typical Roman house of the area would have looked like in the 1st century BC, and still has vestiges of mosaics and paintings. The city boasts an Anfiteatro Romano (Roman Amphitheatre), one of the country's largest. Unfortunately it is within military barracks and closed to the public. Wander along Via dell'Anfiteatro, off Piazza Garibaldi, in search of a glimpse.

An hour-long stroll or an all-day hike is a lovely way to while away an afternoon along the Via del Ponte to the **Ponte delle Torri**, erected in the 14th century on the foundations of a Roman aqueduct. The bridge is 80m high and 230m across, built in an imposing set of 10 arches. Cross the bridge and follow the lower path, Strada di Monteluco, to reach the **Chiesa di San Pietro** (☎ 0743 4 48 82; Loc. San Pietro; admission free; ☯ 9.30am-11am & 3.30-6.30pm). The 13th-century façade, the main attraction of the church, is liberally bedecked with sculpted animals.

ROCCA ALBORNOZIANA
The **Rocca Albornoziana** (☎ /fax 0743 22 30 55; Piazza Campello; single ticket €6, combined ticket to Rocca & museum €7.50; ☯ 10am-8pm summer & weekends, 10am-1pm & 3-6pm late Mar-Jun, Sep & Oct, 10-11.45am & 2-4.15pm Mon-Fri, 10am-4pm Sat & Sun Nov-Feb), an example of a Cardinal Albornoz–built fortress from the mid-14th century. Cardinal Albornoz led Pope Innocent VI's forces in the fight to take back control of Umbria. He fostered the building of many of the *rocche* (fortresses) in the area, including the one still standing in Narni (p391), the ruins of one in Orvieto (p368), and one in Perugia (p321) that was destroyed in an uprising against the Pope just three years after it was built. The monstrosity dominates the city. For hundreds of years, until as recently as 1982, Spoleto's *rocca* was used as a high-security prison housing such notables as Pope John Paul II's attempted assassin, Ali Agca. It now hosts open-air concerts (most notably during the Spoleto Festival) and a museum displaying local history.

In 2007, the Rocca became home to the **National Museum of the Dukedom of Spoleto** (☎ /fax 0743 22 30 55; Piazza Campello; single ticket €6, combined ticket to Rocca & museum €7.50; ☯ 10am-7pm Thu-Sun) which houses historical information as well as artwork from Spoleto's *pinacoteca*, which will remain closed for several years.

SPOLETO

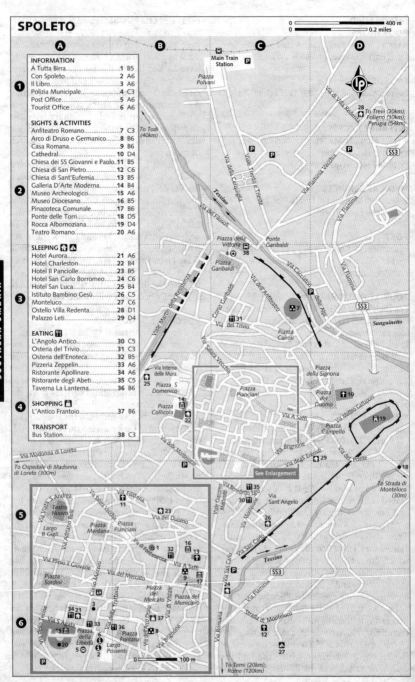

INFORMATION	
A Tutta Birra...........................1	B5
Con Spoleto............................2	A6
Il Libro.....................................3	A6
Polizia Municipale....................4	C3
Post Office..............................5	A6
Tourist Office..........................6	A6

SIGHTS & ACTIVITIES	
Anfiteatro Romano....................7	C3
Arco di Druso e Germanico.......8	B6
Casa Romana...........................9	B6
Cathedral...............................10	D4
Chiesa dei SS Giovanni e Paolo.11	B5
Chiesa di San Pietro...............12	C6
Chiesa di Sant'Eufemia...........13	B5
Galleria D'Arte Moderna.........14	B4
Museo Archeologico................15	A6
Museo Diocesano...................16	B5
Pinacoteca Comunale..............17	B6
Ponte delle Torri....................18	D5
Rocca Albornoziana................19	D4
Teatro Romano......................20	A6

SLEEPING	
Hotel Aurora.........................21	A6
Hotel Charleston...................22	B4
Hotel Il Panciolle...................23	B5
Hotel San Carlo Borromeo......24	C6
Hotel San Luca.....................25	B4
Istituto Bambino Gesù...........26	C5
Monteluco...........................27	C6
Ostello Villa Redenta............28	D1
Palazzo Leti.........................29	D4

EATING	
L'Angolo Antico.....................30	C5
Osteria del Trivio...................31	C3
Osteria dell'Enoteca...............32	B5
Pizzeria Zeppelin...................33	A6
Ristorante Apollinare..............34	A6
Ristorante degli Abeti.............35	C5
Taverna La Lanterna..............36	B6

SHOPPING	
L'Antico Frantoio...................37	B6

TRANSPORT	
Bus Station..........................38	C3

MUSEUMS & CHURCHES

The stunning **cathedral** (Santa Maria Assunta; ☎ 0743 44 307; Piazza del Duomo; ☑ 7.30am-12.30pm & 3-6pm summer, 7.30am-12.30pm & 3-5pm winter) in Spoleto was consecrated in 1198 and remodelled in the 17th century. The Romanesque façade is fronted by a striking Renaissance porch. In the 11th century, huge blocks of stone salvaged from Roman buildings were put to good use in the construction of the rather sombre bell tower. The mosaic floors are from a 12th-century reconstruction effort. Inside, the first chapel to the right of the nave (Chapel of Bishop Constantino Eroli) was decorated by Bernardino Pinturicchio, and Annibale Carracci completed an impressive fresco in the right transept. Check out the apse's fresco *Life of the Virgin Mary*, done by Filippo Lippi and his assistants, Fra Diamante and Piero Matteo d'Amelia (who painted a starry sky on the Sistine Chapel ceiling 20 years before Michelangelo covered it up). Lippi died during the commission. Lorenzo de' Medici travelled to Spoleto from Florence and ordered Lippi's son, Filippino, to build a mausoleum for the artist. This now stands in the cathedral's right transept.

The spectacular closing concert of the Spoleto Festival is held on the piazza, in front of the cathedral.

On Via Filitteria, you'll come across the tiny and ancient **Chiesa dei SS Giovanni e Paolo** (☑ 10am-1pm & 3-8pm Jun-Sep, sporadically in winter), an example of a pre-Romanesque church, built with Roman ruins above an older church, and consecrated in 1174. If it's open, check out the earliest depiction of the Archbishop of Canterbury Sir Thomas Becket's martyrdom. If it's closed, you can still see the 13th-century fresco of *Our Mary with Saints* above the door.

The 12th-century **Chiesa di Sant'Eufemia** (☎ 0743 23 10 22; Via A Saffi; adult/child €3.10/1.55; ☑ 10am-12.30pm & 3.30-7pm summer, 10am-12.30pm & 3.30-6pm winter) is within the grounds of the Archbishop's palazzo. It is notable for its *matronei* – galleries set high above the main body of the church to segregate the female congregation. The admission price is for the attached Museo Diocesano.

To check out more modern artwork, head towards the **Galleria D'Arte Moderna** (☎ 0743 464 34; Palazzo Collicola; ☑ 10.30am-1pm & 3-5.30pm Wed-Mon 16 Oct-14 Mar, 10.30-1pm & 3.30-7pm Wed-Mon 15 Mar-15 Oct; adult/child €4/3) an homage to Spoleto's

commitment to its ongoing artistic support. The Italian sculptor Leoncillo has a dedicated room here.

The **Pinacoteca Comunale** is under restoration for several years, but much of its artwork has been moved to the new National Museum of the Dukedom of Spoleto (p379) in the interim. Check with the tourist office or any museum to locate its new spot (possibly in the Rocca Albornoziana).

Festivals & Events

The Italian-American composer Gian Carlo Menotti conceived the **Festival dei Due Mondi** (Festival of Two Worlds) in 1958. Now simply known as the **Spoleto Festival**, it has given the town a worldwide reputation and spawned a sister festival in Charleston, South Carolina.

Events at the festival, held over three weeks from late June to mid-July, range from opera and theatre performances to ballet and art exhibitions, in the Rocca Albornoziana, the Teatro Romano at the archaeological museum and the cathedral, among other places. A special Spoleto Cinema component shows old and new films, and a fairly new but inventive performance tradition has been to re-enact either famous or historical court proceedings. Tickets cost €5 to €200, but most are in the €20 to €30 range. The most famous performances sell out as early as March or April, but you can still buy tickets that week for many shows. There are usually several free concerts in various churches.

For details, phone ☎ 800 56 56 00 or look for further details and book tickets online at www.spoletofestival.it.

Sleeping

The city is well served by cheap hotels, *affittacamere* (rooms for rent), hostels and camp sites. Expect significantly higher prices during the festival.

BUDGET

Monteluco (☎ /fax 0743 22 03 58; www.geocities.com /monteluco2002; Loc. San Pietro; per person €4.50-6.50, per tent €4.50-6.50, per vehicle €2-7; ☑ Apr-Sep) This leafy, simple camp site is just behind the Chiesa di San Pietro. It's a good 15- to 20-minute walk uphill from the town centre and less than 1km from the aqueduct and several good hiking trails. The restaurant is good enough to attract the locals.

Ostello Villa Redenta (☎ 0743 22 49 36; www.vil laredenta.com; Via di Villa Redenta 1; dm/d incl breakfast €18-24/42-55; **P**) Pope Leone the Twelfth slept here. Literally. The 17th-century home is set within a quiet park just outside the historic centre and comes complete with a bar, breakfast and private bathroom in each room. Reception is open from 8am to 1pm and 3.30pm to 8pm.

Hotel Il Panciolle (☎ /fax 0743 4 56 77; Via del Duomo 4; s €30-50, d €35-65) Comfortable enough for those used to nicer hotels and a deserving splurge for hostellers, this Spoleto mainstay is in a good position between the cathedral and the Piazza del Mercato. The rooms facing the street can be a tad loud. There are hairdryers, TVs and comfortable bedding in all rooms.

Istituto Bambino Gesù (☎ 0743 402 32; Via Sant'Angelo 4 at Via Monterone; s €18-36, d €36-70, all incl breakfast) The combined age of these enterprising nun-B&B proprietors might be older than the 16th-century convent itself. Get in touch with your monastic side in these bare-bones cells, no more than a bed, dresser and postage stamp–sized bathroom. But the price is right, the views are amazing and the dead silent, pitch black nights will guarantee a good night's sleep.

Hotel San Carlo Borromeo (☎ 0743 22 53 20; www .geocities.com/sancarloborromeo; Via San Carlo; s €25-5, d €30-70, tr €50-100, all incl breakfast; **P** **⊠** **▣**) The least atmospheric of the hotels listed, the convenience, price and free car park make it a safe bet. The back rooms are quieter and have a view of Monteluco, but all are clean, functional and spacious.

MIDRANGE

Hotel Aurora (☎ 0743 22 03 15; www.hotelauroraspoleto .it; Via Apollinare 3; s €40-65, d €55-100, tr €70-115, all incl breakfast; **▣**) Just off Piazza della Libertà, the Aurora is central and offers fabulous value. Opened in 1958 to coincide with the Spoleto Festival, the Aurora has been hosting satisfied artists and performers ever since. Staff are friendly and will help you plan your Spoleto itinerary. Some rooms have pleasant balconies and breakfast is excellent.

Hotel Charleston (☎ 0743 22 00 52; www.hotelchar leston.it; Piazza Collicola 10; s €40-75, d €52-135, tr €99-160, all incl breakfast; **P** **⊠** **▣**) With a sauna, fireplace and an outdoor terrace, the Charleston is an enticing location in both winter and summer. Named after Charleston, South Carolina (home of a sister Spoleto Festival), the hotel is covered in distinguished modern art

and provides wine tastings or apéritifs every evening. The 17th-century building has been thoroughly renovated with double-paned windows and some rooms come with VCRs or bathtubs. Internet access (per hour €6) is also available. The wood-beamed attic suite is worth the splurge. Parking costs €10.

TOP END

Palazzo Leti (☎ 0743 22 49 30; www.palazzoleti.com; Via degli Eremiti 10; s €150, d €200, ste €260-320, incl breakfast; **P** **⊠**) In the southeast part of town facing the hills, this former noble palace exudes romance and charm down to the last detail, from the delicate breakfast china to the historical oak and wrought-iron furnishings. With the view and perfect silence, you'll feel like you're staying in the country, but you're a three-minute walk from the centre of Spoleto. Parking will set you back €13 the first night, and €7 subsequent nights.

Hotel San Luca (☎ 0743 22 33 99; www.hotelsanluca .com; Via Interna delle Mura 21; s €95-170, d €110-240, ste €210-300, incl breakfast; **P** **⊠**) Practically perfect hospitality is one of the main draws of the Zuccari family's (p344) second hotel. With enough services to rival any of the five-stars in Umbria (sound-proofed rooms, babysitting, laundry service), San Luca has an atmosphere that is rather relaxed, enough to cater to bicyclists and walking tours. Pastel tones and antique furnishings inside complement the 17th-century manicured outdoor garden.

Eating

Spoleto is one of Umbria's main centres for the *tartufo nero* (black truffle), which you'll often find shaved over pasta. On Via dell'Arco Druso is a gathering of five shops selling meat, bread, sauces and wine, perfect to pick up supplies for a picnic.

Pizzeria Zeppelin (☎ 0743 4 77 67; Corso Giuseppe Mazzini 81; pizzas & snacks €0.80-3; ⊙ 10.30am-9.30pm) A meeting point in town, here you can get a filling slice of pizza for less than €1, plus check your email (per hour €3).

Osteria dell'Enoteca (☎ 0743 22 04 84; Via A Saffi 7; tourist menu €15; ⊙ Wed-Mon) Extremely fit waiters carry dishes up and down a curving iron staircase into this 12th-century tavern. Diners sit on dark wood benches under a high-stone ceiling surrounded by rows and rows of local wines from which to choose. Dishes are typical of the area – *strangozzi alla spoletina* ('shoelace' pasta in a tomato, garlic and chilli sauce, €6.20), truffle omelette (€6.20) – and priced to allow at least one or two meals while in town.

Taverna La Lanterna (☎ 0743 4 98 15; Via della Trattoria 6; tasting menus around €15; ⏰ Thu-Tue) A great place with extremely reasonable prices in the town centre, La Lanterna serves a variety of Umbrian pasta dishes. Tasting menus include vegetarian offerings for €11, regular for €13, and porcini and tartufo for €15.

Osteria del Trivio (☎ 0743 4 43 49; Via del Trivio 16; €25; ⏰ Wed-Mon, closed Jan) Strings of garlic and dried peppers grace the walls of this most homey of homestyle restaurants. This is a great place to try the *strangozzi alla spoletina*, and the antipasti and stuffed artichokes are legendary.

L'Angolo Antico (☎ 0743 4 90 66; Via Monterone 109; meals €26; ⏰ Tue-Sun) In a neighbourhood restaurant just outside the main city is this family-run ristorante and pizzeria, with a few suits of armour thrown in for good measure. Nothing fancy on the menu, just good filling *strangozzi alla spoletina* and *scallopine al limone* (pork in a lemon sauce).

Ristorante degli Abeti (☎ 0743 22 00 25; Via Benedetto Egio 3/5; meals €27; ⏰ Wed-Mon) Get your red meat and cream fix here. Not the place for dieters or vegetarians, the menu offers sinfully rich piles of artery thickeners, such as *pappardelle con cinghiale e tartufo* (pasta with wild boar and truffles) and *prosciutto di cinghiale* (ham with wild boar).

Ristorante Apollinare (☎ 0743 22 32 56; Via S Agata 14; tasting menus incl vegetarian €30-48; ⏰ Wed-Sun) A delight for the senses, Apollinare is an extraordinary culinary experience set amid ancient 12th-century walls and low oak beam ceilings lit by flickering candlelight. The menu changes seasonally, but you can choose to go with one of its tasting menus – vegetarian, truffle or traditional – or choose from its nouvelle menu. Somehow this restaurant manages to figure out that squid-ink pasta does go with pesto and crayfish, and rabbit feels quite at home in a black-olive sauce. No matter what, save room for dessert.

Shopping

Gathered along Via dell'Arco Druso are several shops that sell locally produced meats, wines or delicacies.

L'Antico Frantoio (☎ 0743 49 893; Via dell'Arco Druso 8) Sells plenty of pasta, *lenticchie* (typical Castelluccian minilentils), wine, oil and cheese for

a great gift or picnic. Each town in Umbria has several of these gourmet goods stores, but here the fiery owner, Sandra, makes many of her own sauces. Try anything with *tartufi* (truffles), olive or *carciofi* (artichokes). She will carefully package and FedEx any purchases you make to anywhere in the world.

Getting There & Around

BUS

The local **Società Spoletina di Imprese Trasporti** (SSIT; ☎ 0743 21 22 09; www.spoletina.com) buses depart from the near the train station. Long-distance buses are rare as the train is so convenient, but you'll need a bus to get to Norcia and the Valnerina (€4.80, one hour, six daily) or Cascia (€4.80, one hour 10 minutes, six daily). Buses to Monteluco run in summer only (€0.80, 15 minutes, hourly).

To reach town from the train station, take city buses A, B or C for €0.80 (make sure the bus reads 'Centro').

TRAIN

Spoleto is on a main train line so it's extremely easy to reach from just about anywhere. Trains from the main **train station** (☎ 0743 4 85 16; Piazza Polvani) connect with Rome (€7.10 to €11.60, 1½ hours, hourly), Perugia (€3.70, one hour, nine daily – take care not to land on one of the €9.10 Eurostars) or Assisi (€2.80, 40 minutes, hourly).

NORCIA

pop 4971

As the jumping-off point to the Valnerina and Monti Sibillini, venerable Norcia more than delivers its fair share of impressive churches and museums, but that's not the reason most people come here. No, visitors make it this far for the pigs. And the wild boar. And the lentils, cheese, ham, prosciutto, chocolate, *farro* (spelt), mushrooms and, of course, black truffles. To learn more about the art of hunting truffles, see the boxed text on p170.

Norcia is known throughout Italy and the world as a capital of pork butchery. In fact, the word *norcineria* is now used to denote butchers specialising in pork products. The techniques used in Norcia date back to Roman times when the harsh terrain led area inhabitants to focus on animal husbandry as the main food source. The town was also put on the world map as the birthplace of St Benedict in 480 AD, the patron saint of Europe.

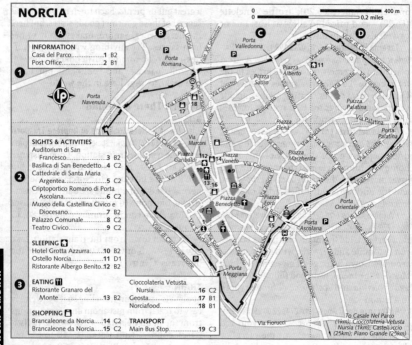

NORCIA

INFORMATION
Casa del Parco..................1 B2
Post Office..................2 B1

SIGHTS & ACTIVITIES
Auditorium di San
   Francesco..................3 B2
Basilica di San Benedetto...4 C2
Cattedrale di Santa Maria
   Argentea..................5 C2
Criptoportico Romano di Porta
   Ascolana..................6 C2
Museo della Castellina Civico e
   Diocesano..................7 B2
Palazzo Comunale..........8 C2
Teatro Civico..................9 C2

SLEEPING
Hotel Grotta Azzurra.......10 B2
Ostello Norcia..................11 D1
Ristorante Albergo Benito..12 B2

EATING
Ristorante Granaro del
   Monte..................13 B2

SHOPPING
Brancaleone da Norcia.....14 C2
Brancaleone da Norcia.....15 C2

Cioccolateria Vetusta
   Nursia..................16 C2
Geosta..................17 B1
Norciafood..................18 B1

TRANSPORT
Main Bus Stop................19 C3

To Casale Nel Parco
(1km); Cioccolateria Vetusta
Nursia (1km); Castelluccio
(25km); Piano Grande (25km)

Orientation

Norcia is almost entirely flat, a rarity in Umbria. The main gate for Norcia is the Porta Ascolana, also known as the Porta Massari, which is where buses arrive. Most of Norcia is pedestrian only, but there are many pay car parks around the city walls, including one near Porta Ascolana.

Information

Bianconi Hospitality (www.bianconi.com) Serving Norcia-bound tourists for 160 years now, the family's hospitality group website includes information on its hotels and restaurants as well as truffle hunts and activities in the Valnerina and Monti Sibillini.

Casa del Parco (☎ 0743 81 70 90; Via Solferino 22; ⏰ 9.30am-12.30pm & 3-6pm Mon-Fri, 9.30am-12.30pm & 3.30-6.30pm Sat & Sun) Offers tourist information and plenty of Monti Sibillini information, including guided trips, public transportation to the area, detailed walking maps and local products. During the summer, ask about low-priced English-language excursions throughout Monti Sibillini.

Geosta (☎ 0743 82 84 70; Via Foscolo 10; ⏰ 9am-12.50pm & 3.45-7.20pm Tue-Sun; per 30min €1) Currently the only internet spot in the town centre, it also has a

superb collection of local maps and books, and outdoor gear.

Norcia (www.norcia.net) Private tourist information.

Post office (next to Porta Romana)

Sights & Activities

The **Basilica di San Benedetto** (Piazza San Benedetto) is an impressive show of architectural know-how. Named after St Benedict, patron saint of Europe, who was born in Norcia, it was built in the shape of a Latin cross with a polygonal apse. The bell tower dates back to 1389 and its portico is Gothic. Frescoes inside the church date to the 16th century, including *Resurrezione di Lazzaro* (Resurrection of Lazarus) by Michelangelo Carducci (not *the* Michelangelo, but one from Norcia) and *San Benedetto e Totila* (St Benedict and Totila) by Filippo Napoletano, completed in 1621. If you're in town on a Sunday, be sure to stop in at 5.30pm or 7.45pm, when Benedictine monks from the attached monastery chant in the crypt.

The **Museo della Castellina Civico e Diocesano** (La Castellina Diocesan Civic Museum; ☎ 0743 81 70 30; Piazza San Benedetto; adult/concession €4/3; ⏰ 10am-1pm & 3-5pm winter, 4-6pm summer) contains a small collection of Roman artefacts and local artwork. It is open late some nights in August. The admission price also gains you entrance to the **Criptoportico Romano di Porta Ascolana** (Roman Crypt of Porta Ascolana), which is a remnant of a small Roman necropolis.

Next to the museum is the **Cattedrale di Santa Maria Argentea** built in 1560 but modified after several earthquakes in the 1700s. The weighty wooden doors are original. Works by several Flemish masters grace the walls. Also on Piazza San Benedetto is the **Palazzo Comunale**, parts of which date back to the 14th century. Its bell tower dates to 1713.

Feel the love at the **Teatro Civico** (☎ 0743 81 60 22; Piazza Veneto; ☺ 11am-1pm & 5-7pm for free tours), a beaux arts building dating from 1872 which was rebuilt by dedicated Nursine (residents of Norcia) after a fire in 1952. There are also performances at the **Auditorium di San Francesco** (☎ 0743 816 44 88; Via Renzi).

Festivals & Events

Truffle lovers, foodies and mooches should head to Norcia on the last weekend in February and the first weekend in March for the **Mostra Mercato del Tartufo Nero**, where dozens of Italian merchants sell (and offer samples of) the best Italian food has to offer.

Sleeping

BUDGET

Ostello Norcia (☎ 349 300 20 91; www.montepatino.com; Via Ufente 1/b; dm incl breakfast €15) Brought to you in conjunction with the Casa del Parco folks,

---

ONE-STOP ORGANIC HOLIDAY

our pick **Casale Nel Parco** (☎ /fax 0743 81 64 81; www.casalenelparco.com; Loc. Fontevena 8; s €50-60, d €100-120, half-board s €70-80 d €130-150, full board €170-190, extra person €30-35; P ☺) Only 1km from Norcia towards Castelluccio, this working organic *agriturismo* grows its own lentils, spelt and vegetables (which you can sample at dinner). Swim in the terracotta-tiled pool under the eye of snow-capped Monte Patino, ride the horses through the foothills of Monti Sibillini or ask your hosts to arrange any outdoor activity you can imagine. Fourteen rustic and romantic double rooms are individually designed.

---

the walls of this former hospital for the poor are covered with everything you'll need to know for your trip into the Valnerina and Monti Sibillini, that is, if you haven't booked an excursion through them yet. Fifty-two tidy rooms come with two to 10 beds. Try calling ahead to book as it closes intermittently during the day and often fills up with school groups on outings. Bed sheets included.

Ristorante Albergo Benito (☎ 0743 81 66 70; www .hotelbenito.it; Via Marconi 5; s/d/tr incl breakfast €50/75/85) Located perfectly in the centre of town, it's a friendly one-star hotel with eight modest rooms. Nothing fancy, but the rooms are tidy and quiet. The attached restaurant (below) is excellent.

MIDRANGE

Hotel Grotta Azzura (☎ 0743 81 65 13; www.bianconi .com; Via Alfieri 12; s €37-88, d €44-125; ☺) A suit of armour greets guests in the reception of this 18th-century palazzo. The family-run hotel can be a fabulous deal during the week and low season, and is steeped in the area's history. Cross-vaulted rooms are stately if a bit dark, complete with carved ceilings and recently upgraded bathrooms. This hotel has the most personality by far, and you can still take advantage of the activities the group offers: babysitting, evening events, gym classes, a sauna and outdoor activities, like truffle hunts.

Eating

The town is full of *norcinerias* – butchers serving Norcia-produced dried meats. In fact, the word *norcineria* is now used to mean a butcher throughout all of Italy. Famous food items from the area also include *cinghiale*, lentils and *pecorino* cheese.

Ristorante Granaro del Monte (☎ 0743 81 65 13; Via Alfieri 12; meals €28) One of the most famous restaurants in Umbria for visitors, it has been open daily for 150 years running. It is a tad touristy, but the food is still excellent and comes in great piles of porcini mushrooms, sausages and prosciutto, truffles and *cinghiale*. In the winter, sit inside next to the grand fireplace in the enormous banquet-sized interior, and in summer, relax on the pleasant outdoor dining area. Its signature dish is *filetto tartufato del cavatore*, a veal dish sautéed in butter, black truffles and red wine – as rich as it is delicious.

Ristorante Albergo Benito (☎ 0743 81 66 70; Via Marconi 5; meals €30; ☺ Tue-Sun) This simple but

---

BE THANKFUL FOR UMBRIAN OLIVE OIL

Most visitors to Umbria notice the bread right away. Many words have been used to describe it: namely 'bland', 'hard' and 'dry'. But Umbrians are intensely proud of their bread, partly due to the historical significance. In 1540, Pope Paul III levied a salt tax on Umbria. The hardy and self-reliant peasants refused to pay, and began baking bread without salt. They soon found out unsalted bread didn't spoil as easily, and spiffed up quickly when moistened with olive oil, topped with tomatoes, or added to soup or salad. Be sure to try the delicious bruschetta (toasted bread topped with olive oil, tomatoes, truffles, artichokes etc) or *panzanella* (bread salad), but try to keep your appetite for your meal, not the bread bowl.

---

delicious restaurant within the hotel of the same name (p385) offers many dishes served with local meats and truffles.

Shopping

Norcia is lined with shops selling local products, cheeses and every conceivable piece of pig in every conceivable form of pork product. Be careful, though: you can't ship meat to most countries.

Norciafood (☎ 0743 82 83 62; www.norciafood.com; Via dei Priori 38) This is one of the largest and most complete Norcineria and local produce shop. It ships to anywhere in the world and you can order many of their products on the website.

Brancaleone da Norcia (☎ 0743 82 83 11, 0743 81 75 15; www.gustusitaliano.com; Corso Sertorio 17 or Via Roma 24) A savvy shop specialising in locally produced products of every sort, size and type – cheese, lentils, jam, and every conceivable cut of pork known to humankind. Once you're home, order anything you want from their website.

Cioccolateria Vetusta Nursia (☎ 0743 81 73 70, shop 0743 82 80 70; Viale della Stazione 41/43) A kilometre outside Norcia on the road to Castelluccio you'll pass what looks like a boring warehouse. Step inside and you'll find the best prices on a huge selection of chocolate, wine, lentils and local (non-meat) products. Best of all, there is always something available to taste. There's also a smaller and more expensive shop in town at Via Mazzini 6.

Getting There & Away

The closest train station is in Spoleto, so the best way to get to Norcia is by bus or car. The main bus stop is near Porta Ascolana. **SSIT** (☎ 0743 21 22 11; www.spoletina.it) runs trips to Norcia from Spoleto (€4.40, one hour, five daily) and Perugia (€6.80, two hours, one daily at 2.10pm).

You can travel to Castelluccio only once a week, and Norcia is the town to do it from. The bus leaves Norcia at 6.25am and 1.30pm on Thursday only (€3.20, 40 minutes). It originates in Castelluccio, returning at 7.20am or 2.20pm, so if you just wanted to take a drive through the region, you could technically buy a return ticket and take it straight through.

MONTI SIBILLINI

Monti Sibillini is one of those places it would be great to discover by accident, but there's no way you're going to haul yourself up from Norcia (if you make it to Norcia at all) unless you hear how beautiful this area is.

This area is really, really, really beautiful. Really. Go. Even during summer, its jagged peaks keep a healthy dusting of snow. Mt Vettore – the highest peak in Monti Sibillini – stands at 2476m. In May and June, infinite expanses of wildflowers blanket the Piano Grande, the great plain surrounding Castelluccio. Wolves run free, icy streams flow and fairies dance. Well, so the story goes. During the Middle Ages, the Sibillini mountains were known throughout Europe as a place that held demons, necromancers and fairies. A woman named Sybil was said to live in a cave and tell fortunes. These days, the area is home to peregrine falcons, royal eagles and porcupines (brought over in the last few decades). Eighteen hundred botanical species have been counted just in this one area.

Before going off into the Monti Sibillini, you can pick up a host of maps at the Casa del Parco (p384) in Norcia, depending on how strenuous or leisurely you want to be. Any level of activity is possible here, spanning from day paths to week-long survival treks circling the mountain chain. The office has a lot of useful information available on different kinds of inexpensive guided trips in English, as well.

For information, try the official **Parco Nazionale dei Monti Sibillini** (www.sibillini.net).

Castelluccio

Castelluccio looks impossible. The crumbling village sits atop a lonely hill-top like an outpost in the middle of the vast expanse of the Piano Grande. It's difficult enough these days to traverse the dozen kilometres (at least) over treacherous mountain passes to reach the nearest village in any direction, especially during winter when temperatures can reach -30ºC, but Castelluccio was even more isolated in the past and as such, has stayed relatively poor.

The hamlet now boasts a smattering of small eateries and a few places to stay, but what has put it on the map is the Castelluccio *lenticchie*: small, thin-skinned legumes that keep many of the hundred or so permanent residents in business and many Umbrian bellies warm and full during the winter. The town is also famous for its *pecorino* and ricotta cheeses.

During the day, head out in any direction to hike, ski, hang-glide or go horseback riding. Or, wander the perimeter of the main square (the area around the car park) to chow down in small shops selling all sorts of Castelluccian goodies. Since the nightlife consists mostly of chasing goats around dilapidated stone buildings, a good night's sleep is practically guaranteed.

INFORMATION

The Casa del Parco (p384) in Norcia has information about the town of Castelluccio.

ACTIVITIES

Pro Delta (☎ 0743 82 11 56, 339 563 54 56; www.prodelta .it; Via della Fate 3, Castelluccio) is one of the most well-respected hang-gliding institutions in Europe and has a solid reputation for safety. A basic five-day hang-gliding or paragliding course costs €400 and refresher courses start at €120. Those with a sense of adventure but neither time nor money can take a two-person paragliding and hang-gliding ride for €25 to €70. Check the requirements page of its website before arriving for a course.

Another school is **Fly Castelluccio** (☎ 0736 34 42 04; www.flycastelluccio.com; Via Copernica 12, Ascoli Piceno), in the neighbouring region of Le Marche. It offers weekend, five- or 10-day elementary courses in paragliding and hang-gliding, as well as paramotoring.

For horseback riding, contact **Associazione Sportiva Piangrande** (☎ 0743 81 72 79; Castelluccio), which is open from Easter to October, and on weekends in winter. The organisation offers half- and full-day treks throughout Monti Sibillini, plus bicycle tours of the region. Mountain-bike riders should pick up the *Pedalling in the Park* brochure at any Casa del Parco office.

SLEEPING & EATING

Agriturismo Locanda dè Senari (☎ 0743 82 12 05; www .agriturismosenari.it; Via della Bufera; B&B per person €40, subsequent nights per person €35; Mar-Oct) This *agriturismo* is housed in an old barn in the heart of the old town. There are just five rooms in the time-worn stone building, but all are modern and well designed. The downstairs restaurant (meals €24) is the liveliest place in town. The owners serve all the products from their nearby farm here – spelt, lentils, ricotta cheese, beef and salami.

Albergo Sibilla (☎ 0743 82 11 13; Via Piano Grande 2; s €29-36, d €45-60; P) Offers very basic rooms with rudimentary bathrooms. But they're clean and it's whisper quiet at night. The view is the reason you're staying here (that, and, well, it's one of the only hotels in town). There's a decent restaurant downstairs, so consider the half-board option.

Taverna di Castelluccio (☎ 0743 82 11 58; Via Dietro la Torre 6; meals €22.50; Thu-Tue Easter-Oct, daily in August) A ramshackle edifice on the outside, but the hearty, filling meals is what brings the hanggliders and paragliders out by the wingful. The dish to try, of course, is the lentil soup, but truffle frittatas and *farro* (spelt) soup round out the territory's offerings.

GETTING THERE & AWAY

You can travel to Castelluccio only once a week, and Norcia is the town to do it from. The bus leaves Norcia at 6.25am and 1.30pm on Thursday (€3.20, 40 minutes). It originates in Castelluccio, returning at 7.20am or 2.20pm, so if you just wanted to take a drive through the region, you could technically buy a return ticket and take it straight through.

VALNERINA

Forget all those softly rolling hillsides and delicate vineyards gracing much of the rest of Central Italy. The landscape in the Valnerina is a geographically feral contrast to the nearby time-worn topography. Named for the

SOUTHERN UMBRIA

valley of the Nera River, the ancient flow created steep valleys and jagged mountains, and millennia of isolated history has placed hidden monasteries and castles throughout. The entire area has been nominated as a Unesco World-Heritage site, although it remains one of the most overlooked spots in Umbria. Outside of the wildly popular Cascata delle Marmore waterfalls, the Valnerina shyly beckons travellers with its unequalled beauty. Those with their own transportation (do not even consider coming here without) will have the back roads (and even the main highways) all to themselves.

Information

Associazione Gaia (☎ 338 767 83 08; www.asgaia.it; Via Cristoforo Colombo 1/a, Foligno) Specialises in rafting trips, but it also offers environmental education, mountain biking, horseback riding and free climbing. Before each rafting trip commences, it offers a very informative small introductory course on the natural surroundings of the Corno River.

Rafting Umbria (☎ 0742 231 46, 348 351 17 98; www.raftingumbria.it; Via Santi Brinati 2, Foligno) A full-service outdoor activity centre offering much more than rafting. Activities include canoeing, kayaking, horseback riding, free climbing, mountain biking, white-water rafting, orienteering and survival skills. Based out of Foligno this outfit arranges rafting trips in the Valnerina on the Corno and Nera Rivers, bicycling in Monti Sibillini and free climbing in Ferentillo.

www.valnerinaonline.it Look up information on accommodation, activities, events and dining in English or Italian.

Cascata delle Marmore

Don't let the tourist trap entrance to this attraction scare you off (except on weekends in August – then you should run screaming). These waterfalls are the highest in Europe, and are a truly amazing sight to behold. The Romans created them in 290 BC when they diverted the Velino River into the Nera River. These days, the waterfall provides hydroelectric power to the region. If you are without a car, it is worth catching a bus out to see it, particularly to witness the arrival of the water after it has been switched on. If you need to to travel from Terni out to these falls, jump on local bus 7.

Whenever the waterfalls are operational, the SS209 (connecting Terni and Perugia to Norcia and Ferentillo) and the SS79 (connecting Terni and Perugia to Piediluco and

---

ROAD TRIP: VALNERINA

The Valnerina is easily accessed as a day trip from Spoleto, Terni or Norcia, and is only a little over an hour from Trevi, Foligno, Narni or Todi. The SS395 from Spoleto and the SS209 from Terni join with the SS320 and then the SS396, which passes through Norcia. The best way to see the area is to take a day trip along the SS209, starting at **Cascata delle Marmore** (left) in the morning, visiting Ferentillo and its **Mummy Museum** (below) after its 2.30pm afternoon opening time and ending up at **Il Cantico** (opposite) in San Pietro in Valle for a memorable dinner.

Rieti) come to a virtual standstill. There are four car parks throughout the area. Plan on staying a while, as the area surrounding the falls is equally attractive.

The falls operate on a bizarrely complex schedule that probably isn't even accurate. Just about any tourist office in Umbria will have the schedule for the waterfall, but the local tourist offices – Terni, Narni, Spoleto, Norcia and Perugia – are most likely to know the correct data, or you can call ☎ 0744 629 82. The falls are completely closed in December, January and February. The best time to see them is between 10am and noon, or 3pm or 4pm up until 9pm or 10pm in the summer, during holidays and on Sundays. Opening hours are even more restricted on Saturdays and weekdays.

The skittish and the completely insane are both welcome at **Centro Canoe e Rafting Le Marmore** (☎ 330 75 34 20; www.raftingmarmore.com; Via Carlo Neri), based in Terni. One can try 'hydrospeeding' – the white-water equivalent of bobsledding – or take what is called a 'soft rafting' excursion down the Nera, more appropriate for all ages and skill levels.

Ferentillo

As you head from the waterfalls north up the SS209 you'll see a set of medieval walls placed precariously over a hill above this quiet town set in the midst of the fluvial Valnerina.

Fans of the macabre will have a deathly good time at the goosebump-inducing **Museo delle Mummie** (Museum of the Mummies; ☎ 0743 543 95; Via delle Torre; adult/concession €3/2; ☉ 9am-12.30pm & 2.30-7.30pm Apr-Sep, 10am-12.30pm & 2.30-6pm Oct & Mar,

10am-12.30pm & 2.30-5pm Nov-Feb), reached through an eerie subterranean 4th-century crypt. You'll find a collection of ancient Ferentillian mummies – glorified desiccated corpses, really – in various stages of decay, mummified naturally with a process of salt, ammonia and mushrooms. Dozens of mummies – one, a visiting 19th-century Chinese doctor – sit, stand or lie down, some still clothed, others with a full set of teeth or hair, a mother and child, and the ever-popular display of disembodied heads.

The second thing Ferentillo is known for is its rock climbing. You can contact certified rock-climbing guide Kathleen Scheda at **Duka Duka Outdoors** (☎ 0765 6 32 02; dukadukaoutdoors@libero.it) to arrange climbing expeditions. Kathleen's family owns a B&B just across the border in Lazio called **La Torretta** (☎/fax 0765 6 32 02; www.latorrettabandb.com; Casperia, Lazio; s/d/f €60/80/140). It's in a medieval town about an hour from Rome and close to the best climbing spots in Lazio and Umbria. The B&B has a two-night minimum stay and offers one-week rock-climbing trips, as well as cooking courses and hiking excursions.

Ostello Il Tiglio (☎ 0744 38 91 04; www.umbriahostels.org; Via Abruzzo; dm €14.50, f per person with bathroom €17; P) is perfectly situated to reach many different parts of the Valnerina, Norcia and La Cascata delle Marmore for river rafting and rock climbing. It's a small hostel with just 25 beds, but perfectly outfitted for jaunts into the nearby area. Breakfast is €1.60, dinner is €9 and staff will even pack you a lunch for €7!

Le Due Querce (☎ 0744 78 14 41; www.bellaumbria.net/agriturismo-Leduequerce; Via del Piano 5; d/tr/q €50/70/90, campingper person/tent €6/1.50; P) is a full-service *agriturismo*, camp site and horseback-riding stables, next to the Nera River. It produces eggs, olive oil, cheese and truffles, and can set you up to do every outdoor sport in the Valnerina.

our pick **Ristorante Piermarini** (☎ 0744 78 07 14; www.saporipiermarini.it; Via Ancaiano 23; meals €46; Tue-Sat, Sun lunch, bookings required for lunch Tue-Fri) Off the beaten track but on a well-signed back road, the Piermarini farm estate provides an elegant backdrop for extravagant cookery, featuring home-grown olive oil, grains and truffles from the nearby hills. A far cut above the home-style cooking found in most roadside establishments, the restaurant features refined local cuisine, heavily seasoned with truffles, along with expert service and upscale presentation. A most worthy destination for gastronomes and oenophiles, with at least 2½ hours for a meal.

San Pietro in Valle

There is some serious history going on at San Pietro in Valle (St Peter Abbey) in the town of Valle, just 6km north of Ferentillo. Evidence suggests it was a pagan temple before two wandering Syrian hermits happened upon it in the 5th century. The interior of the abbey has pre-Giotto frescoes from the Roman and Lombard epochs.

The **Residenza d'Epoca Abbazia San Pietro in Valle** (☎ 0744 780 129; www.sanpietroinvalle.com; SS209 Valnerina, km 20; s €98-109, d €129-139, ste €175-189; open around Easter-Oct; P), also known as a hotel, is a special place, away from the crowds. Rooms have been upgraded quite a bit since their days as medieval nunnery cells. A few have stone fireplaces or breathtaking views over the cloisters and the surrounding valley; ask for any last-minute discounts. The hotel owners can give you hiking maps of the area and set you up with all sorts of adventurous activities. It serves an enormous breakfast of freshly baked bread and home-made preserves on the abbey's outdoor patio. There is a free sauna for guests.

The attached restaurant **Il Cantico** (☎ 0744 78 00 05; meals €31; mid-Mar–Oct) is tucked under the abbey in a centuries-old subterranean stone vault. Seasonal dishes include crayfish ravioli with Trasimeno bean soup, pumpkin flan with pecorino sauce and truffles, and pigeon breast in Sagrantino wine sauce, all made with fresh, local ingredients. A great bet is to order one of the four enormous tasting menus: vegetarian (€35), rivers and lakes (€40), Valnerina specialities (€38) or meat (€40).

CREEPY UMBRIA

Visit one of these places for a hair-raising experience:

- See medieval corpses frozen in time at the **Museo delle Mummie** (opposite) in Ferentillo
- Get a history lesson on the Battle of Trasimeno and how to beat the Romans in **Tuoro** (p358)
- Visit **Narni Sotterranea** (p391) to see an Inquisition prisoner's desperate graffiti

TERNI

pop 104,938

There are only two reasons to come to Terni – passing through on your way to the Valnerina, Norcia and Monti Sibillini or because you're an art historian. Terni is a major industrial city, virtually obliterated in WWII bombing raids and subsequently rebuilt. Known as 'the steel city' or 'the Manchester of Italy', its modern factories used to attract tourists in the early 1900s.

Terni's **tourist office** (☎ 0744 42 30 47; info@iat .terni.it; Viale Cesare Battisti 7; ☺ 9am-1pm & 3-6pm Mon, Tue, Thu & Fri) is south of the main train station and just west of Piazza C Tacito, near Largo Don Minzoni.

Art lovers should stop by the **pinacoteca** (☎ 0744 45 94 21; Via del Teatro Romano 13; adult/concession €4/2.50; ☺ 10am-1pm & 3-7pm) to have a look at one of the more important remaining works by Piero Matteo d'Amelia, Pala dei Francescani. He was the most important artist of his time but has been surpassed in history as his finest work, a certain Vatican chapel's ceiling, was painted over by some newcomer named Michelangelo.

One of Terni's charms is its devotion to that famous Umbrian pastime, the festival. Its most famous home-town hero is St Valentine, who was the bishop of Terni until Placidius Furius, on orders of Emperor Aurelius, got really angry and had St Valentine executed in AD 269. Well after Valentine's martyrdom, a legend was created. It was said that he would often give gifts of flowers from his own garden to his young visitors. Two of these visitors fell in love and married, forever linking St Valentine with love. Now, a huge feast engulfs the city on 14 February, but the entire month is dedicated to love and romance.

From Terni, you can catch an ATC Terni bus to Perugia (€6.90, 1¼ hours, three daily) and Narni (€1.80, 30 minutes, every other hour with a gap between 10am and 1.30pm). If you arrive in Terni by train and need to get to the bus station on Piazza Europa, or vice versa, catch local bus 1 or 2.

NARNI

pop 20,054

While Umbria is called the 'Green Heart of Italy', the town of Narni could be called the true heart of Italy. It's the closest town to the geographic centre of the Italian peninsula, a symbolic position not lost on its inhabitants. Umbria is one of the more rural provinces in Italy, and Narni exudes the friendly, laid-back charm that's so pervasive throughout the southern part of Umbria. You're not just imagining it: people here *are* friendlier.

As one Narni local puts it, 'We have the bread, but we don't have the teeth'. He's referring to the amazing array of tourist sites – a 13th-century hill-top *rocca* guarding mightily over the town; the Narni Sotterranea, a subterranean world of caves that used to house Inquisition prisoners; churches and palaces galore – but practically no tourist structure. The *rocca* is difficult to get to and Narni Sotterranea is only open on public holidays, Sundays and a few Saturdays (the entrance is through a day-care centre playground). However, the tourist board just published its first Narni map, available in English, which will help ensure you don't miss its bread for lack of teeth.

History

Narni became a Roman stronghold in the 2nd century BC as the Via Flaminia ran from Rome to Rimini through Narni. Its importance grew partly because of the Nera River, which flowed at the bottom of Narni's great hill. The town developed into a *comune* (city-state) as early as the 11th century but was partially destroyed in the 14th century by northern mercenaries on their way home from sacking Rome. After rebuilding, Narni regained its status as a centre for art and goldsmithing, and held great artistic prominence throughout the Renaissance.

Orientation

Narni has two historic centres: the quieter Piazza dei Priori, which houses the tourist office and Palazzo del Podestà; and Piazza Cavour, home to the cathedral. Just outside the main town gate – **the Arco Romano** – is Piazza Garibaldi, along the back of the cathedral, where you'll find restaurants, cafés and the bus stop. Everything is a short walk from these two, except for the *rocca*, which is either a drive or a pretty decent hike up the hill. At the bottom of the hill flows the Nera River, where the Roman Ponte d'Augusto lies.

Information

EMERGENCY

Police station (☎ 0744 71 52 34; Via Portecchia)

INTERNET RESOURCES

Bella Umbria (www.bellaumbria.net/narni) The best private tourist information on Narni.

Narnia (www.narnia.it)
Narnia Comune (www.comune.narni.tr.it) The government website for Narni.

MEDICAL SERVICES
Hospital (☎ 0744 74 01; Via Cappuccini Nuova)

TOURIST INFORMATION
Tourist office (☎ 0744 71 53 62, 0744 74 72 47; www.comune.narni.tr.it; Piazza dei Priori 3; ⊙ 9.30am-12.30pm daily, 4.30-7pm Mon-Tue, 3.30-7pm Wed-Sun)

Sights
Plan your visit to Narni around the concise opening hours of the tortuously fascinating **Narni Sotterranea** (Narni Subterranean; ☎ 0744 72 22 92; www.narnisotterranea.it; Via San Bernardo 12; admission €5; ⊙ tours 10.15am, 12.15pm, 3.15pm, 4.15pm Sun & public holidays, 3pm & 6pm Sat Apr-Oct). The 1½ hour tour (in Italian, English or both) guides you through millennia of history, starting with a look into Roman plumbing and an underground Romanesque frescoed church, and moving on to an Inquisition prisoner's cell from 1759 and the torture devices with which he might have been familiar. Skulls and bones abound throughout the tour. The subterranean was rediscovered in 1979 on the advice of an older town resident whose grandfather had heard the stories passed down for centuries. The current archaeological director rents a tranquil apartment outside of town, **Podere del Cardinale** (p393), and guests or visitors might be able to lend a hand during the week for the ongoing archaeological excavations. In addition to the above hours the subterranean is also open weekdays during the Corso all'Anello and Ferragosto, or by appointment during the week.

Above the subterranean is the **Chiesa di San Domenico** where the Dominican inquisitors preached love and kindness when they weren't inquisiting and torturing. The Sotterranea's archaeologist is spending several years excavating the floors under the church. There was a pathway recently discovered that led the monks from the church into the subterranean. Search for the hidden symbols – a Templar 'rosy' cross (a cross hidden in a four-sided rose) and the sun and the moon, the Lombard symbols for the beginning and the end.

Above town is the fortress **La Rocca Albornoz** (admission €3; ⊙ 11am-7pm summer, 10am-5pm winter, weekends & holidays; Ⓟ)), built by Cardinal Albornoz, who was the heavy charged with switching Narni from a free *comune* to a papal-controlled state in the 13th century. The pope needed an imposing bastion to guard against the pro-Emperor Ghibellines and to scare the people into submission. Some original frescoes still exist, but its use as a prison for hundreds of years took its toll on the building. The climb up the tower stairs can be treacherous but it is well worth it for the 360-degree perfect Umbrian views when you get to the top. La Rocca now opens its doors to choirs and orchestras and has a collection of photos from its medieval festival. Also housed

---

NARNI/NARNIA

One might notice the mythical setting of Narnia from CS Lewis' *The Chronicles of Narnia* bears a striking etymological similarity to the town of Narni, and even more remarkably like its old Roman name, Narnia. When, in summer, you see the Disney cruise line bus drive through town, you'll realise the moniker isn't just a passing resemblance.

While researching Roman history at Oxford, CS Lewis was inspired by several descriptions of the ancient town of Narnia. He most likely remembers the name from reading books by Livy or Pliny the Elder, which described a stunning Roman village with beautiful villas and baths. In fact, Lewis showed his biographer, Walter Hooper, the ancient atlas in which he'd underlined the town name. The biographer eventually made a literary pilgrimage to Narni in the 1990s with his godson.

Although CS Lewis never visited, *Narnese* (residents of Narni) like to point out the similarities between mythical and historical Narnia. Narni's symbol is the flying griffin, and fans of the movie will undoubtedly remember the flying gryphons. In the fourth nave on the right side of the **Cathedral di San Giovenale** (above/) lies the rather creepy remains of Beata Lucia, Blessed Lucy. At the **Palazzo di Comune** (above), look for the stone lion statue, Narni's own Aslan. And if you head down the Via Flaminia towards the **Ponte d'Augusto** (above) stop off at the halfway point to hunt for the pre-Roman stone altar, similar to the one where Aslan was sacrificed.

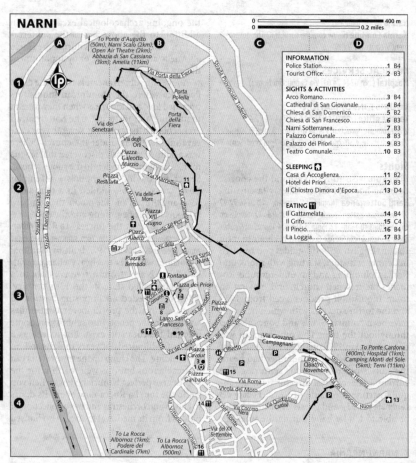

NARNI

is a fascinating motorcycle collection, including a 1906 foldable motorcycle, a rare surviving joint venture from Aermacchi (a popular Italian manufacturer) and Harley Davidson. Imagine the bomber helmet you might have worn sitting in the 1938 BMW sidecar. Contact the tourist office for information.

The Romans built the **Ponte d'Augusto**, a bridge on the ancient route of the Via Flaminia, in 27 BC. The bridge now has only one remaining arch, but it's not everyday you see a giant Roman arch.

Around what was the Roman forum is now the municipal and social centre of Narni. The **Palazzo dei Priori** (10am-1pm & 3-7pm) construction is attributed to Gattapone in 1275. Look up at the balcony called the *loggia colpire,*

from where a town crier used to yell the equivalent of the evening news. Across the street from the Palazzo dei Priori is the **Palazzo Comunale** (0744 74 72 69; Piazza dei Priori 1; admission free; 10am-1pm Mon, 10am-1pm & 4-7pm Tue-Sun summer, to 6pm Tue-Sun winter), a 13th-century building formed by the union of three towers. If no-one is inside, you can take a peek in the council chamber to see the *Pala di Ghirlandaio*, a representation of the coronation of the Virgin Mary. In the courtyard is the Roman statue of a lion, Narni's own version of Aslan from *The Chronicles of Narnia*. The 12th-century **Cathedral di San Giovenale** (Piazza Cavour; 7.30am-12.30pm & 3.30-7pm) is dedicated to Narni's patron saint, San Giovenale, who became the first bishop of Narni in AD 386. You'll see the remains of Beata Lucia, who received the stigmata, and now reminds visitors to Narni of Lucy Pevensie, one of the four children in *The Chronicles of Narnia*.

The **Teatro Comunale** (☎ 0744 72 63 62; Via Garibaldi; admission free; ☺ 4-7pm Sat, 9am-1pm & 4-7pm Sun) is a glorious 19th-century theatre that can accommodate up to 350 patrons. You can visit it for free on the weekends, and it's also a lovely place to see a performance. Make sure you make an appointment first.

The simple **Chiesa di San Francesco** (Via Aurelio Saffi) was built several years after the death of St Francis on the same site of a place where the Assisian himself had briefly lived.

The geographic centre of Italy is just outside Narni at the **Ponte Cardona** (☎ 0744 72 22 92), a Roman bridge that is the only remnant of an old Roman aqueduct dating to the 1st century AD. It's off the Via Flaminia heading south towards Terni. Call for information or to book a guided tour.

Abbazia di San Cassiano is an imposing abbey dating back to the 11th century, built in the plan of a Greek cross. It's thought to have been the first Benedictine abbey constructed in the area.

Festivals & Events

Corso all'Anello (The Race for the Ring) The town's major festival of the year is held from the end of April to the beginning of May. The town goes all out for this festival. As a rare foreign tourist, you will be welcomed with open arms. There are all sorts of feasts, competitions and performances by the Anerio Choir, an ancient choir formed by Palestrina, who was one of the founders of baroque music. The race itself is held on the second Sunday of May.

International Folklore Festival Held from mid-July to mid-August, this festival sees folklorist groups from all over the world perform nightly at the Piazza dei Priori.

Sleeping

Narni has very few hotels but the options available are quite good, including one of Umbria's best religious accommodation options, a peaceful oasis outside of town and a fabulously central hotel.

BUDGET

Camping Monti del Sole (☎ 0744 79 63 36; montisole@libero.it; Str di Borgaria 22, SS Flaminia, Km 80.800; per person €6-7, per tent €5-6, per car €2-3; ☺ Easter-Sep; P ☒) This camp site, 5km south of Narni, has a pool, restaurant and tennis courts. It's

surrounded by forested grounds. Camp sites have electric hookups for campers.

Casa di Accoglienza (Suore di Santa Anna; ☎ 0744 71 52 17; www.istituto-santanna.com; Via Gattemelata 74; student dm €15, s €19-21, d €34-38, all without bathroom) Go on, take a look from the garden's stone balcony. It's OK to cry. Really. It's that beautiful. Located along the city's ancient walls but walking distance to the centre, the quiet nun's quarters are as simple as you might expect, but the 14th-century building, tranquil garden and outlandishly stunning views are enough to bring tears to anyone's eyes.

Podere del Cardinale (☎ 0744 71 70 31; www.podere delcardinale.com; Strada di Massa Bassa 7, Taizzano; per person €20-35) Archaeology buffs will most definitely enjoy staying at this absolutely charming country house. The owner is also the director of the Narni Sotterranea and during the week he often does digs there, and gladly invites guests along. The house itself is down a dirt road surrounded by olive trees. There's a gigantic wood-burning adobe oven that takes up half the living room. The furniture is what country chic strives to be: ancient gnarled farmhouse tables, huge wooden beds and a homey fireplace that makes this more of a retreat than a hotel. With a kitchenette, solar-powered shower and sofa bed, the rooms can accommodate up to four comfortably. Roberto can also give you a tour of a nearby Romanesque church with Templar inscriptions and point you to horseback-riding facilities.

MIDRANGE

Hotel dei Priori (☎ 0744 72 68 43; www.loggiadeipriori .it; Vicolo del Comune 4; s €48-55, d €60-75, incl breakfast; ☒) In the centre of town is a fantastic three-star hotel, located in a 15th-century building with contemporary amenities – hairdryer, TV, minibar. It's got 17 beautiful rooms with incredible views, and some with balconies, but the penthouse *camere di torre* (tower room) is the *piece de resistance*, with a balcony that overlooks the entire valley. Inside its walls is the charming restaurant, La Loggia.

Il Chiostro Dimora d'Epoca (☎ 0744 76 02 07; www .hotelminareto.com; Via dei Cappuccini Nuovi 32; s €50, d €65-75, incl breakfast; P ☒) Located at the top of the city, where the view is as good as it gets from anywhere in Umbria. Built in 1603 as the new friary of a band of Cappuccini monks, the cloisters eventually fell into disrepair and it was turned into a holiday spot in 1878 for a local army commander, and in 2003 refurbished as a hotel with a restaurant and conference facilities. Plenty of historic touches remain – like antique four-poster beds and wrought-iron chandeliers hung from low stone and mortar ceilings – but contemporary touches add comfort.

Eating

Il Grifo (☎ 0744 72 66 25; Via Roma 3; meals €21.50, ☑ Thu-Tue) Specialising in Umbrian and international cuisine, this large restaurant's view is as enticing as the food. Set along the outer walls of the city, the large plate glass-windows overlook the green valley below. Try the sinfully rich gnocchi with black truffles and *taleggio* cream sauce (€10) or the pizzas (€4.50 to €5). A very simple tourist menu costs €12.90.

La Loggia (☎ 0744 72 27 44; Vicolo del Comune 4; meals €23) Owned by the Hotel dei Priori, this restaurant serves excellent dishes at even better prices. Bright-yellow walls and small tables set in front of an open fireplace make for an intimate dinner. The menu blends typical Umbrian dishes with intricate flavours, such as lamb with artichokes (€11) or pork with juniper berries (€8).

Il Pincio (☎ 0744 72 22 41; Via del XX Settembre 117; meals €24; ☑ Thu-Tue) Located under a beautiful old nobleman's palace is this restaurant that you might simply walk by if you didn't know part of it was literally inside a grotto. Ask chef Leonardo Passone to suggest a bottle of wine, and you'll soon be circling down a staircase into his famed wine cellar. Try the pasta with zucchini flowers.

Il Gattemelata (☎ 0744 71 72 45; Via Pozzo della Comunità 4; meals €27; ☑ Tue-Sun) Named after the *capitano di ventura* (mercenary captain) Il Gattemelata, this simply decorated restaurant serves wonderful meals that are a little more imaginative than the typical Umbrian cuisine. You can try dishes such as ravioli with smoked cheese in herb-infused butter (€8). However, the dish you can't leave without trying is the chocolate mousse pyramid dessert, flambéed with essence of vermouth. You can order from two tasting menus that feature foods served during medieval times.

Entertainment

Open Air Theatre (☎ 0744 75 11 97; www.narniopera.it; Parco dei Pini, Piazza Rossellini, Narni Scalo; tickets €12-170, average performances €30-60, reduced prices for under-26s & over 65; ☑ performances May-Sep) Built specifically for the Narni Opera Open Air concert series

is the 1840-seat, this brand-new theatre puts on world-class performances in a stunning outdoor setting, reminiscent of a Roman theatre. While opera is the main draw, the theatre also hosts a fine array of jazz, classical and world-music performances. In the low-season, performances switch back to the Teatro Comunale (see Sights p393).

Getting There & Away

ATC Terni (☎ 0744 71 52 07) buses leave from Piazza Garibaldi, just outside the main gate. From Narni, you can travel by bus to Amelia (€1.80, 30 minutes, nine daily from Piazza Garibaldi, plus another 10 from Narni Scalo), Terni (€1.80, 30 minutes, almost hourly with a gap between 10.30am and 1pm) and Orvieto (€5.20, one hour and 20 minutes, five daily). To get to Perugia, switch in Terni (€6.90, 1½ hours).

To get to Narni from the A1 autostrada, take the Magliano Sabina exit if you're coming from the south. Take the Orte exit if you're coming from the north.

AMELIA
pop 11,090

Few other words describe this town as aptly as 'sweet'. Perhaps 'quaint', 'delightful' or 'adorable' come close. It's a tiny little village, unassuming and unspoiled, with one of the oldest histories in Umbria. The legend goes that Amelia was founded by a mythological king named Ameroe in the 12th century BC. Latin texts mention the existence of Amelia as a settlement as early as the 11th century BC (four centuries before Rome was founded). A good chunk of the original walls (believed to have been constructed sometime around the 6th century BC) can still be seen by the theatre, but much of the wall is of newer construction. You know, the 4th century BC.

For even more sweetness, take your sweetie down 'Girl-Kissing Alley' or try the town's delicacy, *fichi girotti*, an Amerino snack of fig and chocolate. Locals vie with Narnians for the friendliest people in Italy and, knowing Umbria, they just might invent a festival testing that theory one day.

Orientation

The town is still a walled city, with several *porte* (doors) leading in and out. The main entrance is the Porta Romana. Just outside of it is the tourist office, parking facilities, the bus station and several cafés (some selling *fichi girotti*). Signs posted in front of monuments are all listed in Italian and English, so it's easy to get around.

Information

For information on the town, try www.amelia.it.

Pro Loco Città di Amelia (☎ 0744 98 25 59; web.tiscali.it/proloco.amelia; Piazza Augusto Vera 8; ☯ 9.30am-12pm & 4-7pm Mon-Fri, 9.30am-12pm Sat)

Tourist office (☎ 0744 98 14 53; info@iat.amelia.tr.it; Porta Romana; ☯ 3.30-6.30pm Mon, 9am-12.30pm Tue-Sat 15 Sep-30 May, 9.30am-12.30pm & 3.30-6.30pm rest of year) Bypass this office for the more helpful Pro Loco.

Sights

Amelia is almost entirely surrounded by pre-Roman polygonal walls, possibly dating back to the 6th century BC. The huge stones have held together without mortar for over 2500 years. Piazza Matteotti was the site of an ancient Roman forum.

Don't miss the fascinating **Museo Archeologico di Amelia** (Archaeological Museum & Art Museum; ☎ 0744 97 81 20; www.sistemamuseo.it in Italian; Piazza Augusto Vera 10; adult/concession €5/4; ☯ 10.30am-1pm & 3.30-6pm Fri-Sun Oct-Mar, 10.30am-1pm & 4-7pm Tue-Sat Apr-Jun & Sep, 10.30am-1pm & 4.30-7.30pm Tue-Sun Jul-Aug), with its famous bronze statue of Germanico, Roman captain and adopted son of Tiberius. Over 2m high, this almost fully restored statue is covered in armour featuring Achilles' ambush of Troilus in the Trojan War. You'll also find a painting by one of Amelia's most famous residents, Piermatteo d'Amelia. Piermatteo was instrumental in securing Christopher Columbus the three ships he used to discover America and was also the painter of the original Sistine Chapel ceiling.

An **ancient Roman cistern** (☎ 0744 97 84 36; ☯ 4.30-7.30pm Sat, 10.30am-12.30pm & 4.30-7.30pm Sun Apr-Sep, 3-6pm Sat, 10.30am-12.30pm & 3-6pm Sun Oct-Mar) goes underneath Piazza Matteotti from what is now a private house to the youth hostel.

If you're with your darling be sure to walk down from Piazza Matteotti past the Palazzo Municipale to Vicolo Baciafemmine (Girl-Kissing Alley), so named because its narrowness has been known to cause passers-by to get close enough to let their passions run amok.

In 1783 Amelia's Theatrical Society (comprised of the middle class and bourgeoisie) decided that their hamlet needed some culture. They banded together and built the **Teatro Sociale** (☎ 0744 97 83 15; Via del Teatro), turning the

theatre into the most important gathering spot in town. The moving wings still work on the original wood wheels. Domenico Bruschi frescoed the ceiling and booths in 1886. Most of the concerts begin at 8pm.

From the theatre, go to Via della Valle to get the best look at the Mura Megalitiche, stone walls built by the Etruscans in the 6th century BC. The rougher the texture, the older the stone. The builders didn't have mortar, but the walls were constructed well enough so that we can still see them.

The **Chiesa di San Francesco** (☎ 0744 97 81 20; ☯ 10am-noon & 3-6.30pm) was originally built in the 13th century, but most of the architecture now is from the 15th and 20th century. The façade is from 1406, and is decorated in the Romanesque and Gothic styles.

Since 872, there has been a religious institution on the site of the current **cathedral** (☯ 10am-noon & 3-6.30pm). The cathedral has been rebuilt after several disasters, and is certainly not the most impressive in Umbria, but there are several paintings and sculptures of interest inside. Next to the cathedral is the **Torre Civica**, which was built in 1050. Like many towers that were built in the medieval period, it was constructed on a dodecagonal (12-sided) plan based on the symbolic importance of the number 12 (12 apostles, 12 signs of the zodiac).

Courses

If you're looking for somewhere easy-going to learn Italian, try **Eurolinks** (☎ 0744 98 18 60; www.eurolinkschool.com; Viale Rimembranze 48), which runs live-in classes at all levels from €660 per week for a double room in a farmhouse to €1232 for two weeks full board staying with a local family. It also arranges wellness retreats, cooking courses, and tours of local wineries and *frantoio* (olive mills).

Festivals & Events

Amelia knows how to throw a party during its medieval *manifestazione* (event), the **Palio dei Columbi**. Every August, teams comprised of neighbourhood residents vie against each other in competitions recorded in the municipal records from the 14th century. Knights and crossbowmen are paired up to attempt to shoot an arrow through a target, which then sets free a dove. Practically every resident of the town is in full costume. The wooden doors you see on the Porta Romana are closed only on this day each year.

Sleeping

It's rather amazing, but there is not one hotel or B&B in the entire town centre of Amelia. Thankfully, there's a fabulous hostel with family rooms as good as any hotel. Check with the Pro Loco (or the tourist office, but they're generally not as friendly or helpful) as to any new B&Bs or accommodation outside the town walls.

Ostello per la Gioventù Giustiniani (☎ 0744 97 86 73, 339 261 03 98; www.ostellogiustiniani.it; Piazza Mazzini 9; dm/f per person incl breakfast €16/18; ☽ 8-10am & 4pm-midnight 1 Apr-30 Sep; ☐) Whether bunking in a dorm room or with a friend in a two- or four-person family room, you'll appreciate the relaxing nature of this most comfortable of hostels. Double oak doors add to your sense of privacy. Lockout is virtually all day, so make sure you call ahead for a bed. An HI card is required, but can be issued upon arrival.

Eating

Be sure to try the local sweet *fichi girotti* at any shop in town. It's kind of like eating the hardened insides of a fig biscuit mixed with chocolate and nuts.

Osteria dei Cansacchi (☎ 0744 97 85 57; Piazza Cansacchi 4; meals €22; ☽ Thu-Tue) Set in a medieval atmosphere, this restaurant combines two excellent local delicacies by serving *bistecche di cinghiale e porcini* (wild boar with porcini mushrooms). Pizza is a good and inexpensive bet here, but the fish comes most highly recommended. For an excellent pasta dish, try the *tagliata tartufo*, home-made local pasta with black truffles.

La Gabelletta (☎ 0744 98 21 59; Str Tuderte Amerina 20; meals €25) Its signature dish is *pappardelle al sugo di lepre* (pasta with wild hare sauce).

Getting There & Away

Amelia is serviced by ATC Terni. Buses leave from in front of the main gate. From Amelia, nine buses travel daily to the centre of Narni, plus another 10 to Narni Scalo and the train station (€1.80, 30 minutes). Buses also travel to Orvieto (€4.40, one hour and 10 minutes, seven daily; check with the driver as to whether the bus stops at the train station or Piazza Cahen) and Terni (€2.80, one hour, 16 daily). To get to Perugia, switch in Terni.

Getting Around

Bypass the paid parking near the city-centre and head towards the tourist office. Veer right into the little street along the city walls. At the end of this road, head left under the bridge to find a free car park. The entire town is within walking distance.

AROUND AMELIA

The area surrounding Amelia is known as the Amerino and has an untold amount of little treasures, natural and cultural. Holm-oak groves, ilex trees, and an ample amount of rivers and interesting geological terrain make this area worthy of a country drive. But Sundays and public holidays – when the museums are open and the rest of Umbria is closed – is the best time to visit.

In nearby Alviano you'll find the Lago di Alviano and Oasi di Alviano, which is more marshland than lake, formed when Lago di Corbara was dammed, and now a bird habitat. To go on a quest to learn about the *capitani di ventura*, journey to the **Museo Storico Multimediale Bartolomeo d'Alviano e i Capitani di Ventura** (☎ 0744 90 50 28, infoline 199 194 114; ☽ 10.30am-12.30pm year-round & 4.30-7.30pm Jul-Aug, 4-7pm Apr-Jun & Sep, 3-6pm Oct-Mar or by appt), which shares a castle with the Museo della Civiltá Contadina (Museum of Agricultural Heritage). Bartolomeo d'Alviano was a *capitani di ventura*. The Alviano family held a lot of clout over the centuries and was instrumental in building the Orvieto cathedral. Bartolomeo was so famous as a *capitano di ventura* that his likeness was minted on a Venetian coin.

CARSULAE

The most complete example of a Roman city in Umbria, **Carsulae** (☎ 0744 33 41 33; adult/concession €4.40/3.30; ☽ 8.30am-7.30pm 25 Mar-Sep, 8.30am-5.30pm Oct-24 Mar) isn't quite the size of Pompeii or Rome, but it does offer some spectacular Roman history in a beautiful setting. During the reign of Augustus in the 3rd century BC, Romans built the strategically important Via Flaminia. Carsulae was one of the many outposts systematically built along this Roman version of a highway. It was on the part of the road that joined Narnia to Vicus Martis Tudertium (Narni to the Todi region), so when reconstruction started on a more easterly route, Carsulae fell into decline. Then, barbarians from the north began using this part of the road to head towards Rome, and Carsulae had no chance.

To arrive here, take the road to Perugia from Terni. Look for the sign indicating SS75/San Gemini and you'll then see signs for Carsulae. The closest place to spend the night around Carsulae is in San Gemini.

Directory

CONTENTS

ACCOMMODATION

Prices for accommodation quoted in this book are intended as a guide only. Accommodation rates fluctuate wildly; Tuscany is more expensive than Umbria, while prices across the board can double during summer weekends and festivals. Rates are at their lowest during the low season from January to early March and November to mid-December: in Florence many hotels close for two weeks in January.

High season – July and August – sees choice accommodation booked up months ahead. The same goes for holidays such as Easter or Christmas and the two weeks surrounding Ferragosto (15 August) when holidaying Italians are out in force. Through the entire busy season – June to early September – an advance reservation definitely eases arrival.

BOOK ACCOMMODATION ONLINE

For more accommodation reviews and recommendations by Lonely Planet authors, check out the online booking service at www.lonelyplanet.com. You'll find the true, insider lowdown on the best places to stay. Reviews are thorough and independent. Best of all, you can book online.

Arriving late? Call ahead to ensure your host keeps your room.

In this book, 'budget' describes accommodation where a double with private bathroom costs a maximum of €70 a night, 'midrange' doubles €70 to €150 and 'top end' upwards of €150 a night.

Agriturismo

The most insightful way of discovering the region; see p309 for a complete low-down on what *agriturismo* (farm stay accommodation) really means and a selection of the region's best.

B&Bs

Small, family-run guesthouses offering bed and breakfast (B&B) in the intimacy of a private home make a handsome alternative to hotels. Many offer double rooms with a private bathroom and a copious breakfast greets guests in the morning. Several are listed in this guide and hundreds more can be found on the internet.

Camping

Camping is extremely popular, but costs can add up: separate charges for each adult, child, car, tent, caravan, motorcycle, dogs and so on makes it far from dirt-cheap – count on €30 to €40 for two adults, car and tent on a site near Florence; €20 to €25 for equivalent happy campers elsewhere in Tuscany and Umbria.

Most *campeggi* (camp sites) are a good trot from town, so public-transport users should factor in extra time for long walks or extra costs for bicycle rentals, buses or camp-site pick-ups. Camping rough is generally not permitted.

TCI publishes *Campeggi e Villaggi Turistici* (€20), an annual guide listing 2243 camp

PRACTICALITIES

■ Italy uses the metric system for weights and measures.

■ Videos use the PAL image registration system.

■ Plugs have two or three round pins so bring an international adapter; the electric current is 220V, 50Hz.

■ Gem up on Italian news with leading national dailies, *Corriere della Sera* (www.corriere.it in Italian) or Rome's centre-left *La Repubblica* (www.firenze.repubblica.it in Italian), which puts out a Florence edition. Regional broadsheet, Florence-based *La Nazione,* also runs national news, as does Turin's *La Stampa* (www.lastampa.it in Italian). *Corriere dell' Umbria* (www.corr.it in Italian) is the main Umbrian read.

■ News, views, culture and classifieds fill the English-language pages of biweekly newspaper, the *Florentine* (www.theflorentine.net), freely distributed at select hotels, restaurants and bars in Florence. *Toscana News* (www.toscananews.com) and sister publication *Chianti News* (www .chiantinews.it) cover the region in English.

■ Tune in to state-Italian RAI-1 (1332AM or 89.7FM), RAI-2 (846AM or 91.7FM) and RAI-3 (93.7FM) for classical and light music with news broadcasts; Radio 105 (www.105.net in Italian) airs contemporary and rock music throughout Italy out of Milan.

■ Watch the box: Italy's commercial stations are Canale 5, Italia 1, Rete 4 and La 7, alongside state-run RAI-1, RAI-2 and RAI-3.

sites across Italy. The Istituto Geografico de' Agostini publishes a less-glossy equivalent (€19.90). Online, see www.campeggitalia.com and www.camping.it.

Convents & Monasteries

Many of the 50-odd convents and monasteries scattered about the region offer some form of accommodation to outsiders. Monk-like

TOP TEN ONLINE RENTAL RESOURCES

For sites dealing exclusively with farm and other *agriturismi* properties, see p309; a couple listed share a go-slow, think-green philosophy.

■ www.florenceandtuscany.com

■ www.i-escape.com

■ www.justtuscany.com

■ www.knowital.com

■ www.merrygoround.org

■ www.responsibletravel.com

■ www.slowtrav.com

■ www.solemar.it

■ www.tourism-in-tuscany.com

■ www.viatraveldesign.com

rooms are far from luxurious, but they are quiet and clean. You almost always need to call or email ahead, and there is usually a two-night minimum stay and a curfew of around 10.30pm or 11pm. A handy resource, available in good travel bookshops in the region, is *Guida ai Monasteri d'Italia,* by Gian Maria Grasselli and Pietro Tarallo (€9.90); otherwise tourist offices have lists.

Hostels

Most hostels in the region are run by Rome-based Italian hostelling association **Associazione Italiana Alberghi per la Gioventù** (AIG; ☎ 06 487 11 52; www.ostellionline.org), affiliated with Hostelling International (HI). Only members can stay but hostels do sell one-night stamps (€3) and/or annual HI membership cards (€18).

Accommodation is usually in segregated dormitories and beds cost around €15 per night. Some hostels offer family rooms at a higher price. In the summer months you should book in advance, especially in Florence and Perugia. It is usually necessary to pay before 9am on the day of your departure, otherwise you could be charged for an additional night.

Hotels

Italian hotels are strictly regulated and classified on a scale of one to five stars. Most trade as an *albergo* (hotel), although smaller, cheaper, family-run places might well call themselves *locande, affittacamere* or *pensione*.

One-star hotels are basic and usually tout one or two shared bathrooms on a corridor. Standards at two-star places are slightly higher, with most rooms these days at least having a private sink, toilet and shower. Arrive at three stars and you can expect stylish up-to-the-minute rooms with TV (flat-screen in the trendiest joints), telephone, wi-fi and/or internet access (right), modern bathroom and a lift to whisk up you and your bags; that said, quality can still vary dramatically. Four- and five-star hotels are sometimes part of a group of hotels, and offer facilities such as room service, laundry, restaurant, fitness centre perhaps and so on at an appropriately high price.

Use rates quoted in this book – the lowest and highest price year-round for a standard double – as a guide only. Prices peak in Florence and on Elba in July and August, when some hotels, especially along the beach, may impose a multinight stay. Many hotels do not have *camera singola* (single rooms) as such; rather singletons pay a slightly lower price for the use of a double room with *camera doppia* (twin beds) or double with *camera matrimoniale* (double bed).

Unless stated otherwise, rates do not include breakfast.

Rental Accommodation

Finding rental accommodation in the cities or countryside can be daunting and time-consuming. Rental agencies can assist (for a fee); the Tuscany and Umbria regional tourist offices (p409) have lists; and there's a plethora of websites online touting short- and long-term apartment and villa rental in the region: a one-room apartment with kitchenette in Florence or Perugia costs anything from €400

> **WHAT THE COMPUTER ICON MEANS**
>
> Throughout this guide, only hotels and other types of accommodation that have an actual computer for guests to access the internet are flagged with a computer icon like this: ⌨ ; those that are wi-fi friendly, but have no computer, are not.

---

to €800 a month, and renting or sharing a room or studio starts at €200. Renting elsewhere is cheaper.

You can also look for rental ads in advert rags, such as Florence's *La Pulce* and *Panorama* or Perugia's *Cerco e Trovo*.

Rifugi

Those planning to hike in the Apennines can bunk down in a *rifugio* – a mountain hut kitted out with bunk rooms sleeping anything from two to a dozen or more people – usually run by **Club Alpino Italiano** (CAI; www.cai.it in Italian). Half -board (dinner, bed and breakfast) is often available. Most open mid-June to mid-September, although some at lower altitudes may remain open longer. Always call ahead, or have someone do so for you, to check that the *refugio* you are hiking to is (a) open; (b) has a bed for you. In addition to CAI *rifugi*, there are a handful of privately run ones and the occasional *bivacchio* – a rock-bottom basic, unstaffed hut.

Student Accommodation

Those planning to study in the region can often organise accommodation through the school or university they will be attending. Options include a room with an Italian family, or a share arrangement with other students in an independent apartment. If you're willing to chance it, you can look through newspapers and on university notice boards after you've

---

HOTEL PARKING

Parking at rural and suburban accommodation is rarely a problem – unlike in larger towns and Florence where parking is, in short, nightmarish. In towns many three-star-plus hotels offer parking either on-site or give guests a validation for a nearby public car park. In Florence practically no hotels have parking of their own (those so lucky to do so are flagged in this book with a Ⓟ icon) but rather offer guests the option of overnight parking in the nearest public car park (€18 to €24) or for valet service (€24 to €50), ie a friendly man in uniform escorts your vehicle to/from the same car park for you. The more stars in the hotel melting pot, the higher the parking charges. In hostels and smaller establishments in the city, you are, quite simply, on your own.

VILLAS & FARMHOUSES

Be it hanging in a hammock strung between poplars, dropping off beneath medieval frescoes or rising with the sun amid rolling hills, there is no better way to revel in the extraordinary peace and tranquillity of rural Tuscany and Umbria than by renting a villa, farmhouse or medieval hill-top village house.

Dreamy properties are as rife as vines. Rentals can be short- (some, but not all, can be rented per night, particularly in low season), medium- (one to four weeks) or long-term (more than a month); and there is ample chance to pick 'n' choose from those little luxuries in life that too many holidays require – infinity swimming pool, Jacuzzi, butler service, private chef, air-conditioning and so on.

Those in search of down-to-earth simplicity are equally spoilt for choice: organic farms are plentiful, many renovated with respect to original structures and using wholly natural materials. Heating is partially solar, pools in some instances are filtered naturally by aquatic plants and many have herb gardens. Farm produce (fruit, vegies, honey, olive oil, wine) is biodynmic and for sale, allowing self-catering guests to create their own splendid Tuscan feasts.

Prices range wildly, but split per person per night can work out very good value. An apartment in a villa or farmhouse for up to two people costs upwards of €500 a week; most four- to eight-bed properties fall in the €800 to €2000 per week range. Many property owners live on site, speak English and are a font of local knowledge; contacting them directly to organise your rental inevitably saves the expense of an agency, of which the following include our favourites:

Cottages to Castles (☎ 01622-77 52 36; www.cottagestocastles.com) Enticing collection of properties from this UK company, with agents in New Zealand, Australia, South Africa, the US, Israel and across Europe.

Cuendet (☎ 0577 576 330, see website for toll-free numbers; www.cuendet.com) A large-scale operation since 1974 with several European offices, this Italian company in Monteriggioni Siena manages hundreds of villa rentals in Umbria and Tuscany; also arranges wine- and oil-tasting, golf, bike tours, cooking courses and hot-air ballooning.

Italian Villas (☎ 1-888-214 2170, international 1-514-908-8907; www.villaescapes.com) US-based company, managing several hundred villas and *agriturismi* in Italy catering to all price ranges.

Summer's Leases (☎ 0845-230 2223; www.sumlea.com) From a Real McCoy Medici villa with domestic help, cook and air-con to a straightforward studio for two in central Siena, this small London-based agency is a Tuscan and Umbrian specialist.

Traditional Tuscany (☎ 01553-810003; www.traditionaltuscany.co.uk) Specialist company in Norfolk, UK, with a wide range of villas and apartments in Tuscany and Umbria; car rental, activity holidays and last-minute special offers online.

Tuscan Way (☎ 800 766 2390; www.tuscanway.com) Based in the US, Tuscan Way has a slew of Tuscan villa apartments on its books; some organise cooking courses.

Tuscany Now (☎ Tuscany 0207 684 8884; www.traditionaltuscany.co.uk) Born in a family home just outside Florence, this Tuscan and Umbrian specialist with offices in Florence and London lets you search for your dream villa by four clever categories: honeymoon, luxury, secure pool and no need for a car.

Veronica Tomasso Cotgrove (☎ 020-7267 2423; www.vtcitaly.com) Period properties to rent and buy in Tuscany and Umbria, hand-picked by London-based Veronica. Highly recommended.

Windows on Tuscany (☎ 055 26 85 10; www.windowsontuscany.com) The property arm of the Florentine Salvatore Ferragamo fashion-house empire, this Florence-based agency handles some of Tuscany's most prestigious rental properties.

arrived. Many hostels and B&Bs give a weekly discount.

BUSINESS HOURS

Shops are generally open 9am to 1pm and re-open in the afternoon from 3.30pm or 4pm to 7.30pm or 8pm Monday to Friday, but in main towns and cities it's increasingly popular for shops to remain open all day. Bank hours are generally from 8.30am to 1.30pm and 3pm to 5pm on weekdays, but times can vary. Post offices open 8.30am to 1.30pm Monday to Friday and for several hours in the afternoon. In large towns, they might open on Saturday morning. Pharmacies open 9am to 12.30pm and 3.30pm to 7pm Monday to Friday, and are open on Saturday and Sunday mornings. It is the law that one pharmacy in every town has to stay open on the weekend, and all other pharmacies list that location on their front door.

Restaurants usually serve from 12pm to 2.30pm and 7.30pm to 10pm. Bars usually open at 8am until the early hours. The law requires restaurants to close one day a week, but some ignore this rule and others close two days a week. Nightclubs open their doors at about 10pm but don't fill up until midnight.

CHILDREN

Most places happily accommodate children, with *agriturismi* and hotels usually supplying baby cots (free) and/or an extra bed (€25 to €35) for younger children. Few offer baby-sitting services though. Kids aged under 12 get discounts on public transport, museum and gallery admissions etc, and those aged under three are almost always free.

Small mouths are welcomed with open arms in restaurants. In larger towns many serve a special children's menu; those that don't go out of their way to cater to younger children's needs – serving a half-portion of pasta, dividing one portion between two, serving it at the same time as the adults' *antipasti,* supplying smaller hands with teaspoons and so on. The ritual basket of bread brought to the table at the start of every meal can temporarily appease hungry-kid grumps and grumbles but be warned, its lack of salt has been known to provoke severe tantrums in certain bread-mad five year olds. Despite such royal service, not that many restaurants have high chairs bizarrely.

Car seats can be hired with rental cars for a sometimes extortionate fee, but if you plan to do a lot of travelling you might be better off taking your own (which will almost certainly be more comfortable than the nonadjustable, sparsely cushioned seats usually provided); if you are flying, check your luggage allowance.

Farmacie (pharmacies) sell baby formula in powder or liquid form as well as sterilising solutions. Disposable nappies are widely available at supermarkets and pharmacies. Fresh milk is sold in cartons in supermarkets, corner shops and in bars touting a 'Latteria' sign: carrying a couple of emergency bottles of UHT milk is a good idea, not only because it doesn't need to be refrigerated prior to opening, but because it can also be found in screw-lid plastic bottles – way more practical for travelling than a carton.

Packing a pair of armbands or other inflatable floating device can be a life-saver for those with young children staying in a hotel or *agriturismi* with a swimming pool. Not all pools have shallow ends and very few are gated or closed in with a security fence to prevent wandering toddlers wandering in unaccompanied. An ample supply of water-resistant high-factor sunscreen, a robust sun hat, kid-friendly insect repellent and cream should your child be attacked by mosquitoes are other summer essentials. Depending where you are staying, a cot mosquito net might be useful for young babies.

For more information, see Lonely Planet's *Travel with Children.*

CLIMATE CHARTS

Tuscany and Umbria enjoy a typically Mediterranean climate, with a mean annual temperature of around 15°C. Summertime, especially in the cities, can be oppressive and

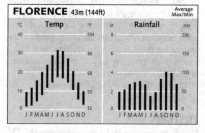

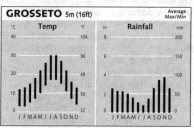

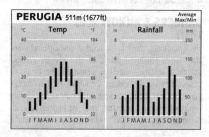

LETTER TO LONELY PLANET

I was crossing the piazza at Santa Maria Novella on the way to the train station in Florence last Friday morning when a very well-dressed 'Italian gentleman on his way to work' walked past me and pointed out gunk dripping down the front of the luggage I was wheeling behind me. My natural response was 'Gross! What's that?', and when he kindly offered me a tissue to clean it off, I took it rather than reaching into my own shoulder bag…which I stupidly set down to clean up the mess. He's the one who squirted the stuff (looked like runny baby cereal) on my luggage and then distracted me while his accomplice took off with my bag. This will hopefully help other travellers, since the US Consulate in Florence tells me it has become a very popular method of separating tourists from their valuables.

Janet C, USA

---

hot, with temperatures reaching a sweaty 35°C. For more information on when to go, see p17.

COURSES

Tuscany and Umbria are hot spots for those keen to twist their tongue around Italian; Florence, Perugia and Siena draw thousands of eager students. Universities and private schools provide all levels and types of language courses, many offering accommodation with families. Painting, ceramic, art history and restoration, sculpture, architecture, fashion, design, cooking and wine (p76) courses are equally widespread.

Online, find a slew of schools at www.it-schools.com.

CUSTOMS

Goods brought in and exported within the EU incur no additional taxes, provided duty has been paid somewhere within the EU and the goods are for personal consumption. There is no longer duty-free shopping within the EU; you have to be leaving Europe.

Coming from non-EU countries, duty-free allowances (for adults) are: 200 cigarettes, 50 cigars, 1L of spirits, 2L of wine, 50g of perfume, 250ml of eau de toilette and other goods up to the value of €183. Anything over the limit must be declared and paid for.

DANGERS & ANNOYANCES
Theft

Pickpockets and bag snatchers operate in the more touristy parts of the bigger cities, at train stations and in some of the coastal resort towns. Invest in a money belt to keep your important items safe, and pay attention to what's going on around you. In Florence and around train stations and tourist areas, watch out for groups of dishevelled-looking women and children, especially two or three together, holding some sort of distracting diversion such as a pile of papers or even a baby. Children as young as six or seven might be employed in the sleight-of-hand thefts, one of which is to have several children make a commotion in front of you or ask for money while an adult sneaks behind and cuts your bag straight off your back or shoulder. Never underestimate their skill – they are as fast as lightning and very adept. As soon as you notice a suspicious ruckus, hold on tight to all your possessions.

Parked cars, particularly those with foreign number plates or rental-company stickers, are also prime targets for thieves. Never leave valuables in your car, and make sure you are adequately insured. See p420 for more details. In case of theft or loss, always report the incident to the police within 24 hours and ask for a statement, otherwise your travel insurance company may not pay out.

Traffic

Italian driving varies dramatically between city and country, but expect to stay on your toes at all times. The city is fast, chaotic and not overly friendly to pedestrians. Crossing the street can be a life-threatening event, as Italians would rather swerve around a pedestrian than (god forbid) stop and wait. Scooter drivers often act more like bicyclists and it's not uncommon to see them driving on a footpath or going the wrong way down a one-way street. Always look both ways before crossing a street.

Driving in the countryside can be substantially more relaxing, but is not without its share of anxiety-provoking moments. Even secondary roads that look rather substantial on a map can be windy little two-lane roads.

DISCOUNT CARDS
Senior Cards
Seniors over 60 or 65 (the age limit depends on what you are seeking a discount for) can get many discounts simply by presenting their passport or ID card as proof of age.

Student & Youth Cards
These cards can get you worthwhile discounts on travel, and reduced prices at some museums, sights and entertainment spots. The International Student Identity Card (ISIC), for full-time students, and the International Teacher Identity Card (ITIC), for full-time teachers and professors, are issued by more than 5000 organisations around the world – the organisations are mainly student travel related, and often sell student air, train and bus tickets. In Australia, the USA or the UK, try **STA Travel** (www.statravel.com).

Anyone under 26 can get a Euro26 card. This gives similar discounts to the ISIC and is issued by most of the same organisations. See www.euro26.org for details.

Centro Turistico Studentesco e Giovanile (CTS; www.cts.it) youth and student travel organisation branches in Italy can issue ISIC, ITIC and Euro26 cards.

CTS Florence (☎ 055 324 50 78; Via Luigi Gordigliani 56)
CTS Perugia (☎ 075 584 83 09; Via Orazio Antinori 57)
CTS Pisa (☎ 050 220 03 47; Via San Bernardo 53)
CTS Siena (☎ 0577 285008; Via Bandini Sallustio 21)

Note that many places in Italy give discounts according to age rather than student status. An ISIC may not always be accepted without proof of age (eg passport).

EMBASSIES & CONSULATES
Italian Embassies & Consulates
Several countries have consulates in more than one city; check with the main consulate's website to find the one closest to you.
Australia (☎ 02-6273 3333; www.ambcanberra.esteri .it; 12 Grey St, Deakin, Canberra, ACT 2600)
Canada (☎ 416-977 1566; www.constoronto.esteri.it; 136 Beverley St, Toronto, Ontario M5T 1Y5)
France (☎ 01 49 54 04 10; www.ambparigi.esteri.it; 51 rue de Varenne, 75343 Paris)
Germany (☎ 030 254 400; www.ambberlino.esteri.it; Hiroshmastr 1, 10785 Berlin)
Ireland (☎ 01-660 1744; www.ambdublino.esteri.it; 63-5 Northumberland Rd, Dublin 4)
New Zealand (☎ 04-4735 339; www.italy-embassy .org.nz; 34-8 Grant Rd, PO Box 463, Thorndon, Wellington)

Netherlands (☎ 070-302 1030; www.italy.nl; Alexander-straat 12, 2514 The Hague)
UK (☎ 020-731 222 00; www.embitaly.org.uk; 14 Three Kings Yard, London W1K 4EH)
USA (☎ 212-439 8600; www.consnewyork.esteri.it; 690 Park Ave, New York, NY 10021)

Embassies & Consulates in Italy
There are few consulates in Florence; most countries have an embassy (and often a consulate too) in Rome.
Australia (☎ 06 85 27 21; www.italy.embassy.gov.au; Via Antonio Bosio 5, Rome)
Canada (☎ 06 85 44 41; www.dfait-maeci.gc.ca /canada-europa/italy; Via Zara 30, Rome)
France Florence (Map p103; ☎ 055 230 25 56; Piazza Ognissanti 2); Rome (☎ 06 686 011; www.france-italia.it; Piazza Farnese 67)
Germany Florence (Map p103; ☎ 055 29 47 22; Lungarno Amergio Vespucci 30); Rome (☎ 06 49 21 31; www .rom.diplo.de; Via San Martino della Battaglia 4)
Ireland (☎ 06 697 91 21; www.ambasciata-irlanda.it; Piazza di Campitelli 3, Rome)
Netherlands Florence (☎ 055 475 249; www.olanda .it; Via Cavour 81); Rome (☎ 06 3228 6002; Via Michele Mercati 8)
New Zealand (☎ 06 441 71 71; www.nzembassy .com/italy; Via Zara 28, Rome)
UK Florence (Map pp100-1; ☎ 055 28 41 33, emergency 06 4220 2603; consular.florence@fco.gov.uk; Lungarno Corsini 2); Rome (☎ 06 4220 0001; consular.rome@fco .gov.uk; Via XX Settembre 80a)
USA Florence (Map p103; ☎ 055 266 951; http://florence .usconsulate.gov; Lungarno Amerigo Vespucci 38); Rome (☎ 06 4 67 41; http://rome.usembassy.gov; Via Vittorio Veneto 119a)

FOOD & DRINK
This section covers the nuts and bolts of dining and drinking. For a portrait of culinary culture, history and cuisine, see the Food & Drink chapter, p66.

Meal prices quoted within Eating listings of this guide are the average price you can expect to pay for a *primo* (first course, usually of pasta), *secondo* (main meat or fish course, *dolci* (dessert) and a 0.25L of house wine. Naturally meals in each respective place can cost a lot more or a lot less, depending on what you order.

We've used the term 'budget' to describe places where you can eat the above for less than €20; 'midrange' places cost between €20 and €45 a head, while a 'top-end' restaurant costs anything upwards of €45.

Eating places generally display their menu outside, although many have an additional board featuring that day's specials. Some of the smaller, most endearing and authentic trattorie simply have the day's market-dictated menu chalked up on a blackboard or rely on the waiter to tell you what's cooking. Generally speaking, if a place is full and loaded with locals, you should dine well. Treat any place featuring a menu translated into several languages and starring spaghetti Bolognese, lasagne and a fixed *menu turistico* as just that – a place geared first and foremost at the region's less-discerning tourist trade. For typical opening hours, see p400.

Fast food is slow and takes the form of a *panini* (sandwich) standing up at a bar, pizza *al taglio* (by the slice), tripe from a street cart in Florence (p137), or a cake or sugar doughnut from one of the region's many delectable *pasticcerie* (cake shops).

Vegetarians won't go hungry in this agricultural region where stuffed zucchini flowers, white beans dressed in olive oil and a bounty of other vegetable-based dishes titillate meat-free tastebuds. Be aware that many sauces contain meat or animal stock.

Vegans are in for a much tougher time. Cheese is often added on top of dishes or in many sauces, so you have to say *'senza formaggio'* when you order. Many types of pasta are made with eggs.

For dining with children, see p401.

Drinks

Italian beers tend to be crisp, light Pilsener-style lagers, which younger Italians guzzle down with a pizza. Morena, Moretti, Peroni and Nastro Azzurro are all very drinkable and cheaper than imported varieties. If you want a local beer, ask for a *birra nazionale* in a bottle or *alla spina* (on tap).

Tap water is perfectly drinkable, but Italians generally drink bottled *acqua minerale* (mineral water) – *frizzante* (sparkling) or *naturale* (still) – which rarely costs more than €2 in a restaurant for a litre bottle.

Tè (tea) is not big. Those who do drink it only do so late afternoon in the company of a few *pasticcini* (small cakes). If warm doesn't suit your taste, ask for it *molto caldo* (very hot) or *bollente* (boiling).

Serious etiquette surrounds coffee, easily Europe's best.

GAY & LESBIAN TRAVELLERS

The age of consent for homosexuals in Italy is 16 and homosexuality is well tolerated in larger cities, including Florence, Pisa and Perugia. On the Tuscan coast, Versilia and Torre del Lago have a lively gay scene, best expressed by **Friendly Versilia** (www.friendlyversilia.it), a summer campaign that encourages gays and lesbians to revel in Torre del Lago's fun-in-the-sun frolics from late April to September.

Online, www.gayfriendlyitaly.com (connected to the Italian-language site www.gay

---

DINING LEXICON

Places to eat come in all shapes and sizes in this food-driven part of Italy where it pays not to judge purely by appearance: the best meal of your travels could well be in the open air, on a farm or in a dingy old restaurant with cheap paper tablecloths. Bars meanwhile, far more than a drinking hole, double as the fastest food joint you'll find in these increasingly slow climes (p21) as locals grab a *panini* (sandwich) standing up chatting with friends.

In a nutshell, this is what you can expect:

Enoteca Wine bar; similar to an *osteria* (restaurant focussing on wine), but focused purely on a lengthy wine list with a few homemade dishes or cold appetisers thrown in to keep munchies at bay.

Fiaschetteria Tuscan fast food: serves small snacks, sandwiches and the like, usually at the bar over a glass of wine or two.

Osteria or hosteria Restaurant focussing on wine – atmospheric and intimate with good wholesome home cooking.

Pizzeria Just that.

Ristorante Generally too upmarket to fit into any of the above categories; think a line-up of cutlery and table cloths of the starched white rather than disposable paper variety.

Tavola calda Literally 'hot table', cooking up cheap, preprepared meat, pasta and vegetable dishes served buffet style; help yourself.

Trattoria Casual, relaxed, usually family-owned restaurant, serving local fare.

COFFEE LEXICON

Know what to order when:

Un caffè Literally 'a coffee', meaning an espresso and nothing else.

Caffè corretto Espresso with a dash of grappa or other spirit.

Caffè doppio Double espresso shot.

Caffè freddo Long glass of cold, black, sweetened coffee.

Caffè freddo amaro Former minus the sugar.

Caffè granita Sweet and strong, traditionally served with a dollop of whipped cream.

Caffè latte Milkier version of a cappuccino with less froth.

Caffè lungo Literally 'long coffee', also called *caffè Americano;* an espresso with extra water run through the grinds to make it mug-length (and occasionally bitter).

Cappuccino Espresso topped with hot, frothy milk, only drunk by Italians at breakfast and during the morning *(never* after meals).

Cappuccino freddo Bit like an iced coffee, popular in summer.

Cappuccino senza schiuma Cappuccino minus the froth.

Espresso Short sharp shot of strong, black coffee, perfectly acceptable any time of day but the *only* coffee to end a meal with.

Latte macchiato Warmed milk 'stained' with a spot of coffee.

Macchiato 'Stained' coffee'; an espresso with a dash of cold milk.

Macchiato caldo/freddo Espresso with a dash of hot, foamed/cold milk.

.it) helps with information on tour groups and gay-friendly hotels, and runs a homophobia rating system of Italian cities. Gay-friendly bars and clubs can be tracked down at www .gayfriendlyitaly.com or through local gay organisations, such as Italian gay association **ArciGay** (☎ 051 649 30 55; www.arcigay.it) or Florence-based **Azione Gay e Lesbica** (☎ 055 67 12 98; www .azionegayelesbica.it in Italian: Via Pisana 32r). See p148 for more on Florence's gay and lesbian scene.

HOLIDAYS
School Holidays

Avoid Tuscany and Umbria in mid-August when most Italians take their holidays, school kids in tow. Beaches are overly crowded and many restaurants and shops are closed, especially during the week of Ferragosto (15 August). The Easter break (Settimana Santa) is another busy holiday period when many schools take pupils on cultural excursions. Museums and places of interest may be more crowded than usual. Allow for long queues and be sure to make hotel reservations in advance, especially on weekends.

Public Holidays

In addition to these national public holidays, individual towns celebrate the feasts of their patron saints with their own public holidays; see regional chapters for details.

New Year's Day (Anno Nuovo) 1 January

Epiphany (Befana) 6 January

Easter Sunday (Pasqua) March/April

Easter Monday (Pasquetta) March/April

Liberation Day (Festa della Liberazione) 25 April – marks the Allied victory in Italy, the end of the German presence and Mussolini

Labour Day (Festa del Lavoro) 1 May

Foundation of the Italian Republic (Festa della Repubblica) 2 June

Assumption of the Virgin (Ferragosto) 15 August

All Saints' Day (Ognissanti) 1 November

Day of the Immaculate Conception (Concezione Immaculata) 8 December

Christmas Day (Natale) 25 December

St Stephen's Day/Boxing Day (Festa di Santo Stefano) 26 December

INSURANCE

See p423 for health insurance and p413 for car insurance.

Travel Insurance

A travel-insurance policy to cover theft, loss and medical problems is a good idea. Some policies specifically exclude dangerous activities, which can include scuba diving, motorcycling, even hiking.

You may prefer a policy that pays doctors or hospitals directly rather than you having to pay on the spot and claim later. If you have to claim later, ensure you keep all

COPIES

All important documents (passport data page and visa page, credit cards, travel insurance policy, air/bus/train tickets, driving licence etc) should be photocopied before you leave home. Leave one copy with someone at home and keep another with you, separate from the originals.

documentation. Check that the policy covers ambulances or an emergency flight home. Paying for your airline ticket with a credit card often provides limited travel accident insurance. Ask your credit card company what it's prepared to cover.

INTERNET ACCESS

Logging on can be hard work for wi-fi users in Tuscany and Umbria where public wi-fi access points remain few and far between. In Florence and other larger towns, more and more cafés with free wi-fi are opening every day; look for the gaggle of portable-computer users filling practically every table. Check sites like www.wifinder.com and www.wi-fihotspotlist.com for wi-fi hotspots regionwide.

Internet cafes are fairly abundant in towns and cities; they are listed under Information in the regional chapters. Expect to pay €3 to €5 per hour and don't forget your passport – a recent (much-ridiculed) antiterrorism law requires internet cafés to take a photocopy of your passport before they allow you online access.

If you're using your laptop, check it is compatible with the 220V current in Italy; if not you will need a converter. You'll also need a telephone plug adaptor. Having a reputable global modem will prevent access problems that can occur with PC-card modems brought from home.

If you do not go with a global Internet Service Provider (ISP; such as AOL), make sure your ISP has a dial-up number in Italy or sign up for a short-term account with an Italian internet provider, such as www.tiscali.it.

For useful travel websites, see p18.

LEGAL MATTERS

For many Italians, finding ways to get around the law is a way of life. Some Italians are likely to react with surprise, if not annoyance, if you point out that they might be breaking a law.

Few people pay attention to speed limits and many motorcyclists and drivers don't stop at red lights – and certainly not at pedestrian crossings. No-one bats an eyelid about littering or dogs pooping in the middle of the footpath, even though many municipal governments have introduced laws against these things. But these are minor transgressions when measured up against the country's organised crime, the extraordinary levels of tax evasion, and corruption in government and business.

The average tourist will probably have a brush with the law only if they are unfortunate enough to be robbed by a bag snatcher or pickpocket.

Drink Driving

The legal limit for blood-alcohol level is 0.05%. Random breath tests are carried out by the authorities, and penalties can range from an on-the-spot fine to the confiscation of your licence.

Drugs

Italy's drug laws are lenient on users and heavy on pushers. If you're caught with drugs that the police determine are for your own personal use, you'll be let off with a warning (and, of course, the drugs will be confiscated). If, instead, it is determined that you intend to sell the drugs, you could find yourself in prison. It's up to the police to determine whether or not you're a pusher, since the law is not specific about quantities. The sensible option is to avoid illicit drugs altogether.

Police

The *polizia* (police) are a civil force and take their orders from the Ministry of the Interior, while the *carabinieri* (military police) fall under the Ministry of Defence. There is a considerable overlap of their roles, despite a 1981 reform intended to merge the two forces.

The *carabinieri* wear a navy-blue uniform with a red stripe and drive navy-blue cars that also have a red stripe. Their police station is called a *caserma* (barracks).

The police wear powder-blue trousers with a fuchsia stripe and a navy-blue jacket, and drive light-blue cars with a white stripe and 'polizia' written on the side. Tourists who want to report thefts, and people wanting to get a residence permit, will have to deal with them. Their headquarters are called the *questura*. This is where you get your *permesso di soggiorno* (permit to stay; see p410).

Other varieties of police in Italy include the *vigili urbani,* basically traffic police, who you will have to deal with if you get a parking ticket, or your car is towed away; and the *guardia di finanza,* who are responsible for fighting tax evasion and drug smuggling.

In an emergency, just go to the nearest people in uniform. Even if they're not the right uniforms, they'll know who to contact.

Italy has some antiterrorism laws that could make life difficult if you happen to be detained by the police. You can be held for 48 hours without a magistrate being informed and you can be interrogated without the presence of a lawyer. It is hard to obtain bail and you can be held legally for up to three years without being brought to trial.

MAPS

Those motoring around Tuscany and Umbria will find the Istituto Geographico de Agostini's spiral-bound, 100-page *Atlante Turistico Toscana* (1:200,000) with 32 pages of city maps, 30 pages of regional maps and 14 pages of itineraries indispensable; local bookshops in the region sell it. In the UK and US, the road atlases for Italy published by the AA are likewise invaluable, if less detailed, for the region.

The AA also publishes regional maps for Tuscany and Umbria, as does Michelin whose excellent orange-jacketed *Tuscana, Umbria, San Marino, Marche, Lazio and Abruzzo* (1:400,000) includes two Florence city maps.

One of the best maps of Umbria is the Touring Club Italiano's *Carta Regionale* 1:200,000, a greenish topological foldout map available for free at most tourist offices and many hotels. It marks many features that make it extremely helpful: tertiary/dirt roads and sites of interest, including sanctuaries, Etruscan tombs, grottos, ruins and monasteries. On the reverse side are maps of major tourist towns, such as Perugia, Castiglione del Lago and Todi. Most maps of Umbria are combined with either Le Marche or Tuscany, except Mappe Iter's Umbria 1:200,000 *Carta Turistica e Automobilistica* (€6). (A note about the terrain: 94% of Umbria is hilly. Industrial complexes have taken advantage of the remaining flat 6%, so if you want attractive landscapes, don't go towards anything white

on your map, but the flat areas directly around Perugia or Terni. Bevagna and Montefalco are exceptions.)

The city maps in this book, combined with tourist-office maps, are generally adequate to get you around. Many bookshops, with good selections of maps and guidebooks, are listed in each section.

The quality of city maps available commercially varies considerably, depending on the city. Most tourist offices stock free maps of their city, and commercial maps of larger cities are available from newsstands and bookshops. For suggestions on maps for the other main cities covered in this book, refer to each destination.

Tuscany and Umbria are great destinations for those who love the outdoors. Edizione Multigraphic publishes a couple of series designed for walkers and mountain-bike riders, scaled at 1:50,000 and 1:250,000. Where possible you should go for the latter. Ask for the *Carta dei Sentieri e Rifugi* or *Carta Turistica e dei Sentieri.* Another publisher is Kompass, which produces 1:50,000 scale maps of Tuscany and the surrounding areas. Occasionally you will also come across useful maps put out by the Club Alpino Italiano (CAI). For cycling enthusiasts, Verlag Esterbauer produces a *Cycling Tuscany: Cycle Guide and Map,* a spiral-bound 1:100,000 guide detailing the best cycling spots in the region.

Those planning a driving holiday should consult the AA's *Best Drives: Tuscany & Umbria,* which contains hand-picked car tours, essential motoring tips and specially designed maps.

MONEY

The euro has been the official currency of Italy since 2002. One euro is divided into 100 cents or centimes, with one, two, five, 10, 20 and 50 centime coins. Notes come in denominations of five, 10, 20, 50, 100, 200 and 500 euros. Euro notes and coins issued in Italy are valid throughout the other 11 countries in the euro zone: Austria, Belgium, Finland, France, Germany, Greece, Ireland, Luxembourg, the Netherlands, Portugal and Spain.

Exchange rates are given on the inside front cover of this book and a guide to costs can be found on p17.

ATMs

Automatic Teller Machines (ATMs) – known as *bancomat* in Italian – are the cheapest and

DIRECTORY

most convenient way to get money. ATMs are situated in virtually every town or half-way populated village in Tuscany and Umbria (though are more scarce in rural areas), and usually offer an excellent exchange rate. Many are linked to the international Cirrus, Plus and Maestro networks so that you can draw on your home account. Cash advances on credit cards are also possible at ATMs, but incur charges.

It's not uncommon for Italian ATMs to reject foreign cards for no reason whatsoever. If this happens, try a few branches or another day, and always make sure you're not down to your last *centesimi*. PIN codes need to be four digits.

Cash

You always get a better exchange rate in-country, though it's a good idea to arrive with enough local currency to take a taxi to a hotel if you have to. Carry as little cash as possible while travelling around. Bear in mind however that many smaller establishments (including some hotels) only accept cash.

Credit & Debit Cards

Credit and debit cards are convenient, relatively secure and will usually offer a better exchange rate than travellers cheques or cash exchanges. Visa and MasterCard (Access or Eurocard) are widely accepted; American Express (AmEx) cards are useful at more up-market establishments, and allow you to get cash at AmEx offices and certain ATMs. In general, all three cards can be used in shops, supermarkets, for train travel, car rentals, motorway tolls and cash advances. Don't assume that you can pay for a meal or a budget hotel with a credit card – inquire first.

Getting a cash advance against a credit card is usually an expensive way to go as fees (and interest) are charged. Debit card fees are usually much less.

For lost cards, these Italy-wide numbers operate 24 hours:
AmEx (☎ 800 914 912) The AmEx office in Florence (p95) can arrange on-the-spot replacements.
Diners Club (☎ 800 864 064)
MasterCard, Eurocard & Access (☎ 800 870 866)
Visa (☎ 800 819 014)

Travellers Cheques

Travellers cheques can be cashed at most banks and exchange offices (bring your pass-port as proof of identity). AmEx, Thomas Cook and Visa are the most widely accepted brands in this region. Those in euros are less likely to incur commission on exchange than other currencies: AmEx and Thomas Cook don't charge commission, but other exchange places do.

POST

Italy's **postal service** (www.poste.it) is notoriously slow, unreliable and expensive. If you're sending a package, you might want to send your things home using DHL or FedEx. Shops such as Mail Boxes Etc can be found in most major towns.

Francobolli (stamps) are available at post offices and authorised tobacconists (look for the official *tabacchi* sign: a big 'T', often white on black). Main post offices in the bigger cities are generally open from around 8am to at least 5pm; many open on Saturday morning too. Tobacconists keep regular shop hours.

Postcards and letters up to 20g sent by airmail cost €1 to Australia and New Zealand (zone 3), €0.85 to the USA, Asia and Africa (zone 2), and €0.65 within Europe (zone 1); mail weighing between 20g and 50g costs €1.80, €1.50 and €1.45 respectively. Within Italy, a letter up to 20/50g costs €0.60/1.40. You can also send express letters (*posta prioritaria*) and registered letters (*raccomandata*) at additional cost. Charges vary depending on the type of post and weight of the letter. Normal airmail letters can take up to two weeks to reach the UK or the USA, while a letter to Australia will take between two and three weeks. The service within Italy is not much better: local letters take at least three days and up to a week to arrive in another city.

SHOPPING

Some tour groups hit Tuscany simply to shop at the orgy of designer factory outlets on the outskirts of Florence (see p151) and the exclusive collection of boutiques selling leather goods, jewellery, clothes, shoes and handmade paper in central Florence (see p149). Be warned, though: despite supposed discounts of up to 70% at the outlets, prices are still high, especially for those coming from Canada and the US.

Umbria is Italy's ceramics capital, Deruta being particularly renowned for its centuries-old majolica technique (p333).

SOLO TRAVELLERS

Florence aside, there might not be the large numbers of solo travellers as in other places with an established backpacking culture, but those travelling alone will experience few problems in Tuscany and Umbria: you should not feel out of place and you certainly won't be made to feel uncomfortable. As with anywhere in the world, the same common-sense rules apply: avoid unlit streets and parks at night, and ensure your valuables are safely stored.

Single-room accommodation can be hard to find (you could well end up in a double; p397), although those on a tight budget could consider hostel accommodation.

TELEPHONE

Privatised **Telecom Italia** (www.telecomitalia.com) is Italy's largest phone company and its orange public pay phones are liberally scattered all over the place – on the street and in train stations, some big stores and unstaffed Telecom centres. Most only accept *carte/schede telefoniche* (phone cards), sold at post offices, tobacconists, newspaper stands and Telecom offices for €5 and €10 (snap off the perforated corner before use), although you might stumble upon the odd relic that still accepts coins. Most phones have clear instructions in English.

Telephone numbers change often in Italy, so check the local directory for up-to-date information. *Numeri verdi* (free phone numbers) usually begin with ☎ 800 (some start with ☎ 199 and ☎ 848). For directory enquiries within Italy, dial ☎ 12.

Mobile Phones

Italy uses GSM 900/1800, compatible with the rest of Europe and Australia, but not with the North American GSM 1900 or the totally different system in Japan (some North Americans have GSM 1900/900 phones that do work here).

If you have a GSM phone, check with your service provider about using it in Italy: beware of calls being routed internationally (very expensive for a 'local' call). Better still, once you arrive in Italy, sign up at any mobile-phone store for a pay-as-you-go plan. Pop in an Italian SIM card, buy *ricarica* minutes (prepaid minutes) and gab all you want, for about €0.20 within Italy and €0.60 to North America. Italy's main providers are **TIM** (www

.tim.it), **Omnitel Vodaphone** (www.190.it), **Wind** (www .wind.it) and **H3G** (www.tre.it in Italian).

Mobile-phone numbers always start with a three-digit prefix, such as ☎ 330, ☎ 339, ☎ 347 etc – never a zero.

Phone Codes

The international access code is ☎ 00 and the country code is ☎ 39.

Telephone numbers comprise a one- to four-digit area code starting with zero followed by a number of four to eight digits. Area codes are an integral part of all telephone numbers and must always be dialled. When making domestic and international calls always dial the full number, *including* the initial zero.

TIME

Italy operates on a 24-hour clock. It is one hour ahead of GMT/UTC. Daylight-saving time starts on the last Sunday in March, when clocks are put forward one hour. Clocks are put back an hour on the last Sunday in October.

TOURIST INFORMATION

Practically every village and town has a tourist office of sorts (listed under the relevant towns and cities throughout this book), operating under a variety of names but most commonly known as Pro Loco. It might deal with a town only or in some cases the surrounding countryside too. In the provincial capitals, Azienda di Promozione Turistica (APT) offices provide information on the provinces. English and French are widely spoken in Tuscany, but not in Umbria where you might well – even in tourist hotspots like Perugia or Assisi – struggle to understand or make yourself understood. Larger tourist offices often respond to written and telephone information requests.

Regional tourist offices, closed to the public but offering a wealth of information, itineraries and brochures online:

Tuscany (☎ 055 43 82 111; www.turismo.toscana.it; Via di Novoli 26, Florence)
Umbria (☎ 075 57 59 51; www.english.umbria2000.it; Via Mazzini 21, Perugia)

TRAVELLERS WITH DISABILITIES

Tuscany and Umbria are far from easy for travellers with physical disabilities. Cobblestone streets pave many towns in the region and are a darn nuisance for wheelchair users, as are many older public buildings (including many hotels and monuments), which have either a lift the size of a pocket handkerchief or no lift at all. Wheelchair-accessible ramps are likewise something of an enigma.

While some cities are making strides in the right direction, Assisi outpaces the lot: Go to www.assisiaccessibile.it (in Italian) to read a paraplegic Assisian's assessment of the wheelchair accessibility of the city's hotels, restaurants and monuments. In northern Umbria, Città di Castello is refreshingly free of hills and has several hotels with access for people with disabilities.

Another excellent resource is **Accessible Italy** (www.accessibleitaly.com), which publishes an on-line catalogue of accommodation suitable for travellers with disabilities, and organises both small group tours and independent travel for customers with physical or visual disabilities. It can coordinate an entire holiday, including airport pick-up and hotel reservations, and it also provides a listing of accessible monuments.

The Italian State Tourist Office in your country may be able to provide advice on Italian associations for the disabled and what help is available in the country. It may also carry a small brochure *Services for Disabled People*, published by the Italian railways, which details facilities at train stations and on trains. There's an airline directory that provides information on the facilities offered by various airlines on the disability-friendly website www.everybody.co.uk.

VISAS & PERMITS

The following information on visas was correct at the time of writing, but restrictions and regulations can change. Use the following as a guide only, and contact your embassy for the latest details. You may want to visit the websites of **Lonely Planet** (www.lonelyplanet .com), for useful links and up-to-date information, or the **Italian Ministry of Foreign Affairs** (www.esteri.it), for updated visa information, including links to every Italian consulate in the world and a list of nationalities needing a visa.

TOP TEN TOURS

Be it an intimate trek for adventuring cyclists or a cattle-call bus tour led by an umbrella-wielding leader shouting into a microphone, the options for organised travel to Tuscany and Umbria are endless. Travellers from any country can join the following tours:

Arblaster & Clarke (☎ 01730-893 344; www.arblasterandclarke.com) Wine tours with VIP tastings at local wineries by specialist British wine-tours operator.

ATG Oxford (☎ 01865-315 678; www.atg-oxford.co.uk) With an impressive commitment to sustainable tourism, this company offers small walking, cycling and cultural tours, and arranges 'footloose' trips for independent walkers. Choose between comfortable strolls, grand hotels and wine-tasting or rugged hikes through mountains.

Backroads (☎ 800 462 2848; www.backroads.com) Family biking, easy biking or walking 'n cooking tours are what this outstanding US-based tour company is best at.

Beach's Motorcycle Adventures (☎ 1 716 773 4960; www.beachs-mca.com) Two-week motorcycling tours through Tuscany and Umbria's winding, scenic roads by US specialist. Riders need a motorcycle licence, preferably an international one.

Cyclists' Touring Club (☎ 0870-873 00 60; www.ctc.org.uk) This UK club can help you plan your own bike tour or organise a guided one for you.

Elderhostel (☎ 877-426-8056; www.elderhostel.org) Adults aged 55 or more and their companions (of any age) can join forces for an educational and adventurous look into Tuscan and Umbrian art, nature and culture.

Explore Worldwide (☎ 01252-760000; www.exploreworldwide.com) One of several companies in the UK offering well-priced organised walking tours in Tuscany.

GAP Adventures (☎ 800 465 5600; www.gapadventures.com) Hike, bike and raft the region or pursue a gourmand's dream with this Canadian outfitter: active tours made up of max 12 'Great Adventure People' is its market.

Headwater (☎ 01606-720033; www.headwater.com) UK-based Headwater lures an active set with its gourmet getaways, rural retreats and walking/cycling tours in the Florentine hills, around Siena and so on.

Martin Randall (☎ 020-8742 33 55; www.martinrandall.co.uk) Art, architecture, archaeology, gastronomy, history and music tours organised by the UK-based specialist take a cultured set around Michelangelo's Florence, Puccini's Trooe del Lago, Lucca's art and architecture of Lucca.

Be sure to understand the difference between a visa and a *permesso di soggiorno* (see below). A visa gets you into the country and a *permesso di soggiorno* (permit to stay) allows you to stay. To apply for a visa, visit an Italian consulate in your home country. To apply for a *permesso di soggiorno,* apply at a *questura* (police station) within eight days of your arrival.

Permits

EU citizens do not need permits to live, work or start a business in Italy. They are, however, advised to register with a *questura* if they take up residence – in accordance with an anti-Mafia law that aims at keeping an eye on everyone's whereabouts.

PERMITS TO STAY

EU citizens do not require a *permesso di soggiorno*. All other *stranieri* (foreigners) staying in Italy for more than eight days are supposed to report to the police station to receive a *permesso di soggiorno.* Tourists staying in hotels are not required to do this.

A *permesso di soggiorno* only becomes a necessity if you plan to study, work or live in Italy. Obtaining one is never a pleasant experience; it involves long queues and the frustration of arriving at the counter only to find you don't have the necessary documents.

The exact requirements change: depending on what type of *permesso di soggiorno* you're applying for, you might need to bring with you anything from eight extra passport-sized photos to a vial of the blood of a six-toed cat born on a Tuesday. In general you need at least: a valid passport (if possible containing a visa stamp indicating your date of entry into Italy); a special visa issued in your own country if you are planning to study; four passport-size photographs; and proof of your ability to support yourself financially. You can apply at the *ufficio stranieri* (foreigners' bureau) of the police station closest to where you are staying.

WORK PERMITS

Non-EU citizens wishing to work in Italy will need to obtain a *permesso di lavoro* (work permit). If you intend to work for an Italian company and will be paid in euros, the company must organise the *permesso di lavoro* and forward it to the Italian consulate in your country – only then will you be issued an appropriate visa.

If non-EU citizens intend to work for a non-Italian company or will be paid in foreign currency, or wish to go freelance, they must organise the visa and *permesso di lavoro* in their country of residence through an Italian consulate. This process can take many months, so look into it early.

Visas

Italy is one of 15 countries that have signed the Schengen Convention, an agreement where 13 of the original EU member countries (except the UK and Ireland), plus Iceland and Norway, have agreed to abolish checks at common borders. Legal residents of one Schengen country do not require a visa for another Schengen country. In addition, nationals of a number of other countries, including all other EU countries (including the UK) and Switzerland do not require a visa. Citizens of the US, Canada, Australia, Ireland, Japan, New Zealand and Mexico can stay for up to 90 days without a visa. There are several dozen countries whose citizens require tourist visas, including Bosnia and Hercegovina, Peru, India and South Africa. Check with your nearest Italian consulate.

All non-EU nationals (except those from Iceland, Norway and Switzerland) entering Italy for any reason other than tourism (such as study or work) should contact an Italian consulate, as they may need a specific visa. They should also insist on having their passport stamped on entry as, without a stamp, they could encounter problems when trying to obtain a residence permit *permesso di soggiorno.*

STUDY VISAS

Non-EU citizens who want to study at a university or language school in Italy must have a study visa. These visas can be obtained from your nearest Italian embassy or consulate. You will normally need confirmation of your enrolment and payment of fees, as well as proof of adequate funds to be able to support yourself. The visa will then cover only the period of the enrolment. This type of visa is renewable within Italy, but, again, only with confirmation of ongoing enrolment and proof that you are able to support yourself (bank statements are preferred).

TOURIST VISAS

The standard tourist visa is the Schengen visa, valid for up to 90 days. A Schengen visa issued by one Schengen country is generally valid for travel in all other Schengen countries. However, individual Schengen countries may impose additional restrictions on certain nationalities. It is therefore worth checking the visa regulations with the consulate of each Schengen country you plan to visit.

It's mandatory to apply for a visa in your country of residence. You can apply for no more than two Schengen visas in any 12-month period, and they are not renewable inside Italy. For more information see www .eurovisa.info/SchengenCountries.htm.

WOMEN TRAVELLERS

Tuscany and Umbria are not dangerous regions for women, although many women travelling alone will sometimes find themselves with unwanted attention from local and foreign men. This attention is usually nothing more than whistles or overly long stares, but women travelling alone will want to keep an eye open for more sinister attention, especially in nightclubs or discos.

As in many parts of Europe, women travelling solo may at times find it difficult to be left alone. It is not uncommon for Italian men of all ages to try to strike up conversations with foreign women who just want to drink a coffee or are trying to read a book in the park. Usually the best response is to just ignore them, but if that doesn't work, politely tell them that you are waiting for your *marito* (husband) or *fidanzato* (boyfriend) and, if necessary, walk away. Florence can be a pain in this way, especially in the bars. It can also be an issue in some of the coastal resorts and on Elba.

Avoid becoming aggressive as this almost always results in an unpleasant confrontation. If all else fails, approach the nearest member of the police.

Avoid walking alone on deserted and dark streets, and look for centrally located hotels within easy walking distance of places where you can eat at night. Lonely Planet does not recommend hitchhiking, and women travelling alone should be particularly wary of doing so.

WORK

It is illegal for non-EU citizens to work in Italy without a work permit (p411), but obtaining one can be time-consuming. EU citizens can work in Italy, but they still need a *permesso di soggiorno* (p411) from the main *questura* in the town where they have found work.

Baby-sitting and au pair work is possible if you organise it before you come to Italy. *The Au Pair and Nanny's Guide to Working Abroad* by Susan Griffith and Sharon Legg is a useful guide.

The easiest source of work for foreigners is teaching English, but even with full qualifications a native English speaker might find it difficult to secure a permanent position. Most of the larger, more reputable schools only hire people with a *permesso di lavoro,* but the attitude of the schools can become more flexible if the demand for teachers is high and they come across someone with good qualifications. The more professional schools will require at least a Teaching English as a Foreign Language (TEFL) certificate. It is advisable to apply for work early in the year, in order to be considered for positions available in September (language-school years correspond roughly to the Italian school year: late September to the end of June).

Some people pick up private students by placing advertisements in shop windows and on university notice boards. Rates of pay vary according to experience.

Some travellers are able to pick up kitchen and bar work in the more touristy restaurants, particularly in Florence.

Further reading resources include *Work Your Way around the World* and *Teaching English Abroad,* both by Susan Griffith, and *Live & Work in Italy* by Victoria Pybus and Huw Francis, or *Living, Studying & Working in Italy* by Travis Neighbor and Monica Larner.

Transport

CONTENTS

GETTING THERE & AWAY

ENTERING & LEAVING THE COUNTRY

As an alternative to air travel, arriving by car, bus or train will leave a lighter carbon footprint. Entering Italy is relatively simple. If you are arriving from a neighbouring EU country, you do not require a passport check.

Italian airports, as everywhere, have tightened up on security measures, especially when you leave the country. Plan to arrive around two hours before an international flight. Check the current policy regarding restrictions on hand luggage, any electronic items and liquids before you travel, as these regulations are subject to change. Many airlines now allow only one piece of hand luggage on board – so if you're also carrying a handbag you'll need to pop it inside your main hand luggage. At the time of writing, there were severe restrictions on taking liquids, gels and foams in hand luggage. To avoid any delays, simply pack such items in your hold baggage and only keep essential liquids (such as baby milk or medicines – if you have a prescription you will probably be permitted to carry the liquid) for your hand luggage.

Flights, tours and rail tickets can be booked at www.lonelyplanet.com/travel_services.

Passport

All citizens of EU member states can enter Italy with their national identity cards (except the British, who haven't got around to them yet). All non-EU nationals must have a valid passport. If applying for a visa, check that the expiry date of your passport is at least some months off. See p410 for more information about obtaining a visa.

An entry stamp may not be made in your passport, but if you plan to remain in the country for an extended period or wish to work, you should insist on having one. Without a stamp non EU-nationals could encounter problems when trying to obtain a *permesso di soggiorno* – in effect, permission to remain in the country (see p411).

AIR

Whatever your point of departure, competition between the airlines means you should be able to pick up a reasonably priced fare to Italy. In particular, budget companies fly in from many European cities and standard carriers, such as Alitalia and British Airways, often offer comparably low fares.

High season for air travel to Italy is June to September. Shoulder season will often run from mid-September to the end of October and again in April. Low season is generally November to March, but fares around Christmas and Easter often increase or are sold out well in advance.

THINGS CHANGE...

The information in this chapter is particularly vulnerable to change. Check directly with the airline or a travel agent to make sure you understand how a fare (and ticket you may buy) works and be aware of the security requirements for international travel. Shop carefully. The details given in this chapter should be regarded as pointers and are not a substitute for your own careful, up-to-date research.

CLIMATE CHANGE & TRAVEL

Climate change is a serious threat to the ecosystems that humans rely upon, and air travel is the fastest-growing contributor to the problem. Lonely Planet regards travel, overall, as a global benefit, but believes we all have a responsibility to limit our personal impact on global warming.

Flying & climate change

Pretty much every form of motorised travel generates CO_2 (the main cause of human-induced climate change) but planes are far and away the worst offenders, not just because of the sheer distances they allow us to travel, but because they release greenhouse gases high into the atmosphere. The statistics are frightening: two people taking a return flight between Europe and the US will contribute as much to climate change as an average household's gas and electricity consumption over a whole year.

Carbon offset schemes

Climatecare.org and other websites use 'carbon calculators' that allow travellers to offset the level of greenhouse gases they are responsible for with financial contributions to sustainable travel schemes that reduce global warming – including projects in India, Honduras, Kazakhstan and Uganda.

Lonely Planet, together with Rough Guides and other concerned partners in the travel industry, support the carbon offset scheme run by climatecare.org. Lonely Planet offsets all of its staff and author travel.

For more information check out our website: www.lonelyplanet.com.

Airports & Airlines

Pisa's increasingly important **Galileo Galilei airport** (PSA; ☎ 050 50 07 07; www.pisa-airport.com) is the most convenient destination for Tuscany and Umbria. From it, more than 20 airlines serve nearly 50 national and international destinations.

From the small **Amerigo Vespucci airport** (FLR; ☎ 055 37 34 98; www.aeroporto.firenze.it), just outside of Florence, Meridiana flies to/from Amsterdam and London (Gatwick), while Lufthansa serves Frankfurt and Air France serves Paris (Charles de Gaulle).

From Umbria's even tinier **Sant'Egidio airport** (PEG; ☎ 075 59 21 41; www.airport.umbria.it), on the outskirts of Perugia, there are flights to/from Milan (Malpensa) and London (Stansted; Ryanair).

Most long-haul flights use Rome's **Leonardo da Vinci** (Fiumicino; FCO; ☎ 06 659 51; www.adr.it) or Milan's **Malpensa** (☎ 02 748 522 00; www.sea-aero portimilano.it) airports.

Airlines flying into the region:

Air Berlin (AB; hub Nuremberg; ☎ 848 39 00 54; www .airberlin.com)

Air France (AF; hub Paris; ☎ 848 88 44 66; www .airfrance.com)

Air One (AP; hub Rome; ☎ 199 20 70 80; www .flyairone.it)

Alitalia (AZ; hub Rome; ☎ 06 22 22; www.alitalia.it)

British Airways (BA; hub Heathrow; ☎ 199 712 266; www.ba.com)

Delta (DL; ☎ 848 78 03 76; www.delta.com; hub Atlanta)

EasyJet (U2; hub Luton; ☎ 899 67 89 90; www.easyjet .com)

Jet2 (LS; hub Leeds Bradford; ☎ 199 309 240; www .jet2.com)

Lufthansa (LH; hub Frankfurt; ☎ 199 400 044; www .lufthansa.com)

Meridiana (IG; hub Olbia; ☎ 199 111 333; www .meridiana.it)

Ryanair (FR; hub London Stansted; ☎ 899 67 89 10; www.ryanair.com)

Thomsonfly (TOM; hub Coventry; ☎ 02 36 00 3582; www.thomsonfly.com)

Tickets

World aviation has never been so competitive, and the internet is fast becoming the easiest way to find reasonably priced seats.

Full-time students and those under 26 have access to discounted fares. You have to show a document proving your date of birth or a valid International Student Identity Card (ISIC) when buying your ticket. Other cheap deals are the discounted tickets released to travel agents and specialist discount agencies. Most major newspapers carry a Sunday travel section with ads for these agencies, often known as brokers in Europe and consolidators in the US.

Check the websites directly for budget carriers, such as Ryanair, Jet2 and Easyjet. Be on the alert; many aren't as low cost as their come-on publicity alleges, once you factor in taxes and fuel charges. Some even charge for hold luggage (Ryanair, for example, slaps on a minimum of €6 per piece).

Major travel websites that can offer competitive fares:

Cheap Flights (www.cheapflights.com)
Ebookers.com (www.ebookers.com)
Expedia (www.expedia.com)
Kayak (www.kayak.com)
Last minute (www.lastminute.com)
Orbitz (www.orbitz.com)
Priceline (www.priceline.com)
Travelocity (www.travelocity.com)

Australia

Flights between Australia and Europe generally make a stop in one of the Southeast Asian capitals. The major players are Qantas and British Airways. Also well worth considering are Malaysia Airlines and the **Star Alliance** (www.staralliance.com) carriers, such as Thai Air, Singapore Airlines or Austrian Air.

Quite a few travel offices specialise in discount air tickets. Some travel agencies, particularly smaller ones, advertise cheap air fares in the travel sections of weekend newspapers, such as the *Age* in Melbourne and the *Sydney Morning Herald*.

STA Travel (☎ 134 782; www.statravel.com.au) has offices in all major cities and on many university campuses. **Flight Centre** (☎ 133 133; www.flight centre.com.au) has offices throughout Australia.

Canada

Alitalia has direct flights between Toronto and Milan. Air Transat (www.airtransat.com) flies nonstop from Montreal to Rome in summer. Scan the budget travel agencies' advertisements in the *Toronto Globe & Mail, Toronto Star* and *Vancouver Province*.

Air Canada flies daily from Toronto to Rome, direct and via Montreal and Frankfurt. British Airways, Air France, KLM and Lufthansa all fly to Italy via their respective home countries.

Canada's main student travel organisation is **Travel Cuts** (☎ 866 246 9762; www.travelcuts.com), which has offices in all major cities.

Mainland Europe

All national European carriers offer services to Italy. The larger ones, such as British Airways, Air France, Lufthansa and KLM, have representative offices in major European cities. Italy's national carrier, Alitalia, has a huge range of offers on all European destinations. Several airlines, including Alitalia, Qantas and Air France, offer cut-rate fares between cities on the European legs of long-haul flights.

But usually the cheapest way to go is aboard one of the burgeoning number of low-cost airlines.

Air Berlin (www.airberlin.com) Berlin.
Air One (www.flyairone.it) Munich, Frankfurt, Hamburg, London.
Clickair (www.clickair.com) Valencia.
Central Wings (www.centralwings.com) Krakow, Warsaw.
Sky Europe (www.skyeurope.com) Prague, Bratislava, Budapest, Vienna.
SN Brussels Airlines (www.flysn.com) Brussels.
Vueling (www.vueling.com) Barcelona, Madrid and Seville.
Wizz Air (www.wizair.co) Bucharest, Sofia.

Virgin Express (www.virgin-express.com) has a whole host of flights out of Brussels, including five daily flights to Rome. Details of its offices in Belgium, Denmark, France, Germany and Greece can be found on the website.

New Zealand

Singapore Airlines flies from Auckland through Singapore to Rome's Fiumicino airport – sometimes with more than one stop. New Zealand Air flies via London. The *New Zealand Herald* has a travel section in which travel agencies advertise fares. **Flight Centre** (☎ 0800 24 35 44; www.flightcentre.co.nz) has a central office in Auckland and many other branches throughout the country. **STA Travel** (☎ 0800 47 44 00; www.statravel.co.nz) has offices in Auckland, as well as in Hamilton, Palmerston North, Wellington, Christchurch and Dunedin.

UK & Ireland

The cheapest air route between the UK or Ireland and Italy is the no-frills way. EasyJet flies to Pisa from London (Gatwick) and Bristol. Its other northern Italian destinations are Milan (Malpensa and Linate), Rome, Turin, Rimini and Venice. Its main competitor is Ryanair, who flies to both Pisa and Perugia. In nearby regions, Ryanair also serves Milan, Parma,

Rome, Bologna, Genoa, Venice, Rimini, Verona and Ancona. Some of these routes are seasonal. Prices vary wildly according to season and depend on how far in advance you can book them.

The two national airlines linking the UK and Italy are British Airways and Alitalia. Both have regular flights to Pisa. Other Italian destinations that they share include Rome, Milan, Bologna, Venice and Verona.

Discount air travel is big business in London. Advertisements for many travel agencies appear in the travel pages of the weekend newspapers, such as the *Independent* and the *Guardian* on Saturday and the *Sunday Times*, as well as in publications such as *Time Out*, the *Big Issue* and *Exchange & Mart*.

STA Travel (☎ 0870 160 0599; www.statravel.co.uk) and **Trailfinders** (☎ 020 7292 18 88; www.trailfinders .com), both of which have offices throughout the UK, sell discounted and student tickets.

Most British travel agents are registered with Association of British Travel Agents (ABTA). If you have paid for your flight with an ABTA-registered agent who then goes bust, ABTA will guarantee a refund or an alternative.

USA

Delta Airlines and Alitalia have nonstop daily flights from New York's JFK airport to Rome's Fiumicino and Milan's Malpensa airports, while Continental (www.continental.com) flies nonstop to both from Newark. American Airlines (www.aa.com) flies from Chicago and JFK to Rome.

Discount travel agencies in the USA are known as consolidators. They often advertise in Sunday newspaper travel sections, especially in the *New York Times,* the *Los Angeles Times,* the *Chicago Tribune* and the *San Francisco Chronicle.*

STA Travel (☎ 800 781 4040; www.statravel.com) has offices in Boston, Chicago, Los Angeles, New York, Philadelphia and San Francisco. Fares vary wildly depending on season, availability and a little luck. **Discover Italy** (☎ 866 878 74 77; www.discoveritaly.com) offers flight-, hotel- and villa-booking services.

Discount and rock-bottom options from the USA include charter, standby and courier flights. Stand-by fares are often sold at 60% of the normal price for one-way tickets. **Courier Travel** (☎ 303 570 7586; www.couriertravel.org) is a comprehensive searchable database for courier and standby flights.

You might find it cheaper to take a cut-price flight to London, then make a cheap no-frills hop onwards to Pisa or another major Italian airport. Low-cost transatlantic flyers include **Zoom** (www.flyzoom.com), **Aer Lingus** (www .aerlingus.com) and **Jetblue** (www.jetblue.com).

LAND

There are plenty of options for reaching Tuscany and Umbria by train, bus or private vehicle. If time does not equal money, bus travel is the cheapest option, but it takes significantly longer and is less comfortable than travelling by train.

Border Crossings

The main points of entry to Italy are the Mont Blanc Tunnel from France at Chamonix, which connects with the A5 for Turin and Milan; the Grand St Bernard tunnel from Switzerland, which also connects with the A5; and the Gotthard tunnel from Switzerland. The brand-new, 34km-long Swiss Lötschberg Base Tunnel, the world's longest beneath land, connects with the century-old Simplon tunnel into Italy. To the east, the Brenner Pass from Austria leads to the A22 to Bologna. All are open year-round. Mountain passes are often closed in winter and sometimes even in autumn and spring, making the tunnels a more reliable option. Make sure you have snow chains if driving in winter.

Regular trains on two lines connect Italy with the main cities in Austria, Germany, France and Eastern Europe. Those crossing the frontier at the Brenner Pass go to Innsbruck, Stuttgart and Munich. Those crossing at Tarvisio in the east proceed to Vienna, Salzburg and Prague. Trains from Milan head for Switzerland, then on into France and the Netherlands. The main international train line to Slovenia crosses near Trieste.

Bus

Eurolines (www.eurolines.com) is a consortium of European coach companies that operates across Europe with offices in all major European cities. Italy-bound buses head to Milan, Rome, Florence, Siena or Venice and all come equipped with on-board toilet facilities (necessary for journeys such as London to Rome, which take about 30 hours). Its multilingual website gives comprehensive details of prices, passes and travel agencies throughout Europe where you can book tickets. There are discounts for seniors and travellers under 26 years.

Another option is the backpacker-friendly **Busabout** (☎ 020 7950 1661; www.busabout.com), which covers at least 60 European cities and towns with a hop-on, hop-off pass – the shortest is a six-stop ticket. Its season runs from May to October and buses usually leave between large cities every other day. In Tuscany, its buses call by Florence, Siena and Pisa. You can book onward travel and accommodation aboard the bus or on its website.

Car & Motorcycle

Coming from the UK, you can take your car across to France by ferry or via the Channel Tunnel on **Eurotunnel** (☎ 08705 35 35 35; www.eurotun nel.com). The latter runs at least 10 crossings (35 minutes) daily between Folkestone and Calais year-round. You pay for the vehicle only and fares vary according to time of day, season and advance purchase, starting at £49 one way.

For breakdown assistance both the British **RAC** (☎ 0800 55 00 55; www.rac.co.uk) and **Automobile Association** (AA; ☎ 0800 085 28 40; www.theaa.com) offer comprehensive cover in Europe. In the US, try **AAA** (www.aaa.com) or contact the automobile association in your own country for more information.

In Italy, assistance can be obtained through the **Automobile Club Italiano** (ACI; ☎ 803 116, 24hr information 02 66 165 116; www.aci.it in Italian).

Every vehicle travelling across an international border should display a nationality plate of its country of registration.

Train

Florence is an important hub, so it's easy to get to Tuscany and Umbria from many points in Europe. The *Thomas Cook European Timetable* has a complete listing of train schedules. It's updated monthly and available from Thomas Cook offices worldwide for about €15. It is always advisable, and sometimes compulsory, to book seats on international trains to and from Italy. Some of the main international services include transport for private cars – an option worth examining to save wear and tear on your vehicle before it arrives in Italy.

Consider taking long journeys overnight, as a sleeper fee for around €20 costs substantially less than a night in a hotel.

Train timetables at stations generally display *arrivi* (arrivals) on a white background and *partenze* (departures) on a yellow one. Imminent arrivals and departures are also signalled on electronic boards.

For more information, see p421.

SEA

Ferries connect Italy with its islands and countries all over the Mediterranean. However, the only options for reaching Tuscany directly by sea are the ferry crossings to Livorno from Sardinia, Corsica and Sicily. See p218 for more details.

For a comprehensive guide to all ferry services into and out of Italy, check out **Traghettionline** (www.traghettionline.com in Italian). The website lists every route and includes links to ferry companies, where you can buy tickets or search for deals.

GETTING AROUND

Most towns and cities in the region have a reasonable bus service, but you'll probably find that amenities and places of interest are usually within walking distance. You buy town bus tickets from newsagents, *tabacchi* (tobacconists) or kiosks before travelling and validate them in the machine on board.

Buses and trains connect Pisa's Galileo Galilei airport with Pisa and Florence, while buses link Amerigo Vespucci airport, just outside Florence, with central Florence. Buses from Piazza Italia coincide with flights at Perugia's Sant'Egidio airport.

Taxis are widely available. It's sensible to use only the official taxis, which are easily identifiable.

BICYCLE

Cycling is a national pastime in Italy. You cannot take bikes onto the autostrada.

Bikes can be taken on any train carrying the bicycle logo. The cheapest way to do this is to buy a separate bicycle ticket (€3.50, or €5 to €12 on Intercity, Eurostar and Euronight trains), available even at the self-service kiosks. You can use this ticket for 24 hours, making a day trip quite economical. Bicycles that are dismantled and stored in a bag can be taken for free, even on night trains, and all ferries allow free bicycle passage. Check out p410 for organised bicycle tours and p88 for areas that offer the most satisfying pedalling.

TRANSPORT

TRANSPORT

Hire

There are bikes available for rent in most Italian towns and many rental places offer both city and mountain bikes. Rental costs for a city bike start at around €10/30 per day/week.

Purchase

If you shop around, bargain prices for basic bikes are about €120 for a standard machine to €210 for a mountain bike with 16 gears. Check university bulletin boards for used bicycles.

BOAT

Regular ferries connect Piombino with Elba. On Elba, summertime trips depart from Portoferraio for the island of Capraia, and from both Porto Azzurro and Marina di Campo for the tiny island of Pianosa. From Livorno, ferries run to Capraia via the prison island of Gorgona. You can reach the island of Giglio from Porto Santo Stefano on the mainland. See the relevant chapters for more details.

BUS

Although trains are the most convenient and economical way to travel between major towns, a bus is often the best link between small towns and villages. For a few intercity routes, such as the one between Florence and Siena, the bus is your best bet.

Dozens of different companies offer a multiplicity of itineraries. Most reduce or even drop services on holidays and weekends, especially Sundays. Local tourist offices normally carry bus timetables or will call the companies for you.

In larger cities, ticket companies often have offices at the bus terminal. In some villages and even good-sized towns, you pick up your ticket from a bar near your stop or on the bus itself. Turn up on time; in defiance of deep-seated Italian tradition, buses are almost always punctual.

Lazzi runs buses from Florence to parts of Tuscany, mostly in the northwest, including Pisa, Lucca and Pistoia. The CAP and Copit companies also serve towns in the northwest. In Umbria, look out for the companies ATC and SSIT, which serve southern Umbria, and APM, which covers Perugia, Assisi and the north.

You can purchase tickets at most *tabacchi* and newsstands, or from ticket booths and dispensing machines at bus stations. Some larger cities offer good-value daily tourist tickets.

CAR & MOTORCYCLE

The north–south autostrada, signed by a white A followed by a number on a green background, slices through the region. This apart, you'll mostly be driving on the wider web of *strade statali*. They're represented by 'S' or 'SS' and vary from four-lane, toll-free highways to two-lane roads. Even thinner are the *strade provinciali*, which connect smaller communities, then the string-thin *strade locali*, which might not even be paved. Seek them out; they often lead you to the most enticing, least-frequented places.

When driving in Italy always carry proof of vehicle ownership or your rental-car papers.

Automobile Associations

The **Automobile Club d'Italia** (ACI; ☎ 803 116; www .aci.it in Italian; Via Colombo 261, Rome) is a driver's best resource in Italy. It has a dedicated 24-hour phone line for foreigners looking for emergency assistance, weather conditions or simply tourist information.

To reach the ACI in a roadside emergency, dial ☎ 803 116 from a land line or ☎ 800 116 800 from a mobile phone. Foreigners do not have to join, but instead pay a per-incident fee. Having a broken-down vehicle towed to the nearest mechanic shop will set you back about €150.

Bringing Your Own Vehicle

Cars entering Italy from abroad need a valid national licence plate and an accompanying registration card.

Driving Licence

All EU member states' driving licences are fully recognised throughout Europe. Drivers with a non-EU licence are supposed to obtain an International Driving Permit (IDP) to accompany their national licence. An IDP, issued by your national automobile association, costs around €10 and is valid for a year. People

---

WHERE TO PARK

Parking spaces outlined in blue are designated for paid parking. White or yellow outlines almost always indicate reserved parking or residential permits needed. You buy your ticket at a machine that's usually a few metres from wherever you've parked and display it in the front window.

who have held residency in Italy for one year or more must apply for an Italian driving licence. To hire a car or motorcycle you need to produce your driving licence.

Fuel & Spare Parts

Italy has a good network of petrol and repair stations. For fuel, you have three choices: petrol (benzina), unleaded petrol (benzina senza piombo) and diesel (gasolio). Petrol costs around €1.30 per litre and diesel a little less, at about €1.15.

For spare parts, check with a repair shop or call the 24-hour ACI motorist assistance number ☎ 803 116. You'll probably be connected to an operator who speaks English.

Hire

Tourist offices and most hotels can provide information about car or motorcycle rental. To rent a car you must be at least 25 years old and you need a credit card.

Many car-rental agencies expect you to bring the car back with a full tank of petrol and will charge astronomically if it's not. Make sure you understand what is included in the price (unlimited kilometres, tax, insurance, collision damage waiver and so on).

CAR

Following are among the most competitive multinational and Italian car-hire agencies:

Avis (☎ 199 100 133; www.avis.com)
Budget (☎ 800 472 33 25; www.budget.com)
Europcar (☎ 199 307 030; www.europcar.com)
Hertz (☎ 199 112 211; www.hertz.com)
Italy by Car (☎ 091 639 3120; www.italybycar.it) Partners with Thrifty.
Maggiore (☎ 199 151 120; www.maggiore.it) Partners with Alamo and National.

A fun way to get around Italy is by renting a camper van. If you are travelling for more than a few weeks, it can be more cost effective to buy, then sell back the vehicle. Check **IdeaMerge** (www.ideamerge.com), where you can lease or buy vehicles.

MOTORCYCLE

You'll have no trouble hiring a small Vespa or moped. There are numerous rental agencies in cities where you'll also be able to hire larger

ROAD DISTANCES (KM)

	Arezzo	Assisi	Carrara	Cortona	Florence	Livorno	Lucca	Orbetello	Orvieto	Perugia	Pisa	Pistoia	Prato	Siena	Spoleto	Viareggio
Assisi	96															
Carrara	198	317														
Cortona	28	72	237													
Florence	80	172	122	109												
Livorno	195	266	72	224	115											
Lucca	155	243	52	184	74	45										
Orbetello	175	222	247	215	180	175	216									
Orvieto	104	87	282	94	156	264	230	118								
Perugia	78	38	256	30	153	268	227	204	86							
Pisa	175	263	57	203	95	20	21	190	246	245						
Pistoia	115	208	92	143	35	85	45	215	204	190	65					
Prato	99	189	109	128	19	95	55	199	188	170	84	20				
Siena	65	124	153	99	70	130	140	116	134	109	110	105	81			
Spoleto	133	49	355	108	249	336	307	197	80	78	323	284	248	187		
Viareggio	180	266	30	206	97	41	25	195	250	247	21	69	89	123	325	
Volterra	111	175	135	151	75	69	74	168	186	161	65	108	88	52	239	86

TRANSPORT

TRANSPORT

motorcycles for touring. The average rental cost for a 50cc scooter is around €20/150 per day/week.

Most agencies will not rent motorcycles to people aged under 18. Many require a size-able deposit, and you could be responsible for reimbursing part of the cost of the bike if it is stolen.

You don't need a licence to ride a moped under 50cc. The speed limit is 40km/h, you must be 14 or over and you can't carry pas-sengers. To ride a motorcycle or scooter up to 125cc, you must be aged 16 or over and have a licence (a car licence will do). For motorcycles over 125cc you will need a motorcycle licence. Helmets are compulsory for motorcyclists and their passengers, whatever the size of the bike.

On a motorcycle, you can ride freely in the heart of cities such as Florence that have re-stricted traffic areas. Traffic police generally turn a blind eye to motorcycles or scooters parked on footpaths. There is no lights-on re-quirement for motorcycles in daylight hours.

Check out p410 for information on mo-torcycle tours.

Insurance

Third-party motor insurance is a minimum requirement in Italy. If your vehicle is regis-tered outside Italy, you need an International Insurance Certificate, also known as a Carta Verde (Green Card); your car-insurance com-pany will issue this. Also ask it for a European Accident Statement form, which can simplify matters in the event of an accident. Never sign statements you don't understand – insist on a translation.

Purchase

Rock-bottom prices for a reasonable car that won't break down instantly will run about €2000 to €3000. The cost of a second-hand Vespa ranges from €200 to €700.

To find vehicles for sale, look in the classi-fied sections of newspapers or go to an online auction site such as www.ebay.it.

Road Rules

Italians, like all mainland Europeans, drive on the right side of the road and overtake on the left. On three-lane roads, the middle lane is reserved for overtaking. At crossroads and roundabouts, give way to traffic from the right, unless otherwise indicated.

The driver and all passengers must wear a seatbelt, wherever fitted. If you're caught with it unbuckled, you're in for a hefty, on-the-spot, non-negotiable fine. Children under 12 must travel in the back seat, and those under four must use child seats.

A warning triangle (to be used if you have a breakdown) is also compulsory. Rec-ommended accessories are a first-aid kit, spare-bulb kit and fire extinguisher. If your car breaks down at night, take great care if you get out of the vehicle. You could be fined steeply unless you wear an approved yellow or orange safety vest (available at bicycle shops and outdoor stores).

Traffic police conduct random breath tests. If you are involved in an accident while you are under the influence of alcohol, the penalties are severe. The blood-alcohol limit is 0.05%. Speeding fines are determined by how many kilometres you are caught driv-

PASSING

You might call it passing or overtaking, but Italians call it a national pastime. On first glance, it seems as if the overtaker is going to be reunited soon with an undertaker, but there are actually a few rules in place.

The major hard-and-fast rule is: stay in the right lane unless you're passing or going Italian-driver-on-three-espressos fast!

Italians joke that they don't use their rear-view mirrors when driving. This means that you don't have to, either. When a driver is on your tail at 160km/h, it's not your responsibility to pull over or slow down. If they want to pass, they will have to wait until it is safe (or not seriously dangerous) to do so. If they pass when another car is passing on the opposite side of the road, you can manoeuvre gently to the right with a turn signal indicator to allow the cars not to car-een into each other, but that's your only choice.

When you pass, make sure you have your left-turn signal on. Wait until the solid yellow middle line turns into dots or dashes. Don't even think about passing on a curve. Oh, yes, and make sure there isn't a car coming from the opposite direction.

ROAD SIGNS

You can save yourself a degree of grief in Tuscany and Umbria by learning what some of the many road signs mean:

- *entrata* – entrance (eg onto an autostrada)
- *incrocio* – intersection/crossroads
- *lavori in corso* – roadworks ahead
- *parcheggio* – car park
- *passaggio a livello* – level crossing
- *rallentare* – slow down
- *senso unico* – one-way street
- *senso vietato* – no entry
- *sosta autorizzata* – parking permitted (during times displayed)
- *sosta vietata* – no stopping/parking
- *svolta* – bend
- *tutte le direzioni* – all directions (useful when looking for the town exit)
- *uscita* – exit (eg from an autostrada)

ing over the speed limit – they can reach up to €260.

Drivers usually travel at high speeds in the left-hand fast lane on the autostrada, so use that lane only if you need to pass other cars. There's a toll, which can be paid by credit card, to use the autostrada. For up-to-date information on road tolls and passes, call the **Società Autostrade** (☎ 840 04 21 21; www.autostrade.it in Italian) or consult its comprehensive website.

In built-up areas the speed limit is usually 50km/h, rising to 90km/h on secondary roads, 110km/h (caravans 80km/h) on main roads and up to 130km/h (caravans 100km/h) on the autostrada.

Motoring organisations in various countries have publications that detail road rules for foreign countries. If you get an IDP, it should also include a road rules booklet. The website www.drivingabroad.co.uk has some useful tips and background information for driving in Italy.

HITCHING

Hitching is rare in Tuscany and Umbria. Locals never hitch, and you might find yourself stranded for hours on end.

TAXI

You can usually find taxi ranks at train and bus stations, or you can telephone for radio taxis. It's best to go to a designated taxi stand, as it's illegal for taxis to stop in the street if hailed. If you phone a taxi, bear in mind that the meter starts running from the moment of your call rather than when it picks you up.

TRAIN

The train network throughout Tuscany and Umbria is widespread so you can get to most tourist areas by train, with relatively few exceptions (such as the Chianti region in Tuscany and Monti Sibillini in Umbria). A Regionale or Interregionale train stops at nearly all stations, while faster trains such as the Intercity (IC), call only at major towns and cities.

Trenitalia (☎ 800 89 20 21 Italian speaking; www.trenitalia.com) is the partially privatised state train system, which runs most of the services in Italy. We indicate the few other private Italian train lines within relevant sections.

In Umbria, there's an extremely helpful free **information source** (☎ 800 51 21 41; www.trasporti.regione.umbria.it) for regional train, bus and ferry details. You will rarely be connected to someone who speaks English, but usually, if your number is in Italian and you can tell them the city, they'll patiently tell you the prices and departure times.

Most Italian train stations have either a guarded left-luggage office or self-service lockers. The guarded offices are usually open 24 hours or 6am to midnight and charge around €3 per 12 hours for each piece of luggage.

VALIDATE, VALIDATE, VALIDATE!

Almost all trains (and several bus) journeys require passengers to validate their tickets *before* boarding. You just punch them in the yellow *convalida* machines installed at the entrance to all train platforms. On local buses and trains run by some private railway companies, you validate your ticket on the bus or train itself. Getting caught freeloading or with a ticket that hasn't been validated risks a fine of up to €50. This is paid on the spot to an inspector who will be kind enough to escort you to an ATM if you don't have the cash on you. Don't even think about trying the *'Ma sono turista!'* line; it won't wash.

TRAIN ROUTES

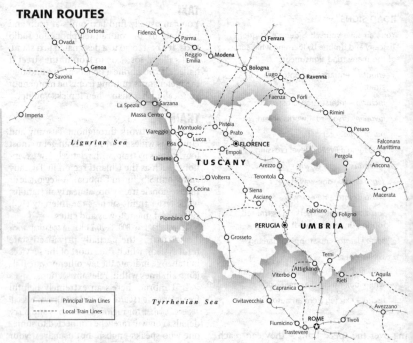

Principal Train Lines
Local Train Lines

Classes & Costs

There are 1st and 2nd classes on most Italian trains; a 1st-class ticket costs just under double the price of a 2nd-class one. There are special deals for families and group travel.

To travel on Intercity you pay a supplement (€3 to €16), determined by the distance you are travelling. If you are simply travelling to a town a stop or two up the line, check whether the short journey on the train you're thinking of requires a supplement. You might arrive 10 minutes earlier, but pay €5 or more for the privilege. Check up-to-date prices of routes on www.trenitalia.com.

Reservations

Reservations on trains are not essential but without one you may not be able to find a seat on certain trains. Bookings can be made when you buy your ticket, and usually cost an extra €3.

You can make train bookings at most travel agencies and in many cases on the internet. Alternatively, you can buy your ticket on arrival at the station. Most have automatic machines that accept both cash and credit cards.

Train Passes

If you're just travelling within Tuscany and Umbria, train travel is inexpensive and a train pass doesn't make financial sense.

If you are planning to travel more widely, Trenitalia offers a variety of passes. These include the free Cartaviaggio Smart. Armed with this, those aged from 12 to 26 can then buy a Ticket Sconto Smart, which has a 10% discount (25% discount for international tickets). If you get the Cartaviaggio Relax (also free) and are over 60, you can buy a Ticket Sconto Relax (€30; free for those over 75), which entitles you to discounts of 15% on 1st- and 2nd-class tickets and 20% on couchettes. Children who are aged between four and 12 years are entitled to receive a 50% discount; those who are under four travel free.

The Trenitalia Pass allows four to 10 days of travel within a two-month period. Only available to nonresidents, it's on sale at all major train stations or through a travel agent in your home country. Prices for four/six/eight/ten days of 2nd-class travel are €174/210/246/282.

Health

CONTENTS

BEFORE YOU GO

While Tuscany and Umbria have excellent health care, prevention is the key to staying healthy while abroad. A little planning before departure, particularly for pre-existing illnesses, will save trouble later. Bring medications in their original, clearly labelled, containers. A signed and dated letter from your physician describing your medical conditions and medications, including generic names, is also a good idea. If carrying syringes or needles, be sure to have a physician's letter documenting their medical necessity. If you are embarking on a long trip, make sure your teeth are OK (dental treatment is particularly expensive in Italy) and take your optical prescription with you.

INSURANCE

If you're an EU citizen, arm yourself with the European Health Insurance Card, a handy piece of plastic, valid for two years, that entitles you to emergency treatment throughout the EU. Order online or through your local health office. This card supersedes the E111 form that previously entitled you to treatment within the EU.

Citizens from other countries should find out if there is a reciprocal arrangement for free medical care between their country and Italy.

If you need health insurance, get a policy that covers you for the worst possible scenario, such as an accident requiring an emergency flight home. Find out in advance if your insurance plan will make payments directly to providers or reimburse you later for overseas health expenditures.

RECOMMENDED VACCINATIONS

No jabs are required to travel to Italy. The World Health Organization (WHO), however, recommends that all travellers should be covered for diphtheria, tetanus, measles, mumps, rubella and polio, as well as hepatitis B.

INTERNET RESOURCES

The WHO's publication *International Travel and Health* is revised annually and is available online at www.who.int/ith/. Other useful websites include www.mdtravelhealth.com (daily health recommendations for every country), www.fitfortravel.scot.nhs.uk (general travel advice), www.ageconcern.org.uk (advice on travel for the elderly) and www.mariestopes .org.uk (information on women's health and contraception).

IN TRANSIT

DEEP VEIN THROMBOSIS (DVT)

Blood clots may form in the legs during plane flights, chiefly because of prolonged immobility; the longer the flight, the greater the risk. The chief symptom of DVT is swelling or pain of the foot, ankle or calf, usually but not always on just one side. When a blood clot travels to the lungs, it may cause chest pain and breathing difficulties. Travellers with any of these symptoms should immediately seek medical attention. To prevent the development of DVT on long flights you should walk about the cabin, contract your leg muscles while sitting, drink plenty of fluids, and avoid alcohol and tobacco.

JET LAG

To avoid jet lag try drinking plenty of non-alcoholic fluids and eating light meals. Upon arrival, get exposure to natural sunlight and readjust your schedule (for meals, sleep etc) as soon as possible.

IN TUSCANY & UMBRIA

AVAILABILITY & COST OF HEALTH CARE

If you need an ambulance anywhere in Italy, call ☎ 118. For emergency treatment, go straight to the *pronto soccorso* (casualty) section of a public hospital, where you can also get emergency dental treatment.

Excellent health care is readily available throughout Italy but standards can vary. Pharmacists can give valuable advice and sell over-the-counter medication for minor illnesses. They can also advise when more specialised help is required and point you in the right direction. In major cities you are likely to find English-speaking doctors or a translator service available.

TRAVELLERS' DIARRHOEA

If you develop diarrhoea, be sure to drink plenty of fluids, preferably in the form of an oral rehydration solution such as Dioralyte. If diarrhoea is bloody, persists for more than 72 hours or is accompanied by fever, shaking, chills or severe abdominal pain, you should seek medical attention.

ENVIRONMENTAL HAZARDS
Heatstroke

Heatstroke occurs following excessive fluid loss with inadequate replacement of fluids and salt. Symptoms include headache, dizziness and tiredness. Dehydration is already happening by the time you feel thirsty – aim to drink sufficient water to produce pale, diluted urine. To treat heatstroke drink water and/or fruit juice, and cool the body with cold water and fans.

Hypothermia

Hypothermia occurs when the body loses heat faster than it can produce it. As ever, proper preparation will reduce the risks of getting it. Even on a hot day in the mountains, the weather can change rapidly, so carry waterproof garments, wear warm layers and a hat, and inform others of your route. Hypothermia starts with shivering, loss of judgment and clumsiness. Unless rewarming occurs, the sufferer deteriorates into apathy, confusion and coma. Prevent further heat loss by seeking shelter, warm dry clothing, hot sweet drinks and shared body warmth.

Bites, Stings & Insect-Borne Diseases

Tuscan beaches are occasionally inundated with jellyfish. Their stings are painful but not dangerous. Dousing in vinegar will deactivate any stingers that have not fired. Calamine lotion, antihistamines and analgesics may reduce the reaction and relieve pain.

Italy's only dangerous snake, the viper, is found throughout Tuscany and Umbria. To minimise the possibilities of being bitten, always wear boots, socks and long trousers when walking through undergrowth where snakes may be present. Don't put your hands into holes and crevices, and be careful when collecting firewood. Viper bites do not cause instantaneous death and an antivenin is widely available in pharmacies. Keep the victim calm and still, wrap the bitten limb tightly, as you would for a sprained ankle, and attach a splint to immobilise it. Seek medical help, if possible with the dead snake for identification. Don't attempt to catch the snake if there is a possibility of being bitten again. Tourniquets and sucking out the poison are now comprehensively discredited.

Always check all over your body if you have been walking through a potentially tick-infested area as ticks can cause skin infections and other more serious diseases such as Lyme disease and tick-borne encephalitis. If a tick is found attached, press down around the tick's head with tweezers, grab the head and gently pull upwards. Avoid pulling the rear of the body as this may squeeze the tick's gut contents through the attached mouth parts into the skin, increasing the risk of infection and disease. Lyme disease begins with the spreading of a rash at the site of the bite, accompanied by fever, headache, extreme fatigue, aching joints and muscles, and severe neck stiffness. If untreated, symptoms usually disappear but disorders of the nervous system, heart and joints can develop later. Treatment works best early in the illness – medical help should be sought. Symptoms of tick-borne encephalitis include blotches around the bite, which is sometimes pale in the middle, and headaches, stiffness and other flu-like symptoms (as well as extreme tiredness) appearing a week or two after the bite. Again, medical help must be sought in these instances.

Leishmaniasis is a group of parasitic diseases transmitted by sandflies and found in coastal parts of Tuscany. Cutaneous leishmaniasis affects the skin and causes ulceration and disfigurement; visceral leishmaniasis affects the internal organs. Avoiding sandfly bites by covering up and using repellent is the best precaution.

TRAVELLING WITH CHILDREN

Make sure children are up to date with routine vaccinations and discuss possible travel vaccines with your doctor well before departure as some vaccines are not suitable for children under a year old. Lonely Planet's *Travel with Children* includes travel health advice for younger children.

WOMEN'S HEALTH

Emotional stress, exhaustion and travelling through different time zones can all contribute to an irregular menstrual pattern.

If using oral contraceptives, remember some antibiotics, diarrhoea and vomiting can stop the pill from working. Time zones, gastrointestinal upsets and antibiotics do not affect injectable contraception.

Travelling during pregnancy is usually possible but always consult your doctor before planning your trip. The most risky times for travel are during the first 12 weeks of pregnancy and after 30 weeks.

SEXUAL HEALTH

Condoms are readily available but emergency contraception is not, so take the necessary precautions.

HEALTH

Language

Italian is a Romance language related to French, Spanish, Portuguese and Romanian. The Romance languages belong to the Indo-European group of languages, which includes English. Indeed, as English and Italian share common roots in Latin, you'll recognise many Italian words.

Modern literary Italian began to develop in the 13th and 14th centuries, predominantly through the works of Dante, Petrarch and Boccaccio – all Tuscans to a man – who wrote chiefly in the Florentine dialect. The language drew on its Latin heritage and many dialects to develop into the standard Italian of today. Although many dialects are spoken in everyday conversation, standard Italian is the national language of schools, media and literature, and is understood throughout the country.

While standard Italian was essentially born out of the Florentine dialect, anyone who has learned Italian sufficiently well will find many Florentines surprisingly hard to understand, at least at first. Whether or not they have their own localised nonstandard vocabulary you could argue about at length, but no-one can deny the peculiarity of the local accent. Here, and in other parts of Tuscany, you are bound to hear the hard 'c' pronounced as a heavily aspirated 'h'. *Voglio una cannuccia per la Coca Cola* (I want a

straw for my Coca Cola) in Florence sounds more like *voglio una hannuccia per la Hoha Hola!* Over the regional border in Umbria, you'll be spared the anomalies of Tuscan pronunciation, and understanding the local accent should be a lot easier.

You need to be aware that many older Italians still expect to be addressed in the third-person polite form, *Lei* instead of *tu*; using *Lei* is a bit like using the terms 'he/she', rather than 'you' in English (you may hear something similar in royal dramas where a King or Queen is addressed directly, but in the third person). It is also not good form to use the greeting *ciao* when addressing strangers, unless they use it first; it's better to say *buon giorno* (or *buona sera*, as the case may be) and *arrivederci* (or the more polite form, *arrivederla*). We've used the polite address for most of the phrases in this guide. Use of the informal address is indicated by (inf). Like other Latin-based languages, Italian has both masculine and feminine forms (in the singular they often end in 'o' and 'a' respectively). Where both forms are given in this guide, they are separated by a slash, with the masculine form first.

Lonely Planet's *Italian Phrasebook*, packed with practical phrases and simple explanations, fits neatly into your pocket.

PRONUNCIATION
Vowels

Vowels are generally more clipped than in English:

a	as in 'art', eg *caro* (dear); sometimes short, eg *amico/a* (friend)
e	short, as in 'let', eg *mettere* (to put); long, as in 'there', eg *vero* (true)
i	short, as in 'it', eg *inizio* (start); long, as in 'marine', eg *vino* (wine)
o	short, as in 'dot', eg *donna* (woman); long, as in 'port', eg *ora* (hour)
u	as the 'oo' in 'book', eg *puro* (pure)

Consonants

The pronunciation of many Italian consonants is similar to that of their English counterparts. Pronunciation of some consonants depends on certain rules.

c	as the 'k' in 'kit' before **a**, **o** and **u**; as the 'ch' in 'choose' before **e** and **i**
ch	as the 'k' in 'kit'
g	as the 'g' in 'get' before **a**, **o**, **u** and **h**; as the 'j' in 'jet' before **e** and **i**
gli	as the 'lli' in 'million'
gn	as the 'ny' in 'canyon'
h	always silent
r	a rolled 'rr' sound
sc	as the 'sh' in 'sheep' before **e** and **i**; as 'sk' before **a**, **o**, **u** and **h**
z	as the 'ts' in 'lights'; at the beginning of a word, it's most commonly as the 'ds' in 'suds'

Note that when **ci**, **gi** and **sci** are followed by **a**, **o** or **u**, the 'i' is not pronounced unless the accent falls on the 'i'. Thus the name 'Giovanni' is pronounced jo-*va*-nee.

A double consonant is pronounced as a longer, more forceful sound than a single consonant.

Word Stress

Stress is indicated in our pronunciation guide by italics. Word stress generally falls on the second-last syllable, as in spa-*ghet*-ti, but when a word has an accent, the stress falls on that syllable, as in cit-*tà* (city).

ACCOMMODATION

I'm looking for a ...	*Cerco ...*	*cher*·ko ...
guesthouse	*una pensione*	*oo*·na pen·*syo*·ne
hotel	*un albergo*	oon al·*ber*·go
youth hostel	*un ostello per la gioventù*	oon os·*te*·lo per la jo·ven·*too*

Where is a cheap hotel?
Dov'è un albergo a buon prezzo? — do·ve oon al·*ber*·go a bwon *pre*·tso

What is the address?
Qual'è l'indirizzo? — kwa·*le* leen·dee·*ree*·tso

Could you write the address, please?
Può scrivere l'indirizzo, per favore? — pwo *skree*·ve·re leen·dee·*ree*·tso per fa·*vo*·re

Do you have any rooms available?
Avete camere libere? — a·*ve*·te *ka*·me·re *lee*·be·re

I'd like (a) ...	*Vorrei ...*	vo·*ray* ...
bed	*un letto*	oon *le*·to
single room	*una camera singola*	*oo*·na *ka*·me·ra *seen*·go·la
room with two beds	*una camera doppia*	*oo*·na *ka*·me·ra *do*·pya

double room	*una camera matrimoniale*	*oo*·na *ka*·me·ra ma·tree·mo·*nya*·le
room with a bathroom	*una camera con bagno*	*oo*·na *ka*·me·ra kon *ba*·nyo
to share a dorm	*un letto in dormitorio*	oon *le*·to een dor·mee·*to*·ryo

How much is it ...?	*Quanto costa ...?*	*kwan*·to *ko*·sta ...
per night	*per la notte*	per la *no*·te
per person	*per persona*	per per·*so*·na

May I see it?
Posso vederla? — *po*·so ve·*der*·la

Where is the bathroom?
Dov'è il bagno? — do·ve eel *ba*·nyo

I'm/We're leaving today.
Parto/Partiamo oggi. — *par*·to/par·*tya*·mo *o*·jee

CONVERSATION & ESSENTIALS

Hello.	*Buongiorno.*	bwon·*jor*·no
	Ciao. (inf)	chow
Goodbye.	*Arrivederci.*	a·ree·ve·*der*·chee
	Ciao. (inf)	chow
Good evening.	*Buonasera.*	bwo·na·*se*·a
(from early afternoon onwards)		
Good night.	*Buonanotte.*	bwo·na·*no*·te
Yes.	*Sì.*	see
No.	*No.*	no
Please.	*Per favore.*	per fa·*vo*·re
	Per piacere.	per pya·*chay*·re
Thank you.	*Grazie.*	*gra*·tsye
That's fine/ You're welcome.	*Prego.*	*pre*·go

| Excuse me. | *Mi scusi.* | mee *skoo*·zee |
| Sorry (forgive me). | *Mi scusi/ Mi perdoni.* | mee *skoo*·zee/ mee per·*do*·nee |

What's your name?

| *Come si chiama?* | *ko*·me see *kya*·ma |
| *Come ti chiami?* (inf) | *ko*·me tee *kya*·mee |

My name is ...

| *Mi chiamo ...* | mee *kya*·mo ... |

Where are you from?

| *Da dove viene?* | da *do*·ve *vye*·ne |
| *Di dove sei?* (inf) | dee *do*·ve *se*·ee |

I'm from ...

| *Vengo da ...* | *ven*·go da ... |

I (don't) like ...

| *(Non) Mi piace ...* | (non) mee *pya*·che ... |

Just a minute.

| *Un momento.* | oon mo·*men*·to |

DIRECTIONS

Where is ...?

| *Dov'è ...?* | do·*ve* ... |

Go straight ahead.

| *Si va sempre diritto.* | see va *sem*·pre dee·*ree*·to |
| *Vai sempre diritto.* (inf) | va·ee *sem*·pre dee·*ree*·to |

Turn left.

| *Giri a sinistra.* | *jee*·ree a see·*nee*·stra |

Turn right.

| *Giri a destra.* | *jee*·ree a *de*·stra |

at the next corner

| *al prossimo angolo* | al *pro*·see·mo *an*·go·lo |

at the traffic lights

| *al semaforo* | al se·*ma*·fo·ro |

behind	*dietro*	*dye*·tro
in front of	*davanti*	da·*van*·tee
far (from)	*lontano (da)*	lon·*ta*·no (da)
near (to)	*vicino (di)*	vee·*chee*·no (dee)
opposite	*di fronte a*	dee *fron*·te a

SIGNS

Ingresso/Entrata	Entrance
Uscita	Exit
Informazione	Information
Aperto	Open
Chiuso	Closed
Proibito/Vietato	Prohibited
Polizia/Carabinieri	Police
Questura	Police Station
Gabinetti/Bagni	Toilets
Uomini	Men
Donne	Women

EMERGENCIES

Help!

| *Aiuto!* | a·*yoo*·to |

There's been an accident!

| *C'è stato un incidente!* | che *sta*·to oon een·chee·*den*·te |

I'm lost.

| *Mi sono perso/a.* | mee *so*·no *per*·so/a |

Go away!

| *Lasciami in pace!* | la·*sha*·mi een *pa*·che |
| *Vai via!* (inf) | va·ee *vee*·a |

Call ...!	*Chiami ...!*	kee·*ya*·mee ...
	Chiama ...! (inf)	kee·*ya*·ma ...
a doctor	*un dottore/ un medico*	oon do·*to*·re/ oon *me*·dee·ko
the police	*la polizia*	la po·lee·*tsee*·ya

beach	*la spiaggia*	la *spya*·ja
bridge	*il ponte*	eel *pon*·te
castle	*il castello*	eel kas·*te*·lo
cathedral	*il duomo*	eel *dwo*·mo
island	*l'isola*	*lee*·so·la
(main) square	*la piazza (principale)*	la *pya*·tsa (preen·chee·*pa*·le)
market	*il mercato*	eel mer·*ka*·to
old city	*il centro storico*	eel *chen*·tro *sto*·ree·ko
palace	*il palazzo*	eel pa·*la*·tso
ruins	*le rovine*	le ro·*vee*·ne
sea	*il mare*	eel *ma*·re
tower	*la torre*	la *to*·re

HEALTH

I'm ill.

| *Mi sento male.* | mee *sen*·to *ma*·le |

It hurts here.

| *Mi fa male qui.* | mee fa *ma*·le *kwee* |

I'm ...	*Sono ...*	*so*·no ...
asthmatic	*asmatico/a*	az·*ma*·tee·ko/a
diabetic	*diabetico/a*	dee·a·*be*·tee·ko/a
epileptic	*epilettico/a*	e·pee·*le*·tee·ko/a

I'm allergic ...	*Sono allergico/a ...*	*so*·no a·*ler*·jee·ko/a ...
to antibiotics	*agli antibiotici*	a·lyee an·tee·bee·o·tee·chee
to aspirin	*all'aspirina*	a·la·spe·*ree*·na
to penicillin	*alla penicillina*	a·la pe·nee·see·*lee*·na
to nuts	*ai noci*	a·ee *no*·chee

| antiseptic | *antisettico* | an·tee·se·*tee*·ko |
| aspirin | *aspirina* | as·pee·*ree*·na |

condoms	preservativi	pre·zer·va·tee·vee
contraceptive	contraccetivo	kon·tra·che·tee·vo
diarrhoea	diarrea	dee·a·re·a
medicine	medicina	me·dee·chee·na
sunblock cream	crema solare	kre·ma so·la·re
tampons	tamponi	tam·po·nee

60	sessanta	se·san·ta
70	settanta	se·tan·ta
80	ottanta	o·tan·ta
90	novanta	no·van·ta
100	cento	chen·to
1000	mille	mee·le

LANGUAGE DIFFICULTIES

Do you speak English?
Parla inglese? — par·la een·gle·ze

Does anyone here speak English?
C'è qualcuno che — che kwal·koo·no ke
parla inglese? — par·la een·gle·ze

How do you say ... in Italian?
Come si dice ... — ko·me see dee·che ...
in italiano? — een ee·ta·lya·no

What does ... mean?
Che vuol dire ...? — ke vwol dee·re ...

I understand.
Capisco. — ka·pee·sko

I don't understand.
Non capisco. — non ka·pee·sko

Please write it down.
Può scriverlo, per — pwo skree·ver·lo per
favore. — fa·vo·re

Can you show me (on the map)?
Può mostrarmelo — pwo mos·trar·me·lo
(sulla pianta)? — (soo·la pyan·ta)

NUMBERS

0	zero	dze·ro
1	uno	oo·no
2	due	doo·e
3	tre	tre
4	quattro	kwa·tro
5	cinque	cheen·kwe
6	sei	say
7	sette	se·te
8	otto	o·to
9	nove	no·ve
10	dieci	dye·chee
11	undici	oon·dee·chee
12	dodici	do·dee·chee
13	tredici	tre·dee·chee
14	quattordici	kwa·tor·dee·chee
15	quindici	kween·dee·chee
16	sedici	se·dee·chee
17	diciassette	dee·cha·se·te
18	diciotto	dee·cho·to
19	diciannove	dee·cha·no·ve
20	venti	ven·tee
21	ventuno	ven·too·no
22	ventidue	ven·tee·doo·e
30	trenta	tren·ta
40	quaranta	kwa·ran·ta
50	cinquanta	cheen·kwan·ta

PAPERWORK

name	nome	no·me
nationality	nazionalità	na·tsyo·na·lee·ta
date of birth	data di	da·ta dee
	nascita	na·shee·ta
place of birth	luogo di	lwo·go dee
	nascita	na·shee·ta
sex (gender)	sesso	se·so
passport	passaporto	pa·sa·por·to
visa	visto	vee·sto

QUESTION WORDS

Who?	Chi?	kee
What?	Che?	ke
When?	Quando?	kwan·do
Where?	Dove?	do·ve
How?	Come?	ko·me

SHOPPING & SERVICES

I'd like to buy ...
Vorrei comprare ... — vo·ray kom·pra·re ...

How much is it?
Quanto costa? — kwan·to ko·sta

I don't like it.
Non mi piace. — non mee pya·che

May I look at it?
Posso dare un'occhiata? — po·so da·re oo·no·kya·ta

I'm just looking.
Sto solo guardando. — sto so·lo gwar·dan·do

It's cheap.
Non è caro/cara. — non e ka·ro/ka·ra

It's too expensive.
È troppo caro/a. — e tro·po ka·ro/ka·ra

I'll take it.
Lo/La compro. — lo/la kom·pro

Do you accept credit cards?
Accettate carte — a·che·ta·te kar·te
di credito? — dee kre·dee·to

I want to	Voglio	vo·lyo
change ...	cambiare ...	kam·bya·re ...
money	del denaro	del de·na·ro
travellers	assegni dee	a·se·nyee dee
cheques	viaggio	vee·a·jo

more	più	pyoo
less	meno	me·no
smaller	più piccolo/a	pyoo pee·ko·lo/la
bigger	più grande	pyoo gran·de

I'm looking for ...	Cerco ...	cher·ko ...
an ATM	un Bancomat	oon ban·ko·mat
a bank	un banco	oon ban·ko
the church	la chiesa	la kye·za
the city centre	il centro	eel chen·tro
the market	il mercato	eel mer·ka·to
the museum	il museo	eel moo·ze·o
the post office	la posta	la po·sta
a public toilet	un gabinetto	oon ga·bee·ne·to
the tourist	l'ufficio	loo·fee·cho
office	di turismo	dee too·reez·mo

TIME & DATES

What time is it?	Che ore sono?	ke o·re so·no
It's (one o'clock).	È (l'una).	e (loo·na)
It's (8 o'clock).	Sono (le otto).	so·no (le o·to)
When?	Quando?	kwan·do
today	oggi	o·jee
tomorrow	domani	do·ma·nee
yesterday	ieri	ye·ree
in the morning	di mattina	dee ma·tee·na
in the afternoon	di pomeriggio	dee po·me·ree·jo
in the evening	di sera	dee se·ra

Monday	lunedì	loo·ne·dee
Tuesday	martedì	mar·te·dee
Wednesday	mercoledì	mer·ko·le·dee
Thursday	giovedì	jo·ve·dee
Friday	venerdì	ve·ner·dee
Saturday	sabato	sa·ba·to
Sunday	domenica	do·me·nee·ka

January	gennaio	je·na·yo
February	febbraio	fe·bra·yo
March	marzo	mar·tso
April	aprile	a·pree·le
May	maggio	ma·jo
June	giugno	joo·nyo
July	luglio	loo·lyo
August	agosto	a·gos·to
September	settembre	se·tem·bre
October	ottobre	o·to·bre
November	novembre	no·vem·bre
December	dicembre	dee·chem·bre

TRANSPORT
Public Transport

What time does	A che ora parte/	a ke o·ra par·te/
the ... leave/	arriva ...?	a·ree·va ...
arrive?		
(city) bus	l'autobus	low·to·boos
(intercity) bus	il pullman	eel pool·man
plane	l'aereo	la·e·re·o
train	il treno	eel tre·no

I'd like a ...	Vorrei un	vo·ray oon
ticket.	biglietto ...	bee·lye·to ...
one way	di solo andata	dee so·lo an·da·ta
return	di andata e	dee an·da·ta e
	ritorno	ree·toor·no
1st class	di prima classe	dee pree·ma
		kla·se
2nd class	di seconda	dee se·kon·da
	classe	kla·se

I want to go to ...		
Voglio andare a ...	vo·lyo an·da·re a ...	
The train has been cancelled/delayed.		
Il treno è soppresso/	eel tre·no e so·pre·so/	
in ritardo.	een ree·tar·do	

the first	il primo	eel pree·mo
the last	l'ultimo	lool·tee·mo
platform (two)	binario (due)	bee·na·ryo (doo·e)
ticket office	biglietteria	bee·lye·te·ree·a
timetable	orario	o·ra·ryo
train station	stazione	sta·tsyo·ne

Private Transport

I'd like to hire	Vorrei	vo·ray
a/an ...	noleggiare ...	no·le·ja·re ...
car	una macchina	oo·na ma·kee·na
4WD	un fuoristrada	oon fwo·ree·
		stra·da
motorbike	una moto	oo·na mo·to
bicycle	una bici(cletta)	oo·na bee·chee·
		(kle·ta)

Where's a service station?
Dov'è una stazione — do·ve oo·na sta·tsyo·ne
di servizio? — dee ser·vee·tsyo
Please fill it up.
Il pieno, per favore. — eel pye·no per fa·vo·re
I'd like (30) litres.
Vorrei (trenta) litri. — vo·ray (tren·ta) lee·tree
diesel
gasolio/diesel — ga·zo·lyo/dee·zel
petrol
benzina — ben·dzee·na
Is this the road to ...?
Questa strada porta — kwe·sta stra·da por·ta
a ...? — a ...
(How long) Can I park here?
(Per quanto tempo) — (per kwan·to tem·po)
Posso parcheggiare qui? — po·so par·ke·ja·re kwee
Where do I pay?
Dove si paga? — do·ve see pa·ga
I need a mechanic.
Ho bisogno di un — o bee·zo·nyo dee oon
meccanico. — me·ka·nee·ko

ROAD SIGNS

Dare la Precedenza	Give Way
Deviazione	Detour
Divieto di Accesso	No Entry
Divieto di Sorpasso	No Overtaking
Divieto di Sosta	No Parking
Entrata	Entrance
Passo Carrabile/Carraio	Keep Clear
Pedaggio	Toll
Pericolo	Danger
Rallentare	Slow Down
Senso Unico	One Way
Uscita	Exit

The car/motorbike has broken down (at ...).
La macchina/moto	la *ma·kee·na/mo·to*
si è guastata (a ...).	see e gwas·*ta·*ta (a ...)

The car/motorbike won't start.
La macchina/moto	la *ma·kee·na/mo·to*
non parte.	non *par·*te

I have a flat tyre.
Ho una gomma bucata.	o oo·na *go·*ma boo·*ka·*ta

I've run out of petrol.
Ho esaurito la benzina.	o e·zo·*ree·*to la ben·*dzee·*na

I've had an accident.
Ho avuto un incidente.	o a·*voo·*to oon een·chee·*den·*te

TRAVEL WITH CHILDREN
Is there a/an ...?
C'è ...?	che ...

I need a/an ...
Ho bisogno di ...   o bee·*zo·*nyo dee ...
  baby change room
  un bagno con fasciatoio   oon *ba·*nyo kon fa·sha·*to·*yo
  car seat
  un seggiolino per   oon se·jo·*lee·*no per
    bambini   bam·*bee·*nee
  child-minding service
  un servizio di   oon ser·*vee·*tsyo dee
    babysitter   be·bee·*see·*ter
  children's menu
  un menù per bambini   oon me·*noo* per bam·*bee·*nee
  (disposable) nappies/diapers
  pannolini (usa e getta)   pa·no·*lee·*nee (*oo·*sa e *je·*ta)
  formula (infant milk)
  latte in polvere   *la·*te in *pol·*ve·re
  (English-speaking) baby-sitter
  un/una baby-sitter   oon/*oo·*na be·bee·*see·*ter
    (che parli inglese)   (ke *par·*lee een·*gle·*ze)
  highchair
  un seggiolone   oon se·jo·*lo·*ne
  potty
  un vasino   oon va·*zee·*no
  stroller
  un passeggino   oon pa·se·*jee·*no

Do you mind if I breastfeed here?
Le dispiace se allatto	le dees·*pya·*che se a·*la·*to
il/la bimbo/a qui?	eel/la *beem·*bo/a kwee

Are children allowed?
I bambini sono	ee bam·*bee·*nee so·no
ammessi?	a·*me·*see

Also available from Lonely Planet:
Italian Phrasebook

LANGUAGE

Glossary

abbazia – abbey
aeroporto – airport
affittacamere – rooms for rent (relatively inexpensive and not part of the classification system)
agriturismo – farm-stay accommodation
albergo – hotel
alimentare – grocery shop
alloggio – lodging (relatively inexpensive and not part of the classification system)
alto – high
ambulanza – ambulance
anfiteatro – amphitheatre
appartamento – apartment, flat
arco – arch
autobus – local bus
autostazione – bus station/terminal
autostop – hitching
autostrada – motorway, highway

baldacchino – canopy supported by columns over the altar in a church
basilica – Christian church with a rectangular hall, aisles and an apse at the end
battistero – baptistry
benzina – petrol
biblioteca – library
bicicletta – bicycle
biglietteria – ticket office
biglietto – ticket
biglietto cumulativo – combined ticket that allows entrance to a number of associated sights
binario – platform
borgo – ancient town or village

cabinovia – two-seater cable car
calcio – football
camera doppia – room with twin beds
camera matrimoniale – double room with a double bed
camera singola – single room
campanile – bell tower
campeggio – camping
campo – field
cappella – chapel
carabinieri – military police
carnevale – carnival period between Epiphany and Lent
carta d'identità – identity card
carta telefonica – phonecard (also *scheda telefonica*)
cartolina (postale) – postcard
casa – house, home
castello – castle

cattedrale – cathedral
cava – quarry
cena – evening meal
centesimi – cents
centro – city centre
centro storico – (literally, 'historical centre') old town
chiaroscuro – (literally, 'light-dark') artistic distribution of light and dark areas in a painting
chiesa – church
chiostro – cloister; a covered walkway around a quadrangle, which is usually enclosed by columns
circo – oval or circular arena
codice fiscale – tax number
colle – hill
colonna – column
comune – equivalent to a municipality; town or city council; historically, a commune (self-governing town or city)
contado – district around a major town (the area surrounding Florence was known as the *contado di Firenze*)
contrada – town district
convalida – ticket-stamping machine
coperto – cover charge
corso – main street, avenue
cortile – courtyard
cupola – dome

deposito bagagli – left luggage
distributore di benzina – petrol pump (see also *stazione di servizio*)
duomo – cathedral

enoteca – wine bar

farmacia – pharmacy
ferrovia – train station
festa – festival
fiore – flower
fiume – river
fontana – fountain
foro – forum
francobollo – postage stamp
fresco – painting method in which watercolour paint is applied to wet plaster
funicolare – funicular railway
funivia – cable car

gabinetto – toilet, WC
golfo – gulf
grisaille – technique of monochrome painting in shades of grey

grotta – cave
guardia di finanza – fiscal police

HI – Hostelling International

intarsio – inlaid wood, marble or metal
isola – island

lago – lake
largo – (small) square
lavanderia – laundrette
lavasecco – dry-cleaning
lettera – letter
libreria – bookshop
lido – beach
locanda – inn, small hotel (relatively inexpensive and not part of the classification system)
loggia – covered area on the side of a building; porch
lungomare – seafront road, promenade

macchia – scrub, bush
mare – sea
mercato – market
monte – mountain, mount
motorino – moped
municipio – town hall
museo – museum

navata centrale – nave; central part of a church
navata laterale – aisle of a church
nave – ship
necropoli – (ancient) cemetery, burial site

oggetti smarriti – lost property
ostello per la gioventù – youth hostel
osteria – simple, trattoria-style restaurant, often with a bar

palazzo – palace; a large building of any type, including an apartment block
parco – park
passaggio ponte – deck class
passeggiata – traditional evening stroll
pensione – small hotel
permesso di lavoro – work permit
permesso di soggiorno – residence permit
piazza – square
piazzale – (large) open square
pietà – (literally, 'pity' or 'compassion') sculpture, drawing or painting of the dead Christ supported by Madonna
pinacoteca – art gallery
piscina – pool
poltrona – (literally, 'armchair') airline-type chair on a ferry
polyptych – altarpiece consisting of more than three panels (see also *triptych*)

ponte – bridge
porta – door, city gate
portico – walkway, often on the outside of buildings
porto – port
presepio – nativity scene
profumeria – perfumery
pronto soccorso – first aid
pullman – long-distance bus

questura – police station

rifugio – mountain hut, alpine refuge
rocca – fort

sagra – festival (usually with a culinary theme)
sala – room in a museum or a gallery
santuario – sanctuary
scalinata – flight of stairs
scavi – excavations
scheda telefonica – phonecard
servizio – service fee
spiaggia – beach
spiaggia libera – public beach
stazione – station
stazione di servizio – service/petrol station (see also *distributore di benzina*)
stazione marittima – ferry terminal
strada – street, road
superstrada – expressway; highway with divided lanes (but no tolls)

tabaccheria/tabaccaio – tobacconist's shop/tobacconist
teatro – theatre
telefonino – mobile phone
tempio – temple
terme – thermal bath
tesoro – treasury
torre – tower
torrente – stream
traghetto – ferry
trattoria – simple restaurant
triptych – painting or carving over three panels, hinged so that the outer panels fold over the middle one, often used as an altarpiece (see also *polyptych*)

ufficio postale – post office
ufficio stranieri – (police) foreigners' bureau
uffizi – offices

via – street, road
via aerea – airmail
via ferrata – climbing trail with permanent steel cables to aid walkers, usually in a hilly area
vicoli – alley, alleyway
vigili urbani – traffic police, local police

Saints Glossary

Italy has some 3500 recorded saints, who give their names to towns, villages, *vias* (streets) and *viales* (boulevards). You'll frequently come across apostles, such as San Giovanni (St John) and San Pietro (St Peter), or international stars like San Giorgio (St George), the dragon slayer, and San Sebastian, pierced by arrows and perpetually suffering.

Here are some of Tuscany and Umbria's home-grown *santi* (saints):

Sant'Agnese di Montepulciano (1268–1317) – b Graciano near Montepulciano, Tuscany. Appointed abbess when only 20, cured illnesses simply by her presence and could multiply loaves when the convent bakery ran short. A sweet-scented liquid dribbled from her hands and feet long after her death.

San Benedetto (c 480–547) – b Norcia, Umbria. Patron: Europe, cavers, farmers. Good against: witchcraft, gall stones, nettle rash. St Benedict divided his life between directing his monastery and living as a hermit. He was the founder of the Benedictine order.

San Bernadino di Siena (1380–1444) – b Massa Maritima, Tuscany. Patron: advertising, communications. Good against: compulsive gambling, chest complaints. Urging listeners to fling objects of temptation into 'bonfires of vanities', his public preaching attracted thousands. In later life, he became head of the Franciscan order in Italy.

Santa Caterina di Siena (1347–80) – b Siena, Tuscany. Patron: nurses, firefighters. Good against: sickness, sexual temptation. Her 300-plus surviving letters are considered masterpieces of early Tuscan literature. Now somewhat dispersed – her head and right thumb in Siena, body in Rome and foot in Venice.

Santa Chiara (1194–1253) – b Assisi, Umbria. Patron: goldsmiths, telephone, TV. Good against: sore eyes, bad weather. A devotee of St Francis, St Clare founded the order that still bears her name. Members go barefoot and mostly observe silence.

San Filippo Neri (1515–95) – b Florence, Tuscany. Patron: Rome, US special forces. Founded a lay fraternity to support impoverished pilgrims visiting Rome.

San Francesco (1182–1224) – b Assisi, Umbria. Patron: animals, merchants, the environment. Good against: fire. After a wild youth, St Francis assumed extreme humility and founded the Franciscan order of friars. He lived with animals, cared for lepers and received stigmata, which bled during the last years of his life.

Santa Rita (1381–1457) – b Spoleto, Umbria. Patron: parents, widows. Good against: desperate cases, difficult marriages. Widowed after an abusive marriage, spent 40 years as a nun. The deep, unhealing gash on her forehead was reputedly caused by a thorn from Christ's crucifixion.

Sant'Ubaldo (c 1100–60) – b Gubbio, Umbria. Patron: sick children. Powerful against: demonic possession, migraines. Except for a brief period of study in Vienna, lived all his life in his home town, where, revered for both his fervour and humility, he served as abbot of the local monastery.

Santa Zita (1218–72) – b Monsagrati, near Lucca, Tuscany. Patron: servants, waiters. Good against: losing keys. Became a domestic servant when only 12 and spent her whole life in service, where she would share her meagre rations with the poor. One day, when her master accused her of stealing the bread that bulged beneath her apron, Zita gave it a shake and out tumbled flowers.

The Authors

NICOLA WILLIAMS

For Nicola, a British journalist, living in France for the last 10 years (in a hillside home with Lake Geneva view in Haute-Savoie), has meant it's an easy getaway to Italy, where she's spent years eating her way around and revelling in its extraordinary art heritage and vibrant landscapes. When not working, she can be found in the Alps skiing, strolling in Paris, or flitting between family in Britain and Germany. Nicola wrote the first edition of *Milan, Turin & Genoa* for Lonely Planet and updated a tasty chunk of Tuscany for Lonely Planet's *Italy* guide, alongside a Florentine chunk of this book. She has worked on numerous other Lonely Planet titles.

LEIF PETTERSEN

In 2003 Leif Pettersen was 'Kramered' into abandoning an idiot-proof career with the Federal Reserve Bank of Minneapolis and embarked upon an odyssey of travel writing. Despite a dubious grasp of grammar, he managed modest success by deluging hapless editors with material so raw that a trilingual international support group was formed to cope with the situation. Good coffee, cheap wine and gnarly old stuff has driven Leif to visit over 100 Italian cities and eat in over 300 restaurants in just a few years. He writes an almost-award-winning, 'slightly caustic' blog at KillingBatteries.com, where he dishes on travel writing, Romania, Italian internet, Berlin and Jesus.

ALEX LEVITON

Alex updated her original Umbria chapters for the third edition of this guide in a row, partly from a Perugian medieval apartment on Via Ritorta. She wrote her first book when she was four years old, about how a frog felt to be green. Once slightly more mature, Alex developed an addiction to independent travel, picked up a master's degree in journalism from UC Berkeley, and spent a decade falling in love with Italy's food, history, culture and landscape. She's been writing for Lonely Planet since 2002. For two years Alex was mostly transient, but by the time you read this, she should be settled in Oakland, California, with her kitty Romeo and new husband Matt.

ALISON BING

When not scribbling notes in church crypts and methodically eating her way across the Italian countryside, Alison contributes to Lonely Planet's *Italy* guide, as well as art publications, including Italy's *Flash Art*. She divides her time between San Francisco and a hilltop town on the border of Tuscany, where she compensates for admittedly suspect regional loyalties (she wrote *Best of Milan* 2, and partner Marco Marinucci is Roman) with a distinctly local appetite for truffles and ramshackle stone buildings. Alison holds a bachelor's degree in art history and a masters degree from the Fletcher School of Law and Diplomacy, a joint programme of Tufts and Harvard Universities – perfectly respectable diplomatic credentials she regularly undermines with opinionated culture, a commentary for newspapers, magazines and radio.

MILES RODDIS

This is Miles' fourth Italian Job for Lonely Planet, this time written, frustratingly, from the comfort of his office. Writing mostly about Mediterranean lands, he lives just across the water in Valencia, Spain, and has authored or contributed to more than 25 Lonely Planet titles including *Europe on a Shoestring, Mediterranean Europe, Western Europe, France, Walking in France, Spain* and *Walking in Spain*.

Behind the Scenes

THIS BOOK

This 5th edition was updated by Nicola Williams, Alex Leviton, Alison Bing, Leif Pettersen and Miles Roddis. The previous edition was updated by Miles Roddis and Alex Leviton. The book was commissioned in Lonely Planet's London office, and produced in Melbourne by the following:

Commissioning Editor Paula Hardy
Coordinating Editor Alison Ridgway
Coordinating Cartographer Helen Rowley
Coordinating Layout Designer Yvonne Bischofberger
Managing Editor Geoff Howard
Managing Cartographer Mark Griffiths
Managing Layout Designers Adam McCrow, Celia Wood
Assisting Editors Sasha Baskett, Carly Hall, Rosie Nicholson, Kristin Odijk
Assisting Cartographers Anita Banh, Csanad Csutoros
Assisting Layout Designers Indra Kilfoyle, Wibowo Rusli, Jacqui Saunders

Cover Designer Pepi Bluck
Colour Designers Yvonne Bischofberger, Indra Kilfoyle
Project Manager Rachel Imeson
Language Content Coordinator Quentin Frayne

Thanks to Sin Choo, Jennifer Garrett, Mark Germanchis, Laura Jane, Lisa Knights, John Mazzocchi, Lyahna Spencer

THANKS
NICOLA WILLIAMS

The graciousness, good-humour and overwhelmingly hospitality and eagerness to help of the many people I interviewed during my travels cannot be emphasised enough: In Florence, thank you to Tuscan chef Fabio Picchi, comic actress Maria Cassi, and assistant Miriam Zamparella (Teatro del Sale); Umberto Montano (Alle Murate); music expert Daniele Pallardini (Plasma); perfumer Lorenzo Villoresi; Roberta Berni (Florence Tourist Board); Dr

BEHIND THE SCENES

LONELY PLANET: TRAVEL WIDELY, TREAD LIGHTLY, GIVE SUSTAINABLY

The Lonely Planet Story

The story begins with a classic travel adventure: Tony and Maureen Wheeler's 1972 journey across Europe and Asia to Australia. There was no useful information about the overland trail then, so Tony and Maureen published the first Lonely Planet guidebook to meet a growing need.

From a kitchen table, Lonely Planet has grown to become the largest independent travel publisher in the world, with offices in Melbourne (Australia), Oakland (USA) and London (UK). Today Lonely Planet guidebooks cover the globe. There is an ever-growing list of books and information in a variety of media. Some things haven't changed. The main aim is still to make it possible for adventurous individuals to get out there – to explore and better understand the world.

The Lonely Planet Foundation

The Lonely Planet Foundation proudly supports nimble nonprofit institutions working for change in the world. Each year the foundation donates 5% of Lonely Planet company profits to projects selected by staff and authors. Our partners range from Kabissa, which provides small nonprofits across Africa with access to technology, to the Foundation for Developing Cambodian Orphans, which supports girls at risk of falling victim to sex traffickers.

Our nonprofit partners are linked by a grass-roots approach to the areas of health, education or sustainable tourism. Many projects we support – such as one with BaAka (Pygmy) children in the forested areas of Central African Republic – choose to focus on women and children as one of the most effective ways to support the whole community.

Sometimes foundation assistance is as simple as helping to preserve a local ruin like the Minaret of Jam in Afghanistan; this incredible monument now draws intrepid tourists to the area and its restoration has greatly improved options for local people.

Just as travel is often about learning to see with new eyes, so many of the groups we work with aim to change the way people see themselves and the future for their children and communities.

Angelo Tartuferi (Galleria degli Uffizi); Jade (McRae Books); and Fiamma Davenport. Thank you to Doreen and Carmelo (Hotel Scoti) for putting me in touch with Florentine nobles Niccolò Rosselli del Turco and Francesco Carlo Griccioli; to Marco (Hotel Dali) for his out-of-town tips; and to Alessio & Asumi (Hotel Cestelli) whose outstanding dining and drinking recommendations readily compete with this guide! Elsewhere in Tuscany, grazie mille to Guido Manfredi for an eye-opening stay at Barbialla Nuova; to Imperio and the ever faithful Toby for coming up trumps with truffles; Cosimo Gericke and Birte at Fattoria Rignana (fabulous fabulous), Giadi & Graziano at Podere Castellare, and Katie and Giancarlo Caldesi. At home a flurry of heartfelt thanks to my parents Ann and Paul Williams, to Matthias for holding the fort while I was gone, and to Niko and Mischa for valiantly tested every gelateria in Florence.

ALEX LEVITON

Heartfelt thanks to friends in Italy – Carlo Rocchi Bilancini, Zach Nowak, Fabiano and Katya, and Roberto Nini. Thanks especially to Federico Bibi and the folks at the Centro Agro Alimentare. Mille grazie to helpful tourist boards: Spoleto, Castiglione del Lago, Gubbio and Orvieto. Props go to on-the-road research helpers Matt Reagan, Leif Pettersen, Olufunke Moses and LP five-timer Len 'Il Muffino' Amaral and back-home write-up supporters Rah Bickley and Jennifer Brunson. A kiss on both cheeks for the in-house crack editing team of Paula Hardy, Fayette Fox, Alison Ridgway and Rosie Nicholson, and cartographers Helen Rowley and the incomparable Mark Griffiths.

ALISON BING

Mille grazie e tanti baci a: Le mie famiglie a Roma & Stateside: the Bings, Ferrys, & Marinuccis; Editorial guru Paula Hardy, who turns ordinary guidebooks into rollicking romps through the countryside; Superheroic coordinating author Nicola Williams, with her mystical powers to turn a phrase and save the day under the Tuscan sun without even breaking a sweat; The Melbourne mavens Imogen Bannister and Bruce Evans; Art cognoscenti Massimo Bartolini and Flash Art editor Chris Sharp; and ma sopra tutto Marco Flavio Marinucci, who makes every adventure worthwhile.

LEIF PETTERSEN

Foremost thanks goes to Miles Roddis, whose notes, coaching and singular wit turned what might have been a suicidal assignment into something wonderful. Also, I'd have been lost without

my patient, supportive Tuscany and Umbria cohorts Alison Bing, Alex Leviton and Nicola Williams all of whom displayed such brilliance during this gig that it scared me a little. Paula Hardy and Fayette Fox in London for all variety of problem solving and damage control. Giangiacomo and Laura in Torricella for arranging food, lake-front shelter and unfettered internet access. Doug and Jenny Mills for their email updates. Susan Scott in San Gimignano for all that basilica stuff. Alessia in Sansepolcro for all that Sansepolcro stuff. The 'Slow Food representative' in Portoferraio for the outstanding recommendations. Jena in Montalcino for making me stop working for five minutes to enjoy some Brunello. My driving companions on Elba. Catalina for the rejuvenating bottles of duty-free Bailey's. And the entire Italian police force who kindly ignored those 187 brazen driving and parking infractions. I heart Pooky Pants.

OUR READERS

Many thanks to the travellers who used the last edition and wrote to us with helpful hints, useful advice and interesting anecdotes:

Mike Anderson, Warren Berlinger, Judy Consden, Carol Cruickshank, Daniel Engström, Dave Gahan, Steven James, Katie Johnson, Sandra & Marvin Kohn, Theo Meyer, Antti Niemistö, Ashley Peeler, Guus Stoelinga, Sharon V, Julie Williams,

ACKNOWLEDGMENTS

Many thanks to the following for the use of their content:

Globe on title page ©Mountain High Maps 1993 Digital Wisdom, Inc.

Internal photographs:

p12 Atlantide Phototravel/Corbis; p10-11 (#3) Franco Cogoli/SIME; p10 (#4) Guido Cozzi/4Corners Images; p8 (#1) Colin Dutton/Grand Tour/Corbis; p11 (bottom, right) La Cucina Caldesi, London; p8-9 (#9) Maurizio Rellini/SIME; p10 (#1) Massimo Ripani/SIME; p9 (#3) Stefano Scatà/SIME All other photographs by Lonely Planet Images, and p5 Jeff Cantarutti; p6 Jenny Jones; p7 (#2, #5) Dallas Stribley; p8 (#4) Nick Tapp; p11 (#5) Barbara Van Zanten.

All images are the copyright of the photographers unless otherwise indicated. Many of the images in this guide are available for licensing from Lonely Planet Images: www.lonelyplanetimages.com.

Index

000 Map pages
000 Photograph pages

000 Map pages
000 Photograph pages

INDEX

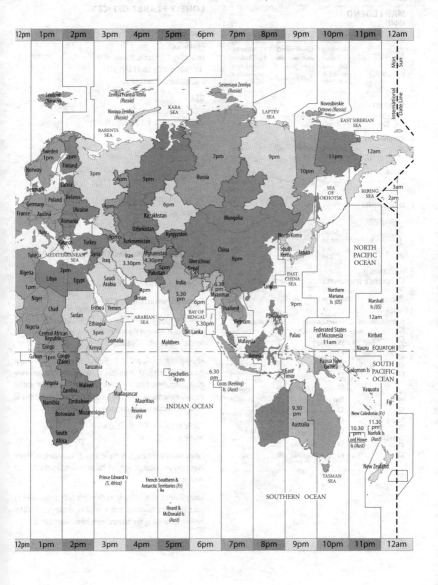

MAP LEGEND

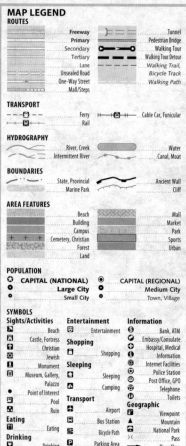

ROUTES

Freeway	Tunnel
Primary	Pedestrian Bridge
Secondary	Walking Tour
Tertiary	Walking Tour Detour
Lane	Walking Trail,
Unsealed Road	Bicycle Track
One-Way Street	Walking Path
Mall/Steps	

TRANSPORT

Ferry	Cable Car, Funicular
Rail	

HYDROGRAPHY

River, Creek	Water
Intermittent River	Canal, Moat

BOUNDARIES

State, Provincial	Ancient Wall
Marine Park	Cliff

AREA FEATURES

Beach	Mall
Building	Market
Campus	Park
Cemetery, Christian	Sports
Forest	Urban
Land	

POPULATION

✪ **CAPITAL (NATIONAL)**	⦿ CAPITAL (REGIONAL)
● **Large City**	● Medium City
○ Small City	○ Town, Village

SYMBOLS

Sights/Activities	Entertainment	Information
Beach	Entertainment	Bank, ATM
Castle, Fortress	**Shopping**	Embassy/Consulate
Christian	Shopping	Hospital, Medical
Jewish		Information
Monument	**Sleeping**	Internet Facilities
Museum, Gallery,	Sleeping	Police Station
Palazzo	Camping	Post Office, GPO
Point of Interest		Telephone
Pool	**Transport**	Toilets
Ruin	Airport	**Geographic**
Eating	Bus Station	Viewpoint
Eating	Bicycle Path	Mountain
Drinking	Parking Area	National Park
Drinking	Petrol Station	Pass
Café		River Flow
		Waterfall

LONELY PLANET OFFICES

Australia
Head Office
Locked Bag 1, Footscray, Victoria 3011
☎ 03 8379 8000, fax 03 8379 8111
talk2us@lonelyplanet.com.au

USA
150 Linden St, Oakland, CA 94607
☎ 510 893 8555, toll free 800 275 8555
fax 510 893 8572
info@lonelyplanet.com

UK
2nd Floor 186 City Road,
London EC1V 2NT
☎ 020 7106 2100, fax 020 7841 9001
go@lonelyplanet.co.uk

Published by Lonely Planet Publications Pty Ltd
ABN 36 005 607 983

© Lonely Planet Publications Pty Ltd 2008

© photographers as indicated 2008

Cover photograph: Il Palio, Piazza del Campo, Siena, Paolo Sacchi/
Getty Images. Many of the images in this guide are available for licensing from Lonely Planet Images: www.lonelyplanetimages.com.

Printed by Hang Tai Printing Company
Printed in China